P9-DUA-366

Second Edition

Corrections in the United States

A Contemporary Perspective

DEAN J. CHAMPION

Minot State University

Prentice Hall
Upper Saddle River, New Jersey 07458

rspective /

HV9471.C47 1998 97-26177
364.6'0973—dc21 CIP

Acquisition Editor: Neil Marquardt
Editorial Assistant: Jean Auman
Managing Editor: Mary Carnis
Project Manager: Linda B. Pawelchak
Prepress and Manufacturing Buyer: Ed O'Dougherty
Cover Director: Jayne Conte
Cover Design: Miguel Ortiz
Cover Art: Terry Qing / FPG International
Electronic Art Creation: Asterisk Group
Marketing Manager: Frank Mortimer Jr.

This book was set in 10.5/12 New Century Schoolbook
by Stratford Publishing Services and was printed and bound
by RR Donnelley & Sons Company.
The cover was printed by Phoenix Color Corp.

Reprinted with corrections June, 1999

Printed in the United States of America

10 9 8 7 6 5 4 3 2

ISBN 0-13-293937-1

Prentice-Hall International (UK) Limited, *London*
Prentice-Hall of Australia Pty. Limited, *Sydney*
Prentice-Hall Canada Inc., *Toronto*
Prentice-Hall Hispanoamericana, S.A., *Mexico*
Prentice-Hall of India Private Limited, *New Delhi*
Prentice-Hall of Japan, Inc., *Tokyo*
Prentice Hall Asia Pte. Ltd., *Singapore*
Editora Prentice-Hall do Brasil, Ltda., *Rio de Janeiro*

In memory of my big brother,
Frank Gilbert Champion
1927–1997

Contents

Preface

Corrections in the United States: A Contemporary Perspective is about the punishment phase of the criminal justice system. When crimes are committed and suspects are apprehended, prosecuted, and convicted, correctional agencies take over. Corrections is the vast collective of persons, agencies, and organizations that manages criminals. The most visible part of corrections is prisons and jails. The most notorious prisons have been popularized by the media. Prison names such as San Quentin, Alcatraz, Sing Sing, Leavenworth, Attica, and Marion are familiar to the general public. But prisons and jails, though important, are only two parts of the larger corrections mosaic. Another part of corrections manages offenders who either have been granted early release from prison or have been convicted but not incarcerated. Community correctional agencies are increasingly popular as nonincarcerative alternatives for probationers and parolees. One reason for their popularity is that they are more cost-effective than prisons and jails. In some instances, less serious offenders are not prosecuted, but rather are diverted from the criminal justice system. They also are managed by certain corrections agencies for a specified period.

Today, correctional agencies and organizations are facing several significant challenges. Rising crime rates and greater numbers of criminal prosecutions are responsible for record high prison and jail populations that are outpacing new prison and jail construction. Overcrowding is inevitable, and it fosters living conditions that are both intolerable and unconstitutional. In recent years, a "litigation explosion" has occurred by which prisoners have filed thousands of lawsuits against prison and jail administrators and correctional officers. Inmate rights is an increasingly important issue.

This book is divided into four parts, each examining several elements of corrections. Part I examines the history of corrections in the United States and contrasts several important philosophies that have influenced correctional reforms during the last century. A brief overview of the criminal justice system is provided, with an emphasis on the interrelatedness of the police, prosecution, courts, the sentencing process, and the final correctional phase. Offenders are profiled and different sentencing schemes are discussed as are contemporary issues associated with sentencing systems.

Various correctional alternatives are examined, including diversion and probation. Diversion programs are intended to be front-end solutions to the case processing of criminal defendants. Low-risk first-offenders are usually considered good candidates for diversion, by which their cases are resolved through various alternatives involving civil procedures rather than criminal ones. Both standard and intensive probation programs are examined in detail. A brief history of probation is also presented.

Part II distinguishes between jails and prisons. A history of jails in the United States is provided as are jail functions and a profile of jail inmates. Contemporary jail problems are also explored, including jail overcrowding, the quality of jail personnel, jail suicides, the prevalence of AIDS, and the provision of health-care services. Various jail reforms are described, including jail privatization, the overhaul of existing jail architecture, and the emergence of new-generation, direct-supervision jails. Jail officer recruitment and training are examined as well as the administration of jail programs. Jails and prisons are contrasted, and their major differences are described. In recent years, jails have assumed various prison functions, and this development has exacerbated existing jail problems. The history of prisons in the United States is described as are several contemporary issues associated with these types of institutions. Highlighted here are several important issues concerning the administration and operation of correctional facilities. The rights of prisoners are discussed, including the increasingly important role of the jailhouse lawyer and related legal issues that often prompt civil and criminal lawsuits filed by inmates against institutional staff.

Part III focuses on parole and community-based corrections programs. Parole is defined and a brief history of parole developments in the United States is presented. Included here are the philosophy and goals of parole programs. Parolees are also profiled. Whenever parolees and/or probationers violate one or more conditions of their conditional program, their respective programs may be revoked. The revocation process is described, including some of the landmark U.S. Supreme Court decisions relating to such revocation actions. In most states, parole boards function to determine one's early release eligibility. This decision making involves anticipating one's future potential for public risk or dangerousness. Some of the instruments and techniques used in risk assessment are described. The nature and functions of parole boards are examined. Various types of parole board actions are described, including an overview of some of the programs into which prospective parolees may be directed. The quality of decision making in probation and parole actions is assessed according to rates of recidivism among probationers and parolees. Recidivism rates are measured in different ways, and different types of recidivists are profiled.

Another key dimension of postinstitutional activity is community corrections. Viewed as a viable alternative to prison and jail overcrowding, community corrections and intermediate punishments are increasingly popular in most jurisdictions. The goals and functions of community corrections programs are described, along with several key issues involved in their emergence and establishment. Several intermediate punishments are discussed in some detail, including home confinement, electronic monitoring, furloughs and work/study release, halfway houses, and community residential centers. Technology is creating a more sophisticated client management environment, and some of the more recent technological developments are presented.

Part IV describes the individual who performs probation functions—the probation officer. Since there are overlapping duties and responsibilities associated with both probation and parole officers, these roles are considered simultaneously. Often, the same individuals supervise both probationers and parolees. Thus, selection and recruitment of both probation and parole officers involve similar qualifications and skills. The education, training, and role performance of these officers are highlighted. In addition, some of the ways caseloads are assigned officers are described. Probation and parole work can be stressful, and stress often leads to burnout. Some of the factors that contribute to stress and burnout are examined, together with some of the strategies officers use to combat and/or overcome them.

Also described in Part IV is the increasingly important role of volunteers and paraprofessionals who become involved in correctional work. Some of the legal liabilities of volunteers and paraprofessionals are addressed. More offenders with special needs are being supervised, both in institutions and communities. Clients with special needs include those who are alcohol or drug dependent, the mentally ill, sex offenders, those with AIDS and other communicable diseases, and offenders with various physical handicaps. Communities have been responsive to meeting these offender needs in diverse ways.

Another component of Part IV is an examination of women in corrections. Nearly 10 percent of all inmates and probationers/parolees are women. Women's prisons are generally different from male facilities in several important ways. And female offenders have different needs than their male counterparts. Some of the major differences in male and female inmates and clients are discussed. Included are selected issues relating to women's prisons, such as the problem of inmate mothers, vocational/educational programs for women, and the general problem of co-correctional facilities.

Juvenile corrections is also described. A brief overview of the juvenile justice system is presented, together with the leading cases that have shaped it over the years. Various types of community corrections programs for juveniles are discussed as are probation and parole programs and revocation actions.

As helpful study aids at the ends of chapters, questions that are designed to help students review important chapter features are included. These questions are also useful as a means of studying chapter contents. Key terms are listed and have been boldfaced throughout each chapter. Additionally, these key terms have been defined and listed in a comprehensive glossary. Each chapter also contains several suggested readings for those desiring to learn more about specific chapter subject matter for class report preparation and general research investigations on particular topics. An extensive up-to-date reference list is also included. Students will find these references helpful in their own research projects on various corrections topics.

I wish to thank the following reviewers for their helpful comments on this edition: Howard Abadinsky, St. Xavier College; Ted Alleman, late of Pennsylvania State University; George Evans, William Rainey Harper College; and Ken Kerle, American Jail Association.

My appreciation is also extended to those who provided some of the photos for this book, including Corky Stromme, chief of security, North Dakota State Penitentiary; Lt. Darrell Theurer, North Dakota State Penitentiary; Darin Egge, Steve Whitesell, Rodney L. Tryhus, Bryan M. Durham, DeVawn Beckman, Kari Sage, William A. Brown, and Jay Laudenschlager, Minot (N.D.) Police Department; Scott Kast, Minot State University; Thom Mellum, Penny Erickson, Deryl Martin, Deb Armstrong, Deanna Flagstad, Corie A. Delzer, Laura Forbes, Jeremy Mattison, Glennis Knudsvig, Donald Williams, Ward County (N.D.) Jail; and Jarrett Wold, Eric Pinnick, Jordan Hendershot, and Zach Schultz of Minot, North Dakota.

Dean J. Champion

1

An Introduction to Corrections: Philosophy, Goals, and History

CHAPTER OUTLINE

OVERVIEW

- Riots in U.S. prisons increased by 50 percent between 1994 and 1995. Nearly 280 disturbances were reported in 1995 compared with 186 disturbances in 1994 (*Corrections Compendium*, 21 [June]:9, 1996).
- Inmate suicides in U.S. prisons and jails increased between 1994 and 1995 to 160, a jump of 14 percent (*Corrections Compendium*, 21 [June]:11, 1996).
- A total of 6,860 staff assaults were reported in 1995 by 39 different prison systems in the U.S., a 25 percent increase in staff assaults over the previous year (*Corrections Compendium,* 21 [June]:11, 1996).
- In October 1994 a federal judge ruled that prisoners may perform satanic rituals in their cells. The judge held that the federal prison rule barring devil worship is unconstitutional, saying that "We ought to give the devil his due." The judge declared the satanic ceremony a "religious" service (Associated Press, "A Right to Rituals?" *Minot [N.D.] Daily News*, October 18: 1994:A4).
- Attaining greater amounts of education while in prison tends to reduce an inmate's chances of recidivating or committing new offenses. In 1996 Congress moved to withdraw funding for Pell Grants, a major source for funding inmate education (*Corrections Compendium*, "Corrections Education and Pell Grant Funding," 20 [December]:11, 23, 1996).

Corrections is in trouble and haunted by many problems. And these problems are getting worse. One pervasive and continuing problem is jail and prison overcrowding. As overcrowding both continues and increases, other jail and prison problems are created and/or aggravated. The annual growth rate of offenders entering correctional facilities and institutions is considerably greater than the growth rate of the U.S. population. Between 1985 and 1995, state and federal prison populations increased by 121 percent. During the 1990–1995 period, the state and federal prison population grew by 38 percent, while the U.S. population grew by only 4.7 percent (Gilliard and Beck, 1996:2; *World Almanac Books*, 1996:388). Projections are that by the year 2002, the prison inmate population will increase by another 43 percent (Wees, 1996a:1).

By 1997, nearly 6 million persons were under some form of correctional supervision in the United States. This compares with 5.1 million persons who were under some form of correctional supervision in 1994 and 5.3 million persons in 1995 (Associated Press, 1995:A3; Department of Justice, 1996:1). About 30 percent of these persons were incarcerated in local, state, and federal jails and prisons. Supervising these offenders were over 408,711 personnel in adult and juvenile corrections (American Correctional Association, 1996a:xlii–xliii, xliv–xlv, xlvi). About 50 percent of these were correctional officers, and about 10 percent of all personnel worked in juvenile corrections. There were 1,977 administrators of adult and juvenile correctional facilities. The median ratio of inmates to correctional officers was 4.25, or 4.25 inmates per correctional officer. The median turnover among correctional officers was 11 percent for 1995 (American Correctional Association, 1996a).

Whatever the *causes* of crime, our courts are glutted with record numbers of criminal cases and U.S. prisons and jails are well above their maximum capacities. Even the Federal Bureau of Prisons exceeded its maximum capacity of federal inmates by more than 25 percent in 1995 (Camp and Camp, 1995a:36–37). Many local, state, and federal incarcerative facilities are under federal court order to reduce their inmate populations to healthier and safer levels. Most correctional programs and facilities are inadequately staffed and underfunded. One result is that offenders frequently leave these programs without receiving proper treatment or assistance and quickly return to crime as a way of life. Thus, a vicious cycle perpetuates and aggravates many types of correctional problems.

This chapter is an introduction to corrections in the United States and has three objectives. First, *corrections* is defined and a brief history of corrections is presented. Second, several contrasting *correctional philosophies* are described. Third, several important *functions of corrections* are outlined and discussed, together with an examination of certain correctional alternatives and reforms.

CORRECTIONS DEFINED

The term *corrections* means many different things to the average citizen. Some of these connotations have created several myths about what corrections is and does. Ideally, criminals assigned to correctional agencies are *corrected*. That is, they are punished and reformed. However, a significant part of corrections is unrelated to punishment or reformation. In fact, some experts question whether *any* correctional institution corrects or reforms (Walker, 1989).

Corrections is the vast number of persons, agencies, and organizations that manage accused, convicted, or adjudicated criminal offenders and juveniles. Although prisons and jails are the most visible correctional institutions, the vast majority of correctional personnel, agencies, and organizations are less obvious and blend in with many other community agencies and organizations. A fifth of all convicted criminals are placed in jails and prisons. The remainder of all offenders are involved as **clients** in a variety of community programs and services that manage offenders in different ways. When prison inmates are granted early release from incarceration, or *paroled,* or if convicted offenders are given nonincarcerative sentences, such as probation, they are usually supervised by **parole officers, probation officers,** or public and private agencies for varying periods (Henderson and Simon, 1994). These offenders live within the community, lead reasonably normal lives, are employed in diverse occupations or professions, support their dependents, and otherwise blend in with other community residents. The conditions of their supervision (e.g., observance of curfews, periodic drug or alcohol tests, and random checks of their residences) are only a few of the unobtrusive program rules and regulations that differentiate them from others in their communities.

The services provided by correctional agencies are diverse. While correctional institutions manage primarily those persons convicted of crimes, other categories of offenders are supervised as well. Those charged with minor offenses in some communities (e.g., shoplifting, petty theft, vandalism, public drunkenness) may be placed in **diversion programs.** These programs are usually operated by correctional employees and are designed to monitor program participants for short probationary periods. If offenders in these programs obey the rules and comply with all conditions of their diversion programs, they usually avoid further involvement with prosecutors and the courts and their records are often expunged.

When persons are arrested by law enforcement officers for more serious crimes or for violations of local ordinances such as loitering or freeway hitchhiking, they are usually confined in jails temporarily for investigation and released, or they may be charged with one or more crimes. Sometimes important witnesses are housed in jails until they are called to testify in criminal trials. When juveniles are arrested or cited for whatever reason, they, too, may be placed in jails or detention facilities temporarily until their disposition can be properly managed by juvenile authorities. Thus, corrections is *not* limited to the management of adult offenders.

The public view of corrections has been influenced significantly by the media. Sensationalized portrayals of prison life in newspapers, on television, and in motion pictures, coupled with isolated incidents such as the killing of two prison correctional officers at the maximum security federal penitentiary in Marion, Illinois, in 1983 and the 1971 inmate rioting at Attica, New York, have done little to dispel public myths about prisons and their rehabilitative effectiveness. Prisons house "dangerous" persons. Charles Manson, leader of the "Manson cult" of the late 1960s and convicted murderer of actress Sharon Tate and others; David Berkowitz, the "Son of Sam" who methodically and brutally dispatched many victims with a .44 magnum revolver; and Sirhan Sirhan, convicted assassin of Robert Kennedy, are only a few of the many nefarious figures who are confined in U.S. prisons. Manson and Sirhan have become eligible for early release in recent years, but parole boards have consistently denied their parole requests. Despite the notoriety and dangerousness of these offenders, most prisons and many jails are relatively safe custodial institutions. The likelihood of inmate escapes is rare, although they do occur occasionally. More serious offenders are usually placed in maximum-security areas, space permitting, where they are closely monitored by correctional officers either directly or through closed-circuit television cameras.

Despite public relations campaigns and the mass distribution of informative materials by correctional officials and organizations, offenders and the programs designed to manage and help them both inside and outside of prison walls are grossly misunderstood by many citizens. Few people want prisons in their communities, and even fewer citizens like the idea of having community-based offender services operating in their neighborhoods to house criminals while they are on work release, furloughs, parole, or probation (Turner and Petersilia, 1996). Some citizens are terrified by the idea of criminals roaming freely within their communities.

Former Massachusetts Governor Michael Dukakis was a presidential candidate in 1988. At the time, the Massachusetts Department of Corrections operated a furlough program for selected nonviolent inmates by which some inmates would be granted periodic unescorted leaves from prison. One especially violent inmate, Willie Horton, was granted one of these furloughs, although he was clearly ineligible for such a program. While on one of these furloughs, Horton committed several violent crimes in his community and the public was enraged. Horton was quickly apprehended, but Governor Dukakis was blamed for this incident, and his political career as a presidential candidate was seriously impaired. Horton's name became synonymous with the liberal "soft-on-criminals" perspective espoused by various prisoner's rights groups, and the public reacted by rejecting the use of furloughs as a rehabilitative measure. Therefore, corrections usually suffers the serious disadvantage of having an unfavorable public image (Anderson, 1995).

EARLY ORIGINS OF CORRECTIONS

Imprisonment as a punishment is found in ancient Greece and Rome. In 640 B.C., the **Mamertine Prison** was constructed by Ancus Martius. This was a vast series of dungeons constructed under the main sewer of Rome called the **Cloaca Maxima,** and it housed a variety of offenders (Carter, Glaser, and Wilkins, 1985:4). In addition to this facility, rock quarries and strong cages were often used by the Romans and others to incarcerate political dissidents, social misfits, and criminals (Johnston, 1973).

Religion and Corrections

The role of religion in the development of prisons and punishments is particularly evident from ancient times through the Middle Ages (Skotnicki, 1991). The Spanish Inquisition, a religious tribunal reorganized after earlier thirteenth-century inquisitions to suppress and punish nonconformists for assorted heresies, existed for many years and was widely feared as a severe sanctioning medium. Joan of Arc (1412–1431) was an early victim of such inquisitions and was burned at the stake for alleged witchcraft. She had professed to have visions from God instructing her to lead the French people away from British occupation and control. A bothersome troublemaker for the British (a fact that was more likely the reason for her execution than allegations of witchcraft), Joan of Arc was pronounced innocent by the pope in 1456, and she was declared a saint in 1920.

Religious institutions have influenced the structure and functioning of punishment systems in many countries throughout the world including the United States. Religious nonconformists were often confined in dungeons for long periods in order to induce them to recant their dissident religious beliefs. The Apostle Paul was confined under a type of "house arrest" during which time he was given the opportunity of repenting and appealing to his captors for forgiveness. Until the Middle Ages, wrongs committed against the state and citizens were frequently handled privately under the principle of **lex talionis** or the law of retribution or retaliation. Revenge was the usual remedy, particularly during the feudal period.

During the Middle Ages, particularly in Scotland and England, the first examples of what are currently recognized as elements of contemporary corrections began to appear (Cameron, 1983). Although there was little administrative organization or coordination among cities and counties and their incarcerative facilities, large numbers of debtors' prisons existed to confine those who couldn't pay their bills. Many debtors died in prison, because they or their families or friends were unable to pay for their release (Harding et al., 1985). Debtors' prisons were not correctional institutions in any sense, primarily because no efforts were made by guards and others to "correct" or rehabilitate the inmates.

These penal facilities also housed social misfits and criminals and were exclusively designed to segregate them from society. Again, no consideration was given to offender treatment or rehabilitation. These early institutions were principally custodial (Cameron, 1983). Conditions under which prisoners were confined were miserable, inasmuch as it was deemed "wasteful" to feed and clothe outlaws who were either going to die a natural death or be executed anyway. The Church of England was particularly adept at punishing persons for vague crimes such as offenses against morality (Harding et al., 1985). Thus, it is important to recognize that early uses of prisons and other incarcerative facilities were exclusively punishment-centered and not synonymous with what is currently meant by corrections.

Scottish and English prisons eventually were transformed into profitable enterprises by influential mercantile interests. In the 1500s houses of correction were nothing more than slave labor camps designed to exploit prison labor and produce marketable goods cheaply. **Bridewell Workhouse** was established in 1557 to house London's undesirables, although more often than not, these facilities were designed to train prisoners to acquire special skills and where they would labor as craftsmen in the service of private interests (American Correctional Association, 1983). This thinly disguised private profiteering was passed off as work for the development and improvement of an offender's social skills and moral habits (Dobash, 1983). Interestingly, whenever there was an excess in the labor supply, execution was often used as a punishment. In later years, England transported many vagrants, petty criminals, and dissidents to the American colonies as **indentured servants.** Indentured servants were obligated to work for certain wealthy businessmen for seven-year periods. In some respects, indentured servants were the voluntary equivalent of the involuntary slave pattern that emerged in the United States in the early 1800s. However, indentured servants entered into these servile work arrangements for a period of years in exchange for the cost of their passage to the American colonies. After their period of servitude, they were granted freedom, whereas black slaves and their offspring remained slaves for life or until slavery was abolished at the end of the Civil War.

Banishment and Other Punishments

Banishment. Regardless of the primitiveness of any society, sanctions have always been applied against offenders who violate societal rules. Imprisonment has not always been the primary punishment of choice in most social systems. In Biblical times, **banishment** was frequently used and often amounted to capital punishment. Food and shelter would be denied those banished within a distance of 400 or 500 miles, thus dooming them to certain death. In later centuries, banishment was used for other purposes. Probably the first recorded case in which banishment was used as a punishment was Adam and Eve (Duff and Garland, 1994).

During the eighteenth and nineteenth centuries, banishment was used as a punishment in various Chinese provinces, such as in Xinjiang (Waley-Cohen, 1991). The Chinese ranked banishment second only to death as the most serious punishment they could impose. Eventually, the Chinese used banishment as a form of colonization for newly discovered regions. The use of convicts as colonists was also economically expedient, since China could profit from low-cost colonial goods.

Banishment has also been used in recent times (Palmer, 1991). In 1993, for instance, two Everett, Washington, teenagers, Simon Roberts and Adrian Guthrie, were banished to a desolate Alaska island for several months as their punishment for a 1993 robbery (Associated Press, 1994:A7). Tlingit Indian tribal law governing these youths decreed that banishment should be imposed, and the courts did not intervene to prevent their banishment. The youths were forced to live in one-room cabins heated with wood-burning stoves. They were given shotguns, an ax, a pitchfork, a knife, and some other basic tools to survive off of the land. They ate wild foods supplemented by fish and canned food. The banishment and solitary living were intended to transform them and cause them to feel remorse and regret. Additionally, a milder form of banishment is **parental banishment,** where some parents of delinquent youths have expelled children from their homes more or less permanently (Borgman, 1986). This "Don't come home again!" phenomenon is occurring with increasing frequency.

Transportation. During the post-Reformation period and the next few centuries, England found it practical to export through banishment large numbers of prisoners to their possessions in remote parts of the world. Between 1600 and 1776, England exported thieves, vagrants, political undesirables, and religious dissidents to the American colonies through **transportation,** a form of banishment (Rusche and Kirchheimer, 1939). Although estimates vary, 2,000 or more convicts were transported to the American colonies during this period (Sellin, 1980).

Transportation was either a temporary or permanent removal of an offender from England, coupled with a condition that the offender would never return to England or would not return within a specified time period. When the American colonies separated from British domination, England sought other locations to banish some of their offenders. From 1788 to 1868, over 160,000 prisoners were exiled through banishment or transportation to Australia or Africa for work in labor colonies (American Correctional Association, 1983).

Corporal Punishment. Besides banishment, England and many other countries used *corporal punishments* as sanctions for various offenses. **Corporal punishment** is the infliction of pain on the body by any device or method. Corporal punishment included branding, flogging, dismemberment, stretching on a device known as "the rack," and other forms of mutilation. Pickpockets and thieves often had their hands cut off and adulterers would be branded with the letter "A" on their arms or faces. Perjurers or liars would lose their tongues. Stocks and pillories were also used for the public display of offenders. Stocks and pillories were wooden frames through which one's head and hands would protrude. Offenders would be made to stand in these devices for several days for such obscure offenses as lying or spousal disobedience (Duff and Garland, 1994; Murphy, 1992). Execution was also a common sanction for minor offenses. In the early 1800s, England used the death penalty as punishment for over 200 crimes ranging in seriousness from murder to disturbing the peace (Pike, 1968).

Early penal philosophy stressed punishment for deterrence, retribution, and revenge. Theoretically, potential wrongdoers in France would be deterred from crime if they believed there was a good chance they would be caught and beheaded by the guillotine. Ideally, prospective thieves, robbers, and murderers would be deterred if they knew corporal punishments such as mutilation or death would be inflicted. Convicted offenders suffering corporal tortures would think seriously about the unpleasant consequences if they committed new offenses. In the United States today, capital punishment in two thirds of all states exists, in part as a form of vengeance against those who kill others. While the deterrent value of capital punishment is questionable, the vengeance and retribution functions of the death penalty are undeniable (Haas, 1994).

Enlightenment and Social Reforms

During the 1700s and early 1800s, several French, English, and Italian philosophers and social reformers achieved prominence through their criticisms of corporal punishments. One of the more influential humanitarians was the Frenchman **Montesquieu** (Charles-Louis de Secondat, Baron de La Brède et de Montesquieu, 1689–1755). He was a lawyer, philosopher, and writer whose book, *The Spirit of the Laws*, criticized the French penal code and inhumane punishments suffered by prisoners. Montesquieu believed that punishments should fit the crimes committed and that more humane conditions should be provided for incarcerated offenders (Johnson and Wolfe, 1996).

Another French philosopher and social critic, **Voltaire** (François-Marie Arouet Voltaire, 1694–1778) was appalled by French injustices meted out to criminals. Voltaire believed that judges were capricious in their sentencing practices. Secret trials were conducted and equal protection under the law for citizens was nonexistent. A less influential French encyclopedist and anarchist, Denis Diderot (1713–1784), also campaigned strongly for penal reforms.

English penal philosophy during the late 1700s was influenced by **Jeremy Bentham** (1748–1832). His work, *An Introduction to the Principles and Morals of Legislation*, described a scheme whereby the punishment inflicted would offset the pleasure offenders achieved from their crimes. His hedonistic reasoning was that criminals engage in crime for pleasure. Thus, a utilitarian philosophy would be useful in deterring crime by minimizing or eliminating the pleasures offenders derived from wrongdoing. Criminals would therefore calculate the gains and losses or pleasures and pains associated with criminal conduct. Offenders would be deterred from crime by rational thought, because they would believe that punishment would likely be swift, certain, and painful. Bentham also advocated several reforms and architectural changes that are still used today. He pioneered the "panopticon" or circular design for prisons by which correctional officers may monitor many offenders from one central location (Skolnick, 1995).

The most influential writer of that period was **Cesare Beccaria** (Cesare Bonesana, Marchese di Beccaria, 1738–1794), an Italian jurist and economist. Beccaria developed the **classical school of criminology.** The classical school is a synthesis of penal philosophies that derive largely from Montesquieu and Voltaire. This philosophy assumes that persons are rational beings, act on the basis of reason and intelligence, and are capable of being responsible for their own behavior. Accordingly, punishment should be rational and fitting for whatever crimes are committed. Like Voltaire,

Beccaria was aware of judicial tyranny and injustice and the torturous corporal punishments that included dismemberment, branding, stoning, and crucifixion. His 1764 work, *An Essay on Crimes and Punishments*, contained the basic elements of the classical school (Beirne, 1994), including the following:

1. The best approach to crime is prevention rather than punishment. Prevention is maximized by establishing legal codes which define prohibited behaviors and the punishments for them.
2. Law serves the needs of society rather than enforces moral virtues. Therefore, law should be limited only to the most serious offenses.
3. All persons should be considered innocent until proven guilty.
4. Punishment should be swift and certain, with no regard for offender personalities or social characteristics.
5. Since those who violate the law should be punished, their punishment should be retributive. The degree of retribution should fit the seriousness of the crime.

Several of Beccaria's principles have been incorporated into the present-day jurisprudence of many countries. When his ideas were first suggested, they were considered antithetical toward the existing legal system. Legal rights and privileges were most often extended to those with wealth, property, and political influence, while those without wealth or political power were often denied the same rights. Many of the founders of the U.S. Constitution were influenced by Beccaria's ideas, and the statutory language of some of our current criminal laws reflects Beccaria's thinking (Hirsch, 1992).

While an in-depth discussion of the reasons for the philosophical shift from corporal punishment of offenders toward more humanitarian treatment is beyond the scope of this chapter, several explanations for this shift can be noted briefly. Langbein (1976) indicates there are clear social and economic bases for criminal punishments. Less advanced societies that lack proper facilities to house, feed, clothe, and monitor offenders tend to use corporal punishments, including inflicting pain or mutilation. When societies become more sophisticated and develop the means to house and supervise offenders, shifts occur in the types of punishments offenders receive. Incarceration in these societies is more the rule than the exception. Langbein indicates that the police and courts were often used as instruments of social control by which the wealthy could preserve their wealth and status and isolate themselves from the poor. Since corporal punishments were more often inflicted on the poor rather than on the rich, this unfairness in the administration of justice was sensed by various interest groups and criticized by them.

In this context of social and legal inequality, Beccaria may not have been quite the humanitarian he appeared to be. Some experts have suggested that Beccaria's classical school of criminology advocated equal access to legal rights primarily for the purpose of controlling citizen unrest and preventing revolution (Krisberg, 1975). Interestingly, the radical school of criminology and penology argues that basic inequalities continue today just as they existed during the time of Beccaria, and for many of the same reasons (Beirne, 1994; Norrie, 1991). The radical view is that economic and political groups create laws that perpetuate their possession of wealth and property and preserve the socioeconomic status quo.

Regardless of their motives, Beccaria and Voltaire were instrumental in shaping the future correctional policies and philosophies of several countries including the United States. Also influential in bringing about major correctional changes were religious groups such as the Quakers. Additionally, corporal punishments had failed to reduce crime or to deter offenders from committing new offenses (Johnson and Wolfe, 1996; Norrie, 1991).

THE HISTORY OF CORRECTIONS IN THE UNITED STATES

There are several uniquely American innovations associated with corrections in the United States. However, many U.S. penal practices were also derived from procedures and policies developed by other countries. The system of punishments used during the American colonial period was patterned after English penal methods, largely because most colonists emigrated from England and continued those punishment practices most familiar to them. However, there were several important differences. England continued to execute large numbers of misfits and political and religious nonconformists because of their labor supply excesses, whereas the American colonies reserved execution only for the most serious offenses. The colonists perpetuated the pillory, flogging, mutilations, branding, and even banishment (to the West known as "the wilderness") as corporal solutions to crime and as sanctions for other forms of deviant behavior. Banishment to the Western territories meant almost certain death at the hands of hostile Indians who dominated these territories and were intolerant of intruders.

A comprehensive description of corporal punishments used by the early American colonists has been provided by Earle (1969). One punishment was the **ducking stool**, whereby offenders were placed in a chair at the end of a long lever and dunked in a nearby pond until they almost drowned. These offenders were often town gossips or wife beaters. Branding irons were also used to brand both serious criminals and petty offenders. Thieves were branded with a "T," while drunkards were branded with a "D."

These punishments continued to be used in the colonies until the Quaker and founder of Pennsylvania, **William Penn,** commenced several correctional reforms in 1682. Under the **"Great Law of Pennsylvania,"** Penn abolished corporal punishments and gradually introduced fines and incarceration in facilities known as jails, named after their **gaol** (pronounced "jail") British counterparts. Penn commissioned each county in Pennsylvania to establish jails to accommodate offenders. Local constables or sheriffs were appointed to administer these county jails.

The "sheriff" concept emerged in the aftermath of the Norman Conquest, the conquest of England by the Normans in 1066. William the Conqueror introduced the feudal system that lasted for several centuries. During this period, England counties known as "shires" were administered by "reeves" or political appointees. Reeves collected the taxes, kept the peace, and operated gaols on behalf of the king. In effect, each "shire" had a "reeve" or peace officer, and eventually these terms combined into "sheriff" (shire-reeve). Today the sheriff designation denotes the chief law enforcement officer of many U.S. counties in different states.

Penn's ideas about correctional reform were unpopular with Pennsylvanians, and when Penn died in 1718, his colony quickly reverted to corporal punishment. Pillories were reestablished, floggings and lashings were reinstituted, and other corporal punishments were reintroduced. Every colony practiced these punishment methods for many decades preceding the Revolutionary War.

Adamson (1984) divides penal developments in the United States after 1790 into six distinct periods:

1. Postrevolutionary period, 1790–1812
2. Recession following the war of 1812
3. Jacksonian period, 1812–1837
4. Mid-century period, 1837–1860
5. Postbellum South, 1865–1890
6. Industrial Northeast, 1865–1914

These periods coincide with U.S. economic, political, and social conditions and trends. Prison policies were often modified as the demand for cheap labor increased. In fact, many early jails and prisons in the United States were designed to exploit prisoners and secure forced slave labor. Profits from prison labor often were diverted to wealthy interests in the private sector. Prisoners were given sufficient food for survival and strength to produce goods for others.

An example of private profiteering from prison labor is North Carolina's state prison operations during the period 1741–1868 (Hawkins, 1984). Private business interests were largely in control of North Carolina inmates, because both state and local governments attempted to evade the responsibility for their confinement and maintenance. From the end of the Civil War to 1933, the responsibility for containing North Carolina's inmate population gradually shifted from private enterprises to state legislature-approved operations, although prison labor continued to be exploited by North Carolina as a revenue source (Hawkins, 1984). However, North Carolina was not alone in its prison exploitation of inmate labor. Oklahoma and Louisiana were two of several other states that had histories of exploiting prisoner labor, not only for greater revenue, but also for political patronage (Conley, 1982).

At the federal level, offender sentences in early U.S. district courts were served in their entirety. Early release from prison was unknown.

However, between 1790 and 1815, the federal inmate population escalated, and prison officials were faced with a dilemma that continues to be the most serious corrections problem—overcrowding. Soon, federal district judges were permitting prison administrators to grant prisoners early release or parole, simply to make room for new and more serious prisoners. Sometimes prison administrators made these decisions on their own without court approval. State prisons and local jails were both experiencing overcrowding problems during this period, despite the fact that by 1840, the national inmate population was only 4,000. Thirty years later in 1870, the national inmate population had grown to 33,000, which meant that there were about 83 inmates for every 100,000 persons in the United States. Prison and jail construction had not paralleled the growing inmate population.

In 1870, the **National Prison Association** was founded. **Rutherford B. Hayes** (a later U.S. president) was selected as its first president. During the next few years, its name was changed to the **American Prison Association.** As its membership increased, it was eventually renamed the **American Correctional Association** (ACA) in 1954 (American Correctional Association, 1983). By early 1997, the ACA had a membership of over 20,600 members, more than double the 9,000 members enrolled a decade earlier in 1987 (American Correctional Association, 1996a; telephone communication, November 1996). These members represent a cross-section of many corrections-related professions including correctional officers, teachers, prison and jail administrators, probation/parole officers, and court personnel. When originally formulated, the goals of the ACA were to (1) provide technical assistance to correctional institutions, (2) provide training and publications to any interested agency, (3) work toward establishing a national correctional philosophy, and (4) design and implement high correctional standards and services (American Correctional Association, 1983). These remain ACA goals.

Probation and parole were established as nonincarcerative strategies for managing offenders during the early 1800s. Evidence of the early use of parole is found in the 1820s, while probation was used informally during the 1830s in selected jurisdictions. By 1944, all states had parole. **Parole** is the early release of inmates from incarcerative sentences that were originally imposed by judges. This decision is usually, though not always, made by parole boards consisting of prison administrators, other correctional personnel, and prison psychiatrists or group counselors. Probation is a sentence in lieu of incarceration. Offenders are assigned to probation officers or to community programs in which they must comply with several stringent conditions. Probationers are responsible to judges for their conduct during their probation period, while parolees are accountable to the parole boards.

Several authorities have contended that corrections is at a "crossroads" today (Martinson, 1976; McShane and Williams, 1996; Welch, 1995). Rising crime rates together with numerous correctional experiments have led some experts to conclude that "nothing works" (Martinson, 1974). The late

Robert Martinson (1976) noted caustically that the history of corrections is a graveyard of abandoned fads. His own disenchantment with the current state of the art in corrections has generated much debate among correctional professionals and others about the proper role of corrections in the United States. To understand the debate and why it persists, several contrasting and often competing correctional philosophies must be examined.

CORRECTIONAL FUNCTIONS AND GOALS

Most authorities agree that corrections oversees the punishment of criminals. However, disagreement persists about *how* and *why* offenders should be punished. Several functions of corrections have been identified. These include (1) retribution, (2) deterrence and prevention, (3) incapacitation or isolation, (4) rehabilitation, (5) reintegration, and (6) control.

Retribution

Retribution or revenge is probably the oldest goal of corrections. It is rooted in the ancient doctrine of *lex talionis* or an "eye for an eye and a tooth for a tooth" (Packer, 1968:37–38). Retribution means "getting even." The death penalty is the ultimate retribution, and it has been used in many countries as retribution for serious crimes such as murder and kidnapping. As we have seen in nineteenth-century England, many less serious offenses such as theft and burglary were punishable by death (Duff and Garland, 1994).

Corporal punishments practiced by England and the American colonies were based on retribution. Among Beccaria's complaints about the legal system was that punishments imposed for crimes often far exceeded the seriousness of them. The major character in the novel *Les Miserables* was sentenced to twenty years of hard labor for stealing a loaf of bread to feed his starving family. This and other fictional portrayals of punishments in the 1700s and 1800s were real reflections of life in those times.

Today, the **retributionist philosophy** is apparent in the sentencing practices of U.S. courts, decisions of state legislatures, and rules and regulations of various correctional programs. Restitution, fines, and victim compensation for losses, pain, and suffering resulting from crimes are common punishments in many jurisdictions (Duff and Garland, 1994). Offenders are required to perform hundreds of hours of public service as restitution to the state in partial payment for the losses resulting from their crimes. Although it is not invoked on a large scale, the death penalty is used in many states as the punishment for first-degree murder. The Florida execution of serial murderer Ted Bundy in January 1989 was hailed by many of the families of his victims as "just" punishment. However, other relatives of his victims were opposed to death as a punishment for Bundy on any grounds. Thus, there is considerable disagreement about whether this punishment form should be used as a retributive criminal sanction (Bedau, 1992; Haas, 1994; Murphy, 1992).

BOX 1.1 Chain Gangs for Women?

The Case of Sheriff Joe Arpaio

If you don't know about Sheriff Joe Arpaio, Maricopa County (Phoenix), Arizona, by now, you will after this. Sheriff Arpaio plans a female chain gang. Scheduled for September 21, 1996, Maricopa County sheriff's deputies and armed volunteers will be monitoring both male and female chain gangs of prisoners along Phoenix, Arizona, highways.

The idea of chain gangs is certainly not new. However, the use of chain gangs was nonexistent for many decades until Alabama renewed their use in 1995. Since then, Florida and Arizona have followed suit by pioneering the regeneration of chain gangs on their highways.

Chain gangs consist of 15 inmates each, actually chained together at the ankles, that perform various types of work each day along state highways and county roads. Typical chores include picking up trash, painting over graffiti, and breaking rocks. Leg irons hold the chains in place, limiting the movement of any given prisoner. Thus, it is impossible while working on a chain gang for a single prisoner to run away from the rest of the inmates. Armed supervision of inmates discourages inmate fights or other forms of misconduct.

More than a few observers regard Joe Arpaio's actions as "attention-grabbing," and the media have been quick to give considerable coverage to his chain gangs. But Joe "doesn't believe in discrimination in [his] jail system." The sheriff says that "I feel that women should be treated just like men. These women will be placed in the same areas where I place the men, out in the streets of Phoenix where everyone can see them."

Chain gangs are popular with at least some of the inmates. In August 1996, Sheriff Arpaio had 34 volunteers signed up for chain gang duty. According to some inmates, it gets them "outside" doing something, rather than remaining in cramped cells or "tent cities" doing nothing.

Chain gangs in Arizona are also distinctive. Sheriff Arpaio dresses his inmates in traditional black and white striped uniforms. These horizontal stripes set them apart from everyone else and remind us of the 1920s and old movies in which prisoners in stripes were chased by the Keystone Cops.

Are chain gangs unconstitutional? Not according to Sheriff Arpaio. Also, the American Civil Liberties Union has investigated Maricopa County as well as counties in Alabama and Florida where chain gangs are used. Louis Rhodes, state director of the American Civil Liberties Union, said that Sheriff Arpaio likes to come up with "headline-grabbing" gimmicks, and that this is just the latest one. Rhodes says that "[Arpaio's] ideas are basically harmless. They aren't illegal or unconstitutional, [but] they end up wasting a lot of time and taxpayer money."

Sheriff Arpaio has already attracted considerable media attention by banning cigarettes, coffee, and *Playboy* magazines from his Maricopa County Jail. Justice Department officials have said that in the past some of Sheriff Arpaio's officers have been found to use excessive force with certain county inmates, although the sheriff himself says that "I'm not worried about the hits. This is the right thing to do. I want to put them on the streets because I want everybody to see them, especially the prospective criminals."

continued

What do you think of chain gangs? Do you think that public humiliation of the type this sort of chain gang activity inspires is a deterrent to potential criminals? Why or why not? Would you favor the use of chain gangs in your own state? If you were a criminal, would you want to be placed on a chain gang?

Source: Adapted from Associated Press, "Chain Gang Women: Nation's Toughest Sheriff to Put Nation's First Female Chain Gang to Work." *Minot (N.D.) Daily News*, August 26, 1996:A1, A5.

Deterrence and Prevention

Another goal of punishment is **deterrence.** The rationale underlying deterrence is that if punishment is sufficiently severe enough for crimes, offenders will be deterred from committing those crimes. Thus, **prevention** is a major concomitant of deterrence. However, extensive research on the severity of punishment as a deterrent to crime has been disappointing. Nothing seems to deter offenders from committing crimes, not even capital punishment (Clear, 1994; Walker, 1989). Both incarcerative and nonincarcerative correctional strategies have been found ineffective for reducing crime in most U.S. jurisdictions (Sigler and Lamb, 1995). Evidence for this view is found in rising crime rates that are disproportionately higher than the corresponding general population increase (Maguire and Pastore, 1996). Furthermore, many criminals who have already been punished for previous offenses continue to commit new crimes (Cavanagh, Boyum, and Nambiar, 1993; Niskanen, 1994).

Incapacitation (Isolation)

Isolating criminals from society through confinement or incarceration is the most direct method of crime prevention (Champion, 1994; Mande, 1992). **Incapacitation** means the restriction of movement or liberty. For many offenders, incapacitation is psychologically painful, and it is seen by the public as a legitimate correctional function (LeClair and Guarino-Ghezzi, 1991). Although public sentiment is difficult to gauge accurately by any poll, some evidence indicates that incapacitating criminals through incarceration is seen as a mechanism for social defense (Palmer, 1992). Containing offenders in prisons and jails means that they cannot harm others or damage their property. Such isolation is viewed as beneficial and as a sound defensive strategy that the public can use to combat crime. However, many criminals remain undetected, unapprehended, and unrestrained. Thus, the defensive value of incarceration may be limited or overrated.

The "maxi-maxi" federal penitentiary at Marion, Illinois, houses the "baddest of the bad" among criminals. Only the most dangerous federal offenders are sent there for confinement. Jack Henry Abbott, twice-convicted murderer and former inmate of Marion, calls the facility "the belly of the beast" (Abbott, 1981). Social and recreational programs are nonexistent and prison officials make no pretense at rehabilitation. Their sole objective is incapacitating dangerous offenders. The philosophy at Marion is to psychologically emasculate inmates by stripping their egos, crushing their insolence, and forcing them to conform to the strictest rules ever implemented in modern American penology (*U.S. News and World Report*, 1987:23). For 23 hours a day, all prisoners are kept in solitary confinement. There is no communal dining, no prison industry, no group recreation, no visiting entertainment, no educational classes, no trustees, no contact visits with relatives, no church services. If prisoners don't like it, tough luck. Their condition is one of "total helplessness" (1987:23).

Some experts contend that incarceration of any kind serves little remedial purpose and offenders frequently emerge from correctional institutions "uncorrected" regardless of the programs they are provided (Martinson, 1974; McShane and Williams, 1996). Although Robert Martinson was one of the more severe critics of American corrections, he mellowed in later years by not entirely abandoning rehabilitation as a valid and useful correctional aim (Martinson and Wilks, 1977).

One explanation for the ineffectiveness of prison programs as rehabilitative tools is that they are coercive and closely linked with the incentive of the early release if prisoners participate in them (Nagel, 1984). Thus, whatever therapeutic value they may hold for inmates is lost through their coercive element. Nagel (1984) says that although incarceration is grave punishment, it does not necessarily follow that punishment is the major business of corrections. In his analysis of the history of U.S. prisons and their role as either instruments of corrections or social revenge, Nagel says that the American people have consistently defined the major priority of prisons as the rehabilitation of offenders rather than revenge. However, in recent years the public may have abandoned the correctional ideal in favor of the more primitive, revenge-oriented correctional aim. This shift has no doubt been stimulated by public disenchantment with the ineffectiveness of prisons and jails in modifying offender behaviors away from antisocial modes toward more socially acceptable conduct. In more than a few U.S. jurisdictions, such as Michigan and California, the continued ineffectiveness of prisons is illustrated by rising rates of recidivism among parolees (Austin, 1989; Michigan Council on Crime and Delinquency, 1993). However, some experts dispute the claim that corrections is generally ineffective as a crime deterrent (Palmer, 1992).

Rehabilitation

Rehabilitation has always been promoted as a key correctional goal. However, the effectiveness of corrections as a rehabilitative medium has been controversial (Wright, 1995). At times, experts are inclined to dismiss the rehabilitative value of prisons, whereas at other times, other experts reaffirm it (Holton, 1995; Wright, 1995). The National Congress on Penitentiary and Reformatory Discipline convened in Cincinnati, Ohio, in 1870, and rehabilitation through reformation was officially recognized as a valid and useful correctional function. However, almost a century earlier, in 1787, the Quakers had established the Philadelphia Society for Alleviating the Miseries of Public Prisons. Although this was private philanthropy, the goals it espoused paralleled closely those of the 1870 National Congress. They considered the main objective of jails and prisons to be reformation, not retribution. Religious instruction in the Quaker faith and elementary education were key elements of the Quaker jail plan.

The **Walnut Street Jail** in Philadelphia mentioned was constructed in 1776 to handle the overflow from the already overcrowded High Street Jail. Primarily through the efforts of the religious reformer and physician **Dr. Benjamin Rush** (1745–1813), the Quakers successfully incorporated their ideas into the organization and operation of the Walnut Street Jail with positive results. Prisoners worked at various tasks by which a portion of their wages was applied to pay for court costs, fines, and inmate maintenance. Gardening was permitted, and inmates grew much of their own fresh fruit and vegetables.

A century later in 1876, the **Elmira Reformatory** in New York was established and administered by **Zebulon Brockway** (1827–1920), an advocate of rehabilitation and reformation. Although historians disagree about the true rehabilitative value of the Elmira Reformatory, it is undisputed that the reformatory movement was greatly stimulated by Brockway and his management philosophy (American Correctional Association, 1983; Pisciotta, 1983). Between 1876 and 1920, a fourth of the states used the Elmira model for their own construction and operation of reformatories. Like Elmira, these institutions emphasized educational training and the cultivation of vocational skills as worthwhile inmate activities to facilitate their eventual rehabilitation and reformation.

During the lawless decades and the Prohibition Era of the 1920s and 1930s, prison populations increased beyond their capacities dramatically. Prison overcrowding has always interfered with the proper administration of educational and vocational programs and the Prohibition Era was no exception. Unable to operate their prison rehabilitative programs effectively, many officials discontinued these programs or offered them on a limited scale to small numbers of prisoners. During the next several decades, the public grew increasingly disenchanted with these rehabilitation programs.

During the 1960s, 1970s, 1980s, and well into the 1990s, changes in sentencing and correctional practices were introduced in an effort to stem the rising tide of crime. The courts were considered too lenient on offenders. Parole was discontinued in several states. Incarcerative punishments were increased for certain types of offenses. Sentencing practices have been modified by state legislatures so that the emphasis today is adjusting punishments to fit crime seriousness. Thus, several of Beccaria's ideas have been revived and applied to contemporary offender sentencing (Beirne, 1994; Hirsch, 1992; Norrie, 1991).

Reintegration

Reintegration as a punishment goal is particularly relevant for offenders who have been incarcerated for long prison terms. Prison life means strict adherence to rules and regulations that are alien to community residents on the "outside." Prisons foster their own subculture among inmates, and this subculture is pervasive and long lasting (Sykes, 1958; Wright, 1995). For some incarcerated offenders, especially those with undiagnosed mental illnesses, the adverse effects of prison life can be critical to their future adjustment. Certain symptoms of mental illness may manifest themselves in ways that cause prison officials to overclassify some mentally ill persons and place them in maximum-security settings in which they will not receive the institutional treatment they deserve (Miller and Metzner, 1994). Such persons may eventually emerge from prison life with impressions of themselves that are much worse than when they were initially confined. Thus, some of the adverse effects of labeling are highlighted in such mental illness cases. One alternative used by some states to counter these adverse labeling effects of prisonization is to reduce for some offenders the average lengths of stays in prison settings (Ball, 1991).

Because the suddenness of freedom is so overwhelming, many inmates find it difficult to adjust to life outside of prison when they are released. The highly regimented and violent milieu of prison environments is so coercive that many parole-eligible inmates are more than a little anxious about the prospect of living with minimal restrictions in community settings (Silberman, 1995). Aiding their transition back to community living are halfway houses (McCarthy and McCarthy, 1997). **Halfway houses** are community-based centers or homes operated either by the government or privately and which are designed to provide housing, food, clothing, job assistance, and counseling to ex-prisoners and others (McCarthy and McCarthy, 1997). Parole officers assume some supervisory responsibility as well, and many of these officers perform networking functions to assist parolees in their community adjustments. Parole officers have become service brokers, whereby contacts between their parolee-clients and various community services are arranged for the parolee's benefit and improvement (Cosgrove, 1994).

Besides the use of direct parole or early release, many prison systems gradually accustom parole-eligible inmates for the outside world through a variety of prerelease programs. Within prisons, inmates have the opportunity to acquire vocational skills and earn academic degrees (Washington State Department of Corrections, 1993). Some of these inmates may be permitted to attend classes at nearby colleges or universities during their last year or so before being paroled (Johnson, McKeown, and James, 1994). Psychological services, vocational and employment counseling, and experiences intended to heighten one's self-awareness and responsibility also contribute to enhancing one's community adjustment prospects (DeBerry, 1994).

Control

Another contemporary goal of corrections is to **control** offenders through intensive supervision or monitoring (Holton, 1995). Every year, large numbers of offenders are released into communities in which intensive supervision programs exist. Some of these programs involve **shock incarceration,** where some offenders are placed in jail for up to 130 days and then placed on probation. The "shock" experience of confinement is intended to acquaint these clients with the undesirability of confinement (Hunter, 1993). While the public is generally skeptical of the value of such programs and naturally apprehensive about having convicted felons roaming their streets freely, the other alternative is increasingly costly incarceration. Society currently lacks the resources and means to lock up all offenders and is reluctant to pay the price of such large-scale incarceration.

The criminal justice process has often been compared to an hydraulic system. As pressure is increased or decreased in one area, other related areas respond to the pressure accordingly. The analogy for corrections is that as more criminals are sentenced to incarceration, jails and prisons cannot possibly contain all of them within constitutionally safe limits. One consequence is that probation and parole officers must assume greater responsibility for supervising the larger numbers of offenders assigned to them (Glaser, 1994; Sharbaro and Keller, 1995). Alleviating some of an officer's supervisory burden are **day reporting centers,** which are considered a part of intermediate sanctions. In Orange County, California, probationers may live at home while on probation, but they must report regularly to a day reporting center where their daily activities are closely monitored by staff (Diggs and Pieper, 1994).

Considerable experimentation has been undertaken in various dimensions of corrections (Montgomery et al., 1994; Palumbo and Petersen, 1994). This experimentation has often involved different programs with diverse components or elements, varying the levels of supervision or control over offenders, and a variety of other control strategies (Cronin, 1994; Sharbaro and Keller, 1995). In the 1990s, more intensive supervised probation programs and boot camps for more youthful offenders have been promoted strongly as viable interventions that have the best chance of deterring offenders and reducing recidivism (Burns and Vito, 1995; Glaser, 1994; Polsky and Fast, 1993; Poole and Slavick, 1995). Programs that attempt to equip clients with useful skills to make them more employable also are positively viewed by experts (Leiber and Mawhorr, 1995; Sametz, Ahren, and Yuan, 1994). However, some experts caution that despite this considerable experimentation and programming to rehabilitate, control, and reintegrate offenders, the growth of corrections has not been particularly beneficial either socially or economically (Clear, 1994). The effectiveness of correctional programs and program evaluation generally is difficult to assess because vast differences in program planning and implementation make outcome assessment either premature or unreliable or both (Clear, 1994; Palumbo and Petersen, 1994; Palmer, 1995).

SOME CORRECTIONAL MODELS

The functions of corrections are best understood by examining several competing philosophies of punishment. These philosophies have evolved into *models* and schemes used to construct and operate various correctional programs. A close inspection of any correctional program usually reveals the influence of a particular correctional model. Each model makes different assumptions about criminals and the reasons they become criminals, the logic being that if a specific process exists whereby persons become criminals, then there must be a specific remedy or solution that will counter or reverse this process. Five models are examined. These are (1) the medical or treatment model, (2) the rehabilitation or reform model, (3) the community model, (4) the just deserts or retribution model, and (5) the justice model.

The Medical or Treatment Model

The **medical or treatment model** assumes that criminal behavior is the result of psychological or biological conditions that can be treated. If we accept this premise of the medical model—that criminals are criminals because they have particular biological or psychological conditions or problems—then the identification of cures is vital to remedying these criminal behaviors.

The medical model was officially recognized by the National Prison Association in 1870 through its Declaration of Principles. Moral regeneration of criminals was emphasized through the administration of appropriate treatments. Thus, researchers sought psychiatric and biological solutions. Because it was believed that improved physical health provided a basis for criminal reform, experiments were conducted in which offender diets were controlled. And psychiatrists examined thousands of prisoners, attempting to find significant psychological clues to explain their criminal condition.

One of the most obvious applications of the medical model is for criminals who are also substance abusers. In many of these cases, criminal behavior is triggered by one's need for drugs and thus the money to purchase them. Therefore, if proper medical treatment is applied such that the need for drugs either can be modified chemically, or withdrawn, then the conditions activating the criminal conduct will no longer exist. Unfortunately, many drug abusers who go through drug treatment programs and therapy have high relapse rates (Dawson, 1992). Even use of the medical model to control the spread of AIDS in the Federal Bureau of

Prisons has been hampered by nonmedical factors such as active legal efforts by vested interest groups to protect AIDS patients from public knowledge of their disease (Wilbur, 1991). Thus, the problems of crime attributable to drug abuse or controlling the spread of AIDS among prisoners are not solved as easily as we might think. The medical model does have its limitations.

Group therapy, behavior modification, and counseling have been considered essential tools to effect behavioral changes (Sullivan, 1990). However, because few significant long-range behavioral changes among prisoners have been observed over the years, correctional personnel became disenchanted with the medical model. Popular up until the 1950s, the medical model was eventually replaced by more popular explanations and solutions (Cosgrove, 1994).

The Rehabilitation (Reform) Model

Closely related to the treatment or medical model is the **rehabilitation (reform) model**. This model stresses rehabilitation and reform. Although rehabilitation may be traced to William Penn's work in correctional reform, the most significant support for the rehabilitation orientation came in 1876 from Zebulon Brockway's Elmira Reformatory. Federal recognition of rehabilitation as a major correctional objective did not occur, however, until the Federal Bureau of Prisons was established on May 14, 1930. And though the first federal penitentiary was built in 1895 in Leavenworth, Kansas, it took 35 more years for an official federal prison policy to be devised. The original mandate of the Bureau of Prisons called for rehabilitating federal prisoners through vocational and educational training as well as with the traditional individualized psychological counseling that was associated with the treatment model. In later years, encounter groups, group therapy, and other strategies were incorporated into federal prison operations and policy as alternative rehabilitative methods.

Between 1950 and 1966, more than 100 prison riots occurred in federal and state facilities. In 1993, 21 state systems reported 186 riots; 277 riots were reported in 40 jurisdictions; 402 riots were reported by these same jurisdictions in 1995 (these figures do not include Florida or California, two of the largest inmate population jurisdictions) (Bryan, 1995:2; Taylor, 1996:9–10). These escalating incidents suggest to prison officials that the rehabilitation model is not as effective for reforming prisoners as has been believed.

This model has other weaknesses as well. Similar to the treatment model that preceded it, the rehabilitation model stresses *individual* treatment or reform, and as a result inmate sanctions have often been individualized. This means that those who have committed similar offenses of equal severity might receive radically different rehabilitation or punishment. The inequity of this individualized system is apparent, and in many jurisdictions such inequities in the application of sanctions have been associated with race, ethnicity, gender, or socioeconomic status (Spelman, 1994; Sullivan, 1990)

The Community Model

The **community model** is a relatively new concept based on the correctional goal of inmate reintegration into the community (Duguid, 1992). Sometimes called the *reintegration model,* the community model stresses offender adaptation to the community. The primary strengths of the community model are that offenders are able to reestablish associations with their families and they have the opportunity to work at jobs at which a portion of their wages can be used for victim restitution, payment of fines, and defrayment of program maintenance costs. Furthermore, offenders may participate in psychological therapy or educational and vocational programs designed to improve their work and social skills.

The community correctional model also encourages citizen involvement in offender reintegration (Pitts, 1992). Paraprofessionals often assist probation officers in their paperwork. Community volunteers also assist offenders by performing cleaning and kitchen work. With such community support, offenders have a better chance of adapting to community life. In recent years, operators of community-based offender programs have been keenly aware of the importance of cultivating links with the community, especially with community leaders (McCarthy and McCarthy, 1997).

The "Just Deserts" or Retribution Model

The **just deserts model** or **deserts model** emphasizes punishment that fits the severity of the crime. In this respect, Beccaria's ideas are evident in the development of just deserts as a punishment goal. Offenders should get what they deserve. Therefore, retribution is an important component. The just deserts model dismisses rehabilitation as a major correctional aim. It alleges that offenders ought to receive punishments that are equivalent to the seriousness of their crimes. If rehabilitation occurs during the punishment process, this is not undesirable, but it is also not essential (Glaser, 1994).

Applying the just deserts philosophy, offenders sentenced to prison would be placed in custody levels that fit the seriousness of their crimes. Petty offenders who commit theft or burglary might be sentenced to minimum-security facilities or "honor farms" with few guards and fences. Accordingly, robbers, rapists, and murderers would be placed in maximum-security prisons under close supervision. If offenders are sentenced to probation, their level of supervision would be adjusted to fit their offenses. The more serious the offense, the more intensive the supervision.

The just deserts model has emerged in recent years as a popular alternative to the rehabilitation model that has influenced correctional programs for many decades. Penal and sentencing reforms among jurisdictions are currently consistent with the just deserts approach. Public pressure for applying just deserts in judicial sentencing, including greater severity of penalties imposed, has stimulated the "get tough on crime" movement.

The Justice Model

Like the just deserts model, the **justice model** rejects rehabilitation as the major objective of punishment. By the same token, sentencing disparities for offenders convicted of similar crimes are opposed. A key proponent of the justice model is David Fogel (1975), who argues that all persons should receive equitable treatment under the law. Sentencing disparities attributable to race, ethnic origin, gender, or socioeconomic status should not to be tolerated.

Again, Beccaria's ideas are among the basic assumptions of the justice model. Offenders should be punished for their crimes (just deserts), and these punishments should vary according to the crime's seriousness. An offender's prior record should be considered as an important factor in giving punishment for current offenses. The principle of distributive justice should be the basis for administering punishments, and these punishments should reflect what the community believes is fair punishment (Skolnick, 1995). Everyone is responsible for his or her own conduct. Through rational thought, persons decide whether to commit crimes. Those who decide to commit offenses are blameworthy, and the state must ensure that they are appropriately punished. Deterrence and rehabilitation are not essential. The public deserves to be protected, however, and thus the sanctions imposed should be within constitutionally permissible severity ranges. Punishment guidelines for all criminal offenses should be established and adhered to by the courts (Johnson and Wolfe, 1996; Norrie, 1991).

Fogel (1979, 1981) has endorsed the principle of justice as fairness. Sentencing for crimes should be scaled proportionately according to the crime's seriousness. The justice model is also based on the fundamental concept that sanctions should be influenced by past, proven criminal behavior rather than on predictions of future illegal acts. In this respect, the justice model requires a backward-looking perspective in applying sanctions (Duff and Garland, 1994). Sanctions should be clear, explicit, and highly predictable (Beirne, 1994). This would overcome the indefiniteness associated with rehabilitation-oriented and individually based sentencing schemes currently used by judges in a majority of jurisdictions.

CORRECTIONAL REFORMS

The history of corrections is a history of reforms (Strazzella, 1996). The Quakers sought extensive reforms in Pennsylvania and other colonies in the 1700s and have continued their efforts well into the twentieth century. These reforms were directed at inhumane prison conditions to eliminate and alleviate inmate suffering. Several religious and other philanthropic interests have both engaged in social experiments and instituted innovations.

In his analysis of the history of sentencing reforms in the United States, David Rothman (1983) has described in great detail specific time periods associated with different punishment emphases. During the period 1790 to 1820, the wholesale use of capital punishment was gradually replaced by lengthy incarceration. By 1870 and during the next few decades, offender imprisonment became less popular as rehabilitation and reform gained prominence. During 1900 to 1960, rehabilitation programs dominated the correctional scene, and sentencing patterns were closely identified with and influenced by the idea of rehabilitation as the major correctional objective. In recent years, there has been a major shift toward justice-oriented sentencing schemes. Despite these major reforms in corrections and sentencing, their effectiveness has been debated by experts.

Some observers say that sentencing reform laws were originally conceived to prevent or decrease crime and crime rates and to reduce incarceration rates. However, in most jurisdictions under existing sentencing reforms, crime rates have continued to climb and prison and jail populations have escalated (Wicharaya, 1995). For example, California and many other states have revised their laws to include a "Three Strikes and You're Out!" provision, which means that if offenders commit three or more serious felonies, they will receive mandatory life prison terms. Despite this "get tough" posturing by California and other states, no discernible effect on the crime rates in these jurisdictions has resulted from this new sentencing provision (Benekos and Merlo, 1993).

Quite often, policymakers create sentencing reforms before thinking through their long- range impacts or implications. The results are often disastrous. In many jurisdictions, sentencing reform laws have driven overcrowding in jails and prisons further upward, with little or no meaningful planning about how these inmate population increases can be accommodated (Texas Criminal Justice Policy Council, 1993). Yet other experts say that new sentencing laws are only indirectly responsible for rising inmate populations (Marvell and Moody, 1991).

Some experts have attacked policymakers for promoting changes in sentencing laws for their cosmetic value rather than for any direct crime prevention benefits they might have (Fabelo, 1994; Thomas, 1994). Politicians often take credit for implementing get tough policies so that they appear anti-criminal and tough on crime. But the implemented reforms often create more problems than they resolve (Reitz et al., 1993).

The United States is not unique in making sweeping changes in sentencing policies. Other countries, such as the United Kingdom, Canada, Sweden, and Australia, have implemented similar sentencing reforms. In many instances, these countries have not achieved the desired effects of their sentencing reforms and have abandoned them (Ashworth, 1993).

Present problems of prison and jail overcrowding raise serious questions about policies and reforms that will increase prison and jail inmate

BOX 1.2 Sex, Lies, and Videotape: Richard Speck in Retrospect

The Case of Richard Speck on Candid Camera

Richard Speck died in 1991 of a heart attack. He was 49. He was convicted and sentenced to death for the murders of eight Chicago nurses on July 14, 1966. His death sentence was commuted to life imprisonment following the *Furman v. Georgia* (1972) case. Up until his death, Speck maintained that he did not know he had killed the nurses and that he was under the influence of drug-induced amnesia.

In May 1996, a videotape surfaced that had been made of Richard Speck while he was a prisoner at Stateville Correctional Center in Springfield, Illinois. Why the tape surfaced then is unclear. What is perfectly clear, however, is the fact that Speck is shown on the videotape snorting cocaine and smoking marijuana, having oral and anal sex with other prisoners, and bragging about his murders.

Prison officials were shocked to learn of the videotape's existence. It was obviously made by Speck and some of his friends while confined. Speck admitted that he committed the killings of the nurses. He said to the camera at one point, "If they only knew how much fun I was having in here, they would turn me loose." The tape was more than a minor embarrassment for Illinois corrections officials and raised questions about how closely Speck was monitored while confined. "To use cocaine, smoke marijuana, to have explicit sexual contact with who knows how many people, that's a disaster," said Republican Representative Peter Roskam. "And if that's happening, it doesn't matter what watch it's happening on, that's not what the taxpayers are bargaining for." Although lawmakers do not have the power to prosecute anyone for the videotape, they can investigate and recommend appropriate punitive actions.

Apparently, Speck and two other inmates gained access to an area with video equipment reserved for staff training. The two-hour tape was almost exclusively pornographic, with Richard Speck as the starring attraction. At the time, Speck was serving eight consecutive 50 to 150 year life terms. He had been denied parole on seven previous occasions. He had always maintained that he didn't know that he had committed the murders, since he allegedly was under a drug-induced amnesia at the time. The tape soundly discredits his former contention. He was one of the nation's most notorious serial killers. Speck was a painter while in prison, with the freedom to move about from one prison area to another, without continual supervision.

In view of this latest revelation about Richard Speck, should corrections officials tighten security to disallow persons such as Speck the freedoms he was permitted? Should persons under a sentence of life imprisonment be permitted the degree of freedom Speck was permitted? What safeguards should be taken to prevent such an event in the future?

Source: Adapted from Associated Press, "Prison Video of Speck Using Drugs, Having Sex Surprises Jail Officials." *Minot (N.D.) Daily News*, May 14, 1996:A5.

populations rather than decrease them. Originally intended to reduce sentencing disparities among federal judges, the U.S. Sentencing Commission's guidelines for federal offenders in 1987 and the scheduled abolition of the U.S. Parole Commission have been labeled by some critics as aggravating federal prison overcrowding in future years rather than alleviating the problem (Alschuler, 1989). In 1976, for example, Maine abolished parole. But soon, Maine prisons became overcrowded, and Maine officials had to devise alternative strategies such as good-time adjustments to compensate for an escalating inmate population. Despite the bad luck Maine had with its parole abolition, 10 other jurisdictions since 1976 abolished parole. These include Minnesota (1980), Florida (1983), Federal Bureau of Prisons (1984), Washington (1984), Oregon (1989), Delaware (1990), Kansas (1993), Arizona (1994), North Carolina (1994), and Virginia (1995) (Camp and Camp, 1995a:11).

During the 1990s, architects and correctional officials have been working to devise new schemes for prison construction, organization, and operation. But new prison and jail construction does not solve the overcrowding problem. We fill our jails and prisons as fast as they are built (Keve, 1991; Maguire and Pastore, 1996). This fact has caused criminal justice professionals to examine nonincarcerative alternatives such as community-based programs, especially for those designated as low-risk offenders. Experiments are underway in most states to target the most successful programs for managing growing offender populations (Wooldredge, 1996). While it is presently unknown where these reforms are leading, few critics question the need for them. Considerable disagreement exists among correctional experts over which sentencing systems are best, which nonincarcerative alternatives are most workable and fair to both society and offenders, and how much discretion prosecutors, judges, and corrections officials should have in decisions affecting offender life chances (Griset, 1991; Kalstein, McCornock, and Rosenthal, 1992).

KEY TERMS

American Correctional Association
American Prison Association
Banishment
Beccaria, Cesare
Bentham, Jeremy
Bridewell Workhouse
Brockway, Zebulon
Classical school of criminology
Clients
Cloaca Maxima
Community model
Control
Corporal punishments
Corrections
Day reporting centers
Deterrence
Diversion programs
Ducking stool
Elmira Reformatory
Gaol
"Great Law of Pennsylvania"
Halfway houses

Hayes, Rutherford B.
Incapacitation (isolation)
Indentured servants
Just deserts model
Justice model
Lex talionis
Mamertine Prison
Medical or treatment model
Montesquieu, Charles-Louis de Secondat
National Prison Association
Parental banishment
Parole
Parole officers
Penn, William
Prevention
Probation officers
Reform model
Rehabilitation
Rehabilitation model
Reintegration
Retribution
Retributionist philosophy
Rush, Dr. Benjamin
Shock incarceration
Transportation
Voltaire, François-Marie Arouet
Walnut Street Jail

QUESTIONS FOR REVIEW

1. What is meant by *lex talionis?* What function of corrections seems most closely associated with *lex talionis?*
2. Compare the medical or treatment model with the rehabilitation model. What are some of their respective strengths and weaknesses? Why have these models been criticized in recent years?
3. What is meant by corrections? Are juveniles processed by correctional personnel?
4. What were some significant accomplishments of William Penn and the Quakers?
5. What are four functions of corrections? Which function do you think is the most relevant for our society today? Why do you think this?
6. What is the "just deserts" model? What are some of its characteristics? Why do you think the just deserts model has become more popular than the rehabilitation model?
7. What are the major assumptions and ideas associated with the justice model? How has the justice model influenced our sentencing practices? Give an example.
8. How were Beccaria, Voltaire, and Montesquieu influential in helping to bring about penal reforms?
9. What were four corporal punishments used by American colonists in the 1600s and 1700s? Describe them.
10. What significant events in the 1800s influenced the corrections field and helped to bring about more humanitarian corrections practices and punishment methods?
11. What is the community model and how is it related to offender reintegration?

SUGGESTED READINGS

Conley, John A. *The 1967 President's Crime Commission Report: Its Impact 25 Years Later.* Cincinnati, OH: Anderson Publishing Company, 1994.

Durham, Alexis M., III. *Crisis and Reform: Current Issues in American Punishment.* Boston: Little, Brown and Company, 1994.

Pollock-Byrne, Joycelyn M. *Ethics in Crime and Justice: Dilemmas and Decisions* (2nd ed.). Belmont, CA: Wadsworth Publishing Company, 1994.

Vito, Gennaro F., and Ronald M. Holms. *Criminology: Theory, Research, and Policy.* Belmont, CA: Wadsworth Publishing Company, 1994.

Walker, Samuel. *Sense and Nonsense about Crime and Drugs: A Policy Guide* (3rd ed.). Pacific Grove, CA: Brooks/Cole Publishing Company, 1994.

2

Classifying Offenders and Locating Corrections in the Criminal Justice System

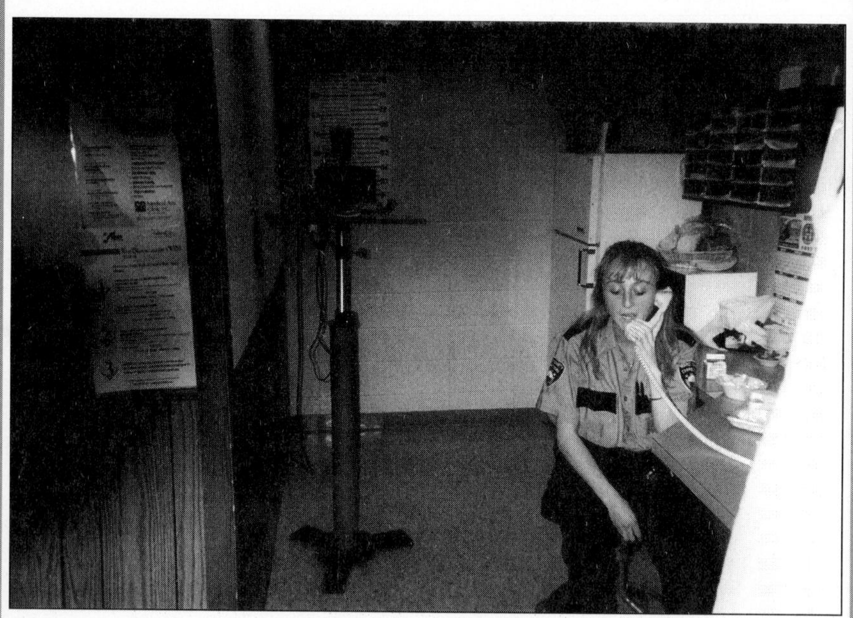

CHAPTER OUTLINE

OVERVIEW

This chapter is about the **criminal justice system** and the role of corrections in it. Major components of the criminal justice system are highlighted. Emphasized is the *interrelatedness* among criminal justice agencies and personnel, given that decisions made in one part of the system influence decisions made in another part of it.

When offenders enter corrections, they are classified in various ways. To understand the nature and purposes of correctional classification, we must first describe the types of offenders who enter corrections. These include traditional offender categorizations such as first-offenders and property and violent offenders. Other offender categories are described, including drug/alcohol dependent offenders, the mentally ill, sex offenders and child sexual abusers, physically handicapped offenders, and those with AIDS and other communicable diseases.

The chapter concludes with a description of the corrections organization at the local, state, and federal levels. Some organizational independence is apparent; however, similar to the criminal justice system, all corrections agencies are intertwined in various ways.

THE CRIMINAL JUSTICE SYSTEM: AN OVERVIEW

The sources of our criminal laws are diverse. The criminal statutes of state and federal jurisdictions are partially rooted in custom. Legislatures enact many of our laws. State supreme courts as well as the U.S. Supreme Court interpret these laws and how they ought to be applied. Sometimes, court interpretations of particular laws may lead to the creation, elimination, or revision of existing laws. Whatever the origins of our criminal laws, an elaborate apparatus exists that oversees their enforcement. Three major criminal justice system components are (1) law enforcement, (2) the prosecution and courts, and (3) corrections. A simplified version of the criminal justice system is shown in Figure 2.1

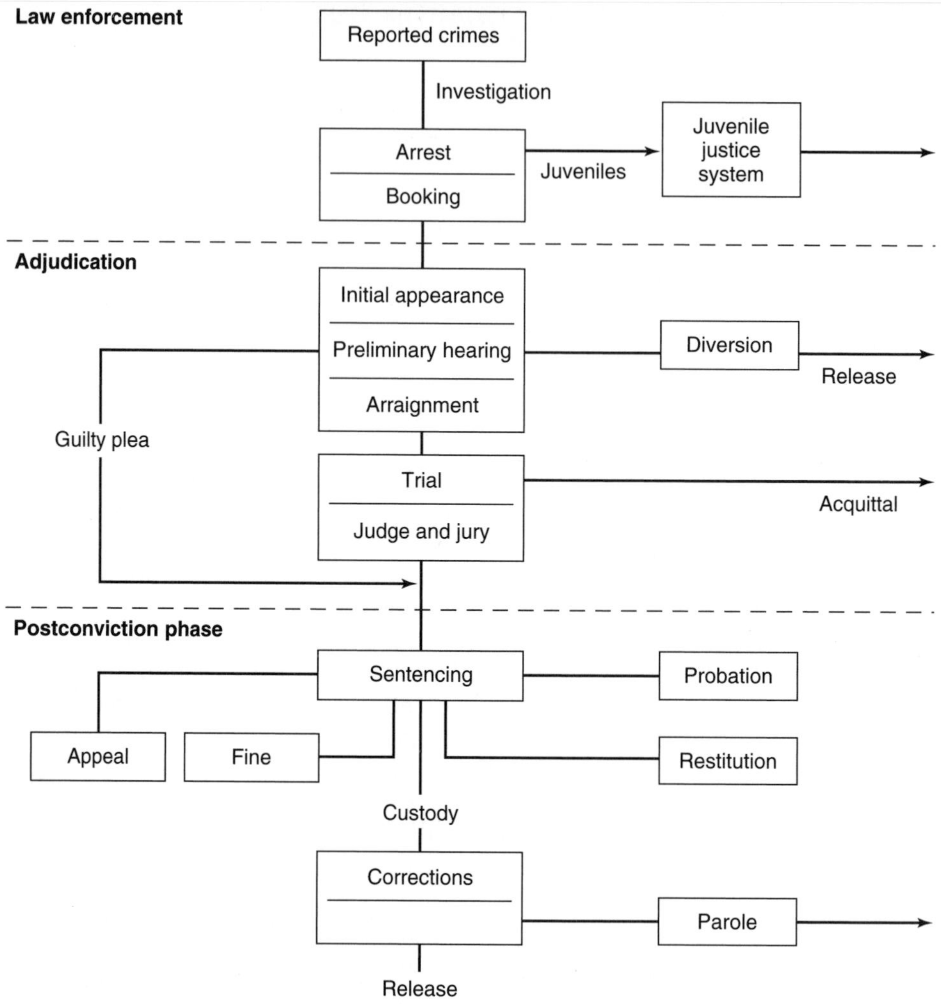

FIGURE 2.1. An overview of the criminal justice system. (*Source:* George Cole, *American System of Justice*. Belmont, CA: Wadsworth Publishing Company.)

Law Enforcement

The largest and most visible component of the criminal justice system is **law enforcement**. Most conspicuous are the uniformed police officers and highway patrol who, among their other responsibilities, issue traffic tickets and citations, respond to neighborhood complaints, settle domestic disputes, investigate reports of crimes, apprehend criminals, and perform myriad other tasks.

In 1993, there were 17,120 local police and sheriff's agencies and departments in the United States (Reaves and Smith, 1996:1). Table 2.1

TABLE 2.1 Employment by State and Local Law Enforcement Agencies in the United States, 1993

Type of Agency	Number of Agencies	Number of Employees: Full-Time: *Total*	Full-Time: *Sworn*	Full-Time: *Civilian*	Part-Time: *Total*	Part-Time: *Sworn*	Part-Time: *Civilian*
Total	17,120	828,435	622,913	205,522	87,875	42,890	44,985
Local police	12,361	474,072	373,554	100,518	58,146	28,186	29,960
Sheriff	3,084	224,236	155,815	68,421	19,660	11,048	8,612
State police	49	76,972	51,874	25,098	845	228	617
Special police	1,626	53,155	41,670	11,485	9,224	3,428	5,796

Note: Special police category includes both state-level and local-level agencies. Consolidated police-sheriff agencies are included under local police category. Data are for the pay period that included June 30, 1993.

Source: Bryan A. Reaves and Pheny Z. Smith, *Sheriff's Departments.* Washington, DC: U.S. Bureau of Justice Statistics, 1996:1.

shows a breakdown of the numbers of police and sheriff's departments by state and type of agency for 1993.

The national average for all cities is 21 officers per 10,000 residents. Geographically, the highest rate of officers to population occurs in the Northeastern states where there are 28 officers per 10,000 residents. The lowest rates occur in the Western states where there are 16 officers per 10,000 inhabitants (Reaves, 1993:7, 1996:1).

All law enforcement officers in the United States are sworn to uphold the law in their respective jurisdictions. **Jurisdictions** are simply areas of authority in which law enforcement officers or judges have the power to make arrests and judgments against criminals (Black, 1990). Jurisdictions are most often geographical territories, although jurisdiction might also refer to the power of a court to hear certain kinds of cases. A separate system of juvenile courts exists that has jurisdiction over juveniles, and juvenile judges are not empowered to decide cases involving serious crimes committed by adults.

Less obtrusive law enforcement agencies include the Federal Bureau of Investigation or FBI, the Bureau of Alcohol, Tobacco, and Firearms, the Drug Enforcement Administration, the Criminal Investigation Division of the Internal Revenue Service, the U.S. Customs Service, the Secret Service, the U.S. Marshals Service, and the Immigration and Naturalization Service, which includes the Border Patrol (Torres, 1985). Police departments and county sheriff's offices vary considerably in their sophistication and size throughout the United States. A small county sheriff's office may consist of one or two deputies, while the New York City Police Department has over 28,000 uniformed officers to police its boroughs. Law enforcement officers in these different jurisdictions also vary in their professional training and in other qualities as well (Maguire and Pastore, 1996:42–43).

Arrest and Booking. When law enforcement officers arrest criminal suspects, these suspects are "processed" by being taken to a local jail or before a magistrate and **booked.** Booking involves photographing suspects, fingerprinting them, and obtaining other personal background data. Arrests are logged in a formal record including the time, place, and circumstances associated with the suspect's apprehension. See Figure 2.1 for an overview of the criminal justice system.

The Prosecution and the Courts

City, county, state, and federal **prosecutors** represent the interests of their jurisdictions. When someone allegedly violates criminal laws and is apprehended, district attorneys or prosecutors examine the facts in the case and decide whether to take further action. Prosecutors consider the strength of evidence, the circumstances of the crime and its seriousness, and the criminal history of defendants in making this decision (Maryland General Assembly Department of Fiscal Services, 1994).

Initial Appearance. Following booking, those suspected of criminal activity are entitled to an **initial appearance** before a judicial official. Those to be charged with major or minor crimes must be brought before a judge or magistrate "without undue delay" so that they may be informed of the criminal charges filed against them. The initial appearance may have been brought about by a grand jury indictment or presentment, a criminal information filed by prosecutors, or from bench **warrants** issued by judges. The purposes of the initial appearance are to advise suspects of their legal rights and the charges against them and to provide them with an opportunity to make provisions for bail.

Bail. Bail is a surety (either a fixed monetary sum or a guarantee of payment from responsible persons or organizations) to obtain the release of a suspect under arrest and to assure the court that the defendant will appear at trial later to face the criminal charges filed. **Bail bondspersons,** who post bail for various suspects, are located near jails. The **bail bond** is a written guarantee from the bonding company that the suspects charged with offenses will appear later to face those charges in court. For minor traffic violations, the bail often equals the fine accompanying the offense. For more serious charges, bail, if granted, is adjusted upward accordingly. In capital cases and exceptional crimes, bail is denied. This is because defendants either pose a danger to themselves or to others or are likely to flee the jurisdiction to avoid prosecution. Persons denied bail are placed in **preventive detention** until their trials begin. They remain incarcerated unless they are acquitted. Preventive detention for both juveniles and adults is constitutional (*Schall v. Martin*, 1984; *United States v. Salerno*, 1987).

Preliminary Hearing or Examination. For especially serious crimes, a **preliminary hearing** or **examination** is held. The purpose of these hearings is to establish whether there is probable cause to continue cases against defendants and bring them to trial. The preliminary hearing does not establish one's guilt, but rather, the government is obliged to show probable cause that a crime was committed and the defendant committed it. Thus, some evidence is presented to convince judges or magistrates that reasonable cause exists to pursue the case. A defendant may decide to waive the preliminary hearing. If this is done or if the preliminary hearing is held and probable cause is established, the next stage is the arraignment.

Arraignment. An arraignment is held within a short time after the preliminary hearing. The **arraignment** is a formal proceeding by which (1) the formal charges against defendants are stated, (2) defendants enter a plea to the charges, and, (3) depending upon the plea, a trial date is determined.

Suspects who plead guilty to criminal charges save the government a lot of time and the expense of conducting a trial to determine their guilt. Over 90 percent of all criminal convictions for both minor and major offenses are obtained through guilty pleas entered at or near the time of arraignment (Lanier and Miller, 1995). Usually, the prosecution has engaged in **plea bargaining** with the accused. A plea bargain is a negotiation between the prosecution and defendant (as well as the defendant's attorney) in which the state desires a guilty plea in exchange for some prosecutorial concession. This concession may be a recommendation for leniency from the judge, a reduction of more serious charges to lesser ones, or an offer to place offenders on probation rather than incarcerate them. A plea of "not guilty" usually leads to a trial to determine the guilt of the accused.

Trial. Trials are adversarial proceedings during which a judicial examination and determination of facts may be made by either a judge or jury (Black, 1990:1504–1505). Depending upon the seriousness of the charges and the possible penalties if the defendant is convicted, the trial may be conducted by the judge or a jury may be impaneled. Trials in which one's guilt is determined by the judge are **bench trials** or trials by the bench (judge). If defendants request a jury to determine their guilt rather than rely on the judge's decision, a **jury trial** is conducted. Jury trials originated in early England in 1220 (Cockburn and Green, 1988).

There are approximately 90,000 criminal trials by jury conducted in the United States annually (Maguire and Pastore, 1996:497–499). This is about one fifth the number of *all* jury trials annually. If the defendant is entitled to a jury trial based on the seriousness of the offense(s) alleged but wishes the judge to hear and decide the case, the right to trial by jury may be *waived voluntarily.* In 1992, for instance, there were 820,662 felony convictions in state courts due to plea bargaining. This accounted for 92 percent of all state court felony convictions (Maguire and Pastore, 1996:497). The remaining 8 percent of the felony convictions were from jury trials (37,593) and bench trials (35,376).

Juries consist of one's peers in the community, but investigators have shown biases in jury composition attributable to race, gender, and socioeconomic status (Golash, 1992; Ogletree, 1994). A "screening" process is ordinarily conducted in all jurisdictions whereby both the prosecution and defense are permitted to excuse certain persons from serving on the jury for various reasons (Iowa Equality in the Courts Task Force, 1993). Sometimes judges permit the adversaries to question prospective jury members about their biases and prejudices about the case and the defendant. Prospective jurors may be *challenged* for cause if they demonstrate bias either for or against the defendant or if they are related by blood to the accused. Relatives of the judge, law enforcement officials, and other persons closely related to the case are likewise excused from serving on juries (Middendorf and Luginbuhl, 1995).

The trial consists of evidence and arguments presented by the prosecution and defense that are used to persuade juries or judges concerning the guilt or innocence of the defendant. Evidence is presented, witnesses are called, and many questions are asked with the ultimate aim of discovering the truth about the crime and the defendant's relation to it.

Trials vary in their length and complexity. The evidence presented, as well as the witnesses, may be challenged or questioned. Witnesses called by one side are cross-examined by the other side. The judge or jury must decide about the credibility of the evidence presented and the truthfulness of each witness who testifies. If the verdict is "not guilty," the defendant is discharged and exits the criminal justice system. If the prosecutor proves the guilt of the defendant beyond a reasonable doubt, the judge or jury returns a "guilty" verdict. When defendants are convicted, they are sentenced and are turned over to corrections for further processing and punishment (Babcock et al., 1993).

Corrections

A finding of guilt means that a sentence must be imposed by the judge. Each criminal statute carries maximum penalties of incarceration and fines, and judges may impose these maximum sentences if they decide to do so. Judges exercise discretion in sentencing at local, state, and federal levels. However, maximum penalties provided by law are seldom invoked. Judges take into account mitigating and aggravating circumstances when determining offender sentences. Mitigating circumstances lessen the punishment imposed. Age may be a mitigating factor. Punishment is often lessened for especially young or especially old offenders. Whether defendants cooperated with police, whether no physical harm was inflicted on one or more victims, and their mental status are additional mitigating factors or circumstances. Aggravating circumstances include whether serious injury or death resulted from the defendant's actions, whether the offender was on probation or parole at the time the new crime was committed, and whether

BOX 2.1 Sterilization as Drug Use Punishment?

The Case of Cheryl Richard

It happened in Youngstown, Ohio. Cheryl Richard, 24, was found guilty of drug use in a local municipal court. Because Richard was nine months' pregnant with her fourth child, Municipal Court Judge Patrick V. Kerrigan gave her the choice of either serving three months in jail, a $750 fine and two years' probation, or to undergo a sterilization operation by which her fallopian tubes would be tied. In the latter scenario, Richard would still be placed on probation for two years and required to have counseling.

Cheryl Richard elected to have the sterilization operation. The judge said, "I'm not punishing her for her lifestyle, but I'm recognizing she can't seem to break out of crime and drug dependency unless some drastic measures are taken." Richard waived her right to an attorney and pleaded guilty in early February 1995 to two counts of possession of crack-cocaine pipes and one count each of disorderly conduct and possession of marijuana. Richard told Judge Kerrigan that she had used cocaine regularly.

Should sterilization be allowed as a proper punishment for a woman who is pregnant and deliberately uses a drug substance known to harm fetuses? Was the judge right to give her the choice of jail or sterilization? Was the sentencing choice coercive?

Source: Adapted from Associated Press, "Woman Chooses Sterilization Over Jail." *Minot (N.D.) Daily News*, February 12, 1995:A2.

the crime was especially violent. These factors are not inclusive but simply serve to illustrate the sorts of facts judges consider when sentencing offenders (Daly, 1994).

Assisting judges in their evaluations of offenders and in determinations of the most appropriate sentences are probation officers (Lanier and Miller, 1995). These correctional personnel often prepare **presentence investigation reports** containing much valuable information about the offender. Information about their social acquaintances and family stability, income potential, prior record, and other factors is contained in these reports.

A collection of agencies and personnel managing a large and growing offender population, corrections is influenced either directly or indirectly by virtually every other criminal justice system component. This interrelatedness is easily illustrated. When law enforcement officers (e.g., detectives, FBI, Border Patrol, Secret Service) make arrests, they book and confine suspects in jails or other local holding facilities. Depending upon the level of arrest activity of these officers, local jail populations may become quickly overcrowded (Babcock et al., 1993).

Jails also furnish housing for those awaiting trial under preventive detention (Cornelius, 1997). On an average day in California jails, for example, about half of the inmates are being held in pretrial custody. To complicate the jail overcrowding picture even further, some of the inmate overflow from already overcrowded state and federal prisons is boarded in local jails through state and federal contractual arrangements with local jail authorities (Santa Clara County Office of the County Executive Center for Urban Analysis, 1994). In 1994, for instance, Louisiana, Texas, Virginia, West Virginia, Mississippi, New Jersey, Tennessee, and Idaho held more than 10 percent of their prison populations in local jails (Bryan, 1996:1). Many local jails, especially Texas jails, have contracts with other state and federal correctional agencies to house certain numbers of prisoners who cannot otherwise be accommodated by existing prison space (Bryan, 1996:1; Welch, 1990).

Prison inmate populations are affected directly by prosecutorial and judicial actions. An infrequently used statute of many states is an **habitual offender law** or **repeat offender law** that provides mandatory incarceration, often life imprisonment, for those convicted of three or more serious crimes. One reason for its limited use is that it would add immeasurably to existing prison populations if invoked whenever it could be invoked. Prosecutors often use the habitual offender statute to their advantage as a lever to obtain guilty pleas from defendants during the plea bargaining process.

These habitual offender statutes have been given additional credence by the federal government and the passage of the Crime Bill of 1994. One part of this crime bill provides that short-term federal money will be given to states that adopt tougher sentencing policies and provide longer prison terms for offenders. In response, North Dakota and several other states revised their current sentencing practices so that new convicted offenders will have to serve at least 85 percent of their sentences before they can be considered parole-eligible. Previously, prisoners could be considered for parole in North Dakota after serving as little as 25 percent of their maximum sentences. North Dakota was not altogether different from other states in this respect, with Tennessee inmates and those in several other states serving about 29 percent of their maximum sentences (Tennessee Sentencing Commission, 1995). However, inmate overcrowding problems are imminent if North Dakota and other states with these sentencing provisions abide by them. Eventually, these prison populations will exceed their operating capacities. Thus new prison construction will be required to house increasing numbers of convicted felons or the new sentencing law will have to be changed again. This “on again, off again” phenomenon has already occurred, most notably in California.

Some states with similar “get tough” sentencing provisions have incurred immense prison overcrowding problems. In 1994, for example, California enacted a “Three Strikes and You’re Out” sentencing provision that prescribed 25-years-to-life sentences for persons convicted of a third felony (American Correctional Association, 1996b:1). However, on June 20, 1996, the California Supreme Court overruled the "Three Strikes and You're Out" sentencing mandate. The high court ruled that judges who believe the law is too harsh have the authority to impose lighter sentences at their discretion. In 1996 about 14,000 criminal cases in California were affected by the California Supreme Court ruling.

There is considerable sentencing discretion among state and federal judges to impose a wide range of punishments for various offenses. Judges may sentence convicted offenders to either jail or prison or some form of probation. A majority of convicted offenders avoid incarceration, however, because judges attempt to use alternative sanctions whenever possible. Nonincarcerated offenders are managed by probation officers and other probation personnel. Although ideal caseloads for probation officers (the number of offenders that can be properly monitored by any probation officer) range from 25 to 50, many of these officers have caseloads of 200 or more (American Correctional Association, 1994). Because the quality of their contact with probationers is affected directly by their ability to have face-to-face contact with these probationers regularly, probation is often judged unfairly as an ineffective deterrent to crime. Probation departments are often the last in line for additional funding to create new positions to handle larger numbers of offenders. Few agencies or courts consider the negative implications of giving understaffed and underfunded probation departments increasing numbers of persons to supervise (Minnesota Probation Standards Task Force, 1993).

Those who view the criminal justice system as a process rightly note that decision making in one sector of the system does not require the approval or endorsement of other system components (Babcock et al., 1993). Prison officials are far removed from police officers who make arrests and have no input on the level of arrest activity by one police department or another. In addition, prosecutors are not obligated to account to judges and others for why they decline to prosecute certain defendants and persist in prosecuting others. While many judges receive information from local jails and prisons about their ability to accommodate more sentenced offenders before making an incarceration decision, this is an exception to the general lack of coordination between judges and facilities. Ordinarily, little systematic feedback or logical coordination exists between the different parts of the criminal justice system. The inconsistent and often devastating results of this general lack of coordination are well-known and heavily documented (Cromwell and Killinger, 1994; Lanier and Miller, 1995; Ray, 1994).

Corrections is the final link in the criminal justice systemic chain and therefore suffers the consequences of all decisions made by other criminal justice organizations, agencies, and individuals, regardless of the rationality of those decisions. This is a difficult burden to bear, because corrections is unilaterally dependent upon other agencies for the size of the offender population it must manage (Gottfredson and Gottfredson, 1988).

TYPES OF OFFENSES

Misdemeanors and Felonies

Crimes are divided into two general categories: *misdemeanors* and *felonies*.

Misdemeanors. Misdemeanors are minor or petty offenses. These offenses carry less severe penalties than major crimes or felonies. Misdemeanor offenses may result in fines and/or incarceration for less than one year. **Misdemeanants,** or those who commit misdemeanors and are incarcerated, usually spend their period of incarceration in a local jail. Examples of misdemeanors include making a false financial statement to obtain credit, prostitution, shoplifting, and trespass.

Felonies. Felonies are major crimes that carry more severe penalties. Usually, statutory penalties associated with felonies are fines and/or incarceration in a state or federal prison for one or more years. Felonies include arson, murder, rape, burglary, robbery, vehicular theft, and aggravated assault. Both misdemeanor and felony convictions create criminal records for offenders. In some jurisdictions, there is a third class of crimes known as **summary offenses.** These are petty crimes and ordinarily carry penalties of fines only. In addition, convictions for these petty offenses will not result in a criminal record. Examples of summary offenses are speeding or dumping litter from an automobile on a public highway.

Each state has a set of criminal statutes different from other states. Acts defined as crimes in one state may not be crimes in other jurisdictions. Because of these interstate differences, it is difficult to apply standard criteria suitable for defining misdemeanor and felony offenses across all states. Furthermore, felony offenders often enter guilty pleas to less serious misdemeanors in exchange for leniency or some other prosecutorial concession (McDonald, 1985). Thus, portrayals of serious crime in the United States will be flawed by this and other technical inaccuracies. Box 2.2 shows eight Index Offenses used annually by the Federal Bureau of Investigation to chart crime trends in the United States. Definitions of these crimes are also provided.

Violent and Property Crimes

Crimes also may be distinguished according to the categories **violent crimes** and **property crimes.** Violent crimes usually involve injury to one or more victims. Violent crimes include robbery, aggravated assault, homicide, and rape. Property crimes are considered nonviolent because their commission does not ordinarily cause physical injuries or death to crime victims. Examples of property crimes are larceny, burglary (of an unoccupied dwelling), and vehicular theft.

BOX 2.2 Definitions of Eight Index Offenses from the Uniform Crime Reports 1996

1. Murder and nonnegligent manslaughter: the willful (nonnegligent) killing of one human being by another.
2. Forcible rape: the carnal knowledge of a female forcibly and against her will.
3. Robbery: taking or attempting to take anything of value from the care, custody, or control of a person or persons by force or threat of force or violence and/or by putting the victim in fear.
4. Aggravated assault: the unlawful attack by one person upon another for the purpose of inflicting severe or aggravating bodily injury.
5. Burglary: the unlawful entry of a structure to commit a felony or theft.
6. Larceny-theft: the unlawful taking, carrying, leading, or riding away of property from the possession or constructive possession of another.
7. Motor vehicle theft: the theft or attempted theft of a motor vehicle.
8. Arson: any willful or malicious burning or attempt to burn, with or without intent to defraud, a dwelling house, public building, motor vehicle or aircraft, or personal property of another.

Source: Federal Bureau of Investigation (1996). *Uniform Crime Reports 1996.* Washington, DC:U.S. Department of Justice, Federal Bureau of Investigation.

The *Uniform Crime Reports* and the *National Crime Victimization Survey*

Two official sources of national crime statistics are the ***Uniform Crime Reports (UCR)*** and the ***National Crime Victimization Survey (NCVS).*** The *UCR* is an annual report of crimes by most law enforcement agencies throughout the United States. City police departments and county sheriff's departments report crime in their jurisdictions to the Federal Bureau of Investigation. The *UCR* previously distinguished between **crimes against the person** and **crimes against property**. These distinctions indicated whether victims were directly involved when the crime was committed. Therefore, a robbery was a crime against the person because one or more victims were involved and had something of value taken from them forcibly. Vehicular theft was a crime against property because thieves usually stole unattended automobiles. Today the *UCR* uses *violent crimes* and *property crimes* for their classifications.

The *NCVS* is a survey of crime reported by crime victims. A random number of people are asked semiannually whether they have been victimized by criminals. From these reports, criminologists and others are able to determine the frequency of different kinds of crime in various jurisdictions. The *NCVS* estimates of the amount of crime in the United States are almost four times the amount of crime reported by the *UCR*. There are several explanations for this difference.

BOX 2.3 1995 Crime Rate Down from 1994

The Case of the Fluctuating Crime Rates: What Do They Mean?

- Rapes decreased almost 18 percent from 432,700 to 354,670
- Robbery fell 14 percent from 1.3 million to 1.1 million
- Assault declined 8 percent, down from 9.1 million to 8.4 million
- Purse snatchings were down 18 percent, from 488,930 to 402,590
- Property crimes dropped by 5.6 percent, from 31 million to 29.3 million

Does all of this mean that crime in the United States is decreasing? Have law enforcement officials made a difference in fighting crime? Is the Crime Bill effective? Yes and no.

During the presidential election campaign in 1996, crime and crime trends were important issues for political candidates. Neither major political party candidate made strong declarations about whether this 1994 to 1995 crime decrease was caused by anticrime legislation, however.

Crime experts say that the decline in the number of violent crimes began in 1992, interrupting a rising trend that had existed since the mid-1980s. Jan Chaiken, Director of the Department of Justice Bureau of Justice Statistics, says that the economy and the aging of the population have done much to account for the crime decrease. Jack Levin at Northeastern University in Boston says that "the baby boomers have matured into their 30s and 40s, that they are mellowing out, perhaps aging gracefully, and they are graduating out of high-risk violence and property crimes into white collar crimes, fraud, and embezzlement."

Jim Fyfe, criminal justice professor at Temple University, says that right now, we are at a point at which there are fewer people in the crime-prone years, ages 16 to 24. But we can expect crime to increase over the next 10 years, because there will be significant increases in the numbers of persons in this age bracket. At the same time, says Fyfe, the better the economy, the less violent we are.

Do you think that crime in the United States has really decreased? Is there much hope for a continuing crime decrease, especially if we anticipate growing numbers of persons in the high-crime age range of 16 to 24? How accurate are Bureau of Justice Statistics figures?

Source: Adapted from Associated Press, "Violent Crime Down 9 Percent Last Year." *Minot (N.D.) Daily News*, September 18, 1996:B6.

The *UCR* and *NCVS* collect different kinds of information about the prevalence of crime in the United States. Neither source is categorically accepted by professionals as the most accurate reflection of the true amount of crime that occurs annually (Wells and Rankin, 1995). Both sources of crime information are flawed by various methodological deficiencies, but they are the best indicators we have about how much crime exists from year to year. For example, the *UCR* is criticized because (1) not all law enforcement agencies report crime regularly to the FBI; (2) different definitions are assigned by different states and localities for essentially the same criminal offenses; (3) a great deal of crime remains unreported; (4) if several crimes are committed by a single offender, only the most serious crime is logged and reported to the FBI for its annual statistical compilation; (5) the number of arrests in various cities and towns may be the result of stringent or lax law enforcement practices, sometimes explained by mandates from mayors or city councilpersons to police commissioners or captains to "do more about crime" during election years; and (6) the number of arrests is not indicative of the number of those actually convicted of crimes. Again, there are varying levels of police enforcement in selected areas, and suspects often are arrested and later released without charges being filed.

The *NCVS* discloses much *unreported* crime (Lohr and Liu, 1994; Wells and Rankin, 1995). When crime victims are interviewed and asked why they do not report certain crimes committed against them to police, they indicate that police won't be able to do anything about it anyway, or that the items stolen weren't worth reporting, or that they believe that police will be apathetic in handling their complaints (U.S. Bureau of Justice Statistics, 1994). In rape cases, many rapes are unreported because the rapist is either a friend, family member, or someone known to the family. Fear of reprisal deters some rape victims from reporting these incidents (Bachman and Taylor, 1994).

Acknowledging these limitations, we can use information from the *UCR* and *NCVS* as crude indicators that are descriptive of crime trends. We also can glean from these statistics a fairly accurate profile of the types of crimes committed in various jurisdictions. While the actual amount of crime in the United States remains unknown, it is likely that both of these sources are *underestimates* rather than *overestimates*. Table 2.2 shows arrest rate trends for Type I offenses between the years 1971 and 1993 based on information supplied to the FBI by local law enforcement agencies (Maguire and Pastore, 1996:395).

The *UCR* displays crime statistics according to Part I and Part II offenses. Part I offenses are **index crimes**, because they are used as barometers of crime trends generally. These index offenses are also exclusively felonies in all jurisdictions—local, state, or federal. Part II offenses may include some felonies, but most are misdemeanors or lesser offenses. Table 2.3 shows the estimated Part I and Part II arrests by offense charged for 1993 as reported to the FBI. The first grouping of offenses in Table 2.3, from murder and nonnegligent manslaughter to arson, represent the Type I offense listing, whereas the remaining offenses shown, ranging from "Other assaults" to "Runaways" are Part II offenses.

Figure 2.2 shows a **crime clock** that illustrates the frequency of different kinds of crime according to some time frame such as seconds or minutes. If we take the total number of robberies or murders in a given year and divide this figure into the total number of days, minutes, or seconds during the year, we will get an idea of how frequently different crimes occur.

Figure 2.2 shows that a violent crime is committed every 17 seconds

TABLE 2.2 Arrest Rates (per 100,000 inhabitants) by Offense, 1971–1993 (rate per 100,000 inhabitants)

	Total Crime Index[a]	Violent Crime[b]	Property Crime[c]	Murder and Non-negligent Manslaughter	Forcible Rape	Robbery	Aggravated Assault	Burglary	Larceny-Theft	Motor Vehicle Theft	Arson
1971	897.1	175.8	721.4	9.4	10.7	65.4	90.3	202.9	434.2	84.2	—
1972	881.5	186.5	695.0	9.4	12.1	68.1	97.0	196.0	423.1	76.0	—
1973	883.4	187.3	696.1	9.3	12.4	65.7	99.9	204.1	415.6	76.4	—
1974	1,098.0	219.7	878.3	10.3	13.3	80.9	115.2	254.1	544.2	80.0	—
1975	1,059.6	206.7	852.9	9.2	12.3	72.4	112.8	250.7	535.1	67.1	—
1976	1,016.8	193.1	823.7	8.0	12.4	62.8	109.8	231.8	528.8	63.1	—
1977	1,039.4	202.7	836.7	9.0	13.5	64.2	116.0	238.1	527.8	70.9	—
1978	1,047.6	215.5	832.2	9.1	13.6	68.3	124.4	234.6	523.6	74.0	—
1979	1,057.2	212.5	844.7	8.9	14.3	63.9	125.4	228.8	536.8	70.2	9.0
1980	1,055.8	214.4	841.4	9.0	14.1	67.0	124.3	230.4	539.8	62.3	8.9
1981	1,070.0	216.8	853.2	9.5	14.0	68.8	124.5	228.4	558.8	57.0	9.0
1982	1,148.9	236.9	912.0	9.9	15.1	73.7	138.2	232.9	612.1	58.0	9.0
1983	1,071.9	221.1	850.8	9.0	15.0	66.8	130.3	207.1	582.5	52.6	8.6
1984	1,019.8	212.5	807.3	7.6	15.8	60.4	128.8	185.9	561.4	51.9	8.2
1985	1,046.5	212.4	834.0	7.8	15.7	59.3	129.6	188.1	580.7	56.9	8.3
1986	1,091.8	234.5	857.3	8.1	15.7	62.6	148.1	189.2	595.6	64.7	7.8
1987	1,120.1	233.8	886.4	8.3	15.5	60.9	149.1	185.3	621.0	72.5	7.5
1988	1,123.5	243.8	879.7	8.6	15.1	58.9	161.2	175.6	615.4	81.0	7.7
1989	1,173.1	268.6	904.4	9.0	15.3	66.9	177.4	178.4	627.3	91.4	7.3
1990	1,203.2	290.7	912.5	9.5	16.0	70.4	194.8	176.3	641.4	87.0	7.7
1991	1,198.8	293.0	905.8	9.8	16.0	73.3	194.0	173.1	639.8	85.1	7.9
1992	1,162.4	300.5	861.9	9.1	15.6	71.9	203.8	168.6	605.5	80.3	7.6
1993	1,131.6	302.9	826.8	9.5	15.2	71.7	206.5	158.0	584.4	78.8	7.5

[a] Includes arson beginning in 1979.
[b] Violent crimes are offenses of murder, forcible rape, robbery, and aggravated assault.
[c] Property crimes are offenses of burglary, larceny-theft, motor vehicle theft, and arson.

Source: U.S. Department of Justice, Federal Bureau of Investigation, *Crime in the United States, 1971,* p. 116; *1972,* p. 120; *1973,* p. 122; *1974,* p. 180; *1975,* p. 180; *1976,* p. 173; *1977,* p. 172; *1978,* p. 186; *1979,* p. 188; *1980,* p. 192; *1981,* p. 163; *1982,* p. 168; *1983,* p. 171; *1984,* p. 164; *1985,* p. 165; *1986,* p. 165; *1987,* p. 165; *1988,* p. 169; *1989,* p. 173; *1990,* p. 175; *1991,* p. 214; *1992,* p. 218; *1993,* p. 218 (Washington, DC: USGPO). Table adapted by SOURCE-BOOK staff.

TABLE 2.3 Estimated Number of Arrests[a] by Offense Charged, United States, 1993

Offense Charged	Arrests
Total[b]	14,036,300
Murder and nonnegligent manslaughter	23,400
Forcible rape	38,420
Robbery	173,620
Aggravated assault	518,670
Burglary	402,700
Larceny-theft	1,476,300
Motor vehicle theft	195,900
Arson	19,400
Violent crime[c]	754,110
Property crime[d]	2,094,300
Total Crime Index[e]	2,848,400
Other assaults	1,144,900
Forgery and counterfeiting	106,900
Fraud	410,700
Embezzlement	12,900
Stolen property; buying, receiving, possessing	158,100
Vandalism	313,000
Weapons; carrying, possessing, etc.	262,300
Prostitution and commercialized vice	97,800
Sex offenses (except forcible rape and prostitution)	104,100
Drug abuse violations	1,126,300
Gambling	17,300
Offenses against family and children	109,100
Driving under the influence	1,524,800
Liquor laws	518,500
Drunkenness	726,600
Disorderly conduct	727,000
Vagrancy	28,200
All other offenses (except traffic)	3,518,700
Suspicion (not included in total)	14,100
Curfew and loitering law violations	100,200
Runaways	180,500

[a] Arrest totals based on all reporting agencies and estimates for unreported areas.
[b] Because of rounding, figures may not add to total.
[c] Violent crimes are offenses of murder, forcible rape, robbery and aggravated assault.
[d] Property crimes are offenses of burglary, larcency-theft, motor vehicle theft, and arson.
[e] Includes arson.

Source: U.S. Department of Justice, Federal Bureau of Investigation, *Crime in the United States, 1993* (Washington, DC: USGPO, 1994), p. 217.

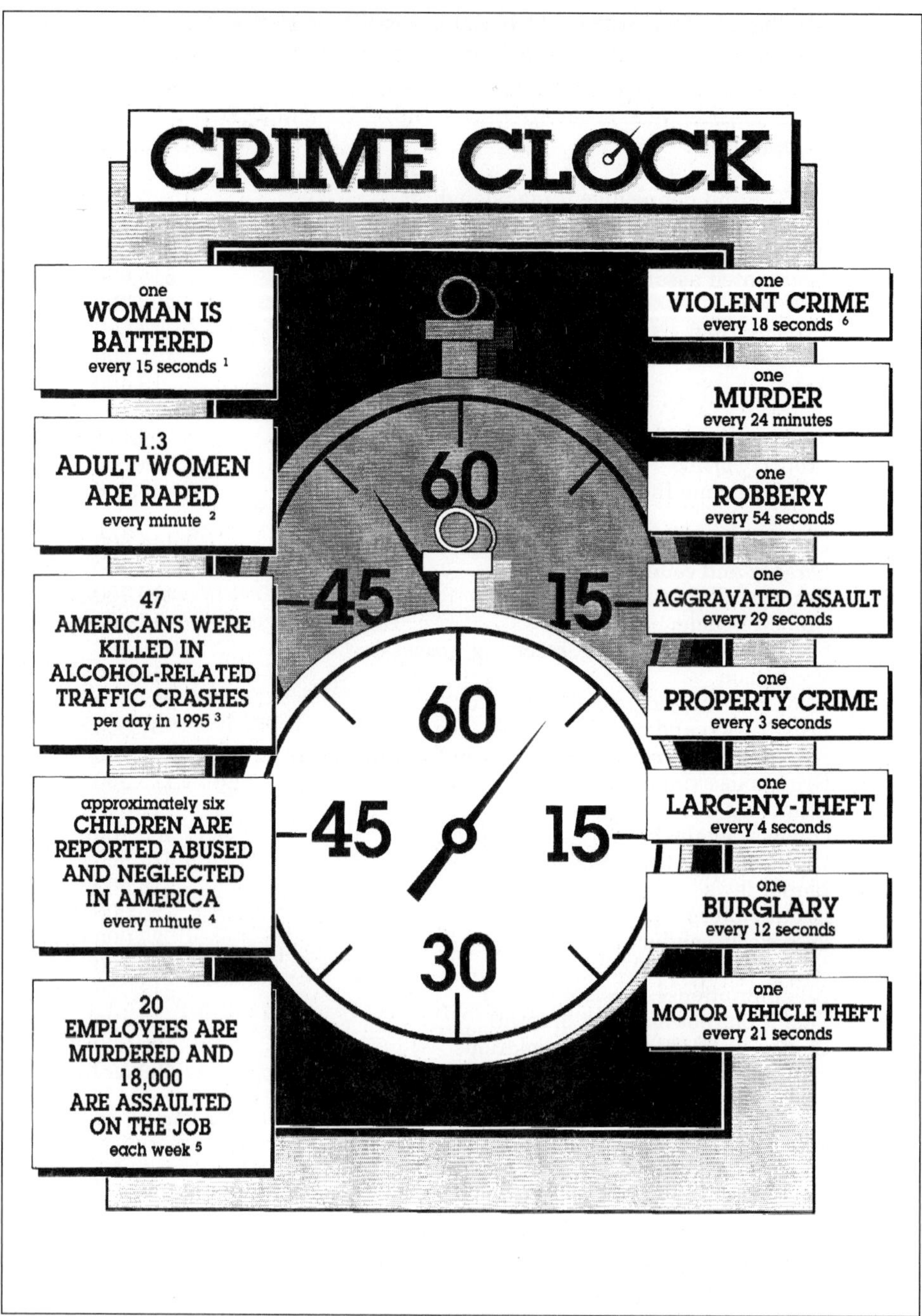
CRIME CLOCK
one
WOMAN IS
BATTERED
every 15 seconds 1
1.3
ADULT WOMEN
ARE RAPED
every minute 2
47
AMERICANS WERE
KILLED IN
ALCOHOL-RELATED
TRAFFIC CRASHES
per day in 1995 3
approximately six
CHILDREN ARE
REPORTED ABUSED
AND NEGLECTED
IN AMERICA
every minute 4
20
EMPLOYEES ARE
MURDERED AND
18,000
ARE ASSAULTED
ON THE JOB
each week 5
60
45
15
30
one
VIOLENT CRIME
every 18 seconds 6
one
MURDER
every 24 minutes
one
ROBBERY
every 54 seconds
one
AGGRAVATED ASSAULT
every 29 seconds
one
PROPERTY CRIME
every 3 seconds
one
LARCENY-THEFT
every 4 seconds
one
BURGLARY
every 12 seconds
one
MOTOR VEHICLE THEFT
every 21 seconds

FIGURE 2.2 Crime clock. (*Source:* Left column, top to bottom: 1. American Medical Association, 1991; 2. National Victim Center and Crime Victims Research and Treatment Center, 1992; 3. Mothers Against Drunk Driving, 1992; 4. Based on National Committee for Prevention of Child Abuse data, 1993; 5. All statistics in the right column are derived from the Federal Bureau of Investigation, 1992. Compiled by the National Victim Center.)

in the United States. This does not mean that Chicago, Illinois, or Miami, Florida, or Minot, North Dakota, or Des Moines, Iowa, are cities in which crimes are committed every 17 seconds. Rather, these figures are *averages of the incidence of crime nationwide* for the entire year. These figures are informative, however, because they permit us to see the incidence of various offenses relative to other offenses. They also permit us to determine crude trends for specific crimes quarterly, annually, or according to some other time standard.

CLASSIFYING OFFENDERS

Classifying offenders is more complex than it appears (Hanson, Steffy, and Gauthier, 1993). Objectively classifying criminals according to their crimes is one way of differentiating between offenders. Felons are in one category, misdemeanants are in another. Further simplified breakdowns are possible where the *UCR's* index offenses such as robbery, larceny, aggravated assault, arson, or burglary are used. Classification schemes are used by prison and jail authorities to decide which **level of custody** is most appropriate for particular prisoners. Placing prisoners in optimum custody levels enables officials to control their institutions more effectively and to regulate the level of inmate violence (McCorkle, Miethe, and Drass, 1995). Psychological inventories such as the **Minnesota Multiphasic Personality Inventory (MMPI)** are often used in assessments of inmate personalities to make more effective placement decisions (Hanson et al., 1993). Such devices are believed to be helpful in predicting an inmate's future adjustment, institutional performance, and postrelease recidivism (Motiuk, Motiuk, and Bonta, 1992).

In recent years, the incidence of AIDS (acquired immune deficiency syndrome) among prisoners has increased (Brien and Harlow, 1995:1). Confirmed AIDS cases in federal and state prisons more than doubled from 1,682 cases in 1991 to 3,765 cases in 1993 (Brien and Harlow, 1995:3). One way of transmitting AIDS is receiving blood from others who have AIDS. Anal intercourse among prisoners is often linked with the transmission of this deadly virus. Semen contains the AIDS virus as well, and oral–genital contact may result in new AIDS victims among inmates. Thus, those diagnosed as having AIDS are often segregated from those who do not test positively for this virus (National Research Council Panel on the Understanding and Control of Violent Behavior, 1990).

Increasing numbers of prison and jail inmates are women (Benson et al., 1995). As more women enter corrections, special problems are created relating to how and where such offenders will be accommodated (Paulus and Dzindolet, 1993). More creative solutions are required as the jail and prison inmate population grows and continues to be more diverse (Kyle, 1995; Perkins, Stephan, and Beck, 1995).

Corrections officials also want to know which offenders should be placed in maximum-security custody and which ones should be confined in minimum-security facilities (Buchanan, Unger, and Whitlow, 1988; Champion, 1994). Certain prisoners pose a physical threat to other prisoners and should be isolated from them (U.S. Bureau of Justice Statistics, 1994). Sometimes prisoners can endanger themselves and are potential suicide risks (Crane, 1992:2). Other prisoners are low risk and are cheaper to supervise, often requiring only minimal supervision by one or two correctional officers (Walters, 1991). Classification is an ongoing process, because offenders are reassessed periodically to determine whether their custody level should be changed or their treatments modified (Marshall, Eccles, and Barbee, 1993). Violent and high-risk offenders continue to be those most frequently targeted for institutional interventions, but we have not devised effective long-term treatment strategies as yet (Serin, 1994).

Traditional Offender Categorizations

Most criminals fit into a limited number of standard classifications used by corrections professionals. These classifications are useful for investigating settings within which criminals are placed, whether those settings are jails, prisons, or probation/parole programs (A. Roberts, 1994). Besides violent and low-risk offenders, two additional classifications include (1) first-offenders and (2) recidivists and career criminals.

First-Offenders. **First-offenders** are those who commit one or more crimes but have no previous history of criminal behavior. There is nothing especially unique about first-offenders. They may commit violent crimes or property crimes. They may be male or female. They may be old or young. They may or may not have records as juvenile delinquents. No useful blanket generalizations can be made about first-offenders other than the fact that they have no previous criminal history. However, even this statement may be inaccurate. For example, a first-offender in Colorado may have a prior record in Utah or California. Additionally, first-offenders may have committed previous crimes and escaped arrest. Depending on the sophistication of the police administration in the jurisdiction in which offenders are arrested, computer checks with other jurisdictions may or may not disclose whether any offender has a prior criminal history.

In 1967, the FBI established the National Crime Information Center (NCIC). The NCIC permitted information sharing among the various states about people wanted for different crimes (Haglund, 1993). The NCIC is also used to locate missing and identified persons (Bell, 1993; Haglund, 1993). Currently, most large urban police departments are connected with NCIC or are linked to other local jurisdictions to share information about wanted criminals. But despite these computer advances, many offenders with prior records are processed annually as first-offenders in certain jurisdictions (Eckstrand, 1993). First-offender status is associated with leniency in sentencing and correctional treatment. If the first-offender is incarcerated, the period of incarceration tends to be shorter than the sentence of a criminal who commits the same crime but has a prior record. Of course, not all first-offenders receive leniency. Those who commit particularly serious or violent crimes such as aggravated rape or murder or who inflict serious injury on victims during the commission of their crimes receive less leniency in treatment by prosecutors and the court.

Those first-offenders who commit only the offense for which they were apprehended and prosecuted and who are unlikely to commit future crimes are called **situational offenders** (Haskell and Yablonsky, 1974). Situational offenders commit serious crimes or petty offenses. Usually the situation creates the unique conditions leading to the criminal act. A heated argument between husband and wife over something trivial may lead to the death of one of the spouses. Serious financial pressures or setbacks may prompt situational offenders to commit robbery or theft. Situational offenders seldom need rehabilitation or counseling, and they respond favorably to authorities whether on probation or incarcerated. Precisely because of the uniqueness of their act and their lack of criminal histories, it is difficult to prescribe treatment for them. Jail and prison officials often consider some of these situational offenders good candidates for early release and believe that they contribute unnecessarily to overcrowding.

Recidivists and Career Criminals. Besides first-offenders and situational criminals, some offenders continue to commit new offenses. Even after they have been apprehended, prosecuted, and incarcerated, a fairly large number of offenders continue their criminal activity when released. Various experts report recidivism rates as high as 70 percent among those who have been granted early release from incarceration in different state prisons (Bowker, 1995; Hanson, Scott, and Steffy, 1995). Although there are disagreements among experts about how this phenomenon ought to be defined, **recidivism** is "the reversion of an individual to criminal behavior after he or she has been convicted of a prior offense, sentenced, and (presumably) corrected" (Maltz, 1984:1).

An extensive analysis of studies of recidivism reveals many usages of the term. Thus, according to Maltz's definition, a **recidivist** is an offender who reverts to criminal behavior after being convicted of a prior offense. However, recidivists may also be (1) parolees who violate one or more terms of their parole and are returned to prison; (2) probationers who violate one or more terms of their probation and are sentenced by the judge to jail or prison; (3) those who fail to complete their rehabilitation or vocational/technical training programs; (4) those who are rearrested for new offenses but not necessarily convicted; (5) those simply "returned to prison"; or (6) those who are convicted of new offenses (Anderson, Gibeau, and D'Amora, 1995; Troia, 1993).

Career criminals are those offenders who earn their living through crime (Reckless, 1961). They go about their criminal activity in much the same way workers or professional individuals engage in their daily work activities. Career criminals often consider their work as a "craft," because they acquire considerable technical skills and competence in the performance of crimes. Reckless (1961) suggests that career criminals expect occasionally to get arrested and convicted as one of the risks of their criminal behavior. The career criminal has been epitomized by Edwin H. Sutherland's description of the professional thief (1972).

Special Types of Offenders

Correctional agencies must manage a wide range of offenders including those with special problems. While the list of special problems offenders may have is extensive, this discussion will be limited to (1) drug/alcohol dependent offenders, (2) mentally ill offenders, (3) sex offenders and child sexual abusers, (4) physically handicapped offenders, and (5) offenders with AIDS and other communicable diseases.

Drug/Alcohol Dependent Offenders. Drug and alcohol abuse is highly correlated with crime (Babcock et al., 1993). In 1992, for instance, a survey of prison inmates revealed that two out of three said that they had used drugs as frequently as once a week or more while committing crimes (Bureau of Justice Assistance, 1992:3). About 40 percent of the inmates arrested for drug offenses reported that they were trying to get money for drugs when they were arrested. Cocaine use, for instance, has increased over the years for both jail and prison inmates. Over 25 percent of all inmates were under some form of drug or alcohol influence when they committed their conviction offenses (Bureau of Justice Assistance, 1992:3).

The Bureau of Justice Assistance reports that over 75 million people in the United States have used drugs in their lifetime. During any given month, 12 million persons have used illicit drugs (Bureau of Justice Assistance, 1992:26). One of the leading causes of correctional program failures is drug and/or alcohol dependencies (Langan, 1994; Zamble and Quinsey, 1991).

Those with drug or alcohol dependencies present several problems to correctional personnel (Morris and Wilkinson, 1995). The most prevalent types of problems linked with drugs and alcohol among inmates involve discipline, aggression, and insubordination (Van Voorhis, 1994). Often, jails are unequipped to handle their withdrawal symptoms, especially if they are confined for long periods (Kratcoski, 1994). The symptoms themselves also are frequently dealt with rather than the social and psychological causes for these dependencies (Morris and Wilkinson, 1995). Thus, when offenders go through an alcohol detoxification program or are treated for drug addiction, they leave the program and are placed back into the same circumstances that originally caused the drug or alcohol dependencies.

The pervasiveness of drug and alcohol problems among jail and prison inmates has caused several national organizations to experiment with a variety of drug/alcohol treatment programs (Kassebaum and Chandler, 1994). These programs have been implemented in all types of correctional facilities (Tunis et al., 1996:i). Available evidence suggests that drug treatment programs currently offered in these correctional facilities can impact recidivism, perceptions of self-efficacy, and mood states such as depression

BOX 2.4 Drug Arrests Up Among College Students

Campus Drug Use Escalating

A report by the *Chronicle of Higher Education* has disclosed that drug use among college students is escalating. Between 1993 and 1994, for instance, there were 6,138 drug violations reported on American college campuses. This is a 23 percent increase over drug use reported for 1992. Between 1992 and 1993, a 34 percent increase in drug use was observed and reported, and a 46 percent increase in drug use among students occurred between 1991 and 1992.

Alcohol consumption and arrests involving underage drinking also increased dramatically during the same periods. In 1994, for instance, there were 15,923 liquor-related offenses reported among college students, an increase of about 5 percent over 1993.

Authorities suggest that the rise in drug use among college students is attributable, in part, to the fact that more private colleges are gaining arrest authority for their campus law enforcement officers. The University of Delaware Public Safety Director and President of the International Association of Campus Law Enforcement Administrators, Douglas F. Tuttle, said that while campuses have had laws in the past forbidding the use of drugs and alcohol among students, officers on many campuses lacked arresting authority. Vested with greater arrest powers, these officers can now function to enforce these laws that were not enforced as rigorously in past years.

Other campus crimes included the following:

19 murders in 1994 compared with 15 in 1993
1,001 forcible sex offenses, up 12 percent from 892
1,375 robberies, up less than 1 percent from 1993
3,049 aggravated assaults, down 3 percent from 3,140
19,172 burglaries, down 7.4 percent from 20,693
6,624 auto thefts, down 8.2 percent from 7,219
Number of weapons violations remained the same, at about 1,500

Source: Adapted from Associated Press, "Report:Drug Arrests Up at Colleges." *Minot (N.D.) Daily News*, April 21, 1996:A2.

and anxiety (Tunis et al., 1996:i). The following list includes some of the drug treatment programs reporting favorable results (Tunis et al., 1996:i–ii):

1. Jail Education and Treatment (JET) Program, Santa Clara County, California
2. Deciding, Educating, Understanding, Counseling and Evaluation (DEUCE) Program, Contra Costa County, California
3. Rebuilding, Educating, Awareness, Counseling, and Hope (REACH) Program, Los Angeles County, California
4. Substance Abuse Intervention Division (SAID) Program, New York City Department of Correction
5. New Beginnings, Westchester County, New York

Jails and prisons do not always insulate inmates from continued drug or alcohol abuses. Some drug treatment programs attempt to integrate community services with offender needs and jail and prison interventions. The Treatment Alternatives to Incarceration Program (TAIP) was designed and initiated in Texas to intervene in the cycle of substance abuse and crime by linking the criminal justice system with the treatment community (Maring and Eisenberg, 1993). The components of this program include screening, assessment and referral to recommend appropriate treatment, and a continuum of services. Those who have participated in the TAIP program have exhibited low rearrest rates (Maring and Eisenberg, 1993).

Because the use of illegal substances is prevalent enough in state and federal prisons, the Federal Bureau of Prisons revised its regulations permitting random urinalyses of high-risk inmates who are known to have been involved with drugs prior to their incarceration. The abuse of drugs is not strictly confined to inmates. It has been found that corrections employees are often about as likely as prisoners to abuse drugs. Most state, local, and federal agencies conduct routine urinalyses to detect and/or deter drug abuse among corrections employees as well as inmates (Ellsworth, 1985:13).

Mentally Ill Offenders. It is estimated that of the 7 million people jailed annually for short periods of incarceration about 600,000 are mentally ill (Judiscak, 1995). On any given day, 86 percent of our nation's jails hold mentally ill individuals for varying periods (Cornelius, 1997:31). The mentally ill exhibit a range of mental problems from psychoses and emotional disruptions to dysfunctions in their abilities to work with or relate to others.

The short-term confinement purpose of jails means that often these facilities are not equipped or prepared to provide adequate or relevant treatment for those inmates with serious mental disorders. Many jail and prison suicides are linked with the mental illnesses of inmates unable to cope with confinement (Camp and Camp, 1995b:61–64). In 1993, for example, suicides among jail inmates were the second leading cause of jail inmate deaths. There were 234 jail inmate suicides (Bureau of Justice Statistics, 1995).

Mentally ill inmates also exhibit a high degree of socially disruptive behavior. This disruptive behavior occurs not only during confinement, but also later when these inmates are discharged (Miller and Metzner, 1994). Such inmates often behave in ways atypical to the general jail/prison population. Because they respond differently to commands, they are unfairly disciplined for alleged insubordination, when in fact their undiagnosed illness is responsible for their peculiar behaviors. In addition to their behavioral peculiarities, mentally ill inmates often cannot deal with the stresses of confinement; they may pose a danger to themselves, other inmates, or jail/prison staff; and their symptoms may worsen if they are untreated (Cornelius, 1997:31).

Further, inadequate staffing makes diagnoses of inmates and their problems difficult. In many jurisdictions, treatment services and programs for mentally retarded offenders have low priority. Mentally ill individuals tend to be incarcerated disproportionately. When in prison, they tend to mask their limitations and are highly susceptible to prison culture and inmate manipulation (Maryland Governor's Office of Justice Administration, 1995). They also are often unresponsive to traditional rehabilitation programs available to other inmates. They present correctional officers with unusual discipline problems that are unlike those of other inmates (Kratcoski, 1994). Advocates for assisting developmentally disabled inmates argue that proper classification systems should be devised to identify them. Furthermore, these individuals need appropriate legal representation along with consideration of dispositional alternatives other than incarceration (Byrne and Taxman, 1994).

Since 1968 a deinstitutionalization movement has occurred in the United States whereby mentally ill offenders are increasingly shifted from institutional to community care (Byrne and Taxman, 1994; Maryland Governor's Office of Justice Administration, 1995). The Americans with Disabilities Act has further stimulated jails and prisons to establish more effective mental health screening mechanisms, so that those with mental disabilities can be evaluated and treated (Cornelius, 1997:32). Psychiatric examinations and screenings are conducted on a regular basis in virtually every state jurisdiction today (Miller and Metzner, 1994). Some follow-up research suggests that while those with psychotic or neurotic symptoms tend to get arrested and jailed more frequently, little evidence exists to indicate that such persons will commit disproportionately greater numbers of violent offenses when released compared with the general jail inmate population (Teplin, Abram, and McClelland, 1994). Teplin and her colleagues say that much of the adverse publicity received by the jailed mentally ill is the result of unwarranted stereotyping. Presently, almost every diagnosed mentally ill offender receives some form of correctional counseling or treatment (Kratcoski, 1994). However, many incarcerated mentally ill persons remain undiagnosed despite our best efforts to identify and classify them (Miller and Metzner, 1994).

Both state and federal court intervention has resulted in several major changes in jail and prison operations and the early detection of those who might be mentally ill. For example, the Mentally Retarded Offender Program was established within the Texas Department of Corrections to identify entering offenders who might have psychological disorders. Offenders diagnosed as mentally retarded or ill are separated from the general prison population and placed in isolated and sheltered units where they can receive appropriate treatment (Texas Criminal Justice Policy Council, 1993). This action by Texas and other jurisdictions is consistent with a U.S. Supreme Court ruling in the case of *Estelle v. Gamble* (1976). This ruling stated that deliberate indifference by prison authorities to serious medical disorders of prisoners violates the Eighth Amendment as *cruel and unusual punishment*. Thus, corrections administrators in Texas and other states have made significant efforts to provide for effective initial

BOX 2.5 Not Guilty by Reason of Insanity

The Case of Reuben Harris

Soon Sin, a New York City 63-year-old seamstress, was standing on a subway platform at the Herald Square subway station in midtown Manhattan one morning. The subway train approached. Suddenly, and without warning, Sin felt herself being catapulted from the platform onto the tracks of the onrushing subway train. She was killed instantly.

Onlookers were horrified at what they had seen. A 44-year-old man, Reuben Harris, had been lurking behind Ms. Sin shortly before the subway train's arrival. Then he pushed her onto the tracks where she was killed. Several pedestrians wrestled Harris to the ground and held him for police.

When Harris was arrested, he was charged with murder. A jury trial followed. Harris's attorney, Harvey Fishbein, entered a plea of insanity on behalf of his client. Fishbein observed that Harris was an escaped mental patient and was not responsible for his actions. Fishbein further claimed that Harris was psychotic and didn't know what he was doing. The prosecution painted Harris as a cold-blooded killer who was very much in possession of his faculties.

Subsequent testimony in court revealed that Harris had been hospitalized on 17 previous occasions for assorted mental problems. When Harris was caught for killing Ms. Sin, he gave police a babbling, childlike confession that was videotaped. The jury was shown the videotaped confession, which showed Harris in a childlike state giving what they felt was a disjointed and babbling confession, as Fishbein had indicated. They viewed the videotape three times before returning a verdict of not guilty by reason of insanity. Harris was placed in a hospital for the criminally insane with the time of his subsequent release unspecified.

Should the insanity plea be permitted in any case involving violence or murder? What burden must the state bear in overcoming an insanity defense once it is raised? Was Harris sane or insane when he killed Ms. Sin? What were Ms. Sin's rights to be protected from persons like Reuben Harris?

Source: Associated Press, "Jury Rules that Man Who Gave Woman Deadly Subway Shove is Insane." *Minot (N.D.) Daily News*, April 12, 1996:A2.

classifications of offenders and to deal with those diagnosed as mentally ill or retarded (Texas Criminal Justice Policy Council, 1993).

Sex Offenders and Child Sexual Abusers. Receiving special emphasis from corrections are **sex offenders,** including child sexual abusers. Some experts classify these offenders the same as criminals who are mentally ill and deserve special services (American Correctional Association, 1995). Because many sex offenses are committed against victims known by the offender as a friend or family member, a large number go unreported to the police. Thus, it is impossible to obtain an accurate picture of the actual number of sex offenders in the United States.

Sex offenders make up about 9 percent of the prison population in the

United States (Lotke, 1996:2). About 20 percent of all state prison inmates have reported victimizing children. More than half of all violent crimes committed against children have involved child victims under the age of 12. Two thirds of all prisoners convicted of rape or sexual assault had committed their crime against a child (Greenfeld, 1996:1). While a majority of child sexual abusers are men, a small but significant number of child sexual abusers are females, and these numbers are growing (Allen, 1991; Allen and Lee, 1992; Wakefield and Underwager, 1991).

Child sexual abusers are adults who involve minors in virtually any kind of sexual activity ranging from intercourse with children to photographing them in lewd poses (Milner, 1992; Milner and Robertson, 1990). Over 3 million cases of general child abuse and neglect were reported in 1993 alone, and the actual number of *unreported* cases is no doubt much higher (Vachss, 1996:5). Although the true amount of child sexual abuse in the United States annually is unknown, it is estimated that at least 3 million children are sexually victimized (Langan and Harlow, 1994; Lloyd, 1992). It is also estimated that 90 percent of all child sexual abuse cases are never prosecuted (B. Smith, 1995; Widom, 1995).

Sex offenders, especially child sexual abusers, pose significant problems for jail and prison authorities. A majority of sex offenders have histories of being abused as children (Milner and Robertson, 1990; Oregon Department of Corrections, 1995; Song and Lieb, 1995). Child sexual abusers are often abused themselves by other inmates when their crimes become known to others. Other sex offenders become the prey of stronger inmates who use these offenders for their own sexual satisfactions. Because of limited resources and space, jail and prison officials cannot segregate these offenders effectively from other inmates.

Evidence suggests that most jurisdictions are imposing harsher sentences on sex offenders of all types. In Oregon, for example, offenders convicted of rape and sodomy averaged 40 months in prison in 1986. In 1992, the average sentences served for such offenders increased to 71 months (Martin and Hutzler, 1994). Furthermore, when Oregon sex offenders are released back into their communities after they have served their sentences or have been paroled, a November, 1993 legislative mandate requires community notification through the *Oregon sex offender community notification law.* Community notification includes door-to-door distribution of flyers, posting of the offender's home, newspaper articles, community meetings, and television or radio announcements (Oregon Department of Corrections, 1995).

In nearby Washington, sex offenders may participate in the **Special Sex Offender Sentencing Alternative Treatment** (SSOSA), which is a community-based treatment program. Between 1985 and 1991, 1,373 adult sex offenders who entered this program were compared with a sample of sex offenders who did not participate in it. Recidivism rates were considerably lower for program participants. The results were favorable (Song and Lieb, 1995).

In other jurisdictions, such as Minnesota, the results of some community-based sex treatment programs have not been as successful. For

BOX 2.6 Child Sex Abuser Wants to Be Castrated

A Case of Preventive Medicine and the Law

Larry Don McQuay, 32, of Rusk, Texas, is not an especially good person. He is a convicted child molester. In 1989 he was convicted of sexually molesting a 6-year-old San Antonio, Texas, boy and has served six years of an eight-year sentence. During his confinement, McQuay has written numerous times to victims' rights groups, warning them that if he were ever released from prison, he would "do it again." Often, he signed his letters "child molesting demon." In a recent letter to others, McQuay said he is "doomed" to strike again and this time, kill. He requested castration!

The Texas Board of Pardons and Paroles has made little comment on McQuay's request. The Chairman of the Board of Pardons and Paroles for Texas, Victor Rodriguez, has said, however, that McQuay's request was considered, but that the state cannot perform this procedure because it is considered "elective surgery." In addition, Texas is barred from making castration a condition of parole.

In the meantime, McQuay has admitted to committing child sexual molestation over 240 times in the past and that these crimes have never been reported or detected. McQuay believes that he will progress to even more violent sexual aggression against boys if he is released without being castrated. The Texas Board of Pardons and Paroles has responded by noting that McQuay can pursue independently his request for castration with various medical agencies if he wishes. Many volunteers have come forward with offers to pay for McQuay's castration, because they don't want him to sexually abuse others.

McQuay was to be placed in a halfway house under "close supervision." However, halfway houses are located in residential areas within communities, and the monitoring capacity of such facilities is extremely limited and closely connected to adequate staffing. It is acknowledged that staff members cannot monitor McQuay or his whereabouts 24 hours a day, however.

Some authorities contend that even if McQuay were to be castrated, he is still left with the physical capacity to do harm to, even kill, young boys if permitted freedom to roam about freely in the community. Therefore, they say, castration will not prevent McQuay from his own predicted violence. Authorities are prevented from acting against McQuay on the basis of his threats that he will probably harm others. Ordinarily, police cannot act unless an overt illegal act is committed or is in the process of being committed. Otherwise, our nation's jails would be overflowing with those making threats against others but who have no intention of following through on those threats. The situation is much like a restraining order in a marital dispute. Parties are supposed to abide by restraining orders, by which one spouse is forbidden by law from seeing or being in the physical presence of the other spouse. However, many deaths and serious injuries have been inflicted on spouses whose other spouses were under restraining orders prohibiting contact. The law can only do so much to protect citizenry.

How should the community respond to McQuay? Should convicted child sexual abusers be castrated or physically altered in some other way so as to remove their propensity to commit sexual violence against children? Should the laws about connecting castration or sterilization to one's probation or parole be changed? How would you deal with McQuay and his request?

Sources: Associated Press, "Texas Delays Release of Convicted Pedophile." *Minot (N.D.) Daily News*, April 3, 1996:A7; Associated Press, "State Wants Molester Castrated." *Minot (N.D.) Daily News*, April 6, 1996:A12.

instance, between 1981 and 1992, the number of child sexual abuse convictions in Minnesota tripled. About 70 sex treatment programs had been established in Minnesota by 1993. Over 2,600 outpatients had been treated by one or more of these programs. About half of all clients did not complete these programs successfully. Program operators suggested that the effectiveness of these programs could be greatly improved by more adequate staffing and client supervision, which was considered less than adequate during experimental periods (Minnesota Program Evaluation Division Office of the Legislative Auditor, 1994). However, psychological counseling and other services for sex offenders are expensive (Watson and Stermac, 1994). Depending upon the regimen, the average cost of treating sex offenders under intensive supervised probation in communities ranges between $5,000 and $15,000 annually (Lotke, 1996:3).

Physically Handicapped Offenders. Those offenders with physical handicaps are a neglected but growing part of the offender population. Some offenders are confined to wheel chairs and, therefore, special facilities must be constructed to accommodate their access to probation or parole offices or community-based sites. Other offenders have hearing or speech impairments that limit them in various ways. For instance, Counselor Kay McGill of the Rehabilitation Services Division of the Georgia Department of Human Resources, has described her role in dealing with certain handicapped parolees (*Georgia Parole Review,* 1990). One of her parolee-clients was described as suffering from tinnitus, an inherited condition involving a constant roaring in one's head and sound that is amplified and unfiltered. The client had difficulty holding a job and suffered from depression and insecurity stemming from his tinnitus condition. McGill arranged for her client to acquire a job that involved working with an electronics program with low noise levels and some isolation. In the general case, the Georgia Rehabilitation Services Division is an agency whose mission is to get its clients functioning at an optimal level so that they may adjust more normally within their communities (*Georgia Parole Review,* 1990:176).

Physically challenged offenders often require greater attention from their parole officers (POs). Acquiring and maintaining employment is sometimes difficult for persons with different types of physical handicaps, such as the parolee-client managed by Kay McGill. Many POs become brokers between their own agencies and community businesses that are encouraged to employ certain clients with special problems. Community volunteers are increasingly helpful to probation and parole agencies with physically handicapped clients.

AIDS: A Growing Problem. **AIDS (acquired immune deficiency syndrome)** is a growing correctional problem (Brien and Harlow, 1995). In 1993 it was estimated that there were 21,538 inmates infected with HIV in U.S. prisons (about 2.4% of the federal and state prison inmates). The actual number of AIDS cases was 3,765 or 0.4 percent, and these cases were doubling about every 8 to 10 months (Brien and Harlow, 1995:1). AIDS is particularly prevalent among jail and prison inmates (Hammett, 1992; Martin and Zimmerman, 1992). Inmates living in close quarters are highly susceptible to the AIDS virus because of the likelihood of anal-genital or oral-genital contact. An examination of 31 large city and county jail systems, 50 correctional departments, and the Federal Bureau of Prisons in 1993 disclosed 3,500 deaths attributable to AIDS (Hammett et al., 1994). Since the mid-1980s, AIDS education in incarcerative settings has been expanded to provide inmates with a greater understanding of the causes and spreading of this disease (Marcus, Amen, and Bibace, 1992).

If AIDS is prevalent and increasing among jail and prison inmates, then it is prevalent and increasing among probationers and parolees as well (Lurigio, Bensinger, and Laszlo, 1990). In view of the various circumstances under which AIDS has been transmitted in recent years, from saliva or blood residue from dentists and others working in different health professions, probation and parole officers have perceived that their risk of being infected with the AIDS virus has increased greatly. Many probationers and parolees are former drug offenders. Drug-dependent clients represent a special danger, because AIDS is known to be easily transmitted when drug addicts share needles used to inject heroin and other substances. Thus, there have been increased efforts to coordinate AIDS treatment between prison and community-based corrections agencies in recent years (Durham, 1994; Luciani et al., 1994).

Within jails and prisons, either voluntary or mandatory AIDS testing has been undertaken. While the U.S. Supreme Court has not ruled definitively on the constitutionality of such mandatory testing, the results of these tests have been favorable in limiting the spread of AIDS in selected jurisdictions (Jacobs, 1995). For correctional officers who must work around inmates with AIDS, there is marked apprehension. A survey of correctional officers has revealed that requiring inmates to undergo AIDS testing would assuage their own feelings while working within a potentially medically dangerous population (Mahaffey and Marcus, 1995). At the same time, educational programs have been or are being established in various jurisdictions for the purposes of enabling correctional officers to learn more about how HIV is transmitted and to dispel some of the myths associated with AIDS (Florida Office of the Auditor General, 1993; Luciani

BOX 2.7 Man Bites Police Officer

The Case of Ronald Riggins

It happened in Gainesville, Florida, in November 1993. Ronald Riggins, 33, was scuffling with police during a 911 response. As Riggins wrestled with police, he bit one of the officers on the finger. After he bit the officer, he looked at the officer, smiled and said, "I have AIDS." The police officers arrested Riggins immediately thereafter and charged him with third-degree attempted murder.

At Riggins's subsequent trial, police testified about his behavior and statements. It turned out that Riggins was indeed HIV-positive and that he had AIDS. The officer bitten by Riggins, Mason Byrd, subsequently was examined by physicians and tested negative for HIV. Byrd told the court, however, that there was considerable anguish during the months following the biting incident and not knowing for certain whether he had been infected with AIDS. "I spent weeks and months wondering if that bullet was going to hit me," said Byrd when interviewed.

Riggins was sentenced to ten years in prison following his third-degree attempted murder conviction. He was also convicted of two felony counts of resisting arrest. He received two five-year sentences to run concurrently with the other ten-year sentence.

Were these sentences proper under the circumstances? Should persons who have deadly diseases be charged with attempted murder if they intentionally attempt to give others these diseases?

Source: Adapted from Associated Press, "HIV-Positive Man Sentenced to 10 Years for Biting Officer." *Minot (N.D.) Daily News*, March 24, 1995:A2.

et al., 1994; Mahaffey and Marcus, 1995). Certainly AIDS education is a major issue in contemporary corrections (Durham, 1994).

CORRECTIONS AND OFFENDER MANAGEMENT

Supervising dangerous offenders doesn't always mean supervising offenders who will endanger others. Sometimes offenders pose dangers to themselves. Some offenders who are mentally ill may pose threats to themselves as well as to others. Many of those released from jails and prisons exhibit signs or characteristics of mental illness and should receive needed treatment from one or more community agencies. However, not all communities have the capacity to deal with these offenders. Mentally ill offenders may engage in self-destructive acts. They may also be unwilling to be referred to a mental health agency for treatment. In Delaware County, Pennsylvania, for instance, a study was conducted to determine the extent to which mentally ill persons of all kinds come to the attention of police. Further, the study explored the response of interested community agencies in meeting these mentally ill offender needs (Bonovitz, 1980). Delaware police department information disclosed that the mentally ill pose a significant problem for police officers. Police officers are faced with having to classify mentally ill persons initially, and then they must determine where these offenders should be taken. It is not always the case that these persons are shuffled back to jails. Rather, community mental health agencies exist to treat these persons in limited ways. The study highlighted serious gaps in the community social services network, at least in Delaware County, Pennsylvania.

Supervising high-risk offenders may pose other risks. Some offender-clients are dangerous and/or have a high likelihood of program failure (Pepino et al., 1993). These persons need closer supervision or monitoring than other offenders on standard probation (Dickey and Wagner, 1990; Lawrence, 1991). Some experts suggest high-risk offender intervention strategies that incorporate accountability and acceptance of responsibility with law internalization and community expectations (Lawrence, 1991).

THE ORGANIZATION OF CORRECTIONS

State Corrections Organizations

State Prison Systems and Departments of Corrections. There is considerable variation among states in their correctional organization and operations. No state is required to follow any federal correctional system or plan, and as a result a mixture of agencies and organizations is found when examining differences among state correctional apparatuses. Two examples of states with similar numbers of correctional officers and probation/parole officers are Utah and Oregon. In 1995, Oregon had 2,088 personnel in their adult correctional system, with 1,091 correctional officers. In contrast, Utah had 1,810 personnel and 938 correctional officers (American Correctional Association, 1996a). Despite these correctional personnel similarities, there are significant differences between the two states regarding numbers of parolees, probationers, and inmates in their correctional facilities.

In 1995, Utah had about half as many prison inmates (3,448) compared with Oregon (7,886). Utah had about a fourth as many convicted offenders on probation compared with Oregon (8,478 compared with 39,725) (American Correctional Association, 1996a). However, Utah had about one fifth of the parolees (2,731) compared with Oregon's parolee population (15,019). One explanation is that Utah has a statute restricting the length of probation terms and limits the use of probation to less serious types of crimes (Maguire and Pastore, 1996). Yet overall, there were 62,630 Oregon inmates, probationers, and parolees under the supervision of 1,091 correctional officers, compared with about a fourth as many inmates, probationers, and parolees (14,657) under the supervision of 938 correctional officers in Utah in 1995 (American Correctional Association, 1996). Despite the lopsided inmate/client-to-correctional officer ratio between Oregon and Utah, Oregon's correctional operating budget was less than twice as large as Utah's, $177 million compared with $107 million in 1995. One interpretation is that Oregon spends considerably less per prisoner/inmate than does Utah.

The correctional organization of the two states also varies in complexity. Oregon has a Department of Corrections that provides correctional services through Institutions. The Department of Human Resources provides juvenile correctional services through the Oregon Youth Authority. Within Institutions, there are 12 correctional facilities including a penitentiary, six correctional institutions, a women's correctional center, two correctional facilities, and a camp. Under Juvenile Services there are two training schools and five correctional camps.

In contrast, Utah has a Department of Corrections that administers five correctional facilities and a women's facility. In addition, there are six regional field offices and six community corrections centers. The Department of Human Services is broken down into a Division of Youth Corrections and a Youth Parole Authority. The Division of Youth Corrections is further subdivided into three regions managing thirteen youth centers and three assessment units. Utah has a youth parole board, whereas Oregon does not. However, there are nearly *four times as many wardens and superintendents* of adult correctional facilities in Utah compared with Oregon.

Oregon has a five full-time member Board of Parole appointed by and answerable to the governor for parole decisions. Utah has a Board of Pardons and Parole consisting of three full-time board members who have full parole, pardon, and commutation authority over all sentenced prisoners. The decision-making authority of Utah board members is autonomous and uninfluenced (American Correctional Association, 1996a:380–387, 461–467). In both state jurisdictions, considerable autonomy and responsibility is given to individual counties for administering detention centers, holdover facilities, and community corrections programs. These responsibilities also include the construction and operation of local jails to house a variety of offenders. Some of these differences between Oregon and Utah are shown in the accompanying list.

These differences suggest that it is difficult to devise an officer-client formula or ratio that can be applied across all state jurisdictions. Compared with Utah and Oregon, Maine has only a Department of Corrections, which administers the Maine State Prison, three adult correctional centers, and a youth center. Maine's Division of Probation and Parole is a part of the Department of Corrections and has six districts. Because Maine abolished parole in 1976, the parole board convenes to hear exclusively the remaining pre-1976 cases. In 1985, there were only four parolees in Maine (Department of Justice, 1996:1–6). More or less elaborate correctional organizations are associated with the remaining states.

Because of the fragmented nature of local and state correctional agencies and organizations, the operation of programs and services frequently suffers. Many state and local correctional agencies make little, if any, effort to coordinate their activities. An absence of effective and efficient planning is more the rule than the exception. It would be misleading to feature the correctional organization and arrangement of one state as an ideal for others to follow. The volume of offenders varies greatly among the different state and local jurisdictions. Types of offenders also vary. However, a careful examination of the correctional organization of various states will tell us much about the centralized or decentralized nature of these organizations.*

	Oregon	Utah
Number of prisoners (1995)	7,886	3,448
Number of probationers (1995)	39,725	8,478
Number of parolees	15,019	2,731
Total prisoners/probationers/parolees	62,630	14,657
Number of correctional officers (1995)	1,091	938
Number of personnel in adult system	2,088	1,810
Board of Pardons and Paroles	Five full-time members appointed by and answerable to governor	Three full-time members who make autonomous decisions
Number of wardens/superintendents for adult facilities	8	29
Penitentiaries	1	1
Correctional centers	11	12
Youth correction facilities	1	1
Youth parole board	Yes	No
Youth paroling authority	No	Yes
Women's correctional facility	1	1
Co-correctional facilities	1	2
Regional offices	1	6
Operating budget	$177,259,424	$107,461,000

In the Oregon and Utah example of correctional organizations, Utah has a more decentralized system, whereas Oregon's correctional agencies are more centralized. The Utah Board of Pardons and Parole can make decisions independent of the intervention of others such as the governor. In contrast, the governor of Oregon can intervene at will and countermand any decision made by the Oregon Board of Parole. This power relation is

*American Correctional Association, 1996a:xiv–xv, xxii, xlii–xliii, xliv–xlv, 380–387, 461–467; Department of Justice, 1996:1–7; Gilliard and Beck, 1996:1–4).

underscored by the fact that the governor may appoint and terminate parole board members at will. *Generally, the greater the decentralization of power relative to offender management, the more difficult it is for effective coordination between organizations to occur.* Table 2.4 illustrates the fragmentation of corrections among the states.

Wyoming is one of the most centralized states, with four major administrative organizations to oversee all correctional operations. The Wyoming Department of Corrections is responsible for the management of all penal institutions. A Division of Field Services operates all probation and parole activities. The Board of Parole recommends sentence commutations to the governor and controls good-time awards. Finally, the Department of Family Services oversees all juvenile functions (American Correctional Association, 1996a:505–506). Most of the other states have decentralized systems, because so many different boards and departments have jurisdictional authority over various facets of their corrections operations.

Federal Corrections

Organizationally, the **U.S. Department of Justice** exercises administrative control over all federal correctional agencies and organizations including (1) the Federal Bureau of Prisons, (2) the U.S. Parole Commission, (3) U.S. courts, and (4) the U.S. Sentencing Commission.

The Federal Bureau of Prisons. The **Federal Bureau of Prisons** (BOP) was established in 1930 by Congress (U.S. Federal Bureau of Prisons, 1993, 1994). By 1995, the BOP operated 71 correctional institutions arranged according to level of custody from maximum-security penitentiaries such as the one at Marion, Illinois, to minimum-security prison camps like Allenwood Federal Prison Camp at Montgomery, Pennsylvania (American Correctional Association, 1996a:508–550).

Organization of Federal Bureau of Prisons

Director (Dr. Kathleen M. Hawk)

Administration Division

(budget development, execution, capacity planning, design and construction, facilities management, finance, management support, procurement and property, site selection and environmental review, trust fund)

Community Corrections and Detention Division

(community corrections, detention services, National Office of Citizen Participation)

Correctional Programs Division

(correctional services, chaplaincy services, psychology services, correctional programs, inmate systems management)

TABLE 2.4 Probation/Parole/Aftercare Service Providers (as of June 30, 1994)

	Number Board Members[a]	Adult Paroling Authorities	Adult Parole Services	Adult Probation Services	Juvenile Parole/Aftercare Services	Juvenile Probation Services
AL	3	Bd Pardons & Paroles	Bd Pardons & Paroles	Bd Pardons & Paroles	Co Counts	Dept Youth Svcs ($ only) & Co Cts
AK	5 (PT)	Bd Parole	Dept Corrections	Dept Corrections	No parole/aftercare	DHSS/Div Family & Youth Svcs[b]
AZ	7	Bd of Exec Clemency	Bd of Exec Clemency	State Courts	DYTR/Parole Admin	State Courts
AR	7 (PT)[1]	Post-Prison Transfer Board	Bd C&Cmty Pun/Dept Cmty Pun[b]	Bd C&Cmty Pun/Dept Cmty Pun[b]	Courts/DHS/Youth Svcs Bd	Courts/DHS/Youth Svcs Bd
CA	9	Bd Prison Terms	YAC/DOC/Par & Cmty Svcs Div	Co Courts	YAC/DYA/Parole Svcs & Cmty Corr	Co Courts
CO	7	Bd Parole	DOC/Div Adult Parole Supv	Judicial Dept	DHS/Div Youth Svcs	Judicial Dept
CT	11 (PT)[2]	Bd Parole	DOC/Div Op/Cmty Svcs	Office Adult Prob	Dept Children & Families	Superior Court Juv Matters/ Family Div
DE	5 (PT)[2]	Bd Parole	DOC/Div Cmty Svcs	DOC/Div Cmty Svcs	DSCYF/Div Youth Rehab/Cmty Svcs[b]	DSCYF/Div Youth Rehab/Cmty Svcs[b]
DC	5	Bd Parole	Bd Parole	DC Superior Ct/Social Svcs Div	DHS/YS Admin/Bu of Ct & Cmty Svcs	DC Superior Ct/Social Svcs Div
FL	7	Parole Cmsn	DOC/Prob & Parole Svcs[b]	DOC/Prob & Parole Svcs[b]	DHRS/Juvenile Justice	DHRS/Juvenile Justice
GA	5	Bd Pardons & Paroles	Bd Pardons & Paroles[b]	DOC/Cmty Corr Div	DHR/Dept Ch Youth Svcs & Co Courts	DHR/Dept Ch Youth Svcs & Co Courts
HI	3 (PT)[2]	Paroling Authority	Paroling Authority/Field Svcs	State Judiciary/Prob Ofc	DHS/OYS/Yth Corr Facil/Cmty Svcs	State Judiciary/Family Courts
ID	5 (PT)	Cmsn for Pardons & Parole	DOC/Div Field & Cmty Svcs	DOC/Div Field & Cmty Svcs	DHW/Bur of Juv Justice	DHW/Bu of Juv Justice/Co Courts
IL	12	Prisoner Review Bd	DOC/Cmty Svcs Div[b]	Judicial Circuits/Prob Div	DOC/Juv Div/Juv Field Svcs	Judicial Circuits/Prob Div
IN	5	Parole Bd	DOC/Parole Svcs Section	Judicial/County Courts	DOC/Parole Svcs Section	Judicial/County Courts
IA	5 (PT)[2]	Bd Parole	DOC/Div Cmty Corr Svcs	DOC/Div Cmty Corr Svcs	DHS/Div Adult, Children & Family Svcs	Judicial Districts
KS	5	Parole Bd	DOC/Cmty Field Svcs[b]	Judicial Districts/Ct Svcs Div	DSRS/Youth & Adult Svcs	Judicial Districts/Ct Svcs Div
KY	7	Parole Bd	DOC/Cmty Svcs & Facil/Div PP	DOC/Cmty Svcs & Facil/Div PP	CHR/DSS/Div Family Svcs	CHR/DSS/Div Family Svcs
LA	7	Bd Parole	DPSC/Div Prob & Parole[b]	DPSC/Div Prob & Parole[b]	DPSC/Ofc Youth Development	DPSC/Ofc Youth Development
ME	5 (PT)	Parole Bd[3]	DOC/Div Prob & Parole	DOC/Div Prob & Parole	DOC/Div Prob & Parole	DOC/Div Prob & Parole
MD	7	Parole Cmsn	DPSCS/Div Parole & Prob	DPSCS/Div Parole & Prob	Dept Juv Svcs	Dept Juv Svcs
MA	8	Parole Bd	Parole Bd	Office of Cmsnr Prob/Courts	DYS/Bur Cmty Svcs	Office of Cmsnr Prob/Courts
MI	10	Parole Bd	DOC/Field Op Admin	DOC/Field Op Admin & Dist Cts	DSS/Office Delinq Svcs/Co Cts	DSS/Office Delinq Svcs/Co Cts
MN	4 (PT)[4]	DOC/Office Adult Release[b]	DOC/Prob Par Supv Rel[b]/ Co Cts or CCA	DOC/Prob Par Supv Rel[b]/ Co Cts or CCA	DOC/Prob Par Supv Rel[b]/ Co Cts or CCA	DOC/Prob Par Supv Rel[b]/ Co Cts or CCA
MS	5	Parole Bd	DOC/Cmty Svcs Div	DOC/Cmty Svcs Div	DHS/DYS/Cmty Svcs Div	DHS/DYS/Cmty Svcs Div
MO	5	Bd Prob & Parole	DOC/Bd Prob & Parole	DOC/Bd Prob & Parole	DSS/Div Youth Svcs & Jud Circuits	Judicial Circuits
MT	3 (PT)	Bd Pardons	DCHS/CD/Prob & Parole Bureau	DCHS/CD/Prob & Parole Bureau	Dept Family Svcs/Corr Div	Judicial Districts
NE	5	Bd Parole[b]	DCS/Adult Parole Admin[b]	NE Prob System	DJS/Juv Parole Admin[b]	NE Prob System
NV	6	Bd Parole Cmsnrs	DMV/Div Parole & Prob	DMV/Div Parole & Prob	DHR/YCS/Youth Parole Bureau	District Courts
NH	5 (PT)	Bd Parole	DOC/Div Field Svcs[b]	DOC/Div Field Svcs[b]	DHHS/DCYS/Bur Children	DHHS/DCYS/Bur Children
NJ	9	Parole Bd	DOC/Bureau Parole	The Judiciary/Prob Div	DOC/Bureau Parole	The Judiciary/Prob Div
NM	4	Adult Parole Bd	CD/Prob & Parole Div	CD/Prob & Parole Div	CYFD/Cmty Svcs Div	CYFD/Cmty Svcs Div
NY	19	Bd Parole	Div Parole	Div Prob & Corr Alt/Co Courts	Exec Dept/Div for Youth/Div Parole[b]	Exec Dept/Div Prob & Corr Alt/Courts
NC	5	Parole Cmsn	DOC/Div Adult Prob & Parole	DOC/Div Adult Prob & Parole	Admin Office Courts/Juv Svcs Div	Admin Office Courts/Juv Svcs Div
ND	3 (PT)	Parole Bd	DCR/Div Parole & Prob	DCR/Div Parole & Prob	DCR/Div Juv Svcs[b]	DCR/Div Juv Svcs[b]/Supr Cts
OH	11[5]	DRC/Div Parole & Cmty Svcs/ Ad Parole Auth & Parole Bd	DRC/Div Parole & Cmty Svcs	DRC/Div Parole & Cmty Svcs & Co Courts	DYS/Div Courts, Par, & Cmty Svcs[b]	Co Court
OK	5 (PT)	Pardon & Parole Bd	DOC[b]	DOC[b]	DHS/OJJ/Juvenile Svcs Unit[b]	DHS/OJJ/Juvenile Svcs Unit[b]
OR	4	Bd Parole & Post Prison Supv	DOC/Cmty Corrections	DOC/Cmty Corrections	DHR/CSD/Juv Corr Svcs	Co Courts
PA	5	Bd Prob & Parole[b] & Co Cts[6]	Bd Prob & Parole[b] & Co Cts	Bd of Prob & Parole[b] & Co Cts	Co Courts	Co Courts
RI	6 (PT)	Parole Bd	DOC/Div Rehab Svcs	DOC/Div Rehab Svcs	DCYF/Div Juv Corr Svcs	DCYF/Div Juv Corr Svcs

SC	7 (PT)	Bd Prob, Parole, & Pardon Svcs	Dept Prob, Parole, & Prdn Svcs	Dept Prob, Parole, & Prdn Svcs	Dept Juv Justice/Cmty Div	Dept Juv Justice/Cmty Div
SD	6 (PT)	Bd Pardons & Paroles	DOC	Unified Judicial Sys/Ct Svcs Dept	Unified Judicial Sys/Ct Svcs Dept	United Judicial Sys/Ct Svcs Dept
TN	7	Bd Paroles	BP/Parole Field Svcs[b]	DOC/Div Field Svcs[b]	DYD/Div Prob[b]	DYD/Div Prob[b]
TX	18	Bd Pardons & Paroles	TDCJ/PPD/Parole Supv	TDCJ/Cmty Jus Asist Div/Dist Cts	TYC/Cmty Svcs Div/Ofc Par Supv[b]	Co Courts
UT	5	Bd Pardons	DOC/Div Field Operations	DOC/Div Field Operations	DHS/Div Youth Corr	Juv Courts
VT	5 (PT)	Bd Parole	AHS/DOC	AHS/DOC	AHS/DSRS[7]	DSRS/Div Social Svcs
VA	5	Parole Bd	DOC/Div Cmty Corr	DOC/Div Cmty Corr	Dept Youth & Fam Svcs[b]	Dept Youth & Fam Svcs[b]
WA	3	Indeterminate Sent Review Bd	DOC/Div Cmty Corr	DOC/Div Cmty Corr & Co Cts	DSHS/Juv Rehab Admin	Co Courts
WV	3	Parole Board	DPS/Div Corrections	DPS/DOC & Judicial Circuits	DPS/DOC (Compact) and courts	DPS/DOC (Compact), Jud Circuits[8]
WI	5	Parole Cmsn	DOC/Div Prob & Parole	DOC/Div Prob & Parole	DHSS/Div Yth Svcs/Co Soc Svcs Depts	Co Social Svcs Depts
WY	7 (PT)	Bd Parole	DOC/Div Field Services	DOC/Div Field Services	Dept Family Svcs	Dept Family Svcs/Co Munic Depts
US	9	Parole Cmsn[b]	Admin Ofc of US Courts	Admin Ofc of US Courts/Div of Prob		

[a] All members serve full-time unless coded "PT."
[b] Accredited by Commission on Accreditation for Corrections.

1. AR—3 full-time, 4 part-time.
2. Chairman serves full-time; members part-time.
3. ME—Parole Board hears pre-1976 cases of parole. Flat sentences with no parole under criminal code effective 5/1/76.
4. MN—Executive Officer & three Deputy Executive Officers (CCA Cmty Corr Act.)
5. OH—Plus 15 hearing officers.
6. PA—The Board of Probation and Parole administers adult services when sentence is over 2 yrs; county courts when sentence is 2 yrs or less.
7. VT—No functional juvenile parole system. Children in custody go into placement and eventually return to community under supervision of caseworker.
8. WV—Under state statute, juv release is judicially, rather than administratively, determined and is considered probation.

The following states have one or more independent county, municipal or city departments: CO, GA, IN, KS, KY, LA, MO, NE, NY, OK, TN, WY.

All Boards are independent except MD, MI, MN, OH, TX.

Source: 1996 ACA Directory. Laurel, MD: American Correctional Association, 1996.

General Counsel and Review

(Office of General Counsel, legislative and correctional issues, commercial branch, equal employment opportunity, freedom of information/privacy, ethics, rules, administrative remedies, National Legal Training Center, Staff Training Academy)

Health Services Division

(Office of Medical Director; systems, policy, planning and evaluation, health services program)

Human Resource Management Division

(labor-management relations, affirmative action, national recruiting office, examining, conference coordinator, security and background investigation, training operations, field training services, employee relations, human resources management information system, human resource research and development, policy and professional development, pay and position management, staffing)

Industries, Education and Vocational Training

(corporate management; ombudsman; management information systems, management control system, project group, human resources, plans and policy, products, marketing, procurement, engineering, financial management education, training and recreation, inmate work programs, competition, activation)

Support Divisions

Information, Policy and Public Affairs Division

(public affairs, security technology, national policy review, archives, external liaison, documents control, research and evaluation information systems)

National Institute of Corrections

(technical assistance, grants, National Academy of Corrections, National Jail Center, Information Clearinghouse)

Program Review Division

(Office of Assistant Director, program review branch, program analysis branch, internal control branch, competition advocacy program, office of strategic planning)

Regional Offices: Mid-Atlantic (Annapolis Junction, MD), North Central (Kansas City), Northeast (Philadelphia), South Central (Dallas), Southeast (Atlanta), and Western (Dublin, CA)

In 1995, the Federal Bureau of Prisons had a budget of $2.3 billion, with $1.5 billion in salaries and $800 million in administration/operations (American Correctional Association, 1996:xvi). There were 100,250 federal inmates in 1995, with 38,506 federal probationers and 59,136 federal parolees (Department of Justice, 1996a:5–6). Total 1995 Federal Bureau of

Prisons personnel were 25,515, with 10,248 of these as corrections officers (American Correctional Association, 1996a:xlii–xliii, xliv–xlv).

The U.S. Parole Commission. When the Federal Bureau of Prisons was conceived in 1930, the **U.S. Parole Commission** (USPC) was also established. It was originally called the U.S. Board of Parole (Runda, Rhine, and Wetter, 1994). The USPC is under the administrative control of the U.S. Department of Justice and is responsible for the management and monitoring of all federal prisoners who are released on parole or mandatory release. The USPC is responsible for the classification and placement of parolees and for maintaining reports on their progress. To accomplish these tasks, federal probation officers are used as field supervisors. These probation officers are employed by the various U.S. district courts and manage federal probationers as well as parolees (American Correctional Association, 1996a:551). In addition, these probation officers manage federal probationers and report to their respective district courts on offender progress while on probation (Powers, 1992). In 1995 there were three regional offices of the USPC.

The Administrative Office of U.S. Courts. The **Administrative Office of U.S. Courts** oversees U.S. Pretrial Services Officers and Probation Officers in 94 judicial districts (Administrative Office of U.S. Courts, 1995). Pretrial Services Officers conduct pretrial release investigations for persons charged with federal offenses and supervise defendants released pending final disposition and those placed on pretrial diversion (American Correctional Association, 1996a:552). U.S. probation officers also conduct presentence investigations for U.S. district court judges on offenders who are awaiting sentencing.

The U.S. Sentencing Commission. An independent agency in the judicial branch, the **U.S. Sentencing Commission,** consisting of nine members (seven voting members), is charged with promulgating mandatory sentencing guidelines for federal judges to use when sentencing convicted federal offenders. Created under the Comprehensive Crime Control Act of 1984, the Commission's goals include reducing unwarranted disparity in sentences for offenders who commit similar offenses and ensuring fairness and certainty in sentencing. New sentencing guidelines created by the U.S. Sentencing Commission went into effect on November 1, 1987. The guidelines and related sentencing provisions determine the appropriate sentence based on the specific characteristics of the offense and the offender. If incarceration is imposed, the guidelines specify a range of months from which judges must choose a specific sentence. By statute, offenders sentenced under the new guidelines are not parole-eligible. Additional responsibilities of the Commission include ongoing monitoring, amendment, and sentencing education responsibilities. The Commission members are presidential appointees with the advise and consent of Congress. The U.S. Attorney General and chair of the U.S. Parole Commission also sit on the Commission as nonvoting ex officio members.

KEY TERMS

Administrative Office of U.S. Courts
AIDS (acquired immune deficiency syndrome)
Arraignment
Bail
Bail bond
Bail bondspersons
Bench trial
Booking
Career criminals
Child sexual abusers
Crime clock
Crimes against the person
Crimes against property
Criminal justice system
Federal Bureau of Prisons
Felonies
First-offenders
Habitual offender law
Index crimes, index offenses
Initial appearance
Jurisdictions
Jury
Jury trial
Law enforcement
Level of custody
Minnesota Multiphasic Personality Inventory
Misdemeanant
Misdemeanors
National Crime Victimization Survey
Plea bargaining
Preliminary hearing or examination
Presentence investigation reports
Preventive detention
Property crime
Prosecutors
Recidivism
Recidivist
Repeat offender law
Sex offenders
Situational offenders
Special Sex Offender Sentencing Alternative Treatment
Summary offenses
Trials
Uniform Crime Reports
U.S. Department of Justice
U.S. Parole Commission
U.S. Sentencing Commission
Violent crime
Warrants

QUESTIONS FOR REVIEW

1. What are the major components of the criminal justice system? Describe the nature of their interdependency with one another.
2. How does increasing or decreasing the number of arrests by local law enforcement officers affect other criminal justice system components?
3. Why is there some controversy over whether the criminal justice system is regarded as a “process” rather than a “system”?

4. What is booking? Differentiate between a preliminary hearing and an arraignment.
5. If a defendant goes to trial, what are their trial options?
6. Is everyone entitled to a jury trial when charged with crimes? What are some restrictions?
7. What correctional bureaus and commissions are administered by the U.S. Department of Justice?
8. Do all states have the same correctional systems? In what respects are there differences among state systems, if any?
9. Are states obligated to follow the federal correctional organizational structure in their own corrections planning? Is there any relation between federal correctional organization and local/state correctional organization? What is the relation, if any? Give an example.
10. Why is the centralization of correctional organizations an important factor when examining the effectiveness of state or local corrections agencies?
11. What are some of the responsibilities of the U.S. Parole Commission?
12. Differentiate between felonies and misdemeanors. Are all felonies violent crimes? Why or why not?
13. What are some differences between violent and property crimes? Give examples of each.
14. What is recidivism? How it is measured?
15. How much child sexual abuse is there in the United States?
16. Why are drug/alcohol dependent inmates poor risks for parole?
17. How prevalent is drug abuse among inmates and correctional staff in prisons and jails?
18. What are two treatment programs for sex offenders? To what degree do they appear to be effective?
19. In what respects are sex offenders and mentally ill offenders similar?

SUGGESTED READINGS

Champion, Dean J., and George E. Rush. *Community-Oriented Policing.* Upper Saddle River, NJ: Prentice Hall, 1997.

Inciardi, James A. *Drug Treatment and Criminal Justice.* Thousand Oaks, CA: Sage, 1993.

Messner, Steven F., and Richard Rosenfeld. *Crime and the American Dream.* Belmont, CA: Wadsworth Publishing Company, 1994.

Neubauer, David W. *America's Courts and the Criminal Justice System* (5th ed.). Belmont, CA: Wadsworth Publishing Company, 1995.

Walker, Samuel, Cassia Spohn, and Miriam DeLane. *The Color of Justice: Race, Ethnicity, and Crime in America.* Belmont, CA: Wadsworth Publishing Company, 1995.

3

Sentencing and Sentencing Issues

CHAPTER OUTLINE

OVERVIEW

- Mitzi Horton, 31, was the housekeeper for 84-year-old Vernon Laughon. She took Laughon on a drive to buy liquor one afternoon. She stopped the car, choked Laughon until he passed out, dragged his body from the car and put it in the trunk, and then drove around for the next two days spending Laughon's money. A tip from someone who heard Laughon inside the car trunk alerted police to investigate, eventually discovering Laughon and learning of Horton's deed. Horton was convicted of abduction and robbery and sentenced to 12 years in prison. Was this a reasonable sentence? (Adapted from Associated Press, "Woman Gets 12 Years in Prison for Locking Boss in Car Trunk." *Minot (N.D.) Daily News,* May 23, 1996:A2).
- Henry Stepney is 42 years old and lives in Miami, Florida. Stepney is a career criminal and has been convicted of over 50 burglaries. In 1996, Stepney was caught stealing 22 toilet paper rolls from a company and was convicted and sentenced to life imprisonment. Was this a reasonable sentence? (Adapted from Associated Press, "Man with 51 Prior Arrests Gets 40 Years for Stealing Toilet Paper." *Minot (N.D.) Daily News,* September 30, 1996:A2).
- In Fargo, North Dakota, William Hart approached an attorney, Cliff Rodenburg, who was exiting the local YMCA. Hart drew a .357 magnum revolver and shot Rodenburg five times. Rodenburg survived, but Hart was convicted of attempted murder and sentenced to life imprisonment. Was this a reasonable sentence? (Adapted from Associated Press, "Hart Sentenced to Life in Prison." *Minot (N.D.) Daily News*, November 2, 1996:B5).
- "Let's get violent criminals off of city streets and away from the public. Let's get tough on crime." That's what California Governor Pete Wilson said of the "Three Strikes and You're Out" law that California enacted in the early 1990s. The intent of the law was to target violent criminals who were recidivists, who committed three or more violent crimes. They would automatically receive life imprisonment under the new law. However, in 1996 it was revealed that 85 percent of those sentenced under the new "get tough" California laws are persons who have committed nonviolent offenses such as drug possession, burglary, and petty larceny. Do mandatory life sentences for repeat offenders deter career criminals and violent recidivists? (Adapted from Associated Press, "'Three Strikes' Striking Out." *Minot (N.D.) Daily News,* March 8, 1995:A5).

- In 1991, a lone gunman in Visalia, California, walked into a courtroom and tried to kill Judge Howard Broadman with a .38 revolver. His bullets missed Broadman by inches. His motive—he was upset over a sentence the judge had imposed earlier on Darlene Johnson. Johnson was a 27-year-old mother of four children, expecting a fifth child. She had been convicted of child abuse and placed on probation by Judge Broadman. But Broadman ordered that she have a device implanted in her body that would render her incapable of having any children for at least five years. Some persons thought the judge stepped "over the line" when imposing this conditional sentence. Was this sentence fair? Did the judge step over the line? (Adapted from Michael Ryan, "Did the Judge Go Too Far?" *Parade Magazine*, September 1, 1991:8).

We are often perplexed over the types of sentences criminals receive. In some cases, we might applaud judges for "doing the right thing" and imposing what *we* think are "just" sentences. In other cases, we may feel strongly that the sentencing judge didn't do enough to punish the offender. We might read about a woman in Ottawa, Ohio, who steals over $400,000 from her church and who receives a sentence of two years. We know that she will probably only serve one year at the most and that this will be followed by her conditional release into the community (Associated Press, May 18, 1996:A6). What sentence would you impose on someone who steals nearly a half million from a church? We might also read about a man in Seattle, Washington, who steals $40 and gets life without parole (Klass, 1994:A1, A6). This seemingly excessive sentence may appear to us to be unwarranted. But not all crimes and their punishments match up closely with the amounts of money stolen or embezzled. Many other factors and circumstances cause judges to increase or decrease accordingly the punishments they impose. These and the real scenarios presented earlier are indicative of the diversity of sentencing among U.S. judges.

This chapter is about sentencing. It describes various types of sentencing systems used today in various U.S. jurisdictions. **Sentencing** is the penalty phase of the criminal justice system in which incarcerative and nonincarcerative punishments are imposed. Every criminal statute in every jurisdiction is accompanied by possible fine and incarceration guidelines.

The sentencing process is described, commencing with a description of pretrial alternatives available to prosecutors and judges. Several sentencing systems are identified and discussed. By either legislative mandate or court request, presentence investigation reports are prepared for particular offenders and are used during sentencing hearings. These reports are prepared by probation officers. Such reports and their contents and functions will be described.

Next we will examine judicial sentencing discretion and the latitude many judges have in sentencing convicted offenders. Some of the examples presented above describe creative sentences that judges have imposed. The criteria for sentencing offenders will be discussed, including the risk or dangerousness posed by particular offenders to their communities and the seriousness of their crimes. The chapter concludes with an examination of several sentencing issues. Such issues include the convicted offender's right to due process, judicial sentencing disparities, the resources of correctional institutions and their limitations, and jail and prison overcrowding.

PRETRIAL ALTERNATIVES

When offenders are arrested and charged with crimes, this does not mean that they will automatically be prosecuted for those crimes. Police officers may decide to give suspects warnings rather than arrest them. An arrest means extensive paperwork for arresting officers, and thus only more serious offenders are brought to jail for booking. Police officers and other law enforcement officials exercise some discretionary authority in deciding when to make an arrest and which offenses will be alleged.

A "funneling effect" occurs between the time of arrests and when offenders are convicted. Figure 3.1 shows how this funneling effect operates. For every 1,000 felonies committed in the United States annually, about 540 are reported to police. Investigation by police, detectives, and others results in 65 arrests. Of these 65 arrests, 36 defendants will be convicted and only 17 will be sentenced to incarceration in a jail or prison. In probabilistic terms, this means about 25 percent of all arrests result in conviction with incarceration.

Arrests of suspects by law enforcement officers or officials create cases that are presented to prosecutors. On the basis of the facts and evidence

FIGURE 3.1 Funneling effect. (*Source:* George Cole, *American System of Justice.* Belmont, CA: Wadsworth Publishing Company, 1986).

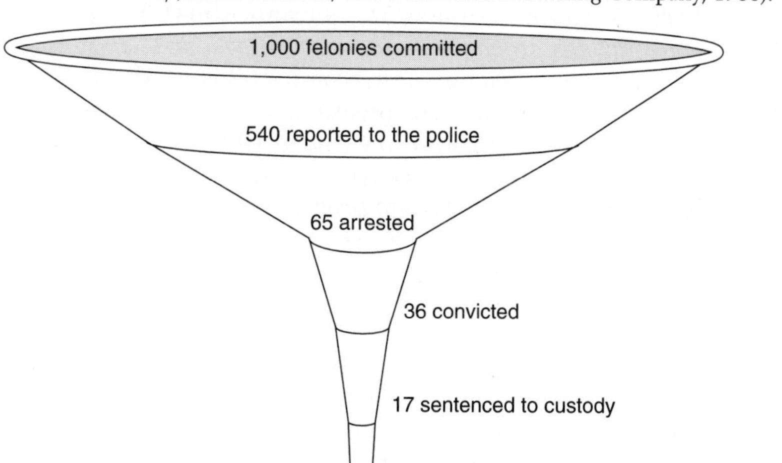

associated with these cases, prosecutors decide whether to prosecute. Prosecutors at local, state, and federal levels have extraordinarily broad discretionary powers about the cases they will drop and those they will pursue. There are few statutory restraints on prosecutorial discretion, and prosecutors do not have to account to anyone for this prosecutorial discretion. Many prosecutors will recommend the pretrial release of certain defendants charged with crimes. **Pretrial release** is permitting defendants to remain in their communities until the date of their forthcoming trials. Those granted pretrial release are usually considered to be good risks. Pretrial releasees have strong community ties, are not considered a danger to themselves or others, and are unlikely to flee the jurisdiction. During 1992, for example, an estimated 63 percent of all state defendants charged with felonies were granted pretrial release (Reaves and Perez, 1994:1). Many jurisdictions with pretrial release report low rates of **failure to appear,** where defendants do not show up when their trials or court appearances are scheduled (Goodman, 1992; Maryland General Assembly Department of Fiscal Services, 1994).

Case Prioritizing, Prosecutions, and Dismissals

Prosecutors may decline to prosecute certain criminal cases. Prosecutors want to have a strong record of convictions, and convictions are usually obtained where substantial evidence exists against the accused. Where evidence is weak or where the police violated one or more constitutional rights of defendants in their arrests, or where witnesses are unwilling or unable to testify against the accused, prosecutors may dismiss the criminal charges.

Cases such as date rape are especially difficult to prosecute. Many date-rape incidents never are reported to police (Vicary, Klingaman, and Harkness, 1995; Ward and Dzuiba-Leatherman, 1994). The victims may be embarrassed to appear in court in front of others, or they may be intimidated by the defendant (Fisher and Sloan, 1995). If the defendants are friends, dates, or family members, questions arise about whether the sexual assault was invited and voluntary (Stan, 1995). Furthermore, the statistics do not favor rape victims in court. In major U.S. cities annually, of *all* rape cases brought to the attention of prosecutors, *only 11 percent* are prosecuted, and the conviction rate in these cases is quite low (Vachss, 1994).

Several national surveys of the charging practices of prosecutors have revealed that prosecutors *do* prioritize the cases they will prosecute (Chaiken and Chaiken, 1987). Most often prosecuted are career criminals and violent recidivists. For less serious property offenders and instances of weak cases, deferred prosecution or outright dismissals of such cases occurs in 51 percent of all cases (Dawson, Smith, and DeFrances, 1993:1). Diversion is used about 44 percent of the time for first-offenders. In many jurisdictions, prosecutors will divert large numbers of cases for civil disposition through alternative dispute resolution.

Alternative Dispute Resolution

For relatively minor criminal offenses, another option increasingly used by the prosecution is **alternative dispute resolution** (ADR), a community-based, informal dispute settlement between offenders and their victims (Palumbo, Musheno, and Hallett, 1994). A tavern brawl may result in arrests of brawlers and criminal charges of aggravated assault. These cases could consume valuable court time if a trial were held. However, if the offenders and victims agree, ADR can sometimes be used to dispose of these cases quickly and informally, mutually satisfying the parties involved.

ADR means the direct participation of the victim and offender, with the aim of mutual accommodation for both parties (Hengstler et al., 1994). The emphasis of ADR is upon restitution rather than punishment. ADR has a direct impact on alleviating court calendars and reserving valuable court time for only the most serious types of cases (Clarke et al., 1994). Thus, speeding up criminal case processing is one functional outcome from the greater use of ADR (American Bar Association, 1994). However, some experts believe that ADR fails to penalize true criminals for the crimes they have committed. ADR is seen by some as a type of decriminalization, while others perceive it to be a reasonable alternative to more costly criminal prosecutions (Maine Commission to Study the Future of Maine's Courts, 1993; McWilliams et al., 1993). Chapter 4 explores alternative dispute resolution in greater detail.

Diversion

Another strategy prosecutors may use is **diversion,** which removes a case from the criminal justice process and obligates defendants to comply with various conditions (American Bar Association, 1994). Divertees are placed on a type of probation. It is expected that defendants will engage in good conduct during the diversionary period, although other conditions may be imposed. Divertees may be required to perform an amount of public service or pay restitution to their victims. The period of diversion may range from six months to two years or more. Successful completion of diversion results in a reexamination of the case by prosecutors. The charges against defendants often are dismissed and their records may be expunged. They exit the criminal justice system as though they had never committed a crime.

Plea Bargaining

Plea bargaining is a preconviction agreement whereby a guilty plea is entered by defendants in exchange for some concession from the prosecution. The concession may be a reduction in the seriousness of the original charges filed, a request for leniency in sentencing, or even the promise not to make any recommendation to the judge about the sentence to be imposed (McDonald, 1985). Thus, defendants who plea bargain reasonably expect that such bargaining will result in more favorable dispositions of their cases than if they were tried in court (LaFree, 1985). Plea bargaining was declared constitutional in the case of *Brady v. United States* (1970) (See Box 3.2).

Over 90 percent of all criminal convictions are obtained through plea bargaining (Dawson et al., 1993). Some states, such as Alaska, have abolished plea bargaining, although it continues to be used informally among prosecutors in jurisdictions in which it has been banned (Carns and Kruse, 1991; Marenin, 1995). Other jurisdictions have adopted sentencing schemes that have drastically modified the use of plea bargaining. For instance, the federal government established sentencing guidelines in 1987, and the amount of plea bargaining in U.S. district courts has declined from 65 percent to about 17 percent per year (U.S. Sentencing Commission, 1991).

There are four kinds of plea bargaining. **Implicit plea bargaining** occurs when the defendant pleads guilty with the expectation of receiving a more lenient sentence from the judge. **Judicial plea bargaining** occurs when the judge makes a specific offer of a sentence to the defendant in exchange for a guilty plea. A third type is **charge reduction bargaining**—prosecutors offer to reduce or drop certain charges in exchange for the defendant's guilty plea to a less serious offense. Finally, **sentence recommendation plea bargaining** occurs when the prosecutor suggests or recommends a particular sentence for the defendant in exchange for the guilty plea. In the United States, the latter two types of plea bargaining are the most common.

Plea bargaining has proponents and opponents. Those favoring its say that valuable court time is saved when defendants plead guilty. Also, the greater leniency in offender sentencing from plea bargaining compared with harsher sentences imposed through trial convictions is attractive. The defendant also benefits by saving legal fees. Another advantage is that the prosecution is spared the task of having to prove the case against the defendant beyond a reasonable doubt. However, plea bargaining has been criticized as contributing to sentencing disparity according to gender. A study of 9,966 felony theft cases and 18,176 felony theft cases was undertaken to determine whether any sentencing disparities could be detected according to one's gender. It was determined that females with no prior record were more likely than similar males to receive charge reductions, and that this advantage enhanced women's chances for receiving probation (Farnworth and Teske, 1995). Yet some experts contend that the sheer bureaucratic nature of large urban prosecutors' offices has minimized sentencing disparities attributable to gender and other factors such as race (Dixon, 1995).

Opponents of plea bargaining claim it is inherently coercive and that defendants needlessly waive their constitutional rights (Pohlman, 1995).

BOX 3.1 Changing Pleas in the Middle of the Stream

The Case of Carl Sidney Race

It happened in Miles City, Montana, on the night of October 21, 1995. Someone broke into the home of Claude and Reta Wyman at Kinsey, a few miles northeast of Miles City. Claude Wyman was shot in the stomach as he approached the back door to see who drove up. His sister-in-law, Reta Wyman, was then shot, as well as the couple's two sons, Jeff, 32, and Paul, 28. Kerosene was poured over the bodies and the house was set on fire. However, Claude and Jeff managed to crawl away from the burning house. They later made their way to a nearby farm where they reported the incident to police.

It turned out that the assailant was identified as Carl Sidney Race, 49, the brother-in-law of Reta Wyman. Both Claude and Jeff Wyman later identified him as the killer. Following the murders, Race fled from Montana and went to Texas. He was the subject of a nationwide manhunt for several days, and then he was seen and arrested near Corpus Christi, Texas, on October 28. He was subsequently extradited to Montana where he faced double-murder charges as well as two charges of attempted murder.

Initially, Race told police that he had stayed at the home of a Williston, North Dakota, family in July and again in October 1995. At first he claimed amnesia and that he couldn't remember what he had done or where he had been on the night he allegedly murdered the Wymans. However, under police questioning, he eventually broke down and admitted to the shootings of all four family members.

"I left my car running, I got out with my shotgun and I went into the house. Claude was heading towards me, I shot him. And then Jeff and Paul jumped up and headed towards me and I shot 'em, both of 'em. And then I shot Reta," said Race. Race had been married to Reta's sister, Nancy, and the two were undergoing a bitter divorce at the time. According to Race, he believed that the Wymans were largely responsible for the breakup of his family and that is why he decided to kill them.

At first, Race pleaded "not guilty" to the murder charges. However, following negotiations with the prosecutor's office in Montana, Race changed his plea to "guilty." When asked why he changed his plea, Race replied, "Because I got a plea bargain and because I did it." The prosecution agreed not to seek the death penalty against Race in exchange for his guilty plea to the murders. Custer County, Montana, Attorney Garry Bunke said that it was difficult offering Race the plea bargain. But he did so because of the years of anguish a capital trial and extended death penalty appeals would have on the survivors and their families. Bunke said that he expects Race to spend the rest of his life in prison.

Should the Montana prosecutor have sought the death penalty against Race? Do you think that the murders were premeditated under these circumstances? What punishment would you impose on Race if you were the judge? Should prosecutors be permitted to downgrade the seriousness of a murder simply to avoid protracted appeals in death penalty cases?

Source: Adapted from Associated Press, "Race Changes Plea to Guilty in Family Murders." *Minot (N.D.) Daily News*, May 21, 1996:B4.

BOX 3.2 Three Plea Bargaining Cases

Brady v. United States, 397 U.S. 742, 90 S.Ct. 1463 (1970). Brady and a codefendant were charged with kidnapping. The offense carried a maximum penalty of death. Brady initially entered a "not guilty" plea, but his codefendant pleaded guilty under a plea bargain arrangement. When Brady learned that his companion had confessed and agreed to testify against him, Brady changed his plea to guilty, in exchange for a lengthy prison sentence. Brady knew that if the case proceeded through trial, the death penalty could have been imposed by the jury. After he received a 50-year sentence, it was commuted to 30 years. In any case, Brady appealed, claiming that his plea of guilty was involuntarily given, that he did so only to avoid the possible imposition of the death penalty. The U.S. Supreme Court upheld Brady's conviction and sentence, saying that the guilty plea was not coerced. The U.S. Supreme Court said a plea of guilty is not invalid merely because [it is] entered to avoid the possibility of a death penalty. Thus, the U.S. Supreme Court said that although Brady's plea of guilty may well have been motivated in part by a desire to avoid a possible death penalty, we are convinced that his plea was voluntary and intelligently made and we have no reason to doubt that his solemn admission of guilt was truthful.

North Carolina v. Alford, 400 U.S. 25, 91 S.Ct. 160 (1970). Alford was indicted for first-degree murder. A subsequent plea agreement was approved wherein Alford entered a guilty plea to second-degree murder in exchange for life imprisonment in lieu of the death penalty in the event of an unfavorable guilty verdict. The judge imposed a 30-year term. A lower appellate court held that Alford's plea of guilty had been involuntary, because it had been prompted by a fear of the death penalty. The U.S. Supreme Court heard the case and reversed the lower court, letting the 30-year term stand. The U.S. Supreme Court said that an accused may voluntarily, knowingly, and understandingly consent to the imposition of a prison sentence even though he is unwilling to admit participation in the crime, or even if his guilty plea contains a protestation of innocence, when, as here, he intelligently concludes that his interests require a guilty plea and the record strongly evidences guilt. The significance of this case, known as the "Alford plea," allows defendants to enter a *nolo contendere* plea that is in their best interests (e.g., avoiding a likely death penalty through a jury trial); thus, accused persons may be unwilling to admit guilt, but they may also waive their right to a jury trial and accept a sentence such as that arranged through a plea bargain.

Bordenkircher v. Hayes, 434 U.S. 357, 98 S.Ct. 663 (1978). A defendant's rights were not violated by a prosecutor who warned that not to accept a guilty plea would result in a harsher sentence. Hayes was indicted for check forgery in Fayette County, Kentucky. The punishment for such an offense was from 2 to 10 years, while an Habitual Offender Statute carried a mandatory life imprisonment sentence upon conviction. Hayes also had several prior felony convictions, thus he qualified as an habitual offender and could be prosecuted under this statute. The prosecutor told Hayes that if Hayes pled guilty to the forgery charge, the prosecutor would not charge Hayes with the Habitual Offender Statute violation. Hayes decided to plead "not guilty" and was convicted of the forgery charge. Furthermore, the prosecutor brought habitual offender charges against Hayes, and he was ultimately convicted and sentenced to life imprisonment. He appealed, alleging that he had been coerced by the prosecutorial threat of an habitual offender prosecution. The U.S. Supreme Court disagreed with Hayes and said that it is not a violation of due process for prosecutors to threaten defendants with other criminal prosecutions so long as the prosecutor has probable cause to believe that the accused has committed an offense defined by statute. The case significance is that prosecutors may use additional charges as threats in plea bargaining with criminal defendants as long as there is a basis for these charges. It would be improper and unconstitutional, for instance, if a prosecutor threatened to bring charges against a defendant for which there was no basis or probable cause.

Defendants should have the opportunity of having their cases aired in the courtroom and decided by impartial juries or judges. Also, where plea bargaining is permitted, prosecutorial and judicial abuses of one's due process rights may occur. Prosecutors often are coercive in their use of the plea bargaining tool. **Overcharging** is a common tactic by which the prosecutor files numerous charges against a defendant stemming from a single incident. Sometimes more charges as well as more serious charges are filed, even when the prosecutor lacks sufficient evidence to support a conviction (McConville and Mirsky, 1995).

Sometimes this strategy is called **prosecutorial bluffing** because the prosecution does not expect to obtain a conviction against the defendant on all charges. The idea is to overwhelm defendants and to scare them into guilty pleas by threatening severe penalties. This prosecutorial practice raises ethical and moral questions. While it is unknown how often prosecutors engage in overcharging defendants with crimes, it occurs with great frequency in many jurisdictions and myriad factors impact the plea bargaining outcome (Myers and Reid, 1995).

The judge usually approves the plea agreement and imposes the sentence contemplated by all parties. Although it is unusual for judges to depart markedly from the terms of plea agreements, they may impose more severe penalties on offenders. However, judges either impose the sentence contemplated by the plea agreement or may even decrease the severity of the original agreement terms (McConville and Mirsky, 1995; Pohlman, 1995).

THE SENTENCING PROCESS

Types of Sentencing Systems

In 1992, more than 900,000 felony convictions were obtained in state courts (Langan and Graziadei, 1995:1). About 44 percent of these convicted felons were incarcerated in state prisons, whereas about 26 percent were confined in local jails. Between 1988 and 1992, the sheer volume of felony convictions rose by 34 percent, with aggravated assault and drug trafficking cases accounting for this increase (Langan and Graziadei, 1995:1). For every one of these felony convictions, sentences were imposed by judges according to one of several sentencing schemes. Table 3.1 shows the average and median sentence lengths imposed for selected felony offenses among state prison inmates for 1992.

There are four basic sentencing systems currently used by U.S. courts as alternatives. These include (1) indeterminate sentencing, (2) determinate sentencing, (3) presumptive sentencing or "guidelines-based" sentencing, and (4) mandatory sentencing.

Indeterminate Sentencing. Indeterminate sentencing is used by a majority of state courts (Langan and Graziadei, 1995:1-2). **Indeterminate sentencing** occurs when the judge sets upper and lower limits on the time to be served, either on probation or in jail or prison. If offenders are incarcerated under indeterminate sentencing, a parole board determines their early release. Usually, offenders must serve at least the *minimum sentence* as prescribed by the judge before parole can be granted. This is known as the **minimum/maximum sentence.** An example of indeterminate sentencing might be where a judge sentences an offender to "not less than 1 year nor more than 10 years" for robbery. The offender must serve at least one year of this sentence before a parole board can grant early release. Indeterminate sentencing provides a strong inducement for inmates to behave well while confined. Inmates who disrupt the prison or jail or who otherwise cause correctional staff or other inmates problems will seriously jeopardize their early-release chances. Inmates who are continually disruptive may never be paroled. But after they serve their *maximum sentence* of 10 years, the state must release them.

Another version of indeterminate sentencing is **fixed indeterminate sentencing.** Under this scheme, judges sentence offenders to a single prison term that for all practical purposes is treated as the maximum sentence. The implied minimum might be zero for all sentences, one year for all sentences, or a fixed proportion of the maximum (Koppel, 1984:2). In either the minimum/maximum or fixed indeterminate sentencing systems, parole boards determine an inmate's early-release date.

Determinate Sentencing. In the last few decades, all states have revised or reformed their sentencing schemes (Kaune, 1993). In nearly half of all state jurisdictions, a shift has occurred from indeterminate to determinate sentencing (Key, 1991; Marvell and Moody, 1991; A. Roberts, 1994). Determinate sentencing prescribes that judges fix the term of an offender's incarceration that must be served in full, less any **good-time credits** that might be applicable (Koppel, 1984:2). Good-time credits are days earned and deducted from one's maximum sentence as the result of good institutional behavior (Davis, 1990a).

For example, in 1990, most U.S. state correctional systems awarded either 15 days, 20 days, or 30 days a month off of an inmate's maximum sentence for every 30 days served in prison. Thus, if an inmate was sentenced to a maximum of 10 years, under a 30-day-per-month good-time scenario, it is possible that the inmate would serve only half of the original

TABLE 3.1 Lengths of Felony Sentences Imposed by State Courts, by Offense and Type of Sentence, 1992

Most Serious Conviction Offense	Maximum sentence length (in months) for felons sentenced to			
	Incarceration			
	Total	Prison	Jail	Probation
Mean				
All offenses	53 mo	79 mo	7 mo	47 mo
Violent offenses	95 mo	125 mo	8 mo	52 mo
Murder[a]	238	251	10	78
Rape	130	164	8	71
Robbery	101	117	11	62
Aggravated	56	87	7	45
Other violent[b]	55	88	6	52
Property offenses	45 mo	67 mo	7 mo	47 mo
Burglary	56	76	8	55
Larceny[c]	34	53	7	43
Fraud[d]	44	69	6	44
Drug offenses	43 mo	67 mo	6 mo	48 mo
Possession	32	55	4	45
Trafficking	50	72	8	51
Weapons	36 mo	55 mo	6 mo	38 mo
Other offenses[e]	32 mo	53 mo	6 mo	42 mo
Median				
All offenses	24 mo	48 mo	5 mo	36 mo
Violent offenses	60 mo	84 mo	6 mo	36 mo
Murder[a]	252	288	10	60
Rape	72	108	6	60
Robbery	66	84	9	60
Aggravated	24	60	6	36
Other violent[b]	24	60	4	36
Property offenses	24 mo	42 mo	5 mo	36 mo
Burglary	36	48	6	36
Larceny[c]	18	36	4	36
Fraud[d]	24	36	3	36
Drug offenses	24 mo	48 mo	5 mo	36 mo
Possession	12	36	3	36
Trafficking	36	48	6	36
Weapons	16 mo	36 mo	4 mo	24 mo
Other offenses[e]	12 mo	28 mo	4 mo	36 mo

Note: Means exclude sentences to death or to life in prison. Sentence length data were available for 854,592 incarceration and probation sentences.
[a] Includes nonnegligent manslaughter.
[b] Includes offenses such as negligent manslaughter, sexual assault, and kidnapping.
[c] Includes motor vehicle theft.
[d] Includes forgery and embezzlement.
[e] Composed of nonviolent offenses such as receiving stolen property.

Source: Patrick Langan and Helen A. Graziadei, *Felony Sentences in State Courts, 1992*. Washington, DC: U.S. Department of Justice, 1995:2.

maximum sentence of 10 years. Essentially, an inmate would have an equivalent amount of time deducted from his sentence for every month or year served. A five-year incarcerative period would earn five years' worth of good-time credit. Under this determinate sentencing scheme, good-time credit accumulations would determine one's specific release date. This is a key reason such a scheme is called **determinate sentencing**, because inmates know approximately when they must be released from custody.

The state with the most generous good-time credit allocation is Alabama, which permitted 75 days of good-time credit for every 30 days served. Prior to 1988, Oklahoma provided 137 days of good-time credit for every 30 days served. The U.S. Federal Bureau of Prisons provides up to 54 days a year for every year served (Davis, 1990a).

The basic distinction between indeterminate and determinate sentencing is that judges must impose a fixed sentence under determinate sentencing, and early release is governed by the accumulation of good-time credit; under indeterminate sentencing, parole boards make early-release decisions following a minimum-maximum sentence imposed by the sentencing judge (Griset, 1994). Theoretically, at least, determinate sentencing reduces or minimizes the abuse of judicial and parole board discretion in determining early release for inmates. It is arguable, however, whether judicial discretion has been affected seriously by determinate sentencing (Griset, 1995; A. Roberts, 1994; Stolzenberg, 1993).

Presumptive or "Guidelines-Based" Sentencing. One way of making sentencing more objective is to establish a sentencing commission to study sentencing and its deterrent effects. The use of sentencing commissions was first proposed in the United States in the early 1970s, with the first sentencing commission being established in 1978 (Tonry, 1993). Sentencing guidelines have reduced disparities and gender differences in sentencing in most jurisdictions where they have been established (Tonry, 1993).

The U.S. Sentencing Commission and 18 other state jurisdictions such as Minnesota have shifted to **presumptive** or **guidelines-based sentencing** schemes (*Corrections Compendium*, 1994b:7; Tonry, 1993). Presumptive sentencing is based upon predetermined guidelines accompanying each offense. For instance, the presumptive guidelines formulated by the U.S. Sentencing Commission arrange offenses into 43 levels, with 6 criminal history categories. Table 3.2 shows these guidelines according to offense seriousness level, criminal history category, and the range of punishment of incarceration (expressed in terms of months).

A formula is used to arrive at the specified range of numbers of months imposed by the sentencing judge. The formula is based on an offender's prior record or criminal history, mitigating and/or aggravating circumstances, the length of previous incarcerations, and other factors. For example, the base offense level for the crime, insider trading, is "8." Transporting a minor for the purpose of prostitution has a base offense level of "16." From here, the level is increased by one of several possible aggravating circumstances such as the amount of money involved or whether victim

TABLE 3.2 Sentencing Guidelines (months)

Offense Level	Criminal History Category I 0 or 1	II 2 or 3	III 4, 5, 6	IV 7, 8, 9	V 10, 11, 12	VI 13 or more
1	0–1	0–2	0–3	0–4	0–5	0–6
2	0–2	0–3	0–4	0–5	0–6	1–7
3	0–3	0–4	0–5	0–6	2–8	3–9
4	0–4	0–5	0–6	2–8	4–10	6–12
5	0–5	0–6	1–7	4–10	6–12	9–15
6	0–6	1–7	2–8	6–12	9–15	12–18
7	1–7	2–8	4–10	8–14	12–18	15–21
8	2–8	4–10	6–12	10–16	15–21	18–24
9	4–10	6–12	8–14	12–18	18–24	21–27
10	6–12	8–14	10–16	15–21	21–27	24–30
11	8–14	10–16	12–18	18–24	24–30	27–33
12	10–16	12–18	15–21	21–27	27–33	30–37
13	12–18	15–21	18–24	24–30	30–37	33–41
14	15–21	18–24	21–27	27–33	33–41	37–46
15	18–24	21–27	24–30	30–37	37–46	41–51
16	21–27	24–30	27–33	33–41	41–51	46–57
17	24–30	27–33	30–37	37–46	46–57	51–63
18	27–33	30–37	33–41	41–51	51–63	57–71
19	30–37	33–41	37–46	46–57	57–71	63–78
20	33–41	37–46	41–51	51–63	63–78	70–87
21	37–46	41–51	46–57	57–71	70–87	77–96
22	41–51	46–57	51–63	63–78	77–96	84–105
23	46–57	51–63	57–71	70–87	84–105	92–115
24	51–63	57–71	63–78	77–96	92–115	100–125
25	57–71	63–78	70–87	84–105	100–125	110–137
26	63–78	70–87	78–97	92–115	110–137	120–150
27	70–87	78–97	87–108	100–125	120–150	130–162
28	78–97	87–108	97–121	110–137	130–162	140–175
29	87–108	97–121	108–135	121–151	140–175	151–188
30	97–121	108–135	121–151	135–168	151–188	168–210
31	108–135	121–151	135–168	151–188	168–210	188–235
32	121–151	135–168	151–188	168–210	188–235	210–262
33	135–168	151–188	168–210	188–235	210–262	235–293
34	151–188	168–210	188–235	210–262	235–293	262–327
35	168–210	188–235	210–262	235–293	262–327	292–365
36	188–235	210–262	235–293	262–327	292–365	324–405
37	210–262	235–293	262–327	292–365	324–405	360–life
38	235–293	262–327	292–365	324–405	360–life	360–life
39	262–327	292–365	324–405	360–life	360–life	360–life
40	292–365	324–405	360–life	360–life	360–life	360–life
41	324–405	360–life	360–life	360–life	360–life	360–life
42	360–life	360–life	360–life	360–life	360–life	360–life
43	Life	Life	Life	Life	Life	Life

Source: U.S. Sentencing Commission, *U.S. Sentencing Guidelines.* Washington, DC: U.S. Government Printing Office, 1987.

injury resulted from the crime. Thus, an offender convicted of insider trading but with no prior record is in offense level 6 and criminal history category I. Where these values intersect in the body of Table 3.2 shows the number of months possible incarceration, 0 to 6 months in this instance. The judge may sentence the offender to probation ("0") or a maximum of 6 months. Career offenders are always placed in category VI, regardless of the offense level associated with the crime they have committed.

Several states including Minnesota have adopted presumptive sentencing guidelines for judges to follow. Tennessee groups offenses into various ranges such as a Range I offense or a Range II offense. Class X felonies are also identified with accompanying serious punishments. Rather complex calculations are used by Tennessee judges in arriving at the sentence imposed on offenders. If they are recidivists, a separate set of calculations is necessary to determine numbers of years or months of incarceration. Table 3.3 shows 19 states and the U.S. Federal Bureau of Prisons sentencing guidelines, when they were enacted, and whether judges can depart from them.

Presumptive sentencing guidelines supposedly curb judicial discretion by obligating judges to stay within certain boundaries (expressed in terms of months) when sentencing offenders. The intent of presumptive guidelines is to create greater consistency among judges in the sentences they impose on different offenders convicted of the same offenses under similar circumstances. However, a proviso exists whereby judges may depart from these statutory ranges by as much as a year or more (Purdy and Lawrence, 1990). If judges impose a harsher or milder sentence, they must usually furnish a written explanation and justification for these departures (*Corrections Compendium*, 1994b:8).

The results of presumptive sentencing among state jurisdictions are mixed (Tonry, 1993). In New York, for instance, it was determined that sentences were often more a product of judges' attitudes and defendant race and socioeconomic factors. Since new sentencing guidelines have been imposed, improper sentencing considerations have been reduced because sentencing has become more systematic for similar offense categories (Griset, 1995). In Minnesota, although new presumptive guidelines were introduced in 1980, irregular sentencing patterns have been observed in subsequent annual follow-ups showing that sentencing uniformity and proportionality have varied on a year-by-year basis (Key, 1991; Stolzenberg, 1993).

Despite massive sentencing reforms, the percentage of prison sentences among convicted state felons has not changed much. About 44 percent of all convicted felons received incarceration in 1988 as well as in 1992 (Langan and Graziadei, 1995:7). The average prison sentence was 6½ years in 1992, the same as it was in 1988. However, the imprisonment of drug traffickers rose from 41 percent in 1988 to 48 percent in 1992. It has been suggested that while these various sentencing schemes may not have changed the overall sentence lengths of state prison inmates, sentencing disparities have been minimized in more than a few jurisdictions (Stolzenberg, 1993). Stolzenberg (1993) has found, for example, that in Minnesota

TABLE 3.3 State and Federal Systems Using Sentencing Guidelines

System	Year Guidelines Enacted	Guidelines Set by:	Can Guidelines Be Changed Without a Change in the Law?	Guidelines Enacted to:	Sentence Limits Based on:	Can Judge Depart from Guidelines?	# Available Prison Beds Considered?	Are Alternatives Covered in Guidelines?
Alaska	Presumptive and mandatory minimums enacted in 1980.	State law	No. However, judges may have discretion based on past history, mitigating or aggravating circumstances.	Provide more equal sentencing.	Circumstances of the offense and offender's past record.	Yes. Judges may have discretion based on past history, mitigating or aggravating circumstances.	No	No
Arkansas	1993 (effective Jan. 1, 1994).	State law; sentencing commission	Yes. Sentencing commission may change recommended sentence lengths and dispositions pursuant to the Administrative Procedures Act which requires legal notice and public hearings.	Provide more equal sentencing; relieve prison overcrowding; eliminate discretionary parole.	Circumstances and ranking of the offense; offender's past record; social history.	Yes	No	Yes. Regional punishment facilities (RPF) for nonviolent offenders; as well as probation, suspended sentence and jail.
Florida	Oct. 1, 1983; restructured Jan. 1994.	State law; sentencing commission	No	Provide more equal sentencing; eliminate discretionary parole; devise and implement a uniform sentencing policy.	Circumstances of the offense, offender's past record; level of victim injury.	Yes	No	Yes. Probation, community control and county jail.
Kansas	1993	State law	No	Provide more equal sentencing; eliminate discretionary parole; control need for capacity expansion.	Circumstances of the offense, offender's past record.	Yes	No	Yes. Probation, community corrections, shock incarceration.
Louisana	1992	State law; sentencing commission	Yes. Revisions, approved by the sentencing commission, are promulgated according to the Administrative Procedures Act	Provide more equal sentencing; increase turnover/reduce length of incarceration rather than numbers incarcerated.	Circumstances of the offense, offender's past record.	Yes	No	Probation, intensive supervision, periodic and home incarceration, community service, treatment, economic sanctions, privilege denial.
Maryland	1983	State law; sentencing commission	Yes	Provide more equal sentencing throughout the state.	Circumstances of the offense, offender's past record.	Yes	No	No
Michigan	1984	Administrative order of State Supreme Court	Yes. Revisions can be made based on Sentencing Guidelines Committee recommendations.	Provide more equal sentencing throughout the state	Circumstances of the offense, offender's past record.	Yes, but the Judge must give reason on record.	No	No
Minnesota	1980	Sentencing commission	Yes. Commission can amend the guidelines, but must hold a public hearing. Most changes must be reviewed by the legislature.	Provide more equal sentencing, eliminate discretionary parole, provide proportionality in sentencing and coordinate sentencing policies with correctional resources to ensure available prison space for violent and repeat offenders.	Circumstances of the offense, offender's past record.	Yes	No	No

(table continues)

TABLE 3.3 (continued)

System	Year Guidelines Enacted	Guidelines Set by:	Can Guidelines Be Changed Without a Change in the Law?	Guidelines Enacted to:	Sentence Limits Based on:	Can Judge Depart from Guidelines?	# Available Prison Beds Considered?	Are Alternatives Covered in Guidelines?
New Mexico	Not available	State law	No	Provide more equal sentencing throughout the state.	Circumstances of the offense, offender's past record & social history.	No	No	Yes. Intensive supervision, community corrections.
New York	1965	State law	No	Ensure that certain types of offenders receive certain minimum terms of imprisonment	Offender's social history.	No	No	Yes
North Carolina	1993	State law	No	Relieve prison overcrowding, eliminate discretionary parole.	Circumstances of the offense, offender's past record.	No, but discretion is allowed within guidelines.	No	Yes. Intensive supervision, electronic house arrest, boot camp, residential facility, community penalties plan.
Oregon	1989	State law	Yes. The Sentencing Guidelines Board may change guidelines between legislative sessions. However, if the legislature does not adopt the changes, the rule must be rescinded.	Provide more equal sentencing, eliminate discretionary parole, impose longer sentences for serious offenders, use prison for those convicted of violent and other person crimes.	Circumstances of the offense, offender's past record.	Yes	No	Yes, probation.
Pennsylvania	1978—created. 1982—in effect.	Sentencing commission	Yes. Proposed guidelines go through a public hearing, then submitted for legislature's approval. If not vetoed, revisions become effective 90 days after submission.	Provide more equal sentencing and harsher sentences.	Offense circumstances, offender's past record, minimum sentence length recommendations, enhancements for deadly weapon possession and drug trafficking to minors.	Yes, with written justification.	No	Yes. Intermediate punishments include electronic monitoring, drug treatment, intensive probation, etc.
Rhode Island	Not available	State law and benchmarks	Yes	Provide more equal sentencing throughout the state.	Circumstances of the offense, offender's past record, and social history.	Yes	No	Yes. R.I.G.L.12-19-23.1 sentence and execution - intermediate sanctions. (Not with benchmarks.)
Tennessee	Nov. 1989	State law; sentencing commission	No	Provide more equal sentencing; relieve prison overcrowding.	Circumstances of the offense, offender's past record. First-degree murder is sentenced not to sentencing grid, but to first-degree murder statute.	No	No	No
Virginia	Jan. 1, 1991	Sentencing commission	No	Provide more equal sentencing throughout the state.	Circumstances of the offense, offender's past record, and social history	Yes	No	Yes. I.S.P., electronic monitoring, bootcamp, Community Diversion incentive, probation.

Washington	1984	State law; sentencing commission	No	Provide more equal sentencing, eliminate discretionary parole.	Offender's past record, legislativity determined offense seriousness, and associated factors such as use of a deadly weapon.	Yes	No	Yes. Certain first-time offenders may receive jail time and/or treatment instead of prison.
Wisconsin	1984	State law; sentencing commission	Yes. Guidelines are designed to be revised through the administrative rule-making process.	Provide more equal sentencing throughout the state or jurisdiction; encourage proportionality in sentencing.	Circumstances of the offense, offender's past record. Also, social history under aggravating or mitigating circumstances.	Yes, as long as reasons for deviation are noted.	No	Yes
Federal Bureau of Prisons	1987	Sentencing commission	Yes. U.S. sentencing commission promulgates changes, which become effective if not vetoed by Congress.	Provide more equal sentencing; eliminate discretionary parole.	Circumstances of the offense, offender's past record.	Yes. But then sentence can be appealed.	No	Yes. Home confinement, split sentences, probation.

Source: Corrections Compendium (1994b:9–11).

BOX 3.3. Man Convicted of Raping Four-Year-Old

The Case of Willie Robinson, Child Rapist

It was a warm evening, February 24, 1992, in Montgomery, Alabama. The little four-year-old girl was playing in her living room with her brothers and sisters. Her parents were away and her babysitter, Willie Robinson, 41, was there to protect her. Her parents came home late, asked if there were any problems, and Willie said "No. Everything went just fine."

Two weeks later, the four-year-old girl began itching in her genital area. Her parents inspected her and discovered irritated skin, sores, and other indications of an infection. Rushing her to a physician, they found that their four-year-old daughter had gonorrhea! When doctors and investigating police asked the little girl who touched her, she said "Willie did." Police brought in Willie Robinson for questioning.

At first, Robinson denied having any sexual contact with the little girl. But later, he recanted when authorities and doctors discovered that he actually had gonorrhea. Further, other tests showed that Robinson was AIDS-infected, and that possibly he had transmitted the AIDS virus to the little girl through his sexual contact with her.

District attorneys charged Robinson with rape. Prior to his trial, prosecutors obtained videotaped testimony from the four-year-old girl. She described in great detail what Robinson did to her during the evening of February 24, 1992, while he was babysitting her. They wanted to charge Robinson with attempted murder as well as rape, but they could not prove that Robinson knew that he had the AIDS virus at the time of the sexual assault. Robinson was subsequently tried twice. The first trial resulted in a mistrial because the jury could not agree whether to convict Robinson of first-degree rape or a lesser charge, according to the jury forewoman.

Robinson was convicted on Tuesday, May 21, 1996, of the rape of the four-year-old. The little girl died a month earlier at age 7. She died of AIDS.

Should Robinson be punished for the four-year-old's murder? Although he was convicted of rape, should the judge enhance Robinson's sentence because Robinson gave the little girl AIDS?

Source: Adapted from Associated Press, "Man Convicted of Raping 4-Year-Old." *Minot (N.D.) Daily News*, May 23, 1996:A2.

there has been a 22 percent reduction in disparity for the nonprison/prison outcome and a 60 percent reduction in sentencing inequality for the length-of-prison decision.

Mandatory Sentencing. A **mandatory sentencing** system requires the judge to impose an incarcerative sentence, often of a specified length, for certain crimes or for particular categories of offenders (Koppel, 1984:2). There is no option of probation, suspended sentence, or immediate parole eligibility. Michigan and many other states have mandatory sentencing provisions for specific offenses, such as using a dangerous firearm during the commission of a felony. Michigan adds two years to whatever sentence judges might impose otherwise. For example, if the conviction offense is armed robbery, the judge may impose a sentence of 5 to 10 years. However, an additional mandatory two-year sentence is imposed to run *consecutively* with the 5 to 10 year sentence as a punishment for using a dangerous weapon. Thus, if the offender becomes parole-eligible after serving six years of his sentence, then an additional two-year sentence must be served in its entirety before parole can be considered by the parole board. Clearly, Michigan wants offenders who commit felonies not to use dangerous weapons. Mandatory sentencing is intended to deter them from using such weapons.

Michigan is not alone. Most states have mandatory penalties for particular offenses. The most well-known mandatory penalty is life imprisonment for being convicted as an habitual offender. Recidivists, especially those who commit violent crimes, are targeted by "three-strikes-and-you're-out" legislation, such as that enacted in California. Offenders convicted of a third felony may receive life imprisonment as a mandatory sentence. However, California's prison and jail overcrowding problems are such that finding space for offenders convicted under the new three-strikes law will be impossible. Greenwood et al. (1994) say that although violent crime would be reduced by as much as 34 percent under such a mandatory sentencing scenario, the actual cost of imprisoning many minor felons may be too much for citizens to bear.

Some critics are quite outspoken about mandatory sentencing laws. Forer (1994) contends that mandatory sentencing should be abolished outright, because it has not deterred serious offenders from reoffending. Furthermore, Forer says that extensive prison overcrowding has resulted from mandatory sentencing policies. Arizona is typical of how enforcement of mandatory sentencing statutes can drive up the inmate population. Due to mandatory sentencing in Arizona, a typical committed offender can expect to serve 5.1 years before being released (Fischer and Thaker, 1992). The average expected percentage of the sentence to be served is 74.6 percent compared with an average of 31.6 percent in other states. Similar sentencing policy–sentence length associations have been observed and criticized in other jurisdictions, such as Delaware (Rodriguez-Labarca and O'Connell, 1993).

Another charge leveled against mandatory sentencing is that the criminal statutes targeted for mandatory sentences are typically associated with street crimes. Street crimes are overrepresented by criminals in the lower socioeconomic levels, and thus there is inherent class discrimination whenever such mandatory laws are implemented (Shilton et al., 1994). Interestingly, Fox (1989:144–145) has presented one of the best analyses of sentencing guidelines by noting that generally they have targeted, intentionally or unintentionally, powerless and marginal groups in American society. This observation is supported by the work of Shilton et al. (1994) where similar evaluations of mandatory sentencing schemes have been made.

The Federal Violent Crime Control and Law Enforcement Act of 1994 and Sentencing Reforms. Also known as the Federal Crime Bill and the 1994 Anti-Crime Bill, the Federal Violent Crime Control and Law

Enforcement Act of 1994 was designed to accomplish many things, including putting more police officers on the streets, investigating and experimenting with new crime prevention techniques, and exploring ways of attacking gangs and juvenile delinquency (Curry, 1994; Webb, 1995). The Crime Bill was also intended to modify the present sentencing practices and policies of individual states and to get tough on criminals. One way of getting tough on criminals would be to impose more severe sentences on them and to make offenders serve greater portions of their sentences. Short-term federal monies would be made available to any state agreeing to ensure that sentenced offenders would have to serve at least 85 percent of their maximum sentences. In 1996 the average sentence was about 33 percent of the maximum sentence imposed. Making offenders serve at least 85 percent of their maximum sentences would cause most inmates to be confined for longer periods than they presently serve.

But this aspect of the Crime Bill has its drawbacks, particularly the problem created by greater prison and jail overcrowding. In states such as North Dakota, for example, in the past offenders have served about 40 percent of their maximum sentences. Thus, if a 10-year sentence was imposed, offenders were ordinarily paroled after serving 4 years. But under the Crime Bill, inmates would have to serve 8½ years of a 10-year sentence, or 85 percent of the maximum sentence imposed. While the North Dakota State Penitentiary did not have an overcrowding problem in 1995, by 1996 there were indications that the operational capacity of the penitentiary was being exceeded. Some legislators were toying with the idea of new prison construction for North Dakota, which would impose a substantial tax burden on state residents. It doesn't take a lot of math to project growing inmate populations in those states accepting federal money. Because the federal money given to states is only short-term money, the burden of paying for additional prison and jail space eventually shifts to taxpayers, many of whom already feel overtaxed.

Sentencing Hearings

For almost every serious felony conviction, a sentencing hearing is held. This hearing is usually scheduled six to eight weeks following one's conviction. A **sentencing hearing** is a formal proceeding where the sentencing judge hears pleadings and arguments from both the prosecution and defense to either impose the maximum sentence under the law or show leniency by imposing a lesser sentence. Sentencing hearings may be conducted exclusively by the judge or with a jury. In murder cases where the death penalty might be imposed, juries find defendants guilty in a first phase, deliberating at the conclusion of a trial. Then the same juries must convene again in a second phase, the sentencing hearing, and determine whether the death penalty should be imposed.

Sentencing hearings are usually held in the same courtrooms where

BOX 3.4 Washington Test Case on Three-Strike Law

Three Strikes and You're Out, Larry Fisher!

What sort of punishment should you receive from a court when you rob a sandwich shop in Bellingham, Washington, and get $151 for your trouble? In Larry Fisher's case, he got life imprisonment. What happened? Aren't robbers supposed to get 5- or 10-year sentences?

Washington enacted a Three Strikes and You're Out law in 1994. This law was designed to put teeth into the state's criminal justice system and sentencing procedures. Under this law, persons convicted of three or more felonies are automatically sentenced to life imprisonment. Larry Fisher, 35, was the second person to be sentenced to life imprisonment under this new law.

Larry Fisher was sent to a state home for juvenile incorrigibles when he was 12. His lawyer, Chad Dold, said that Fisher was "trained to fail" when he went through the various bureaucratic chains as a Washington youth. "Fisher is not intelligent or patient enough to negotiate the bureaucracy for help, and so he often takes the fastest route to obtain what he needs," said Dold. "He's a loser, but he's not a violent felon in the sense of what Washington residents thought of when they passed this law," he added.

Interestingly, Washington was in a prison capacity crisis in 1994. The Washington State prison system was holding 33 percent more inmates than their prisons were designed to hold. Thus, adding Larry Fisher, a nonviolent felon, to this overcrowded situation will only aggravate it. Many politicians agree that the Three Strikes laws they propose are targeted primarily at those felons who harm, injure or kill others—violent felons. They do not necessarily have in mind nonviolent felons, although robbery is considered a violent crime, regardless of the money yielded from the act.

Some judges believe that the Three Strikes law handicaps them. One expert, Eric Sterling of the Criminal Justice Policy Foundation, said that "the three strikes law handcuffs judges, that they say the judge is too stupid to know who deserves a long sentence and who doesn't deserve one." But others say that regardless of the felony committed, whether it is a violent or nonviolent one, it is still a felony. Something drastic needs to be done to deter criminals from committing felonies of *any* kind.

Larry Fisher's prior record includes sixteen previous convictions, six of which were for felonies. Thus, Fisher is not exactly a three-time loser. He has been in and out of the system enough to know that further crime will yield greater punishment. He did not learn this lesson well, because he continued to commit felonies after six prior convictions. Two of these convictions were for robbing his grandfather of $360 and taking $100 from a pizza parlor.

Is the Three Strikes law a sufficient crime deterrent? Is a life sentence for persons such as Larry Fisher a "just" punishment? Should we consider the impact upon jail and prison inmate populations whenever we change sentencing policy? Should we place violent or nonviolent felons on probation if they cannot adequately be housed in incarcerative facilities? What do you think?

Source: Adapted from Robert Davis, "Wash. Case Is a Test for '3 Strikes' Law." *USA Today*, June 21, 1994:A4.

the convicted offender's trial was conducted. Defense counsel may present friends and relatives of the offender who can testify about the offender's past, his good qualities, and his likelihood of behaving in a law-abiding fashion in the future. An attempt is made by the defense to influence the judge so that a lighter sentence will be imposed. Significant others in the convicted offender's past are called to make favorable remarks about the offender. However, the prosecution is able to call as witnesses against the offender the victims and their relatives and friends. These persons can make statements and give testimony about why the judge should impose the maximum sentence. They can speak out against showing the offender any leniency.

For instance, Richard Allen Davis, 42, was convicted in June 1996 of kidnapping and murdering 12-year-old Polly Klaas in Petaluma, California, on October 1, 1993 (Associated Press, 1996:A4). In August 1996, a sentencing hearing was held for Davis to determine whether he should receive life without parole or the death penalty. Polly Klaas's father, Marc Klaas, spoke in favor of Davis's execution. Many other relatives and friends of Polly Klaas spoke out against any leniency for Davis. Davis showed his contempt for the proceedings by making vulgar gestures at television cameras. At one point, Davis spoke on his own behalf, apologizing to the Klaas family in open court. But he ruined this exhibition of contrition by insinuating that Polly Klaas had been sexually abused by her own father and that she had disclosed this "fact" to Davis shortly before he killed her. Davis was sentenced to death (Locke, 1996:A1).

Essentially, sentencing hearings enable both victims and offenders an opportunity to be heard (Alexander and Lord, 1994). In the Davis hearing, the event was clearly cathartic for the family and close friends of Polly Klaas. In less emotionally charged hearings, some victims and their families may actually ask the judge to show the offender leniency. In short, the victims and/or the friends and family of victims may speak about how the offender's crime has affected their lives. The loss of a loved one is most grievous, and statements can be given to indicate the extent of this loss. For convicted offenders, sentencing hearings provide them with a brief forum to show judges that they have accepted the responsibility for their own actions and that they are sorry. While their apologies cannot replace the loss of life, they can attempt to mitigate or lessen the harshness of the penalty contemplated by the sentencing judge.

Besides hearing from the defense and prosecution orally, letters and other documents are introduced both for and against convicted offenders. Psychiatrists may provide additional testimony, either favorable or adverse to offenders. Judges also request the preparation of presentence investigation reports. These documents, usually prepared by probation officers at court request or order, are submitted to the judge during the interval between conviction and the sentencing hearing. Thus, an additional written statement, evaluation, and recommendation is a part of the documentation judges consider when imposing sentences.

THE PRESENTENCE INVESTIGATION (PSI) AND REPORT

The **presentence investigation (PSI) report** is an informational document prepared by a probation officer that contains personal data about convicted offenders, the conviction offense(s), and other relevant data, such as the following:

1. Name
2. Address
3. Prior record including offenses and dates
4. Date and place of birth
5. Crime(s) or conviction offense and date of offense
6. Offender's version of conviction offense
7. Offender's employment history
8. Offender's known addiction to or dependency on drugs or alcohol or controlled substances of any kind
9. Statutory penalties for the conviction offense
10. Marital status
11. Personal and family data
12. Name of spouse and children, if any
13. Educational history
14. Any special vocational training or specialized work experience
15. Mental and/or emotional stability
16. Military service, if any, and disposition
17. Financial condition including assets and liabilities
18. Probation officer's personal evaluation of offender
19. Sentencing data
20. Alternative plans made by defendant if placed on probation
21. Physical description
22. Prosecution version of conviction offense
23. Victim impact statement prepared by victim, if any
24. Codefendant information, if codefendant is involved
25. Recommendation from probation officer about sentencing
26. Name of prosecutor
27. Name of defense attorney
28. Presiding judge
29. Jurisdiction in which offense occurred
30. Case docket number and other identifying numbers (e.g., Social Security, driver's license, etc.)
31. Plea
32. Disposition or sentence
33. Location of probation or custody

"Presentence investigation reports are written summaries of information obtained by the probation officer through interviews with the defendant and an investigation of the defendant's background" (Drass and Spencer, 1987:280). An alternative definition is that PSI reports are "narrative summaries of an offender's criminal and noncriminal history used to aid a judge in determining the most appropriate decision as to the offender's sentence for a crime" (Clear, Clear, and Burrell, 1989:2). These documents are often partially structured in that they require probation officers to fill in standard information about defendants. PSIs also contain summaries or accounts in narrative form, highlighting certain information about defendants and containing sentencing recommendations from probation officers (Drass and Spencer, 1987:280). In some instances, space is available for the defendant's personal account of the crime and why it was committed.

Presentence investigation reports are prepared from the facts stemming from investigative efforts by probation officers. Although there is considerable variation in the nature and complexity of PSI reports among jurisdictions, most PSI reports should contain the following items (Black, 1990:1184):

1. Complete description of the situation surrounding the criminal activity
2. Offender's educational background
3. Offender's employment history
4. Offender's social history
5. Residence history of the offender
6. Offender's medical history
7. Information about the environment to which the offender will return
8. Information about any resources available to assist the offender
9. Probation officer's view of the offender's motivations and ambitions
10. Full description of the defendant's criminal record
11. Recommendation from the probation officer as to the sentence disposition

Regardless of whether convictions are obtained through plea bargaining or a trial, a PSI is often conducted on instructions from the court. This investigation is sometimes waived in the case of negotiated guilty pleas, because an agreement has already been reached between the prosecution and defense on the case disposition and nature of sentence to be imposed.

Functions and Uses of PSI Reports

Why Are PSI Reports Prepared? No standard format exists among the states for PSI report preparation. The PSI report was adopted formally by the Administrative Office of the U.S. Courts in 1943. Since then, the PSI has been revised several times. The 1984 version reflects changes in correctional law that have occurred in recent decades. Prior to 1943, informal reports about offenders were often prepared for judges by court personnel. Probably the earliest "informal" PSI was prepared in 1841 by **John Augustus**, the father of probation in the United States.

Although the U.S. Probation Office represents federal interests and not necessarily those of particular states, their PSI report functions are very similar to the general functions of PSI reports in most states. The PSI report for the U.S. district courts and the U.S. Probation Office serves at least five important functions (Administrative Office of U.S. Courts, 1984:1):

1. To aid the court in determining the appropriate sentence for offenders
2. To aid probation officers in their supervisory efforts during probation or parole
3. To assist the Federal Bureau of Prisons and any state prison facility in the classification, institutional programming, and release planning for inmates
4. To furnish the U. S. Parole Commission and other parole agencies with information about the offender pertinent to a parole decision
5. To serve as a source of information for research

Providing information for offender sentencing is the primary function of a PSI. It continues to be an important function, because judges want to be fair and impose sentences fitting the crime. If there are mitigating or aggravating circumstances that should be considered, these factors appear in the report submitted to the judge.

Aiding probation officers in their supervisory efforts is an important report objective because proper rehabilitative programs can be individualized for different offenders. If vocational training or medical help is needed, the report suggests this. If the offender has a history of mental illness, psychological counseling or medical treatment may be appropriate and recommended. This information also is helpful to ancillary personnel who work in community-based probation programs and supervise offenders with special problems such as drug or alcohol dependencies. PSIs assist prisons and other detention facilities in their efforts to classify inmates appropriately. Inmates with special problems or who are handicapped physically or mentally may be diverted to special prison facilities or housing where their needs can be addressed by professionals. Inmates with diseases or viruses such as AIDS can be isolated from others for health purposes.

The fourth function of federal PSIs is crucial in influencing an inmate's parole chances. In those jurisdictions in which parole boards determine an inmate's early-release potential, PSIs are often consulted as background data. Decisions about early release are often contingent upon the recommendation of the probation officer contained in the report. Finally, criminologists and others are interested in studying those sentenced to various terms of incarceration or probation. Background characteristics, socioeconomic information, and other relevant data assist researchers in developing explanations for criminal conduct. Research efforts of criminologists and those interested in criminal justice also may be helpful in affecting the future design of prisons or jails. Special needs areas can be identified and programs devised that will assist offenders with their various problems. Because most inmates will eventually be paroled, research through an examination of PSIs may help corrections professionals devise more effective adaptation and reintegration mechanisms, permitting inmates to make a smoother transition back into their respective communities.

When Are PSI Reports Conducted? In all felony convictions in local, state, and federal trial courts, a PSI usually is conducted between the time an offender is convicted and the date of the sentencing hearing. These reports are designed to assist judges in their sentencing decisions. The Administrative Office of the U.S. Courts uses standardized PSIs that include five core categories that must be addressed in the body of the report. These are (1) the offense, including the prosecution version, the defendant's version, statements of witnesses, codefendant information, and a victim impact statement; (2) prior record, including juvenile adjudications and adult offenses; (3) personal and family data, including parents and siblings, marital status, education, health, physical and mental condition, and financial assets and liabilities; (4) evaluation, including the probation officer's assessment, parole guideline data, sentencing data, and any special sentencing provisions; and (5) recommendation, including the rationale for the recommendation and voluntary surrender or whether the offender should be transported to the correctional institution on his own or should be transported by U.S. Marshals.

Who Prepares PSI Reports? When requested by federal district judges, PSI reports are usually prepared within a 60-day period from the time judges make their requests. While there is no standard PSI report format among states, most PSIs contain similar information. PSI reports are usually prepared by probation officers. Although it was much more informally prepared contrasted with contemporary PSI reports, John Augustus has been credited with drafting the first one in 1841. It has been estimated that there are over 1 million PSI reports prepared by probation officers annually in the United States (Cohn and Ferriter, 1990:15-17). Figure 3.2 (p. 98) shows a short form of a PSI for the North Dakota Probation and Parole Department.

Specific duties of probation officers relating directly to PSI report preparation include the following:

1. Probation officers prepare presentence investigation reports at the request of judges.
2. Probation officers classify and categorize offenders.
3. Probation officers recommend sentences for convicted offenders.
4. Probation officers work closely with courts to determine the best supervisory arrangement for probationer-clients.
5. Probation officers are a resource for information about any extralegal factors that might impact either positively or adversely on the sentencing decision.

Clear et al. (1989:173–175) note that there are three legal approaches to PSI report preparation. In at least 23 states, PSI report preparation is *mandatory* for all felony offense convictions (Clear et al., 1989:175). They note that other factors may initiate PSI report preparation in these jurisdictions, such as when incarceration of a year or longer is a possible sentence, when the offender is under 21 or 18 years of age, and when the defendant is a first-offender. In nine states, statutes provide for mandatory PSI report preparation in *any* felony case where *probation* is a possible consideration. When probation is *not* a consideration, then the PSI report preparation is optional or discretionary with particular judges (North Carolina Administrative Office of the Courts, 1988). Finally, in seventeen states, a PSI report is totally discretionary with the presiding judge. Clear et al. indicate an example of various state policies about the preparation of PSI reports (Clear, Clear, and Burrell, 1989:174):

New Jersey

PSI report—required in all felony cases; suggested in misdemeanor cases involving one or more years' incarceration

Connecticut

PSI report—mandatory for any case in which incarceration is one or more years

Pennsylvania

PSI report—mandatory for any case in which incarceration is one or more years

District of Columbia

PSI report—required unless offenders waive their right to one with court permission

California

PSI report—mandatory for all felony convictions; discretionary for misdemeanor cases

Arizona

PSI report—mandatory for any case in which incarceration is a year or more; may be ordered in other cases

Texas

PSI report—totally discretionary with the judge

Can Private Organizations Prepare PSI Reports? Yes. Sometimes PSIs are prepared by private corporations or individuals. Criminological Diagnostic Consultants, Inc., Riverside, California, founded by brothers

PRE-SENTENCE INVESTIGATION REPORT I
NORTH DAKOTA PAROLE AND PROBATION DEPARTMENT
SFN 16394 (7-88)

County	File No. (s)		Date PSI Ordered
Judge	States Attorney		Date PSI Due
Defense Attorney	☐ Appointed	☐ Retained	Date PSI Completed

Name (Court Records)	Date of Birth	Race	Sex
Name (Alias)	Place of Birth		
Offense			
Address		Telephone No.	
Lives With (Name)	Relationship		
☐ OWNS ☐ RENTS ☐ House ☐ Apartment ☐ Room	How Long At This Address?		
Marital Status	Gross Monthy Income -All Sources	Number of Dependents	
Occupation	Social Security No.	NDSID No.	
Employer		How Long Employed	
Previous Employer		How Long Employed	
Reason For Leaving			
Education			
Military Service (Branch & Dates)	Type of Discharge		
Current Physical Condition			
☐ Drug Use ☐ Mental / Emotional Problems ☐ Alcohol Use (Give details under comments)			

PRIOR RECORD (USE REVERSE SIDE IF NEEDED FOR ADDITIONAL SPACE)

Date	Offense	Arresting Agency	Disposition

COMMENTS AND RECOMMENDATIONS (Community Service and/or Treatment Proposals, etc.):

MANDATORY ATTACHMENTS:
Criminal Information
Law Enforcement Investigation Report
Victim Impact Statement (If applicable)

Probation / Parole Officer Date

FIGURE 3.2 Short-form presentence investigation report.

PRIOR RECORD (USE REVERSE SIDE IF NEEDED FOR ADDITIONAL SPACE)			
Date	Offense	Arresting Agency	Disposition

Offense and Penalty Classification	Days In Custody
Date of Offense	Arresting Agency
Co-defendants and disposition	
Victim	Address

DEFENDANT'S VERSION OF CRIME

INVESTIGATING OFFICER'S VERSION OF CRIME

OTHER INFORMATION (Reputation, Attitude, Leisure time activities, Associates, etc.)

COMMENTS AND SENTENCING ALTERNATIVES (Community Service and/or Treatment Proposals, etc.):

MANDATORY ATTACHMENTS:
Criminal Information / Complaint
Law Enforcement Investigation Report
Victim's Impact Statement (If applicable)

Probation / Parole Officer　　　　Date

William and Robert Bosic, is a corporation that prepares privately commissioned PSIs for defense attorneys and others (Kulis, 1983:11). William Bosic is a former prison counselor and probation officer, while his brother, Robert, is a retired police officer. Their claim is, "we don't do anything different than the probation department; we just do it better." The average cost of a government-prepared PSI report is about $250, while privately prepared PSIs cost from $200 to $2,000 or more. The cost varies according to the PSI contents and thoroughness of the investigation and whether psychiatric evaluations and other types of tests of offenders are made. Increasing numbers of PSI reports are being prepared privately, often by ex-probation officers or others closely related to corrections.

The advantages of privately prepared PSI reports are that the preparers can slant the facts about the offender and the offense in such a way as to increase the chances of leniency from sentencing judges. Public servants, probation officers, may not take the time to include mitigating details about the offense. Therefore, when offenders can afford to have PSI reports prepared, they are at an advantage in that the judge will likely see "their side" more clearly. However, no one knows how much value judges place on PSI reports, regardless of who prepares them.

How Long Does It Take to Prepare PSI Reports? PSI report preparation may take as little as a few hours, with the majority of PSI reports, however, taking several working days to prepare properly. Investigative time and interviewing must be factored in when considering how long probation officers require to complete reports for any particular offender. In many jurisdictions, it is not unusual to discover that over half of a probation officer's time is spent preparing such reports. It takes time for officers to verify one's employment, check educational records, interview family members, obtain victim and/or witness information, analyze court records, review police reports of the arrest and crime details, and a host of other bits and pieces of necessary and relevant information. This activity is only a preliminary step in the process of PSI report preparation. Then officers must sit down and type up these reports. Many probation agencies do not have adequate secretarial staff to whom such information can be dictated and subsequently converted into a written report by someone else. Thus, probation officers must often write their own reports. Knowing how to type or use a word processor or computer is an essential skill for probation officers to acquire.

How Confidential Are PSI Reports? California permits an examination by the public of any PSI report filed by any state probation office for up to 10 days following its filing with the court. Under exceptional circumstances, however, even California courts may bar certain information from public scrutiny if a proper argument can be made for its exclusion. Usually, a good argument would be potential danger to one or more persons who have made statements or declarations in the report. Further, some witnesses or information-givers do so only under the condition that they will remain anonymous.

Ordinarily, only court officials and others working closely with a particular case have a right to examine the contents of these reports. All types of information are included in these documents. Convicted offenders are entitled to some degree of privacy relative to a PSI report's contents. The federal government requires the disclosure of the contents of PSI reports to convicted offenders, their attorneys, and to attorneys for the government at least 10 days before actual sentencing (18 U.S.C., Sec. 3552(d), 1997). At state and local levels, this practice varies, and the PSI report may or may not be disclosed to the offender. Under 18 U.S.C., Fed.R.Cr.Proc. 32(c)(3)(B) (1997), some information in the PSI may be withheld from the defendant. The report may contain confidential information such as a psychiatric evaluation or a sentencing recommendation. The presiding judge determines those portions of the PSI report to be disclosed to offenders and their counsels. Anything disclosed to defendants must also be made available to the prosecutors.

In some jurisdictions, these provisions have been interpreted to mean that convicted offenders should have greatly restricted access to these PSI reports. Many federal prisoners have filed petitions under the **Freedom of Information Act** (FOIA) in order to read their own PSI reports in some judicial districts (Shockley, 1988). This Act makes it possible for private citizens to examine certain public documents containing information about them, including IRS information or information compiled by any other government agency, criminal or otherwise.

The Offender's Sentencing Memorandum and Version of Events

An essential part of the PSI report is the offender sentencing memorandum. **Sentencing memorandums** are a written account of how and why the crime occurred, including the offender's explanation and apology. This memorandum is especially crucial in most sentencing decisions, because the offender uses this occasion to accept responsibility for the crime committed. This is an obligatory component and must be written convincingly. If judges honestly believe that offenders have accepted the responsibility for their actions and are ready to accept the consequences, then they might impose a more lenient sentence. Too many convicted offenders blame others: "I had a bad childhood; my mother and father beat me!"; "I was sexually abused as a child"; "Society did this to me. It's society's fault that I'm here"; "Everybody was against me, and no one gave me a chance." The classic line from convicted offenders is, "I'm not guilty; I'm really innocent; I shouldn't be punished." When judges see or hear offenders make these claims, this is a clear indication that the offenders have *not* accepted responsibility for the crimes. Of course, there *are* innocent convicted offenders out there who express righteous indignation over their plight—but they can't do much about it except appeal the verdict. In the meantime, judges must sentence them and rely in part on the information they put in their sentencing memorandum.

Victim Impact Statements and the Victim's Version of Events

Many U.S. jurisdictions today request victims of crimes to submit their own versions of the offense as a victim impact statement (Umbreit, 1994). The **victim impact statement** is a "statement made by the victim and addressed to the judge for consideration in sentencing. It includes a description of the harm inflicted on the victim in terms of financial, social, psychological, and physical consequences of the crime. It also includes a statement concerning the victim's feelings about the crime, the offender, and a proposed sentence" (Erez and Tontodonato (1990:452–453). Victim participation in sentencing is increasingly encouraged, and a victim impact statement is given similar weight to the offender's version of events. Although victim participation in sentencing raises certain ethical, moral, and legal questions, indications are that victim impact statements are used with increasing frequency and appended to PSI reports in various jurisdictions (Bazemore, 1994:19–20).

Victim impact statements may be in the form of an attachment to a PSI report in which victims provide a written account of how the crime and offender influenced them. Victims may also make a speech or verbal declaration during the offender's sentencing hearing. This is ordinarily a prepared document read by one or more victims at the time offenders are sentenced (Erez and Tontodonato, 1990:453; Erez et al., 1994). The admission of victim impact statements is controversial. Defense attorneys may feel that these statements are inflammatory and detract from objective sentencing considerations. Victim impact statements may intensify sentencing disparities in certain jurisdictions with sentencing schemes that rely more heavily on subjective judicial impressions than in those jurisdictions in which more objective sentencing criteria are used, such as mandatory sentencing procedures or guidelines-based sentencing schemes. Proponents of victim impact statements believe that such statements personalize the sentencing process by showing that actual persons were harmed by certain offender conduct. In addition, victim's rights advocates contend that victims have a moral right to influence one's punishment (Alexander and Lord, 1994). In recent years, the U.S. Supreme Court ruled that victim impact statements are constitutional in *Payne v. Tennessee* (1991). (See Box 3.5.)

Some evidence suggests that victim impact statements have little or no effect on sentencing severity in those jurisdictions in which victims spoke out against their victimizers. An investigation of 293 cases in which victim impact statements were given showed little if any difference, given the nature of the conviction offense and the usual punishments imposed by judges (Davis and Smith, 1994a). Thus, sentencing decisions were made apart from a consideration of victim impact statements during sentencing hearings. When imposing sentences, judges relied more upon the offender's

BOX 3.5 Victim Impact Statements

On the Constitutionality of Victim Impact Statements

Booth v. Maryland, 482 U.S. 496, 107 S.Ct. 2529 (1987). Booth was convicted of first-degree murder in a Baltimore, Maryland, court. During his sentencing hearing, a victim impact statement (VIS) was read so that his sentence might be enhanced or intensified. Following the sentence of death, Booth appealed, alleging that the VIS was a violation of his Eighth Amendment right against cruel and unusual punishment. The U.S. Supreme Court agreed and said that during sentencing phases of capital murder trials, the introduction of VISs is unconstitutional. Among its reasons cited for this opinion, the U.S. Supreme Court said that VISs create an unacceptable risk that a jury may impose the death penalty in an arbitrary and capricious manner. Thus, VIS information may be totally unrelated to the blameworthiness of the offender. However, the U.S. Supreme Court changed its mind in *Payne v. Tennessee.*

Payne v. Tennessee, 501 U.S. 808, 111 S.Ct. 2597 (1991). Payne was convicted of a double murder. At the sentencing hearing, Payne introduced various witnesses on his behalf to avoid the death penalty. During the same hearing, the victims' relatives introduced their victim impact statement, pressing the jury to impose the death penalty on Payne. The death penalty was imposed and Payne appealed, contesting the introduction of damaging evidence and opinions expressed in the victim impact statement. The U.S. Supreme Court upheld Payne's death sentence, holding that victim impact statements do not violate an offender's Eighth Amendment rights. The significance of this case is that it supports and condones the use of victim impact statements against convicted offenders during sentencing hearings.

prior record and crime seriousness. Victim impact statements did not produce sentencing decisions that reflected more clearly the effects of crime on particular victims (Davis and Smith, 1994a).

The *fact* of victim involvement in the sentencing process, whether such involvement actually persuades judges to impose harsher penalties on offenders, seems to produce greater satisfaction among victims with the criminal justice system. A sample of 293 victims showed that their perceptions of involvement in the sentencing process were sufficient to increase their satisfaction that justice was served by the sentences imposed (Davis and Smith, 1994b). The cathartic impact of having an opportunity to speak out against convicted offenders does much to assuage the feelings of the victim.

What Is the Influence of PSI Reports on Judicial Sentencing Decisions? Judges may treat the PSI the same way they treat plea agreements. They may concur with probation officer sentencing recommendations, or they may ignore these reports. However, because most convictions occur through plea bargaining, the only connection a judge usually has with the defendant before sentencing is through the PSI report. In federal district

BOX 3.6 Birth Control as Crime Prevention?

The Case of Debra Ann Forster

What should you do with a woman who leaves two toddlers, ages 6 months and 18 months, alone in a sweltering apartment for three days? Lynch her? How about sterilization?

Maricopa County Superior Court Judge Lindsay Ellis Budzyn heard just such a case. A woman, Debra Ann Forster, 18, of Mesa, Arizona, was charged with leaving her two sons alone for three days in a sweltering apartment. When Forster appeared before the judge, her excuse was unacceptable. The judge found her guilty and imposed the following sentence: Debra Forster must use birth control for her remaining childbearing years.

As a way of checking to see that the court order is obeyed, Forster is required to periodically provide written evidence to her probation officer. Forster was married at age 15. She said that she had been overwhelmed by the job of taking care of her two boys after her marriage broke up. Both children, as well as a daughter born in March 1988, have since been adopted by others through a state agency.

The sentence was applauded by many Arizona residents who condemned Forster's actions as abominable. However, the American Civil Liberties Union and the Catholic Church protested her sentence as unusually harsh. According to the ACLU, the state has no right to interfere in Forster's freedom to become pregnant.

How would you decide? What should Forster's punishment be? Because Forster has proved to be incapable as a parent, do you believe her "creative" sentence from the judge was fair?

Source: Adapted from "Inconceivable Sentence," *Time*, June 6, 1988:27.

courts, judges may decide not to order PSIs if they feel there is sufficient information about the convicted offender to "enable the meaningful exercise of sentencing discretion, and the court explains this finding on the record" (18 U.S.C., Rule 32(c)(1), 1997). Sometimes defendants may waive their right to have a PSI report prepared as long as the court approves.

It would be foolish to conclude that PSI reports have *no* impact on judicial sentencing decisions. The contents of PSI reports furnish judges with a detailed account of an offender's prior record. However, the influence of socioeconomic, gender, and racial or ethnic differences on judicial attitudes and sentencing severity is pervasive, although we do not know for sure how heavily these factors influence particular judges. Most judges weigh heavily one's prior record when imposing prison terms or nonincarcerative alternatives. Many judges believe themselves to be fair and impartial when imposing sentences on offenders of different genders or races; however, their actions strongly suggest that these variables *do* influence their decisions, although the impact of these variables is not consistent for judges across all jurisdictions (Brantingham, 1985; Figueira-McDonough, 1985; Pollack and Smith, 1983). Good predictors of sentence type and sentence length are case facts, offender characteristics such as age, educational level, and employment history, and prior record of other criminal activity (Brantingham, 1985). Crime seriousness and victim injury also figure prominently when judges calculate the most appropriate sentences for offenders (Champion, 1988a; 1988c).

Judges have considerable sentencing power under most sentencing schemes. Mandatory sentences must be imposed on offenders for specific conviction offenses, although prosecutors decide in advance which crimes will or will not be prosecuted. Judges see only the conviction offense rather than any other charges that have been dropped. The fairest scenario for convicted offenders is for judges to have a knowledge of both the bad and good information about offenders and their crimes. Bad information (unfavorable to offenders) is often expressed as aggravating circumstances, while good information (favorable to offenders) consists of mitigating circumstances. These circumstances are most often detailed in the PSI report.

AGGRAVATING AND MITIGATING CIRCUMSTANCES

Aggravating Circumstances

Aggravating circumstances are those circumstances that may intensify the severity of punishment. Listed below are some of the factors considered by judges to be "aggravating":

1. Whether the crime involved death or serious bodily injury to one or more victims
2. Whether the crime was committed while the offender was out on bail facing other criminal charges
3. Whether the offender was on probation, parole, or work release at the time the crime was committed
4. Whether the offender was a recidivist and had committed several previous offenses for which he/she had been punished
5. Whether the offender was the leader in the commission of the offense involving two or more offenders
6. Whether the offense involved more than one victim and/or was a violent or nonviolent crime
7. Whether the offender treated the victim(s) with extreme cruelty during the commission of the offense
8. Whether the offender used a dangerous weapon in the commission of the crime and the risk to human life was high

Whenever PSI reports or sentencing hearings disclose one or more aggravating circumstances about the offender or crime committed, judges are likely to intensify the punishment imposed. This might mean a longer sentence, incarceration instead of probation, or a sentence to be served in a maximum-security prison rather than a minimum- or medium-security institution. Mitigating circumstances may influence judges to be lenient with offenders and place them on probation rather than in jail or prison. A sentence of a year or less may be imposed rather than a five-year term, for example.

Mitigating Circumstances

Mitigating circumstances are those circumstances considered by the sentencing judge to lessen the crime's severity. Some of the more frequently cited mitigating factors in the commission of crimes might be the following:

1. Offender did not cause serious bodily injury by his/her conduct during the commission of the crime
2. Convicted defendant did not contemplate that his/her criminal conduct would inflict serious bodily injury on anyone
3. Offender acted under duress or extreme provocation
4. Offender's conduct was possibly justified under the circumstances
5. Offender was suffering from mental incapacitation or physical condition that significantly reduced his/her culpability in the offense
6. Offender cooperated with authorities in apprehending other participants in the crime or in making restitution to the victims for losses suffered
7. Offender committed the crime through motivation to provide necessities for himself/herself or his/her family
8. Offender did not have a previous criminal record

Judges weigh the mitigating and aggravating circumstances involved in an offender's conviction offense. If the aggravating circumstances outweigh the mitigating ones, then the judge is justified in intensifying sentencing severity. If the mitigating circumstances outweigh the aggravating ones, then judges may exhibit greater leniency in their sentencing decision. Judges have considerable discretionary power when sentencing offenders. How particular aggravating or mitigating circumstances might be evaluated are highly individualized according to particular judges. More than a few judges are especially severe when sentencing child sexual abusers, for example. They may impose especially harsh sentences even though there may be extensive mitigating circumstances, simply because they don't like child sexual abusers. Other judges have similar inclinations, depending upon the nature of the offense and attitude of the offender. Besides these factors, judges also consider the risk or dangerousness posed by particular offenders. If judges contemplate placing some of these convicted offenders on probation and allowing them freedom to move about within their communities, then these judges will want to have some objective criteria to assist them in their probation decision. Since the early 1980s, the use of risk instruments and predictors of dangerousness have become increasingly important components in judicial sentencing decisions.

RISK ASSESSMENT AND INSTITUTIONAL PLACEMENT

What are *dangerousness* and *risk?* Dangerousness and risk refer essentially to the same phenomenon. Dangerousness and risk indicate propensities to cause harm to others or oneself. Risk (or dangerousness) instruments are screening devices intended to distinguish between different types of offenders for purposes of determining initial institutional classification, security placement and inmate management, early-release eligibility, and the level of supervision required under conditions of probation or parole. Most state jurisdictions and the federal government refer to these measures as *risk instruments* rather than *dangerousness instruments* (Illinois has a dangerousness designation; Illinois Department of Corrections, 1988). States vary considerably on the format and content of such measures.

Sentencing and parole decisions are based on multiple factors that include the projected risk of the offender and the danger posed to citizens if probation or parole is granted. For example, Leslie Van Houten, a convicted murderer of actress Sharon Tate and others in the late 1960s and a former member of the Charles Manson "family," has been eligible for parole in California for several years. However, the parole board has consistently denied her request for parole on the basis of her suspected risk to the public if released. It is likely in Van Houten's case, however, that there is a *hidden agenda* that explains her parole denials. Her conviction offenses and how they were committed were so heinous that it is unlikely that she will *ever* be paroled, despite the likelihood that she probably will never reoffend if released.

Generally, risk or dangerousness predictions are most often based on instruments devised by social researchers (Gottfredson and Tonry, 1987). Each is methodologically flawed, and no instrument yet devised can be used with absolute confidence when sentencing offenders (Monahan, 1984). However, it is well-known that long-term predictions of future dangerousness are used throughout the criminal justice process in investigation, pretrial detention, bail, sentencing, prison administration, and early-release decisions (Morris and Miller, 1985).

Risk assessment measures are used for the purpose of determining probabilities that inmates, probationers, or parolees will pose a risk or a danger to themselves or to others (Champion, 1994). These probabilities are subsequently used for placement, program, and security decision making. Needs measures and instruments enable corrections personnel and administrative staffs to highlight client weaknesses or problems that may have led initially to their convictions or difficulties. Once problem-areas have been targeted, specific services or treatments might be scheduled and provided.

Risk and needs instruments were increasingly used during the 1960s (Spieker and Pierson, 1989:6). Some risk measures were used with juvenile offenders. Subsequently, numerous behavioral and psychological instruments were devised and used for the purpose of assessing client risk or inmate dangerousness. The Minnesota Multiphasic Personality Inventory (MMPI), consisting of 550 true-false items, was originally used in departments of corrections for personality assessments. This instrument is still applied in many correctional settings by researchers such as Edwin Megargee. These researchers have extracted certain items from the MMPI for use as predictors of inmate violence and adjustment (Megargee and Carbonell, 1985). Classifications such as Megargee's are often designated as *MMPI-based assessments or classifications.* Applications of scales such as Megargee's have received mixed results and evaluations. Some studies show that these scales do not predict one's future behavior very well (Megargee and Carbonell, 1985).

Much of the early work with risk instruments involved juvenile delinquents. For instance, Quay devised a relatively simple typology of delinquent behavior, classifying delinquents into four categories: undersocialized aggression, socialized aggression, attention deficit, and anxiety-withdrawal-dysphoria (Quay and Parsons, 1971). Juveniles would complete a self-administered questionnaire and their personality scores would be quickly tabulated. Depending upon how certain juveniles were classified, a variety of treatments would be administered to help them. Later, Quay (1984) created **AIMS (Adult Internal Management System).** Quay also used a self-administered inventory, the Correctional Adjustment Checklist and the Correctional Adjustment Life History (Sechrest, 1987:302–303). His adult typology consisted of five types of inmates: aggressive psychopathic, manipulative, situational, inadequate-dependent, and neurotic-anxious. Sechrest (1987:303) and others (Spieker and Pierson, 1989) consider AIMS more of an inmate management tool rather than a rehabilitative or treatment-centered one, however.

The **I-level classification** system, which refers to the Interpersonal Maturity Level Classification System, was originally devised by Sullivan, Grant, and Grant (1957). It is based on a combination of developmental and psychoanalytic theories and is administered by psychologists or psychiatrists in lengthy clinical interviews (Spieker and Pierson, 1989). Clients are classified as being at particular "I levels," such as I-1, I-2, and so on, up to I-7. Each I level is a developmental stage reflecting one's ability to cope with complex personal and interpersonal problems. The higher the I level, the better adjusted the client, according to its proponents. In recent years, several jurisdictions have devised special risk assessment devices for females (Spieker and Pierson, 1989:7-8). For instance, Illinois developed and implemented a female initial classification instrument in January 1984 (Illinois Department of Corrections, 1988). Actually, the Illinois instrument devised for female offender classification is very similar to the one used to classify male offenders.

State corrections departments began to create and apply risk assessment schemes in the mid-1980s. For example, Arizona created its first Offender Classification System manual in 1986 (Arizona Department of Corrections, 1991). Most jurisdictions are currently revising or have recently revised their risk and needs instruments (Champion, 1994). An example of a classification instrument is shown in Figure 3.3, the Alaska

Classification Form for Sentenced Prisoners. In addition to routine information about prisoners and their identifying numbers, ages, and types of cases, this form also includes whether there are any detainer warrants for the named prisoner. A **detainer warrant** is issued by another state and indicates that the named inmate is wanted, usually for other criminal charges. Thus, it is important for prison officials to know whether a given prisoner is wanted by one or more states elsewhere. "Wanted" prisoners do not especially want to be extradited to other jurisdictions following their incarceration in an Alaska prison. Therefore, they are deemed greater risks than inmates who do not have detainer warrants against them.

The Alaska Classification Form for Sentenced Prisoners also measures the severity of the conviction offense; the time to a firm release date or parole; numbers and types of prior convictions; history of violent behavior; present security level; involvement with drugs or alcohol; record of disciplinary infractions while confined; responsibility demonstrated by the inmate; and "family/community," which is an indication of whether there is a familial or community support system for the inmate when paroled. Many states have classification instruments such as the one used by Alaska. Among other things, the Alaska Classification Form enables prison officials to determine which custody level (e.g., minimum-, medium-, or maximum-security custody) is most appropriate for particular inmates. Officials may use the instrument to increase or decrease an inmate's current custody level. These assessments are conducted regularly, such as every six months or year. *Overrides* are options to prison officials who may agree or disagree with an inmate's score and potential placement in one custody level or another.

Classification and Its Functions

Several important functions are served by classification instruments:

1. Classification systems enable authorities to make decisions about appropriate offender program placements.
2. Classification systems help to identify one's needs and the provision of effective services in specialized treatment programs.
3. Classification helps determine one's custody level if confined in either prisons or jails.
4. Classification helps to adjust one's custody level during confinement, considering behavioral improvement and evidence of rehabilitation.
5. While confined, inmates may be targeted for particular services and/or programs to meet their needs.
6. Classification may be used for offender management and deterrence relative to program or prison rules and requirements.
7. Classification schemes are useful for policy decision making and administrative planning relevant for jail and prison construction, the nature and number of facilities required, and the types of services to be made available within such facilities.

STATE OF ALASKA **DEPARTMENT OF CORRECTIONS**

Classification Form for Sentenced Prisoners

(1) ______________________ (2) ______________________
Institution Prisoner Name

(3) ______________________ (4) ______________________
Date Date of Birth

(6) ______________________ (6) ______________________
Type of Case: Regular or Exception OBSCIS Number

SECTION A SECURITY SCORING

1. Type of Detainer:

0 = None 3 = Class C Felony 7 = Unclassified or
1 = Misdemeanor 5 = Class B Felony Class A Felony [ ] 1

2. Severity of Current Offense:

1 = Misdemeanor 3 = Class C Felony 7 = Unclassified or
5 = Class B Felony Class A Felony [ ] 2

3. Time to Firm Release Date:

0 = 0-12 months 3 = 60-83 months
1 = 13-59 months 5 = 84 + months ______________ [ ] 3
Firm Release Date

4. Type of Prior Convictions:

0 = None 1 = Misdemeanor 3 = Felony [ ] 4

5. History of Escapes or Attempted Escapes:

	None	+15 Years	10-15 Years	5-10 Years	-5 Years	
Minor	0	1	1	2	3	
Serious	0	4	5	6	7	[ ] 5

6. History of Violent Behavior:

	None	+15 Years	10-15 Years	5-10 Years	-5 Years	
Minor	0	1	1	2	3	
Serious	0	4	5	6	7	[ ] 6

7. SECURITY TOTAL [ ]

8. Security Level:

Minimum = 0-6 points Medium = 7-13 points Maximum = 14-36 points

SECTION B CUSTODY SCORING

1. Percent of Time Served:

3 = 0 thru 25% 5 = 76 thru 90%
4 = 26 thru 75% 6 = 91 plus % [ ]

FIGURE 3.3 Alaska Classification Form for Sentenced Prisoners.

2. Involvement with Drugs and/or Alcohol:

2 = Current 3 = Past 4 = Never [ ]

3. Mental/Psychological Stability:

2 = Unfavorable 4 = No referral or favorable [ ]

4. Type Most Serious Disciplinary Report:

1 = Major 3 = Low Moderate 5 = None
2 = High Moderate 4 = Minor [ ]

5. Frequency of Displinary Reports:

0 = 5 + Reports 2 = 1 Report
1 = 2 - 4 Reports 3 = None [ ]

6. Responsibility Prisoner has Demonstrated:

0 = Poor 2 = Average 4 = Good [ ]

7. Family/Community:

3 = None or Minimal 4 = Average or Good [ ]

---

8. CUSTODY TOTAL: [ ]

---

9. Custody Change Scale:

Prisoner's Present Security Level	Consider Custody Increase if Points	Continue Present Custody if Points	Consider Custody Decrease if Points
Minimum	11-19 Points	20-22 Points	23-30 Points
Medium	11-19 Points	20-24 Points	25-30 Points
Maximum	11-19 Points	20-27 Points	28-30 Points

10: ______________________ ______________________
PRESENT CUSTODY RECOMMENDED CUSTODY

11. Administrative/Program Considerations:

1. Release Plans
2. Medical
3. Psychiatric
4. Education
5. Special Treatment
6. Ethnic/Cultural Consideration
7. Overcrowding
8. Judicial Recommendation
9. Residence

12. Explanation:

SECTION C INSTITUTION ACTION

---

1. Recommendation/Justification______________________

---

2. Recommendation based on: _______Points Total _____Management Override

3. Community Custody Provisions (if applicable):______________________

(figure continues)

4. Date of Next Review: ______________

5. Chair Person: ______________________
   Member: ______________________
   Member: ______________________

6. Superintendent's Action (if applicable): __________Approve __________Disapprove

Comments:____
____
____

COPY RECEIVED

PRISONER SIGNATURE ______________________ DATE ______________________

Notice to Sentenced Prisoners:

(1) The sentenced prisoner designation is without administrative appeal;
(2) Classification Committee action not referred to nor modified by the Superintendent may be appealed only to the Superintendent, and no higher;
(3) Classification Committee action referred to or modified by the Superintendent, except for transfer, may be appealed to the Regional Director in accordance with 760.01, Appeal Procedures;
(4) Classification Committee action regarding transfer may be appealed directly to the Deputy Commissioner for Operations in accordance with 760.01, Appeal Procedures;
(5) Forms to facilitate an appeal will be provided by institutional staff upon request by the prisoner;
(6) An appeal must be routed through the institutional staff member designated for the purpose of receiving and forwarding classification appeals; and
(7) Any classification action may be commenced pending an appeal, except a transfer to an out-of-state facility.

FIGURE 3.3 ***(continued)***

8. Classification systems enable parole boards to make better early-release decisions about eligible offenders.
9. Community corrections agencies can use classification schemes to determine those parolees who qualify for participation and those who don't qualify.
10. Classification systems enable assessments of risk and dangerousness to be made, generally in anticipation of the type of supervision best suited for particular offenders.
11. Classification schemes assist in decision making relevant for community crime control, the nature of penalties to be imposed, and the determination of punishment.
12. Classification may enable authorities to determine whether selective incapacitation is desirable for particular offenders or offender groupings.

Incarcerative Decisions: Jail or Prison?

Should offenders be placed on probation or in jail or prison? Probation officers make recommendations in their PSI reports. The court considers this recommendation but is not bound by it. A plea agreement may stipulate a particular sentence, and in most instances, judges approve of these stipulated sentences. The just deserts philosophy is a dominant theme in American corrections today; and given the sentences they impose, judges appear

BOX 3.7 Vampire Child Sexual Abusers

The Case of Child Sexual Abuser-Vampire

Jon C. Bush, 27-year-old air-conditioner repairman, is a vampire and child sexual molester in his spare time. When he is not fixing someone's air conditioner, he is biting little girls and having sex with them. It happened in Virginia Beach, Virginia, in September 1996.

Bush was convicted of sexually molesting eight teenage girls as a part of an elaborate vampire game. Bush would dress up as a vampire, complete with artificial vampire teeth, and bite unwitting young girls on the neck. Then he would have sex with them to initiate them into the vampire world. His criminal convictions were for crimes against nature, indecent liberties, and contributing to the delinquency of a minor. The combined sentences could total 100 years in prison.

The girls testified that Bush taught them a game in which he played the leader of a family of ancient vampires. The girls would paint their faces white and lips and fingernails black for excursions to malls or the ocean front. Bush wore snap-on fangs and would walk with his hands folded in an "X" pattern across his chest. The girls were told that they could become vampires if they let him have sex with them and bite them on their breasts, neck, and navels. His bites were considered "marks" and the girls said he bit them "hard." Then they would submit to his sexual advances, which included oral-genital and oral-anal contact, in addition to straight sexual intercourse. The girls ranged in age from 13 to 16.

How would you punish Jon Bush? Should he receive 100 years for his crimes? What kind of information would you provide young teens to help them avoid persons such as Bush? Can this type of sexual misconduct and deviance be averted by any general deterrent program?

Source: Adapted from Associated Press, "'Vampire Family' Leader Convicted of Biting, Sexually Molesting Girls." *Minot (N.D.) Daily News*, September 11, 1996:A2.

to be influenced by this philosophy. Generally, their interest is in imposing sentences on offenders that are equated with the seriousness of the conviction offense. However, some evidence suggests that they are influenced by other factors as well (Kempf and Austin, 1986).

Laws in most states permit pretrial detention of defendants who are considered dangerous (Gottlieb and Rosen, 1984). Judges are not prevented from using risk measures as one of several sentencing criteria. Risk assessment information is treated together with the contents of PSI reports. Some persons oppose the use of risk assessments in sentencing decisions, however, because it is difficult if not impossible to forecast one's dangerousness in any absolute sense (Wilkins, 1985). Morris (1974) suggests that "punishment should not be imposed, nor the term of punishment extended, by virtue of a prediction of dangerousness, beyond that which would be justified as a deserved punishment independently of that prediction."

Offenders Also Have Needs. Offenders who are considered a risk to themselves or others also have one or more needs. Most jurisdictions have developed instruments to assess one's needs. *Needs assessment devices* are instruments that measure an offender's personal/social skills; health, well-being, and emotional stability; educational level and vocational strengths and weaknesses; alcohol/drug dependencies; mental ability; and other relevant life factors, and which highlight those areas for which services are available and could or should be provided. If some offenders are illiterate, they may be placed, either voluntarily or involuntarily, into an educational program at some level, depending upon the amount of remedial work deemed necessary (Oberst, 1988). Psychologically disturbed or mentally ill offenders may require some type of counseling or therapy. Some offenders may require particular medications for illnesses or other maladies.

Risk and needs assessments may be combined in a more lengthy instrument and labeled simply as **risk-needs assessments.** Figure 3.4 shows an Alaska Needs Assessment Survey. This survey solicits information about an inmate's health, intellectual ability, behavioral/emotional problems, alcohol and/or drug abuse, educational level, vocational status, and the nature of one's skills. On the basis of this survey, correctional officials can plan more effectively and place particular inmates into prison programs that may help them improve their educational or vocational skills. Appropriate group or individual counseling or therapy may be provided, if the survey shows a particular need (e.g., alcohol or drug dependency).

However, virtually every risk or needs instrument is inherently flawed. More than a few experts are skeptical about their application in corrections and the types of decisions they encourage officials to make concerning particular prisoners. For instance, Sechrest (1987) says that classification schemes that match certain offenders with specific treatment programs often lack theoretical coherence. Thus, while classifications of offenders result in separate categorizations destined to receive certain treatments and services, considerable variation exists among individual offenders within each category. Therefore, there are frequent mismatches between classification systems and the treatment programs prescribed. For example, checking one category or another in a given need area can make a considerable difference in the lives of offenders who are subsequently placed or misplaced in particular remedial, educational, vocational, or therapeutic programs. Sechrest's criticism is sound, because scales such as the Alaska Needs Assessment Survey often may result in offender/treatment program mismatches and treatment ineffectiveness.

Types of Risk Assessment Instruments

There are three different kinds of risk prediction: (1) anamnestic prediction, (2) actuarial prediction, and (3) clinical prediction (Morris and Miller, 1985:13–14).

STATE OF ALASKA NEEDS ASSESSMENT SURVEY DEPARTMENT OF CORRECTIONS

Prisoner Name:____________________ Institution:________________________ Date:______

Staff member making assessment:____________________; Select best description and enter number at right:

A. HEALTH:

1. Sound physical health, ability, able to function independently.	2. Handicap or illness which interferes with functioning on a recurring basis.	3. Serious handicap or chronic illness, needs frequent medical care.	_____

B. INTELLECTUAL ABILITY:

1. Normal intellectual ability, able to function independently.	2. Mild retardation, some need for assistance.	3. Moderate retardation, independent functioning severely limited.	_____

C. BEHAVIORAL/EMOTIONAL PROBLEMS:

1. Exhibits appropriate emotional responses.	2. Symptoms limit adequate functioning, requires counseling, may require medication.	3. Symptoms prohibit adequate functioning, requires significant intervention; may require medication or separate housing.	_____

NOTE: If number 2, or 3, is most appropriate for this prisoner for A, B, or C. above, obtain a Medical/Psychiatric Records Extract (form 20-807.060) as supplement to this form.

D. ALCOHOL ABUSE:

1. No alcohol problem.	2. Occasional abuse, some disruption of functioning.	3. Frequent abuse, serious disruption, needs treatment.	_____

E. DRUG ABUSE:

1. No drug problem.	2. Occasional abuse, some disruption of functioning.	3. Frequent abuse, serious disruption, needs treatment.	_____

F. EDUCATIONAL STATUS:

1. Has high school diploma or GED.	2. Some deficits, but potential for high school diploma or GED.	3. Major deficits in and/or reading, needs remedial programs.	_____

G. VOCATIONAL STATUS:

1. Has sufficient skills to obtain and hold satisfactory employment.	2. Minimal skill level, needs enhancement.	3. Virtually unemployable, needs training	_____

List Skills:	List Skills:	List possible skills to acquire:
__________	__________	____________________
__________	__________	____________________
__________	__________	____________________
__________	__________	____________________

PROGRAM RECOMMENDATION

1. Housing:____

2. Work assignment:__________________________________

3. Program assignments:______________________________

4. Other:____

FIGURE 3.4 Alaska Needs Assessment Survey.

1. *Anamnestic prediction.* Anamnestic prediction is a forecast of offender future behavior based on past circumstances. If the past circumstances include hanging out with a gang, being a part of a dysfunctional family, being addicted to drugs and/or alcohol, and doing poorly in school and at work, then a comparison is made with present circumstances. If the present (and projected) circumstances are different, then perhaps the offender will behave in law-abiding ways. If the circumstances are the same, then the prediction is that the offender will continue to recidivate. For example, a parole-eligible inmate may tell the parole board that he has a new job waiting for him in a town 100 miles from where he was originally arrested. He no longer corresponds or contacts the gang he was a part of when he was convicted. He no longer is addicted to drugs or alcohol, and he has earned a G.E.D. degree. He has taken several self-improvement courses while in prison and has undergone extensive counseling. The parole board will regard this inmate favorably and probably recommend his early release. This is because his circumstances in the future are different from his circumstances in the past. By the same token, another parole-eligible inmate may say that he resents teachers, hates education, has no job, does not know what he plans to do, still corresponds with his friends and gang members, and will probably go back to using drugs and alcohol. Further, he rejects counseling of any kind and thinks psychiatrists and counselors are "stupid." It is unlikely that his present (and future) circumstances are going to be much different from his past circumstances. His parole will probably be denied.
2. *Actuarial prediction.* Actuarial prediction is based on the characteristics of a segment of offenders who reoffend. If we study the characteristics of a large sample of recidivists who are returned to prison, for example, we may find that they are young, black, uneducated, lacking in vocational skills and training, and come from dysfunctional families. Therefore, when parole boards or judges see new probation- or parole-eligible offenders fit this profile, judges and parole boards tend to respectively place offenders in prisons or jails or deny their early release. Studies of failures or those offenders who recidivate contain descriptions of *aggregate characteristics of persons who have already failed.* Theoretically, others in the future with similar characteristics are deemed more likely to reoffend than those who do not match these aggregate characteristics. However, it seems that program failures often resemble closely those who succeed. But corrections departments focus more on failures than successes when considering persons for parole. Judges are inclined to decide similarly about whether to grant probation or impose an incarcerative sentence.
3. *Clinical prediction.* Clinical prediction is based on the professional training and expertise of those who work directly with offenders. Based on extensive diagnostic examinations, the belief is that the offender will behave in a certain way. The subjectivity inherent in clinical prediction is apparent. The skills of the assessor are critical. However, such prediction is more expensive, because each clinical prediction is individualized. Both anamnestic and actuarial prediction respectively utilize situational factors and general characteristics of *offenders* in forecasting their future risk.

The highest degrees of validity are associated with actuarial and anamnestic predictions (those currently used by parole boards), and these types of prediction are considered more reliable than clinical prediction. Clinical prediction is more of an art and depends on one's experience, training, and association with clients (Floud and Young, 1981:29, 1982). Looking at all three types of prediction, however, we can say that *no prediction method is more or less valid or reliable than the others.* Further, *instrument complexity* does not seem to make much of a difference in the reliability and validity of predictions. Simple instruments seem to have about the same predictive utility as more complex instruments. Few studies, if any, have shown conclusively that more complex instruments are better. We may think that greater complexity should be equated with greater predictive accuracy, but comparisons of the predictive power of more complex instruments compared with simple ones are categorically disappointing.

There are various limitations associated with risk prediction instruments. For instance, Morris and Miller (1985:35–37) have suggested three guiding principles for parole boards to consider when making early-release decisions:

1. Punishment should not be imposed, nor the term of punishment extended, by virtue of a prediction of dangerousness, beyond that which would be justified as a deserved punishment independently of that prediction.
2. Provided this limitation is respected, predictions of dangerousness may properly influence sentencing decisions and other decisions under criminal law.
3. The base expectancy rate of violence for the criminal predicted as dangerous must be shown by reliable evidence to be substantially higher than the base expectancy rate of another criminal with a closely similar criminal record and convicted of a closely similar crime but not predicted as unusually dangerous, before the greater dangerousness of the former may be relied on to intensify or extend his/her punishment.

False Positives and False Negatives

It is impossible to incarcerate all convicted criminals. It is also debatable whether certain offenders should be incarcerated (Spelman, 1994). Therefore, both judges and parole boards exert absolute influence over which offenders will be incarcerated and which ones will be conditionally released, either on probation or parole. Mistakes by judges and parole boards occur frequently, whereby some offenders are released into the community and are deemed not to be dangerous (Farrington, 1992). Nevertheless, these "nondangerous" persons turn out to be quite dangerous, with some offenders committing serious new offenses, including rape, robbery, and murder. By the same token, some offenders are ordered incarcerated by judges or are denied parole by parole boards, because these authorities believe that these particular offenders have a strong likelihood of committing new and serious offenses if they are freed into their communities. But some of these "dangerous" offenders might never commit new crimes if freed. These two scenarios describe a great correctional dilemma. Who should we lock up and who should we release?

False Positives. **False positives** are offenders who are believed to be dangerous or more likely to pose a risk to others; however, these offenders will never reoffend. False positives are unfairly penalized. Often it is because they attained a score on a risk instrument that gave officials the impression that they would be dangerous or pose a risk to others. However, the fallibility of prediction tools is such that considerable *overprediction* occurs. A man who kills his wife in the heat of passion, for example, might never kill again. Circumstances associated with the murder might be that the man, a law-abiding religious person with no prior criminal record, came home unexpectedly one night and found his wife in bed with another man. The outrage and indignation prompted the husband to grab a nearby handgun and kill his wife in the heat of anger. This may be the only time in the man's life when such a crime will ever be committed. If this man were subsequently released, he might never commit another murder. This doesn't mean that we are *excusing* the murder of the man's wife; rather, circumstances were such that it is unlikely that the man will ever be confronted by them again.

Yet false positives rightly object to their extra punishment because of some score they receive on a risk instrument or from a clinical diagnosis. We are penalizing these persons for crimes that they have not yet committed. Their past crimes are often easily explained, but their risk scores may tell a tale quite different from any future misconduct on their part (Farrington, 1992; Gottfredson and Gottfredson, 1992).

False Negatives. **False negatives** are persons predicted not to be dangerous, who are freed into their communities and eventually turn out to be dangerous by committing new serious offenses. We are afraid of false negatives. These are persons with low risk or dangerousness scores. These are persons the correctional system trusts. Again, the obvious fallibility of prediction measures lures us into making the wrong decisions for the right reasons. After all, these persons *did* receive low risk scores on these tests and measures. How much trust should we have in such instrumentation?

When false negatives are placed on probation or parole, and when they commit especially heinous acts, they attract media attention. In Seattle, Washington, a man was serving time for raping a woman. At his sentencing hearing, he vowed that when freed, he would hunt down the woman and kill her for testifying against him. The woman moved to Oregon several years later. She continued to rebuild her life and acquire new friends. Five or six years later, the man was released on parole by Washington. He located the woman and murdered both her and her female companion one afternoon, thus fulfilling his earlier promise. The Washington Parole Board was shaken by this turn of events. The risk measures said that the man was no longer a danger or risk to others. The test said he would not reoffend. Even testimony in his behalf from friends and family was such that the parole board was willing to parole him. But the tragic consequences, the double murder, were mute testimony to the parole board error in his case.

Risk Assessment Device Effectiveness

The sentencing practices and other corrections decisions in most states has led to the factors listed in Table 3.4 (Petersilia and Turner, 1987:158). These factors are ordinarily included in risk/dangerousness measures. Ultimately, *prior record and employment history are the two most frequent factors associated with recidivism.*

When designing any instrument to predict future criminal conduct, two crucial questions are (1) which factors are most relevant in such predictions? and (2) what weight should be given each of these factors? We don't know for sure. Prediction studies and the development of risk assessment instruments are criticized because much work is needed to identify the most important criteria associated with future offending (Gottfredson and Gottfredson, 1990). This does not mean that all of the instruments presently developed are worthless as predictors of success on probation or parole. But it does suggest that these measures are imperfect. Therefore, it may be premature to rely exclusively on instrument scores to decide who goes to prison and who receives probation. But in many jurisdictions, risk assessment scores are used precisely for this purpose (Champion, 1994).

Some Applications of Risk/Needs Measures

One way of highlighting the most common applications of risk/needs instruments by various states is to inspect their own utilization criteria and objectives. The following state utilization criteria are not intended to represent *all* other states or to typify them. Rather, they have been highlighted because of their diverse objectives. For example, Arizona's Offender Classification System (OCS) is designed to assign all offenders to an appropriate institutional setting based on required levels of security/custody and the needs of offenders for productive work, education, and treatment during their incarceration (Arizona Department of Corrections, 1991). Additionally, risk prediction tools, as used by the Colorado Parole Guidelines Commission (1988), serve the following purposes:

1. Concentrating secure management and/or program resources on a specific group of "high need" offenders without reducing public safety
2. Promoting greater understanding of the statistical management of the parole release process
3. Significantly improving predictive accuracy over case review or clinical methods
4. Addressing offender needs as they relate to reoffending in the community

Arizona and Colorado risk prediction instrument goals are related to initial placement decisions and management objectives, including allocat-

TABLE 3.4 Factors Included in Formal Guidelines or Classification Instruments

Factor	Sentencing	Community Supervision	Parole Release
Criminal Record			
No. of parole/probation revocations	b	a	a
No. of adult and juvenile arrests	—	b	c
Age at first arrest	—	—	—
Nature of arrest crimes	—	—	—
No. of adult and juvenile convictions	a	b	a
Age at first conviction		a	c
Nature of prior convictions	a	b	a
Repeat of conviction types	c	—	c
No. of previous felony sentences	—	b	—
No. of previous probation sentences	—	b	—
No. of juvenile incarcerations	—	—	b
No. of jail terms served	—	—	b
No. of prison terms served	—	—	a
No. of incarcerations served	b	—	a
Age at first incarceration	—	—	b
Length of current term	—	—	c
Total years incarcerated	—	—	c
Commitment-free period evidenced	c	b	b
On probation/parole at arrest	b	b	b
Nature of current crime:			
Multiple conviction crimes	b	—	—
Involves violence	a	—	a
Is property crime	—	—	c
Weapon involved	c	—	c
Victim injured	a	—	b
Victim/offender forcible contact	—	—	c
Social factors			
Current age	—	c	c
Education level	—	c	c
Employment history	—	b	c
Mental health status	—	c	—
Family relationships	—	c	—
Living arrangements	—	c	c
Drug use	—	a	b
Juvenile use/abuse	—	b	—
Alcohol use/abuse	—	b	c
Companions	—	c	—
Address change in last year	b	—	—
Attitude	b	—	—
Financial status	c	—	—
Prison behavior			
Infractions	—	—	b
Program participation	—	—	c
Release plan formulated	—	—	c
Escape history	—	—	c

[a] 75 percent or more of those instruments identified used this factor.
[b] 50–74 percent of those instruments identified used this factor.
[c] 25–49 percent of those instruments identified used this factor.

Source: Joan Petersilia and Susan Turner, "Guidelines-Based Justice: Prediction and Racial Minorities." In Don M. Gottfredson and Michael Tonry (eds.), *Prediction and Classification: Criminal Justice Decision Making.* Chicago: University of Chicago Press, 1987.

ing scarce resources most profitably in view of system constraints. It is possible to group these diverse objectives according to several general applications. Thus, for most states, the following general applications are made of risk assessment instruments (Champion, 1994):

1. To promote better program planning through optimum budgeting and deployment of resources
2. To target high-risk and high-need offenders for particular custody levels, programs, and services without endangering the safety of others
3. To apply the fair and appropriate sanctions to particular classes of offenders and raise their level of accountability
4. To provide mechanisms for evaluating services and programs as well as service and program improvements over time
5. To maximize public safety as well as public understanding of the diverse functions of corrections by making decision making more open and comprehensible to both citizens and offender-clients

Selective Incapacitation

Ethical, moral, and legal questions are raised when predictors of dangerousness are used that result in one offender's incarceration and another offender's freedom when similar crimes have been committed (Zimring and Hawkins, 1995). This is selective incapacitation. **Selective incapacitation** is the incarceration of offenders who are believed to be most likely to recidivate and commit new offenses. Those offenders believed to have a low propensity to reoffend are freed, either through probation or parole. A decision to incarcerate offenders largely because of their suspected future criminal conduct is, in effect, a penalty for future behaviors that have not as yet occurred. Obviously, more research is needed before judges and others place their faith in existing prediction instruments to make sentencing decisions. But despite existing pitfalls associated with risk and dangerousness measures, they are used with increasing frequency by the courts during sentencing and by prison officials in their attempts to classify offenders (Gottfredson and Gottfredson, 1988). Morris (1984) suggests several principles that are useful when applied in tandem with judicial sentencing and probation officer PSI recommendations:

1. Clinical predictions of dangerousness should not be relied upon other than for short-term intervention.
2. Decisions to restrict offender autonomy should be made by considering the actual extent of harm that may occur and how much individual autonomy of offenders ought to be limited.
3. Predictions of dangerousness are "present condition," not predictions of particular results.

4. Sufficiency of proof of dangerousness should not be confused with proof beyond a reasonable doubt, clear and convincing evidence, or on a balance of probability.
5. Punishment should not be imposed or extended, by virtue of a dangerousness prediction, beyond that justified as "deserved" punishment independent of that prediction.
6. Provided the previous limitation is respected, dangerousness predictions may properly influence sentencing decisions.
7. The base expectancy rate of criminal violence for the criminal predicted as dangerous should be shown by reliable evidence to be "substantially higher" than the rate for another criminal, with a closely similar crime, but not predicted as unusually dangerous, before greater dangerousness of the former may be relied on to intensify or extend the punishment

SOME SENTENCING ISSUES

No matter which sentencing schemes states or the federal government use, there are an unending list of criticisms leveled against them. Criticisms of one type of sentencing system have led to the establishment or enactment of an alternative sentencing scheme. Eventually, critics will mass evidence to show why the new sentencing scheme is unworkable, and thus a never-ending cycle is set in motion for the constant reassessment of how offenders should best be punished. No one has yet devised a universally acceptable answer to the question of how offenders should be sanctioned and which sentencing system is best (Benekos, 1992).

Numerous sentencing reforms have occurred, however, particularly during the 1970s and 1980s (Cavanagh et al., 1993). For example, Arizona undertook an extensive revision of the Arizona Criminal Code in the mid-1970s. The result was a shift to determinate sentencing in 1978. A follow-up study of the impact of this different sentencing scheme compared with the indeterminate sentencing scheme it replaced involved agency record data for felons sentenced between 1989 and 1990 (N = 4,468); a sample of 1,882 prison inmates; and 604 parolees whose parole programs had been revoked (Institute for Rational Public Policy, Inc., 1991). Whereas the Arizona Criminal Code revision and determinate sentencing practice was intended to provide offenders with anticipated certainty, proportionality, and rationality in their punishment, it was found that determinate sentencing failed to produce these results. Instead, Arizona corrections has reported *more* judicial discretion rather than less, escalating prison costs, and glaring sentencing disparities. These are key problems that determinate sentencing was designed to correct. Some offenders were serving disproportionately longer or shorter sentences than others, controlling for prior record and other salient variables. No apparent "just deserts" or deterrent effects were achieved. Arizona has now gone back to the drawing board to try again with new sentencing reforms (Institute for Rational Public Policy, Inc., 1991).

The sentencing reforms implemented by Arizona and most other states have been prompted by various sentencing issues. These issues include (1) sentencing disparities: race, gender, age, and socioeconomic factors; (2) correctional resources and their limitations; (3) the economics of systemic constraints; and (4) jail and prison overcrowding problems.

Sentencing Disparities: Race, Gender, Age, and Socioeconomic Factors

When judges are accused of unfairness in their sentencing practices, they are quick to take offense and allege that they do not discriminate between convicted offenders according to extra-legal variables such as race, gender, age, and socioeconomic status. Most judges believe that their decisions about offenders are made impartially and are free of any overt bias or prejudice. Interviews with both state and federal judges confirm this (Champion, 1988a; Pollack and Smith, 1983). However, an examination of judicial sentencing patterns in various jurisdictions reveals in some instances substantial disparities in sentencing offenders who have similar records and have been convicted of identical offenses (Stolzenberg, 1993). Even among the federal judiciary, the U.S. sentencing guidelines have failed to curb sentencing disparities according to extra-legal factors (Heaney, 1991; Heaney et al., 1992).

In the federal system, for instance, more power has shifted to prosecutors and probation officers and away from judges. Thus, actors in the federal system exert considerable influence over the life chances of offenders before they are sentenced (Heaney, 1991). Judges are only able to impose sentences based upon the factual information they are provided by the prosecution and U.S. Probation Office. If plea agreements have been worked out in advance and federal probation officers have provided their own "spin" on an offender's conviction offense and the circumstances of it, then judicial discretion in sentencing has obviously been diminished. It is easy to see how earlier decision making in the plea agreement phase of a prosecution can take on extra-legal dimensions and how such decision making is attributable to one's race, ethnicity, gender, age, and/or socioeconomic status (Heaney et al., 1992). The power shift to prosecutors as the result of contemporary sentencing reforms was anticipated by various experts as early as 1975 (Hewitt, 1975).

To encourage greater accountability and democracy among judges during the sentencing process, nationwide parameters for sentencing in similar situations have been recommended, the establishment of requirements for judges to submit written reasons for the sentences selected, and opening up judicial decisions to direct and indirect citizen review (Berlin, 1993; M. Davis, 1992). But such requirements are often unwieldy and not easily implemented. Judicial cooperation is required, and few judges are interested in creating more paperwork for themselves (Stolzenberg, 1993; Heaney, 1991).

BOX 3.8 Man Pretends to Have Cancer, Goes to Prison

The Case of Charles Barry

I've got cancer. Look at me. My hair is falling out. I have blood in my urine. I have frequent seizures. Help me. Give me some money so I can survive.

What's wrong with this picture? Charles Barry, 51, of Canterbury, New Hampshire, gave that line to everyone he met, at his church, at his work, and in his family. For six years Barry pretended to have cancer, and police say he used this ploy to get at least $43,000.

Barry was a used car salesman. He claimed to have kidney, lung, and prostate cancer. His former wife and three stepsons believed him. Most of the residents in the town of Canterbury believed him as well. Barry shaved his head, talked about how awful chemotherapy was and dropped red dye in his toilet to make it appear as though he were bleeding from the bowel or had blood in his urine. Sometimes he slammed his head against the wall, claiming to be having seizures.

The county prosecutor, Arnold Huftalen, said "He's a con man, a convicted liar who will be locked up in a cage for the next year, and that's where he belongs." Barry pleaded guilty in May 1996 to various federal fraud charges in U.S. District Court in Providence, Rhode Island. The charges arose from Barry's acceptance of checks from his employer, Grappone Auto Junction in Concord, New Hampshire, which paid him a full salary after Barry went on to his part-time schedule because of his supposed illness. He also received thousands of dollars in contributions from citizens of Canterbury and from two New Hampshire churches. Barry had been a deacon in the United Community Church of Canterbury and had once told the audience to "use him as an example of how to live with adversity." Now Barry can live with adversity himself, real adversity, in a federal prison. In addition to the 14-month prison sentence, Barry was ordered to perform 200 hours of community service and make restitution to all of his "victims," repaying the $43,000 he obtained under false pretenses.

Do you think the sentence imposed by the judge was fair? Although Barry asked the judge for forgiveness during the sentencing phase of his trial, what should the judge have imposed? How would you punish someone such as Barry, who pretended to have a fatal illness?

Source: Adapted from Associated Press, "Man Who Pretended to Have Cancer Sentenced to Prison." *Minot (N.D.) Daily News*, August 16, 1996:A5.

Correctional Resources and Their Limitations

There is only so much that corrections can do to accommodate the growing and increasingly diverse offender population. New prison and jail construction was originally believed to be a practical way of housing and treating greater numbers of offenders. Indeed, the prison space available in 1993 was 4.5 times greater than the prison space that existed in 1965 (Marvell, 1994:59). Despite this expansion of prison space, we would need *at least four times as much space* as presently exists to accommodate the existing population of offenders who deserves to be incarcerated. Where does the money come from for new prison construction? Prison space isn't cheap. In 1995, for example, the average construction cost per bed was $55,618 for 49 new institutions that were opened in 17 different jurisdictions (Camp and Camp, 1995a:38).

In October 1994, for example, Governor Robert P. Casey of Pennsylvania authorized the expenditure of $60.5 million in contracts for the construction of a new, 640-inmate medium-security state correctional institution near Chester, Pennsylvania (*Corrections Digest*, 1994:27). Unfortunately, by the time this facility is completed (the seventh and last prison constructed in Pennsylvania under a prison-expansion initiative commenced in 1990 to add 10,000 beds to the state correctional system), there will be a continuing demand for more prison space as new offenders are sentenced and enter Pennsylvania corrections. In 1995, the entire Pennsylvania prison system was operating at 122 percent of its existing rated prison capacity (Camp and Camp, 1995a:36–37).

But Pennsylvania is not an anomaly in this respect. In 1995, the *average percent of capacity of U.S. prisons was 115 percent* (Camp and Camp, 1995a:36–37). Several prison systems were even worse. Nebraska was operating at 182 percent of its rated prison capacity, while Ohio operated at 170 percent of its rated prison capacity. Only 16 states were operating at less than 100 percent of their rated prison capacities, and most of these were at nearly 100 percent (Camp and Camp, 1995a:36–37). Despite the immense problems of prison expansion and attempts to accommodate growing numbers of offenders, corrections is usually the last in line for funding by most jurisdictions. In 1995, only 4.8 percent of most state and county budgets were allocated to jails and prisons. Only 1.6 percent of the South Dakota state budget was allocated to corrections in 1995. Oregon corrections received only 1.9 percent of the state budget. New Hampshire corrections received only 1.8 percent of the state budget. This budget allocation includes new prison construction, old prison and jail renovations, jail and prison maintenance and operations, and administrator/officer salaries (Camp and Camp, 1995a:48–49). With these meager budgets and allocations, state correctional agencies are expected to "correct" offenders, educate and rehabilitate them, feed and clothe them, and provide law libraries and research resources, medical staff, individual and group psychological therapy and counseling, and myriad other services.

The Economics of Systemic Constraints

Some experts examine the economics of incarceration by comparing the costs saved by offender incapacitation and crime reduction with the direct cost of prisoner maintenance (Marvell, 1996:1–2). Using a cost-benefit analysis, experts compare the actual costs of prisoner maintenance in prison with the potential cost to victims if these inmates were placed on probation instead. Thus, if we incarcerate Offender A for five years, it will cost X dollars. However, if Offender A is placed on probation and *not* incarcerated, the future crimes Offender A *might commit* are estimated and compared with Offender A's incarceration costs.

Several cost-benefit studies have been conducted to examine whether the cost of incarcerating offenders is worth the benefits accruing to victims and the general public (Cavanagh and Kleiman, 1990; Klass, 1994; Marvell and Moody, 1994). Using data from the latest *National Crime Victimization Survey* and *Uniform Crime Reports*, Marvell and Moody (1994) and Cavanagh and Kleiman (1990) have determined that given the average cost of particular index offenses, such as burglary, theft, auto theft, rape, and robbery, the reduced cost to victims by incarcerating a single offender per year is about $19,000. Additionally, crime entails losses such as suffering by victims' families, increased fear of crime by acquaintances, loss to victims' employers for sick leave, and commercial declines in high-crime neighborhoods (Marvell, 1996:2–3). These costs are estimated at about $18,000 per prisoner per year. Together, the cost savings per prisoner per year is about $37,000. Average incarceration costs per prisoner per year, using 1994 dollars, were about $29,000. Thus, it would appear that the "gain" is about $8,000 per prisoner per year accruing to victims and the general public.

It should be noted that these estimates are impossible to verify in any absolute sense, because we have no way of predicting *which* offenders will commit any particular amount of crime if placed on probation instead of being incarcerated. Marvell (1996), Marvell and Moody (1994), and the other experts who have engaged in such cost-benefit study and speculation respectively conclude that a relatively small number of offenders commit disproportionately high amounts of crime over their criminal careers. Therefore, some type of selective incapacitation is a possible solution to the problem of deciding which offenders should be incarcerated for greater or lesser lengths than others. But the state of the art regarding predicting risk and future dangerousness is not particularly sophisticated even in the late 1990s. Thus, the potential use of selective incapacitation raises more issues than it resolves.

Higgins (1996:8) suggests that at least for the foreseeable future, it appears that correctional systems at all levels—local, state, and federal—will continue to face the twin challenges of providing more beds while competing for scarcer government resources. These conflicting forces will place increasing demands on those working within systems as well as for those providing services to support these programs. Also noted by Higgins is that within the federal prison system, at least, it is ordinarily assumed that the "life expectancy" of a prison facility is between 20 and 30 years. However, most major federal prison construction occurred during the 1930s, and many of today's federal prisons are 60 or more years old. He indicates that it is likely that many of these 60-year-old structures will be with us for perhaps another 60 years or longer. Nevertheless, Higgins is optimistic that new prison construction and design within the federal system will enable the Federal Bureau of Prisons to manage and cope more effectively with the growing population of federal inmates (Higgins, 1996:8). In the future, however, most state and federal officials are exploring less costly community-based approaches to offender management (Nebraska Governor's Task Force on Prison Alternatives, 1993).

Jail and Prison Overcrowding Problems

Jail and prison overcrowding conditions influence judicial discretion in sentencing offenders (D'Allessio and Stolzenberg, 1995; Glaser, 1994). Judges have many sentencing options, including incarceration or a non-jail/prison penalty such as fines, probation, community service, restitution to victims, halfway houses, treatment, or some combination of these; or judges may even suspend or stay the execution of sentences (Kaune, 1993). It is precisely because of this broad range of discretionary options associated with the judicial role as well as the independence of other actors in the criminal justice system that has led jail and prison overcrowding to be the most pressing problem facing the criminal justice system today (Gendreau, 1993; Kaune, 1993).

Judges are not solely to blame for jail and prison overcrowding, however. The responsibility for overcrowding problems is shared also by the police, magistrates, prosecutors, parole boards, jail and prison officials, and even probation personnel (U.S. General Accounting Office, 1993b). Judges must balance several interests in the sentencing process. First, they must consider the offender and the seriousness of the crime committed. Should the offender be incarcerated or sentenced to some nonincarcerative alternative? Second, they must be responsive to both the prosecutor and probation officer and their recommendations, whether such recommendations stemmed from plea agreements or PSI reports. Third, they must consider public interests. Will the public good be served by imprisoning an offender, or will these interests be better served by placing offenders in nonincarcerative probation programs in which they can perform constructive services and possibly become rehabilitated? Finally, what will be the impact upon jail or prison populations if judges sentence offenders to incarceration, even for short periods?

One controversial solution to the problem of prison overcrowding is the exportation of prison inmates to jails, often in other states. For several years, several Texas jails have advertised to accommodate federal and state prisoners from other jurisdictions experiencing overcrowding problems. Ordinarily, state and federal prison inmates do not have a choice in deciding where they will be housed for the duration of their sentences. Many county jails in different states are used to house a portion of their state prison overflow. The Knox County Jail in Tennessee, for example, houses federal and state prisoners serving lengthy sentences together with other offenders convicted of misdemeanor offenses who are serving short jail terms.

Taking advantage of Texas jail space are at least two states, Virginia and Hawaii. In 1995, Virginia placed at least 450 of its prison inmates in Texas jails. In May 1995, Virginia authorities sent an additional 154 prison inmates to Texas to be housed in jails. In 1995, over 100 Hawaii state prison inmates were serving their time in Texas jails (*Corrections Today*, 1995:28–29). Besides using Texas jail facilities, Virginia prison officials were also making use of their own county jail facilities to control their inmate overflow. Some Virginia county sheriffs were not pleased with these arrangements because this meant overcrowding in their own jail facilities.

Following numerous lawsuits filed by inmates and jail officials against the Virginia prison system, a Virginia circuit judge ruled on May 2, 1995, that Virginia was violating the law by "illegally stuffing local jails with felons who should be held in state prisons instead" (*Corrections Today*, 1995:30). Jail officials in Alexandria, Richmond, and Virginia Beach collectively alleged that Virginia was causing their county jails to become overcrowded by ordering state prisoners to be housed in their jail facilities. The ruling from the circuit court meant that Virginia would have to look elsewhere to accommodate its growing inmate population. In 1995, Virginia was operating at 139 percent of its rated prison capacity (Camp and Camp, 1995a:37).

KEY TERMS

Aggravating circumstances
AIMS (Adult Internal Management System)
Alternative dispute resolution (ADR)
Augustus, John
Charge reduction plea bargaining
Detainer warrants
Determinate sentencing
Diversion
Failure to appear
False negatives
False positives
Fixed indeterminate sentencing
Freedom of Information Act
Good-time credits
I-level classification
Implicit plea bargaining
Indeterminate sentencing
Judicial plea bargaining
Mandatory sentencing
Minimum/maximum determinate sentencing
Mitigating circumstances
Overcharging
Plea bargaining
Presentence investigation (PSI) report
Presumptive or guidelines-based sentencing
Pretrial release
Prosecutorial bluffing
Risk-needs assessment
Selective incapacitation
Sentence recommendation plea bargaining
Sentencing
Sentencing hearing
Sentencing memorandum
Victim impact statement

QUESTIONS FOR REVIEW

1. What is meant by alternative dispute resolution? How does it alleviate case processing in the courts?
2. What is diversion? What sorts of offenders are placed in diversionary programs?
3. Identify and define four types of sentencing. What type of sentencing is used most frequently among the states?
4. In what ways do presumptive sentencing guidelines constrain judges in their sentencing discretion?
5. What is plea bargaining? What are four types of plea bargaining? Which are most popular and why?
6. What are some important factors considered by judges when sentencing offenders?
7. What is a presentence investigation report? Who prepares the report and when?
8. What does a presentence investigation report contain? When is it used in the criminal justice process?
9. What are some problems associated with risk predictors and instruments that forecast offender dangerousness?
10. What is selective incapacitation? What are some moral and ethical problems associated with selective incapacitation?
11. How is the success of probation programs often measured? Is this type of measure a true reflection of whether a program is effective?
12. Do sentencing disparities exist among judges? What factors are frequently associated with sentencing disparities? How have presumptive and mandatory sentencing schemes influenced sentencing disparities?

SUGGESTED READINGS

Belknap, Joanne. *The Invisible Woman: Gender, Crime and Justice.* Belmont, CA: Wadsworth Publishing Company, 1995.

Friedrichs, David O. *Trusted Criminals: White Collar Crime in Contemporary Society.* Belmont, CA: Wadsworth Publishing Company, 1995.

Irwin, John, and James Austin. *It's About Time: America's Imprisonment Binge.* Belmont, CA: Wadsworth Publishing Company, 1994.

Merry, Sally Engle, and Neal Milner (eds.). *The Possibility of Popular Justice: A Case Study of Community Mediation in the United States.* Ann Arbor, MI: University of Michigan Press.

van den Haag, Ernest. *Punishing Criminals: Concerning a Very Old and Painful Question.* Lanham, MD: University Press of America, 1994.

Wrightsman, Lawrence S., Michael T. Nietzel, and William H. Fortune. *Psychology and the Legal System.* Belmont, CA: Brooks Cole, 1994.

4
Diversion and Standard and Intensive Supervised Probation Programs

CHAPTER OUTLINE

OVERVIEW

- An old friend of yours meets you while you are shopping in a local grocery store. Your friend says he's in the television repair business and wonders if you would like to buy a new color television set still under warranty, but with some minor defects that he has repaired. He says that the television set was worth $599 new but that you could buy it from him for $100. You visit his home and he helps you load a brand new television set into the back of your van. You notice that the television set is still boxed in its original container. Later, you are visited by detectives who want to see the television you purchased from your friend. They compare the serial number on your television with some serial numbers of televisions stolen from a large appliance warehouse a few weeks earlier. Your television was one of the stolen items. Police arrest you on charges of receiving stolen property.
- You are celebrating your fiftieth birthday and throw a party for your friends in your home. Later in the evening, your 24-year-old son shows up with several younger guests and asks if he can join in the celebration. Engaged in a lively conversation with several of your work associates, you say, "Why not?" and your son's group joins in. At your party you are serving beer, wine, and other drinks, together with various party snacks. Your son's friends have some beer and wine. At about 11:00 PM two police officers knock on your door and you invite them in. They received a complaint from the mother of one of the girls with your son. It seems that she is only 16 years of age, although she appears much older. The police find the girl and determine that she is somewhat intoxicated. You are arrested for contributing to the delinquency of a minor because you served liquor to someone under the age of 18.
- You are a waiter in a local restaurant. You are 22 years old. When you are off duty at 11:00 PM on a Saturday night, you go up to the bar and have two beers. On your way home, you are driving down a two-lane country road leading to some apartments. As you turn the corner into your apartment complex on the poorly lighted street, suddenly you see two persons wrestling in the road directly in front of you. You are only going 20 miles per hour, but you cannot stop in time. You run over and kill the two men. Investigating police arrest you and charge you with vehicular homicide, although your blood-alcohol

level is only .04. The state legal limit for intoxication is .08, and you are not legally drunk. Nevertheless, you killed two persons. Certainly you did not expect to encounter two persons wrestling in the middle of a roadway on a poorly lighted street at 12:00 AM. You have no prior record of arrests for anything. Furthermore, a subsequent investigation discloses that both men were very drunk at the time they were fighting in the middle of the street, having come from a local bar down the road.

If you were the prosecutor, what would you recommend in each of these cases? Receiving stolen property, contributing to the delinquency of a minor, and vehicular homicide are serious offenses, although there seem to be mitigating circumstances in each case. Yet each of these offenses carries statutory penalties that vary in severity. Should those who commit crimes, for whatever reason, escape the full punishment of the law? Should exceptions be made for those who ordinarily obey the law but under the circumstances seem to be victims of the situation?

This chapter is about diversion and probation. Diversion occurs before any formal adjudication of offender guilt and is best described as a type of preconviction probation. Although those granted diversion may never be prosecuted, convicted, or incarcerated, diversion is included here as a part of corrections because in most jurisdictions it is ordinarily administered by various correctional agencies. In contrast, probation is granted after a conviction has been obtained. The history of probation is examined briefly, together with an evaluation of its effectiveness. Community reaction to probation is also treated.

CIVIL ALTERNATIVES: ALTERNATIVE DISPUTE RESOLUTION AND DIVERSION

Alternative Dispute Resolution

An increasingly used option by the prosecution is alternative dispute resolution (ADR). ADR is a community-based, informal dispute settlement between offenders and their victims. Misdemeanants, or those who commit minor crimes, are most often targeted for ADR (Alaska Judicial Council, 1992). However, some first-offender felons might also be included in such programs. More ADR programs are being established throughout the United States annually (Royse and Buck, 1991). ADR is also known as *restorative justice* (Umbreit, 1991:164). ADR involves the direct participation of the victim and offender, with the aim of mutual accommodation for both parties.

The emphasis of ADR is upon restitution rather than punishment. Someone might get drunk in a tavern and break up furniture or assault another patron, one who might also be drunk. The fight leads to property loss for the tavern owner as well as physical injuries to both fighting parties. Grounds exist for a criminal prosecution of the drunk patron who broke furniture and provoked a fight. But under certain circumstances, if both the offender and victim agree, ADR can be used to resolve these crimes by civil rather than criminal means. The drunk patron can agree to pay the damages he caused in the tavern and reimburse the injured patron for any medical expenses and time lost from a job. If both parties agree, the case is concluded and no criminal action is taken. ADR programs have been established in over 100 U.S. jurisdictions, 54 in Norway, 40 in France, 25 in Canada, 25 in Germany, 18 in England, 20 in Finland, 8 in Belgium, and several in Australia (Deichsel, 1991).

When criminal cases are removed from the jurisdiction of criminal courts, not everyone views this alternative favorably (Harrington and Merry, 1988). There are those who insist that criminals should receive their just deserts. North Carolina, for example, has at least 19 mediation programs (Clarke, Valente, and Mace, 1992). How effective are the mediation programs in North Carolina? An evaluation study was conducted comparing several counties with programs with several counties without programs. A sample of 1,421 clusters of cases filed in 1990 that matched eligibility criteria were followed in records of courts and mediation programs. Interviews from complainants and defendants were examined. Of those cases referred, about 59 percent were actually mediated, with nearly all (92 percent) resulting in mediated agreements. Complainants were generally satisfied with the results of such mediation (Clarke et al., 1992).

Victim-Offender Reconciliation Projects

Another type of alternative dispute resolution is victim-offender reconciliation. **Victim-offender reconciliation** is a specific form of conflict resolution between the victim and the offender. Face-to-face encounter is the essence of this process (Roy and Brown, 1992). Elkhart County, Indiana, was the site of a **Victim-Offender Reconciliation Project (VORP)** in 1987. Kitchener, Ontario, was where VORP was officially established in 1974. VORP was subsequently replicated as **PACT** (**Prisoner and Community Together**) in northern Indiana near Elkhart. VORP has several objectives, including: (1) making offenders more accountable for their wrongs against victims; (2) reducing recidivism among participating offenders; and (3) heightening responsibility of offenders through victim compensation and repayment for damages inflicted (Roy and Brown, 1992).

In Genessee County (Batavia), New York, the Sheriff's Department established a VORP in 1983. In Quincy, New York, for instance, the VORP program was named *EARN-IT* and was operated through the Probation Department (Umbreit, 1986:55). More than 25 different states have one or another version of VORP (Umbreit, 1986). One of these sites involved a study of offender recidivism and ADR. During the 1987 to 1991 period an investigation of ADR and its effectiveness was undertaken and the results evaluated (Roy and Brown, 1992). The VORP significantly reduced recidivism among offenders. Both juvenile and adult offenders have been involved in this project over the years. Results suggest that it will be continued. Caution is recommended, however, when interpreting the results of ADR programs in selected jurisdictions, because it is believed that net widening occurs. Thus, a state's political policy agenda is furthered by expanding state control over larger numbers of people (Palumbo et al., 1994).

PRETRIAL DIVERSION

Diversion is the temporary and conditional suspension of the prosecution of a case prior to its adjudication usually as the result of an arrangement between the prosecutor and judge (Fields, 1994:20). Diversion is not new. It has been used as an informal sanction against offenders for many decades. During the mid- to late-1970s, for instance, the Kalamazoo, Michigan, Citizen's Probation Authority (CPA) made deferred prosecution available to 200 to 300 persons per year. Under CPA directives, formal criminal proceedings against these criminal defendants were *conditionally suspended* for one year to allow suspects an opportunity to complete successfully a pretrial period of informal probation supervision. When the informal probationary period was completed, then the individual's record for that offense was expunged. Prosecutorial discretion determined whether particular defendants would be included in the CPA program. In follow-up investigations of those persons who participated in the CPA program, 83 percent of the participants were not involved in further criminal activity, whereas only 17 percent were rearrested for new offenses.

Probably the most informal diversion occurs when police officers exercise discretion and issue warnings to petty offenders rather than arrest them. In these instances, there are no formal records of crimes, and offenders escape any sort of processing in the criminal justice system. Because of the lack of formal records concerning diversion cases and the limited access to such dispositions by only a few criminal justice agencies, no accurate records are available about the true extent of the use of diversion in the United States (Ford and Regoli, 1993; S. Davis, 1994).

Who Qualifies for Diversion?

Divertees, or those placed on diversion, are selected according to whether they are first-offenders and if their crimes are minor ones. Violent offenders and career criminals do not qualify for diversion programs. However, diversion is a likely option for elderly shoplifters (Curran, 1984). If some of those charged with crimes have mental illnesses or are psychologically disturbed or retarded, then they might be diverted into mental health systems in their communities (Davis, 1994). For example, selected numbers of

BOX 4.1 Victimizing the Victimized?

Goetz, the Victim, Gets Victimized Again!

Bernhard Goetz, a victim of an attempted subway mugging in New York in 1984, was sued by his victimizers in 1996. Earlier, Goetz had been a passenger on a New York subway when he was approached and threatened by four black youths. They asked him for money and appeared prepared to assault him if he refused. Goetz pulled out a concealed firearm and shot the four youths, permanently paralyzing at least one of them.

Goetz was tried on attempted murder charges, but he was acquitted. However, he was found guilty of carrying a concealed firearm and sentenced to 8½ months in jail. Following his sentence, several of his victims filed a civil suit, seeking $50 million in damages.

The events leading up to the shooting are disputed. Goetz said that the youths menaced him and demanded money. He was afraid. He acted in self-defense in a situation where he felt his life was threatened. Darrell Cabey, the youth who was shot and paralyzed by Goetz, said that Goetz shot him once, and then Goetz looked down at him and said, "You don't look so bad, here's another." And Goetz shot him again.

Each of the youths had been in trouble with the law in the past. Circumstances and statements from witnesses corroborated Goetz's story about being confronted and asked to turn over his money to the four black youths. However, Cabey's mother, who wasn't there when the event occurred, said that "I just want people to know, the world to know, my son did not do anything to [Goetz]. He was just sitting there. It wasn't a money matter. I want the world to know my son didn't do anything to that man."

In the civil trial occurring in March and April of 1996, Goetz was characterized by the plaintiffs as a "murderous racist who had acted recklessly and without justification" in shooting the four youths. Apparently with an indifferent attitude about the whole affair, Goetz himself made various incriminating remarks when questioned by the plaintiff's attorney. Goetz said that he "wanted to kill them all . . . to gouge their eyes out." "It is as damning a chronicle as one could ever have . . . How much more proof do you need? I don't care how much you award in punitive damages. Bankrupt him. Make sure he never enjoys life as a rich man. Make sure if he wins the lottery, Darrell Cabey wins the lottery."

It is unlikely that alleged victimizer Darrell Cabey will ever collect anything from Goetz. According to New York civil law, Cabey is entitled to 10 percent of Goetz's income for 20 years. While Goetz earned at least $100,000 at one time in the early 1980s, his income dropped to less than $20,000 a year following the subway incident. Goetz was self-employed at the time of the New York judgment against him. In response to the judgment, Goetz said that the youths "were about to rob him" in 1984 when he shot them in self-defense.

Should victimizers be entitled to sue when they are injured by those they victimize? Was this New York court judgment fair to Bernhard Goetz? What message does this send to those in future years who attempt to defend themselves against subway muggers? What do you think about the judgment against Goetz? Was it fair?

Source: Adapted from the Associated Press, "Jury Awards $43 Million in Goetz Trial." *Minot (N.D.) Daily News*, April 24, 1996:A4.

BOX 4.2 Prosecutorial Power

How Much Power Do Prosecutors Have? Too Much!

For several centuries, prosecutors have wielded overwhelming power over those accused of crimes. While the U.S. government has a system of checks and balances, with judicial, executive, and legislative branches, there are *no* checks on prosecutorial power.

Prosecutorial discretion is the power of a prosecutor to pursue charges against those suspected of crimes. The level of proof required for such prosecutions is quite minimal. Some suspects have even pleaded guilty to lesser crimes they never committed, merely to escape being prosecuted and convicted for more serious crimes carrying ominous penalties, such as life-without-parole or death sentences.

While every criminal case is somewhat different from all others, there are some general consistencies that typify the plea bargaining process. Prosecutors threaten to prosecute suspects on more serious charges, but prosecutors are willing to consider guilty pleas to lesser offenses if suspects *cooperate* in prosecutorial investigations of other suspects. Thus, if a conspiracy is alleged, one or more alleged conspirators may find it worth their while to enter guilty pleas to less serious offenses in exchange for assisting prosecutors in their cases against more important suspects. Drug users, therefore, might report their connections to the police in exchange for leniency. Drug dealers, the "connections," might, in turn, give information to incriminate their suppliers, in exchange for lenient treatment.

In 1996, a trial was conducted to try Arkansas Governor Jim Guy Tucker, who was allegedly connected with a Whitewater scandal involving sizable loans for undeveloped land. In exchange for *immunity from prosecution*, a key business associate of Tucker's, Judge Bill Watt, agreed to give incriminating testimony in court against Tucker. Another key witness against Tucker was David Hale, a former business associate. The U.S. Attorney prosecuting Tucker said that Hale's testimony was "highly useful to the government." Hale had previously entered a "guilty" plea to charges that he defrauded the government of $2 million. Instead of serving 10 years in a federal penitentiary and having to pay a $250,000 fine, Hale was given 28 months and fined only $10,000. Another beneficiary of this relatively lenient treatment was Susan MacDougal, who cooperated with prosecutors similarly against Tucker.

The whole point of the "system" is to bring great pressure to bear on defendants to implicate others. But those who plea bargain with prosecutors often are manipulated into telling a story different from the actual events as they knew them to occur. For instance, Bill Watt said, "They want me to lie on Tucker, change the story the way they want it." Amazingly, this parallels precisely what a little-known former defendant testifying against an alleged co-conspirator in Knoxville, Tennessee, was told by an Assistant U.S. Attorney in federal district court: "No, no, no. We don't want you to lie; just let us tell the story our way!"

One of the great paradoxes in government is that judicial discretion is frequently targeted for criticism. Efforts are continually being made to check judicial discretion and limit it. The U.S. sentencing guidelines formulated by the U.S. Sentencing Commission in the late 1980s were intended to limit judicial discretion as a means of promoting fairness and equitable treatment in sentencing. However, almost never is any movement directed toward bridling the discretion of prosecutors. Bill Watt remarked, "These people held within their hands the power to grant you immunity, to release you from the burden of a trial . . . even from the decision to plead guilty or not." As has been aptly conceded by many observers, *you don't get these deals by telling prosecutors you were the only one breaking the law.*

How important is it to monitor prosecutorial discretion? Who should be designated to monitor it? What checks and balances, if any, should exist to prevent prosecutors from abusing their discretion? Do you think prosecutors have too much power?

Source: Adapted from Susan Estrich, "Prosecutor Power." *USA Today*, April 11, 1996:13A.

charged offenders in a Canadian province between 1990 and 1992 were diverted to mental health services on the basis of their (1) minor offense seriousness; (2) court jurisdiction, where the court was remotely located; and (3) psychiatric evaluations and potential for rehabilitation or recovery (Simon Davis, 1994).

Forms of Diversion

Several different kinds of diversionary programs are categorically referred to as **pretrial diversion**. Pretrial diversion programs are either publicly or privately operated. These programs include (1) standard or unconditional diversion, (2) conditional diversion, (3) youth services, and (4) treatment services.

Standard or Unconditional Diversion. All **standard diversion** programs involve one or more conditions. No specific program of treatment is usually indicated. The primary obligations of offenders are to conduct themselves properly, behave as good citizens, and not get into trouble. After a period of six months or a year, the case is reviewed by the prosecutor. Usually, unconditional or standard diversion is distinguished from **conditional diversion** by the number of special conditions added to one's diversion program.

Conditional Diversion. In some instances, divertees have problems with drugs or alcohol or have mental problems. Thus, one or more conditions (e.g., drug treatment, mental health counseling, or observance of curfews and periodic drug/alcohol checks) are required for the diversion. These greater obligations on divertees change one's diversion program from standard or unconditional to *conditional.*

Functions of Diversion

Some of the more important functions of diversion include the following (Law Enforcement Assistance Administration, 1977):

1. To permit divertees the opportunity of remaining in their communities where they can receive needed assistance or treatment, depending upon the nature of the crimes charged
2. To permit divertees the opportunity to make restitution to their victims where monetary damages were suffered and property destroyed
3. To permit divertees the opportunity of remaining free in their communities to support themselves and their families and to avoid the stigma of incarceration
4. To help divertees avoid the stigma of a criminal conviction
5. To assist corrections officials in reducing prison and jail overcrowding by diverting less serious cases to nonincarcerative alternatives
6. To save the courts the time, trouble, and expense of formally processing less serious cases and streamlining case dispositions through informal case handling
7. To make it possible for divertees to participate in self-help, educational, or vocational programs
8. To preserve the dignity and integrity of divertees by helping them avoid further contact with the criminal justice system and assisting them to be more responsible adults capable of managing their own lives
9. To preserve the family unit and enhance family solidarity and continuity

Factors Influencing Pretrial Diversion. Whether any particular defendant is eligible for pretrial diversion is up to individual prosecutors in each jurisdiction. Pretrial diversion is a prosecutorial option. Under most circumstances, diversion may be granted with judicial approval and oversight. Pretrial diversion is *not* a constitutional right available to anyone charged with a crime. Further, whether the crime alleged is a property or violent offense will not automatically qualify or disqualify particular defendants from being considered for pretrial diversion. If we knew the complete population of *all* divertees in the United States, the characteristics of this divertee population would probably encompass all types of criminal offenses. Probably the population would consist mostly of first-offenders, regardless of the nature of their offense. Probably the majority of the population would consist of property offenders or those charged with less serious misdemeanors.

Because diversion is a temporary cessation of a criminal prosecution, where a case is sidetracked most often to a probation department where divertees can be supervised for periods of relatively short duration (e.g., six months to one year), it makes sense that such cases tend to be less spectacular and visible throughout the community. An exhibitionist, for instance, may not pose a danger or immediate threat to community safety, although the exhibitionist's behavior may shock, even insult, passersby. There are probably psychological problems or mental disorders associated with exhibitionist behavior that need to be addressed by the proper community agencies and counseling services (Simon Davis, 1994). Elderly shoplifters who steal trivial items are not serious threats to community safety (Curran, 1984). First-offenders who deliberately overdraw their checking accounts by writing small "insufficient funds" checks are bothersome but do not attract a great deal of attention. Teenagers who race their vehicles on back county roads may not seem to us as serious as someone who might break into our home and steal our valuables or rob us. Many occasional drug users endanger only themselves by their conduct. They might benefit more from a treatment program than incarceration (Hepburn et al., 1992). In short, **offense seriousness** is a consideration in whether diversion should be a prosecutorial option.

Another consideration is **jail or prison overcrowding.** If there are serious overcrowding problems at either local jails or state prisons in which diversion programs exist, then diversion becomes a more attractive consideration for prosecutors, because they would view the diversion option as a temporary, front-end solution to such overcrowding (Broderick et al., 1993). Less serious offenders, especially first-offenders, would contribute unnecessarily to jail or prison overcrowding, especially if their period of diversion is successful and causes them to desist from future criminal conduct.

Are there sufficient resources within the community to operate a diversion program? After all, divertees most often report to or make periodic contact with probation departments and/or courts by furnishing evidence that they have complied or are complying with diversion program requirements. In some communities, the caseloads of probation officers may be such that the additional responsibility for supervising numerous new divertees is overwhelming. It may not be such a good idea to jeopardize the current quality of probation services by overextending current probation officer workloads with additional divertee monitoring.

Not everyone approves of diversion. **Court-watchers** often sit in courtrooms and observe judicial decision making in progress. If they observe judges granting diversion to persons, such as those charged with driving while intoxicated (DWI), they may feel that justice is not being properly dispensed. In Knox County, Tennessee, for example, those first-offenders charged with DWI but whose blood alcohol level was between .10 and .16 (where .10 was the level at which intoxication was presumed) would typically be diverted to a one-year program. The program obligated DWI divertees to send in a monthly report, showing their continued employment and problem-free driving record. They also paid a nominal monthly program maintenance fee. At the end of their year on diversion, they returned to court where the judge dismissed the DWI charges against them and eradicated or expunged the DWI charge from state records. Thus, if such persons were ever stopped by police in future months or years, the state departments of motor vehicles or public safety would have no record of their previous DWI charge. Court- watchers were outraged by this use of diversion. Mothers Against Drunk Drivers (MADD) representatives wrote letters to the local paper, criticizing this diversion leniency. They pressured judges to impose harsher penalties on those charged with DWI and to eliminate the use of diversion for them. Eventually, public pressure caused prosecutors and judges to suspend the diversion program insofar as it applied to DWI cases. Thus, the *nature of the offense* became a major consideration in whether diversion would be granted. No one complained when diversion was used for first-offender exhibitionists or bad-check writers in that same Tennessee jurisdiction. Therefore, diversion itself was not attacked by these interest groups as "wrong"; only certain types of offenses where diversion was applied.

Finally, whether diversion is a consideration depends upon whether it is believed to work in particular cases (Fields, 1994). Diversion involves an amount of trust on the part of the system toward particular divertees. Will those granted diversion show that they can remain law-abiding and not violate this trust? More than a few judges are inclined to impose harsher penalties on those divertees who *fail* during their diversion programs and are subsequently prosecuted and convicted compared with those defendants who are prosecuted and do not become involved in diversion programs.

Profiling Divertees. There are no definitive criteria describing U.S. divertees. Because diversion means a temporary cessation of a criminal prosecution while a conditional program of diversion is undertaken, record expungements after successful completion of programs mean that we have no access to data on divertee characteristics. Of course, we can examine random diversion programs operating in various jurisdictions and solicit client information from program officials. Even this information is sketchy and fails to describe in sufficient detail the characteristics of all of those who participate in diversion programs. However, relevant criteria operating in most jurisdictions in which diversion exists as a prosecutorial option include the following:

1. The age of the offender
2. The residency, employment, and familial status of the offender
3. The prior record of the offender
4. The seriousness of the offense
5. Aggravating or mitigating circumstances associated with the commission of the offense

A majority of divertees are first-offenders and pose a low risk to their supervising officers (DeMore, 1996:34–37). They are typically employed, have relatively stable families, have no serious prior records, and there are often mitigating circumstances associated with their instant offense. While almost all divertees have the ability to pay their monthly maintenance fees for their diversion programs, their inability to pay such fees cannot disqualify them from these programs. Thus, persons of lower socioeconomic status cannot be rejected from diversion programs because of their financial circumstances (*State v. Jimenez*, 1991).

We can also infer something about the characteristics of divertees by examining those criteria that result in one's being *excluded* from diversion programs. For instance, in California diversion programs, the following types of persons are not eligible for diversion (Galvin et al., 1977):

1. Those with prior drug offense convictions, former drug offense divertees, and/or those who traffic in drugs
2. Those convicted of a felony within the previous five-year period
3. Those whose current offense involves violence
4. Those who are past or present probation or parole violators

Diversion Outcomes: What Should Divertees Expect? Essentially two primary outcomes result from the successful completion of a diversion program. One outcome is expungement of one's criminal record relating to the diversion offense. Expungement is offered as an incentive to comply with program requirements for the duration of the program. Once the program is completed, divertees expect that the charges originally filed against them will be expunged and that they will continue to have a crime-free record. For elderly shoplifters in Palm Beach County, Florida, a pretrial diversion program seemed to be an appropriate alternative. During the period 1977 to 1981 83 elderly shoplifters were apprehended and placed in a pretrial diversion program. Only 1 percent of the sample was rearrested later for a new shoplifting offense. These elderly offenders were considered good candidates for the diversion program, and the program was considered successful in modifying their behaviors (Curran, 1984).

In several Canadian cities between 1990 and 1992, 232 criminal suspects with mental disorders were diverted to mental treatment and hospitalization with the understanding that charges against them would be dropped following successful treatment. A majority of these divertees had their records expunged upon receiving the appropriate mental health treatment (S. Davis, 1994).

Another possible outcome is a reduction of charge seriousness or some mitigation of sentence. More than a few jurisdictions cause the charges against successful divertees either to be decreased from a more to less serious misdemeanor or felony, or the actual sanctions imposed by judges upon conviction will be less severe. A divertee may ultimately be convicted of a crime, but the sentence may be one year in jail instead of a five-year prison sentence. For example, Wood and Darbey (1987) describe a Pretrial Diversion Program (PDP) that was administered in Monroe County, New York, for multiple offender DWI defendants. *Prosecutions against these clients were diverted* upon the following conditions:the drivers would surrender their driver's licenses for one year, agree to participate in a treatment plan, and waive their right to a speedy trial. The judge adjourned these cases for a six-month period, during which time the defendant was closely monitored. Satisfactory completion of the program, based upon behavior change and self-learning related to drinking, resulted in a misdemeanor DWI plea. Unfavorable termination from the program resulted in a felony DWI prosecution. In this particular program, Wood and Darbey found no significant recidivism differences between program participants and other defendants subjected to traditional treatment and prosecution.

For those who *fail* to complete their diversion programs successfully (e.g., who test positive for drugs or alcohol, who are rearrested for another crime, who fail to abide by curfew or other technical program conditions), the original criminal charges are reinstated and prosecutors move forward to seek convictions against these defendants. In the Pretrial Diversion Program described above by Wood and Darbey, felony prosecutions were reinstituted against errant defendants.

The Effectiveness of Diversion and Recidivism. Because diversion removes certain cases out of the criminal justice system temporarily and because it *may* result in the expungement of criminal charges against defendants, it is often considered too lenient an option by the skeptical public. However, those who have been granted diversion and have conformed their behaviors to the requirements of the law consider this alternative advantageous in several respects. Offenders may continue their employment without the taint of a criminal conviction. Some diversion programs include victim compensation and restitution by offenders. Therefore, offenders can do much good work while on diversion. There is also the real possibility that treatment programs such as Alcoholics Anonymous (AA) and Treatment Alternatives to Street Crime (TASC) can curb or cure alcohol and/or drug dependencies for many clients.

A benefit to prosecutors is that those cases slotted for diversion have made it possible for them to concentrate their efforts on more important cases. Of course, it has also been suggested that diversion is often used by prosecutors as a weapon against defense attorneys in an effort to elicit guilty pleas from defendants. Defendants themselves often consider diversion a better option than obtaining criminal records. Many offenders return to commit new crimes once their diversionary term is completed. Despite the controversial nature of diversion, it exists in most U.S. jurisdictions today. The prospects are good for its continued use, largely because it diverts large numbers of offenders from lengthy and expensive court processing.

Criticisms of Diversion. The most frequent criticism of diversion is the charge of *net widening.* Diversion "widens the net" by drawing persons into diversion programs who would not be processed by the criminal justice system if the diversion programs did not exist. For example, Hepburn et al. (1992) describe a pretrial diversion program operated in Maricopa County, Arizona, for drug users. Under a general Treatment Alternatives to Street Crime initiative, first-time felony drug users were placed in a drug treatment program in lieu of criminal prosecution. Because of the program's existence, many drug offenders were drawn into the program who would not have been prosecuted by the criminal justice system. While the program itself attracted considerable attention by the media and drug community, the overall results were disappointing. The level of drug use and trafficking in the areas targeted, as well as the recidivism rates among program participants, remained about the same. Perhaps the program was not as selective as it should have been when drawing in prospective serious drug-using clientele.

In some jurisdictions, divertees included those charged with spouse abuse. Violent domestic disturbances are considered serious by most experts. In Indianapolis, Indiana, an experiment was conducted whereby those charged with spouse abuse were temporarily diverted from prosecution to receive treatment and counseling assistance. Record expungements occurred in more than a few cases. Several interest groups, victims-of-domestic-violence representatives, and court-watchers objected to the relatively lenient adjudications in these cases (Ford and Regoli, 1993).

Another criticism is that the application of diversion may be discriminatory. There is inconsistency on how diversion is applied among jurisdictions. Because of the inconsistent application of diversion, some experts have labeled it discriminatory. Socioeconomic, race/ethnic, or gender factors may influence whether diversion will be used or if alleged offenders will be formally charged with crimes and prosecuted. Informal diversion is highly individualized. Alleged offenders are not brought into the criminal justice system but rather are diverted from it, often without participation in any systematic treatment program or penalty.

Summarizing the major criticisms of diversion, we may include the following:

1. Diversion is "soft" on criminals.
2. Diversion is the "wrong" punishment for criminals.
3. Diversion leads to net widening.
4. Diversion excludes female offenders.
5. Diversion ignores "due process."
6. Diversion assumes "guilt" without a trial.

Probation Defined. Nondiverted criminal cases that are prosecuted result in either convictions or acquittals. Frequently, plea bargaining yields guilty pleas in exchange for certain prosecutorial concessions. The vast majority of criminal convictions involve probation as a contingent condition. Standard **probation** is the release of a convicted offender into the community to avoid incarceration under a suspended sentence, with good behavior, and generally under the supervision of a probation officer (Black, 1990:1152).

Standard probation involves minimal contact with a probation officer. A probationer may or may not be expected to report to the probation department monthly. The probationer probably fills out a monthly report.

This report probably includes the probationer's current address, workplace, statement of earned wages, an open-ended question or two about any specific probationer needs that can be met by action on the part of the probation officer, and several other related items. Together with fees ranging from $10 to $50, the report is either hand-delivered or mailed to the probation officer in charge of the offender. The probation officer may or may not have face-to-face contact with the offender. Whereas probation officers sometimes make periodic checks of police records, they rely on the police to keep them advised should their client be arrested or interrogated about new crimes within the jurisdiction.

Standard probationers have most of the same freedoms as other community citizens. Probation is so common in certain jurisdictions that community residents are often unaware that their neighbors are felony probationers under minimal supervision. In California, for example, 1 percent of the entire population is on probation. Standard probation in many jurisdictions may involve a complete absence of supervision of any kind. Even telephone or mail contacts between probation officers and clients are minimal.

In some jurisdictions, the most important aspect of an offender's term of probation is the regular payment of the maintenance fee. Late payments result in officer-initiated contacts with clients. The ever-present threat is the revocation of probation because of client failure to observe one or more technical probation conditions, especially the payment of the monthly maintenance fee. One probationer said his probation officer spent 45 minutes of a one-hour conference at the beginning of the offender's probation term reminding the probationer of the importance of paying this fee. The probationer never saw the officer again until his two-year probationary term was concluded successfully.

Standardless Standard Probation? Regardless of its standardless appearance, standard probation involves conditions to the same extent as standard pretrial diversion. Probationers are expected to adhere to a list of rules and regulations, and most probationers consider their probation terms as true sentences with penalties. For many probationers, however, the intensiveness of supervision may have little deterrent value as a behavioral intervention (U.S. General Accounting Office, 1993a). Several studies involving both adult and youthful offenders have shown that the intensity with which these clients are supervised matters little in whether they will eventually reoffend or recidivate (Elrod and Minor, 1992; Minor and Elrod, 1994; U.S. General Accounting Office, 1993a). In fact, some studies show that intensively supervised offenders had about the same recidivism rates as standard probationers (Orchowsky, Merritt, and Browning, 1994). However, during the terms of their closer supervision, those probationers who were more closely supervised had higher rearrest rates compared with standard probationers. Many of those intensively supervised

BOX 4.3 Judges May Ignore Prosecution Requests for Leniency

The Case of Sentencing a Sexual Predator, David V. Anderson

It happened in Bismarck, North Dakota. A 21-year-old man, David V. Anderson, was arrested after allegedly engaging in various sex acts with a 12-year-old girl. Anderson was a first-offender, but he was labeled as a "sexual predator" after extensive psychological and psychiatric examinations and tests. Anderson's lawyer cut a deal with the state's prosecutor, and they agreed that if Anderson would plead guilty to having sex with a 12-year-old girl, the prosecutor would recommend an 8½ year sentence, with 4½ years suspended.

When Judge James Vukelic saw the plea agreement, he rejected it outright. He sentenced Anderson to eight years in prison, to be followed by ten years of probation. During the probationary period, Anderson would be compelled to be monitored closely and his activities would be greatly restricted. The judge said, "I think the sentence recommended here doesn't go far enough."

Consulting a thick presentence investigation report submitted by a probation officer, Judge Vukelic said: "I don't find anything in here in your favor. Another thing that jumped out at me (in the reports) is how easy it is for you to find victims. We naively assume here in North Dakota that kids are safe." Anderson further admitted to previous rapes of young boys. He had previously been prosecuted in juvenile court on these charges, and his admissions were admitted into his present court record.

Judge Vukelic said that Anderson had resisted treatment for sex offenders and has little or no control over his sexual impulses. He also said that Anderson seems to derive great pleasure from his ability to control his victims. The judge worried that the sex offender treatment wouldn't be successful in Anderson's case, but he ordered Anderson to undergo it anyway at the Bismarck State Penitentiary where Anderson would be confined.

Is Anderson a true sexual predator, with no prior adult convictions? Was the judge right to reject the plea bargain agreement between prosecutors and defense counsel and impose a harsher sentence? Should Anderson be allowed to withdraw his guilty plea and have a jury trial for his offense? How do you think sexual predators ought to be punished?

Source: Adapted from Associated Press, "Judge Doubles Prosecution's Request." *Minot (N.D.) Daily News*, September 6, 1996:A3.

clients were also cited with more technical program, noncriminal violations than standard probationers. This finding simply suggests that if we watch certain probationers more closely than others, we will detect more technical program violations. Thus, for many probationers at least, standard probation functions as an adequate general deterrent to future offending (U.S. General Accounting Office, 1993).

THE HISTORY OF PROBATION IN THE UNITED STATES

Probation means forgiveness or a period of trial, and its use originated in ancient times. Religious and political dissidents were often placed on probation so that their ideas could be brought into line with official church or political policies. Probation originated in the United States in 1841 through the pioneering work of John Augustus (1785–1859), a Boston shoemaker and philanthropist.

Augustus was noted for his affiliation with the Temperance Movement, a religiously based organization dedicated to reforming alcoholics. Together with **Rufus R. Cook** and **Benjamin C. Clark**, other social reformers and philanthropists, Augustus frequented the Boston Municipal Court to offer his services to those charged with public drunkenness and petty crimes. One morning in 1841, Augustus was in the courtroom observing offenders being sentenced by the municipal judge. A man convicted of being a common drunkard was about to be sentenced to the Boston House of Corrections when Augustus intervened and asked the judge to assign the drunkard to his own supervision for three weeks. Augustus guaranteed the man's appearance in court later and agreed to pay all court costs. The judge consented to Augustus's proposal. Three weeks later, Augustus returned with the first "probationer" in the United States. The judge was so impressed with the reformed drunkard that he fined the offender a nominal amount and suspended the six-month sentence. From 1841 to 1859, when Augustus died, he supervised, 1,956 offenders on probation. According to Augustus, only one person ever violated his trust (Lindner and Savarese, 1984).

Although the Boston courts permitted Augustus and others the opportunity of privately supervising certain offenders convicted of petty crimes, these probation efforts were not particularly popular with various vested interests. One group opposed to the early use of probation in Boston were corrections personnel, jailers, and jail administrators. Their opposition had little or nothing to do with the rehabilitative benefits to offenders derived from probation. Quite simply, they were opposed to probation because it decreased their profits from city funds allocated to them for inmate food and housing. Regularly, jail guards and administrators would divert a large portion of Boston funds intended for prisoner food and accommodations. This is one reason why the Boston House of Corrections was regarded by observers as a rat-infested hellhole (Probation Association, 1939).

The public-at-large was not supportive of probation either (Lindner and Savarese, 1984). The press and others considered probation as excessive leniency toward offenders who ought to be punished for their misdeeds. Today, similar criticisms are directed toward the probation concept and programs associated with it (Harris, 1984; Immarigeon, 1985b). Several charitable and religious organizations continued the work of Augustus in Boston and other large cities. Between 1860 and 1900, much of the privately funded philanthropic work in probation was directed at juvenile offenders. The **Boston Children's Aid Society**, sponsored in part by Rufus R. Cook, was established in 1860 and saw to the needs of orphans and other youngsters who did not have adequate adult supervision. Many children were helped by this philanthropy and voluntary work.

In 1878, Massachusetts passed the first probation statute in the United States. The statute authorized the mayor of Boston to hire probation officers and operate a small-scale probation program. The Boston Superintendent of Police was placed in charge of all appointed probation officers. Between 1878 and 1938, 38 states, the District of Columbia, and the federal government passed probation statutes. Table 4.1 shows these states and jurisdictions according to the years when probation statutes were passed.

In the meantime, New York and Chicago were sites of **settlement houses** between 1886 and 1900. Settlement houses were operated privately and furnished food and lodging to wayward or disadvantaged youths. **Jane Addams** established **Hull House** in Chicago in 1889, an experimental settlement house that provided employment assistance and shelter to needy juveniles and others. Addams was instrumental in achieving several impor-

TABLE 4.1 The Adoption of Probation Statutes by Jurisdiction and Year

Year	States/Jurisdictions
1878	Massachusetts
1897	Missouri
1898	Vermont
1899	Rhode Island
1900	New Jersey
1901	New York
1903	California, Connecticut, Michigan
1905	Maine
1907	Kansas, Indiana
1908	Ohio
1909	Colorado, Iowa, Minnesota, Nebraska, North Dakota, Pennsylvania, Wisconsin
1910	District of Columbia
1911	Delaware, Illinois
1913	Arizona, Georgia, Montana
1915	Idaho
1918	Virginia
1921	Washington
1923	Utah
1925	Federal Government
1927	West Virginia
1931	Oregon, Tennessee, Maryland
1934	Kentucky
1937	Arkansas, North Carolina
1938	New Hampshire

Source: Compiled by author.

tant reforms in juvenile laws in Illinois, and she spent many hours helping the children of immigrant families. **James Bronson Reynolds**, an early prison reformer, was the headworker of **University Settlement** in New York City in 1893. Although this settlement was created to provide job assistance and referral services to disadvantaged community residents, it also served as a community-based probation agency to supervise those placed on probation by New York Courts. University Settlement was privately financed and operated in its early years. However, by 1906, New York State had authorized nominal payments to those working with probationers, including University Settlement volunteers. University Settlement was unsuccessful at rehabilitating offenders, largely because it lacked clear goals and a definite purpose, and it was soon forced to close its doors (Lindner and Savarese, 1984).

The federal government formally adopted probation for convicted federal offenders in 1925, although probation in federal district courts was practiced on a limited basis prior to 1925. The administrative control of probation officers was shifted to the U.S. Attorney General in 1930. Ultimately, the responsibility for probation officers was assigned the Administrative Office of the United States Courts. In 1938, Congress passed the Federal Juvenile Delinquency Act, which permitted those juveniles within federal jurisdiction the option of probation. All states had probation statutes by 1957 (Coffey et al., 1974). By 1996, over 3.8 million convicted state and federal offenders were on probation. This figure represents about 2.8 percent of all adults in the United States that were under some form of correctional supervision. Table 4.2 shows all probationers by jurisdiction.

Some indication of the rapid growth of probationers in the United States is provided in Table 4.3. Table 4.3 not only shows the growth of the probation population during the 1980 to 1995 period; for comparative purposes it also shows inmate population growths. Between 1980 and 1995, the probation population grew annually an average of 4 percent. During that same period, the incarcerated population grew an average of 6 percent per year. The population of probationers grew by 176 percent between 1980 and 1995. The population of jail and prison inmates grew by 212 percent during the same period (Department of Justice, 1996:8). Because of prison and jail overcrowding problems, it is anticipated that the probation population and incarcerated offender population will continue to grow in future years at rates similar to those shown in Table 4.3. Figure 4.1 is a graphic portrayal of the total number of persons in the United States under some form of correctional supervision during the period 1980 to 1995. This graph shows both probationers and parolees and jail and prison inmates (Department of Justice, 1996:8).

A PROFILE OF PROBATIONERS

The profile of probationers in the United States is changing annually. Each year, the probation population includes increasing numbers of felony

TABLE 4.2 Adults on Probation, 1995

Region and Jurisdiction	Beginning Probation Population, 1/1/95	During 1995 Entries	During 1995 Exits	Ending Probation Population, 12/31/95	Percent Change in Probation Population During 1995	Number on Probation on 12/31/95 per 100,000 Adult Residents
U.S. total	2,981,400	1,501,589	1,381,636	3,090,626	3.7%	1,593
Federal[a,b]	42,309	18,601	22,404	38,506	—	20
State	2,939,091	1,482,988	1,359,232	3,052,120	3.8	1,573
Northeast	526,375	232,686	214,444	544,620	3.5%	1,402
Connecticut	53,453	37,135	36,081	54,507	2.0	2,201
Maine[c]	8,638	:	:	8,641	†	923
Massachusetts	46,670	34,611	37,601	43,680	−6.4	941
New Hampshire	4,323	3,432	3,408	4,347	.6	509
New Jersey	125,299	59,376	57,552	127,123	1.5	2,125
New York	163,613	45,061	35,175	173,499	6.0	1,276
Pennsylvania	99,524	39,764	32,465	106,823	7.3	1,166
Rhode Island	18,179	9,813	9,314	18,678	2.7	2,483
Vermont	6,676	3,494	2,848	7,322	9.7	1,672
Midwest	642,924	341,567	316,851	671,094	4.4%	1,472
Illinois[c]	104,664	63,862	61,723	109,489	4.6	1,258
Indiana[d]	83,555	:	:	83,555	—	1,936
Iowa	15,902	10,456	9,779	16,579	4.3	783
Kansas[c]	17,256	11,831	7,726	16,547	−4.1	884
Michigan[c]	142,640	68,000	62,338	148,377	4.0	2,110
Minnesota[c]	81,972	55,911	57,131	83,778	2.0	2,490
Missouri[c]	36,295	21,887	18,453	40,595	11.8	1,030
Nebraska	18,639	15,485	14,697	19,427	4.2	1,627
North Dakota	2,036	1,474	1,219	2,291	12.5	486
Ohio[c]	90,190	68,077	59,558	99,603	10.4	1,201
South Dakota	3,874	4,393	4,643	3,624	−6.5	693
Wisconsin[c]	45,901	20,191	19,584	47,269	3.0	1,254
South	1,214,375	618,343	573,402	1,254,817	3.3%	1,846
Alabama[c]	31,284	4,696	4,498	31,416	.4	990
Arkansas	19,606	8,431	5,656	22,381	14.2	1,220
Delaware	15,507	7,395	6,555	16,347	5.4	3,036
District of Columbia	11,306	4,733	5,777	10,262	−9.2	2,334
Florida[c]	247,014	146,989	133,585	255,550	3.5	2,367
Georgia[c]	140,694	69,102	67,228	142,453	1.3	2,699
Kentucky	11,417	5,582	5,500	11,499	.7	398
Louisiana	33,604	11,431	11,282	33,753	.4	1,088
Maryland	76,940	35,530	41,441	71,029	−7.7	1,884
Mississippi	9,042	3,511	2,958	9,595	6.1	496
North Carolina	90,418	49,804	42,301	97,921	8.3	1,815
Oklahoma[c]	26,285	14,195	13,029	27,866	6.0	1,161
South Carolina	40,005	16,643	14,482	42,166	5.4	1,545
Tennessee	34,896	20,431	18,594	36,733	5.3	931
Texas	396,276	200,365	181,144	415,497	4.9	3,119
Virginia	24,089	19,394	19,219	24,264	.7	485
West Virginia[c]	5,992	111	153	6,085	1.6	433

(table continues)

TABLE 4.2 (continued)

Region and Jurisdiction	Beginning Probation Population, 1/1/95	During 1995 Entries	During 1995 Exits	Ending Probation Population, 12/31/95	Percent Change in Probation Population During 1995	Number on Probation on 12/31/95 per 100,000 Adult Residents
West	555,417	290,392	254,535	581,589	4.7%	1,397
Alaska	2,899	960	1,296	2,563	−11.6	619
Arizona[c]	34,365	15,514	10,728	32,532	−5.3	1,076
California	277,655	142,560	133,229	286,986	3.4	1,259
Colorado[c]	39,065	25,042	21,840	42,010	7.5	1,519
Hawaii	13,088	6,620	6,385	13,323	1.8	1,518
Idaho	5,770	6,110	5,711	6,169	6.9	757
Montana	5,656	2,022	1,833	5,845	3.3	922
Nevada	9,410	6,043	5,377	10,076	7.1	890
New Mexico	8,063	7,727	7,514	8,276	2.6	698
Oregon	38,086	13,397	11,758	39,725	4.3	1,695
Utah	7,714	4,136	3,372	8,478	9.9	664
Washington[c]	110,279	58,476	43,640	122,306	10.9	3,048
Wyoming	3,367	1,785	1,852	3,300	−2.0	960

: Not available.
† Less than 0.05%.
— Not calculated.
[a] Defined as persons received for probation directly from court.
[b] The decrease resulted from a review of the statistical database by the Administrative Office of the U.S. Courts, which identified and closed cases that had been coded incorrectly.
[c] Because of nonresponse or incomplete data, the population on December 31, 1995, does not equal the population on January 1, 1995, plus entries, minus exits.
[d] Data are for 12/31/94.

Source: U.S. Department of Justice, 1996:5.

offenders. In 1995, for example, as shown in Table 4.4, 54 percent of all probationers were convicted felons. About two thirds (64%) of all probationers in 1995 were white, with 34 percent black. Those of Hispanic origin represented 14 percent of all probationers. Most probationers were male (79%) (Department of Justice, 1996:8).

THE PHILOSOPHY AND FUNCTIONS OF PROBATION

Philosophy of Probation

The general philosophy of probation can be gleaned from examining the original intent of its pioneer, John Augustus. Augustus wanted to reform offenders. He wanted to rehabilitate common drunks and petty thieves. Thus, rehabilitation was and continues to be a strong philosophical aim of probation. But somewhere over the years, probation changed from how Augustus originally conceived it. Let's look at how Augustus supervised his

TABLE 4.3 Number of Adults Under Community Supervision or Incarcerated, 1980–1995

Year	Total Estimated Correctional Population	Community Supervision		Incarcerated[a]	Percent of U.S. Adults Under Supervision
		Probation	Parole		
1980	1,840,400	1,118,097	220,438	501,886	1.1%
1985	3,011,500	1,968,712	300,203	742,579	1.7%
1990	4,348,000	2,670,234	531,407	1,146,401	2.3%
1991	4,535,600	2,728,472	590,442	1,216,664	2.4
1992	4,762,600	2,811,611	658,601	1,292,347	2.5
1993	4,944,000	2,903,061	676,100	1,364,881	2.6
1994	5,147,100	2,981,400	690,371	1,475,329	2.7
1995[b]	5,357,800	3,090,626	700,174	1,567,000	2.8
Percent change,					
1994–1995	4%	4%	1%	6%	
1980–1995	191	176	218	212	
Annual average change,					
1990–1995	4%	3%	6%	6%	
1980–1995	7	7	8	8	

Note: Counts for probation, prison, and parole are for December 31 of each year. Jail counts are for June 30. Because some persons may have multiple statuses, the sum, of the number of persons incarcerated or under community supervision overestimates the total correctional population. Percent of adults under supervision was computed using the U.S. adult resident population on July 1 of each year.

[a] The incarcerated population count consists of inmates in the custody of jail and prison authorities.

[b] Incarcerated total was estimated and rounded to the nearest 1,000.

Source: Department of Justice, 1996:8.

FIGURE 4.1 Number of persons under supervision per 100,000 adult U.S. residents, 1980–1995. (*Source:* Department of Justice, 1996:8.)

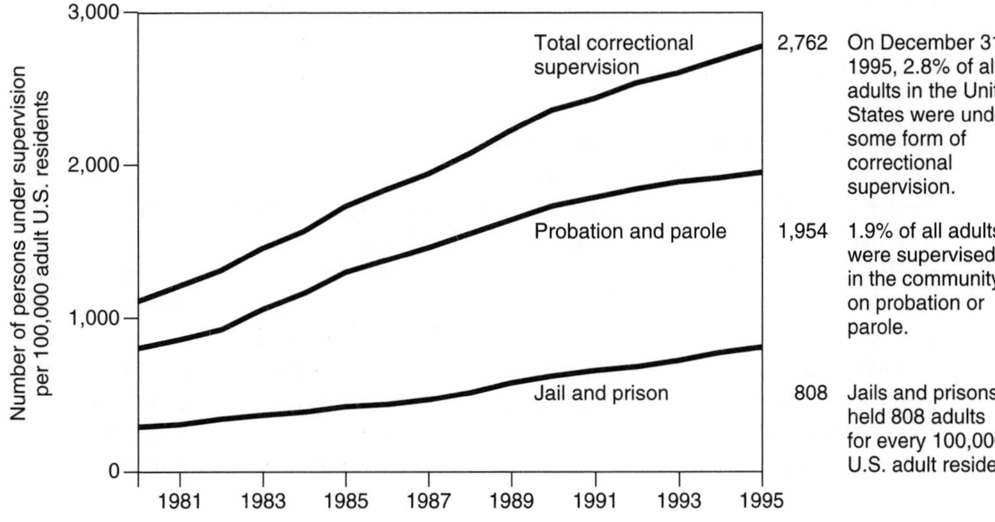

TABLE 4.4 Characteristics of Persons Under Community Supervision, 1995

	Probation	Parole
Number of persons supervised	3,090,626	700,174
Sex		
Male	79%	90%
Female	21	10
Race		
White	64%	50%
Black	34	49
Other	2	1
Hispanic origin		
Hispanic	14%	21%
Non-Hispanic	86	79
Supervision status		
Active	78%	78%
Inactive	8	11
Absconded	10	6
Out-of-State	2	4
Other	2	†
Type of offense		
Felony	54%	—
Misdemeanor	26	—
Driving while intoxicated	17	—
Other infractions	3	—
Sentenced to Incarceration		
More than 1 year	...	94%
1 year or less	...	6

Note: Percentage based on reported data only. Detail may not add to total because of rounding.
† Less than 0.05%.
— Not reported.
... Not applicable.
Source: Department of Justice, 1996:8.

probationers. First, he stood their bail in the Boston Municipal Court. Second, he took them to his home or other place of shelter, fed them, and generally looked after them. He may have even provided them with job leads and other services through his many friendships as well as his political and philanthropic connections. In short, he provided his probationers with fairly intensive supervision and personalized assistance, financial and otherwise.

Augustus supervised approximately 100 probationers a year between 1841 and 1859. We know that Augustus kept detailed records of his client progress. In this respect, he compiled what are now called presentence investigations, although he usually made extensive notes about offenders and their progress after they had been convicted. He showed intense interest in their progress and no doubt many of these probationers were emotionally affected by his kindness and generosity. According to his own assessment of his performance, rehabilitation and reformation were occurring at a significant rate among his clients, and his own efforts were largely responsible.

Present-day probation has become streamlined and bureaucratic. While there are exceptions among probation officers, relatively few take interest in their clients to the extent that they feed and clothe them and look after their other personal needs. No probation officers sit in municipal courtrooms waiting for the right kinds of offenders who will be responsive to personalized attention and care. No probation officers eagerly approach judges with bail bonds and assume personal responsibility for a probationer's conduct, even if for brief periods.

Today, probation officers assess their work in terms of client caseloads and officer/client ratios. Extensive paperwork is required for each case, and this consumes enormous amounts of time (American Probation and Parole Association, 1993:31). If we have strayed far afield from Augustus's original meaning of what probation supervision is and how it should be conducted, it has probably been largely the result of bureaucratic expediency. There are too many probationers and too few probation officers. It is hardly unexpected that the public has gradually become disenchanted with the rehabilitative ideal probation originally promised.

Some experts have characterized today's probation officer as a **ROBO-PO** (Cosgrove, 1994). According to Cosgrove, in the 1970s, rehabilitation was the primary aim of probation supervision. In the 1980s, reintegration replaced rehabilitation as a probation goal. By the end of the 1980s, community needs became primary. Public safety and security caused many probation agencies to devise more effective client supervision strategies. Probation officers in the 1990s acquired a broader range of duties and responsibilities such that the nature of probation work today is multifaceted and more complex (Cosgrove, 1994).

Despite these changes and philosophical shifts in the nature of probation work, the rehabilitative aim of probation has not been entirely rejected. Rather, it has been rearranged in a rapidly growing list of correctional priorities. One dominant, contemporary philosophical aim of probation is **offender control.** If we can't rehabilitate offenders, at least we can devise more effective strategies for controlling their behavior while on probation. Thus, this priority shift in probation's philosophical underpinnings has prompted the development of a string of nonincarcerative intermediate punishments, each connected directly with increased offender control by one means or another. Experts generally agree that the future of probation is closely aligned with the effectiveness of intermediate punishments. And virtually every intermediate punishment established thus far contains one or more provisions for controlling offender behavior (Sluder, Sapp, and Langston, 1994).

Functions of Probation

Probation has the following aims and functions: (1) punishment, (2) deterrence, (3) community reintegration, and (4) crime control.

Punishment. Probation seems to send mixed messages to probationers and the public. Some citizens don't think probation is much of a punishment. They see probationers free from imprisonment, living in their communities, moving about freely. To some citizens, at least, this is the same as *no* punishment (Harlow, Darley, and Robinson, 1995). Some probationers have similar sentiments. However, the courts and a majority of probationers identify with probation as a punishment. It *does* have conditions that limit a probationer's rights. Probationers must allow probation officers entry into their homes or apartments at any time. Often, these probationer-clients must submit to on-the-spot drug and alcohol checks. If probationers are employed, they must maintain a satisfactory work record. Probation officers check up on these things.

Three of the most important factors contributing to the successfulness of probation programs are probationer attitudes, motivation, and good supervision (Ditton and Ford, 1994). The standard requirements of probation are somewhat constraining to most probationers. But most probationers have the strong incentive of avoiding imprisonment by behaving well while on probation (Spelman, 1995).

Deterrence. Experts disagree about the deterrent effect probation serves. The deterrent value of probation is measured most often by recidivism figures among those placed on probation. Because of the low degree of offender control associated with standard probation supervision, recidivism rates are proportionately higher than those associated with those of offenders in more intensively supervised intermediate punishment programs. For instance, Kim (1994) has analyzed the records of 4,398 drug offender probationers and parolees between 1983 and 1989 and followed until 1990. Some of these drug offenders received various types of treatment and counseling in their communities. However, the recidivism rates of both probationers and parolees were similar. But Kim cautions that *selection bias*, or how these drug offenders were initially chosen for inclusion in the study, as well as other nonexperimental aspects of the investigation, may have contributed to the nonsignificant outcome (Kim, 1994). Thus, the deterrent value of probation may vary according to the standard by which deterrence is measured and other factors having to do with study methodology.

Community Reintegration. One benefit of probation is that it permits offenders to remain in their communities, work at jobs, support their families, make restitution to victims, and perform other useful services. It is not so much that offenders need to be reintegrated into their communities; rather, probationers can avoid the criminogenic influence of jail or prison environments (Walker, 1989). In addition, the community reintegration function of probation is most closely associated with its rehabilitative aim. Apart from the idea that retribution deters, probation appears to fulfill at least two distinct reintegrative aims. Probation is a means of providing rehabilitation for society. At the same time, probation assists in the rehabilitation of clients (Chung and Pardeck, 1994).

Crime Control. Precisely how much crime control occurs as the result of probation is unknown. When offenders are outside the immediate presence of probation officers, they may or may not engage in undetected criminal activity (Horn, 1992). Standard probation offers little by way of true crime control, because there is minimal contact between offenders and their probation officers. It is believed that even standard probation offers some measure of crime control by extending to probationers a degree of trust as well as minimal behavioral restrictions. It would be misleading to believe that no monitoring occurs under standard probation supervision. Probation officers are obligated to make periodic checks of workplaces, and conversations with an offender's employer disclose much about how offenders are managing their time. Michigan probation officers, for example, conduct frequent mandatory screenings of probationer-clients for drugs and alcohol (Blevins, Morton, and McCabe, 1996:38–39). Because problem drinkers and others who are drug-dependent tend to have higher reoffending rates than those who don't drink or use drugs, it is especially important for probation officers to supervise effectively this aspect of probationers' lives. The Michigan Alcohol Screening Test is increasingly used by federal probation officers as well. The results have been favorable. Those clients with drinking problems can be given special assistance and placed in the proper programs within their communities. While these programs don't cure everyone, some offenders are helped in ways that deter them from future offending.

Effectiveness of Standard Probation

Probation programs offer nonincarcerative alternatives to offenders. The avoidance of a jail or prison environment and its stigma are considered significant deterrents to future criminal activity. Of course, no program is perfect, and there will always be recidivism among ex-offenders. Thus, it is unrealistic to expect that probation alone will function as the major means of crime control (Conrad, 1984). The major question is how much recidivism is observed before a program is declared ineffective?

During the 1980s, numerous programs were established and experiments designed to effect greater nonincarcerative control over a growing offender population. Because of prison and jail overcrowding in many jurisdictions, solutions have been sought by legislators and others that strike a balance between standard probation, which often involves little or no control over offenders, and total control through confinement. The result has been the creation of a series of **intermediate punishments**, broadly defined as those sanctions that exist on the continuum of criminal penalties somewhere between incarceration and probation (McCarthy and McCarthy, 1997).

The chief distinguishing feature of intermediate punishments is presumably the *high degree of monitoring and control* exerted by program officials over offender behaviors. Other characteristics of intermediate punishments include curfews, which offenders are expected to observe, and frequent monitoring or contact with program authorities, usually probation officers (Petersilia and Turner, 1990b, 1991). The amount and type of frequent monitoring or contact varies with the program, although daily visits by probation officers at an offender's workplace or home are not unusual. The ultimate aim of more intensive supervision over probationers is that their recidivism will be less than those supervised by standard probation supervision methods. This is not always the result, however.

In 1986, three California counties (Los Angeles, Ventura, and Contra Costa) were selected as sites for an experiment involving a sample of 488 high-risk probationers. Probation officers had their caseloads reduced to small sizes; thus, they could give probationers more of their time and supervision. Probationer-clients were expected to work at their jobs; undergo random urine and alcohol testing; perform community service; and pay a portion of their supervisory costs from their earnings. When their probation terms were over, they were studied again after one year had elapsed. Although these offenders received more intensive supervision through increased contacts, monitoring, and drug testing, their recidivism rates were the same as those *not* receiving more intensive supervision. Petersilia and Turner (1990b, 1991) suggest that although the deterrent effect of more intensive supervision did not occur as anticipated, certain benefits accrued to the community. Drug-dependent clients, for instance, received needed treatment and therapy. For some period of time, at least, offenders were monitored closely and did not commit new offenses while under this close supervision.

Petersilia and Turner (1990a, 1992) conducted other research in Oregon and Texas. The Oregon findings appeared to be similar to those of the California study. Recidivism rates among Oregon probationers resulted in many prison placements. In Texas, samples of 221 parolees in Dallas and 458 parolees in Houston were studied between August 1987 through July 1988. Texas officials were especially interested in these offenders because intensive supervised parole might be an effective way of reducing prison overcrowding. However, Petersilia and Turner (1992) observed that more intensive supervision of Texas parolees was about as effective as standard parole. Yet intensive supervised parole in Texas cost about 1.7 times as much as standard parole. Recidivism rates of standard parolees and intensively supervised parolees were about the same. Thus, the desired effects of more intensive supervised probation were not realized, at least in this Texas experiment.

Ideally, intermediate punishments are intended for prison- or jail-bound offenders. Although offenders are given considerable freedom of movement within their communities, it is believed that such intensive monitoring and control fosters a high degree of compliance with program requirements. It is also believed that such intensive supervision acts to deter offenders from engaging in new criminal behaviors. In the following section, we examine several intensive probation supervision programs and assess their effectiveness.

INTENSIVE PROBATION SUPERVISION PROGRAMS

No common standard exists for deciding when a supervision program for probationers becomes intensive (Byrne, 1989; Spelman, 1995). An inspection of "intensive" supervised probation programs in 37 states disclosed a range from two contacts per month by probation officers with offenders in Texas to as many as 32 contacts per month in Idaho (Byrne, 1986:12). For our purposes, **intensive supervised probation/parole** (ISP) consists of the following (adapted from O'Leary and Clear, 1984:19):

1. Small client-officer caseloads, no more than a 10 to 1 ratio
2. Weekly face-to-face contacts between officers and clients
3. Regular field visits at an offender's workplace, perhaps monthly or bimonthly
4. The inclusion of preventive conditions such as regular drug and alcohol testing
5. Swift and certain administrative review and revocation procedures for violating one or more probation conditions

Three programs are examined here. These are (1) the Georgia IPS Model; (2) the New Jersey Model; and (3) the South Carolina Model.

The Georgia IPS Program

Georgia had one of the highest per capita incarceration rates in the United States during the 1970s (Erwin and Bennett, 1987). Prison and jail overcrowding caused Georgia to devise a new and more effective probation program. The Georgia Intensive Probation Supervision (IPS) Program was established in 1982.

Georgia Program Elements. The Georgia program is one of the most strict in the United States (Petersilia et al., 1985:70). Three phases of the program have to do with the level of control, Phase I being the most intensive supervision and Phase III being the least intensive. These standards include the following (Erwin, 1986:17–19):

1. Five face-to-face contacts per week in Phase I (decreasing to two face-to-face contacts per week in Phase III)
2. 132 hours of mandatory community service
3. Mandatory curfew

4. Mandatory employment
5. Weekly check of local arrest records
6. Automatic notification of arrest elsewhere via State Crime Information Network listings
7. Routine alcohol and drug screens
8. Assignment of one probation officer and one surveillance officer to 25 probationers or one probation officer and two surveillance officers to 40 probationers (surveillance officers have corrections backgrounds or law enforcement training and make home visits, check arrest records, and perform drug/alcohol tests among other duties)
9. Probation officer determines individualized treatment (e.g., counseling, vocational/educational training) for offender
10. Probation officer is liaison between court and offender and reports to court regularly on offender's progress from personal and surveillance observations and records

By 1985, 33 out of 45 judicial districts in Georgia were using the ISP program. Between 1982 and 1985, the ISP program had supervised 2,322 probationers (Erwin, 1986:18). Offenders spend from 6 to 12 months under ISP and must pay from $10 to $50 a month as a probation supervision fee (Petersilia, 1987:18).

The Effectiveness of the Georgia ISP Program. Georgia's ISP program thus far has been demonstrated to be effective by demonstrating low recidivism rates among its offender-clientele. Compared with paroled offenders and others supervised by standard probation practices, the ISP participants had systematically lower recidivism rates depending upon their risk classification. Classifications of risk consisted of low risk, medium risk, high risk, and maximum risk. Reconvictions for these groups were 25 percent, 16 percent, 28 percent, and 26 percent, respectively, compared with parolees who had considerably higher reconviction rates for all risk groupings (Erwin, 1986:20). In subsequent years, the Georgia ISP Program has been viewed as a model for other jurisdictions to emulate because of its effectiveness (Byrne, 1990).

The New Jersey Intensive Supervision Program (ISP)

The New Jersey Intensive Supervision Program (ISP) was established in June 1983. Technically it is a form of parole, given that only incarcerated offenders are eligible as possible clients. The program has been influenced by the traditional, treatment-oriented rehabilitation model and is targeted to serve certain less serious incarcerated offenders (Pearson and Bibel, 1986:25).

New Jersey ISP Program Elements. The New Jersey ISP program was established largely in response to chronic overcrowding in New Jersey's prisons and jails (Byrne, 1990; Pearson, 1991). Between June 1983 and December 1985, the ISP has served nearly 600 offenders (Pearson and Bibel, 1986:25). The program's features include the following:

1. Offender participation in the ISP for a term of 18 months.
2. Probation officer contacts with offenders 20 times per month during the first 14 months.
3. During the first 6 months of the program, at least 12 visit are face-to-face between offender and probation officer.
4. Between months 15 through 18, the remaining contacts shall be conducted by telephone.
5. Four out of 20 checks per month will be curfew checks (offenders must be home from 10:00 P.M. to 6:00 A.M. every night).
6. Offenders must be regularly employed during the program.
7. Offenders must pay all fines, victim compensation or restitution, and other miscellaneous fees associated with program maintenance.
8. Random checks are made for drug use (through random urinalysis tests).
9. A probation officer's caseload is 25.
10. Community service work is expected, although this varies according to the seriousness of the offender's conviction offense and individual situation. Current standards call for 16 hours of community service per month, if available.
11. A daily diary must be maintained by the probationer to show accomplishments.

Selection and Participation in the New Jersey Program. Getting into New Jersey's ISP program is on a voluntary basis. Not all volunteers are chosen. For instance, of the 2,400 applications from incarcerated offenders between 1983 and 1985, less than 25 percent were chosen for inclusion in the program (Pearson and Bibel, 1986:26). All applicants had to serve a minimum of 30 days in prison to be considered eligible for the program, and full-time employment had to be arranged within 30 days of a client's acceptance (Pearson and Bibel, 1986:26). In subsequent years, the 30-day minimum incarceration provision has been eliminated. However, almost all participants have served an average of four months in prison (Byrne, 1990; Pearson, 1991).

The selection process consists of seven screening stages. Final decisions on which applicants will be accepted are made by a resentencing panel of Superior Court judges. Reasons for rejecting applicants include first- and second-degree felonies, too many prior felony convictions, prior crimes of violence, and applicant reluctance to comply with ISP provisions (Pearson, 1991). Thus, the New Jersey program is targeted for low-risk offenders with the least likelihood of recidivating.

New Jersey Program Effectiveness. By 1990, over 80 percent of the offenders had made it through the first six months of the program, and those who failed did so primarily because of program rule violations rather than committing new crimes (Byrne, 1990). Furthermore, nearly 100 offenders had been unconditionally released from supervision, and 185 offenders had completed at least one year successfully (Byrne, 1990; Pearson, 1991). The recidivism rate of program participants was well below 30 percent in subsequent follow-ups.

The South Carolina ISP Program

A South Carolina legislative mandate was given in 1984 to establish an ISP program. The South Carolina Department of Probation, Parole, and Pardon Services (DPPPS) was given the responsibility for establishing the ISP program and implementing it. The primary aims of the ISP program were to (1) heighten surveillance of participants; (2) increase parole officer/client contact; and (3) heighten offender accountability. South Carolina started its ISP program as an experimental project. The ISP program goal was to involve 336 probationers during the first year. By 1991, 13,356 offenders had been processed through the ISP program. During that year, South Carolina was supervising 1,589 probationers and 480 parolees (Cavanaugh, 1992:1,5).

Program Elements. All clients in the South Carolina ISP program must pay a $10 per week supervision fee. Supervision fees are not unusual in ISP programs. However, if certain offenders cannot afford to pay these fees, this will not disqualify them from participating. Clients are supervised by intensive agents, who are special probation officers with light caseloads of no more than 35 offenders. Mandatory weekly face-to-face contacts with offenders, together with visits to neighbors, friends, employers and service providers of probationers are critical program elements. Probation officers in the South Carolina program act as liaisons between the private sector and their clients, lining up job possibilities. Thus, POs do some employment counseling when necessary.

Participant Selection. Eligible offenders are classified according to their level of risk and types of needs. Probation officers attempt to individualize program requirements to meet these offender needs. The closeness of offender supervision depends on the risk score achieved by any given client. The goal of DPPPS probation officers is to provide offenders with the proper balance of control and assistance. The ISP program also uses curfews, electronic monitoring, and house arrest or home incarceration elements for certain high-risk offenders. Offenders sentenced to house arrest are in a program called ISP Home Detention and confined to their homes from 10:00 P.M. to 6:00 A.M. They are permitted authorized leaves from home with their probation officer approval. All clientele are subject to random visits from probation officers at any time. Clients must work or attempt to obtain employment, undergo medical, psychiatric or mental health counseling or other rehabilitative treatment, attend religious services, or perform community service work (Cavanaugh, 1992:5–6).

Offender participation in the South Carolina ISP program varies from three to six months. Offenders may be placed on electronic monitoring and must wear an electronic wristlet or anklet for the first 30 days. After successfully completing the first 30-day period of ISP, they are taken off electronic monitoring and are then subject to a 60-day period of simple voice verification. Such verification occurs by telephone, with probation staff calling offenders at particular times to verify their whereabouts. Offenders must give requested information over the telephone, and electronic devices verify whether the voice pattern transmitted matches that of the offender being called. If there are "glitches" in the system, such as a continuous busy signal at the client's home, a probation officer will visit the home immediately to verify the client's whereabouts.

Effectiveness. The ISP program in South Carolina is successful. In 1991 only 13 percent of the 2,000 ISP program clients had their programs revoked. Two percent of the probationers had their programs revoked due to new crimes rather than for technical program violations. For parolees who participated in this program in 1991, 8 percent were revoked for program violations generally, while about 2 percent were revoked because of new crimes (Cavanaugh, 1992:6). Using an arbitrary 30 percent recidivism standard, it should be concluded that the South Carolina ISP program is successful for both its probationers as well as its parolees.

Criticisms of IPS Models

Any ISP program can be faulted because it does not achieve its stated goals (Beck, 1990; Fulton and Stone, 1993:43). Victims may be ignored in probation decision making, and some ISP programs may contribute to net widening by bringing certain offenders under the ISP program umbrella who really do not need to be intensively supervised (Palumbo and Snyder-Joy, 1990). At the same time, many critics praise ISP programs for alleviating prison inmate overcrowding and providing a meaningful option to incarceration (Lemov, 1992:134; Oregon Crime Analysis Center, 1991). One aspect of ISP programs that has drawn some criticism in certain jurisdictions has been the imposition of supervision fees on ISP program clients (Mills, 1992:10). These costs are normally incurred by probationer-clients. Despite the fact that it is unconstitutional to deny any client admission to an ISP program because of a client's inability to pay supervisory fees, there continues to be considerable controversy about requiring such fees generally (DeJong and Franzeen, 1993).

The different ISP programs described have been used by other states as models for their own ISP program development. Several elements of the Georgia model have been adopted by Arizona, Colorado, Illinois, Indiana, Louisiana, Nevada, and North Carolina. The New Jersey model has been partially implemented by Iowa and Kentucky for managing both probationers and parolees. Although states have not copied Georgia or New Jersey precisely in their probation guidelines, their newly developed programs resemble the Georgia and New Jersey Programs to a high degree. In Kentucky, for example, the ISP program is used exclusively with parolees as a condition of their supervision.

Some positive features of the Georgia program are that it has shown low rates of recidivism and it has alleviated prison overcrowding. However, Georgia officials who operate the program may be too selective in which clients can participate in the program. The program includes only those offenders most likely to be successful. With only 29 percent of the offenders exhibiting "maximum risk" scores, it is believed by some critics that the program is self-serving and thus not a true indication of how effective intensive supervised probation can be. The process of selecting only those most likely to be successful clients is known as **creaming**. Dickey and Wagner (1990) say that to be of greatest service, the program should target more offenders who are risks and difficult to manage.

Criticisms of New Jersey's ISP program are that client involvement is strictly voluntary. While volunteers are not *automatically* included in the program, there is an inherent bias introduced. The most serious types of felons are excluded, again reflective of *creaming* such as that seen in the Georgia program. However, the screening process used by New Jersey is considered one of the most rigorous of all existing ISP programs.

The South Carolina ISP program has a low rate of recidivism among its clientele. Compared with the Georgia and New Jersey programs, this program relies on the use of risk assessment instruments for recruiting clients and determining their level of intensive supervision. The South Carolina program element involving the payment of a $10 per week supervision fee is viewed as heightening offender accountability and serves to remind them that they are paying for their crimes. South Carolina probation officers perform liaison functions when they connect their clients with prospective employers. In addition, the combined use of house arrest and electronic monitoring, together with frequent face-to-face visits and checks by supervising parole officers, greatly heightens offender control.

Su Perk Davis (1992a:9) has reported that over 48,000 offenders were under some form of ISP in the United States throughout 41 state jurisdictions in 1992. This represents a 48 percent increase in the number of ISP clients compared with a similar survey conducted in 1988 (Davis, 1992a:9). Table 4.5 shows a distribution of clientele throughout the various states for 1992.

An examination of Table 4.5 shows that the number of offenders supervised under ISP averages about 25. Illinois, Montana, and South Dakota have the smallest ISP PO caseloads of 10 to 12 clients. South Carolina has the largest ISP caseloads at 61 per probation officer. Although ratios were not computed, it is clear that considerable variation exists among the states concerning the proportion of probationers who are in ISP programs compared with the total number of state probationers. Two states with similar total probationers, Georgia (132,000) and New York (139,132) have markedly different numbers of clients on ISP. Georgia has

TABLE 4.5 Summary of State ISP Probationers and Caseloads

State	Number of Probationers[a]	Number of ISP Probationers[b]	Normal Caseloads	ISP Caseloads
Alabama	24,200	180	147	25
Arizona	32,300	2,100	80	25
Colorado	28,700	479	160	20
Connecticut	47,629	160	202	40
Florida	88,640	12,431	120	25
Georgia	132,000	2,795	150	50
Hawaii	3,900	83	160–180	35–40
Idaho	3,194	110	75	25
Illinois	79,411	871	95	10
Iowa	13,580	271	—	20–25
Kansas	15,284	2,342	74	25
Kentucky	9,897	684	60	27
Maryland	88,289	—	142	47
Michigan	46,396	240	110	30
Mississippi	8,139	273	104	28
Missouri	31,319	771	75	20
Montana	625	—	88	10
Nebraska	18,793	318	109	21.5
Nevada	7,561	788	65–75	25–35
New Hampshire	4,100	70	85–95	25–30
New York	139,132	4,800	—	21
North Carolina	86,591	3,033	108	24
North Dakota	1,750	New ISP Program 6/1/92	—	—
Ohio	55,000	3,968	90–120	35–40
Oklahoma	24,871	139	85	—
Oregon	30,000	1,400	85	35–50
South Carolina	30,583	1,804	160	61
South Dakota	3,800	50	75	12.5
Tennessee	20,052	1,119	80	28
Texas	343,382	6,000	40–100	40
Utah	6,542	161	57	15–20
Vermont	6,007	265	97	44
Virginia	22,000	450	70	24
Wyoming	3,500	12	100	25

[a] Numbers of probationers.
[b] Numbers of ISP probationer-clients.

Source: Adapted from Su Perk Davis, "Survey: Number of Offenders under Intensive Probation Increases." *Corrections Compendium,* 17:9–17, 1992a.

about 2,800 clients, while New York has 4,800. Probation department resources are no doubt a factor influencing the actual numbers of probationers who become a part of ISP programs.

There is also considerable variation in client caseloads among the states. There is a caseload low of 40 clients per probation officer in Texas to a high of 202 clients per probation officer in Connecticut. Thus, even under standard probation supervision, some states have probation officer caseloads that are well within the ISP caseload range. It is easy to see from these figures how caseload discussions for either standard or intensive supervised probation and recidivism rates may be subject to widely different interpretations by experts. For instance, if we are discussing standard probation caseloads in Kentucky, someone from South Carolina may think we are referring to ISP PO caseloads, because the normal or standard probation caseload in Kentucky is 60 and the ISP caseload in South Carolina is 61. There are obvious semantic problems here.

ISP Program Components. Several program components are shared among states. These components include electronic surveillance, community sponsorship, payment of probation fees, and split-sentencing, respectively (Wiebush, 1991). Fulton and Stone (1993:43–44) have identified the following criteria as essential program components of ISP programs:

1. High risk/need population targeted for ISP
2. Reliable risk/need instruments used to select clients
3. Small caseloads (no more than 20–30 offenders)
4. Frequent substantive contact with probationers
5. Phase or level system used
6. Systematic case review for program evaluation
7. System of sanctions for program violators
8. Available range of correctional interventions
9. Restitution to victims
10. Community involvement of clients
11. ISP officers as facilitators and advocates
12. Objectives-based management used
13. Sound means of program evaluation

SHOCK PROBATION OR SHOCK PAROLE AND SPLIT SENTENCING

Shock probation or **shock parole** refer to planned sentences by which judges order offenders imprisoned for statutory incarceration periods related to their conviction offenses. However, after 30, 60, 90, or even 120 days of incarceration, offenders are taken out of jail or prison and "resentenced" to probation, provided they behaved well while incarcerated. The "shock" factor relates to the shock of being imprisoned initially. Theoretically, this trauma will be so profound that inmates will not want to return to prison later. Therefore, a strong deterrent factor is associated with these terms.

The key to understanding shock probation is knowing that offenders are not told in advance that they are only being confined for short terms. Judges sentence offenders to "five years in prison (or jail)," and offenders enter confinement *thinking* that they are commencing the first day of a five-year sentence. Suddenly, after 30, 60, 90 or 120 days, they are taken out of confinement and brought before the judge again. The judge suspends the rest of their jail/prison time and imposes probation. Yes, these offenders are relieved. Furthermore, they are "shocked" as they realize they will not have to serve more time in jail.

Ohio introduced the first shock probation law in 1965. Several other states have adopted similar laws in recent years (Friday and Peterson, 1972; Vito, 1978, 1984). In 1988, 1,056 offenders participated in nine shock incarceration programs throughout the country (Yurkanin, 1988:87). By 1994, 41 shock probation programs were being operated in at least 25 states (MacKenzie and Souryal, 1994:1).

The Philosophy and Objectives of Shock Probation

Shock Probation and Crime Deterrence. Ideally, persons who are locked up in jails for brief periods are literally shocked into becoming law-abiding, because they do not want to do more time in jails in the future (Vito, 1984:22). This is because of the unpleasantness of the jail experience. Thus, deterrence is a key objective of shock probation. However, not everyone is affected the same way by short-term incarceration. Depending upon the jurisdiction, the length of jail time varies from one month to four months. For some offenders, this jail time is relatively lenient in view of the crime they have committed.

Shock Probation and Rehabilitation. While shock probation is intended to be traumatic, it is also considered rehabilitative to a degree. After all, shock probationers are ultimately released from jails after serving short jail terms and released into their communities. While in their communities, shock probationers can perform jobs, live with their families, and otherwise lead normal lives. This scenario is much better for their rehabilitation than being confined in prison for one or more years.

Shock Probation and Creative Sentencing. In some cases, judges are encouraged to be creative in their sentencing options. Thus, judges may sentence offenders to short jail terms, followed by the inmate's release into the community. Judges may vary such sentences to include intermittent confinement, such as weekend incarceration. Judges may also add conditions to these sentences, including victim compensation, restitution, community service, counseling, and vocational/educational training.

Shock Probation and Jail/Prison Overcrowding. One result of shock probation in some jurisdictions has been to alleviate some degree of jail and prison overcrowding. Shock probation in South Carolina, for example, has diverted about one third of its offenders from prison during the first few years of its operation since 1987 (South Carolina State Reorganization Commission, 1990). Similar results have been found in other jurisdictions, as shock probation is increasingly used as a front-end solution to jail and prison overcrowding (Vaughn, 1993).

Shock Probation as a Punishment. The fact of locking up shock probationers, even if the periods of confinement are relatively brief, is evidence that some punishment is being imposed. While the incarcerative terms served by shock probationers are not entirely consistent with what the public thinks ought to be served, confinement is equated with punishment. Thus, to that extent, shock probation programs have citizen appeal.

Shock Probation and Offender Needs. When offenders are brought out of jails following short incarcerative terms, judges may impose conditions that include group counseling or individual therapy or treatment for those with special needs. Some offenders are drug- or alcohol-dependent and require medical intervention and assistance as well as employment guidance. The flexibility of shock probation facilitates meeting offender needs more effectively.

Shock Probation and Offender Accountability. The most important components of shock probation programs are those that heighten offender accountability. Offenders who are made to pay restitution to victims or perform some community service are painfully aware of the problems and suffering they have caused others. For many shock probationers, these experiences make them feel more accountable because they are being made to do something constructive to make up for their crimes.

Shock Probation and Community Safety. Citizens want to feel safe. They do not especially like the idea that criminals are being freed within their communities short of serving their full incarcerative sentences. Some citizens do not understand the rehabilitative or reintegrative value of shock incarceration programs. Nevertheless, the corrections system believes that for some offenders, at least, the shock probation option is better in the long run that long-term imprisonment. Thus, only those most likely not to reoffend are included in shock incarceration programs. Typically, these include low-risk first-offenders. It would be inconsistent with shock probation philosophy, for example, to include career criminals or violent offenders in such programs. Some amount of common sense is necessary to understand why certain offenders are included while others are deliberately excluded from program participation.

The Effectiveness of Shock Probation

Extensive research of existing shock probation or shock incarceration programs has been conducted. MacKenzie and Souryal (1994) investigated eight shock probation programs in 1992. These were programs operated in Oklahoma, Georgia, Texas, Florida, New York, Illinois, Louisiana, and South Carolina. They found that the programs shared certain similarities, including rigorous military drills and a daily schedule of physical training and hard labor. In the programs they studied, the program lengths varied from 90 to 180 days. Most participants were youthful male nonviolent offenders with little or no criminal history.

The rates of recidivism for offenders in these shock probation programs were relatively low and varied among the states. A one-year follow-up of the New York program found that only 10 percent committed new crimes and were imprisoned (Clark, Aziz, and MacKenzie, 1994:9). However, in Louisiana, about 43 percent of the shock probation clients did not complete their programs successfully for one of several reasons, including program violations and new crimes (MacKenzie, Shaw, and Gowdy, 1993).

One observation by experts is that the effectiveness of shock probation programs may depend, in part, on who selects shock probationers as clients. In some jurisdictions, judges select offenders, while in other jurisdictions, client selection is the duty of corrections officials. Thus it is entirely possible that less-than-rigorous selection methods may lead to net widening, by which offenders who would never have been incarcerated initially upon conviction are included in shock probation programs anyway, simply because they show the most promise for completing the program successfully. Furthermore, programs vary substantially in the amount of emphasis placed on education, vocational training, discipline, and rehabilitation. All of these factors influence program effectiveness (MacKenzie and Ballow, 1989). Generally, shock probation serves useful rehabilitative and reintegrative purposes. Shock probation programs have been shown to be effective in deterring offenders from recidivating. It is likely that we will see greater expansion of shock probation programs in future years, as more states establish such programs.

BOOT CAMPS

Another program similar to shock probation is shock incarceration or boot camps.

Boot camps are highly regimented, military-like, short-term correctional programs (90–180 days) in which offenders are provided with strict discipline, physical training, and hard labor resembling some aspects of military basic training; when successfully completed, boot camps provide for transfers of participants to community-based facilities for nonsecure supervision. By 1993, boot camps had been formally established in over half of the states (MacKenzie et al., 1995). Boot camps continue to proliferate annually (Cronin, 1994).

Boot camps were officially established in 1983 by the Georgia Department of Corrections Special Alternative Incarceration (SAI). The general idea for boot camps originated some time earlier in the late 1970s, also in Georgia (Parent, 1989b). The usual length of incarceration in boot camps varies from three to six months. During this period, boot camp participants engage in marching, work, and classes that are believed useful in one's rehabilitation (Osler, 1991:34). Usually, youthful offenders are targeted by these programs (Jones and Cuvelier, 1992). In 1993, there were 28 state prison systems operating 43 boot camp programs, with more states planning to establish similar programs (Austin, Jones, and Bolyard, 1993:1). By 1996, there were 32 states and the federal government known to be operating 52 boot camp programs (Bourque, Han, and Hill, 1996:3). Total capacity for 35 federal and state boot camp programs was for 9,304 clients. Nine locally operated boot camp programs for adults had a capacity of 908 clients. The capacity for nine juvenile boot camp programs was 455 (Bourque et al., 1996:3). Table 4.6 shows the characteristics of boot camp programs for 1996.

Table 4.6 indicates that boot camps are increasingly popular among the states. Thirty of the 52 programs shown were opened since 1991. More than 90 percent of these programs are designed for male offenders. The minimal length of these residential boot camps ranges from three months or less to six months.

The Rationale for Boot Camps. Austin et al. (1993:1) suggest the following rationale for boot camps:

1. A substantial number of youthful first offenders now incarcerated will respond to a short but intensive period of confinement followed by a longer period of intensive community supervision.

TABLE 4.6 Characteristics of Boot Camp Programs

	Federal and State[a] (*n* = 35)	Local (*n* = 8)	Juvenile (*n* = 9)
Year Opened			
Prior to 1988	7	0	0
1988–1990	13	2	0
1991–1993	14	6	6
1994	1	0	3
Capacity[b]			
Male	8,678	806	455
Female	626	102	0
Total Capacity	9,304	908	455
Minimum length of residential boot camp			
< 3 months	2	4	1
3 months	15	2	2
4 months	9	0	5
6 months	9	2	1

[a] There were 32 states known to operate boot camps at the time of the study. Since both Georgia and Oklahoma operate two different types of boot camps, they are treated separately in the table.
[b] When a program did not break out male and female capacity, it was counted as being male. Therefore, the female capacities may be undercounted.
Source: Bourque, Han, and Hill, 1996:3.

2. These youthful offenders will benefit from a military-type atmosphere that instills a sense of self-discipline and physical conditioning that was lacking in their lives.
3. These same youths need exposure to relevant educational/vocational training, drug treatment, and general counseling services to develop more positive and law-abiding values and become better prepared to secure legitimate future employment.
4. The costs involved will be less than a traditional criminal justice sanction that imprisons the offender for a substantially longer period of time.

Goals of Boot Camps

The goals of boot camps are to (1) foster rehabilitation/reintegration, (2) promote discipline, (3) deter crime, (4) ease prison/jail overcrowding, and (5) provide vocational, educational, and rehabilitative services.

To Foster Rehabilitation/Reintegration. Boot camps are intended to assist offenders in living in a law-abiding manner with other offenders. Clientele learn to respect one another's property and to be considerate of others.

To Promote Discipline. The military-like regimen of boot camp training instills discipline in most participants. It has been found that many boot camp clientele have never had discipline in their homes and families. They have been disruptive in their schools. Thus, the boot camp experience teaches them about rules and the importance of abiding by them.

To Deter Crime. There is a certain amount of punishment inherent in boot camps. Having to adhere to rigid and demanding physical and educational schedules is something these clients have never had to do. The boot camp experience is a shocking one for most participants. After they have graduated from boot camp, most participants never want to go through boot camp again. The experience is both rewarding and punitive.

To Ease Prison/Jail Overcrowding. It is uncertain as to how much prison and jail overcrowding is alleviated by boot camp programs. It is clear that if the goals of boot camps are followed closely, only prison- or jail-bound offenders should be targeted for boot camp participation. To the extent that such persons are actually singled out for boot camp experiences, then prison and jail overcrowding is eased somewhat. Additionally, the relatively low rates of recidivism of a majority of boot camp participants suggests that most of these former clients will be law-abiding in their future years and not be drawn again into the criminal justice system. Therefore, this should be considered a long-term fringe benefit of boot camp experiences (Tonry and Hamilton, 1995).

To Provide Vocational, Educational, and Rehabilitative Services. An integral part of most boot camp programs is the provision of vocational and educational services for clients. Not only must boot camp clients adhere to strict physical regimens, they must also participate in educational and vocational programs designed to equip them with skills that will make them more employable. Many of these clients were either unemployed or underemployed when they committed their first crimes. If most of these clients can acquire skills that make them more attractive to employers, then they can hold down jobs and provide for their families more effectively. The need to resort to crime to make ends meet will either not exist or be diminished. Employment is almost always a strong factor influencing whether former offenders will reoffend.

A Profile of Boot Camp Clientele

What are the characteristics of those who participate in boot camps? Most boot camp participants are prison-bound youthful offenders convicted of less serious, nonviolent crimes and who have not been previously incarcerated (Parent, 1989b). Depending on the program, there are some exceptions (MacKenzie, Shaw, and Gowdy, 1993:1–3). Participants may either be referred to these programs by judges or corrections departments or they may volunteer. They may or may not be accepted, and if they complete their programs successfully, they may or may not be released under supervision into their communities. Table 4.7 shows the eligibility requirements for the boot camp programs as of 1996.

Although the programs vary in their minimum-age eligibility requirements, the age range targeted for adult boot camps is 25 to 35. Ten programs have no age limitations. Voluntary participation is a requirement for enrollment in 27 of these programs. In addition, those who have prior incarcerations are excluded from 23 of these programs. Those who have committed violent crimes are excluded from 33 of these programs (Bourque et al., 1996:4).

Jail Boot Camps

A 1993 survey disclosed that there were ten jurisdictions operating boot camps through city or county jails (Austin et al., 1993:2). Thirteen other jurisdictions were contemplating boot camps through their jails during the next several years. These **jail boot camps** are short-term programs for offenders in a wide age range. For example, those jail boot camps in New York and New Orleans have age limits of 39 years and 45 years, respectively. Most existing jail boot camps target probation or parole violators who may face revocation and imprisonment.

The age range for inclusion is highly variable among jurisdictions. The jail boot camps are almost equally divided according to whether judges or jail officials select inmates for boot camp participation. Six of the ten pro-

TABLE 4.7 Eligibility Criteria for Boot Camps

Eligibility Requirements	Federal and State ($n = 35$)	Local ($n = 8$)	Juvenile ($n = 9$)
Maximum age			NA[a]
25 or under	7	3	
26–30	8	1	
31–35	7	0	
36–40	3	0	
No limit	10[b]	4	
Maximum sentence			NA[a]
Between 1 and 4 years	9	1	
Between 5 and 10 years	15	1	
Other[c]	11	6	
Requirement that enrollment be voluntary[d]	27	6	3
Exclude those with			
Prior incarceration	23	1	0
Violent crimes	33	6	3

[a] For juvenile programs the maximum age is the age of juvenile court jurisdiction, typically age 17. Minimum ages for these programs are 14 for six programs, 12 or one, 13 for one, and 16 for one. Sentence requirements do not apply.
[b] Includes the federal program, which does not exclude older offenders but does give priority to offenders under age 36, and the Michigan program, which only accepts *probationers* under age 26 but accepts *inmates* of any age.
[c] Includes programs with sentences greater than 10 years and those with no maximums.
[d] Does not include two programs (Arizona and Hidalgo County, Texas) that do not have voluntary requirements but most of the participants do volunteer.
Source: Bourque, Han, and Hill, 1996:4.

grams permit voluntary withdrawal. Finally, all of these jail boot camps have drug education counseling and physical training. Most provide vocational education, work, and general counseling.

Four of these jail boot camps include women in special programs. New York City and Santa Clara, California, operate jail boot camps designed for women. The number of women participants is small (Austin et al., 1993: 4–5). The bed capacity, for instance, ranges from 12 in Brazos, Texas, to 384 in Harris, Texas. The average length of stay ranges from 5 days to 275 days in Ontario, New York, and Orleans, Louisiana, respectively.

The Effectiveness of Boot Camps

Are boot camps or shock incarceration programs successful? Most programs use the recidivism rate standard of 30 percent or less as a measure of program success. If this standard is applied to existing adult boot camp

BOX 4.4 Three Boot Camps Described

The Nevada Program of Regimental Discipline

The Nevada Program of Regimental Discipline was created in 1990. It has the following features (McCorkle, 1995:367–368):

1. 150-day program.
2. Judges select nonviolent male offenders over 18 years of age.
3. Mandatory involvement in boot camps by clientele, where judges defer sentencing and simply order offenders to the program.
4. Seven drill instructors, two substance abuse counselors, and one caseworker for all clients.
5. Physical training daily at 5:15 A.M.
6. Those without high school diplomas must attend G.E.D. classes held at the facility.
7. High school graduates spend each morning at hard labor and close-order drill.
8. All participants must complete 120 hours of drug education classes held in afternoons.
9. All activities are monitored closely by drill instructors.
10. Successful completion of program means a return to court and a three- to five-year probationary sentence; failure to complete program means a period of incarceration in the general inmate population.

The Oregon SUMMIT Boot Camp Program

The Oregon SUMMIT Boot Camp Program was established in 1994. It has the following features (Beers and Duval, 1996:39–53):

1. Six-month program followed by 30-day transitional leave in the community; recidivism rate of 11 percent in one-year follow-up.
2. Participation is voluntary, for both males and females, with an age range of 18 to 40.
3. Excluded from participation are sex offenders, those convicted of first-degree crimes, those with recent escape histories, and those with outstanding detainer warrants.
4. Clients given hot meal on arrival; required to eat all that they take in first meal.
5. Two weeks of "Zero Week" in which clients are oriented to boot camp program concepts and schedule.
6. First two weeks include daily double sessions of physical training, once a day at 5:30 A.M.; purpose of physical education is to teach teamwork, precision, and motivation, with a bonus of enhanced physical fitness.
7. Classroom clothing issued during third week; each 16-hour day begins at 5:30 A.M. with reveille, followed by an hour of physical training, breakfast, flag call, and then day-long work squads or program classes until 3:30 P.M.; then 2-minute showers and dress for community meeting.
8. Daily community meeting from 4:00 to 5:00 P.M., followed by evening flag call, dinner, and then more classes from 6:00 to 9:00 P.M.

9. After a half hour in dormitories to prepare for next day, shine boots, make one phone call per week, and assist peers, lights are out at 9:30 P.M.
10. This schedule is followed 7 days a week for 26 weeks.
11. Program is a modified therapeutic community centered on cognitive change; the idea that changing thinking changes behavior.
12. One and one half hours per week of drug and alcohol education, the Twelve Steps of Alcoholics Anonymous, Narcotics Anonymous, and recovery planning.
13. Each client prepares a detailed and individualized relapse prevention and recovery plan that is shared with the counselor and parole officer and incorporated into the inmate's release plan.
14. Clients memorize the philosophy, community standards, general orders, Twelve Steps to Recovery, general conditions of parole, evaluation categories, and community meeting elements.
15. Clients are evaluated daily by staff in a variety of program areas, including alcohol and drugs, education, self-respect, positive effort, cooperation, following instructions, accepting criticisms, program progress, time management, neatness and cleanliness, military bearing, physical training, positive attitude, safety practices, study habits, treatment comprehension, and personal growth.

The New York Shock Incarceration Program

The New York Shock Incarceration Program was established in 1987. It has the following program elements (Aziz and Clark, 1996:23–24):

1. Two six-month cycles, involving a six-month shock incarceration followed by a six-month intensive parole period.
2. Male and female voluntary participation, with an annual maximum capacity of 3,000 clients age 18 or older.
3. Training in military drill and ceremony, bearing, courtesy, and physical exercise.
4. Each day begins at 5:45 A.M. with 45 minutes of physical exercise and a half-hour run.
5. A 16-hour day includes attending courses in drug and substance abuse education, Alcoholics Anonymous and the Twelve Step Recovery program; day ends at 9:30 P.M.
6. Periodic counseling, both group and individual, to assist in understanding and coping with drug and alcohol dependencies; with 150 group counseling hours in 6 months.
7. Clients observed on a daily and weekly basis by drill instructors, crew officers, network officers, and teachers; individual interviews conducted weekly and staff meetings to discuss client progress.
8. Structured education program for each client, including remedial education, basic high school equivalency classes, and preparation for the G.E.D.; minimum of 12 hours per week of educational instruction for a total of 300 hours of academic classes in six months.
9. Six-month intensively supervised parole program, including group and individual counseling and continued therapy; application of concepts learned first six months during client's reintegration into society.

programs, then the results are not particularly impressive. For example, boot camps operated in Alabama have a 37 percent recidivism rate for boot camp graduates in one-year follow-ups by researchers (Burns and Vito, 1995). A similar aggregate of Alabama parolees who did not participate in boot camp programs had a recidivism rate of 25.7 percent within one year of their release from prison. A boot camp operation in Louisiana reported in 1992 that there were no significant differences in the recidivism of boot camp clientele and Louisiana parolees (MacKenzie, Shaw, and Souryal, 1992). An extensive review of the boot camp literature by Burns (1996:45) indicates that "the finding . . . is that boot camps have had little, if any success in attaining these goals [of lowering recidivism rates]." States such as Washington have reported similar nonsignificant differences in recidivism rates between those placed in boot camps and those paroled through more traditional mechanisms (Poole and Slavick, 1995).

McCorkle (1995) says that while boot camps and shock incarceration programs have grown phenomenally during the 1990s, they have not accomplished the desired effect of reducing recidivism among boot camp participants compared with those subjected to traditional nonincarcerative programs such as parole and probation. However, McCorkle has found that at least some programs, such as the Nevada Program of Regimental Discipline, have *therapeutic integrity*. Therapeutic integrity has to do with the competency and commitment of staff members and their ability to implement the program as originally conceived. Thus, military training as such does not appear to be either a necessary or sufficient element in the rehabilitation of boot camp participants. But McCorkle observed that most boot camp participants changed positively and significantly in their attitudes toward themselves, those around them, and their future (McCorkle, 1995:373).

There are obvious exceptions among states on recidivism rates of boot camp graduates. Among New Hampshire boot camp graduates, for example, Bourque et al. (1996:9) found a recidivism rate of only 17 percent during a two-year follow-up. This compared with a 47 percent recidivism rate among a comparable aggregate of New Hampshire parolees during the same study period. It would seem, therefore, that generalizations about boot camp effectiveness are unwarranted. This is because of the wide diversity of boot camp program elements among the states. Even in those states with high boot camp participant recidivism rates, such as Georgia, the attitude of public officials such as Governor Miller seems to be "I don't give a damn what they say, we're going to continue to do it in Georgia" (Burns, 1996:46). Georgia Governor Miller also said that "Nobody can tell me from some ivory tower that you take a kid, you kick him in the rear end, and it doesn't do any good." And for good measure, the massive allocation of federal resources to boot camp programs from the 1994 Crime Bill have greatly underscored the political support of the federal government. Burns (1996:45) notes that William Jenkins, Jr., the Assistant Director of Justice Issues for the General Accounting Office, has stated that "most people on the Hill believe that boot camps ought to be expanded." For better or worse, this is precisely what is happening in the latter 1990s.

KEY TERMS

Addams, Jane
Boot camps
Boston Children's Aid Society
Clark, Benjamin C.
Conditional diversion
Cook, Rufus R.
Court-watchers
Creaming
Diversion
Hull House
Intensive supervised probation or parole
Intermediate punishments
Jail boot camps
Jail or prison overcrowding
Offender control
Offense seriousness
PACT (Prisoner and Community Together)
Pretrial diversion
Reynolds, James Bronson
ROBO-PO
Settlement houses
Shock parole
Shock probation
Standard diversion
Unconditional diversion
University Settlement
Victim-offender reconciliation
Victim-Offender Reconciliation Project

QUESTIONS FOR REVIEW

1. What is diversion and what are some positive benefits of it for offenders?
2. What are several different forms of diversion? What are their advantages?
3. What is meant by probation? How does standard probation differ from intermediate punishments?
4. What are some functions of probation? How well does probation achieve these functions?
5. Who qualifies for diversion and probation? What are some of the offender characteristics favoring a diversion or probation decision?
6. Who are some of the more important founders and promoters of probation in the United States? What are some of their accomplishments?
7. What is Settlement House? When was it founded? Was it successful? Why or why not?
8. Do all states currently have probation programs? What age group was specifically targeted for probation in its early years?
9. What is alternative dispute resolution? What are its primary advantages?
10. If an offender is diverted for a specific time period, is it always the case that the offender's case will be expunged from the court records upon successful

completion of the diversion program? What are some conditions associated with diversion programs?

11. Who originated probation in the United States? What are probation's philosophical aims? What are some explanations for these aims?
12. How does probation function as a rehabilitative mechanism for offenders?
13. How does prison and jail overcrowding affect the probation population?

SUGGESTED READINGS

American Correctional Association. *Juvenile and Adult Boot Camps.* Lanham, MD: American Correctional Association, 1996.

Barrineau, H.E., III. *Civil Liability in Criminal Justice* (2nd ed). Cincinnati: Anderson Publishing Company, 1994.

Clarke, Stevens H., Ernest Valente, Jr., and Robyn R. Mace. *Mediation of Interpersonal Disputes: An Evaluation of North Carolina's Programs.* Chapel Hill: Institute of Government, University of North Carolina at Chapel Hill, 1992.

Sacco, Vincent F., and Leslie W. Kennedy. *The Criminal Event.* Belmont, CA: Wadsworth Publishing Company, 1995.

5

Jails: History, Functions, and Types of Inmates

CHAPTER OUTLINE

OVERVIEW

- Between October 20, 1987, and December, 1989, 57 suicide attempts were made by inmates of the Jefferson County (Alabama) Jail. Four of these suicide attempts were successful. Families of the deceased inmates filed suit against the jail for failing to monitor inmates so that their suicide attempts could be prevented. In 1992, a federal appeals court ruled that Alabama jails were not required to be "suicide-proof," although they were forbidden to equip each cell with the means whereby inmates could hang themselves. It seems that an iron bar ran across the window of each cell, thus enabling inclined inmates to hang themselves by looping some clothing around the bar and around their necks. Subsequently, the bars in cell windows were covered and no successful suicides (due to hanging) have occurred since in the Jefferson County Jail. (*Tittle v. Jefferson County Commission,* 966 F.2d 606 [11th Cir. 1992])
- Stanley Malinovitz, 38, died from a blood clot in a lung on January 28, 1984, five days after he was arrested for exhibiting bizarre behavior that included shoving an elderly woman to the ground in a Los Angeles shopping mall. Three days later, Malinovitz was found lying naked and dazed in a court holding cell. Municipal Court Commissioner Charles L. Peven postponed his arraignment so that Malinovitz could be taken to the County-USC Medical Center by sheriff's deputies. Instead, the deputies took him to the Men's Central Jail, where they strapped him to an iron cot for 40 hours. He died while strapped to the cot. A jury awarded $2.5 million to Malinovitz's family in April 1990 for the jail negligence. ("Jury Awards $2.5M to Family of Man Who Died in L.A. Jail." *Corrections Compendium* 15:19).

Jails in the United States are one of the most maligned and forgotten components of the criminal justice system (Cornelius, 1996). This chapter is about jails in the United States, their history, evolution, and reforms. With some exceptions, a **jail** is a confinement facility that is usually administered and operated by a local law enforcement agency, such as a county sheriff's office or county department of corrections; jails are intended to confine adults, but they may hold juveniles for brief periods (Cornelius, 1996:1).

Jails are an integral feature of U.S. corrections. In 1995 alone, there were nearly 10 million admissions to and releases from U.S. jails, with an average daily jail population of 509,828 (Gilliard and Beck, 1995:10). This was approximately 93 percent of the rated jail capacity of 545,763. Between 1985 and 1990, the jail inmate population increased by about 50% from 285,010 to 408,075. And again, between 1990 and 1995, there was a 25 percent increase in the U.S. jail inmate population (Gilliard and Beck, 1995:10–11).

In most jurisdictions, this population increase has created serious overcrowding problems in city and county jails. In turn, jail overcrowding has been directly or indirectly responsible for numerous inmate deaths and extensive violence, much offender litigation challenging, among other things, the constitutionality of the nature of their confinement and treatment, and administrative and/or supervisory problems of immense proportions.

This chapter lists and discusses significant historical events that have shaped the course and development of jails. Some of the more important functions of jails will be presented. Jail inmates represent a cross-section of all offender categories, and jail inmates are profiled. Specific types of jail inmates are described, including pretrial detainees, misdemeanants, state and federal prisoners, mentally retarded or ill, drug- or alcohol-dependent persons, and juveniles.

THE HISTORY OF JAILS IN THE UNITED STATES

The term *jail* is derived from the old English term *gaol* (also pronounced "jail"), which originated in A.D. 1166 through a declaration by Henry II of England. Henry II established gaols as a part of the Assize or Constitution of Clarendon (American Correctional Association, 1983:3). Gaols were locally administered and operated, and they housed many of society's misfits. Paupers or vagrants, drunkards, thieves, murderers, debtors, highwaymen, trespassers, orphan children, prostitutes, and others made up early gaol populations. Because the Church of England was powerful and influential, many religious dissidents were housed in these gaols as a punishment for their dissent. This practice continued for several centuries.

Local Political Control

Local control over the administration and operation of jails by shire-reeves in England was a practice continued by the American colonists in later years. Most jails in the United States today are locally controlled and operated in a manner similar to their English predecessors. Thus, political influence upon jails and jail conditions is strong. In fact, changing jail conditions from one year to the next are often linked to local political shifts through elections and new administrative appointments. In addition, the fact that local officials controlled jails and jail operations meant that no single administrative style typified these facilities. Each locality (shire) was responsible for establishing jails, and the way in which jails were operated was left up to local official discretion. Again, current U.S. jail operations in each jurisdiction are characterized by this same individuality of style.

Jails in England were originally designed as holding facilities for those accused of violating local laws. Alleged law violators were held until court could be conducted and the guilt or innocence of the accused was determined. Today, pretrial detainees make up a significant proportion of the U.S. jail population. Shire-reeves made their living through reimbursements from taxes collected in the form of fees for each inmate housed on a daily basis. For instance, the reeve would receive a fixed fee, perhaps 50 or 75 cents per day for each inmate held in the jail. Therefore, more prisoners meant more money for reeves and their assistants. Such a reimbursement scheme was easily susceptible to corruption, and much of the money intended for inmate food and shelter was pocketed by selfish reeves. Quite logically, the quality of inmate food and shelter was very substandard, and jails became notorious because of widespread malnutrition, disease, and death among prisoners.

Workhouses

These cruel and inhumane jail conditions continued into the sixteenth century, when **workhouses** were established largely in response to mercantile demands for cheap labor. A typical workhouse in the mid-sixteenth century was Bridewell, created in 1557. This London facility housed many of the city's vagrants and general riffraff (American Correctional Association, 1983). Jail and workhouse sheriffs and administrators quickly capitalized on the cheap labor these facilities generated, and additional profits were envisioned. Thus, it became commonplace for sheriffs and other officials to "hire out" their inmates to perform skilled and semiskilled tasks for various merchants. While the manifest functions of workhouses and prisoner labor were to improve the moral and social fiber of prisoners and train them to perform useful skills when they eventually were released, most of the monies collected from inmate labor was pocketed by corrupt jail and workhouse officials. This inmate exploitation continued a pattern that was widespread throughout early European corrections (Spierenburg, 1991).

In the New England area and throughout the colonies, jails were commonplace. Sheriffs were appointed to supervise jail inmates, and the fee system continued to be used to finance these facilities. All types of people were confined together, regardless of their gender or age. Orphans, prostitutes, drunkards, thieves, and robbers were often contained in large, dormitory-style rooms with hay and blankets for beds. Jails were great melting pots of humanity, with little or no regard for inmate treatment, health, or rehabilitation.

The Walnut Street Jail

The religious influence of the Quakers in Pennsylvania remained strong following the rejection of Penn's jail reforms. Shortly after the Revolutionary War, the Quakers were able to reinstitute many of Penn's correctional philosophies and strategies through the creation in 1787 of the **Philadel-**

phia Society for Alleviating the Miseries of Public Prisons. This society was made up of many prominent Philadelphia citizens, philanthropists, and religious reformers who believed prison and jail conditions ought to be changed and replaced with a more humane environment. Members of this Society visited each jail and prison daily, bringing food, clothing, and religious instruction to inmates. Some of these members were educators who sought to help prisoners acquire basic skills such as reading and writing. Although their intrusion into prison and jail life was frequently resented and opposed by local authorities and sheriffs, their presence was significant and brought the deplorable conditions of confinement to the attention of politicians. One particularly disturbing feature of both jails and prisons of that period was the extensive use of common rooms for men, women, and children. Little or no thought was given to housing these inmates in private or separate accommodations.

In 1790, the Pennsylvania legislature authorized the renovation of a facility originally constructed in 1776 on Walnut Street, a two-acre structure initially designed to house the overflow resulting from overcrowding of the High Street Jail. The **Walnut Street Jail** was both a workhouse and a place of incarceration for all types of offenders. But the 1790 renovation was the first of several innovations in U.S. corrections. Specifically, the Walnut Street Jail was innovative because (1) it separated the most serious prisoners from others in 16 large solitary cells; (2) it separated other prisoners according to their offense seriousness; and (3) it separated prisoners according to gender. Therefore, the Walnut Street Jail was the forerunner of minimum-, medium-, and maximum-security prisons in the United States as well as **solitary confinement.**

Besides these innovations, the Walnut Street Jail assigned inmates to different types of productive labor according to their gender and conviction offense. Women made clothing and performed washing and mending chores. Skilled inmates worked as carpenters, shoemakers, and other craftspersons. Unskilled prisoners beat hemp or jute for ship caulking. With the exception of women, prisoners received a daily wage for their labor, which was applied to defray the cost of their maintenance. The Quakers and other religious groups provided regular instruction for most offenders. The Walnut Street Jail concept was widely imitated by officials from other states during the next several decades. Many prisons were modeled after the Walnut Street Jail for housing and managing long-term prisoners.

Jail Developments Since Walnut Street

Information about the early growth of jails in the United States is sketchy. One reason is because there were many inmate facilities established during the 1800s and early 1900s serving many functions and operating under different labels. Sheriffs' homes were used as jails in some jurisdictions, while workhouses, farms, barns, small houses, and other types of facilities served similar purposes in others. Thus, depending on who did the counting, some facilities would be labeled as jails and some would not. Limiting jail definitions only to "locally operated" short-term facilities for inmates excluded also those state-operated jails in jurisdictions such as Alaska, Delaware, and Rhode Island. Another reason for inadequate jail statistics and information was that there was little interest in jail populations.

Another problem was that it was difficult to transmit information from jails and jail inmates to any central location during that period of time. Often, local records were not maintained, and many sheriff's departments were not inclined to share information about their prisoners with others. Streamlined communications systems did not exist, and information was compiled very slowly, if at all. State governments expressed little or no interest in the affairs of jails within their borders, since these were largely local enterprises funded with local funds. Even if there had been a strong interest in jail information among corrections professionals and others, it would have been quite difficult to acquire.

The U.S. Census Bureau began to compile information about jails in 1880 (Cahalan, 1986:73). At 10-year intervals following 1880, general jail information was systematically obtained about race, nativity, gender, and age. Originally, the U.S. Census Bureau presented data separately for county jails, city prisons, workhouses, houses of correction, and leased county prisoners (Cahalan, 1986:73). But in 1923, these figures were combined to reflect more accurately what we now describe as "jail statistics." A special report was prepared by the U.S. Census Bureau entitled "Prisoners, 1923." And in that same year, Joseph Fishman, a federal prison inspector, published a book, *Crucible of Crime,* describing living conditions of many U.S. jails (Cahalan, 1986:73; Reid, 1987:404). Comparisons with 1880 base figures show the jail population of the United States to be 18,686 in 1880, almost doubling by 1990 to 33,093. Table 5.1 shows jail population increases between 1880 and 1995, according to U.S. Census, Law Enforcement Assistance Administration, and Bureau of Justice Statistics sources.

Historically, reports about jail conditions in the United States have been largely unfavorable. The 1923 report by Fishman was based on his visits to and observations of 1,500 jails, and he described the conditions he saw as "horrible" (Reid, 1987:404). More recent reports suggest that these conditions have not changed dramatically since Fishman made his early observations (Thomas, 1988). Of course, there are exceptions, but these are few and far between. It was not until 1972 that national survey data about jails became available. Exceptions include the years 1910, 1923, and 1933, where jail inmate characteristics were listed according to several offense categories. A majority of jail inmates in each of those years had committed petty offenses such as vagrancy, public drunkenness, and minor property crimes (Cahalan, 1986:86). Even since 1972, jail data have not been regularly and consistently compiled.

There are several reasons for many of the continuing jail problems in the United States. While some of these persistent problems will be examined in-depth later in this chapter, it is sufficient for the present to under-

TABLE 5.1 **Jail Population Change, 1880–1995**

Year	Number of Jail Inmates
1880	18,686
1890	33,093
1940	99,249
1950	86,492
1960	119,671
1970	129,189
1980	163,994
1983	223,551
1986	274,444
1987	295,873
1988	343,569
1989	395,553
1990	405,320
1991	428,479
1992	444,584
1993	458,804
1994	490,442
1995	509,828

Sources: Cahalan (1986:76); Perkins, Stephan, and Beck (1995:2); Gilliard and Beck (1996:1, 10).

stand that (1) most of the U.S. jails today were built before 1970, and many were built five decades or more before that; (2) local control of jails often results in erratic policies that shift with each political election, thus forcing jail guards and other personnel to adapt to constantly changing conditions and jail operations; and (3) jail funding is a low-priority budget item in most jurisdictions, and with limited operating funds, the quality of services and personnel jails provide and attract is considerably lower when compared with state and federal prison standards and personnel (Cornelius, 1996).

How Many Jails Are There in the United States?

Currently, no one knows for sure the exact number of jails in the United States at any given time. The primary reason for this uncertainty is that experts disagree about how jails ought to be defined. Some survey researchers count only locally operated and funded, short-term incarceration facilities as jails, whereas other people include state-operated jails in their figures. In remote territories such as Alaska, World War II Quonset huts may be used to house offenders on a short-term basis. Work release centers, farms for low-risk inmates, and other facilities may be included or excluded from the jail definition. Sometimes, *lockups* (drunk tanks, holding tanks) are counted as jails, although these facilities exist primarily to hold those charged with public drunkenness or other minor offenses for up to 48 hours. These are not jails in the formal sense, but rather, they are simple holding tanks or facilities.

Cahalan (1986:92–94) underscores this uncertainty by showing that different federal agencies report vastly different numbers of jails for any given year. For instance, in 1970, the Census of Institutional Population estimated there were 2,317 jails in the United States, whereas the Law Enforcement Assistance Administration reported 4,037 U.S. jails. Furthermore, a 1923 study conducted by the U.S. Census Bureau reported there were 3,469 U.S. jails in operation. And in 1984, the Advisory Commission on Intergovernmental Relations reported that there were 3,493 jails in the United States (Advisory Commission on Intergovernmental Relations, 1984:2). These widely disparate figures are confusing to most readers.

Between 1950 and 1995, the jail population grew by 500 percent. If we use U.S. Department of Justice jail figures for comparative purposes, then there has been a substantial *decrease* in the number of jails in the United States between 1970 and 1994, with 4,037 jails reported in 1970 and only 3,272 jails reported in 1994 (American Jail Association, 1994). If these figures are accurate, then current jail overcrowding is easily explained. How can existing jails accommodate such greater jail inmate population increases? One answer is that many *old* jails have been destroyed or drastically remodeled and expanded, while many new jails have been constructed. Newer jails are generally designed to accommodate several times the number of jail inmates that were accommodated in the old jails.

Because many jails are small, it has been difficult to stimulate interest among local officials to accredit them through certification from any national organization. The American Correctional Association Division of Standards and Accreditation reports that often failure by jail officials and sheriffs to apply for accreditation is due to a lack of funds (Thompson and Mays, 1991). The primary benefits of accreditation include (1) protecting life, safety, and health of both jail staffs and inmates; (2) assessing the strengths and weaknesses of jails to maximize their resources and to implement necessary changes; (3) minimizing the potential for costly, time-consuming litigation through negligence and other liability; (4) enhancing the jail's credibility with courts and the public; (5) achieving professional and public recognition of good performance; and (6) improving staff and inmate morale (Washington, 1987:15).

Most county jails throughout the United States have sought accreditation from organizations such as the American Jail Association and the American Correctional Association. In Texas, for instance, the Texas Commission on Jail Standards was established to develop and enforce standards for all Texas county jails (Allen and Graves, 1990). Recommendations are solicited from both the private sector and various corrections agencies. Many jurisdictions, such as the Orange County (CA) Sheriff's Department, focus upon ways to improve jail officer effectiveness with various forms of jail training (Dedischew and Capune, 1989). And in Florida, various initiatives have been adopted to deal with the problem of chronic jail overcrowding and facility improvement (Florida Legislature Advisory Council, 1993). Private contractors have also been consulted for their input and assistance

BOX 5.1 *Deputy Sheriff Pranks*

The Case of the Mock Executions

What should you do to discipline disorderly jail inmates? In Sacramento County, California, sheriff's deputies thought they had a pretty good answer to that question. On at least three occasions, deputies would take unruly inmates from their cells and place them into a chair, telling the prisoners that they were about to be executed by electrocution. They were supposedly joking.

Some inmates didn't think the prank was funny. Eventually, the pranks came to the attention of Captain Bill Roberts and Sacramento County Supervisor Roger Dickinson. An Internal Affairs investigation disclosed that indeed the pranks did occur as inmates had described. The sheriff's deputies involved were forthright and told what they had done, although, they said, they had been "joking."

It seems that unruly inmates would be taken to a chair resembling one used for actual electrocutions. The prisoner would be strapped into the chair, with a head device, resembling that used in an actual electric chair, attached. The prisoner would then be told that he was going to be electrocuted for not obeying jail rules. Some of the inmates exposed to the fake electric chair were emotionally upset. The deputies involved were suspended and received written reprimands for their misconduct.

How should the behaviors of sheriff's deputies be monitored? Should someone monitor the monitors? What punishments would you impose if you were in charge of these deputies? What steps would you take to ensure inmate compliance with jail rules?

Source: Adapted from Associated Press, "Deputies Face Discipline after Mock Executions." *Minot (N.D.) Daily News,* September 1, 1996:B3.

in alleviating various types of jail problems and in providing certain kinds of services for jail inmates (Robbins, 1988).

In some jurisdictions, studies have been conducted to determine whether there are any definitive patterns associated with the rate of male and female incarcerations (Senese, 1991). Admission records were examined from a large Midwestern jail for a five-year period from 1982 to 1986. There appeared to be a cyclical occupancy pattern in the jail for men and women. It has been suggested that certain peak days can be predicted and that budgeting and staffing needs can be adjusted accordingly, so that jail operations can proceed more smoothly. Thus, both jail operations and staff effectiveness issues are increasingly important because most jails in the U.S. are attempting to meet inmate needs adequately (Senese, 1991).

Jail Admissions and Releases

The number of jail admissions and releases annually is high. Table 5.2 shows adult and juvenile jail admissions and releases in the United States by gender for the years 1989 to 1990.

TABLE 5.2 Annual Jail Admissions and Releases, 1989–1990

	1989	1990
Total Admissions	9,774,096	10,064,927
Adults	9,720,102	10,005,138
Male	8,606,700	8,894,706
Female	1,113,402	1,110,432
Juveniles	53,994	59,789
Male	45,294	51,226
Female	8,700	8,563
Total Releases	9,494,814	9,870,546
Adults	9,442,773	9,811,198
Male	8,367,519	8,723,872
Female	1,075,254	1,087,326
Juveniles	52,041	59,348
Male	43,559	50,913
Female	8,482	8,435

Source: Stephan and Jankowski (1991:2).

The figures in Table 5.2 show a fairly consistent pattern across these years. Between 9 and 10 million people were booked into jails in 1989 to 1990, while about the same number were released. Many of these admissions are repeat offenders who enter jails several times a year. Also, many of these admissions are for periods of only a few hours. Some jail inmates are confined for periods of one year or longer, however. Some of the general characteristics of jail inmates are shown in Table 5.3.

Approximately 90 percent of all jail inmates are males. There are disproportionate numbers of blacks in jails compared with their proportionate distribution in the population. About 44 percent of the jail inmates in 1995 were black, while only about 41 percent were white. Regarding jail inmate

TABLE 5.3 Jail Inmate Characteristics for 1995

Characteristic	Percentage
Gender	
Male	89.8
Female	10.2
Race/Ethnicity	
White	40.1
Black	43.5
Other	16.4
Hispanic	14.7
Non-Hispanic	85.3
Conviction Status	
Convicted	44.0
Unconvicted	56.0

Source: Gilliard and Beck (1996:10–13).

ethnicity, Hispanics accounted for about 15 percent of all jail inmates (Gilliard and Beck, 1996:10–13). About 44 percent of all jail inmates had been convicted of a crime, while 56 percent were unconvicted, either awaiting trial or some other reason (e.g., detainer warrant, probation or parole revocation, protective custody).

FUNCTIONS OF JAILS

The following sections describe the functions of jails.

Holding Pretrial Detainees

Pretrial detainees are those arrested for various offenses who cannot afford or are denied bail and are housed in jails until a trial can be held. In some jurisdictions, such as North Carolina, the duration of **pretrial detention** has lengthened. Thus, there is a greater time interval between the time a person is arrested and tried for an offense. As a result, the North Carolina jail inmate population has increased and has exacerbated existing jail overcrowding problems (Clarke and Coleman, 1993).

Temporarily Housing Witnesses and Short-Term Offenders

Housing Inmates Serving Short-term Sentences. Convicted offenders in local courts are typically housed in jails for periods of less than one year. Maximum incarcerative sentences for misdemeanors in almost every jurisdiction are less than one year. Furthermore, many convicted felons serve short sentences in jails, despite the fact judges may impose longer incarcerative sentences (Gilliard and Beck, 1996).

Holding Witnesses in Protective Custody Prior to Trials. In more serious criminal cases, material witnesses may be housed in jails temporarily until trials can be held (Texas Criminal Justice Task Force, 1989). These witnesses may be reluctant to testify and often are placed in protective custody. In some cases, threats have been made against certain witnesses, and their lives are in jeopardy. The popular image of Mafia organized crime figures disposing of witnesses who can incriminate them or link them with criminal activity is more a reality than a myth. Often, jails are designed so that these witnesses can be segregated from the general inmate population in special areas.

Holding Convicted Offenders Awaiting Sentencing. Convicted offenders awaiting sentencing are usually held in local jail facilities. These offenders may be federal, state, or local prisoners. When these offenders are housed in local jails, the jurisdiction is ordinarily reimbursed for offender expenses from state or federal funds (Alaska Governor's Task Force on Community Jails, 1994).

Temporarily Housing Juvenile Offenders

Although most jails in the United States are designed to accommodate adult offenders, arrested juveniles may be housed in jails for brief periods. A general policy known as the **jail removal initiative** has been used to restrict entry of juveniles into jails whenever jail confinement can be avoided, even if the confinement period is brief. When juveniles must be held in jails for short times, they must be segregated from adult offenders by both sight and sound. Not all jails are able to comply with this stringent initiative, however. Thus, in some jails on occasion, juveniles are celled adjacent to or with adult offenders for brief periods. Based on a survey of local jail populations for 1995, less than 1 percent or 1,870 jail inmates were juveniles (persons of an age specified by state statutes, usually under 18). An additional 6,018 juveniles were being held as adults awaiting criminal prosecutions (Gilliard and Beck, 1996:10).

The confinement of juveniles in jails is often unavoidable. Many youths possess false identification, or they may appear to be much older than they really are. Both male and female runaways may engage in prostitution to earn survival money on city streets. They may be arrested by police and confined in jails temporarily until it can be determined who and how old they really are. When it is discovered that they are juveniles, they are often taken to the available community social services or agencies for subsequent disposition. While some persons oppose the placement of juveniles in jails, even for brief periods, the U.S. Supreme Court has upheld the constitutionality of their temporary jail detention.

In 1984, the U.S. Supreme Court ruled in the case of *Schall v. Martin* that juveniles may be subject to the same pretrial detention as adults, especially if it is the opinion of the court that the juvenile would otherwise pose a risk or danger to society if released. This is preventive detention, and it is designed to control offenders, adult or juvenile, who are high escape risks or who might pose a danger to themselves or others if released from jail prior to trial.

Confinement for Misdemeanants, Drunks, and Derelicts

Holding Indigents, Vagrants, and the Mentally Ill. Jails are generally ill-equipped to handle those with mental or physical disorders (Morris and Steadman, 1994). Often, physicians are available only on an "on-call" basis from local clinics in communities, and no rehabilitative programs or activities exist. Most jails have no facilities such as outdoor recreation yards where inmates may exercise. Vocational, educational, and therapeutic programs are almost nonexistent, because jail inmates are considered short-term occupants. Some jurisdictions have explored the possibility of training police officers to recognize mentally ill arrestees so that they can be diverted from jails to hospitals or mental institutions where they can receive treatment rather than jail confinement (Simonet, 1995:30). How-

BOX 5.2 A Sound Way of Preventing Juvenile Delinquency?

The Case of the Juvenile Justice Advisory Council

What can we do to prevent juvenile delinquency? Probably very little. Juvenile delinquency is pervasive, and it is unlikely that it will ever be eliminated. The most ambitious delinquency prevention programs have always exhibited some amount of recidivism among youthful clientele served.

Despite the delinquency prevention efforts attempted thus far, the Juvenile Justice Advisory Council, a state panel of South Dakota juvenile justice experts, has allocated $400,000 for juvenile delinquency prevention programs in 1997 to bolster state efforts at supervising more closely those youths designated to be "at risk" of becoming delinquent. Approximately $1.1 million in federal money has been allocated for South Dakota juvenile programs. Congress has mandated continuing monies to be expended for various delinquency programs among the states since the passage of the Juvenile Justice and Delinquency Prevention Act of 1974.

Nine youths were placed in South Dakota jails in 1996 compared with 746 juvenile jail inmates in 1987. Laws provide that juveniles shall not be jailed in most instances, especially in locations in which adults are also incarcerated. Thus, it is a prevailing national policy to maintain both sight and sound distances between juveniles and adult offenders in local jails and lockups.

One problem experienced by South Dakota and which is suffered by most other state juvenile detention facilities is a lack of space to accommodate juvenile offenders. In South Dakota, for instance, there are 181 state beds available for juveniles, although contemplated programs and facilities are planned for 366 of them. In 1996 there was a waiting list of over 100 youths to be placed in secure juvenile facilities.

One promising effort at delinquency control and possible prevention is the establishment of supervision programs, whereby community volunteers will be enlisted to assist youths to go straight once they have served time in juvenile detention centers, boot camps, or reform schools. Herm Venekamp, a council member and former head of the State Training School in Plankinton and the Youth Forestry Camp in Custer, South Dakota, said that "We need some type of monitoring system. I think we'd see a lot of young people salvaged."

One theory espoused by various juvenile justice experts is that juveniles who have been adjudicated delinquent are often released back into their original community environments without having experienced any real change in their lives. Thus, it is easy for them to fall back into bad habits because of unstable family situations or mixing with the wrong crowd. If youths are able to receive supervisory assistance from community volunteers, some decrease in the rate of South Dakota delinquency is anticipated. At least the recidivism rate among those youths already processed by the juvenile justice system should be lower.

Do you think that community volunteers will make a significant difference in deterring juvenile offenders from committing new offenses? What kind of program would you devise to help prevent delinquency?

Source: Adapted from Associated Press, "Panel:Supervision of Juveniles is Key." *Minot (N.D.) Daily News,* August 27, 1996:B4.

BOX 5.3 The Constitutionality of Preventive Detention for Adults and Juveniles

United States v. Salerno, 481 U.S. 739, 107 S. Ct. 2095 (1987). Salerno and others were arrested for several serious crimes and held without bail under the Bail Reform Act of 1984 as *dangerous.* Salerno was among the first to challenge the constitutionality of the new Bail Reform Act and its *dangerousness* provision that specifies that persons may be held prior to trial in pretrial detention until such time as their case may be decided. Salerno was subsequently convicted and sentenced to 100 years in prison. He appealed, objecting to and challenging the new Act under the Eighth Amendment "cruel and unusual" punishment provision. The U.S. Supreme Court upheld the constitutionality of pretrial detention and declared that it did not violate one's rights under the Eighth Amendment following a finding of dangerousness on the part of specific criminal defendants.

Schall v. Martin, 467 U.S. 253, 104 S. Ct. 2403 (1984). Juveniles can be held in preventive detention if there is concern that additional crimes may be committed while awaiting court action. The facts are that 14-year-old Gregory Martin was arrested at 11:30 P.M. on December 13, 1977, in New York City. He was charged with first-degree robbery, second-degree assault, and criminal possession of a weapon. Martin lied to police at the time, giving a false name and address. Between the time of his arrest and December 29 when a fact-finding hearing was held, Martin was detained (a total of 15 days). His detention was based largely on the false information he had supplied to police and the seriousness of the charges pending against him. Subsequently, he was adjudicated a delinquent and placed on two years' probation. Later, his attorney filed an appeal, contesting his preventive detention as violative of the Due Process Clause of the Fourteenth Amendment. The U.S. Supreme Court eventually heard the case and upheld the detention as constitutional.

ever, this alternative has generally been found to be prohibitive and unworkable (Lupton, 1996; Wood, 1995).

In recent years, jails have held increasing numbers of persons who are mentally ill or who suffer from some type of mental disorder (Lupton, 1996:49–50). Because jail staff are not ordinarily trained to deal effectively with mentally disordered arrestees, it is often difficult to detect which inmates have mental disorders, which ones are pretending to be mentally ill, and which ones are free of any dysfunctional mental disturbance (Lupton, 1996). Lupton (1996:49) says that mentally ill inmates are highly unpredictable, and that they may abruptly begin to exhibit bizarre behaviors. When jail inmates act in peculiar ways, jail staff often call in mental health professionals to diagnose these inmates. Presently, more than a few jail staff are untrained to deal with these sorts of problems. Thus, some mentally ill inmates are criminalized rather than hospitalized (Judiscak, 1995:9–10).

For larger jails with more services and personnel, physicians and paramedics are available to administer one of several mood-altering medications that will calm disturbed inmates. However, it takes time to report disruptive behavior and to locate staff to make on-the-spot diagnoses of inmate problems. Subsequent to a psychological examination by trained personnel, medications may be ordered for them. These medications are supposed to treat specific mental illnesses temporarily. In jail settings, this means that certain drugs may be prescribed for and administered to particular inmates in the interests of institutional or individual safety. The case of *Washington v. Harper* (1990) involved the right of a prison inmate, Harper, to refuse psychotropic medications under the due process clause of the Fourteenth Amendment. However, the U.S. Supreme Court said that compulsory medication may be administered to unruly inmates of both prisons and jails if their behaviors pose a reasonable threat to institutional safety and order (Glade, 1996).

Holding Prisoners Wanted by Other States Through Detainer Warrants. Jails must often accommodate prisoners wanted by other jurisdictions in other states. Detainer warrants are notices of criminal charges or unserved sentences pending against prisoners (McShane, 1985, 1987). Even though these types of prisoners will eventually be moved to other jurisdictions when authorities from those jurisdictions take them into custody, detainees take up space and time when initially booked and processed.

Holding Probation and Parole Violators. When probationers or parolees are picked up by local authorities and others for alleged violations of the terms of their programs, they are usually taken to jail. Under the law, probationers and parolees are entitled to a hearing on whether their probation or parole conditions have actually been violated. Furthermore, they are entitled to a hearing to determine whether their probation or parole should be revoked (*Gagnon v. Scarpelli,* 1973; *Morrissey v. Brewer,* 1972). These hearings take time to arrange, and in the interim, these prisoners often remain jailed (U.S. Government Printing Office, 1993).

Accommodating State and Federal Inmate Prison Overflow

In some jurisdictions such as Tennessee and Texas state and federal prison authorities enter into contracts or leasing arrangements with local city or county jails to accommodate excessive numbers of state or federal prisoners (Lucas, 1996:9). Texas has contracted with state and federal authorities to house a portion of their prison inmate overflow (Texas Criminal Justice Policy Council, 1993). For example, Denton County Jail in Texas houses 232 Oregon prisoners (Lucas, 1996). What does Denton County get out of it? The county receives about $250,000 per month for inmate maintenance. Oregon inmates don't especially like being confined in a county jail for up to two years. In fact, some Oregon inmates, known as **contract prisoners,**

BOX 5.4 Suspect Gnaws Fingerprints Off to Avoid Identification

The Case of "Bernardo Antonio Reyes"

It happened in Allentown, Pennsylvania. A man was arrested following a police drug investigation. A man was spotted at an Allentown bus terminal as police officers were conducting a drug-training program. The man was asked for identification and produced a passport identifying himself as "Bernardo Antonio Reyes." Police officers then asked "Reyes" if they could search his bag and he agreed. When police searched the bag, they found 280 small bags of heroin. The man was arrested.

While in custody, "Bernardo Antonio Reyes" chewed off most of his finger tips, resulting in a bloody mess for jail officers. Allentown Police Department Sergeant Joseph Stauffer said that "It certainly is a strong indication that somebody somewhere is looking for him," and that perhaps he isn't who he says he is. While the ploy will delay identification of the man, Stauffer said that "we should be able to identify him from what we have."

How can jail inmates be prevented from self-mutilation? What probable cause should police officers have to conduct random searches of luggage and bags of persons waiting in bus terminals?

Source: Adapted from Associated Press, "Suspect Gnaws Fingerprints Off." *Minot (N.D.) Daily News,* September 29, 1996:A2.

have gone on "hunger strikes" and engaged in other disruptive behavior while confined at the Denton County Jail. These incidents have been suppressed. However, once jail officials announced that "no prisoner will be returned to Oregon because of misbehavior, but he will be dealt with according to Denton County Jail rules," the disruptive incidents and protests ended fairly quickly.

Other Miscellaneous Jail Functions

The diversity of functions fulfilled by jails accounts for many of their present problems. A jail in a large city or even a small one must accommodate all types of people. It is apparent that not everyone who is processed through a county or city jail has violated the law. Witnesses may be held to testify later in court against various defendants. Or some juveniles, indigents, and others are held temporarily until a community agency can provide alternative services. Those arrested for public drunkenness may be held overnight, where they will be released the following morning after payment of a fine or some other penalty. Interstate hitchhikers may be picked up by county or city police and taken to jail. It is necessary to log or book each detainee or arrestee, especially in the larger jails where routines have become more formalized. Even in less formal jail settings, people-processing takes time.

The Rabble Hypothesis. Irwin (1985) argues that jails are more likely to receive, process, and confine mostly detached and disreputable persons rather than true criminals. Irwin has referred to such persons as *rabble.* He says that many noncriminals are arrested simply because they are offensive and not because they have committed crimes. Irwin worked as a caseworker in several county jails in San Francisco, California, during the early 1980s, and he based his conclusions on personal observations as well as conversations and interviews with county pretrial release and public defender personnel.

Subsequently, researchers sought to determine whether Irwin's observations were valid. Testing the **rabble hypothesis,** Backstrand, Gibbons, and Jones (1992) studied all bookings at the Multnomah County (Portland, Oregon) Jail for a period of time as well as all bookings in Skamania County, Washington, during a one-week period in 1991. These investigators found that although Irwin may have overstated his case, there was some support for the idea that many jail bookings, at least in these jurisdictions, involved marginal nonserious offenders. The investigators did determine that the greater proportion of bookings involved persons charged with or convicted of serious offenses.

TYPES OF JAIL INMATES

The large volume of people admitted to and released from jails annually, nearly 10 million, together with the average daily jail population of 509,000 in 1995, suggests that most admissions are extremely short-term, probably 24 to 48 hours or less (Gilliard and Beck, 1996). A hitchhiker may be picked up by a state trooper and taken to the nearest jail for a brief investigation. The hitchhiker is warned about local ordinances prohibiting hitchhiking; his name, address (if any), and other information may be recorded for future reference, and the person is soon released. These types of arrests and jail bookings account for many of these 10 million jail admissions. If juveniles are taken to jail because of suspicious behavior, their brief stay before being turned over to their parents is also included in jail admission figures.

Reports received from citizenry about suspicious persons in their neighborhoods or those walking the streets late at night without explanation may result in arrests and temporary detentions during which brief investigations of suspicious people are conducted. Again, these arrests and detentions usually result in releases several hours later. Persons wandering about in high-crime areas of cities are prime targets for arrest by police, especially if they are vagrants or indigents. Those sleeping in alleyways at night or in unoccupied buildings or dwellings are also subject to arrest and detention for violating city or county ordinances.

Pretrial Detainees

Pretrial Detainees and Petty Offenders. In 1995, for instance, over 50 percent of all adults being held in jails were pretrial detainees awaiting trial (Gilliard and Beck, 1996). Most local jurisdictions have established policies governing how long these persons will be detained. Much depends upon the seriousness of the offense and efficiency of the court. Sometimes, court calendars are clogged and inmates must be held beyond periods outlined in city or county policy. In some jurisdictions, a 30-day period is the maximum interval between one's arrest and trial for petty offending and city or county ordinance violations. Inmates may be held for longer periods if sufficient justification exists.

Of the average daily jail inmate population in 1995, the average length of stay for pretrial detainees in a majority of U.S. jails was 67 days (Camp and Camp, 1995b:57). For sentenced prisoners, including federal and state prisoners, the average length of stay in these same jails was 143 days. The average length of stay for *all* jail inmates was 86 days (Camp and Camp, 1995b:57).

Convicted Offenders: Local, State, and Federal Prisoners

As we have seen, some jails currently contract with state and federal prison systems to house a portion of their overflow (Lucas, 1996). In fact, evidence suggests that in recent years, these overflow numbers in U.S. jails have been increasing (Gilliard and Beck, 1996). For example, 26 percent of the jails in those jurisdictions with large jail populations in 1986 held inmates because of state or federal prison overcrowding elsewhere (Kline, 1987). However, in 1990, 52 percent of the jails with large inmate populations held federal and state prisoners (Stephan and Jankowski, 1991:3). Over 60 percent of these jails held federal and state prisoners by 1995 (Maguire and Pastore, 1996). Whereas accommodating state and federal prison overflows increases jail revenues in these jurisdictions, such contracting only serves to aggravate existing jail overcrowding problems in these same jurisdictions (Cole and Call, 1992:36–37).

One of the nation's largest jails, the Shelby County Division of Correction in Memphis, Tennessee, has space available for 3,572 inmates (Schellman, 1996:27). For the past several years, space has been made available for 252 prisoners from the Tennessee Department of Corrections. During the time that Shelby County has made jail space available to state prisoners, there has been an average daily bed occupancy of at least 200 state prisoners (Schellman, 1996:27–28). One of the major problems experienced by state prisoners being held at the Shelby County facility is boredom. Tennessee Department of Corrections inmates most often are not enrolled in a treatment or vocational program. Most do not have a jail job. As a result, they do slow time. Nevertheless, state inmates have blended fairly easily into the general population of jail inmates, and problem incidents have not been frequent.

In some cases, contract prisoners are more trouble than they are worth. In December, 1988, for instance, 50 prisoners from the District of Columbia were shipped to the Spokane County Jail in Washington (Zupan, 1993b:22). Rejecting outright this transfer some 3,000 miles away from their home, the inmates proceeded to threaten and assault jail officers, clog toilets, throw food trays, and destroy other jail property. After only three months, Spokane authorities sent these prisoners back to the District of Columbia.

Drunk and Disorderly Persons, Transients

There were 223,200 convicted offenders serving terms of various lengths in U.S. jails in 1995, according to an annual survey of jails (Gilliard and Beck, 1996:10). A majority of these offenders were serving short terms for convictions of city or county laws. Included in these figures, however, are those prisoners from state or federal facilities representing prison overflow, those being held who are wanted by jurisdictions in other states, and those convicted by federal or state courts and not as yet sentenced.

A large proportion of jail inmates consists of those who are indigent, transients, or vagrants (Rockowitz, 1986). In especially small jail facilities, these people pose additional problems to jail staff because there are no separate facilities for segregating them from serious offenders. Many transients and homeless persons who police regard with suspicion are taken into custody as "mercy bookings," where jail confinement is the only alternative to sleeping in alleyways or on the streets (French, 1986).

Drunks, Vagrants, and Juveniles. Historically, jails have housed a variety of transient persons (e.g., inebriates, trams, travelers) in calabooses or small lockups (Guyon and Green, 1990:58-59). All kinds of people are processed through jails every day. Police officers may bring loiterers and vagrants to jail and hold them temporarily until they can establish their identity and account for their conduct (Shelden and Brown, 1991). These arrests and detentions most often result in releases several hours later. Drunk drivers are taken to jails by police officers every evening, and they are released in the morning after they have sobered up.

The Mentally Ill or Retarded

Work Releasees and the Mentally Ill. Jail services also include managing a certain portion of offenders on work release programs in those jurisdictions that have them. Jail inmates sentenced to work release programs are low risk, and some experts question whether such offenders should be jailed at all. One opinion is that work releasees should be diverted to halfway houses or community-based programs, so that scarce jail space may be used more productively for more serious offenders (Turner and Petersilia, 1996). Also, many jail inmates are mentally ill or retarded (Morris and Steadman, 1994).

Drugs and Other Chemical Dependencies

Drug and alcohol abuse are highly correlated with criminal conduct (Deschenes, Turner, and Clear, 1992). Large numbers of pretrial detainees are characterized as having drug and/or alcohol dependencies (Inciardi, 1993). Furthermore, there is evidence that many offenders suffer from polysubstance abuse (Capodanno and Chavaria, 1991).

Offenders with drug or alcohol dependencies present several problems for correctional personnel (Kraus and Lazear, 1991). Often, jails are not equipped to handle their withdrawal symptoms, especially if they are confined for long periods. In addition, the symptoms themselves are frequently addressed rather than the social and psychological causes for these dependencies. Thus, when offenders go through alcohol detoxification programs or are treated for drug addiction, they leave these programs and are placed back into the same circumstances that originally caused the drug or alcohol dependencies.

One unpleasant side effect of housing drug abusers and alcoholics is that their depression and mood swings while withdrawing from drugs and alcohol make them high suicide risks. It has been estimated that among the general jail population drug and alcohol abusers tend to commit suicide at a rate 16 times greater than persons in the general population (Hayes, 1983). Drug users also are likely to continue using drugs while jailed. Thus, the likelihood of spreading communicable diseases such as AIDS is greatly increased by placing drug-dependent inmates adjacent to one another in jail cells (Harlow, 1993).

Pretrial detainees have often been involved in additional criminality while awaiting trial. Even samples of pretrial detainees who were subjected to periodic drug tests as a specific deterrent were found to have high "failure to appear" rates and rearrests (Britt, Gottfredson, and Goldkamp, 1992). Drug dependencies also account for greater numbers of dropouts and failures among those involved in both juvenile and adult intervention programs (Dawson, 1992). For those on either probation or parole, drug and/or alcohol dependencies present various problems and account for program infractions, rearrests, and general adjustment and reintegration problems (Deschenes et al., 1992; Haddock and Beto, 1988).

Those reentering the community on parole after years of incarceration are especially vulnerable to drug dependencies during the first six months following their release (Nurco, Hanlon, and Bateman, 1992). Individual or group counseling and other forms of therapy are recommended for drug- or alcohol-dependent clients, although many clients are considered treatment-resistant (Dawson, 1992). Since 1972, various community-based treatment programs have been implemented to treat and counsel drug-dependent clients. These community-based programs have been collectively labeled Treatment Alternatives to Street Crime (TASC) and currently are being operated in numerous jurisdictions throughout the United States to improve client abstinence from drugs, increase their employment potential, and improve their social and personal functioning (U.S. Bureau of Justice Assistance, 1988).

Juveniles and the Jail Removal Initiative

The Juvenile Justice and Delinquency Prevention Act of 1974 mandated the removal of juveniles from all adult jails (Frazier and Bishop, 1990:427–429). At the time this Act was passed, the federal government was powerless to force all states to comply with this mandate. Many states and local jurisdictions lacked the means, the need, or inclination to go along with this initiative.

For instance, North Dakota had numerous small jails in which adult inmates were housed. Whenever juveniles were picked up as runaways, truants, or curfew violators, police officers most often took such juveniles to these adult jails. It was convenient and the only place to place these juveniles in secure confinement. Juveniles would be held for prolonged periods until local authorities could decide what to do with them. The North Dakota juvenile courts did not help this situation either. Far into the 1990s, North Dakota juvenile courts sent relatively large numbers of delinquent and status offenders to secure confinement facilities such as the North Dakota Industrial School, the equivalent of a prison for juveniles.

Many other states have followed the same type of North Dakota pattern of placing juveniles in adult jails for varying periods. However, the federal government *did* have some indirect power. One way the federal government could compel states to accept this juvenile jail removal initiative was to withdraw or prevent the flow of federal grant money and research funding into various state corrections projects. Florida, Oklahoma, and Illinois were just a few of the states deciding to comply with this initiative.

In Florida, for example, a target date for implementing the full jail removal initiative and having all juveniles out of Florida jails was 1988. However, by 1988 Florida was not in full compliance with federal rules under the Act. Many juvenile suspects were being held in Florida jails because of processing errors. Some jailers were simply ignorant of federal law. There also were occasional deliberate and flagrant violations by jail officials who knew that they were violating the federal mandate (Frazier and Bishop, 1990). It was determined that for Florida to become fully compliant with the provisions of the 1974 Act, the state would have to (1) set up processing and identification centers for juveniles outside of adult jails; (2) provide education and technical assistance to communities that appear to have systemic problems; (3) change the Florida laws to eliminate any potential federal-state legal conflicts; and (4) give greater sanctioning power to Florida and federal officials to impose harsh sanctions on jail systems found to be in violation of the juvenile jail removal initiative (Frazier and Bishop, 1990).

In Oklahoma, a comprehensive review of youth in custody was undertaken in 1988. It was determined that although Oklahoma jails continued to hold juveniles for brief periods, there had been substantial progress made between 1974 and the 1988 review (Oklahoma Commission on Children and Youth, 1988). By the time of the Oklahoma self-study of its compliance with the provisions of the 1974 Act, it was evident that Oklahoma was making much progress toward full compliance.

And in Illinois, the jail removal initiative became a major correctional priority. Corrections officials attempted to establish juvenile holding facilities apart from adult jails. Illinois created a series of 13 detention centers for juveniles throughout the state. Illinois has 102 counties, however, and funding of these new detention centers became a major problem, one that local officials chose to ignore or oppose (Richeson and Klofas, 1990). One solution to the financing obstacle for more juvenile detention centers was to create **duplex jails** in a so-called **duplex jail model.** Essentially, an existing jail would simply create a separate wing in which only juveniles would be accommodated in secure confinement. The construction costs would be only a fraction of the cost of a juvenile detention center. Interestingly, Illinois officials have established jail removal policies, but local jail officials have been lax in their enforcement.

One source of conflict is the sheriffs themselves, who perceive the jail removal initiative as a loss of power. According to jail funding formulae in different jurisdictions, jails are funded according to their average daily occupancy, whether these inmates are adults or juveniles. It makes little, if any, difference to state funding sources. By diverting youths to separate detention centers not under the control of county sheriffs, the sheriffs perceive a substantial loss in jail revenue. Thus, as Richeson and Klofas (1990) suggest, it will probably take judicial intervention over time to force these recalcitrant counties into compliance with the initiative. Similar problems have been experienced by other states such as Kansas, Kentucky, and Virginia as they attempt to comply with the federal mandate (Harris et al., 1991; Klofas et al., 1991).

The National Council on Crime and Delinquency issued in 1991 a policy statement on holding juveniles in adult jails (National Council on Crime and Delinquency, 1991). Among other policy issues, the Council suggested that adult court jurisdiction should be restricted only to those juveniles age 16 or older; that the incarceration of minors in adult jails, lockups, or other correctional facilities should be prohibited outright; that more modern risk-screening methods should be used whenever youths are arrested initially and to divert youths to the appropriate community agencies rather than to jails; and that the high rate of minority juvenile incarcerations should be halted by allocating resources and services to this target population. There is also a continuing debate about the legality of *any* juvenile being held in adult jails for *any* period, no matter what the charge (Chung, 1991). Other experts have voiced similar concerns about how juveniles are handled when arrested by police (Harris et al., 1991; Thompson and Mays, 1991).

KEY TERMS

Contract prisoners
Duplex jail model
Duplex jails
Jail
Jail removal initiative
Philadelphia Society for Alleviating the Miseries of Public Prisons
Pretrial detainees
Pretrial detention
Rabble hypothesis
Solitary confinement
Walnut Street Jail
Workhouses

QUESTIONS FOR REVIEW

1. How many jails are there in the United States? Why is it difficult to determine precise numbers of jails that exist at any given time?
2. What are some characteristics of jails? How does local political control influence jail policies?
3. What are workhouses? Describe the Bridewell Workhouse.
4. Who was Joseph Fishman and why was his book *Crucible of Crime* so powerful at the time it was published?
5. What are jail conditions like in the United States today?
6. What does accreditation mean for local jails? How does the American Correctional Association function to accredit local jails?
7. What are six functions of jails? Explain the importance of each function.
8. What is meant by the jail removal initiative? Why is it important?
9. Is preventive detention constitutional? Describe two cases, one for adults and one for juveniles, having to do with preventive detention.
10. What is the rabble hypothesis? What does it have to do with jails?

SUGGESTED READINGS

American Correctional Association. *1996 Standards Supplement.* Lanham, MD:American Correctional Association, 1996.

Cornelius, Gary. *Jails in America: An Overview of Issues* (2nd ed.). Lanham, MD: American Correctional Association, 1996.

6

Jail Administration: Officer Training, Inmate Supervision, and Contemporary Issues

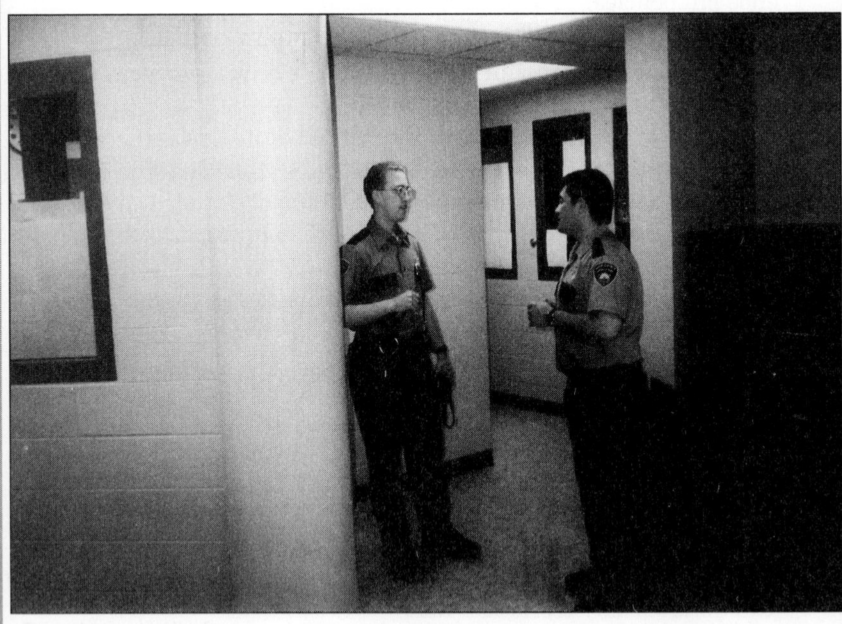

CHAPTER OUTLINE

Overview
Jail Administration
Selected Jail Issues
Jail Reforms
Key Terms
Questions for Review
Suggested Readings

OVERVIEW

- The City of San Francisco was sanctioned in 1991 by a federal court for exceeding a previously determined court-set jail capacity. The contempt of court order by a federal appellate court required San Francisco to pay $300 per inmate per day for each day that its jail facilities exceeded the court-set capacity. San Francisco Jail authorities contended that jail overcrowding was an unforeseeable circumstance and that they had taken "all reasonable steps" to comply with jail population limits ordered by the court. The court declared San Francisco's argument as specious. (*Stone v. San Francisco,* 51 CrL 1406 [9th Cir. 1992])
- John Oviatt was arrested on March 6, 1986, and placed in the Multnomah County, Oregon, Detention Center. He was scheduled to be arraigned two days later, but the court clerk who prepared the docket sheet failed to place his name on it. As a result, it wasn't until June 27 that Oviatt was finally arraigned—a total of 114 days in jail without an arraignment, bail hearing, or trial. The explanation from the county sheriff was that "from time to time" individuals such as Oviatt "slip through the cracks" and remain jailed for prolonged periods. This "crack" turned out to be costly for Multnomah County. Subsequently a federal appellate court awarded Oviatt $65,000 because of the jail's failure to take any action to alleviate its record-keeping problems. (*Oviatt v. Pierce,* 50 CrL 1426 [9th Cir, 1992])
- In Kansas, federal authorities said that the escape of two Dickinson County Jail inmates went unnoticed for eight days! Two men convicted of drug offenses for which they faced mandatory life terms without parole eligibility were being held in the Dickinson County Jail. Using hacksaw blades that had been smuggled into the jail, these men sawed their way out. Their absence wasn't noticed for over a week. A jail supervisor was fired over the incident. The county sheriff, Carl McDonald, said "What I can't live with is the eight days that someone didn't know this happened." (*News Reports,* 1991)

These cases typify the state of the art in many United States jails today. Prisoners are admitted and forgotten. Court-ordered jail improvements are ignored or only partially completed. There are too many inmates for jails to accommodate. Misclassifications of inmates are made. Larger numbers of mentally ill persons are scooped up as a part of jail rabble. Jail suicides continue unabated.

This chapter is about jail organization and administration. In most jurisdictions, sheriffs have the responsibility for selecting jail personnel and establishing jail policies. Jail correctional officer recruitment and training is often haphazard. Almost every county jail has its own training standards, and there is wide variation among U.S. jails in this respect. Thus, the process of selecting and training jail officers is described.

A second part of this chapter identifies and discusses selected jail issues, including the quality of jail personnel; inmate classification problems; jail health-care services; small jails and small-jail problems; jail overcrowding and megajails; and jail suicides. The chapter concludes with an examination of several jail reforms, including court-ordered jail improvements; accommodations for special-needs offenders; jail architecture and aging jails; direct supervision and new-generation jails; vocational and educational services in jails; and the privatization of jail operations.

JAIL ADMINISTRATION

In a majority of jurisdictions, jails are county-operated and funded from local sources. Most large cities in the United States also have jails. These city jails are staffed by the local police department. Thus, a duality of jurisdiction characterizes most city and county jail operations, with sheriffs in charge of county jails and police chiefs in charge of city jails.

There is as much diversity to jail operations as there are jails in the United States. A 1993 survey conducted by the American Jail Association revealed that there were 3,272 jails in cities and counties throughout the United States (Cornelius, 1997:7). Plans were underway for the eventual construction of 350 new jails, while 177 jails were under construction. In 1993, there were 459,804 jail inmates, although this figure had grown to 562,715 inmates by year-end 1994 (Brien and Harlow, 1996:7; Camp and Camp, 1995b:46–47). Besides the obvious diversity in jail operations, there is also increased cultural diversity among jail inmates, thus posing new problems for administrators and jail staff (Garcia, 1993).

Traditionally, the chief executive officer in charge of jail operations is the county sheriff. This is most often an elected position. In most jurisdictions, no special qualifications exist for those who aspire to be sheriffs. They may or may not have previous law enforcement experience (E. Johnson, 1991). Because these posts are most often filled by elected officials, some of these persons may be ex-police officers, ex-sheriff's deputies, ex-restaurant managers, or even ex-school superintendents. While there is a National Sheriffs' Association that disseminates information to its membership about jails and jail problems, there is not much more to foster national sheriff professionalism, unity, or consistency of performance (Senese, 1991). Furthermore, the functions of local jails are gradually changing, causing additional problems for administrators (O'Toole, 1993:8).

Jail Management and Operations

Most jails in the United States are locally operated by sheriff's departments. Thus, local **sheriffs** are responsible for hiring and firing jail staff. In some states, Alaska is one, jail operations are contracted for with the state.

Thus, for many lockups and jails in Alaska, particularly in remote rural regions, a state agency allocates funds and staffs jails, including provisions for housing inmates on short- or long-term bases (Alaska Governor's Task Force on the Contract Jails Program, 1993, 1994). Local jail managers transfer the management and administration of local jails to state agency personnel. New standards are established for jail operations and inmate health and safety. Liability insurance is provided by the state and protects against suits by detainees, public inebriates, the mentally incapacitated, and juveniles in protective custody. The state also provides for jail officer training and education.

Sheriff Responsibilities

Sheriffs are responsible for appointing chief jailers and jail staff. They are also administratively responsible for monitoring the health and safety of jail inmates. But they have other duties as well. They must protect their counties from criminals and do their best to ensure public safety. This requires hiring and retaining deputies who can patrol, make arrests, serve warrants, respond to citizen complaints, keep the peace, and exercise discretion. Given the budgets sheriffs are provided by county authorities, they often find it difficult to attract, hire, train, and retain high-quality deputies to perform these various chores.

Jail Correctional Officer Recruitment and Training

Those hired to perform jail duties frequently have little or no formal training in any kind of law enforcement (Bosarge, 1989). Sheriff's deputies generally receive low pay and have low prestige compared with their officer counterparts on city police forces, although some jurisdictions such as California and Nevada pay their deputy sheriffs much better than average salaries in other jurisdictions. An indication of the low status and prestige of jail correctional officers is that some sheriffs assign their regular deputies to jailer duty as a punishment for violating one or more sheriff's department rules or disciplinary infractions (Pogrebin and Poole, 1988). In some jurisdictions, sheriffs supplement their force of deputies with auxiliary personnel made up of community volunteers. These volunteers receive little or no training in law enforcement. Often, they are assigned correctional duty at the jail, with little or no training in prisoner management (Bosarge, 1989).

Stringent minimal educational requirements are nonexistent, since such requirements would rapidly deplete the ranks of job applicants for correctional officer positions. Minimum educational requirements are often a high school diploma or GED. Whenever jail inmates are permitted visits from families or close friends, jail staff often are unskilled in matters such as search and seizure and the protocol of visitation. With the low degree of security these types of officers create, much contraband is smuggled into jails. Some materials (e.g., knives, saws, or other tools) that reach jail inmates are used to facilitate escapes (Johnson, 1996:39–40; Kalinich and Klofas, 1986).

Jail Officer and Administrative Salaries and Labor Turnover. One major reason that it is difficult for jails to recruit and retain high-quality jail personnel is low pay. In 1995, for example, the average starting salary for jail officers nationwide was $21,542, ranging from a low annual salary of $13,104 in Kenton County, Kentucky, to $66,937 in Montgomery County, Maryland (Camp and Camp, 1995b:15–18). Between 1989 and 1993, there was a 66 percent turnover in jail staff (Perkins et al., 1995:9). Despite these low salaries, some experts think that the recruitment process has been successful at bringing in well-qualified officers and retaining a significant proportion of them in various jurisdictions (Slatkin, 1994:77).

The average jail administrator's salary is $53,460, with a low annual salary of $25,000 in Decatur, Georgia, to a high annual salary of $122,600 in Ventura, California (Camp and Camp, 1995b:19). Average starting lieutenant's salaries were $35,417. Titles for jail administrators vary among jurisdictions. For example, 52 percent of all jail systems in the United States are administered by sheriffs, 19 percent by directors, 10 percent by superintendents, and the rest by wardens, captains, and chief deputies (Camp and Camp, 1995b:7).

Table 6.1 shows a distribution of selected sociodemographic characteristics for U.S. jail staff for 1995. There were approximately 175,000 jail personnel in 1995, with about 70 percent of these performing roles as jail officers. In 1995, about 69 percent of all jail officers were male, while 54 percent were white (Camp and Camp, 1995b; Maguire and Pastore, 1996). However, newly hired jail officers in 1994 indicated that over 75 percent were male and 62 percent were white.

Additionally, 74 percent of all jail officers have been in their positions for two years or less. Approximately 37 percent of all officers are over 30. Interestingly, 80 percent of all jail officers have had some college experience.

Jail Officer Attitudes and Work Performance. Many jails are plagued with morale problems among existing jail staff. In a majority of instances, the "good-old-boy" network seems to operate whereby promotional opportunities and advancements are based on who one knows and not how well one performs (Emerick, 1996:53–54). Such arrangements are often stressful and cause jail officer burnout (Woodruff, 1993). Beyond the traditional bureaucratic network are numerous interrelated and often contradictory factors that work to influence jail-officer role performance. For instance, jail officers must be counselors, diplomats, caretakers, caregivers, disciplinarians, supervisors, and crisis managers simultaneously (Tartaglini and Safran, 1996:43). This role conflict generates a high degree of officer stress, sometimes disabling even the best officers to the point that their work effectiveness is adversely affected.

Problems associated with poor jail-officer morale and training were

TABLE 6.1 **Selected Sociodemographic Characteristics of Jail Personnel for 1995, Including 1994 Hires**

Characteristic	Percentage
Gender	
Male	68.9
Female	31.1
Race/Ethnicity	
White	54.4
Nonwhite	45.6
1994 Hires	
Male	75.4
Female	24.6
White	62.0
Nonwhite	38.0
Education	
High school or less	20.0
Some college	58.0
College graduate, +	22.0
Length of Time in Jail Corrections	
Less than 1 year	36.0
1–2 years	38.0
3–4 years	18.0
5 or more years	8.0
Age	
21 or younger	15.0
22–25	22.0
26–30	26.0
31–40	19.0
40+	18.0

Source: Maguire and Pastore (1996); Camp and Camp (1995b); Gilliard and Beck (1996); Perkins, Stephan, and Beck (1995).

highlighted earlier by Ken Kerle (1985). Kerle has indicated that poor training of jail employees, the lack of clear jail policies, and unequal wages among male and female officers are impediments to overall jail efficiency and to personal job satisfaction. Kerle notes that opportunities for promotion are often thwarted primarily by relegation of female officers to work only with female inmates. He suggests that behind the effort to hold back the advancement of female jail officers is a political agenda, supported by local officials who believe that female officers lack experience in supervising male prisoners and cannot relate to their particular problems. Many county governments seem reluctant to change, and this reluctance is a substantial roadblock to the promotion of female jail officers. In order for significant change to occur, Kerle believes that more jail administrators will have to give up their former stereotypes of female officers. Strong leadership is the key to the advancement of all qualified jail personnel, according to Kerle (1985). These and similar concerns are voiced by other corrections experts (Pogrebin and Poole, 1988).

BOX 6.1 Will the Real Deputy Sheriff Please Stand Up?

The Case of Michael Picard, Military Policeman, Deputy Sheriff, Army Sergeant, FBI Agent, U.S. Marshal, Defense Department Investigator, Bigamist . . .

He fooled the toughest sheriff in the United States. Michael Picard, if that *is* his real name (and we're not sure!), bluffed his way into the Maricopa County Sheriff's Department and Jail on several occasions. He flashed a deputy sheriff's badge and checked out two female prisoners for "investigation." His investigation consisted of extensive groping and fondling on a secluded street near the jail. The female inmates were eventually returned to the jail, but they elected not to say anything incriminating about "Deputy" Picard.

Picard was an actual Army sergeant and military policeman, according to Army officials at Fort Huachuca in southern Arizona. He worked out of the Phoenix office of Fort Huachuca because, according to him, he needed unspecified medical treatment at nearby Luke Air Force Base. The Army claimed that Picard was "mostly on his own."

When Picard was on his own, he accomplished many things. He married at least three times without ever getting divorced. One of his new wives was a sheriff's deputy performing the job of records clerk. He carried numerous phony IDs, including FBI credentials and badges and cards indicating that he was a U.S. Marshal, a Defense Department investigator, and a host of other identities. Police did not know where he had obtained these IDs and accompanying documentation.

Picard even had Sheriff Joe Arpaio, the chief executive officer of Maricopa County, Arizona, fooled. Joe Arpaio said that his friends introduced him to Picard, at Picard's request. Arpaio said, "I've come across some phony cops in 35 years of law enforcement, but this guy takes the cake." Sheriff Arpaio grabbed media attention by creating tent jails and chain gangs for his jail inmates and dressing them in pink boxer shorts. "Talk about a bizarre case! We're still trying to find out who this guy is," said Arpaio.

There is strong evidence to suggest that Michael Picard was wanted in other jurisdictions for assorted crimes. He even succeeded in having warrants that were earlier issued against him cancelled. In his role as sheriff's deputy, there is no way of knowing for sure how many women he fondled or groped while he checked them out into his custody. It appears that Sheriff Arpaio is in great need of changing the nature of security at the Maricopa County Jail. In the meantime, Michael Picard was charged with forgery, fraudulent schemes, impersonating an officer of the law, and theft. He was held on $2 million bail.

What kinds of safeguards should jails establish to prevent events like these from happening in the future? What punishment would you impose for Picard? Should sexual assault charges be filed against him? What would you do?

Source: Adapted from Associated Press, "Phony Deputy Accused of Assaulting Female Prisoners." *Minot (N.D.) Daily News,* December 12, 1996:A5.

The Mecklenburg County Jail Experience. Some jail administrators and county sheriffs have implemented new awareness programs designed to improve communications between all jail staff. In December 1994, for example, at the Mecklenburg County Jail, Sheriff Jim Pendergraph became the new administrator of a 614-bed direct supervision facility, outfitted with the most up-to-date state of the art security equipment, a massive kitchen designed to feed 10,000 persons, and a centralized agency training facility (Emerick, 1996:53). Immediately Pendergraph sensed that morale among his jail staff was incredibly low. The attrition and labor turnover rate among his jail staff was high, a bad sign. He found that many jail staff were unaware of what was expected of them. They had no idea about how they could be promoted within the system or who to report to for advice and information. Most jail officers simply reported for their 12-hour shifts, stayed there for 12 hours, and left.

Pendergraph decided to change things. In December 1995 he organized small focus groups within his jail. He selected 50 officers at random and divided them into groups of 10. These five groups met for one hour per week for four weeks. They shared information about their work, who they were, what they did, and shared their personal interests outside of the jail. Subsequent meetings led to a venting of complaints, grievances, and concerns. The sheriff met with each group and encouraged all persons to "open up" to the group and to him. He had each group devise a list of problems and possible solutions for them. Subsequently, he involved all jail personnel in decision making affecting their particular areas and brought each officer into a catalyst role. Pendergraph implemented many of the group's suggestions and distributed memos and other communications to advise and inform all jail officers of changes brought about as the result of these focus groups. Thus, he reinforced the idea that individual officers were having significant input in jail affairs.

In 1996, Pendergraph and his officers were working together on other strategic ideas for improving communications within the jail (Emerick, 1996:58). Pendergraph believes that his efforts have been rewarded by more positive attitudes among his staff. Employee morale has improved, and labor turnover has decreased. The good-old-boy network has been replaced with a more objective system of rewards for promotions and recognition.

Upgrading Jail Officer Education and Training. Jails are most frequently staffed by local personnel (Peak, 1995). The actual amount of formal training received by jail officers varies considerably from no training to considerable training (Koren, 1995:43–44). Durkee (1996:58) says that prior to the 1970s, training and education for jail officers in the United States was virtually nonexistent. Subsequently, correspondence courses were offered in jail management. In the 1980s, state and local training services were implemented in various jurisdictions, such as Michigan, where prospective jail officers were given 160-hour basic training courses and experiences through the Michigan Corrections Officers Training Council (Durkee, 1996:60). Some training programs for jail officers have been offered in collaboration with nearby colleges and universities (Heim, 1993;

Klofas, 1993). Lansing Community College in Michigan offers courses in prisoner behavior, first aid, stress management, sexual harassment, ethics, correctional law, booking/intake, cultural diversity, defensive tactics, inmate suicides, and custody/security. All of this formal training is designed to professionalize jail staff and to provide them with a better understanding of jail clientele (Durkee, 1996:59–60).

The Lansing Community College has the following curriculum, which leads to acquiring the County and Local Detention Vocational Certificate:

Code	Title	Credit Hours
WRIT 117	Writing Prep II	4
CJUS 130	Local Detention	3
CJUS 135	Legal Issues in Corrections	3
CJUS 242	Unarmed Defense	3
CJUS 245	Report Writing	2
CJUS 251	Correctional Clients	3
CJUS 255	Human Relations in Criminal Justice (Client Relations)	3
CJUS 001	Special Subjects	4
Total		25

This certificate is designed to provide entry-level skills for the person who wishes to enter the job market as a corrections officer at a jail or local lockup after two semesters of study. Besides this academic preparation, a 160-hour Local Corrections Basic Training program was developed in Michigan in the late 1980s (Durkee, 1996:58). This training provided useful skills for officers who were already employed at one of the local county jails or city police lockups. The training was an important step and signified a substantial upgrading of skills for participating officers (Durkee, 1996:58–59). Similar programs have been incorporated into the curricula at participating colleges and universities in other jurisdictions, such as at Washburn University of Topeka, Kansas (Heim, 1993:18–19).

In recent years, a concerted effort has been made to upgrade and improve the quality of jail correctional officers and other correctional personnel generally (Hahn, 1995; Stohr and Zupan, 1992; Tartaglini and Safran, 1996). Few experts dispute the fact that additional education and training for jail personnel is good and that both their professionalization and self-concepts are bolstered as a result (Koren, 1995:43). Further, additional training will make these officers more effective in dealing with the diversity of inmates entering jails annually. Proposals have been made that specify certain minimal criteria for those monitoring prisoners or jail inmates. In past years, the selection of correctional officers has emphasized physical attributes rather than the behavioral and educational skills these officers should possess to perform their work adequately (Wahler and Gendreau, 1985).

Efforts to remedy jail problems relating to staff quality and operations have been implemented by the American Correctional Association (ACA) and other interested organizations (Shandy, Gardner, and Lyons, 1987). During the 1980s, the ACA established an accreditation program whereby jails and other custodial facilities can obtain certification as having met certain minimal standards. The ACA's Professional Education Council has devised a common curriculum for an associate degree in corrections to meet the needs of beginning correctional officers, including jail guards (Barrington, 1987:120). But few jurisdictions have obligated their sheriffs to comply with these ACA standards (Kiekbusch, 1987).

Emerging on the heels of discussions at the 1970 American Correctional Association Professional Education Council was a formal standardized corrections curriculum approved by the International Association of Correctional Officers (IACO), which has now established minimum standards for corrections-related higher education programs. Since 1990 the IACO has sponsored and approved increasing numbers of standardized curricula in major colleges and universities. Through such formalized programs, corrections institutions in the United States are accredited, and corrections officers acquire a higher degree of professionalization to perform their jobs more effectively (Hahn, 1995:45–47).

The IACO has approved the following correctional officer curriculum as a model for training centers and schools to follow (Hahn, 1995:45–46):

I. *Corrections in the Criminal Justice System:* History; Total Systems Overview; Philosophies and Goals; Police, Courts, and Corrections; Corrections in Institutions and the Community; Contemporary Issues.

II. *Correctional Practices:* Safety, Security and Supervision; Classification and Programming; Institutional Procedures; Jail Operations; Alternatives to Incarceration; Probation and Parole; Contemporary Issues.

III. *Basic Communications in Corrections:* Verbal Skills, Nonverbal Skills and Writing Skills; Cross-cultural Communications; Practical Skills Exercises.

IV. *Offender Behavior and Development:* Types of Offenders; Women's Institutions; Offenders with Special Needs; Origins of Criminal Behavior; Subcultures; Offender Change and Growth; Contemporary Issues.

V. *Juvenile Justice and Corrections:* Distinction from Adult System; Evolution of Juvenile Justice System; Youthful Offender in the Adult System; Legal Issues; Control and Intervention; Current Practices; Contemporary Issues.

VI. *Ethical and Legal Issues in Corrections:* Constitutional Issues; Basics of Criminal Law; Offender Rights and Responsibilities; Staff Rights, Responsibilities and Liabilities; Legal Procedures and Grievances; Professional Ethics; Contemporary Issues.

In 1993, a Commission on Correctional Curriculum in Higher Education was established, comprised of the president of the IACO, the executive directors of the American Correctional Association, the American Jail Association, and the National Sheriff's Association; the commissioner of corrections in the state of Maine; an administrator from the U.S. Bureau of

Prisons; and four academicians (Hahn, 1995:47). The mission of this Commission is as follows (Hahn, 1995:47):

> The mission of the Commission on Correctional Curriculum in Higher Education is to promote recognition of corrections as a profession by ensuring relevant higher education of correctional officers. In support of this mission, this Commission shall (1) evaluate the corrections' curriculum component in programs of higher education offering degrees in criminal justice and related fields; and (2) certify that the standardized curriculum (18 semester hours) recognized by the International Association for Correctional Officers is incorporated in such curriculum.

Jail Standards. By 1995, 25 states have developed and implemented jail standards that address issues of mandatory minimum training (Koren, 1995:45). Most of these states make it mandatory for all jail personnel to participate in annual in-service training. In Kentucky, for example, jail officers must undergo annual training and certification from the state corrections cabinet. Although much of this training is tactical or inmate-control oriented, there have been efforts to provide personnel with a more formal or academic set of skills—communication, crisis intervention, and interpersonal problem solving. As a result, line officers who work in jails that have mandatory standards enjoy more pay and job satisfaction than those working in jails without standards (Koren, 1995:45).

Not only is jail officer training targeted as a key priority, but substantive concerns relating to inmate mental health are also viewed as critical areas for improvement (Clark, 1990:72; Kalinich and Klofas, 1986; Quinlan, 1990). Some attention has been given to diverting certain types of offenders from jails before they become jail problems. In some cases, day reporting centers have been suggested and used for low-risk offenders in lieu of jail incarceration (Diggs and Pieper, 1994; Watts, 1993).

Not all jail-officer improvement takes place in classrooms. In many of the larger jails throughout the United States, occasional inmate disturbances are encountered. Sometimes hostages are taken and the lives of other inmates and correctional officers are jeopardized. On these occasions, jails may have to call in outside agencies to quell such disturbances. However, some jails have created **tactical response teams** to cope with serious jail problems (Webb and Alicie, 1994). Also known as *correctional emergency response teams* or *hostage recovery teams,* tactical response teams are special units trained in various types of hand-to-hand combat, firearms, and other skills to neutralize hostile jail inmates and perform rescue missions within jails (Webb and Alicie, 1994:16–17).

Increased attention is also being paid by different jurisdictions to jail upgrading and systemic improvements (Alaska Governor's Task Force on the Contract Jails Program, 1993; Quinlan, 1990; Travisono, 1990). Many jails have sought to improve services delivery in different areas, such as better food service (Mathews, 1993:59). Fire protection and life safety have also been improved in many jurisdictions (Fitzpatrick and Thomas, 1993:

47). Regular procedures for inspecting jail facilities have been established in many of the larger jurisdictions with desired results. Greater compliance with federal standards for jail operations has been observed (Slatkin, Wimbs, and Sidebottom, 1994:47–48).

Jail Lawsuits. About a third of all jails in the United States are under lawsuit or involved in some type of legal action. A **lawsuit syndrome** seems to be crippling both prison and jail systems (Rowan, 1989:13). Rowan (1989:13) and others (Stohr and Zupan, 1992) believe that many of the jail lawsuits are triggered by insensitive jail officers who bring street attitudes to work with them. **Street attitudes** include failing to work within one's job description and failing to follow established policies and procedures; personal biases and prejudices are included. Rowan believes that jail lawsuits can be minimized by (1) hiring the right staff; (2) providing staff training with greater emphasis on development and self-understanding; and (3) using participatory management in which jail officers are involved more in decision making affecting their work. Professionalizing the jail work force can do much to reduce the incidence of jail lawsuits (Koren, 1995).

In many instances, certain inmates have challenged jail policies that limit their religious practices (Dale, 1991). Telephone systems have been the target of legal challenges by some inmates (Alese, 1993:41). Older inmates may require special handling, although jail staff may not be sufficiently trained to recognize some of the problems that afflict older inmates (Potter, 1991:47). Some inmates require special religious artifacts to perform their rituals, while others require special diets and are forbidden from eating certain kinds of foods. Under various theories, different constitutional amendments have been used to launch successful lawsuits against both prisons and jails. Thus, it is critical that jail officers receive some training in the rights of inmates under their control (Dale, 1991:39–40).

In addition, it is important that jail officers know how much *force* to apply when moving prisoners from place to place within jails. Various lawsuits have been filed against jail administrators under the theory that these administrators have failed to train their officers adequately. In some cases, jail inmates who suffer physical injuries may not receive immediate treatment because some jail officers may not believe that they are injured or simply ignore these injuries. Thus, these inmates may sue under a theory of **deliberate indifference.** Many of these lawsuits are successful and underscore the importance of acquainting jail staff with the use of physical force for any institutional purpose (Drapkin and Klugiewicz, 1994a, 1994b). Critical contact points between jail officers and inmates include (1) stabilizing inmates with handcuffs or other restraint devices; (2) monitoring inmates, debriefing; (3) searching inmates; (4) escorting inmates; (5) transporting inmates (e.g., to hospitals or schools); and (6) turnover (e.g., turning inmates over to other authorities, such as state corrections officials, for movement to other facilities) (Drapkin and Klugiewicz, 1994b).

Private Jail Operations. Considerable attention has been given in recent years to the constitutionality of jail operations and jail environments generally. Privatization of jails and some prisons in the United States has occurred whereby private enterprises contract with state or local governments to provide supervisory and operational services in lieu of publicly authorized organizations. While some persons oppose privatization and question the constitutionality of it relating to *any* correctional enterprise, there is nothing inherently unconstitutional about private organizations operating and managing prisons or jails. Private interests are authorized by state departments of corrections to act on their behalf and under their scope of authority, and thus they are vested with the necessary credentials to run correctional institutions (Collins, 1994; Houston, 1994).

SELECTED JAIL ISSUES

The leading cause of court-ordered inmate population reductions or jail improvements is jail overcrowding (A. Roberts, 1994; Welsh, 1990, 1993b). Whenever any jail population exceeds its rated or design capacity, overcrowding occurs. Most jails in the United States, especially those in larger jurisdictions, have serious overcrowding problems. In 1995, U.S. jails were operating at 93 percent of their rated capacity (Gilliard and Beck, 1996:11). The sheer density of jail inmate populations generates a milieu for fostering increasing numbers of assaults among inmates and other problems requiring special intervention by jail staff (Sechrest, 1991). There are many other problems caused by jail overcrowding. Beyond overcrowding, growing offender populations require more effective management and supervision (Garcia, 1993; Watts, 1993; Welsh, 1993b).

This section briefly examines six jail issues cited by correctional experts as major problems. This list is not exhaustive. It seeks to highlight certain issues that either aggravate other jail problems or that are themselves growing problems. These issues include (1) the quality of jail personnel; (2) inmate classification problems; (3) health-care services for jails; (4) small jails and small-jail problems; (5) jail overcrowding and megajails; and (6) jail suicides.

The Quality of Jail Personnel

Corrections is the fastest growing profession in the criminal justice field (Hansen, 1995:37). Because of intense prison overcrowding and the increasing incapacitation of offenders, even for brief periods, jails have experienced a disproportionately high amount of strain. The average daily population of jails is increasing annually, given that jails are used as holdover sites until inmates can be transferred to prisons (Hansen, 1995:37). This strain has greatly increased the need for competent jail supervisors (Ford, 1993). Today's jail supervisor may have to perform one or all of the following responsibilities (Hanson, 1995:37):

1. Setting and maintaining jail standards
2. Keeping up with changes in modern jail operations
3. Conducting routine jail inspections
4. Assisting jail administrators with policy changes
5. Providing proactive risk management to reduce liability
6. Training and mentoring line staff

Ken Kerle (1995:5), managing editor of *American Jails,* says that supervision in the world of corrections encompasses a much wider area than the vast majority of government agencies and businesses operating today. Line officers in jails are supposed to supervise and manage inmates. But competent inmate management and supervision are acquired only through an effective training program in which various skills are transmitted. Kerle believes that jail managers and staff should receive more training relative to ethics and responsibility, human relations skills, progressive staff discipline, and jail management techniques. All too often, Kerle indicates, jail supervision of inmates is nothing more than monitoring cell blocks every half hour or so. Giving staff more responsibilities for managing inmates means greater participatory management. Empowering more staff to act on their own, especially when accompanied by more effective human relations training, can do much to improve staff effectiveness and make jail organization and operation run more smoothly (Kerle, 1995:5).

Gary Cornelius (1995) has written extensively about the nature of the training jail supervisors and staff receive. Cornelius has encouraged jail staff to adopt a **human services approach** during their periods of inmate supervision. First, jail staff must recognize that there is considerable inmate diversity and that this diversity goes well beyond ethnic, racial, and gender differences. Many jail inmates cannot handle being confined, some constantly complain, and some anger easily. Coupled with overcrowding, budget constraints, manipulative inmates, and lawsuits, these different dimensions of jail supervision and inmate diversity make inmate management more complicated than it might appear (Cornelius, 1995:62).

Cornelius suggests that one approach for jail officers to adopt is to accept inmates as human beings and not just entities housed in cells for particular time periods. Jail officers will profit more from their work if they view themselves as human service providers rather than "keepers." Inmates have needs, human needs, and jail officers are in the position of supervising these inmates in ways that will minimize disruptions and other inmate problems. Thus, Cornelius indicates that jail officers should be more sensitive to inmate issues and immediate needs by doing the following (1995:63):

1. *Providing goods and services:* Frustrations and tensions among inmates can be reduced to the extent that jail officers can provide inmates with their basic necessities, such as food, clothes, clean linens, and proper medication.

2. *Helping inmates to adjust:* All inmates feel powerless, anxious, or depressed at given times. Human service-oriented officers take the time to talk with inmates, check on them, and make sure that they are all right. These officers must *listen* to inmates. If there are potential fights brewing, jail officers can intercede and mediate.
3. *Providing referrals and advocacy:* In bureaucratic and overcrowded inmate environments, officers can assist inmates by permitting them telephone calls or putting them in touch with certain inmate services, counseling, or consultation.
4. *Being a part of a helping network:* Jail officers should be a part of a team that performs various mental health, classification, and program functions. They should attempt to reduce fear and tension in the jail environment.
5. *Avoiding the power struggle:* If inmates want to be argumentative, jail officers should not take this type of encounter personally; rather, they should remain calm, take a mature attitude, and walk away, telling such inmates that he or she will return when the inmate acts more appropriately. Many inmates are highly manipulative and know the right buttons to push to trigger defensive reactions from jail staff. These provocations can be minimized with the right type of jail officer response.

There are three essential components in jail inmate control: effective planning, close cooperation with other criminal justice system components, and the development of an array of intermediate sentencing options and alternatives to pretrial incarceration (Keating and Lopes, 1993:35). Planning is crucial to maximizing a jail's effectiveness. Good jail managers can anticipate future jail growth and potential problem areas. They can take a proactive approach to imminent overcrowding by developing tools to analyze their inmate population (Keating and Lopes, 1993:40). Jail supervisors form the foundation of effective jail operations. Good supervisors need to be thoroughly familiar with jail operations as well as have exceptional interpersonal skills. The right kinds of supervisors can make all the difference in the world in whether a jail is effective or ineffective (Lieberg, 1995:32–33). Poor supervision leads to employee dissatisfaction and poor security (Kaup, 1995:21; Sigurdson, 1996:9–11).

Jail Training Programs. One way of equipping jail staff with useful skills that will improve their supervisory effectiveness is to establish jail officer training programs. Local universities are often the ideal sites for such training programs. At Winona State University in Minnesota, for example, a useful training program was established for jail officers. This program was the first higher education program certified by the International Association of Correctional Officers. A grant from the National Institute of Justice assisted the university in acquiring the staff and developing an appropriate curriculum. The program stressed applied or practical experiences as well as theory (Flynt and Ellenbecker, 1995:57–58).

In Texas, the Texas Jail Association cooperated with Stephen F. Austin State University in Nacogdoches to initiate the most comprehensive jail training program in the organization's history (Boyd and Tiefenwerth,

1995:59). The ongoing program provides a 40-hour annual jail officer certification that includes training in verbal and nonverbal communication skills and the proper use of force. The topics covered are handling mentally ill inmates/confinees; HIV/AIDS inmates; cultural sensitivity; security procedures; correctional officer stress; and recognition and reduction, among other relevant areas (Boyd and Tiefenwerth, 1995:60). Updating existing programs is encouraged, especially as the jail work environment becomes more complex technologically and the use of computers increases (Roush, 1993:54–55).

Cornelius (1996:51–52) notes that in 1990 at least 120 hours of correctional training were required of most state correctional officers. By 1993, an average of 5.7 weeks of training was required of these officers. A 1994 survey found that jail officers in 143 jurisdictions were required to have about 7 weeks of training or 282 hours of jail "basics." For jail officers, Cornelius specifies that the American Correctional Association recommends training in each of the following subject areas:

1. Security procedures: key control, head counts, searches
2. Inmate supervision
3. Use of force regulations/procedures
4. Report writing
5. Inmate rules, regulations, discipline, due process
6. Inmate rights and responsibilities
7. Emergency procedures: fire, escape, hostages
8. Weapons training: firearms, nonlethal weapons
9. Interpersonal communications/relations
10. Inmate social/cultural lifestyle
11. Constitutional law and legal issues
12. Ethics
13. Suicide prevention
14. Special management for inmates (mentally ill)
15. On the job training

By 1995, Cornelius found that 130 jail systems required 238 hours of preservice training of all jail officers. Subsequently, an annual average of 31 hours of training was required of all jail officers in these participating jail jurisdictions in courses offered by the Criminal Justice Institute (Cornelius, 1996:52). One additional facet of jail officer training has increasingly included how to deal with AIDS inmates as well as those with tuberculosis, hepatitis, and other diseases.

Managing Offenders from Other Jurisdictions. Managing offender populations from other jurisdictions is another facet of jail-officer training that is increasingly important. As we have seen, more jail systems in the United States are making space available to state prisoners from other jurisdictions. The Albany County Jail and Penitentiary in New York is one example. The Albany County Jail has an average daily inmate population of 783 and a capacity of 834 (Szostak, 1996:22). The jail began to receive prisoners from other jurisdictions in the mid-1970s. The outside inmate population grew steadily each year. Apart from the financial rewards of accepting prisoners from other jurisdictions, the jail has had to become increasingly diverse in its approach to managing inmate problems and dealing with controversial inmate issues. Substantial expansion of the Albany County Jail was undertaken during the 1980s and early 1990s, although the increased revenue generated by accommodating prisoners from other jurisdictions helped to offset construction costs. But jail officers have had to receive extra training. With appropriate planning and staff improvements, the Albany County Jail has been both profitable and effective at inmate management (Szostak, 1996:24).

Working with Other Jail Officers. Working around other jail officers is also an important dimension of staff effectiveness. Jail officers must acquire a respect for one another and get along. If there are tensions among jail officers, often these tensions will be sensed by jail inmates, triggering interpersonal problems. Interactions between jail officers of different genders may be difficult under certain circumstances. Occasionally, some officers will harass others because of their gender (Gurian, 1994:29). It is imperative for all jails to have in place workable sexual harassment statements and policies to minimize or prevent such instances from ever occurring. Specific two- or three-day **gender courses** have been implemented in some jurisdictions, such as the one pioneered by the Washington Criminal Justice Training Commission in Spokane, Washington (Gurian, 1994:33).

Inmate Classification Problems

A contemporary jail issue is how effectively to measure and classify jail inmates so that they can be managed in optimum ways, given existing jail resources and personnel (Poklemba, 1988; Sechrest, 1991). Some persons believe that because jails are *intended* to be short-term facilities, the classification of jail inmates is not particularly important. This may be especially true for many small county jails. Short periods of confinement of several days would not seem to warrant any type of elaborate classification procedure. However, growing numbers of jails are housing more diverse types of offenders for longer periods. In many jurisdictions, prisoners are housed for periods of one or two years, even longer. Thus, it is imperative that jails in which inmates are housed for longer periods have functional classification procedures established and implemented to promote smoother jail operations and inmate control.

Since the early 1980s, there have been concerted efforts by many of the nation's jail systems to devise more effective inmate classification procedures (Brennan and Wells, 1992:59). Such procedures have been consistent with the movement to professionalize jail environments and to provide for more effective staffing and inmate control mechanisms. An early program was operated in Michigan in 1981. It was known as the Community Justice Alternatives and was operated in a 10-county region. The services provided by this program included offender support services such as self-help programs; substance abuse education; employability and life skills; and reentry job placement.

In mid-1984 Michigan jail officials devised an experimental Jail Inmate Classification System (JICS) to be used as a decision tree for screening incoming inmates. The screening instrument for incoming inmates was designed to detect medical and suicide risks and to justify some type of temporary cell assignment and observation. Eventually, computerized and automated versions of these screening procedures were devised to accommodate growing numbers of inmates. The Michigan project yielded a standardized classification system that was being used in over 25 jail jurisdictions by 1992. The JICS instruments have been used successfully throughout Michigan to facilitate jail organization and planning. Brennan and Wells (1992:50) have suggested the following benefits of jail inmate classification:

1. Provide greater inmate safety
2. Provide greater staff safety
3. Provide greater public safety
4. Provide for greater equity, consistency, and fairness among inmates and where they are placed
5. Provide for more orderly processing and discipline
6. Protect the agency against liability
7. Provide data for planning, resource allocation, and greater jail efficiency

The project also promoted the Michigan Jail Population Information System, which is a statewide reporting system for Michigan jail inmates. The system is being used to monitor trends and patterns of jail use (Brennan and Wells, 1992:61). Figure 6.1 illustrates how different dimensions of jail safety and operations are linked with inmate classification.

The Santa Clara County Jail (California) has implemented **B.A.C.I.S. (Behavior Alert Classification Identification System** (Stack and

FIGURE 6.1 Michigan jail population information system. (*Source:* Brennan and Wells, 1992:50)

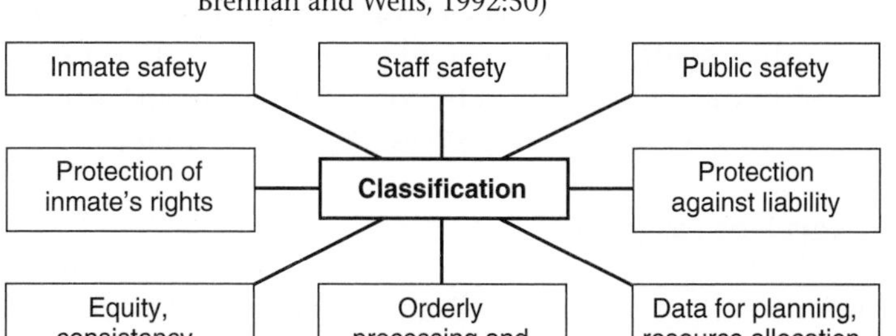

Dixon, 1990:45). According to Stack and Dixon (1990:45–46), classification systems must identify inmates within the jail to ensure that the appropriate housing decision is made. Classification systems based entirely on risk factors are inadequate because they will not result in appropriate inmate placement for new direct supervision styles. B.A.C.I.S. begins at intake, with booking personnel separating medically and mentally ill inmates from the main population and segregating assaultive, high-escape risk, and extreme protective custody inmates into high-security housing units. The overall objective of B.A.C.I.S. is the safety and security of the facility, staff, and inmates. During the first 72-hour period of an inmate's entry into jail, the following happens:

1. Custody staff report on in-custody behavior.
2. Classification admissions/orientation staff evaluate prior risk assessments, administer psychological behavioral instruments, and document in-custody behavior.
3. A recommended classification code is established.

An examination is also made of behavior factors based upon psychological instrumentation; housing placement; a custody profile/risk assessment; judicial status (inmate's judicial status at time of assessment or reassessment); special conditions (identifies special handling, protective custody, medical and mental health, gang status); and bail and current tracking of an inmate's bail amount (Stack and Dixon, 1990:46). Stack and Dixon report that since B.A.C.I.S. was implemented, the incidence of jail inmate violence, extortion, and gang activity has decreased substantially, and jail operations are running more smoothly.

The American Jail Association has established specific resolutions to improve jail operations and to provide for more effective inmate processing and safety. Among the principles espoused by the American Jail Association is the provision for better inmate classification and orientation (Ingley, 1993:7). Increasing numbers of jail jurisdictions have attempted to fulfill this objective in different ways. For instance, the Multnomah County (Oregon) Jail created a population release matrix system (Wood, 1991:52). This matrix cross-tabulates an inmate's offense seriousness with the inmate's prior record and other factors. A score is yielded that enables jail officers to place particular inmates in the best jail surroundings for a particular supervision level. Behavior alerts include assaultiveness, escape risk, unstable personality system, gang membership, and other psychological problems. Therefore, jail staff can supervise and transport inmates more safely, and overall jail security is enhanced (Wood, 1991:53).

Health-Care Services for Jails

Because of the increasing longevity of jail inmates and the changing composition of the jail inmate population, a greater need for health services has been created (Smith, Imhof, and Taylor, 1994). Communicable diseases such as tuberculosis and AIDS have caused increased concern among jail officials as they attempt to devise methods for controlling the spread of these and other diseases (U.S. National Commission on Acquired Immune Deficiency Syndrome, 1991; U.S. Department of Health and Human Services, 1992). It has been found, for instance, that jail and prison populations are three times more likely to have tuberculosis and other related diseases than the general population. But because of the confined nature of the inmate population, appropriate management methods can be implemented to provide for greater disease control, surveillance, containment, and assessment (U.S. Department of Health and Human Services, 1992).

One solution to improving the general health standards of jails is to liaison with local health and medical services to arrange for long-term contracting. Because health-care costs are increasing, it is important for jail staff to plan effectively to provide for nursing and medical services for those inmates suffering from various injuries and illnesses. On-site pharmacy services may be required, especially for some of the nation's largest jail systems. Correctional health and detention administrators can conduct cost evaluations of needed services and plan accordingly. In Maricopa County, Arizona, such planning has been implemented effectively. A workbook has been produced to provide jail officials with jail health-care costs and guidelines (Maricopa County, Arizona, Correctional Health Services, 1991).

In some jails, exercise programs have been established to alleviate the boredom and routine of jail living. Physical exercise was found to be effective in decreasing inmate psychological stress and depression in several Missouri jail sites (Libbus, Genovese, and Poole, 1994). Existing jails without adequate facilities for exercise and other recreational activities have been encouraged by the federal government to make structural changes with supplemental funds (U.S. General Accounting Office, 1991a).

In those jails in which inmates who tested positive for HIV are housed, separate and segregated facilities have been established for the purpose of isolating healthy inmates from sick ones (Harlow, 1993; Messing, 1991). Such segregation facilities have been found to be constitutional as well as useful for the effective administration of treatments and medications (U.S. National Commission on Acquired Immune Deficiency Syndrome, 1991). Professional societies such as the American Medical Association have recommended the establishment of more effective screening mechanisms for early detection of medical problems and sexually transmitted diseases (American Medical Association, 1990).

Beyond HIV and tuberculosis, there are many other types of medical problems that characterize large numbers of jail inmates. Many of them are drug- or alcohol-dependent (Inciardi, 1993). Thus, adequate screening mechanisms must be in place to determine which entering inmates should receive priority for treatment of their particular chemical dependencies (Messing, 1991). Cornelius (1997:29) estimates that at least 58 percent of all entering jail inmates annually are chemically dependent on either drugs or alcohol or both.

Many of the larger jails have established detoxification programs, 12-step programs such as Alcoholics Anonymous, and group or individual therapy for specific offenders (Ragghianti, 1993). Some of these programs involve educational presentations to inform those who are chemically dependent of ways to cope with these dependencies (Inciardi, 1993).

Small Jails and Small-Jail Problems

Jails are unique institutions in criminal justice and American society (Mays and Thompson, 1988:422). According to jail experts, **small jails** have a rated capacity of 10 or fewer inmates. In the 1983 National Jail Census, there were 355 jails that met this "small jail" criterion. Using 1997 jail figures, this is about 12 percent of all U.S. jails. Actually, Mays and Thompson (1988:424) note that about 85 percent of all U.S. jails house fewer than 100 inmates at any given time, while 74 percent house fewer than 49 inmates, and 56 percent house 25 or fewer inmates. Other experts say that small jails are those housing 50 or fewer inmates (Siedschlaw, 1992:41).

Most of these local jails have no on-site medical facilities. For medical services and health needs, local agencies are used on an "as needed" basis. Screening procedures for entering inmates are almost nonexistent. Thus, the potential for suicide and other threats to inmate well-being are greatly increased. Death rates, suicide rates, and homicide rates in small jails are many times larger than their large-jail counterparts (Mays and Thompson, 1988:429).

Small jails are plagued with assorted health and safety problems (Crabtree, 1993; Sluder and Sapp, 1994). Because of these problems, there is greater risk for liability suits filed against counties in which such jails are located. The bases for lawsuits range from unconstitutional housing conditions to mistreatment and misconduct by jail staff. The fact that such jurisdictions often lack financial resources to adequately equip their jails does not provide much defense against such lawsuits by jail inmates and their families.

A key problem confronting small jails is how to separate juveniles from adult offenders. Small jails often do not have elaborate housing and segregation facilities. Rather, they are equipped with a few general holding cells for overnight occupants. Inmate security problems are chronic and persistent. Compared with larger jails, smaller jails are dangerous places (Mays and Thompson, 1988:436–437). In Meade County, Sturgis, South Dakota, a small jail was originally commenced as a mom-and-pop operation (Kaiser, 1994:77). The family resided in quarters connected to the jail. Mom did the laundry and helped keep the kids in line. Dad was responsible for processing inmates and dealing out discipline whenever required. In the mid-1980s the Meade County Jail was renovated and updated. Juveniles were held during a four-year period (1985–1989), but they posed more problems than existing jail staff could handle. When they came into the custody of Meade County jail officers, they were separated from adult inmates. However, they were from homes where they were not welcome; they had so much unspent energy that they spent most of it fighting among themselves in jail cells. They destroyed anything they got their hands on. Eventually, Meade County Jail refused to accept juvenile offenders, even for short periods, because of their destructive propensities (Kaiser, 1994:81).

Pete Garza, Jr. (1994:71) provides some interesting insight into how at least one small jail is operated. After three days of training, Garza was placed as the sole jail officer in charge of 22 prisoners and 6 work releasees in the Sunnyside Jail near Yakima, Washington. Garza says that there were 18 beds allocated for male prisoners, and 4 beds allotted to female prisoners. However, there were seldom any female offenders in his facility. At one point in time, Garza's jail became overcrowded as the result of having to accommodate additional prisoners from an adjacent jurisdiction. New arrestees would be taken to the Sunnyside Jail where they would be held. The Washington State Highway Patrol entered into an agreement with the Yakima County Sheriff's Office providing that arrestees would be held for up to 30 days in the Sunnyside Jail. After 30 days, these prisoners would be transferred to the Yakima County Jail by a van.

At the same time, judges would see the same offenders again and again appearing in court before them. Disgusted with the high rate of recidivism among these persons, judges would impose longer jail sentences on them. This meant that the Sunnyside Jail would have to accommodate *more inmates* for *longer periods.* Eventually, Garza was able to hire 1½ more deputies to assist him. Despite this additional personpower, jail inmates could not be continually supervised by jail officers. During some evening hours, the only supervision maintained over inmates was a closed-circuit camera in the dispatcher's office. The dispatcher then became a jail officer by default. Garza notes that his budget was never increased during the overcrowding period: "We were running the same budget size as we were when we had only three prisoners. During the first and second year, we ran out of money to run the jail" (Garza, 1994:71).

The Sunnyside Jail was equipped with only one shower, located on the male side of the jail. The shower lacked water pressure so that hot water was inadequate. If female offenders were jailed, then in order for them to shower, the complete male inmate population had to be moved from that portion of the jail to another area during the female showering period. The city attempted to provide Sunnyside Jail with additional jail space. However, a small building provided by the city lacked metal doors that had been removed earlier. Garza tracked down the metal doors that were being used by a local farmer to plow his fields. Garza negotiated the return of the metal doors, which were then welded back into place to secure jail inmates in the newly created space. While all of this was going on, Garza had to contend with the fact that the city police department had taken over two cells in the original jail area for office space, shared with the parks department. Two other cells had been converted into a kitchen and a detective's office. Garza eventually succeeded in freeing up this space for jail use exclusively.

Garza's frustrations with the system are quite apparent in his account of his jail officer experience. Evidence from other sources suggests that Garza's experiences are not unique to Sunnyside Jail (Hoefle, 1995; Oldenstadt, 1994).

Jail Overcrowding and Megajails

Jail overcrowding is the major cause of inmate lawsuits in federal and state courts (Pontell and Welsh, 1994). In California, for instance, lawsuits against jail systems last an average of 55 months. Whenever litigation is favorable for inmates, court orders are issued against general jail operations. In 79 percent of the cases involving county jails in California during the years 1975 to 1989, for instance, overcrowding was the most frequently cited problem to be rectified by court action. Other issues cited in these lawsuits included inadequate medical care, sanitation problems, hygiene, access to courts, food services, and ventilation (Pontell and Welsh, 1994).

In many jurisdictions, police arrest policies have been changed to ease jail overcrowding. Thus, police officers are less inclined to take minor offenders to jail for less serious infractions because these persons would exacerbate existing overcrowded jail conditions (Welsh, 1993b).

However, no matter how much planning jail officials can muster, there is no way to predict correctly optimum jail capacity from one day to the next. There is some seasonal variation in jail inmate populations. But there are frequent unpredictable peaks in jail inmate populations that must somehow be accommodated (Murray and Bell, 1996:61). Overall averages of daily jail occupancy are deceptive, because unanticipated peak occupancy periods cannot be predicted. Nevertheless, jail officials are expected to accommodate rising and falling inmate populations no matter how unusual these daily fluctuations.

In Washington state, for example, a persistent jail overcrowding problem was partially resolved through effective planning and interaction between jails and the courts. A jail capacity study was conducted to explore ways that could maximize the use of existing jail space and beds. Three strategies were examined: (1) increase capacity and accommodate the added demand; (2) reduce admissions and lengths of stay and mitigate the effects of demand; or (3) add correctional options and divert demand to other types of placements (Murray and Bell, 1996:62). Experiments in several Washington counties showed that increasing the use of bail in minor offense cases greatly alleviated jail overcrowding. Police officers were advised not to bring the following types of persons to these jails: (1) out-of-county misdemeanant warrant arrests; (2) misdemeanor charges, except those required under the district court bail schedule or state law; and (3) traffic charges other than driving under the influence. With this policy in effect, the Spokane County Jail admission rate decreased by 29 percent. Further, many postconviction misdemeanants and traffic offenders were diverted from jail, while the average length of stay for the average jail inmate was decreased from 14 to 12 days. These strategies were effective in controlling the fluctuating inmate population and alleviating serious overcrowding problems (Murray and Bell, 1996:62–63).

Megajails are jails with 1,000 or more beds (Cornelius, 1997:19). In 1995, for example, the nation's 25 largest jails housed 30 percent of all jail inmates. When jails equal or exceed 1,000 or more beds, there are more complex logistical problems that must be dealt with on a daily basis. Greater coordination among the individual parts of such jails is required. Greater formality between jail officers and inmates is expected. Inmate control becomes an increasingly important problem as well. The following breakdown of jail sizes gives us some perspective about how jail capacities are defined (Cornelius, 1997:19):

Megajails = 1,000 or more beds
Large jails = 250–999 beds
Medium jails = 50–249 beds
Small jails = 49 or fewer beds

In some respects, some megajails operate similar to prison systems. These jails are large enough to hire full-time medical and support staff to be on-call for jail inmate emergencies. Greater segregation among prisoners is achieved with more massive jail size. Some of these megajails have their own commissaries, where prisoners may purchase personal items, articles of clothing, and snacks. These jails are also equipped with weight rooms, small tracks, and other amenities usually found in large prison systems. But despite these amenities, megajails can be overcrowded as well, with all of the problems accompanying overcrowding.

Cornelius (1997:64) indicates that during the next decade, megajails will generate the following:

1. Epidemics of AIDS and tuberculosis
2. Expansion of jail industries
3. Diminishing revenues with which to fund jail operations
4. Privatization
5. Increase in inmate programs
6. Continuing searches for alternatives to incarceration
7. Employee incentives
8. Inmate populations becoming more institutionalized and sophisticated

One solution to chronic jail overcrowding is to regionalize jail operations. In Texas, for instance, there are plans to create 10 new jails holding 17,000 inmates to be operated by the Texas Department of Criminal Justice (Harris-George, Jarrett, and Shigley, 1994:19). Texas plans to use private corporations to construct these new jail facilities. Present programming projections are for prisoners who will be accommodated for stays of 90 days. However, Texas officials note that in future years, inmate stay averages will be 2 years or longer. While many Texas citizens oppose the private operation of jails, Texas officials concede that privatization may be the only solution to long-term jail inmate housing and management. In 1990, for instance, 49 of the largest Texas jails were 51 percent over their functional capacity (Harris-George et al., 1994:19).

Jail Suicides

In 1993, 234 inmates killed themselves (Bureau of Justice Statistics, 1995). Cornelius (1997:32) indicates that at least 60 percent of those who killed themselves while jailed were under the influence of either drugs or alcohol. It is not unusual for suicide survivors to sue jail systems for not properly monitoring them. One problem with many jails is that there are insufficient policies in place to govern the supervision of potentially suicidal inmates. In 1995, for example, the following suicide prevention policies were established. The numbers in parentheses indicate the number of jails with such policies (Cornelius, 1997:33):

Jails with *no* suicide prevention policy (317)
Jails with a suicide prevention policy (2,628)
Jails with staff suicide prevention training (1,796)
Jails with risk assessment at intake (2,209)
Jails with "suicide watch" cell (including checks every 10–15 minutes) (2,025)
Live or remote monitoring (1,801)
Special counseling (mental health staff, etc.) (1,885)
Inmate suicide prevention teams (120)
Other methods (remove belts and shoelaces, issue paper gowns, transfer to psychiatric ward) (53)

Besides drugs and alcohol, other factors are responsible for contributing to jail suicides. Many arrestees are shocked or traumatized by the jail experience. Some are embarrassed by the experience and fear social exposure and ridicule. Some experts have suggested *importation* explanations, where jails attract persons more likely to consider suicide. Other explanations include *deprivation,* suggesting great trauma experienced through a loss of freedom or liberty (Haycock, 1991; Stone, 1990).

A national study of jail suicides was completed in 1988 (Hayes and Rowan, 1988). Demographic data were examined for 453 jail suicides in 1985 and 401 in 1986. These data were compared with an earlier study of jail suicides in 1979. Interestingly, Hayes and Rowan found no significant differences among jail suicide victims across the years 1979 to 1986, suggesting that several persistent demographic factors are typically present. They found, for example, that the offense, intoxication, method/instrument, isolation, and length of incarceration have remained virtually unchanged over time. They recommend that most jail suicides can be averted with proper prevention programs that include written rules and procedures, staff training, intake screening, communication among staff members, and

BOX 6.2 On Two Jail Suicides

The Case of John B. Andrews

It happened in Ithaca, New York, in the Tompkins County Jail. John B. Andrews, 31, was arrested on Friday, November 1, 1996, following an indictment for the murder of two high school cheerleaders. The killings were especially heinous. The two 16-year-olds, Sarah Hajney and Jennifer Bolduc, were kidnapped from their home in Dryden, New York, on October 4, where the two were house-sitting for Sarah's vacationing parents. Their remains were eventually discovered. They had been scattered in pieces across central New York.

Andrews was a computer lathe operator. He had been indicted on October 31, 1996, on nine counts of first-degree murder, which made him eligible for the death penalty if convicted. He was to be arraigned on November 6th. The indictment also included 26 counts involving second-degree murder, felony kidnapping, sexual abuse, and burglary.

Andrews' body was found in his jail cell about 3:00 A.M. on Saturday morning, November 2nd. No immediate details were available about how he had committed suicide. Andrews joined a growing list of jail inmates who commit suicide annually. The immediate shock of incarceration, being placed in a small jail cell, and being charged with various capital crimes is a traumatic experience. For some offenders, suicide watches are implemented, by which jail officers keep these inmates separated from others and under continual observation through closed-circuit television cameras. This procedure was not followed in Andrews' case.

What preventive mechanisms should jails follow to prevent suicides and suicide attempts? Some persons may not mourn the passing of John Andrews, since there was overwhelming evidence of his guilt anyway. Some may say that the criminal justice system was spared the expense of a lengthy trial and appeals, which are automatic in death penalty cases. Nevertheless, justice was not entirely served. Is the jail to blame for not monitoring Andrews effectively? What do you think?

The Case of Richard Guthrie

Richard Guthrie, 38, was a member of a Midwestern bank robbery gang who had pleaded guilty to 19 bank holdups in seven states. He was awaiting sentencing and was being held in the Covington County Jail in Kentucky.

Prosecutors earlier had worked out a plea bargain with Guthrie in which he would be sentenced to no more than 30 years in prison for the robberies that occurred in 1994 and 1995. Guthrie agreed to testify against his other gang members in exchange for the prosecutor's leniency. The gang to which Guthrie belonged netted more than $200,000 from banks in Ohio, Iowa, Wisconsin, Missouri, Nebraska, Kansas, and Kentucky. The gang's effort was compared with Jesse James, a historic outlaw who held up banks in the same general area in the 1800s.

On Friday, July 12, 1996, jail officers found Guthrie hanged with a bedsheet that he had secured around the top bars of his jail cell. Guthrie left two suicide notes, one for his public defender and the other to his brother. He could not face life imprisonment and took his own life.

continued

Could jail officers have prevented Guthrie's death? Should sentenced prisoners be placed in special cells? What policies should have been in place at the time Guthrie committed suicide? What do you think?

Sources: Adapted from Associated Press, "Report: Suspect in Slaying of Two Teen-agers Kills Himself in Jail." *Minot (N.D.) Daily News,* November 3, 1996:A2; Associated Press, "Bank Bandit Found Dead in Jail." *Minot (N.D.) Daily News,* July 13, 1996:A2.

human interaction with jail inmates. Thus, jail officers and administrators are admonished to take a proactive role in developing suicide prevention measures. However, other experts say that it is very difficult to develop an effective profile of potential suicide victims and that a more appropriate prevention response would be to build more suicide-resistant jails (Kennedy and Homant, 1988).

JAIL REFORMS

Corrections generally has been undergoing various reforms in recent decades. The inmate litigation explosion has focused the attention of policymakers and others on prisoner rights and the quality of life in jail and prison settings. One result has been court-ordered improvements in jail conditions and inmate population reductions. The commitment of the American Correctional Association and other interested organizations to improve the quality of life for jail inmates extends also to improvements in the quality of correctional officers selected to perform jail tasks. Educational and training programs are now being offered in various jurisdictions for the purpose of providing more effective training of correctional recruits. Two other reforms have achieved a degree of popularity in recent years. These include (1) jail architecture and (2) the privatization of jail management.

Court-Ordered Jail Improvements

Jail overcrowding problems are the most obvious (Etter, 1996; Kinkade, Leone, and Semond, 1995). However, court-ordered jail improvements extend beyond mere jail overcrowding (D'Allessio and Stolzenberg, 1995). For example, Cornelius (1997:26) notes that civil rights suits have targeted numerous areas that have generated court action. These areas include physical security (failure to protect); medical treatment; due process (improper disciplinary hearings); challenges to conviction (invalid sentences); miscellaneous (denial of parole and other reasons); physical conditions (inadequate sanitation, crowding, and other issues); denial of access to courts or attorneys; living conditions (inadequate clothing or other issues); denial of religious expression and visits; racial discrimination; and assault by jail officers.

In 1993, 413 jurisdictions with large jail populations were under court order to correct one or more of the following conditions: crowded living units; recreational facilities; medical services/facilities; visitation policies/procedures; disciplinary policies/procedures; food services; administrative segregation policies/procedures; staffing patterns; grievance policies/procedures; training/education programs; fire hazards; counseling programs; classification of inmates; and library services (Bureau of Justice Statistics, 1995; Cornelius, 1997:21). The fact is that jail inmates do not lose their constitutional rights when entering jails.

Accommodating Inmates with Special Needs

Jail inmates with various types of disabilities are increasingly common (Motiuk et al., 1994). Known as **special-needs offenders,** jail inmates with physical and/or mental disabilities create unique problems for jail officers and staff. These inmates do not always act in predictable ways. They require special care and treatment. Some require continuous medication for their conditions. Others require special facilities, such as ramps, if they are confined to wheelchairs (American Correctional Association, 1993a; Motiuk et al., 1994).

"Problem inmates" often obligate jail staff to become familiar with their problems and how best to deal with them. Thus, jail staff training programs are increasingly including topics pertaining to managing inmates with special needs. Furthermore, architectural plans for new jails are including features that accommodate special-needs offenders (Gauger and Pulitzer, 1991). Some of these architectural improvements are federally mandated through the Americans with Disabilities Act (American Correctional Association, 1993a). This act, passed in 1990, provides protections for disabled inmates and staff who receive government services, programs or activities, including those provided in local jails. Changes might be required in a jail's physical plant, such as the addition of wheelchair ramps and handrails, and changes in procedures or programs that require accommodating disabled inmates, including provision of accessible housing or work (Cornelius, 1997:27).

Jail Architecture: Aging Jails and Facility Deterioration

On June 6, 1993, the oldest jail in the United States closed. This jail was the Litchfield (Connecticut) Correctional Center, constructed in 1812 to hold the prisoners during that war (*Monday Highlights,* 1993). The Litchfield Jail operated for 181 years. It had 16 employees and was constructed of red brick. Officials did not plan on destroying the Litchfield Correctional Center. Rather, they intended to use the old facility as a 30-bed halfway house for women after some extensive remodeling. And scheduled for opening was the 2,400-bed Allegheny County (Pennsylvania) Jail on a 14-acre tract overlooking the city of Pittsburgh (L. Robert Kimball & Associates,

1991). Thus, as jail inmate populations continue to escalate, there is a continuous annual replacement of old jail facilities with new ones.

Recent interest in jail architecture is accounted for, in part, by the concerns of local jurisdictions to use their available jail space more economically for more inmates. In this way, jail overcrowding may be alleviated to some degree, and jail correctional officers will be able to more effectively monitor inmate behavior when "blind areas" are eliminated. Electronic innovations such as closed-circuit television cameras and other devices have been used historically to assist guards in the performance of their prisoner management chores, but more effective jail construction can also mean more direct and effective inmate supervision by officers (DeWitt, 1986a:5).

A new concept in jail design has been implemented for constructing the Pinellas County Jail in Florida. The new jail concept houses 192 inmates in three interconnected, octagonally shaped buildings of a modular design (DeWitt, 1986a:2). Made of precast concrete, the Pinellas Jail is an example of how new jail construction may be implemented at relatively low cost to taxpayers. The structure will eventually reach a height of five stories, the first modularly constructed jail in the nation to achieve that height (DeWitt, 1986a:5). With various components of these jails prefabricated and assembled in other cities, these jails can be completed in less than a year, some in about eight months, ready for use. The initial costs range from $16,000 (one-person cells) to $29,000 (two-person cells). Statistics show that in other jurisdictions, prison and jail construction using more traditional building concepts have ranged from $40,000 to $100,000 per one-person cell (DeWitt, 1986b:1).

Direct-Supervision and New-Generation Jails

Many of the nation's jails were built prior to 1970, and many are 50 years old or more (Senese et al., 1992). These jails are not only architecturally unsound and unsafe, they also are designed so that jail officers cannot always monitor inmate behaviors. One answer to escalating inmate violence is the establishment of jail and prison facilities that permit greater inmate monitoring. A new innovation in inmate management, a hybrid of architectural design and inmate management principles, is the **direct-supervision jail,** sometimes called the **new-generation jail** (Zupan, 1993a:21). Direct-supervision jails are constructed so as to provide officers with 180-degree lines of sight to monitor inmates (Turturici and Sheehy, 1993). Direct-supervision jails employ a podular design. Modern direct-supervision jails also combine closed-circuit cameras to continuously observe inmates when celled (Stohr-Gillmore, Stohr-Gillmore, and Lovrich, 1990:29–30). Correctional officers are in the same "pod" as inmates. These pods consist of secure dormitory-like areas housing approximately 40 inmates. Inmates are monitored 24 hours a day. The first podular, direct-supervision jail was constructed in Contra Costa, California, in 1981 (Hutchinson, 1993:132). It has been found that coercion and threats by inmates against others is minimized and all but eliminated through the direct supervision concept (Stohr-Gillmore, Stohr-Gillmore, and Lovrich, 1990:30). This is because all inmate behavior is subject to correctional officer scrutiny. Also, inmates have fairly direct access to correctional officers in their central work locations. In 1993, there were about 150 direct-supervision jails in the United States, with plans in many jurisdictions for building more of them (Zupan, 1993a:21).

Modular jail designs, or new-generation jails, have been used increasingly in various jurisdictions, especially after early successes with such facilities were reported by Florida officials (Farbstein and Wener, 1986; Kellman, 1983:32). To understand what is meant by new-generation jails, we must first examine earlier jail generations. Cornelius (1996:7) describes the following generations of jails during the last 200 years:

1. *First-generation jails:* These jails are sometimes called "linear." This is because cells are aligned in rows; the correctional officer walks down a central corridor or catwalk; interactions with inmates are usually through food slots or cell bars.
2. *Second-generation jails:* These jails are characterized by officers stationed in a central control booth; inmate housing surrounds the officers; usual observation of inmates by officers is increased, but officer interactions with inmates is very limited.
3. *Third-generation jails (new-generation jails):* These types of jails are characterized as having jail officers placed inside housing units known as "pods"; there are no physical barriers; under this "direct supervision," officers act as inmate behavior managers; jail officers have more supervisory authority in the daily operations of pods.

In Prince George's County, Maryland, a new 335,000 square-foot correctional center was opened in February 1987 based upon a similar modular design of Florida facilities (Saxton, 1987). Prince George's County officials report that their facility has replaced dormitories with single rooms. Furthermore, treatment programming featuring education, vocational training, substance abuse counseling, and alternative aftercare services for special inmates is currently being provided. Enhanced by this new design are prisoner safety and overall manageability (Saxton, 1987:28). Such designs are also instrumental in assisting officials to avoid inmate litigation as well as to improve jail maintenance (Kimme et al., 1986). Many prisons are being fashioned along modular lines as well (DeWitt, 1987).

Many jail administrators believe that a "competent, well-managed staff working in an inadequate, antiquated building is far preferable to a mediocre staff working in a modern, state-of-the-art facility" (Kiekbusch, 1985:134–135). The major recruitment problem is an insufficient quantity of quality personnel to perform correctional officer functions (Huggins, 1986:118). Jails are regarded by many people as the social dumping ground for misfits, misdemeanants, and others (Zupan, 1993a:21). Jails are usually among the lowest funding priorities. This often results in the recruitment of poorly qualified and trained staff. However, the advent of direct supervision jails is a stimulating innovation capable of attracting more competent officers (Turturici and Sheehy, 1993:106).

Vocational/Educational Provisions

Most jails are not equipped to provide inmates with any vocational/technical and educational programs (Tewksbury, 1994). In fact, many prisons lack a broad variety of programs geared to enhance inmate skills and education (Schlossman and Spillane, 1992). This state of affairs seems consistent with the view that the rehabilitation orientation in American prisons is on the decline. For instance, it has been found that for at least some of the major state prison systems, the influence of higher education programs on graduating inmates and their subsequent rates of recidivism has been ineffective (Lockwood, 1989). However, certain programs designed to rehabilitate sex offenders have had positive effects on decreasing offender recidivism (Sapp and Vaughn, 1989). For drug offenders in the U.S. Bureau of Prisons Choice program, the plan of drug treatment and intervention has been regarded as successful. Inmates with drug dependencies are subjected to a 10-month program, including intake/evaluation/follow-up, drug education, skills development, lifestyle modification, wellness, responsibility, and individualized counseling/case supervision (Walters et al., 1992). The emphasis in the Choice program is upon education and the development of cognitive skills rather than on treatment and insight-oriented therapy.

No guarantees exist that all jail inmates with educational deficiencies will enroll in such programs in jails where educational programs are offered. In a suburban Texas county, for instance, courses were offered to jail inmates pertaining to counseling, stress management, and education. High school dropouts and high school graduates were identified and targeted for these different programs. A disappointing 26.7 percent of the high school dropouts enrolled in self-enriching courses or used counseling services. Even the participation rates of high school graduates were low. Only 14 percent of them took advantage of the offered programs (Tobolowsky, Quinn, and Holman, 1991).

In some jails in 13 state jurisdictions, participation in jail or prison educational programs for both men and women is mandatory (Mullen et al., 1996; Winifred, 1996). Of those states making education mandatory, those inmates most frequently targeted have obvious educational deficiencies and do not meet minimum educational criteria. Reduced sentence lengths are offered as incentives to participate in educational programs. The measure of success of such programs is whether inmates continue their education in jail or prison beyond the mandatory minimum (Winifred, 1996). One of the more innovative inmate literacy programs is operated by the Virginia Department of Corrections. Since September 1986, the "No read, no release" program has emphasized literacy achievement at no lower than the sixth-grade level and has made such an achievement part of the parole decision-making process (Oberst, 1988). Results have been favorably viewed by various states. However, in recent years compulsory educational programs in jails and prisons have been subjected to constitutional challenges (Miller and Hobler, 1996).

Some information suggests that those acquiring greater education while in prison have higher percentages of new convictions (Knepper, 1989). A study of 526 inmates who enrolled in prison and jail college and vocational, secondary, and elementary programs were examined according to their postrelease success experiences. While those who had taken college coursework and other skills courses exhibited fewer problems adjusting to life outside of prison, the more educated group had somewhat higher rates of recidivism attributable to new criminal convictions (Knepper, 1989). Admittedly, it is difficult to predict precisely which inmates will be more amenable to treatment than others, although attempts have frequently been made to do so (Armor et al., 1989). It has been found that generally, older and better-educated inmates seem to benefit more from prison educational programs than those younger offenders who perhaps are most in need of such education (Armor et al., 1989).

However, the importance of intervention and educational or vocational training programs should not be rejected outright. For some inmates, these experiences are quite valuable. For instance, the Sandhills (North Carolina) Vocational Delivery System (VDS) is a vocational rehabilitation program offered to offenders ages 18 to 22 (Lattimore, Witt, and Baker, 1990). An experiment was conducted involving 295 youths in an experimental group who participated in the VDS program and 296 youths in a control group who did not participate. A postrelease analysis of the arrest records of both experimental and control group offenders showed that the experimental group had a significantly lower arrest record. Researchers attributed this success to participation in the VDS program, although further research was recommended to improve the reliability of these findings.

The Privatization of Jail Operations

A proposal that has received mixed reactions in recent years is the **privatization** of jail and prison management by private interests (Florida Advisory Council on Intergovernmental Relations, 1993; Kyle, 1995). Few proposals in corrections have ever stimulated as sharply divided opinions as the prospect of privately operated jails (Mullen, 1985:1). Legally, there is nothing to prevent private enterprises from operating prisons and jails as extensions of state and local governments and law enforcement agencies (Thompson and Mays, 1991). Few states have legislation on the subject (Huskey and Lurigio, 1992). Private enterprise must ensure the same minimum standards currently guaranteed by the law and comply with basic constitutional guarantees. In fact, the U.S. Marshal's Service awarded a large contract to two private firms to design, build, and operate a 440-bed detention facility for federal inmates at Leavenworth, Kansas, in 1990 (*Corrections Compendium,* 1990a:21). The contracts were awarded to Nashville-based Corrections Corporation of America (CCA) and the St. Louis-based Correctional Development Corporation (CDC). The detention site was to be operated for an initial one-year period as a maximum-security facility, with the contracts renewable for another four years. The new facility is believed by the U.S. Marshal's Office to save the government considerable money during its operation. Furthermore, it will ease the severe jail overcrowding and free up valuable jail space for federal prisoners awaiting trial, sentencing, or hearings in the greater Kansas City area. It is intended to house both medium- and maximum-security prisoners. The $71 per day per inmate costs are expected to include medical and dental services, food services, and security. CCA and CDC officials believe revenues will exceed $10 million annually. Despite the built-in profit margin, this cost is well below what the government would have spent to accommodate these prisoners in standard government facilities.

Given the fact that many local jails today in the United States are in a state of crisis, private sector intrusion into offender management and jail operations is not entirely unexpected (Ethridge and Liebowitz, 1994:55). An empirical study of sheriffs' attitudes toward privatization was conducted in the summer of 1991 by Ethridge and Liebowitz. Questionnaires were mailed to 254 sheriffs of Texas counties. Of these, 195 sheriffs responded. Sheriffs were asked various questions about privatization and their opinions about it. Among other things, Ethridge and Liebowitz (1994:56) wanted to know sheriffs' reactions to the pros and cons of privatization. The checklist of reasons *against* privatization included:

1. Private companies should not have control of inmates
2. Too expensive for the county
3. Will not relieve the county from liability
4. Inmates will be abused
5. Security risks
6. Government agencies are more efficient and effective
7. Private companies are only interested in making money
8. Danger of company declaring bankruptcy

The reasons *for* privatization included:

1. Relieve overcrowding
2. Save taxpayers money
3. Relieve county of liability
4. Boost local economy—add new jobs
5. Better care for inmates
6. Better classification and evaluation
7. Better rehabilitation

These researchers found that 70 percent of all responding sheriffs were opposed to privatization. Only 25 percent of the sheriffs were for privatization. The primary reasons cited by sheriffs against privatization were that private companies should not have control over inmates; the county would not be relieved of liability; and that privatization would be too expensive. Proponents favored privatization because, they said, it would alleviate jail overcrowding, boost the local economy, and save taxpayers money.

Cornelius (1997:49–50) notes that the privatization issue continues to be hotly debated. As of 1996, at least 110 jails in the United States were under contracts with private agencies for health care. More than a few jails were operated by private corporations. For instance, the Corrections Corporation of America operates Nashville, Tennessee's Metro Davidson County Detention Center, a medium-security facility with a capacity of 1,092 (Cornelius, 1997:49). The debate over privatization continues, as proponents and opponents disagree over the nature, scope, quality of services, and appropriate roles of public and private agencies.

KEY TERMS

B.A.C.I.S. (Behavior Alert Classification Identification System)
Deliberate indifference
Direct-supervision jail
Gender courses
Human services approach
Large jails
Lawsuit syndrome
Medium jails
Megajails
New-generation jails
Privatization
Sheriffs
Small jails
Special-needs offenders
Street attitudes
Tactical response teams

QUESTIONS FOR REVIEW

1. What are some important events in the evolution of jails in the United States?
2. What were some of the original functions of jails?
3. What are the current functions of jails? How do these functions contribute to some of the problems currently confronting jail administrators?
4. What are some of the types of inmates housed in jails?
5. Over 600 jails with large-jail populations are under court order to improve jail conditions. What types of issues are related to these court-ordered jail improvements?
6. What is meant by jail overcrowding? What strategies have been suggested to alleviate jail overcrowding?

7. What problems do mentally ill and retarded inmates pose for jail officials? Why should these persons be problematic for jail officials?
8. What are some recent developments in jail architecture that have become a part of the new generation of jails?
9. What is the volume of admissions to and releases from U.S. jails annually? In what ways does this volume influence jail problems?
10. What efforts are being made by various organizations to improve the quality of correctional officers through changes in recruitment and selection?

SUGGESTED READINGS

American Correctional Association. *Correctional Issues: Jails.* Laurel, MD: American Correctional Association, 1991.

Murphy, Jeffrie G. *Punishment and Rehabilitation* (3rd ed.). Belmont, CA: Wadsworth Publishing Company, 1995.

Welsh, Wayne N. *Counties in Court: Jail Overcrowding and Court-Ordered Reform.* Philadelphia: Temple University Press, 1995.

7

Prisons and Prisoners

CHAPTER OUTLINE

OVERVIEW

- One day, Dip, a cocky bodybuilder with an imposing physique, was walking back to his cell from the showers. He had a towel wrapped around him. He believed that his imposing size would deter any inmates from abusing him. When he reached his cell, another inmate was hiding under his bed and surprised Dip with an exposed erection, trying to watch Dip undress. Dip stormed out of his cell only to find some of the other man's friends waiting for him with homemade knives. Dip was stabbed several times, although his injuries were not fatal. Other inmates called them "Graterford wounds," meaning that his vital parts were still intact. When prison guards arrived, they locked Dip in solitary, charging him with possession of the knife the other inmates used to cut him. It was just another day in B-Block.
- [Sample of prison slang]: "Three homeys played a tip and did a B & E on the humbug. Dudes were stick-up boys, not back-door boosters, so they weren't down with it. Turns out to be a fat take. They find the stash and it's full of gold, rocks, paper, and cash money. After breaking down the tip man, the cutees get to breaking down the gapper, when one of the homeys throws shit into the game and pulls out a gat, talking about, 'I ain't breaking down with no lames.' He plucks one dude and goes to capping the other, but ain't nothing slow about homeboy and he breaks camp."

  English Translation: "Three neighborhood friends followed up on a tipster's information and committed a house burglary on a sudden impulse. These men were armed robbers and not burglars, so they were not familiar with the business. As it turned out, they stole a lot of money. They found a cache full of gold, precious stones, negotiable instruments, and cash. After the man who tipped them off about the house was paid off, the three partners began to divide the money. One of them complicated matters by pulling a gun, saying 'I'm not sharing any money with losers.' He killed one cohort, but the other one was faster and managed to get away."*

This chapter is about prisons, inmates who are incarcerated in prisons, and an overview of selected prison problems. **Prisons** are state or federally

* Both examples adapted from Victor Hassine, Inmate AM4737, *Life Without Parole: Living in Prison Today.* Los Angeles: Roxbury Press, 1996:15, 24–25.

funded and operated institutions to house convicted offenders under continuous custody on a long-term basis. Unlike jails, prisons are completely self-contained and self-sufficient. A social scientist, Erving Goffman (1961), developed the concept *total institution* to describe the environmental reality of prisons and the absolute dominance they have over prisoners' lives. Over the years, prison life has been amply depicted in feature films and catalogued by historians. A rich folklore of American prison culture has been established. However, much of this folklore is mythical and unrelated to the real world of corrections (J. Roberts, 1994).

In 1995, there were 1,026,882 prisoners under the supervision of state prisons, while there were 100,250 inmates under the supervision of the Federal Bureau of Prisons (Gilliard and Beck, 1996:3). The incarceration rate per 100,000 persons doubled between 1985 and 1995 from 313 to 600. Both the state and federal prison systems were operating at an average of 25 percent above their rated capacity in 1995 (Gilliard and Beck, 1996:1). Between 1985 and 1995, the prison and jail inmate population in the United States increased by 113 percent. Also between 1985 and 1995, the proportion of women incarcerated in jails and prisons rose from 8 to 10.2 percent (Gilliard and Beck, 1996:10).

The first part of this chapter examines briefly the history of prisons in the United States. State and federal prisoners are profiled, together with a description of the general functions prisons perform. Prisons are often segregated internally according to various custody levels, depending upon the types of prisoners housed. More serious or dangerous offenders are maintained in separate prisons or prison areas characterized by high custody, whereas less serious, low-risk offenders are maintained under minimum custody. Most prisons "type" entering offenders according to their offense seriousness, and prisoners are assigned different custody levels according to these classifications.

Because prisons are considered long-term incarcerative institutions, they experience problems different from those normally encountered by jail administrators. By the same token, there are some similarities, such as overcrowding and inmate discipline problems. Some of the more important and contemporary prison issues are highlighted and examined. Finally, various prison reforms are presented. In view of the present state of corrections in the United States, the chapter concludes with a consideration of the future of U.S. prisons and jails and the prospects for changes in this correctional area.

THE HISTORY OF PRISONS IN THE UNITED STATES

The development and growth of U.S. prisons was influenced originally by English and Scottish penal methods (American Correctional Association, 1983; Hughes, 1987). Those English and Scottish prisons that did exist to house criminals and others frequently adopted operational policies that were strongly influenced by economic or mercantile interests as well as those of the church. An influential English prison reformer, **John Howard** (1726–1790), was critical of the manner and circumstances under which prisoners were administered and housed. He had been a county squire and later, in 1773, became sheriff of Bedfordshire. He took his job seriously and conducted regular inspections of gaol facilities in his jurisdiction. He found that prisoners were routinely exploited by gaolers, because gaolers had no regular income other than that extracted from prisoners through their labor.

To get new ideas about gaol operations, Howard visited several other countries to inspect their prison systems. He was especially impressed with the Maison de Force (House of Enforcement) of Ghent, where prisoners were well-fed, adequately clothed, and humanely lodged separately during evening hours. He believed that with proper lobbying these ideas could be incorporated into British prisons and gaols. He reported these observations of prisons to the House of Commons in a lengthy and detailed document, and he succeeded in convincing British authorities that certain reforms should be undertaken. In 1779, the **Penitentiary Act** was passed.

The Penitentiary Act provided that new facilities should be created in which prisoners could work productively at hard labor rather than suffer the usual punishment of banishment. Prisoners were to be well-fed, clothed, and housed in isolated sanitary cells. They were to be given opportunities to learn useful skills and trades. Fees for their maintenance were abolished, rigorous inspections were conducted regularly, and balanced diets and improved hygiene were to be strictly observed. Howard did not believe prisoners should be cruelly treated, but he didn't believe they should be coddled, either. He felt they should be given a hearty work regimen (American Correctional Association, 1983:15). Through hard labor and productive work, prisoners could be made to realize the seriousness and consequences of their crimes. Work became a form of penance. Howard's ideas inspired the coining of a new word, "penitentiary," which was synonymous with reform and punishment. Today, penitentiaries in the United States are regarded as punishment-centered rather than reform-centered, as significant philosophical shifts have occurred in American corrections. In any case, Howard's work inspired others, including Dr. Benjamin Rush, to create the innovations pioneered in later years.

The First State Prison

Although authorities disagree about the first state prison, there was an underground prison established in Simsbury, Connecticut, in 1773. This prison was actually an underground copper mine that was converted into a confinement facility for convicted felons (American Correctional Association, 1983:26–27). It was eventually made into a permanent prison in 1790. Prisoners were shackled about the ankles, worked long hours, and received particularly harsh sentences for minor offenses. Burglary and counterfeiting were punishable in Simsbury by imprisonment not exceeding 10 years, while a second offense meant life imprisonment (American Correctional Association, 1983:26).

The Pennsylvania System

Historians consider the Walnut Street Jail to be the first true American prison to attempt the correction of offenders. Compared with the Simsbury, Connecticut, underground prison, a strictly punishment-centered facility, the Walnut Street Jail was operated according to rehabilitative principles. One of the signers of the Declaration of Independence, Dr. Benjamin Rush (1745–1813), was both a physician and a humanitarian. Dr. Rush believed that the purposes of punishment were to reform offenders, to prevent them from committing future crimes, and to remove them from society temporarily until they developed a repentant attitude. Several of Rush's ideas were incorporated into the operation of the Walnut Street Jail, and eventually, the pattern of discipline and offender treatment practiced there became known popularly as the **Pennsylvania System.** Although the Walnut Street Jail Pennsylvania System was widely imitated by other jurisdictions and holds a permanent and important place in the history of American corrections, poor administration and planning caused the jail to fail as a correctional facility during the next few decades (American Correctional Association, 1983:31).

Consistent with his profession as a physician, Rush believed that prisoners should exercise regularly and eat wholesome foods. Thus, he encouraged prisoners to grow gardens where they could produce their own goods. Prisoner-produced goods were so successful at one point that produce and other materials manufactured or grown by inmates were marketed to the general public. Therefore, he pioneered the first prison industry by which prisoners could market goods for profit and use some of this income to defray prison operating expenses.

The Auburn State Penitentiary

In 1816, New York correctional authorities developed a new type of prison, the **Auburn State Penitentiary,** designed according to **tiers,** where inmates were housed on several different levels. The tier system became a common feature of subsequent U.S. prison construction, and today most prisons are architecturally structured according to tiers. The term **penitentiary** is used to designate an institution that not only segregates offenders from society but also from each other. The original connotation of penitentiary was a place in which prisoners could think, reflect, and repent of their misdeeds and possibly undergo reformation (Allen, et al., 1985). Presently, the words "prison" and "penitentiary" are often used interchangeably, because virtually every prison has facilities for isolating prisoners from one another according to various levels of custody and control.

Thus, each state has devised different names for facilities designed to house its most dangerous offenders. Examples include Kentucky State Penitentiary, California State Prison at San Quentin, New Jersey State Prison, North Dakota Penitentiary, and Maine State Prison.

The Auburn State Penitentiary incorporated several features of the old Walnut Street Jail concept such as solitary confinement. Prisoners were housed in solitary cells during evening hours, therefore perpetuating the solitary confinement theme. Solitary confinement is an administrative segregation feature of virtually every major U.S. prison today (Rogers, 1993). However, one innovation was that inmates were allowed to work together and eat their meals with one another during daylight hours. This was known as the **congregate system,** because of the opportunity for inmates to congregate with one another (American Correctional Association, 1983). Dining rooms were fashioned according to large military mess halls, and work areas were large enough to accommodate several hundred inmates.

Auburn Penitentiary also provided for divisions among prisoners according to the nature of their offenses. The different tiers conveniently housed inmates in different offense categories, with more serious offenders housed on one tier and less serious offenders housed on another. Certain tiers were reserved for the most unruly offenders who could not conform their conduct to prison policies. The most dangerous inmates were kept in solitary confinement for long periods as punishment. These periods ranged from a few days to a few months, depending upon the prison rule violated. Therefore, Auburn Penitentiary is significant historically because it provided the minimum-, medium-, and maximum-security designations by which modern penitentiaries are known. Prisoners also were provided with different uniforms, to set them apart from one another. The stereotypical "striped" uniform of prison inmates was a novelty at Auburn that was widely copied as well. Over half of all state prisons patterned their structures after the Auburn system during the next half century, including the style of prison dress and the manner of separating offenders according to their crime's seriousness (American Correctional Association, 1983:49–54). Striped prison uniforms continued until the 1950s, when they were eventually abandoned (American Correctional Association, 1983:54).

One additional feature of the Auburn system was that prisoners helped to defray a portion of their housing and food costs through their labor. Prison officials contracted with various manufacturers and retailers for purchases of prison goods. The prison industry was gradually recognized to be a mutually beneficial enterprise—prison officials could interpret prisoner labor as worthwhile and rehabilitative, and they could also contemplate the possibilities of profits from prison-manufactured goods. These profits not only offset the costs of prisoner housing, but they also enhanced New York State revenues. While some critics may contend that exploitation of prison labor was the primary objective of the work of Auburn inmates, it is also arguable that the skills these prisoners cultivated, for whatever reason, were beneficial and helped them secure employment in various factories when they were eventually released.

Other Early Prison Developments

Between 1816 and 1900, many state prisons were established. One of the first successful prisons was constructed in Cherry Hill, Pennsylvania, in the early 1830s. This prison was considered successful because it was the first to offer a continuing internal program of treatment and other forms of assistance to inmates (Johnston, 1973). The first state penitentiary in Ohio was opened in Columbus in 1834. The largest state prison of that time period was established in Jackson, Michigan, in 1839. By 1996, this State Prison of Southern Michigan contained 1,547 inmates. However, the original building constructed in 1839 had been rebuilt to accommodate larger numbers of inmates in 1926 (American Correctional Association, 1996a:234). Another large state prison was built in Parchman, Mississippi, in 1900. In 1996, it housed 5,453 inmates and had a rated capacity of 6,381 (American Correctional Association, 1996a:246). Louisiana claims one of the oldest state prisons, however, being built in 1866 with a capacity of 4,532 inmates. In 1996, the Louisiana State Penitentiary in Angola housed 4,531 males at nearly 100 percent of its rated capacity of 4,532 (American Correctional Association, 1996a:192).

Besides those prisons constructed in Pennsylvania and New York, many of the early state penitentiaries were built in areas with large populations. For instance, the California State Prison at San Quentin was constructed in 1852. The Illinois State Penitentiary at Joliet was built in 1860. The Massachusetts Correctional Institution at Bridgewater and the Indiana State Prison were constructed in 1855 and 1859, respectively. However, these older prisons were neither constructed nor designed to house equivalent numbers of offenders as were the Louisiana and Mississippi prisons. In 1996, San Quentin housed 5,436 inmates (rated capacity 3,286); the Indiana State Prison housed 1,638 inmates (rated capacity 1,650); the Bridgewater, Massachusetts, facility housed 320 prisoners (rated capacity 337); and the Joliet, Illinois, Correctional Center housed 1,200 inmates (rated capacity 1,340) (American Correctional Association, 1996a:33, 148, 158, 212).

State prisons in other states with smaller populations were established in later years. The Civil War, 1860 to 1865, did much to indirectly change prison structure and purpose, particularly in the South. After the Civil War, many Southern states established prisons that exploited inmate labor through various leasing arrangements with private enterprises as well as with the federal and state governments. This occurred largely because the Southern economy was adversely affected by the abolition of slavery and the drastic depletion of cheap labor. Thus, many inmates of

Southern prisons worked the cotton fields, formed chain gangs to repair state roads, and engaged in other constructive work (Foster, Rideau, and Wikberg, 1991). Outside the South, penal authorities and others became increasingly critical of such prisoner exploitation. Although Southern prisons gradually changed their operating systems to emulate those of the North, East, and West, especially during the 1940s, an element of prisoner exploitation remains throughout their prison industry. However, today prison inmates who engage in manual labor are paid wages commensurate with the work performed. A portion of these wages offsets the cost of inmate accommodations, although inmates may now save a portion of their wages to provide partial support for their dependents or to acquire a nest egg to use when they are eventually released.

Elmira Reformatory

The next major event in American correctional history occurred in 1870 with the creation of the American Correctional Association (ACA). Rutherford B. Hayes, a future U.S. president, was elected to head the organization. The original goals of the ACA were to formulate a national correctional philosophy, to develop sound correctional policies and standards, to offer expertise to all interested jurisdictions in the design and operation of correctional facilities, and to assist in the training of correctional officers. The ACA was originally called the National Prison Association, then the American Prison Association, and finally and more generally, the American Correctional Association.

It is no coincidence that the United States was entering a new era of correctional reform with the establishment of the ACA, and subsequently, Elmira State Reformatory in Elmira, New York, in 1876. Elmira Reformatory was innovative in that it experimented with certain new rehabilitative philosophies espoused by various penologists, including its first superintendent, Zebulon Brockway (1827–1920). Brockway began his correctional career as a clerk at Wethersfield, Connecticut, Prison in 1848 (Eggleston, 1989). Later, he moved to New York to become superintendent of the Albany Municipal and County Almshouse, the first county hospital for the mentally ill and insane. His experience included superintendencies of prisons and houses of correction at various sites in New York and Michigan. Brockway was critical of the harsh methods employed by the establishments he headed, and he envisioned better and more effective treatments for prisoners. He had his chance in 1876 when he was selected to head Elmira Reformatory.

Elmira was touted as the *new penology* and the latest, state of the art scientific advancement in correctional methods (Pisciotta, 1983). Penologists from Scotland and Ireland, **Captain Alexander Maconochie** and **Sir Walter Crofton,** were instrumental in bringing about changes in European correctional methods during the period when Elmira was established in the early 1870s. These men influenced American corrections by introducing the "mark system," whereby prisoners could accumulate good-time credits to be applied against their original sentences. Thus, through hard work and industry, prisoners could shorten their original sentences that earlier had to be served in their entirety (American Correctional Association, 1983:67).

Elmira was truly a reformatory. Concurrent with penal developments in Great Britain and other United Kingdom countries, prisoners were channeled into productive activities of an educational or vocational nature, where their good behavior and productivity could earn them time off for good behavior. The military model was used at Elmira as well; prisoners were trained in close-order drill, wore military uniforms, and paraded about with wooden rifles. This was regarded as one means of instilling discipline in inmates and reforming them. While Brockway didn't invent parole, he saw that it was used frequently as a reward for those who conformed to the new ways of Elmira. Historians credit Elmira Reformatory with introducing the individualization of prisoner treatment and the large-scale use of indeterminate sentencing.

The influence of Maconochie and especially Crofton are apparent in this regard. Crofton had invented indeterminate sentencing by establishing various work stages whereby prisoners could progress, thus shortening their original sentences. In Elmira Reformatory, however, there is evidence that Brockway and his staff resorted to corporal punishments on occasion to emphasize their principles and encourage conformity to reformatory rules and policies. Despite these drawbacks, however, Elmira Reformatory was widely imitated by other states during the next 40 years.

Rehabilitation was not a bad concept theoretically. In fact, it remains as one of correction's continuing goals as a part of general prison reform (Waite, 1993). But prison overcrowding stimulates significant changes in prison operating policies, and criminal justice procedures are changed to accommodate growing numbers of inmates. Of course, forces external to prison settings have always been at work to shape prison policies. For example, economic fluctuations over time have worked to modify the growth and development of prison industries. And prison industries, including the labor generated from inmates, provide training and development opportunities for prisoners that are closely connected with and facilitate rehabilitation (Adamson, 1984). However, no simple causal link exists to prove a definite connection between economic change and modes of penal discipline and labor (Adamson, 1984).

Many prisons have reported greater inmate idleness and violence as a result of greater overcrowding in recent years (Johnson, 1984). Furthermore, many prisons are experiencing declining staff to prisoner ratios. Accordingly, the quality of programs offered to inmates suffers as prison capacities are exceeded through higher conviction rates and changes in sentencing and parole policies. Although the link between prison population growth and program quality is unclear, overcrowding does seem to adversely influence prison practices and policies (Zimmerman, 1986).

STATE AND FEDERAL PRISON SYSTEMS

Each state and political subdivision including counties and cities maintains facilities for housing offenders. There is considerable diversity in the quality of these facilities, the numbers of offenders housed, and the general conditions of confinement. Those convicted of state offenses and sentenced to a period of incarceration are normally maintained in state prisons or correctional centers. Those convicted of violating local criminal laws and sentenced to incarceration are usually housed in city or county jails.

The Federal Bureau of Prisons

Although federal correctional facilities have existed in one form or another since the 1790s, no central authority system existed to administer these facilities until Congress created the Federal Bureau of Prisons in 1930 (U.S. Federal Bureau of Prisons, 1994). Under the direction of the Attorney General of the United States, the Bureau of Prisons was established to manage and regulate all federal penal and correctional institutions; to provide suitable quarters, subsistence, and discipline for all persons charged with or convicted of federal crimes; and to provide technical assistance to state and local governments in the improvement of their own correctional facilities (18 USC, Sec. 4041-4042, 1997). A director oversees five U.S. regions where all federal correctional institutions are located. These regional directors are headquartered in Atlanta, Dallas, Kansas City, Philadelphia, and San Francisco. The director of the Federal Bureau of Prisons in 1997 was Dr. Kathleen M. Hawk (American Correctional Association, 1996a:508).

Because of prison overcrowding and other factors, the federal prison system has not always been able to accommodate adequately all prisoners in its charge. Thus, contractual arrangements are frequently made between the federal government and state and local corrections to house a portion of the federal prisoner overflow. Early challenges by prisoners as to the constitutionality of such contracting upheld the right of the federal government to make such arrangements with states. In 1876, the U.S. Supreme Court declared that as long as a state permits a federal prisoner to remain in its prison and does not object to his detention, he is rightfully detained in custody under a sentence that is lawfully passed (*Ex parte Karstendick,* 1876). States also have the right to refuse to allow the use of their jails and prisons for housing those convicted of federal crimes if they so desire (*Ex parte Shores,* 1912).

In 1996, there were 97 federal correctional institutions, ranging from penitentiaries and prison camps to detention centers, medical centers, and low security facilities (American Correctional Association, 1996a:508–550). These facilities and the dates of their construction are shown in Table 7.1.

Ideally, those convicted of violating federal criminal statutes and sentenced to incarceration are placed in one federal correctional institution or

TABLE 7.1 Development of Federal Correctional Institutions, 1902–1996

Year	Type of Facility
1902	U.S. Penitentiary, Atlanta, GA
1906	U.S. Penitentiary, Leavenworth, KS
1927	Federal Prison Camp, Alderson, WV
1930	Federal Correctional Institution, Petersburg, VA
1930	Federal Prison Camp, Maxwell AFB, Montgomery, AL
1932	U.S. Penitentiary, Lewisburg, PA
1932	Federal Correctional Institution, La Tuna, Anthony, TX
1933	Federal Correctional Institution, El Reno, OK
1933	Federal Correctional Institution, Milan, MI
1933	U.S. Medical Center for Federal Prisoners, Springfield, MO
1938	Federal Correctional Institution, Tallahassee, FL
1940	Federal Correctional Institution, Ashland, KY
1940	Federal Correctional Institution, Danbury, CT
1940	Federal Correctional Institution, Englewood, CO
1940	Federal Correctional Institution, Seagoville, TX
1940	Federal Correctional Institution, Texarkana, TX
1940	U.S. Penitentiary, Terre Haute, IN
1952	Federal Prison Camp, Allenwood, PA
1955	Federal Correctional Institution, Terminal Island, CA
1958	Federal Correctional Institution, Safford, AR
1959	U.S. Penitentiary, Lompoc, CA
1959	Federal Correctional Institution, Sandstone, MN
1962	Federal Prison Camp, Eglin AFB, FL
1963	U.S. Penitentiary, Marion, IL
1968	Federal Correctional Institution, Morgantown, WV
1973	Federal Correctional Institution, Oxford, WI
1974	Federal Correctional Institution, Lexington, KY
1974	Federal Correctional Institution, Pleasanton, CA
1974	Metropolitan Correctional Center, San Diego, CA
1975	Metropolitan Correctional Center, Chicago, IL
1975	Metropolitan Correctional Center, New York, NY
1976	Federal Correctional Institution, Butner, NC
1976	Metropolitan Correctional Center, Miami, FL
1977	Federal Correctional Institution, Memphis, TN
1979	Federal Correctional Institution, Bastrop, TX
1979	Federal Correctional Institution, Talladega, AL
1979	Federal Prison Camp, Big Spring, TX
1979	Federal Prison Camp, Boron, CA
1971	Federal Correctional Institution, Ft. Worth, TX
1980	Federal Correctional Institution, Otisville, NY
1980	Federal Correctional Institution, Ray Brook, NY
1982	Tucson Federal Correctional Institution, Tucson, AR
1983	Federal Prison Camp, Duluth, MN
1984	Federal Correctional Institution, Loretto, PA
1985	Federal Correctional Institution, Phoenix, AZ
1985	Federal Correctional Institution, Black Canyon, AZ
1985	Federal Medical Center, Rochester, MN
1986	Federal Detention Center, Oakdale, LA
1986	Federal Correctional Institution, Oakdale, LA
1988	Federal Correctional Institution, Marianna, FL

(table continues)

TABLE 7.1 (continued)

Year	Type of Facility
1988	Federal Prison Camp, Pensacola, FL
1988	Federal Prison Camp, Yankton, SD
1988	Federal Prison Camp, Bryan, TX
1988	Metropolitan Detention Center, Los Angeles, CA
1989	Federal Correctional Institution, Sheridan, OR
1989	Federal Correctional Institution, Bradford, PA
1989	Federal Prison Camp, Seymour Johnson Air Force Base, Goldsboro, NC
1989	Federal Prison Camp, El Paso, TX
1990	Federal Correctional Institution, Jesup, GA
1990	Federal Correctional Institution, Fairton, NJ
1990	Federal Correctional Institution, Three Rivers, TX
1990	Federal Detention Center, Oakdale, LA
1990	Federal Prison Camp, N. Las Vegas, NV
1990	Federal Prison Camp, Millington, TN
1991	Federal Correctional Institution, Minersville, PA
1991	Federal Medical Center, Lexington, KY
1992	Federal Correctional Institution, Manchester, KY
1992	Federal Correctional Institution, Fort Dix, NJ
1992	Low Security Correctional Institution-Allenwood, White Deer, PA
1993	Federal Correctional Institution-Allenwood, White Deer, PA
1993	U.S. Penitentiary-Allenwood, White Deer, PA
1993	Federal Correctional Institution, Estill, SC
1993	Federal Correctional Institution-Satellite Camp, Bastrop, TX
1993	Federal Prison Camp-Oakdale, Oakdale, LA
1993	Metropolitan Detention Center, San Juan, PR
1994	Federal Medical Center, Ft. Worth, TX
1994	United States Penitentiary, Florence, CO
1994	United States Penitentiary-Adm Max, Florence, CO
1994	Federal Correctional Institution, Greenville, IL
1994	Federal Correctional Institution, Pekin, IL
1994	Metropolitan Detention Center, Brooklyn, NY
1994	U.S. Penitentiary, Florence, CO
1994	U.S. Penitentiary-Admin Max, Florence, CO
1995	Federal Correctional Institution, Florence, CO
1995	Federal Correctional Institution, Coleman, FL
1995	Federal Correctional Institution, Miami, FL
1995	Federal Correctional Institution, Cumberland, MD
1995	Federal Correctional Institution, Waseca, MN
1995	Federal Correctional Institution, Otisville, NY
1995	Federal Correctional Institution, Ray Brook, NY
1995	Federal Correctional Institution, Memphis, TX
1995	Federal Correctional Institution, Beckley, WV
1995	Federal Detention Center, Miami, FL
1995	Federal Detention Center, Tallahassee, FL
1995	Federal Medical Center, Ft. Worth, TX
1995	Low Security Correctional Institution, Coleman, FL
1995	Low Security Correctional Institution, Butner, NC

another, depending upon the nature of the conviction offense, the geographical area within which the federal crime occurred, and space availability. Normally, federal prisoners are housed in federal facilities, state prisoners are housed in state facilities, and local criminals are incarcerated in local facilities.

However, for many decades, some federal and state prisoners have been lodged in local correctional facilities, largely because of overcrowding in federal institutions. Under Title 18, Section 4082 of the U.S. Code (1997), the Attorney General "may designate as a place of confinement any available, suitable, and appropriate institution or facility, whether maintained by the federal government or otherwise, and whether within or without the judicial district in which the person was convicted, and may at any time transfer a person from one place of confinement to another." Also, if space is unavailable in particular localities where federal prisoners are to be housed, the Attorney General is authorized to cause to be erected in the area a house of detention, workhouse, jail, camp, or other place of confinement that can be used to house those convicted of federal crimes (18 USC, Sec. 4003, 1997).

Until 1985, the establishment of new federal penal facilities was sluggish. Between 1985 and 1995, over 50 new federal prisons were constructed. The oldest U.S. Penitentiary still operating is the one in Atlanta, Georgia, constructed in 1902. The smallest U.S. Penitentiary is the U.S. Penitentiary-Admin Max in Florence, Colorado, with a rated capacity of 484, and the largest is in Atlanta, Georgia, with a rated capacity of 1,819. These penitentiaries generally house the most serious federal offenders and those serving the longest sentences. Those federal penitentiaries designated as "Admin Max" house inmates with chronic misconduct problems. Their average stay is 36 months (American Correctional Association, 1996a:518). The federal correctional institutions have varying security levels. The metropolitan correctional centers and camps are designed to house short-term and low-risk federal offenders at all security levels. Federal medical centers are designed for federal prisoners who require medical, surgical, or psychiatric care. The federal prison camps are designed as minimum-security institutions with no fences, with dormitory housing and low staff-inmate ratios. These facilities are program-oriented and focused on work. Finally, federal detention centers are designed to house pretrial detainees and criminal aliens awaiting deportation hearings (American Correctional Association, 1996a:547).

A report on the achievements of the U.S. Federal Bureau of Prisons in 1994 showed that strong policies and procedures were in place for prison response to various types of emergencies, including prison rioting and other disturbances (U.S. Federal Bureau of Prisons, 1994). Six strategic goals were realized, including more effective population management; human resource management; security and facility management; correctional leadership and effective public administration; inmate programs and services; and building partnerships. A subsequent 1995 survey found that among 46 different state departments of corrections, 94 percent of these departments had established similar emergency plans and tactical response teams for countering inmate disturbances (Bryan, 1995).

State Prisons and Prison Administration

Compared with the highly centralized Federal Bureau of Prisons, state prison organization varies greatly among jurisdictions. There are some common elements associated with the internal operations of most federal and state prisons, however. All state prisons as well as comparable federal facilities have **wardens** or **superintendents** who oversee prison operations. These people have various administrative responsibilities, including hiring and firing corrections personnel, implementing new correctional policies, ensuring the safety of all prisoners as well as prison staff, and establishing internal sanctioning systems for dealing effectively with rule infractions by staff or inmates.

Prison administrators come from diverse backgrounds (Cullen, Latessa, and Burton, 1993). Many of these officials lack legal training. Often, former correctional personnel are appointed to warden positions after many years of service in other correctional capacities (Cullen et al., 1993). In view of the increase in prisoner litigation during the 1970s and 1980s, prison administrators have become more adept at developing defensive policies and acquainting their staffs with strategies for avoiding confrontations and situations that eventually result in lawsuits. Many prison administrators have established or helped to establish prisoner grievance committees to deal with many minor prison problems internally rather than through court action.

In 1973, the National Advisory Commission on Criminal Justice Standards and Goals directed its attention to correctional management and identified certain basic problems of correctional organizations. Subsequently, a report was issued that highlighted certain deficiencies as well as several options as possible solutions to these problems. Some of the problems the Commission identified were (1) the lack of coordination and considerable fragmentation among state corrections agencies and services, (2) shifting federal and state resources allocated to corrections, and (3) changing correctional goals from rehabilitation to more punitive policies. The Commission also noted that managing people-processing organizations such as prisons is probably more difficult than managing other public agencies. The fact that dangerous prisoners must be managed adequately and that appropriate programs must be implemented to directly serve their diverse needs means that prison administrators must continually solve logistical and practical problems that never seem to abate.

In the early 1970s, management by objectives was considered the most promising strategy whereby administrators could cope successfully with their various supervisory problems. **Management by objectives** is achieved by effective goal setting and by creating a system of accountability by which one's performance can be measured over time. Thus, with proper feedback from higher-ups, corrections personnel can establish goals and take appropriate action to achieve them. Administrators can facilitate goal attainment by providing an accepting climate and the necessary feedback that permits officers to remedy bad habits and cultivate good ones. But the Commission also observed that prisons ordinarily do not engage in the necessary planning for management by objectives to succeed. Thus, some of the more important needs of prison administrators were highlighted, but no specific paths were outlined by which these needs could be fulfilled (Carter et al., 1985). Complicating the general application of specific managerial strategies is the fact that state prisons vary greatly in their sizes and functions. As we have seen, prison sizes range from a few hundred inmates to 4,500 or more. Managerial strategies that work for smaller institutions may not work for much larger ones (Carter et al., 1985; Kinkade and Leone, 1992).

Most prison administrators are men. In 1995, about 18 percent of all administrative prison staff were women (Camp and Camp, 1995a:70–71). There are no restrictions that would prevent women from occupying these administrative posts. However, there are informal and traditional barriers that often inhibit the hiring of women to warden posts. In 1990, for instance, a *Corrections Compendium* survey disclosed that there were 53 women wardens, superintendents, or administrators overseeing men's correctional institutions, while another 64 women were either deputies or assistant administrators at other men's or coed institutions (Hicks, 1990:7). One of the chief barriers is overcoming resistance from other male administrators responsible for making such appointments (T. Miller, 1996: 16–17).

Once persons are appointed prison wardens or administrators, they do not stay on the job for particularly long periods. For instance, the average length of service for prison wardens in 1995 was about 2.8 years (Camp and Camp, 1995:68). Those wardens with the longest tenure in their posts have served an average of 13.5 years, with one warden in Florida serving for 35 years (Camp and Camp, 1995a:68).

On July 1, 1982, Jennie Lancaster was promoted to warden of the North Carolina Correctional Center for women. She had begun her career by applying for a correctional internship and taking a position with the Polk Youth Center in Raleigh in 1972. Her interest in corrections had been prompted by a criminology course she had taken during her senior year at Merideth College in Raleigh. Later in 1972, she became program supervisor at Ulmstead Youth Center. By 1980, she had become the assistant superintendent for treatment and programs at the North Carolina Correctional Center for Women. Two years later she was promoted to warden (Gursky, 1988:82–83). Lancaster recalled that two years later in 1984, she was faced with one of the most challenging tasks of her life—the supervision of Velma Barfield, a woman who had poisoned her mother and two other people, and was sentenced to death by a North Carolina court. No woman had been executed in the United States since 1962. Barfield's appeals were denied consistently as she sat on death row for six years at the Women's Prison. In May 1984, Barfield's execution was ordered to be carried out within 90 days. A final appeal by Barfield was rejected by the U.S. Supreme Court in September, and a November 2 execution date was set. Barfield was executed as scheduled.

Although the Central Prison in Raleigh, a maximum-security facility for men, performs all executions in North Carolina, Barfield was housed in the Women's Prison until a few days before the date of execution. Warden Lancaster related that this most emotionally upsetting ordeal was especially difficult for her correctional staff. She said that one of her officers lamented, "We got into corrections because we thought we could make a difference in somebody's life. We have a lot of policies and training programs to teach us how to effectively work with inmates, how to encourage them to change, how to reward positive behavior and motivate inmates. Now we're being told we're going to be a part of the death of somebody and we don't know how to do that. We never anticipated this." Neither did Warden Jennie Lancaster (Gursky, 1988:82). It bothered her also that there was a lack of consideration given to the medical, psychiatric, and religious staff who had been working with Barfield and others (Gursky, 1988:78). Thus, as warden, she assumed additional responsibilities for informally counseling correctional officers bothered by the impending execution. In sum, she said that "the greatest irony [is] that the authentic, genuine, caring part of you is coming right to head with the professional responsibility that seems to be asking you to do something totally against what you've been doing" (Gursky, 1988:78).

Because the death penalty does not exist in several states, some wardens and superintendents do not have to face such correctional pressures and responsibilities. However, a host of other problems face these administrators daily. Solutions to these problems, some arising from inmates and others from correctional officers, are not always clear-cut. Professional improvisation is frequently required. Furthermore, it is clear that the types of inmates administrators must supervise influence the nature of supervision practiced. Fixed and limited correctional budgets impose serious constraints that prevent administrators from being fully effective in the performance of their tasks. There is no single administrative style that describes the typical prison warden or superintendent. There is no uniformity among the states or even within them about how each prison facility should be managed and what sort of correctional officer conduct is to be prescribed. For a time in the 1970s, the Law Enforcement Assistance Administration provided monies for correctional improvements, including training for those performing supervisory roles. While some monies continue to be available under different auspices, there is little indication that former expenditures resulted in substantial administrative improvements in prisons generally.

The Total Institution Concept

Erving Goffman (1961) has observed that prisons in the United States are **total institutions.** That is, they are completely self-sufficient and define a closed culture within which inmates interact. The concept of a total institution conveys the idea that prison environments are unique and distinct from other populations, such as might be found in traditional community settings. There are similarities to communities found in prisons, however. There is a hierarchy of authority and power structure among inmates. Besides institutional rules, prisoners establish their own rules by which to conduct themselves. Thus, a culture within a culture, or **prison subculture,** is created. This subculture has its own status structure and authority pattern. In many prisons, inmates fear the informal prison subculture and its reprisals for rule violations more than formal administrative rules and punishments. Intra-inmate retaliation is often fatal.

To understand how inmates behave and why they react in certain ways to external interventions, such as vocational or educational programs and counseling, we must first understand the fabric of their subculture within their total institution (Davidson, 1995; McCorkle et al., 1995). Once we understand their cultural patterns, we have done much to explain why sometimes interventions designed to achieve specific aims, such as rehabilitation, are not particularly successful. However, some experts dispute the idea that prisons are as segregated as they appear to outsiders. Community-prison interactions in certain prisons, particularly in California, cause some prison settings to be less isolated than the total institution concept would imply (Krause, 1992). Later in this chapter, inmate culture is described. Jargon peculiar to inmates is presented as is the way inmate pecking orders are established. It is expected that in such a setting with its own culture, gang formation is one logical consequence. Inmate violence and other incidents are outgrowths of this subculture and the hostility it breeds and perpetuates. Before we examine inmate culture, we note some of the primary characteristics of today's prison populations.

A PROFILE OF PRISONERS IN U.S. PRISONS

Considerable diversity exists among prisoners in state and federal institutions. These differences include the nature and seriousness of their conviction offenses, age, and psychological or medical problems. To cope more effectively with meeting the needs of such diverse offenders, prisons have established different confinement facilities and levels of custody, depending upon how each prisoner is *classified.*

Between 1985 and 1995, a majority of states more than doubled their number of sentenced prisoners (Gilliard and Beck, 1996:1). Overall, state and federal prisoner populations increased by 121 percent between 1985 and 1995. Generally, a 8.7 percent increase occurred in the national prison population between 1994 and 1995 (Gilliard and Beck, 1995:2). Table 7.2 shows federal and state prison population growth between 1985 and 1995. Figure 7.1 graphically portrays this growth for the same period.

State and federal prison populations more than doubled during the 1985 to 1995 period. State and federal prison population growth was highest between the years 1988 and 1989 and between 1985 and 1986. Selected demographic and social characteristics of new prison admissions in 35 states are shown in Table 7.3. Table 7.3 shows all admissions for these states in 1990 together with new court commitments. An inspection of the new court commitments and a comparison with the existing prisoner profile suggests that there is little change from one year to the next in the social and demographic characteristics of new prisoners.

About 92 percent of all prisoners in these states are male, while about 46 percent are black. Hispanics make up about 18 percent of these inmate populations. Regarding the ages of new prison commitments, there is a slight pattern indicating more admissions of younger offenders, although the proportionate differences from one year to the next are not substantial. The median age of these offenders decreased slightly from 28 years to 27 years. The educational level remained about the same among new prison admissions, with the median educational level being the 11th grade.

Table 7.4 shows a profile of all convicted offenders in state courts for 1992. This profile indicates that of the 893,630 convictions, 45 percent of these offenders were incarcerated, whereas 55 percent received probation. More frequently incarcerated were those convicted of violent offenses (58 percent), whereas less than half (43 percent) of all property offenders were incarcerated. Forty-two percent of all convicted drug offenders were incarcerated, whereas 55 percent of all drug traffickers went to prison.

Table 7.5 shows the race of all convicted felons sentenced in state

TABLE 7.2 Change in the State and Federal Prison Populations, 1985–1995

Year	No. of Inmates	Annual Percentage Change	Total Percentage Change Since 1985
1985	487,593	—	—
1986	546,378	12.0	12.0
1987	585,292	7.1	20.0
1988	631,990	7.9	29.6
1989	712,967	12.8	46.2
1990	743,382	4.3	52.4
1991	792,535	6.6	62.5
1992	850,566	7.3	74.4
1993	909,381	6.9	86.5
1994	991,612	9.0	103.4
1995	1,078,357	8.7	121.1

Source: Gilliard and Beck (1995:2).

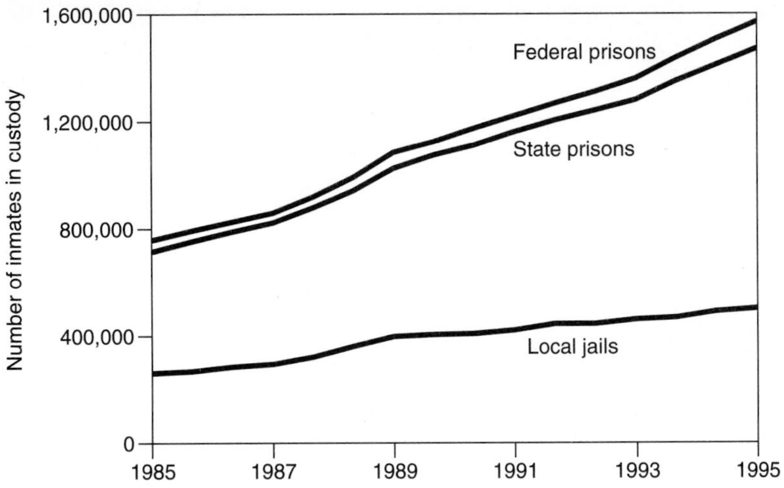

• Since 1985, the total number of inmates in the custody of state and federal prisons and local jails has more than doubled to nearly 1.6 million—an increase of 113 percent.

• On average, the incarcerated population has grown 7.9 percent annually since 1985. The state and federal prison population has grown 8.3 percent annually, while the local jail population has grown 7.0 percent.

• Over the 10-year period, correctional authorities have found beds for nearly 841,200 additional inmates, or the equivalent of almost 1,618 inmates per week.

• At year-end 1985, 1 in every 320 United States residents were incarcerated. By year-end 1995 that ratio had increased to 1 in every 167.

• Since 1985, the nation's prison and jail population has nearly doubled on a per capita basis. In 1995, the number of inmates per 100,000 U.S. residents was 600—up from 313 in 1985.

FIGURE 7.1 Number of inmates in custody, 1985–1995. (*Source:* Gilliard and Beck, 1996:2)

courts for 1992 according to their particular conviction offense (Maguire and Pastore, 1996:408). White offenders accounted for 55 percent of all violent offense convictions, 62 percent of all property offense convictions, and 50 percent of all drug convictions.

Tables 7.6 and 7.7 show *average* and *average maximum* sentence lengths for both state and federal prisoners, according to their conviction offenses. Average prison sentences imposed by state criminal court judges for murder/manslaughter were 251 months, or about 21 years. However, an inspection of Table 7.6 shows that less than half of this time (48 percent) or about 10 years of these murder/manslaughter sentences are served. For violent offenders in state criminal courts, average sentences imposed were

TABLE 7.3 Demographic and Social Characteristics of Prison Admissions in 35 States, 1990

Characteristics	All Admissions	New Court Commitments
Number of Admissions	390,087	268,330
Total	100%	100%
Gender		
Male	92.3	91.6
Female	7.7	8.4
Race		
White	46.0	45.3
Black	53.2	53.9
Other	0.7	0.6
Hispanic origin		
Hispanic	19.5	18.3
Non-Hispanic	80.5	81.7
Age at Admission		
Under 18 years	1.2	1.7
18–24 years	29.6	34.0
25–29 years	25.0	23.5
30–34 years	20.0	18.3
35–44 years	18.7	17.0
45–54 years	4.2	4.1
55 years and older	1.3	1.5
Median Age	28	27
Education		
8th grade or less	16.9%	16.1%
9th to 11th grade	45.6	45.5
High school graduate	29.2	29.6
Some college	8.0	8.4
Other	0.4	0.4
Median education	11th grade	11th grade

Source: U.S. Department of Justice. *National Corrections Reporting Program, 1990.* Washington, DC: U.S. Department of Justice, NCJ-141879, 1993:9.

125 months or about 10 years, while only 48 percent of this time will actually be served. Table 7.7 is a detailed breakdown of average maximum sentence lengths imposed in state and federal courts. Table 7.8 shows the number of prisoners under state and federal jurisdiction for year-ends 1994 and 1995 (Gilliard and Beck, 1996:3).

It is interesting to note that when average federal sentence lengths are compared with average state prison lengths, federal prison lengths are generally *shorter.* However, federal prisoners serve substantially *greater* portions of their sentences compared with state prisoners. This is partially due to the new federal sentencing guidelines that were implemented in 1987. Federal prisoners are limited in the amount of good-time credit they may accumulate per year. They may accrue up to 54 days of good-time credit annually. Further, the 1994 Crime Bill mandated even higher standards, so that in most cases, federal prisoners are required to serve at least

TABLE 7.4 Felony Convictions and Sentences to Probation and Nonprobation in State Courts by Offense, United States, 1992[a]

Most Serious Conviction Offense	1992 Felony Convictions		Percent of Felony Convictions by: Sentence Type Within Offense			Offense Within Sentence Type		
	Total	Probation	Total	Probation	No Probation	Total	Probation	No Probation
All offenses	893,630	493,853	100%	55%	45%	100%	100%	100%
Violent offenses	165,099	69,835	100	42	58	19	14	24
Murder[b]	12,548	1,568	100	13	88	1	(c)	3
Rape	21,655	8,574	100	40	60	2	2	3
Robbery	51,878	145,335	100	28	72	6	3	9
Aggravated assault	58,969	32,783	100	56	44	7	7	7
Other violent[d]	20,049	12,375	100	62	38	2	3	2
Property offenses	297,494	170,043	100	57	43	33	35	32
Burglary	114,630	55,807	100	49	51	13	11	15
Larceny[e]	119,000	70,742	100	60	41	13	14	12
Fraud[f]	63,864	43,855	100	69	31	7	9	5
Drug offenses	280,232	162,603	100	58	42	31	33	29
Possession	109,426	68,709	100	63	37	12	14	10
Trafficking	170,806	93,894	100	55	45	19	19	19
Weapons offenses	26,422	14,663	100	56	45	3	3	3
Other offenses[g]	124,383	76,350	100	62	39	14	16	12

Note: Persons are counted as probation cases so long as their sentences included probation and without regard to whether a term of incarceration was also included. Data on sentence type and conviction offense were available for 892,611 cases of the estimated total of 893,630 convicted felons.

[a] Detail may not sum to total because of rounding.
[b] Includes nonnegligent manslaughter.
[c] Less than 0.5 percent.
[d] Includes offenses such as negligent manslaughter, sexual assault, and kidnapping.
[e] Includes motor vehicle theft.
[f] Includes forgery and embezzlement.
[g] Composed of nonviolent offenses such as receiving stolen property and driving while intoxicated.

Source: U.S. Department of Justice, Bureau of Justice Statistics, *State Court Sentencing of Convicted Felons, 1992,* NCJ-152696 (Washington, DC: U.S. Department of Justice, 1996), p. 30. In Maguire and Pastore (1996:508).

TABLE 7.5 Race of Felons Sentenced to Probation or Nonprobation in State Courts by Offense, United States, 1992[a]

Most Serious Conviction Offense	Percent of Probation Sentences				Percent of Nonprobation Sentences			
	All	White	Black	Other	All	White	Black	Other
All offenses	100%	57%	41%	1%	100%	47%	53%	1%
Violent offenses	100	55	42	3	100	44	55	1
Murder[b]	100	46	53	2	100	40	59	1
Rape	100	70	22	8	100	63	35	1
Robbery	100	39	61	1	100	33	66	1
Aggravated assault	100	55	43	2	100	45	54	1
Other violent[c]	100	73	26	2	100	70	29	1
Property offenses	100	62	36	1	100	54	45	1
Burglary	100	65	33	2	100	55	44	1
Larceny[d]	100	62	37	2	100	52	48	1
Fraud[e]	100	59	41	1	100	56	44	(f)
Drug offenses	100	50	49	1	100	37	63	(f)
Possession	100	50	49	1	100	37	63	(f)
Trafficking	100	51	49	1	100	37	63	(f)
Weapons offenses	100	44	55	1	100	33	66	1
Other offenses[g]	100	68	30	2	100	60	39	1

[a] Detail may not sum to total because of rounding.
[b] Includes nonnegligent manslaughter.
[c] Includes offenses such as negligent manslaughter, sexual assault, and kidnapping.
[d] Includes motor vehicle theft.
[e] Includes forgery and embezzlement.
[f] Less than 0.5 percent.
[g] Composed of nonviolent offenses such as receiving stolen property and driving while intoxicated.

Source: U.S. Department of Justice, Bureau of Justice Statistics, *State Court Sentencing of Convicted Felons, 1992,* NCJ-152696 (Washington, DC: U.S. Department of Justice, 1996), p. 37. In Maguire and Pastore (1996:508).

85 percent of their sentences before their early release can be granted. The good-time credit federal prisoners receive amounts to about 15 percent of their annual sentence lengths (54 days/365 days = 14.8 percent). This explains the 85 percent figure when calculating how much time federal inmates must serve before they are released.

TYPES OF PRISONS AND THEIR FUNCTIONS

There is much diversity among prisoners in state and federal institutions. Differences among them include the *nature* and *seriousness* of their conviction offenses, age, and psychological or medical problems. In order to cope more effectively with meeting the needs of such diverse offenders, prisons have established different confinement facilities and levels of custody, depending upon how each prisoner is classified. **Classification** is the process of separating and confining prisoners according to various criteria,

TABLE 7.6 Average Sentence Length and Estimated Time to Be Served in State and Federal Prison by Offense, United States, 1992 (in months)

Most Serious Conviction Offense	Average Prison Sentences Imposed in 1992[a]			Percent of Sentence Served by Prisoners Released in 1992[a,b]			Estimated Time to Be Served[c]		
	Total	State	Federal	Total	State	Federal	Total	State	Federal
All offenses	79	79	79	45%	43%	76%	36	34	60
Violent offenses	125	125	100	49	48	70	61	60	70
Murder/manslaughter[d]	250	251	153	48	48	70	120	120	107
Rape	163	164	57	56	56	72	91	91	41
Robbery	116	117	99	47	46	69	55	54	68
Aggravated assault	87	87	84	48	48	69	41	41	58
Other violent[e]	54	53	101	47	47	76	26	25	77
Property offenses	66	67	41	43	42	77	28	28	32
Burglary	76	76	63	41	41	80	31	31	50
Larceny[f]	36	36	35	45	45	77	16	16	27
Motor vehicle theft	66	67	29	46	45	73	30	30	21
Other theft	50	50	38	43	43	79	21	21	30
Fraud/forgery[g]	66	69	36	42	38	77	26	26	28
Fraud[g]	68	76	36	48	38[h]	77	28	29	28
Forgery	66	66	35	39	38[h]	74	25	25	26
Drug offenses	70	67	92	45	44	76	31	27	70
Possession	55	55	60	40	40	75	22	22	45
Trafficking	75	72	92	45	45	76	35	29	70
Weapons offenses	57	55	65	60	60	80	35	30	52
Other offenses[i]	52	53	42	50	50	79	26	25	33

[a] Does not include life or death sentences.
[b] State estimates are derived from National Corrections Reporting Program data on first releases (sentences greater than 1 year) from state prisons in 1992. In calculating state estimates, allowance was made for jail time credited by the judge for time served prior to sentencing but no allowance could be made for postsentencing time served in jail awaiting transfer to state prison. Federal estimates are from Federal Justice Statistics Program data on first release (sentences greater than 1 year) from federal prisons in 1992.
[c] Calculated by multiplying sentence length by percent of time served.
[d] Does not include negligent manslaughter.
[e] Includes offenses such as negligent manslaughter, sexual assault, and kidnapping.
[f] Includes motor vehicle theft.
[g] Includes embezzlement.
[h] The 38 percent for the combined category "forgery/fraud/embezzlement" was the basis for this estimate.
[i] Composed of nonviolent offenses such as receiving stolen property and immigration offenses.

Source: U.S. Department of Justice, Bureau of Justice Statistics, *Felony Sentences in the United States, 1992,* Bulletin NCJ-153257 (Washington, DC: U.S. Department of Justice, 1996), p. 9. In Maguire and Pastore (1996:507).

including offense seriousness, prior record, and potential for disciplinary problems.

All prisons in the United States today have classification schemes of one type or another for differentiating among prisoners and assigning them to particular accommodations (Austin and Chan, 1989). The use of such schemes has varying utility depending on the purpose for the initial classification, such as identifying those likely to engage in assaultive or aggressive disciplinary infractions (Van Voorhis, 1993). But regardless of the type

TABLE 7.7 Average Maximum Length of Felony Sentences Imposed by State and Federal Courts by Offense, United States, 1992 (in months)

Most Serious Conviction Offense	Average Maximum Sentence Length for Felons Sentenced to:			
	Incarceration			
	Total	Prison	Jail	Straight Probation
Violent offenses				
Murder/manslaughter[a]				
State and federal	237	250	10	77
State	238	251	10	78
Federal	142	153	7	65
Rape				
State and federal	129	163	8	70
State	130	164	8	71
Federal	41	57	7	38
Robbery				
State and federal	101	116	11	62
State	101	117	11	62
Federal	97	99	8	55
Aggravated assault				
State and federal	56	87	7	45
State	56	87	7	45
Federal	78	84	7	40
Other violent[b]				
State and federal	33	54	6	42
State	32	53	6	42
Federal	75	101	8	41
Property offenses				
Burglary				
State and federal	56	76	7	55
State	56	76	7	55
Federal	55	63	7	34
Larceny[c]				
State and federal	18	36	5	37
State	18	36	4	36
Federal	20	35	7	39
Motor vehicle theft				
State and federal	40	66	6	54
State	40	67	6	54
Federal	20	29	8	51
Other theft				
State and federal	32	50	7	41
State	32	50	7	41
Federal	20	38	7	38
Fraud/forgery[d]				
State and federal	24	66	4	36
State	24	69	3	36
Federal	21	36	8	38

TABLE 7.7 (continued)

Most Serious Conviction Offense	Average Maximum Sentence Length for Felons Sentenced to:			
	Incarceration			
	Total	Prison	Jail	Straight Probation
Fraud[d]				
State and federal	37	68	5	43
State	42	76	5	44
Federal	21	36	5	38
Forgery				
State and federal	46	66	7	45
State	46	66	7	45
Federal	19	35	7	36
Drug offenses				
Possession				
State and federal	32	55	4	45
State	32	55	4	45
Federal	38	60	5	29
Trafficking				
State and federal	54	75	8	51
State	50	72	8	51
Federal	84	92	8	43

[a] Does not include negligent manslaughter.
[b] Includes offenses such as negligent manslaughter, sexual assault, and kidnapping.
[c] Includes motor vehicle theft.
[d] Includes embezzlement.

Source: U.S. Department of Justice, Bureau of Justice Statistics, *Felony Sentences in the United States,* 1992, Bulletin NCJ-153257 (Washington, DC: U.S. Department of Justice, May 1996), p. 8. Table adapted by SOURCEBOOK staff. In Maguire and Pastore (1996:506).

of classification scheme employed by corrections officials in screening their inmates, prisoners are eventually channeled into one of several fixed custody levels. These are minimum-, medium-, and maximum-security.

Minimum-Security Prisons

Minimum-security prisons are facilities designed to house low-risk, nonviolent first-offenders. These institutions are also established to accommodate those serving short-term sentences. Sometimes, minimum-security institutions function as intermediate housing for those prisoners leaving more heavily monitored facilities on their way toward parole or eventual freedom. The Federal Bureau of Prisons operates many minimum-security facilities, including several prison camps at Eglin Air Force Base, Florida, and the Federal Detention Center in Oakdale, Louisiana. Minimum-security state facilities include a subsidiary of the New Jersey State Prison

Table 7.8 Prisoners Under the Jurisdiction of State or Federal Correctional Authorities, by Region and Jurisdiction, Year-End 1994 and 1995

	Total			Sentenced to More Than 1 Year			
Region and Jurisdiction	Advance 1995	Final 1994	Percentage Change, 1994–1995	Advance 1995	Final 1994	Percentage Change, 1994–1995	Incarceration Rate, 1995[a]
U.S. total	1,127,132	1,055,073	6.8%	1,080,728	1,017,059	6.3%	409
Federal	100,250	95,034	5.5%	83,663	79,795	4.8%	32
State	1,026,882	960,039	7.0	997,065	937,264	6.4	378
Northeast	161,815	153,072	5.7%	155,071	146,834	5.6%	301
Connecticut[b]	14,801	14,380	2.9	10,418	10,500	−.8	318
Maine	1,447	1,474	−1.8	1,377	1,401	−1.7	111
Massachusetts[c]	11,619	11,293	2.9	10,633	10,401	2.2	175
New Hampshire	2,014	2,021	−.3	2,014	2,021	−.3	174
New Jersey	27,066	24,632	9.9	27,066	24,632	9.9	340
New York	68,484	66,750	2.6	68,484	66,750	2.6	378
Pennsylvania	32,410	28,302	14.5	32,404	28,294	14.5	268
Rhode Island[b]	2,902	2,919	−.6	1,833	1,854	−1.1	186
Vermont[b,d]	1,072	1,301	—	842	981	—	143
Midwest	193,325	184,508	4.8%	192,252	183,830	4.6%	310
Illinois[e]	37,658	36,531	3.1	37,658	36,531	3.1	317
Indiana	16,125	15,014	7.4	16,046	14,916	7.6	275
Iowa[e]	5,906	5,437	8.6	5,906	5,437	8.6	207
Kansas	7,054	6,371	10.7	7,054	6,371	10.7	274
Michigan[e]	41,112	40,631	1.2	41,112	40,631	1.2	429
Minnesota	4,863	4,575	6.3	4,863	4,575	6.3	105
Missouri	19,139	17,898	6.9	19,139	17,898	6.9	358
Nebraska	3,113	2,711	14.8	3,045	2,667	14.2	185
North Dakota	608	536	13.4	544	501	8.6	85
Ohio	44,677	43,074	3.7	44,677	43,074	3.7	400
South Dakota	1,871	1,708	9.5	1,871	1,708	9.5	256
Wisconsin	11,199	10,022	11.7	10,337	9,521	8.6	201
South	455,143	422,455	7.7%	442,471	415,354	6.5%	478
Alabama	20,718	19,573	5.8	20,130	19,074	5.5	471
Arkansas	9,401	8,643	8.8	9,011	8,517	5.8	360
Delaware[b]	4,802	4,466	7.5	2,980	2,844	4.8	413
Dist. of Col.[b]	9,800	10,949	−10.5	9,042	10,085	−10.3	1,650
Florida[e]	63,879	57,168	11.7	63,866	57,157	11.7	447
Georgia[e]	34,266	33,425	2.5	34,160	32,523	5.0	470
Kentucky	12,060	11,066	9.0	12,060	11,066	9.0	311
Louisiana	25,427	24,063	5.7	24,755	24,063	2.9	568
Maryland	21,453	20,998	2.2	20,450	19,854	3.0	404
Mississippi[c]	13,008	10,930	19.0	12,575	10,606	18.6	464
North Carolina	29,374	23,648	24.2	27,716	23,046	20.3	382
Oklahoma	18,151	16,631	9.1	18,151	16,631	9.1	552
South Carolina	19,611	18,999	3.2	19,015	18,168	4.7	515
Tennessee[c]	15,206	14,401	5.6	15,206	14,401	5.6	287
Texas	127,766	118,195	8.1	123,349	118,195	4.4	653
Virginia	27,710	26,968	2.8	27,523	26,792	2.7	414
West Virginia	2,511	2,332	7.7	2,482	2,332	6.4	136

Table 7.8 (continued)

Region and Jurisdiction	Total			Sentenced to More Than 1 Year			
	Advance 1995	Final 1994	Percentage Change, 1994–1995	Advance 1995	Final 1994	Percentage Change, 1994–1995	Incarceration Rate, 1995[a]
West	216,599	200,004	8.3%	207,271	191,246	8.4%	357
Alaska[b]	3,505	3,292	6.5	2,045	1,934	5.7	339
Arizona[e]	21,341	19,746	8.1	20,291	19,005	6.8	473
California	135,646	125,605	—	131,745	121,084	—	416
Colorado	11,063	10,717	3.2	11,063	10,717	3.2	292
Hawaii[b]	3,560	3,333	6.8	2,590	2,392	8.3	217
Idaho	3,328	2,811	18.4	3,328	2,811	18.4	283
Montana	1,788	1,764	1.4	1,788	1,764	1.4	204
Nevada	7,826	6,993	11.9	7,545	6,993	7.9	482
New Mexico	4,195	3,712	13.0	3,925	3,533	11.1	231
Oregon	7,886	6,936	13.7	6,515	5,935	9.8	206
Utah	3,448	3,045	13.2	3,423	3,028	13.0	173
Washington	11,608	10,833	7.2	11,608	10,833	7.2	212
Wyoming	1,405	1,217	15.4	1,405	1,217	15.4	291

Note: The advance count of prisoners is conducted in January and may be revised. Prisoner counts for 1994 may differ from those reported in previous publications.
—Not calculated because of a change in reporting methods.
[a] The number of prisoners with a sentence of more than 1 year per 100,000 in the resident population.
[b] Prison and jails form one integrated system. All NPS data include jail and prison populations.
[c] Reference date is not December 31. See *NPS jurisdiction notes.*
[d] Since December 31, 1995, only custody counts were reported.
[e] Population figures are based on custody counts.
Source: Gilliard and Beck (1996:3).

at Jones Farm in West Trenton, the Medfield, Massachusetts, Prison Project where inmates work in hospital wards in various capacities, and the Chillicothe, Missouri, Correctional Center for female offenders. In 1995 about 21 percent of all U.S. prison space was for minimum-security classified prisoners (Camp and Camp, 1995a:35).

Minimum-security housing is often of a dormitory-like quality, with grounds and physical plant features resembling a university campus rather than a prison. Those assigned to minimum-security facilities are trusted to comply with whatever rules are in force. States such as California have operated honor farms where prisoners are literally placed on their honor not to attempt escape from what are lightly monitored or unmonitored facilities. Often, correctional officers are present primarily to prevent the public from entering the grounds indiscriminately.

Because of the greater trust administrators place in inmates in minimum-security institutions, these sites are believed to be most likely to promote greater self-confidence and self-esteem among prisoners. The rehabilitative potential of minimum-security inmates is high, whereas those in more secure detention facilities are considered more hard-core offenders and less likely to reform. The emphasis is upon prisoner reintegration into

BOX 7.1 How Easy Is It for Convicted Murderers to Walk Away from Their Prisons?

The Case of Dennis Houle

Dennis Houle, a Native American, was convicted of murder in the shooting death of 16-year-old Sherri Collins in 1980 in Bismarck, North Dakota. Houle was sentenced to 44 years in prison. He was scheduled for parole in January 1998. However, in June 1996, Houle was transferred to a minimum-security prison from the North Dakota State Penitentiary. The minimum-security prison had no fences. It was intended as a reintegrative facility, enabling prisoners to have greater freedom in an effort to make the transition eventually to community living. However, Houle was not content to wait another two years. He simply walked away from the prison compound and disappeared into the Bismarck landscape.

An intensive manhunt was conducted for several days, yielding no results. Eventually, of his own accord, Houle turned himself in, explaining that he had a few things to attend to and never intended to hurt anyone. Houle, at 5'6" and 150 pounds, is not particularly intimidating. However, he does have a history of former escape attempts. In July 1982, he escaped from the prison but was apprehended within minutes of leaving prison property. Warden Tim Schuelzle defended his decision to put Dennis Houle in the minimum-security prison with no fences. Schuelzle said, "He was a problem prisoner his first three or four years here, but I would say over the last 10 years, he's been a model prisoner. I consider him to be someone who had his attitude under control." Despite the fact that Houle eventually turned himself in without incident, the warden considered him dangerous while out of prison. "If you asked me a week ago I would have said no. But knowing that he has this time hanging over his head could make him more dangerous than what you would expect." A conviction for escape from prison is punishable by an additional five years.

Should Houle be made to serve the remainder of his 44-year sentence? Was the warden justified in transferring Houle to minimum-security status, knowing that Houle would eventually be released anyway? What punishment do you think Houle deserves for violating the trust vested in him by prison authorities?

Source: Adapted from Associated Press, "Search Continues for Fugitive." *Minot (N.D.) Daily News,* June 8, 1996:A3.

society. Usually, a wider variety of programs is available to inmates of minimum-security facilities, and there are generally fewer restrictions associated with familial visits. Minimum-security prison space is also the least expensive compared with the costs involved with higher security levels such as medium- or maximum-security space (U.S. General Accounting Office, 1991b).

Medium-Security Prisons

About 27 percent of all state and federal prisons in the United States are medium-security prisons (Camp and Camp, 1995a:35). The Federal Bureau of Prisons uses a six-level scale ranging from Level 1 to Level 6, with Level 1 being a minimum-security facility such as the Federal Prison Camp in Big Spring, Texas, and a Level 6 being a maximum-security facility such as the Marion, Illinois, Penitentiary. Many state prisons or penitentiaries use similar classification schemes for prisoner accommodations. **Medium-security prisons** are really a catch-all, because often both extremely violent and nonviolent offenders are placed in common living areas. Visitation privileges are tighter than in minimum-security institutions and privileges, freedom of movement, and access to various educational, vocational, and/or therapeutic programs are more restricted. However, both state and federal medium-security facilities may offer opportunities for work release, furloughs, and other programs that increase inmates' freedom of movement.

Maximum-Security Prisons

Approximately 19 percent of all U.S. prisons are maximum-security prisons (Camp and Camp, 1995a:35). Ordinarily, those sentenced to serve time in maximum-security facilities are considered among the most dangerous, high-risk offenders. Those with prior records of escape and who are violent crime recidivists often are sentenced to maximum-security institutions. **Maximum-security prisons** are characterized by many stringent rules and restrictions, and inmates are isolated from one another for long periods in single-cell accommodations (Farmer, 1994). Closed-circuit television monitors often permit correctional officers to observe prisoners in their cells or in work areas which are limited. Visitation privileges are minimal. Frequently, these institutions are strictly custodial and make little or no effort to rehabilitate inmates.

One of the most notorious maximum-security penitentiaries ever constructed was the federal facility at Alcatraz in San Francisco Bay. This facility was constructed in 1934; but because of poor sanitation and the great expense of prisoner maintenance, the facility was closed in 1963. During that 29-year span, Alcatraz accommodated over 1,500 prisoners, including Al Capone and Robert "Birdman" Stroud. Escape from Alcatraz was nearly impossible, and of the eight prisoners who attempted escape during that period, only three remain unaccounted for. Maximum-security institutions are typically constructed to discourage escape attempts. Prisoner isolation and control are stressed, and close monitoring by guards either directly or through closed-circuit television reduces prisoner misconduct significantly. There are exceptions, however. In September 1971, the Attica, New York, Correctional Facility became the scene of a prison riot. In the next four days, state police and correctional officers stormed the facility, killing 29 prisoners and 10 officer-hostages. Following the riot, official investigations were conducted to determine why the riot had occurred.

Attica was constructed in 1931, and few physical plant improvements had been made during the next 40 years. Thus, Attica had unhealthy and otherwise poor living conditions. Many prisoner rights were regularly violated by correctional officers. Medical care was inadequate. Prisoners were confined to their cells from 14 to 16 hours a day, and many inmates felt degraded and humiliated with poor food and meager clothing. Less powerful prisoners were customarily assaulted by more powerful inmates. Sodomy was common, and officials were either unable or reluctant to do anything about it.

Attica was located in a rural area of New York. Rural sites for prisons throughout the United States have been common, since many citizens are reluctant to have prisons in their backyards or nearby. Thus, the labor pool from which correctional officers are selected does not contain large numbers of highly educated and disciplined employees. In fact, the poor quality of correctional officers at Attica was cited by an investigative commission later as a contributing factor to subsequent rioting. Correctional officers were inclined to solve disagreements with prisoners by clubbing them about the head regularly rather than talking out problems. Their "billy clubs" or nightsticks were called "nigger sticks," particularly since the all-white prison staff faced a predominantly black-Hispanic inmate contingent (Badillo and Haynes, 1972:26).

Over the years, inmate gangs had formed in Attica. The Black Muslims, La Nuestra Familia, and the Aryan Brotherhood were only a few of the many racially and ethnically related gangs that formed largely for self-protection and prisoner domination, although the Attica inmate population was largely black and Hispanic. Recreational facilities were almost nonexistent, and rehabilitation programs were severely limited or did not exist. Prisoners were permitted to shower once a week. Civil rights issues were prevalent at Attica. For example, Black Muslims, black inmates who adopted the religious philosophy of Islam, were opposed to prison diets that consisted largely of pork. Furthermore, requests for visits by special clergy for Islam and other religions were refused by prison administration. Despite lawsuits by prisoners alleging civil rights violations and other problems, the courts were reluctant to interfere in the affairs of prison operations. In the hot summer months of 1971, several inmate leaders encouraged other inmates to demonstrate peacefully to protest these deplorable conditions. Officials attempted to break up such demonstrations by transferring inmate leaders to other prisons. But the demonstrations continued. Furthermore, several gangs of different ethnic and racial backgrounds pooled their resources and joined forces to protest what they regarded as mutually shared problems.

In early September, confrontations between inmates and correctional officers became more frequent and violent. On September 9, a general riot occurred in the breakfast hall of the facility, and several correctional offi-

BOX 7.2 Inmates Killed in Prison Gang Riots

Black and Hispanic Gangs Clash in Deadly Riot

It happened at the California State Prison in Sacramento. On Friday, September 27, 1996, at least 200 inmates were in an exercise yard when a fight erupted. The maximum-security prison yard became a battleground that lasted for at least 30 minutes. One inmate was killed and 30 others injured when correctional officers were forced to fire shots at the rioting inmates.

Governor Pete Wilson of California was informed of the riot and investigated. He said that the riot was primarily between 100 black and Hispanic inmates. "The gangs were racially organized and this was a fight between the African-American gang and the Latino gang," said Wilson. The dead prisoner was identified as Victor Hugo Flores, 22, who had been convicted of voluntary manslaughter and attempted second-degree murder and was serving an 18-year sentence. Governor Wilson said that prison policy and rules call for guards to fire on inmates only after all other efforts to stop a riot have failed. Numerous handmade weapons were confiscated from inmates following the riot.

What kinds of security measures can be taken to prevent inmates from acquiring dangerous weapons? Do you think that prison overcrowding is a significant factor in inmate rioting? How can inmates be allowed to exercise without fearing incidents such as riots?

Source: Adapted from Associated Press, "Inmate Killed, 13 Prisoners Injured in Clash Between Prison Gangs." *Minot (N.D.) Daily News,* September 29, 1996:A2.

cers were taken hostage. Several of the guard-hostages were beaten savagely by prisoners, and one officer died of his wounds. Prisoners attempted to call attention to their plight by demanding visits with media representatives, lawyers, and other outside observers. Negotiations progressed cautiously as the new commissioner of the Department of Correctional Services, Russell G. Oswald, attempted to meet inmate demands for prison improvements. Those inmates who had rioted also requested amnesty from prosecution, largely because of the officer's death. State officials were not prepared to excuse inmates from this liability.

A poorly organized force of heavily armed state troopers and corrections officers stormed the prison, and within a few minutes, they had regained control of the facility. In the process, the other inmate and hostage deaths noted earlier occurred. Despite these deaths, the nation's attention was focused on Attica as well as on other similar prisons. Would other Atticas occur in the future if similar conditions existed in other prison settings? Many state prisons and correctional facilities implemented vast improvements in their physical plants and made other changes during the next few years to reduce the chances of prisoner rioting. Numerous investigations were conducted by departments of correction in various states during the

1970s. One result of these investigations was that prison administration, the parole concept, and prisons as rehabilitative institutions were widely criticized. It was during the 1970s that major changes occurred, not only in prison organization and administration, but in other areas of the criminal justice system as well. Extensive reforms in criminal processing, sentencing, and inmate treatment were instigated by every state jurisdiction.

Despite the improvements made by various departments of correction among states and the federal government, inmate rioting was not eliminated entirely. Riots in other state and federal prisons have occurred subsequently, some paralleling the terror of Attica. Not all of these riots have been triggered by poor prison conditions, bad food, and civil rights violations, however. Revenge against other inmates who were believed to be government informants and "rats" (those who squeal on others or implicate them in crimes in exchange for leniency for themselves) seemed to be largely responsible for the rioting in the New Mexico penitentiary. The Penitentiary of New Mexico in Santa Fe was overtaken by inmates in February 1980. Inmates formed death squads and systematically killed other prisoners suspected of being informants. One prisoner was beheaded, while others had their legs or arms cut off. Some were even charred beyond recognition with blowtorches. When the rioting was subdued, $80 million in damages to the prison had been sustained, 33 inmates were killed, and nearly 100 others required hospitalization.

In November 1987, the Federal Penitentiary in Atlanta and the federal detention center in Oakdale, Louisiana, were scenes of rioting by large numbers of Cuban inmates. Many Cuban exiles had entered the United States illegally to escape certain death at the hands of Fidel Castro because of their political opposition to his policies. The U.S. government took numerous Cuban refugees into custody. Over 2,400 of them were confined in large buildings on the grounds of the Atlanta penitentiary and the Oakdale facility. Rumors abounded among these Cuban exiles that they were going to be deported back to Cuba. Desperate, fearful, and feeling that they had nothing to lose, Cuban refugees in Oakdale took 28 hostages, while 94 hostages were taken by Cubans in Atlanta.

Although these riots were less costly in terms of lives lost (one inmate was killed in early gunfire), buildings were set aflame and considerable federal property was destroyed. These riots were politically motivated because of the belief by Cuban exiles that they were going to be deported to Cuba. Over 2,400 inmates took part in the rioting. The rioting ended after 11 days and much destruction of government property, after the government agreed not to deport these Cuban refugees back to Cuba. This had been the sole issue. The prisoners contended that they would rather remain in the United States, even behind bars, than face Castro's retaliation. The U.S. government did not agree to provide blanket amnesty for all Cuban refugees, however. But then-Attorney General Edwin Meese agreed to have each case reviewed on its own merits. If government investigations disclosed nothing more than petty crimes or clean prison records, Cuban exiles would not be deported (*Newsweek,* 1987:38).

Rioting in U.S. prisons appears to be increasing despite the newly implemented safeguards and policy changes made by prison administrators to minimize inmate concerns and complaints. Without including either California or Florida, for instance, the rest of the nation's prisons reported 277 riots in 1994, a 49 percent increase in rioting over 1993 (*Corrections Compendium,* 1996b:9). There were 6,860 staff assaults by inmates in 1994 in addition to 62 inmate-on-inmate homicides (*Corrections Compendium,* 1996b:11–12). There were 148 inmate suicides during 1994. Finally, there were nearly 2,300 prisoner escapes from state or federal facilities.

During inmate rioting, staff assaults are commonplace. Jon Taylor reports, for instance, that while he was working in a maximum-security prison, he "survived the crucible of the maximum-security keeps." According to Taylor, "I have been threatened innumerable times, punched with fists, slashed with a razor, bashed with a pipe, and poked with a shiv by other inmates, not to mention being inadvertently shot by a tower guard. Altogether, there are a half dozen scars on my body, with an uncountable number upon my psyche" (Taylor, 1996:1).

The Maxi-Maxi Prison

For the "baddest of the bad," there are prisons such as the Marion, Illinois, Federal Penitentiary. Although this facility is one of the newer federal penitentiaries, constructed in 1963, and is designed to house only 574 inmates, those incarcerated at Marion are considered the very worst prisoners in the system. Those sentenced to Marion are the most violence-prone, are inclined to escape whenever the opportunity arises, and are categorically dangerous. Marion is considered a **maxi-maxi prison,** with restrictions so severe and pervasive as to be unparalleled by any other prison in the United States. It, too, was the scene of a major prison riot in October 1983. Two correctional officers were killed by prisoners in the Control Unit (Mauer, 1985). When the riot was contained, Marion was subject to a general "lockdown," during which every prisoner was subject to solitary confinement and severe restrictions. Maxi-maxi prisons represent about 5 percent of all U.S. penitentiaries (Camp and Camp, 1995a:35).

There is thus a wide range of prisons from those minimum-security, honor farm-type facilities to those close-custody, maxi-maxi penitentiaries like Marion. Depending upon the location of the facility, the composition of prisoners varies greatly as well. In many prisons, gangs form according to particular racial or ethnic patterns. Membership in a gang can mean privileges for individual members, and likewise, nonmembership can expose prisoners to physical and sexual harassment or injury. In the Southwest, for example, where there are large numbers of Hispanic offenders, gangs comprised of different inmates from several ethnic backgrounds have formed within prisons to create rivalries that often lead to violence.

Less violence is associated with minimum-security facilities, although it is not entirely absent (Useem et al., 1995). This is due, in large part, to the fact that inmates are less dangerous and pose the least risk to the safety of correctional officers or other inmates. Each prison setting with its peculiar inmate profile means that wardens or superintendents will be presented with different kinds of problems to resolve (Scully, 1990). Few categorical statements about people management behind prison bars can be made that are applicable to all settings because of the diversity of prison culture.

New Prison Construction: A Growing Medium-Security Trend. Of interest is the fact that in 1994, 49 new institutions were opened in 17 U.S. agencies (Camp and Camp, 1995a:38). A total of 41,227 beds were added in 1994 as a result of this new construction. About 2,514 (6 percent) were maximum security; 30,286 (73 percent) were medium security; and 7,061 (17 percent) were minimum security (Camp and Camp, 1995a:38-39). If this trend in new prison construction continues, the dominant prisoner classification will be medium-security custody. Furthermore, about 50 percent of all renovations and building additions of existing prison space was allocated to medium-security bed space (Camp and Camp, 1995a:39). In 1995, there were 108 new prisons under construction in 24 different jurisdictions. About 124,000 beds were contemplated as a part of this construction, with approximately 58,400 (47 percent) allocated to medium-security custody levels (Camp and Camp, 1995a:40–41).

INMATE CLASSIFICATION SYSTEMS

Religious movements are credited with establishing early prisoner classification systems in the eighteenth century (American Correctional Association, 1983:194). The Walnut Street Jail in 1790 in Philadelphia attempted to segregate prisoners according to age, gender, and offense seriousness. Subsequent efforts were made by penal authorities to classify and separate inmates according to various criteria in many state and federal prison facilities. Adequate classification schemes for prisoners have yet to be devised (Hutton and Miner, 1995; Bohn, Carbonell, and Megargee, 1995). Classification schemes are based largely on psychological, behavioral, and sociodemographic criteria. The use of psychological characteristics as predictors of risk or dangerousness and subsequent custody assignments for prisoners was stimulated by research during the period 1910 to 1920 (American Correctional Association, 1983:196).

No single scheme for classifying offenders is foolproof, although several instruments have been used more frequently than others for inmate classification and placement. The **Megargee Inmate Typology** presumes to measure "inmate adjustment to prison life" (Megargee and Carbonell, 1985). Several items were selected from the Minnesota Multiphasic Personality Inventory (MMPI), a psychological assessment device, to define ten prisoner types and to predict an inmate's inclination to violate prison rules or to act aggressively against others. Basically a psychological tool, the Megargee Inmate Typology has been adopted by various state prison systems for purposes of classifying prisoners into different custody levels. The predictive utility of this instrument is questionable, however. One problem Megargee himself detected was that prisoner classification types based on his index scores change drastically during a one-year period. For some experts, this finding has caused serious questions about the reliability of Megargee's scale. For other experts, however, inmate score changes on Megargee's scale indicate behavioral change, possibly improvement. Thus, *reclassifications* are conducted of most prison inmates at regular intervals to chart their behavioral progress.

Besides Megargee, other professionals have devised useful inmate classification criteria that have not been particularly fruitful (Gottfredson and Gottfredson, 1988; Gottfredson and Tonry, 1987). For example, Goetting and Howsen (1986) found that inmate misconduct is correlated with being young, black, male, having a relatively high number of prior convictions, having been unemployed prior to incarceration, and having been imprisoned for a long period. But descriptions of those who engage in prison misconduct are difficult to apply in screening stages to decide the level of custody inmates should be assigned. Should all young, unemployed, black males with prior records and long sentences be placed in a high level of custody? Undoubtedly, classifications made according to such criteria would be discriminatory and violative of the equal protection clause of the Fourteenth Amendment.

All prisons in the United States have classifications that differentiate between prisoners and cause them to be placed under various levels of custody or security. One of the main purposes for the initial inmate classification is to identify those likely to engage in assaultive or aggressive disciplinary infractions (Wright, 1986a, 1986b). Prisoners are eventually channeled into one of several fixed custody levels known as (1) minimum, (2) medium, and (3) maximum security. These security levels are similar to the types of prisons described earlier in this chapter.

Some experts challenge inmate classification schemes on moral and legal grounds (Gottfredson and Tonry, 1987; von Hirsch, 1985). How inmates are initially classified and subsequently accommodated while in prison may influence directly or indirectly their parole chances (Gottfredson and Gottfredson, 1988). An inmate classified as "maximum-security" may not deserve such a classification, which implies that the inmate is considered dangerous. Furthermore, inmate opportunities for personal development and rehabilitation are adversely influenced by such classifications. On the other hand, those inmates classified as minimum-security have access to a wider variety of prison benefits and programs. They are not monitored as closely and are not considered particularly dangerous. Thus, when these inmates face parole boards, their custody levels may be assets or liabilities. Those prisoners who have been maintained under minimum-security conditions can argue that they have "proven" themselves worthy of release through the trust granted them initially by prison officials. Those inmates maintained under maximum-security conditions likely prejudice parole boards because they have not been granted extensive prison privileges for various reasons.

Because of the instability of present classification instruments, their lack of generalization to prisoners in different jurisdictions, and the lack of instrument validation, serious questions have been raised about the current state of the art in statistical risk prediction (Bohn et al., 1995). Since these risk prediction devices are frequently employed for deciding inmates' levels of custody while incarcerated as well as influencing their parole chances, it seems reasonable that challenges should be made about the quality of these instruments and how they should be used by prison authorities and others.

The controversy over the development and use of inmate classification devices is heightened by those researchers reporting favorable outcomes when such devices are used on selected inmate populations. For instance, the Louisiana Department of Corrections tested two devices designed to predict an inmate's escape risk. Using race, juvenile arrest history, employment history, and selected subscales from the MMPI, researchers found that 54 percent of the escapees and 76 percent of the nonescapees were correctly identified. The report suggested that this escape prediction device could be useful as a screening instrument for evaluating one's escape risk (Shaffer, Bluoin, and Pettigrew, 1985). Other applications of such instrumentation have been fairly successful in predicting mental unit patient adjustment. A study of 57 general population inmates and 64 mental health unit inmates was conducted at the U.S. Medical Center for Federal Prisoners in Springfield, Missouri (Bohn et al., 1995). The classification instrument used was able to differentiate successfully between these two inmate samples. Generally, Bohn, Carbonell, and Megargee found that psychological screenings of new admissions are more useful than attempting to distinguish between those inmates already admitted to the mental health unit. Other experiments with inmates have yielded results consistent with those of Bohn, Carbonell, and Megargee (Hutton and Miner, 1995; Van Voorhis, 1993).

DISTINCTIONS BETWEEN PRISONS AND JAILS

Because prisons are designed to accommodate long-term offenders who usually are convicted of more serious offenses than those housed in jails, several issues are more critical and pressing for prison inmates compared with more short-term jail inmates. But incarceration of any kind has several elements in common. Before examining those issues that are particularly relevant for prisons, it is important to recognize some evident differences between jails and prisons and the types of inmates accommodated by each. While all of the following generalizations have exceptions, most experts would agree they are true:

1. Compared with prisons, jails have a greater diversity of inmates, including witnesses for trials; suspects or detainees; defendants awaiting trial unable to post bail or whose bail was denied; juveniles awaiting transfer to juvenile facilities or detention; those serving short-term sentences for public drunkenness, driving while intoxicated, or city ordinance violations; mentally ill or disturbed persons awaiting hospitalization; and overflow from state and federal prison populations.
2. Compared with prisons, jails usually do not have programs or facilities associated with long-term incarceration such as vocational, technical, or educational courses to be taken by inmates; jail industries; recreation yards; or psychological or social counseling or therapy.
3. Compared with prisons, the quality of jail personnel is lower, with many jail personnel untrained, undertrained, or otherwise less qualified to guard prisoners compared with their counterparts, prison correctional officers.
4. Compared with prisons, jails are not as elaborately divided into maximum-, medium-, or minimum-security areas. Guard towers are not usually found, where armed correctional officers patrol regularly. Jails are ordinarily not surrounded by several perimeters, with barbed wire areas, sound-detection equipment, and other exotic electronic devices.
5. Compared with prisons, jail inmate culture is less pronounced and persistent. There is a high inmate turnover in jails, with the exception of the state and federal convict population.
6. Compared with prisons, the physical plant of jails is poorer, with many jails under court order to improve their physical facilities to comply with minimum health and safety standards.

This list of differences is not exhaustive, and there are also administrative, operational, social, and a host of other features that serve to distinguish prisons from jails. But the major differences occurring in the nature of inmate clientele and length of incarceration mean that certain problem areas seem to have greater relevance for the "average" prison inmate compared with the "average" jail inmate. The issues include (1) prison overcrowding, (2) prison violence and prisoner discipline, (3) prison design and control, and (4) the recruitment and training of correctional personnel.

Functions of Prisons

The functions served by prisons are closely connected with the overall goals of corrections. Broadly stated, correctional goals include deterrence, rehabilitation, societal protection, offender reintegration, just-deserts justice and due process, and retribution or punishment. The following list describes the goals of prisons.

1. *Prisons provide societal protection.* Locking up dangerous offenders or those who are persistent nonviolent offenders means that society will be protected from them for variable time periods. It is not possible at present to lock up all offenders who deserve to be incarcerated. Space limitations are such that we would require at least four or five times the number of existing prisons to incarcerate all convicted felons and misdemeanants. Thus, the criminal justice system attempts to incarcerate those who are most in need of incarceration (Sparks and Bottoms, 1995). Obviously this goal is not realized, since many dangerous offenders are placed on probation annually and many nonviolent offenders are incarcerated. Varying state and federal statutes and prosecutorial practices contribute to sentencing inconsistencies, as well as to peculiar incarceration policies and patterns.

2. *Prisons punish offenders.* Restricting one's freedoms, confining inmates in cells, and obligating them to follow rigid behavioral codes while confined is regarded as punishment for criminal conduct. The fact of incarceration is a punishment compared with the greater freedoms enjoyed by probationers and parolees. Compared with other industrialized nations, the United States has the world's largest incarceration rate (Mauer, 1991). The United States incarcerates 426 persons per 100,000 population, while South Africa incarcerates 333 per 100,000, and the Soviet Union incarcerates 268 per 100,000.

3. *Prisons rehabilitate offenders.* Few criminal justice scholars would agree that prisons are in the prisoner rehabilitation business. There is little support for the view that imprisonment does much of a rehabilitative nature for anyone confined. Nevertheless, many prisons have vocational and educational programs, psychological counselors, and an array of services available to inmates in order that they might improve their skills, education, and self-concept (Wright, 1991). Prisons also have libraries for inmate self-improvement. More often than not, prisons also socialize inmates in adverse ways, so that they might emerge from prisons later as better criminals who have learned ways of avoiding detection when committing future crimes.

Walker (1989) indicates that a majority of inmates who pass through prisons are not rehabilitated in the sense that they will adopt conforming, law-abiding behaviors and offend no more. Prisonization occurs, often through inmate gang socialization (Hunt et al., 1993). Gangs are important components of prison culture, regardless of what officials think about them. Gangs form, in part, for mutual protection from members of other gangs (Stevens, 1994). In this prisonization milieu, inmates cannot help acquiring attitudes and knowledge from other inmates that will improve their criminal skills. Further, many of the vocational and educational programs offered to inmates are ultimately exploited by them. Participation in these programs can look good on an inmate's record, and parole boards are favorably influenced by such inmate activities. Inmates know this, and thus they often participate in a token fashion in various prison programs for the cosmetic value such participation may have in favorable parole-board decision making.

4. *Prisons reintegrate offenders.* It might be argued that moving offenders from higher security levels, where they are more closely supervised, to lower security levels, where they are less closely supervised, helps them understand that conformity with institutional rules is rewarded. As prisoners near their release dates, they may be permitted unescorted leaves, known as *furloughs* or *work release,* where they may participate in work or educational programs and visit with their families during the week or on weekends. These experiences are considered reintegrative. Most prisons have such programs, but they are presumably aimed at certain offenders who are believed to no longer pose a threat to society. Occasionally, officials wrongly estimate the nondangerousness of certain furloughees and work releasees. In any case, the *intent* of reintegrative prison programs is to provide those wanting such programs the opportunity of having them. At least some inmates derive value from such programs, although some experts believe the costs of operating them are far outweighed by the lack of rehabilitation and reintegration that actually occurs.

PRISON CULTURE: ON JARGON AND INMATE PECKING ORDERS

Descriptions of life behind prison walls are abundant (Hunt et al., 1993). During the last five or six decades, several classics have been written depicting prison conditions, prisoner characteristics, and the general nature of prison culture. One of the first objective and systematic studies of inmate culture occurred in 1934 with the publication of *Sex in Prison* by Joseph Fishman. Fishman, a federal prison inspector and consultant, described inmate culture vividly, indicating that prisoners devised a unique language or argot relevant only to them. While he focused upon the prevalence of homosexuality behind prison walls, his work suggested to others a new and rich source in need of social description. In fact, Fishman used the term *subculture* to connote his observations of these unique social arrangements among prisoners.

The concept of a **subculture** is that a separate, smaller social system exists within the larger social system, where the smaller system contains its own special language, status structure, and rewards and punishments. Violence or an inmate's potential for aggression is a key to understanding the pecking order within any prison (Johnson, 1987:75–76). Access to drugs and other scarce contraband is rewarded and results in higher placement in the prisoner status structure, with some inmates labeled as "hustlers" who work the economic system (Irwin, 1970). To understand inmate behaviors, it is essential that the inmate subculture, wherever it is located, be penetrated, described, and understood.

Six years after Fishman's research, Donald Clemmer wrote the classic, *The Prison Community* (1940), which was based on his description of the Menard, Illinois, Penitentiary inmate subculture while he was a correctional officer. His description of the inmate subculture spanned three years and focused upon almost all aspects of inmate life. Especially noteworthy was his description of how new inmates were introduced into the existing prisoner subculture. Immediately upon the arrival of a new "fish" or inmate, other more seasoned inmates would take him aside and acquaint him with the do's and don'ts of life at Menard. This socialization process, whereby new inmates learned through contact with older inmates what the rules were and who controlled the flow of scarce prisoner goods and contraband as well as certain inmate privileges, was referred to by Clemmer as *prisonization* (Gross, 1995). In reality, Clemmer was referring to socialization (i.e., learning through contact with others) applied to the prison setting. Nevertheless, **prisonization** quickly became a popular reference to the phenomenon whereby new prisoners learned the ropes and became acquainted with the customs among the Menard inmates. Clemmer's work stimulated a plethora of subsequent works in which popular writers and criminologists described life among prisoners.

Perhaps the best-known and precedent-setting study of inmate subculture is Gresham Sykes's work, *The Society of Captives* (1958). Sykes has acknowledged the influence of Clemmer and Fishman in his own writings, although Sykes's work attained greater popularity among criminologists and criminal justice professionals over the years. Three reasons for this were that Sykes's description of the New Jersey State Maximum Security Prison in Trenton (1) contained rich descriptions of inmate jargon such as "merchant" (inmates who barter scarce goods for other favors), "rat" (inmates who squeal or tell authorities about illicit activities of other inmates), and "real man" (inmates who are loyal, generous, and tough in their relations with other inmates); (2) described the prevailing inmate code in detail, which outlined behaviors that either would be rewarded or punished by other inmates; and (3) provided a plausible explanation for the inmate propensity to establish solidarity and conformity among their ranks. While the terms Sykes identified as peculiar to the New Jersey State Maximum Security Prison are now dated and unlikely to be used in contemporary prison settings, his work was a masterpiece of detail to be emulated by subsequent investigators.

Three years after Sykes had written about the society of captives, criminologists Clarence Schrag, John Irwin, and Donald Cressey provided alternative typologies of inmate subcultures and advanced contrasting explanations for their emergence. Schrag, for instance, believed that prisoners developed their dispositions toward inmate life before entering prison. Reflecting his sociological background and interests, Schrag emphasized the importance of family socialization and community integration as shaping and developing attitudes of criminals consistent with the roles they eventually acquired when incarcerated. Schrag described inmates as falling into four distinct adaptive categories: (1) right guys (inmates who adhered to the prevailing inmate code); (2) con-politicians (inmates who had influence with correctional officers, had money, or who had access to scarce goods and were therefore in good bartering positions with other inmates; these inmates also had the skill and wit to manipulate other inmates); (3) outlaws (inmates who relied upon force and physical confrontation to get what they wanted from other inmates); and (4) square Johns (inmates who abided by prison rules, accepted their confinement passively, and who participated in prison vocational and educational programs) (Schrag, 1961).

Irwin and Cressey differed from Schrag in that they believed some inmate roles developed within the prison setting or as the result of incarceration, while other roles were imported from the outside (1962). The **importation model** (implying that a part of existing prison culture is imported from the outside by new prisoners) was used by Irwin and Cressey and coincided with Schrag's notion that some inmates adapt to prison life in much the same way as they adapted to life among criminals in their communities. They identified three types of prisoners: (1) thieves (inmates who stick to themselves, avoid trouble, yet attempt to get what they want without getting caught); (2) straights ("do right" and conventional inmates similar to square Johns who do their time, obey the rules, and do not identify closely with any inmate subculture); and (3) convicts (those inmates who attempt to control other inmates and acquire power to achieve their own needs or interests). As will be seen later in this chapter, the gradual formation of inmate gangs along racial or ethnic lines has obscured these early prisoner characterizations and typologies to the extent that it is doubtful that they are universally applicable today, especially in those prisons that have large ethnic or racial inmate populations.

John Irwin's descriptions of life in prisons *(The Felon)* and jails *(The Jail: Managing the Underclass in American Society)* respectively published in 1970 and 1985; McCoy's prison profiles of inmates from the penitentiary at Walla Walla, Washington (*Concrete Mama: Prison Profiles from Walla Walla,* 1981); and Robert Johnson's *Hard Time: Understanding and Reforming the Prison,* (1996) are more recent examples of attempts to describe prison life and culture. *Concrete Mama* is amply illustrated with Washington State Penitentiary inmates under various circumstances, and it is perhaps the best visual portrayal of life in prison that has been published thus far. Many of the photos from this work have been used to illustrate prison scenes in criminal justice-related textbooks and other publications.

The gradual influence of race and ethnicity as variables that have stimulated and heightened inmate cohesiveness and power was noted by participant observer Leo Carroll in his 1974 description of prisoner subculture at "Eastern Correctional Institution (ECI), a small state prison in a highly urban and industrial Eastern state" (Carroll, 1974:11). With the consent of the prison administration, Carroll entered ECI voluntarily for the purpose of observing and talking with prisoners about their experiences. All prisoners knew that Carroll was gathering material for a book. Although Carroll was a white male, he was accepted gradually by inmates of all races and ethnic origins (1974:11). However, his entry into prisoner culture was not entirely problem-free. Inmates regarded him as an inmate advocate and critical of the prison system, while correctional officers at first saw him as a threat for the same reason (1974:11). Eventually he overcame prisoner suspicions and staff resentments and fears.

Carroll found that prisoners formed cohesive associations among themselves primarily along racial lines. A "white Mafia" was comprised of whites and vied for internal power with a black revolutionary group known as the Afro-American Society (Carroll, 1974:197–206). Because Carroll's observations were made on the heels of widespread public protest of the 1960s and dramatic civil rights reforms, the emergence of a strong black inmate organization was a seemingly logical consequence. Carroll also found that both the white Mafia and the black Afro-American Society were united against prison administration and rules, although these groupings also afforded prisoners some degree of protection against assaults by other inmates.

One consistent theme running throughout all of these works is that prison culture exists as an independent entity apart from other society. Erving Goffman labeled prisons as total institutions, totally and completely self-contained communities with their own status systems, regulatory and enforcement agencies and personnel, and other phenomena ordinarily found in outside community life.

Studies have been conducted of inmate subculture in both prisons and jails, although prisons seem to be characterized more often as exhibiting subculture characteristics (Selke, 1993; Silberman, 1995). Each prison has its own inmate subculture, with a highly refined set of rules and regulations. These rules and regulations exist apart from those imposed on inmates by the prison administration. In several respects, these rules are enforced to a greater degree than the enforcement of the so-called official code of conduct prescribed by prison staff.

Unlike jails, where the turnover among inmates is brisk, prisons contain long-term inmates who develop and perpetuate their subculture from one prisoner "generation" to the next. New prisoners, or "fish," are quickly oriented to the prisoner social system, sized up, and are located accordingly within the prisoner social structure (Kane, 1987). An inmate's strength, fighting ability, attractiveness, age, abilities and skills, conviction offense, political and social connections, race, and various other criteria determine where that inmate is placed socially relative to other inmates (Clemmer, 1958).

The influence of prison gangs formed according to racial, ethnic, or even religious affiliation has become increasingly important as a means of perpetuating and preserving inmate subculture (Durham, 1994). Latin gangs in California prisons have established the Nuestra Familia (Our Family), while the United Chicanos and Mexican Mafia have been created in other prison settings (Miller and Rush, 1996). In Texas prisons, for example, gangs formed in the 1980s include the Texas Syndicate, the Texas Mafia, the Mandingo Warriors, and the Self-Defense Family (Beaird, 1986:22). Black inmates have formed the Black Guerrilla Family and Black Muslims. In many respects, these gangs have taken the control of prisoners away from prison administrators. These gangs pose more of a threat to individual prisoners than the sanctions the formal prison system can inflict (Miller and Rush, 1996). The Big Four inmate gangs that started in California prisons and have since spread in factions to correctional facilities in other states (through importation) and even into various communities are the Ayran Brotherhood, Mexican Mafia, Nuestra Familia, and Black Guerrilla Family (Miller and Rush, 1996).

Few experts contest the fact that inmate subcultures exist in virtually every prison (Frazier, 1995). Furthermore, it is conceded generally that these subcultures seem to share common features that operate to control inmate behavior to a high degree. Inmate subcultures are pervasive in prisons internationally, existing in prisons in countries such as Poland, the Netherlands, Canada, Australia, Germany, and Japan (Grapendaal, 1990; Kaminski and Gibbons, 1994; Larsen, 1988; Platek, 1990; Schneider, 1989). The inmate riots at prisons in New Mexico, New York, and Georgia were organized to the extent that a leadership core ordered others to accomplish certain tasks, including the murders of certain inmates believed to be snitches or informants. Much violence among inmates appears prompted by racial or ethnic factors—members of one race or ethnic group seek to protect themselves from members of another group (Benekos and Merlo, 1992; Selke, 1993). Although prison administrations have not acted as yet to implement a segregation program that might help to minimize intra-inmate aggression, such a program has been proposed as one possible solution (Hunt et al., 1993; Stevens, 1994).

SELECTED PRISON ISSUES

Prison Overcrowding

At the heart of many problems associated with prison operations and management is prison overcrowding. Whether a prison is overcrowded is determined by comparing present inmate populations to various criteria such as (1) rated capacity, (2) operational capacity, and (3) design capacity. **Rated capacity** refers to the number of beds or inmates assigned by a rating official to various state institutions. **Operational capacity** is the total number of inmates that can be accommodated based the size of a facility's staff, programs, and other services. **Design capacity** is the optimum number of inmates that architects originally intended to be housed or accommodated by the facility (Greenfeld, 1988:4).

Sometimes it is difficult to make valid comparisons among jurisdictions because each prison system reports prison population excesses using one or more of these different criteria. However, most prisons report their inmate populations according to the system's operating capacity. In 1995, prisons in 51 U.S. agencies were operating at an average of 15 percent over their rated capacities (Camp and Camp, 1995a:36–37). Overall, state prisons were operating between 90 and 170 percent of their capacities in 1995, while the federal prison system was operating at 125 percent of its rated capacity (Camp and Camp, 1995a:36–37). Only six prison systems were not considered to be overcrowded, although *all* of them were above 90 percent of their rated capacities.

Overcrowding in prisons has been linked with violent deaths, suicides, psychiatric commitments, disciplinary infractions, and increased litigation by inmates (Call, 1995b; Kennedy and Homant, 1988). With the increasing threat of AIDS in prison and jail settings, overcrowding is quickly emerging as a most critical issue (S. Williams, 1986). Although several jurisdictions have reported new prison construction to accommodate growing numbers of convicts, official expectations are grim. It is unlikely that by the time new prison construction is completed, sufficient space will be available to house the larger offender population that will need to be housed (Contact Center, Inc., 1987a).

Numerous state and federal prisons contract with local jail authorities to house some of the prison inmate overflow suggests serious prison overcrowding as well (Cole and Call, 1992; South Carolina State Reorganization Commission, 1991). Violent deaths, suicides, psychiatric commitments, and disciplinary infractions have been linked to jail and prison overcrowding (Ruback and Carr, 1993; Sechrest, 1991). Clarke and Coleman (1993) indicate that for the county jail population alone, North Carolina jail inmates increased from 2,032 in 1976 to 8,760 in 1992. Three fourths of these inmates were pretrial detainees. In 1992, North Carolina jails *officially* were not overcrowded, since the rated capacity of the state's jails was 10,146. But North Carolina has had to engage in costly jail construction, where the average cost of each new jail bed is $56,547. There is likely going to be a breaking point in county building construction budgets, since the cost of new prison beds in North Carolina is less than half that of jails, at $25,000 per bed (Clarke and Coleman, 1993).

Many solutions have been suggested to ease jail and prison overcrowding. Some of these solutions are labeled **front-door solutions** because they pertain to policies and practices by criminal justice officials who deal with offenders before and during sentencing. Other solutions are **back-door solutions** by which strategies are suggested to reduce existing prison populations through early release or parole, furlough, administrative release, and several other options (D'Allessio and Stolzenberg, 1995).

Front-door solutions to prison overcrowding typically involve actions by prosecutors and judges and the way they process offenders. Some experts suggest greater use of diversion and/or assignment to community service agencies, where offenders bypass the criminal justice system altogether and remain free within their communities (Glaser, 1994). Greater use of probation by judges and recommendations of leniency from prosecutors have also been suggested, with an emphasis upon some form of restitution, community service, victim compensation, and/or fine as the primary punishment (Jones, 1990). Other solutions include greater plea bargaining where probation is included (Maryland Committee on Prison Overcrowding, 1984); selective incapacitation, where those offenders deemed most dangerous are considered for incarceration (Brennan, 1985); assigning judges a fixed number of prison spaces so that they might rearrange their sentencing priorities and incarcerate only the most serious offenders (South Carolina State Reorganization Commission, 1991); and decriminalization of offenses to narrow the range of crimes for which offenders can be incarcerated (Gottfredson, 1984; Kapsch and Luther, 1985).

Some of the back-door proposals by experts include easing the eligibility criteria for early release or parole (Semanchik, 1990); the administrative reduction of prison terms, where the governor or others shorten originally imposed sentences for certain offenders (Finn, 1984b); modifying parole revocation criteria so as to encourage fewer parole violations (Finn, 1984b); and expanding the number of community programs, including the use of intensive supervised parole for more serious offender groups (Skovron and Simms, 1990; South Carolina State Reorganization Commission, 1991).

Prison Riots, Inmate Violence, and Disciplinary Measures

Prison violence has increased dramatically during the 1990s (Maitland and Sluder, 1996:24). Because of the diversity of races, ethnicities, and ages of jail and prison inmates, coupled with chronic overcrowding, inmate violence is not an unusual occurrence (Ruback and Carr, 1993; Wolfe, Vega, and Blount, 1992). The existence of gangs is conducive to inmate violence and is something officials cannot eliminate (Peat and Winfree, 1992). Interestingly, gang membership in many state prisons accounts for a small proportion of prisoners. But inmate gangs in prison systems such as Texas account for most of the inmate violence. Inmate gang members in Texas make up less than 3 percent of all inmates, but they are responsible for the majority of violence that occurs (Ralph and Marquart, 1992). Every prison has screening mechanisms for new inmates according to standard criteria, but misclassifications frequently occur. Dangerous offenders and the mentally retarded or ill often commit aggressive acts against other inmates (Toch and Adams, 1986). Short of using solitary confinement, most prisons lack policy provisions for segregating different classes of offenders. Correctional standards are being formulated continuously for improving the qual-

BOX 7.3 Inmate Interprison Transfers

The Case of the Displaced Hawaiian Inmates

The Halawa Correctional Facility in Honolulu, Hawaii, has a great way of reducing their overcrowding problem. They export excess prisoners to Texas!

The operating capacity of Halawa Correctional Facility is 2,646. However, in recent years, the actual inmate population has escalated to over 3,200. Prison officials were increasingly concerned about this overcrowding problem, since it seemed things would get worse before getting better. Other Hawaiian prisons could not absorb prisoners from Halawa because of their own existing overcrowding problems.

The Halawa Correctional Facility houses all types of inmates, including medium- and maximum-security ones. Many inmates are violent, including convicted murderer Ronald Ching. While Hawaii has been able to expand its own prison construction over the past several years, it has not been at a pace to keep up with rising numbers of convicted offenders who require prison accommodations.

During the early 1990s, various institutions in other states commenced advertising available jail and prison space to those jurisdictions such as Hawaii in which prison space was difficult to find. One of those advertising was the Newton County Correctional Facility near Houston, Texas. When negotiations were completed between Hawaiian and Texas correctional officials, about 300 Hawaiian prisoners were transferred to the Texas jail. The best estimates are that about $4 million per year will be saved by the State of Hawaii as the result of these interprison transfers of inmates who are to be housed for long terms.

On the first Friday evening after Christmas 1995, 300 prisoners were loaded in buses and transported under heavy security to the Honolulu International Airport, where they were subsequently flown to Houston. Prison officials did not disclose the nature of security used to transfer the prisoners. Also, they did not disclose precisely when the flight would leave carrying the inmates. At the last minute, several inmates were removed from the transfer list and taken back to Halawa Correctional Facility. No explanation was given to the families of these inmates for why this was done.

Not everyone is excited about inmate transfers from Hawaii to other states. Families must now plan long trips for the simple purpose of seeing an imprisoned relative. The inmates themselves are in new environments where they are unfamiliar with many other inmates and away from immediate family members. Yet there is little or nothing that they can do about it. The U.S. Supreme Court declared long ago that prisoners have no right to determine where they will be housed when serving their prison terms for their crimes.

For receiving jails and other correctional facilities, the income derived from other jurisdictions is considerable. In some states, for instance, the average daily expenditure per prisoner is about $20. However, federal and state prisons elsewhere might pay up to $100 or more per day per prisoner in order to ease their own overcrowding problems. Thus, the revenue derived from other jurisdictions, where inmate housing is costly, is considerable.

The idea of housing inmates from other jurisdictions in city or county jails in other states is not new. In the 1960s and 1970s, this practice was observed in states, such as Tennessee, where the Knox County Jail housed federal and state inmates together with Knox County convicted offenders serving short terms. The revenue from state and federal correctional facilities is such that Knox County officials were able to purchase new school buses, hire additional teachers, or acquire new cruisers for the Knox County Sheriff's Department. Thus, not all revenue derived goes into jail improvements or better inmate accommodations.

Some politicians believe that such interstate inmate transfers should not be permitted, because their prisoners may not be treated as well as if they had remained in their own state facilities. This is often true. Ordinarily, jails are not designed to house inmates for long terms. The amenities of jails are usually limited, and gymnasiums, basketball courts, and commissaries are often nonexistent. However, many prison systems throughout the United States are under court order to either build more prison space to accommodate their growing numbers of convicted offenders or to reduce the inmate populations in those facilities deemed overcrowded to the extent that these systems are in violation of inmate constitutional rights to healthy and safe living conditions. While various lawsuits are pending to curb the practice of using jail space in other state jurisdictions to ease the overcrowding problems of various prison systems, it is unlikely that this method of easing overcrowding will ever go away entirely.

Should prisons be permitted to transfer their inmates out of state to ease their own overcrowding problems? Should jails receiving prisoners from other jurisdictions be required to use the additional revenue to improve existing jail conditions? Should states and local jurisdictions be permitted to use their additional inmate revenue for noncorrectional purposes such as school bus purchases or new county cruisers for law enforcement? How would you resolve the present prison overcrowding dilemma?

Source: Adapted from Associated Press, "Hundreds of Inmates Leave for Texas Prison." *The Maui News,* December 28, 1996:A4.

ity of life for inmates and for treating those who need counseling or special services (McGee, Warner, and Harlow, 1985). But policy provisions for ensuring inmate safety from other violent inmates are almost nonexistent. Often, prisoners themselves must be creative and establish their own means of self-protection within prison walls (McCorkle, 1992; Peat and Winfree, 1992).

A national study of state prison inmates indicates that prison rules exist to regulate inmate conduct to ensure orderly operation of the institution and to protect inmates and staff (Stephan, 1989:1). However, in 1986 a national survey of prisoners showed that 53 percent of them had violated one or more prison rules while confined. This study suggests that rule violation is pervasive throughout all prison systems. Generally, only the most visible inmate violence is recognized by prison officials. Many prisoners suffer physical injuries, and these incidents are frequently unreported or unrecorded. Even when correctional officers suspect or observe rule-breaking and certain forms of inmate violence, this behavior is frequently ignored. Some researchers indicate that correctional officers often ignore this misconduct in order to obtain inmate cooperation and compliance with prison rules (Hewitt, Poole, and Regoli, 1984). This fact gives prisoners some degree of psychological control or power over those correctional officers who look the other way when they observe rule infractions.

Some prison violence has been mitigated successfully in various state prisons (Wilkinson et al., 1994). In one South Carolina prison, for example, the rate of violent assaults has been reduced by 18 percent since using an adult inmate management system (AIMS), by which weaker prisoners are segregated from more violent and sexually aggressive prisoners during evening hours. Even though 70 percent of the prisoners in that South Carolina facility have violent offense records, AIMS has the lowest protective custody rate among its inmates in the entire state. Leeke and Mohn (1986) believe that this is because there is greater prisoner participation in special programs as well as greater accessibility of prisoners to security and human services. And in the Washington State Penitentiary at Walla Walla, administrators have trained staff to cope with inmate violence through an approach known as *prevention and reaction* (Buentello et al., 1992). With appropriate staff training, Washington correctional officers are learning to prevent new prisoners from joining prison gangs through various intervention activities (American Correctional Association, 1993b).

An important tool used by prison officials to manipulate prisoners and to control their violent conduct is staff reports and recommendations. Staff reports and recommendations directly influence an inmate's good-time credit. Good-time credits are earned by inmates who obey the prison rules. However, if there is an absence of incentives, such as early-release recommendations by correctional officers or officials based on a prisoner's good conduct, an important incentive for inmates to comply with prison rules is destroyed (Stojkovic, 1986).

Inmate Disciplinary Councils. In recent years, prisoners themselves have formed **inmate disciplinary councils.** These disciplinary councils exist apart from administrative sanctioning mechanisms. They are mechanisms whereby many inmate complaints against other inmates and even correctional officers can be resolved to the satisfaction of most parties (McClellan, 1994). All prisons at the state and federal levels currently have formal grievance procedures. These councils consist of inmates and one or two prison correctional officers. Prisoners believe that the addition of corrections officers provides some objectivity when these councils process inmate grievances. These councils are similar to civil alternative dispute resolution scenarios, in which two grieving parties have their grievances settled by an impartial third party or arbiter. However, some experts see a direct connection between new jail and prison design and a reduction in inmate violence (Cronin, 1992).

Disciplinary infractions in all prisons are common. Racial, ethnic, and age mixtures of all types interact with overcrowding and related factors to stimulate prison violence (Braswell, Montgomery and Lombardo, 1994; Leger and Barnes, 1986). Although almost every prison screens new inmates and classifies them according to standard criteria, misclassifications still frequently occur. Pathological offenders or those who are mentally retarded or ill often respond with aggression to their forced interaction with other inmates (Toch and Adams, 1986). In fact, several prisons have few, if any, provisions for segregating different classes of offenders, although corrections standards are improving annually and the courts are increasingly requiring such segregation for inmate safety (McGee et al., 1985).

Only the most visible prisoner violence comes to the attention of prison officials. Where certain prisoners suffer physical injuries, these incidents are almost always recorded and reported. But much prisoner violence escapes detection by prison correctional officers. And even when officers suspect or observe rule-breaking and certain forms of inmate violence, it is sometimes not reported. It has been suggested by some researchers that correctional officers often do not report the misconduct they observe, because prisoner cooperation and compliance to prison rules depend on the nonreporting behavior of officers (Hewitt et al., 1984). In some respects, this nonreporting gives prisoners psychological power over those correctional officers who elect not to report the violence or infractions that they may observe.

Sexual assaults and psychological harassment are frequent in these high-risk settings (Blumberg et al., 1990), although some researchers believe that our estimates about the incidence of sexual attacks in prisons are exaggerated. A study of sexual violence in the United States Penitentiary at Lewisburg, Pennsylvania, disclosed that only 9 percent of all inmates were actual victims of sexual attacks. Although 29 percent of the inmates reported sexual propositions from other inmates, a majority had not been involved with any kind of inmate sexual misconduct (Nacci and Kane, 1983).

Proposals for reducing inmate violence are about as diverse as the many solutions for alleviating prison overcrowding (Boin and Van Duin, 1995). However, some states such as South Carolina have implemented what appear to be sound classification systems and policies and then have acted aggressively to enforce these policies. As noted earlier, the South Carolina Department of Corrections started using an adult inmate management system (AIMS) in 1984 (Leeke and Mohn, 1986), reducing prison violence at at least one South Carolina prison by 18 percent since using AIMS.

One means whereby prison officials can manipulate prisoners to some degree and control their violent conduct is through staff reports and recommendations for an inmate's early release. Good-time credits may be earned by inmates who obey prison rules and do not engage in serious rule infractions. However, changes in sentencing policies such as the guidelines established by the U.S. Sentencing Commission in 1987 have diminished

BOX 7.4 Sex, Drugs, and Prison

The Case of the Lorton Prison Complex

It is alleged to have happened at the federal Lorton Prison Complex in suburban Virginia. A total of 38 persons were indicted on a variety of charges, including conspiracy to distribute cocaine, cocaine possession, and smuggling drugs into the prison. Two persons were also charged with transporting persons across state lines for purposes of prostitution.

The average citizen might expect some minor deviance and/or criminal conduct to occur in small jails across the United States. Even some larger prisons have reputations for illegal drug use among inmates. However, no one would ever suspect that a Muslim religious sect known as the Moorish Science Temple of America would hold religious meetings within a maximum-security federal prison and permit drug use and illicit sex.

U.S. Attorney Helen Fahey acknowledged that the FBI seized nearly 200 grams of cocaine from prison inmates during the 12-month undercover investigation of illegal drug use among inmates. According to court documents, members of the Moorish Science Temple of America brought to the prison three women who agreed to have sex with inmates for money. One of the inmates videotaped these sexual interludes, although it was not immediately known how a video camera was brought into the facility for that purpose. It was not known whether the women themselves were members of the religious sect.

Both prison correctional officers and prisoners were named in indictments alleging various crimes. The religious sect was able to carry out some of its illicit activity in part because of relaxed prison regulations relating to religious visits to gain access to prisoners in the maximum-security facility.

How should the correctional officers be punished if convicted? If there is such wrongdoing in a federal maximum-security facility such as the Lorton Prison Complex, how much illicit activity of a similar nature occurs in other prisons, either state or federal? What kinds of measures could be taken to prevent such occurrences in the future?

Source: Adapted from Associated Press, "Dozens Indicted in Drugs, Sex Ring at Federal Prison." *Minot (N.D.) Daily News,* September 28, 1996:A11.

the effectiveness of this type of staff control, since prisoners will have to serve all of their original sentences without parole. With an absence of incentives such as early release, or recommendations for a prisoner's early release by correctional officers or officials based on a prisoner's good conduct, a powerful incentive for inmates to comply with prison rules is withdrawn (Stojkovic, 1986).

As mentioned, prisoners themselves in most state and federal facilities have evolved disciplinary councils apart from administrative sanctioning mechanisms whereby many inmate complaints against inmates and even some prison staff can be resolved to most everyone's satisfaction (Kane, 1987; Schafer, 1986).

Prison Design and Control

Some proposals for resolving jail and prison problems are (1) to create new jails and prisons constructed in ways that will conserve scarce space and require fewer correctional officers; and (2) to reconstruct existing facilities to minimize prison violence and house more inmates. Recent prison construction has included increasingly popular modular designs (Marvell, 1996). New modular designs also permit layouts and arrangements of cell blocks to enhance officer monitoring of inmates. But new prison construction is expensive, and many jurisdictions are either unwilling or unable to undertake new prison construction projects (DeWitt, 1987). One idea is to expand existing facilities in order to accommodate larger numbers of prisoners.

The cost of new prison construction can be gauged according to the cost of each new unit or cell per inmate. On the average, 1995 unit costs of prison construction in New York ran between $157,000 (maximum security) and $87,000 (minimum security) per inmate (Camp and Camp, 1995a:46). In Mississippi, unit costs of prison construction in 1995 were $45,000 (maximum security) and $30,000 (minimum security) (Camp and Camp, 1995a:46).

One innovation has been the use of prefabricated designs, thus shortening considerably prison construction time. In Oklahoma, for example, several prison facilities were completed in only nine months, since components could be previously assembled in other locations and transported to the building site without considering the weather variable (DeWitt and Unger, 1987:4).

New jail and prison construction, the renovation or expansion of existing facilities, or the conversion of existing buildings previously used for other purposes, take into account the matter of security and safety for both staff and inmates. Stairwells and areas otherwise hidden from the view of correctional officers encourage inmate sexual or otherwise physical assaults. These areas can either be reduced or eliminated entirely with new architectural designs. It is generally conceded that reducing blind spots or areas not directly visible to officers and other corrections officials helps to reduce the incidence of inmate assaults (Vanyur, 1995).

In some jurisdictions, buildings used previously for other purposes, even school buildings, have been converted to use as minimum- or medium-security facilities by state corrections agencies (Marvell, 1994, 1996). While building conversions must be accomplished selectively and carefully, they do result in substantial savings to penal authorities. Of course, such facilities adapted for incarcerative purposes are often located in communities or near residential areas where the public may object to their reconstruction. Conversion projects usually are more successful when aggressive public relations and citizen education programs are implemented beforehand (Marvell, 1994).

Sexual Exploitation

Sexual assaults and psychological harassment are increasingly a part of the environment of jails and prisons. A study of inmates from a prison in a Midwestern state found that prison violence affects almost every inmate. The fear of victimization is especially pervasive among the inmate population, and this fear substantially and adversely impacts an inmate's well-being (Maitland and Sluder, 1996:26–28). One reason growing numbers of inmates seek out gang attachments is the belief that if they are a part of a gang, their likelihood of being victimized decreases. Although it is difficult to achieve, the best policy correction officials can adopt is to create a prison environment free from psychological and physical victimization (Maitland and Sluder, 1996:29).

Many prisons make special provisions to isolate sex offenders from the general prison population. Not only are these offenders closely monitored while imprisoned, they are also supervised when they subsequently leave the prison environment on parole (Schram and Milloy, 1993). The Washington State Department of Corrections operates the Sex Offender Supervision Project as a means of reducing recidivism among convicted sex offenders and providing relapse prevention training for correctional officers.

Inmates with AIDS and Other Communicable Diseases

In recent years, a growing problem facing prison administrators is the rapid spread of acquired immune deficiency syndrome or AIDS (Harlow, 1993). AIDS is often transmitted sexually, and crowded prisons are prime settings for AIDS epidemics. At year-end 1994, 2.3 percent (22,713) of 999,693 state and federal prisoners were known to be infected with HIV, the virus causing AIDS (Brien and Beck, 1996:1). Actual known cases of AIDS in prison settings nearly tripled from 1991 to 1994, from 1,682 to 4,849 inmates (Brien and Beck, 1996:1).

Solutions to the AIDS problem in prisons have included physical isolation of any prisoner testing positive for the AIDS virus, the distribution of condoms to prisoners who wish to engage in sexual relations with other inmates, and hospitalizing any AIDS carrier. But isolating prisoners with AIDS in special cells is cost-prohibitive. Solitary confinement on a large scale is a luxury many prisons cannot afford. Hospitalizing AIDS prisoners is perceived by some interests as a "coddling" maneuver unrelated to punishment. Condom distribution is perhaps the least expensive alternative. However, prison officials oppose condom distribution among inmates because of their potential use as weapons. Prisoners can fill them with acid or other caustic substances and throw them in the faces of other inmates or at correctional officers. Condoms can also be used to strangle others. Furthermore, since sodomy is prohibited by law in Florida and other states, some officials believe that the distribution of condoms to prisoners would be regarded as condoning sodomy and facilitating it (Williams, 1987:6–7). Yet in some jurisdictions, other officials oppose AIDS testing outright. Sheriff Jim Gondles of the Arlington, Virginia, County Jail claims that the cost of testing every inmate would double the yearly medical budget (Williams, 1987:8). At the present time, no solutions to the AIDS problem among inmates have received widespread approval from correctional officials and politicians.

The Constitutionality of Segregating AIDS-Infected Inmates. There are other problems associated with segregating AIDS-infected inmates from the general population. Many inmates with AIDS feel that they are unfairly discriminated against by such prison policies and that they lose many privileges ordinarily available to other inmates (Feeney, 1995:1). One of the strongest challenges made by AIDS-infected inmates against a state department of corrections occurred in Alabama in 1991. The case, *Harris v. Thigpen,* involved a claim by inmates that the Alabama Department of Corrections segregation policy relating to AIDS-infected inmates served no useful or legitimate penological interest. However, the court ruled in favor of the Alabama Department of Corrections, concluding that the prison setting is alive with high-risk behavior that is conducive to the spread of HIV/AIDS. The courts have ruled similarly in subsequent cases filed against corrections departments by inmates (*Austin v. Pennsylvania Department of Corrections,* 1995; *Gates v. Rowland,* 1994) (Feeney, 1995:2).

KEY TERMS

Auburn State Penitentiary
Back-door solution
Classification
Congregate system
Sir Walter Crofton
Design capacity
Front-door solution
John Howard
Importation model
Inmate disciplinary council
Captain Alexander Maconochie
Management by objectives
Maxi-maxi prison
Maximum-security prison
Megargee Inmate Typology
Medium-security prison
Minimum-security prison
Operational capacity

Penitentiary
Penitentiary Act
Pennsylvania System
Prisonization
Prisons
Prison subculture
Rated capacity
Subculture
Superintendents
Tiers, tier system
Total institution
Wardens

QUESTIONS FOR REVIEW

1. How do jails differ from prisons? Identify some of the more important differences between jail and prison inmates and suggest several ways in which these general differences create problems for both types of incarceration.
2. What is the tier system? Why is it important to corrections in the United States?
3. What is meant by the "congregate system?" Where was it first used?
4. What events seemed to lead to the development of the Elmira Reformatory? Was the Reformatory successful at rehabilitating prisoners?
5. How do U.S. penitentiaries differ from federal correctional institutions and camps? What types of offenders are usually assigned to penitentiaries?
6. What are some general differences between minimum-, medium-, and maximum-security prisons? In what ways are these differences related to prisoner self-esteem and self-confidence?
7. What is meant by inmate subculture? Do all prisons have inmate subcultures? What are some of their functions?
8. What is meant by management by objectives? How do wardens use management by objectives to improve their prison operations?
9. What are some general descriptive characteristics of state and federal prisoners? What proportion of all prisoners are women?
10. How effective are prisoner classification schemes? What are some of the methods whereby prisoners are classified?
11. What is a "lockdown?" How are lockdowns related to prison violence and disorder?
12. What are some front-door solutions to prison overcrowding? What are some back-door solutions?
13. How is prison overcrowding reported? What are some of the criteria for determining whether prisons are overcrowded?
14. How is prison design and architecture related to prisoner discipline and control? How have modular prison construction methods helped to improve prisoner discipline?
15. How are correctional officers influential in preventing or at least decreasing inmate violence? How important is a college education for performing the correctional officer role? What officer characteristics seem to make a difference to prisoners about the way they are supervised?

SUGGESTED READINGS

Anderson, Barry M. *The Death Penalty and Public Opinion: The Example of the State of Iowa.* Bethesda, MD: Austin & Winfield, 1996.

Cromwell, Paul. *In Their Own Words: Criminals on Crime—An Anthology.* Los Angeles: Roxbury Publishing Company, 1996.

Hassine, Victor. *Life Without Parole: Living in Prison Today.* Los Angeles: Roxbury Publishing Company, 1996.

Mays, G. Larry, and Tara Gray (eds.). *Privatization and the Provision of Correctional Services: Context and Consequences.* Cincinnati: Anderson Publishing Company, 1996.

McShane, Marilyn D., and Frank P. Williams, III (eds.). *The Encyclopedia of American Prisons.* Hamden, CT: Garland Publishing Company, 1996.

8

Corrections Administration and the Privatization of Jails and Prisons

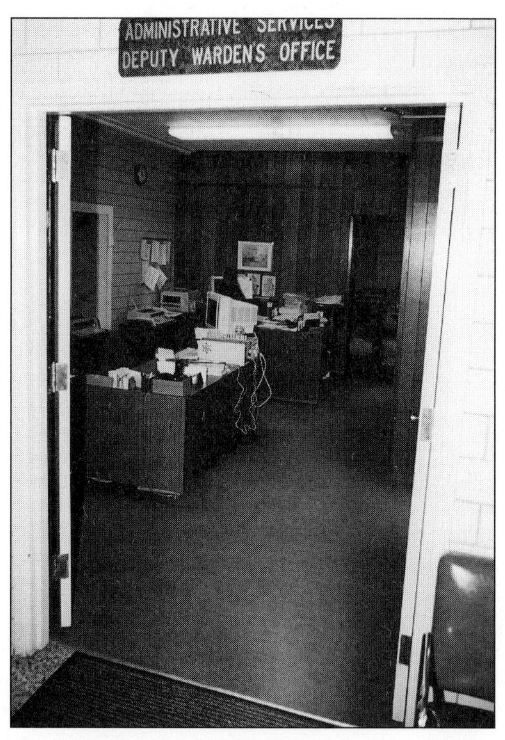

CHAPTER OUTLINE

OVERVIEW

This chapter is about jail and prison administration. Wardens, superintendents, managers, and other administrative personnel who oversee jail and prison operations play a pivotal role in the corrections enterprise. They not only ensure that existing policies established by local, state, or federal authorities are carried out, but they also initiate and come to be identified with their own policies and procedures. Those who manage our correctional institutions are faced with diverse challenges. They are expected to perform many functions and make critical decisions. The decisions made by jail and prison administrators affect both prisoners and staff. Thus, whether jail and prison inmates file large or small numbers of lawsuits often depends upon the nature of jail or prison administration. Whether jail or prison officers perform their work effectively or ineffectively and have high or low job satisfaction frequently depends on the administrative style, leadership, and goal clarity of jail or prison managers. Like captains of large ships, these administrators are responsible for whatever transpires within the scope of their authority. They take the heat when prison riots occur, and they accept the praise when prison operations run smoothly.

Whereas statutory law governs prisoner sentences, and space availability dictates to a great degree where inmates will be housed, administrators exercise considerable discretion about specific inmate conditions while prisoners are in their custody and control. The individuality of administrators is such that no single administrative style typifies all jail or prison operations. Administrative discretion also covers "good time," furloughs, assignment to community centers, and home release (Blumstein, 1988:231). An important administrative function is the selection of quality correctional staff. Furthermore, administrative incentives are important and necessary to motivate correctional officers to perform to their potential. As we have seen, working with prisoners in confinement is stressful, and burnout and other problems lead to labor turnover. Administrators are instrumental in affecting labor turnover one way or the other. Administrative practices relative to staff recruitment, training, and motivation are examined.

THE BUREAUCRATIC MODEL AND LEGAL-RATIONAL AUTHORITY

Jails and prisons are organizations. They aren't Sears and Roebuck, IBM, the Ford Motor Company, the Los Angeles General Hospital, the United Mine Workers Union, or the Tennessee Valley Authority, but they *are* organizations in that they share many features similar to these business and service institutions. To understand jail and prison operations and administration, it is important to understand some basic principles of organizations in general. An early authority on organizational phenomena, Max Weber (1864–1920), introduced the concept of *bureaucracy* to organizational writers and analysts. Weber's original intention was to advance an "ideal type" of organizational structure that would lead to a maximization of organizational effectiveness. He described what effective organizations should be like and the characteristics they ought to possess.

The Bureaucratic Model

Although more elaborate discussions of Weber's **bureaucracy** concept are discussed elsewhere (Champion, 1975; Davis, 1962), the following description lists the essential characteristics Weber devised. The **bureaucratic model** of organizations includes the following:

1. Hierarchical authority, which means an arrangement of supervisors and subordinates with vertical differentiation and a downward flow of power
2. *A priori* specification of job authority and spheres of competence, where each position is clearly specified by a set of predetermined rules and regulations, with duties and responsibilities to be assumed and performed by those assigned different roles, and where no overlapping responsibilities exist
3. Separation of policy and administrative decisions, where officials are obligated to implement policies of the organization apart from their own interests, and where those interests do not conflict with those of the organization as a whole
4. Selection by test, where the most qualified people are selected to perform particular tasks according to their more extensive abilities and skills
5. Appointment and promotion on merit, where those who do the best work are rewarded through promotions to higher positions, and those who deserve recognition are recognized for their particular accomplishments
6. Impersonal relations between superiors, subordinates, and staff, where the abstract rules and regulations can be implemented without interference by personality or interpersonal differences, friendships, or other personal qualities
7. Task specialization, where those performing different roles are selected on the basis of their expertise and have skills that uniquely fit the position as a specialty
8. General rules to govern relations not specified by the above dimensions, where the organization "adapts" to change necessitated by circumstances

internal and/or external to the organization and where the organization may create new policies or rules to apply to new or changing situations.

Weber also suggested that employees (1) ought to view their work as a vocation, (2) should enjoy a degree of social esteem associated with their work performance, (3) should be appointed on merit rather than elected, (4) should plan on holding their position for "life" as a career, and that they (5) should have a fixed salary and security benefits should accrue with each position.

The Human Relations Model

A competing organizational model known as the human relations model was advanced in the early 1930s. The human relations model was developed by Elton Mayo who conducted a series of experiments dealing with factors that affect worker productivity at the Hawthorne plant of the Western Electric Company (Pennock, 1930; Putman, 1930; Roethlisberger and Dickson, 1939). The most important of these factors was the special attention workers received from plant administrators. This factor became known popularly as the "Hawthorne effect," and it helped to highlight the importance of human relations in the workplace.

The principal elements of the **human relations model** include (1) mutual or shared interests between the employer and employees, (2) recognition of individual differences, where employees are "whole" persons and not just impersonal entities with a mass of separate characteristics, and where the group is secondary to the individual in importance, (3) where motivation is critical and the individual must be encouraged through various stimuli to work with others productively toward shared objectives, and (4) human dignity, where workers are shown respect and consideration and are treated as human beings rather than as cogs or interchangeable parts in a large machine (Davis, 1962:14–19).

The human relations model is relevant for correctional institutions and staff. Regarding jail management, Allison (1987:55) says that

> Despite the achievement of management growth and architectural enhancements, problems persist with the development and deployment of midmanagement supervisors . . . correctional facilities are run by people . . . the organization will function no better than the people who work in the organization . . . administrators by their very nature want to promote and experience success throughout their organization . . . networking functions both formally and informally in an organization, and flexibility is its main advantage . . . [the] process is a powerful one and when properly used can allow the organization the opportunity to achieve efficiency and enhance morale for all staff . . . we are dancing to a different tune and believe this tune to be a direct reflection of our management system, tapped midmanagers' resources, and proper use of knowledge and power available in the organization. Clearly, our

> midmanagers [are] leading a successful escape from the jail management blues.

Recent research suggests that a majority of correctional officers enter this profession primarily because of economic necessity rather than a deep-seated commitment to help others, and problems of low morale among corrections staff are abundant (Shannon, 1987:175). While the lack of adequate officer training is often cited as a cause of low morale and poor job performance, an association also exists between administrative laxity, poor leadership, and low morale (Fenton, 1973). Jurik and Musheno (1986: 476–477) have investigated factors associated with serious internal problems of a large correctional facility in the western United States. The link between social and psychological factors and work performance is clear: "We need to identify the personality characteristics of the 'good' [corrections officers] . . . one motivation for upgrading the educational requirements . . . was the hope of recruiting more 'human service-oriented' officers . . . professionalization requires a management style that promotes far greater participation of line personnel in decision-making, particularly decisions related to the fundamentals of client relations and services."

Correctional settings have been criticized for allegedly employing large numbers of unmotivated and unqualified employees, although little evidence exists to show that correctional officer applicants are significantly different from those applying for probation or parole officer positions or jobs related to law enforcement. However, some evidence suggests that informal factors govern promotions and appointments to scarce positions rather than previously demonstrated employee competence through good job performance. Jurik and Musheno (1986:475) add that among correctional officers in some settings, apathy toward work is stimulated by a lack of administrative recognition of work well-done. One officer observes the following: "There are a limited number of advancement slots, and officers wind up competing hard and fast for those. Often, it is who you know. You can work your 'bippy' off and get passed up for someone who isn't worth table salt" (1986:475). They further add that "rare promotional opportunities were extended on the basis of informal favors and alliances," and that these "simply fueled the resentment and frustration of qualified officers who felt that they were being overlooked" (1986:475).

Correctional Settings and the Power Variable

Because of the complex nature of superior-subordinate relations, writers have devised various schemes to differentiate several types of power. Some of the more interesting power schemes have also sought to show the nature of subordinate involvement when compliance to commands is obtained. Two popular power schemes have been developed by French and Raven (1959) and Etzioni (1961). French and Raven have identified five different kinds of power that are found in interpersonal relations between superiors and subordinates. These are (1) **reward power,** where the superior rewards subordinates in different ways or uses the expectation of reward as an incentive for compliance; (2) **coercive power,** where the superior elicits compliance by threatening to punish subordinates if they do not comply; (3) **expert power,** where superiors use their expertise or special knowledge as a device to elicit compliance from subordinates; (4) **referent power,** where friendship is used by superiors to elicit compliance from subordinates; and (5) **legitimate power,** where subordinates comply as the result of a belief that the superior has the right to compel them to do something.

These different kinds of power have prompted others to speculate about the types of involvement elicited from subordinates. For instance, Etzioni (1961) developed a scheme similar to that devised by French and Raven, but where the nature of compliance was more extensively examined and the nature of involvement elaborated. Etzioni described *remunerative, coercive,* and *normative* compliance behaviors. These roughly parallel French and Raven's power types of reward, coercive, and legitimate. But Etzioni went further in his elaboration and discussed the possible implications for subordinates where different types of power were used to elicit compliance. Known as "congruent types," these include (1) *remunerative-calculative,* where subordinates calculate the rewards associated with complying with commands from superiors and act accordingly; (2) *coercive-alienative,* where subordinates comply reluctantly with superiors' requests but are alienated as a result (this is the "coercive" type referred to by Weber); and (3) *normative-moral,* where subordinates consider the position of the superior and regard compliance as natural and "moral."

In prisons and jails, compliance for staff and particularly for inmates is coercive. Prisoners *must* obey superiors, otherwise, punishments of various sorts result (Goodstein and MacKenzie, 1989). The primary means of administrative control in penal institutions of any kind is coercive control. Most prisoners do not comply with prison or jail directives simply because it is moral to do so or because it is the right thing to do. They comply because they are forced to comply. Of course, there is an element of remunerative power involved in these relationships as well, since administrators and officers are in positions to reward inmates in various ways.

In prisons and jails, inmate privileges to engage in one type of behavior or another are highly prized. If inmates fail to abide by institutional rules, they suffer punishments. These punishments most frequently entail a loss of privileges. Access to scarce goods is a privilege, and those prisoners with outside connections and access to scarce goods are able to wield considerable power over other inmates. Yard privileges or access to recreational facilities is also a privilege. Correctional officers are instrumental in whether these privileges are extended or denied, largely because of the reports they file about inmate behavior (Pogrebin and Poole, 1988).

A relationship between inmates and correctional officers also develops along remunerative-calculative lines, where correctional officers may ignore minor infractions of rules or departures from prison policy in exchange for orderly prisoner compliance with other, more important, prison rules. Despite this power advantage, correctional officers possess in relation to inmates, some reports reflect that correctional officers feel somewhat less power in other control areas. Their inability to change inmate behavior for the better, their perceived negative public image, feeling disappointed or disenchanted with correctional work as they originally envisioned it, and lacking sufficient input in policy decision making at higher administrative levels have been cited as associated with these feelings of powerlessness among corrections personnel (Kiely and Hodgson, 1990; Pogrebin and Poole, 1988).

Inmate cooperation is desirable in any prison or jail setting, and it is in the best interests of administrators to do the sorts of things that facilitate inmate cooperation without jeopardizing prison or jail security or compromising existing policies. In fact, compliance assessments of administrators are conducted in many prisons and jails to ensure that statutory or public policies are being enforced. One measure of administrative compliance is an absence of prisoner rioting, work stoppages, or any other form of inmate misconduct (Hawkes, 1985:183). A frequent concomitant of prisoner cooperation is a competent and capable contingent of corrections officers. Administrators have considerable "say" about who is hired and the duties they are subsequently assigned. It is no secret that an often-neglected but important resource in understanding and dealing with inmate problems and potential subsequent litigation is the corrections officer (Smith, 1984:24). The prison or jail administrator depends highly on the available officer pool, however, and is not directly involved in the selection and recruitment of corrections officers.

Power Clusters. Despite the power of prison administrators to make policy changes within their particular prison environments, there are other powerful forces at work to influence, and in some cases control, whatever prison administrators do. Some experts have referred to these powerful forces as power clusters. **Power clusters** are vested interest groups that have a stake in correctional agency organization and operation and that either work alone or in partnership with other groups to bring about a particular end or to ensure that their interests are protected and perpetuated (Wittenberg, 1996:44).

Figure 8.1 shows six different power clusters that appear to "orbit" around a correctional agency. The news media forms a power cluster, just as the executive branch, community, law enforcement, the judiciary, and the legislative branch of government form power clusters. Each of these clusters represents influence. For example, suppose a corrections department establishes a halfway house in a community and forms a liaison between the prison and the halfway house for receiving paroled inmates for community treatment. Some neighborhood residents and city government rep-

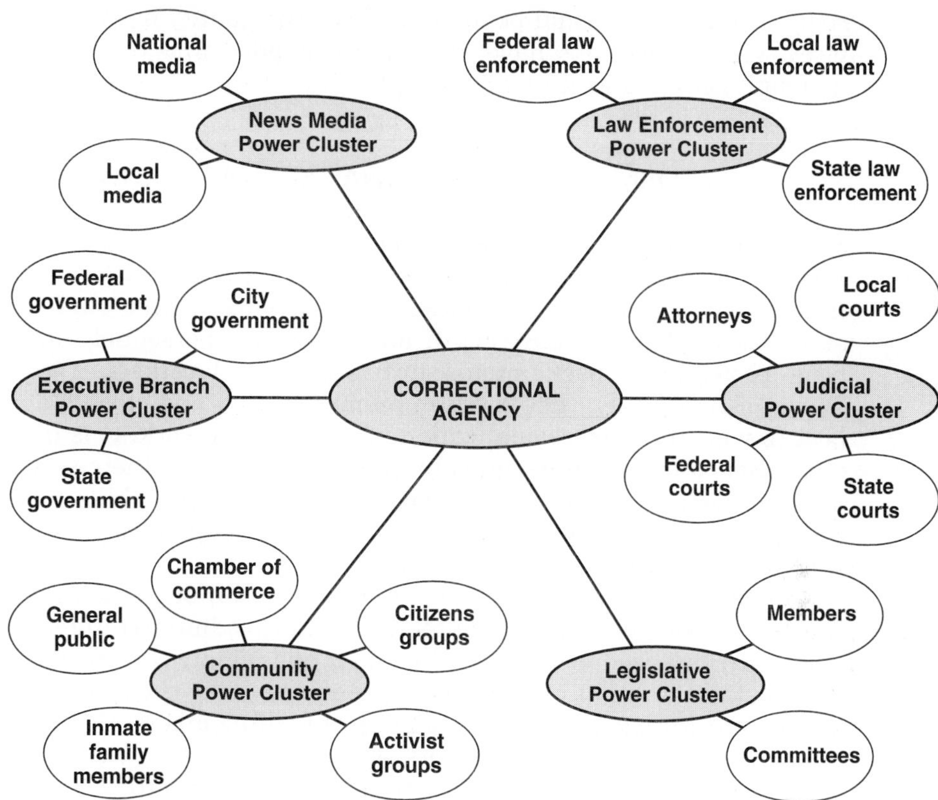

FIGURE 8.1 Power clusters surrounding a typical correctional agency. (*Source:* Wittenberg, 1996:45)

resentatives join forces to oppose the placement of the halfway house in their community. The media fuels the opposition, and the judiciary may provide these other power clusters with injunctive relief, effectively denying the halfway house the right to operate in that particular community (Wittenberg, 1996:44). However, not all power clusters are in an adversary relationship with corrections agencies (Byrne and Brewster, 1993). Some power clusters may assist corrections departments in their siting decision making, and the media power cluster may provide the public with educational information and support (Wittenberg, 1996:44). The fact is that correctional administrators do not operate in a total vacuum. Other factors are at work, whatever we may call them, including power clusters.

During the last three decades, correctional settings have been influenced increasingly by court decrees that mandate jail and prison improvements to make these facilities more inhabitable. Federal district courts have been instrumental in promoting numerous prison reforms. Changes have been ordered on the physical condition of public facilities, staffing, reduction of institutional populations, and the quality of government services. Thus, the courts have effectively intruded into policy making for many prison settings (Fliter, 1993).

FORMS OF CORRECTIONAL ADMINISTRATION

Some experts say that the most common turning point reported among correctional officers relates to problems with prison administration and opening lines of communication between correctional officer staff and their supervisors (Walters, 1987:11). If administrative personnel come largely from professional backgrounds unrelated to corrections, a conceptual Tower of Babel may exist between administrators and officers about how best to view the professionalization of correctional work. It is likely, however, that administrators quickly become attuned to their settings and make necessary adjustments to acquire the necessary skills to facilitate communication between themselves and their employees as well as the inmates.

No particular administrative style fits prison or jail administrators, wardens, managers, or superintendents. Each administrator develops a style individualized to fit the setting, staff, and inmate culture. But because administrators are in key power positions, they may choose to consolidate this power or distribute it among several staff members. Using organizational terminology, administrators either centralize or decentralize the decision-making apparatus of their institutions, and they conduct their administrative affairs according to the power scheme they have fashioned.

Centralization is the limited distribution of power for various administrative decisions among a few staff members at the top of the authority hierarchy in the prison or jail. **Decentralization** is the widespread distribution of power among many staff members, perhaps extending to include some inmates as representatives of the larger prisoner aggregate. Those correctional officers who happen to be employed in a prison or jail facility in which the administrative philosophy is the centralization of decision making will likely feel powerless in influencing prison or jail operations. However, those who work in settings characterized by decentralization probably will be involved to a greater degree in the decision-making process.

The **participation hypothesis** says that those who participate to a greater degree in decision making, especially decisions affecting their own work, may be more satisfied with their jobs and may even be more loyal to the organization. By the same token, those officers who are less involved in decisions affecting their work may be less satisfied and conceivably less loyal (French, Israel, and Aos, 1960). If we were to adopt this framework for assessing correctional officer complaints about their lack of involvement in prison or jail affairs, no doubt much of their behavior would be explained.

The participation hypothesis also applies to inmates. In the last few decades, most prisons and some jails have experimented with inmate councils and committees to hear grievances and have limited input about the operations of their institutions. Grievance committees are fairly commonplace today, and these committees are often helpful at heading off court litigation over incidents that could be resolved internally to most everyone's satisfaction. Grievance committees and inmate councils are also helpful to the extent that they permit prisoner input into how the jails and prisons ought to be operated. This is a valuable source of feedback in a cybernetics organizational context. Prison organization varies among jurisdictions, although the structure shown in Figure 8.2 seems fairly typical of many prison settings. This is a relatively simple organizational arrangement, where different deputy superintendents are responsible for selected dimensions of prison activities, including food services, security, health, and educational programs.

A purely bureaucratic approach to officer recruitment and job performance would suggest that those most capable of performing their roles would be selected initially and that they would orient themselves accordingly toward their different officer chores. They would perform their jobs according to a priori job specifications, and they would maintain impersonal relations between themselves, other correctional officers, and inmates. However, this seldom occurs in the real world of prison and jail life. The interpersonal variable cannot be eliminated from any people-processing institution, especially jails and prisons. Because of this fact, the human relations model has considerable relevance in analyses of correctional officer-prisoner interactions as well as of administrator-correctional officer encounters.

FIGURE 8.2 Formal organization of a prison for adult felons. (*Source:* George Cole, *American System of Criminal Justice,* 5th ed. [Pacific Grove, CA:Brooks/Cole, 1989].)

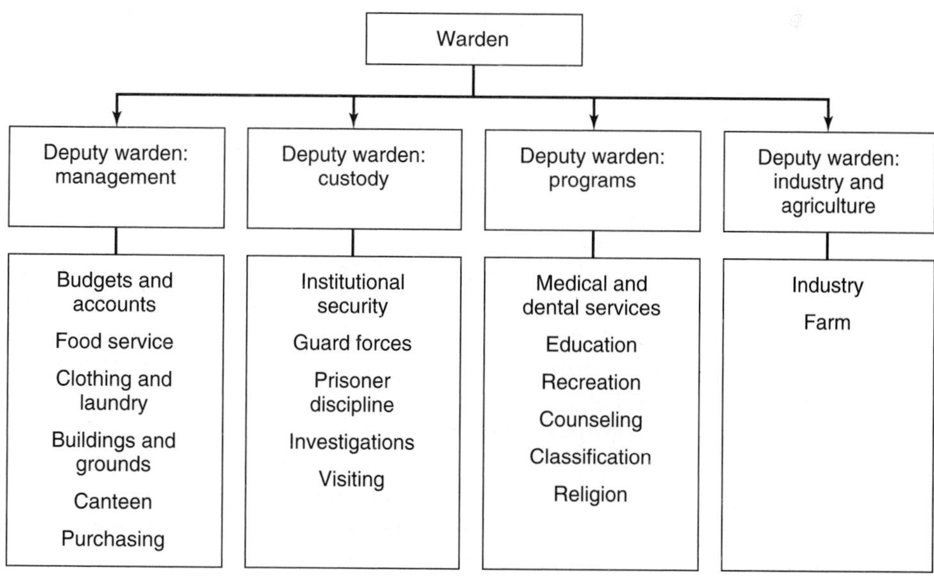

The importance of the human relations element in correctional officer-inmate interactions, however, has been diminished by the use of computer technology in all types of penal institutions (Elchardus et al., 1994; McCulloch, 1990). Locking or unlocking doors, inmate recognition, and other forms of prisoner control are being relegated to a few computer functions, with minimal direct staff involvement or contact with prisoners. Whether this will seriously influence the nature of officer-prisoner relationships in the future cannot be determined presently, but computerized prison settings will no doubt have impacts similar to the depersonalizing effects associated with technological change observed to occur in business or service organizations (Vogel, 1995b).

Four Alternative Prison Management Styles

Barak-Glantz (1986) has described four prison management styles that typify how most prisons are administered by wardens and superintendents. These include (1) the authoritarian model, (2) the bureaucratic-lawful model, (3) the shared-powers model, and (4) the inmate-control model. As Barak-Glantz advises, these models are viewed primarily as "ideal types" in much the same way as Max Weber conceived bureaucracy as an ideal type of organizational model (1986:42).

The Authoritarian Model. The **authoritarian model** is characterized by a high degree of centralized authority and decision making. Wardens limit the amount of authority to a few trusted subordinates. Inmates have virtually no "say" or input about prison operations. This model typified early twentieth-century prisons, although many prisons in the United States today have a similar centralized scheme. Because prisoners have been excluded from any type of decision-making power in this system, it has been attacked repeatedly by civil rights groups. Lawsuits filed by inmates eventually led to the establishment of administrative grievance procedures in all prisons, whereby prisoners may register complaints about their conditions and treatment.

The Bureaucratic-Lawful Model. Departments of Corrections in various jurisdictions have contributed to the bureaucratization of prisons and to the establishment of elaborate chains of command linking prison administrators with their subordinates. Barak-Glantz notes that the evolution and growing importance of civil service and accompanying recruitment regulations have further bureaucratized prison settings. Control is the key to maintaining order in the prison. The courts have also contributed to the orderly and bureaucratic administration of prisons through decisions that acknowledge certain inmate rights. **The bureaucratic-lawful model** stresses inmate rights and a structured avenue for appeals and airings of inmate grievances.

The Shared-Powers Model. An increasingly popular scheme is the **shared-powers model,** in which some degree of decision-making power is extended to inmates as well as to correctional officers and administrators. Reflecting the ideology of rehabilitation, the shared-powers model is apparent in those prisons with strong inmate councils that hear and decide inmate grievances and disputes. Prison officials acknowledge certain inmates possessing the skills and influence to persuade other prisoners to comply with prison policies and rules, as leaders. Some experts have viewed this perspective as *democratizing prisons* (Toch, 1994).

Civil rights decisions by the U.S. Supreme Court pertaining to inmates have contributed to the growth of shared-powers models in many prison settings. Prisoners are treated as citizens with rights that must be respected. Accordingly, administrators and correctional staff oblige inmates by generally following their council decisions, including recommended inmate sanctions. Of course, discretion is always exercised by top prison administrators so that abuses of inmate power will not occur or at least be minimized.

Correctional managers can do much to influence the course of events in their respective institutions. **Total quality management** is a method increasingly used, whereby inmates are viewed more as customers and consumers than as clients (Cohn, 1995:10). Under total quality management, inmates are involved more in the decision making that most directly affects them. In a sense, total quality management is similar to participative management, by which some inmates are given a certain amount of regulatory responsibility and control.

Furthermore, correctional administrators can direct changes that occur in their prisons toward their own ends. Cohn (1995:10) says that ordinary prison administrators tend to react to crises, fail to plan, and view their position as passive, failing to lead the organization. In contrast are those prison managers who are proactive, who view the correctional setting as a system, and who attempt to control its destiny by restructuring the organization of the correctional setting, managing these settings more effectively with total quality management, and using the benefits of technology to make correctional institutions more effective.

Correctional managers can also use their positions to control the proliferation and influence of gangs in prisons. Good intelligence gathering, vigilance, sound operational procedures, and a consistent policy of discipline and firmness will enable officials to maintain control and limit the power and influence of gangs (U.S. National Institute of Corrections, 1991).

The Inmate-Control Model. Under the **inmate-control model,** prisoners form Inmate Government Councils and establish organizations such as the California Union, a prisoner union patterned after those established by Scandinavian prisons (Barak-Glantz, 1986:50). Although the idea of inmate unions is not a novel one, it has encouraged prisoners to act collectively to ensure that their constitutional rights are observed by prison staff. Greater weight is attached to lawsuits in which rights violations of various kinds are alleged that are filed by an inmate collective. Inmate unions have lobbied successfully in some jurisdictions for the abolition of the indeterminate sentence, the establishment of certain worker rights for prisoners including the recognition of minimum wages for work performed, and the right to bargain collectively.

All of these models are found in different U.S. prisons. The model most frequently observed is the bureaucratic-lawful model, although increasingly, the shared-powers model is gaining in popularity. There is a high degree of inmate participation in decision making that is instrumental in achieving and maintaining internal social control. Whereas some administrators don't particularly like or accept this model, they cannot deny that it is somewhat effective for maintaining order and ensuring inmate compliance with most prison regulations.

Other Warden Leadership Styles

Mactavish (1992:162–164) has profiled 283 jail and prison managers from various jurisdictions to establish the first national database in correctional management. Mactavish has used the Myers-Briggs Type Indicator (MBTI) as a means of typifying correctional management behaviors and orientations. These wardens and administrators participated in a 10-day program sponsored by the National Institute of Corrections' Correctional Leadership Development Program. Tables 8.1 and 8.2 show the results of the MBTI applied to the 283 prison managers.

Sixteen personality types are derived from the four preferences. A shorthand version of these types is shown below (Mactavish 1992:164):

1. People are either driven by extroversion, the outer world of actions, objects, and people *or* by introversion, the world of concepts and ideas.
2. People either rely on their five senses to sense the immediate, real practical facts *or* use intuition to consider possibilities and follow their hunches.

TABLE 8.1 Preferences of Correctional Managers

Extroversion 50%	or	Introversion 50%
Sensing 61%	or	Intuition 39%
Thinking 82%	or	Feeling 18%
Judgments 74%	or	Perception 26%

Note that sensing, thinking, and judgment are the most common traits, establishing the STJ profile.

Source: Marie Mactavish, "Are You STJ? Examining Correctional Managers' Leadership Styles." *Corrections Today,* 1992:162.

TABLE 8.2 The 16 Myers-Briggs Profiles

ISTJ Analytical manger, likes facts, details 23%	ISFJ Sympathetic manager, likes facts, details 2%	INFJ People-oriented innovator of ideas 1%	INTJ Logical, critical innovator 10%
ISTP Practical analyzer 5%	ISFP Observant, loyal helper 1%	INFP Imaginative, independent helper 2%	INTP Inquisitive analyzer 5%
ESTP Realistic adapter, stresses material items 1%	ESFP Realistic adapter, stresses human relations 2%	ENFP Warm, enthusiastic change planner 5%	ENTP Analytical change planner 4%
ESTJ Fact-minded, practical organizer 22%	ESFJ Practical harmonizer 4%	ENFJ Imaginative harmonizer 1%	ENTJ Intuitive, innovative organizer 11%

This table places correctional managers in 16 categories and shows which profiles are most common.

Source: Marie Mactavish, "Are You Still STJ? Examining Correctional Managers' Leadership Styles." *Corrections Today,* 1992:162.

3. People either make decisions by thinking, objectively and impersonally, *or* by weighing subjective values and feelings.
4. People either live mostly by judgment, in a decisive, planned, and orderly way, *or* by perception, in a spontaneous and flexible way.

On the basis of the responses of the 182 wardens and prison superintendents, sensing, thinking, and judgment characterize the preferences of correctional managers. Those profiles most common to prison wardens are "analytical manager, likes facts, details," "fact-minded, practical organizer," "intuitive, innovative organizer," and "logical, critical innovator" (Mactavish (1992:164).

Mactavish indicates that most correctional managers prefer using their senses over their intuition as a way of taking in information. They prefer to work with facts, enjoy routines, and prefer to use skills they already have rather than learning new skills. They generally dislike new problems unless they can use a standard procedure for solving them. They prefer to keep things as they are, and when change is necessary, they demand to be convinced of the necessity for change by facts. These findings suggest that most prison administrators follow the bureaucratic model of structuring their own lives as prison managers as well as the lives of the inmates they manage.

PRISON ADMINISTRATOR SELECTION AND TRAINING

Wardens, superintendents, and other prison managers are typically hired or appointed (Maguire and Pastore, 1996:92–93; Camp and Camp, 1995a:68–69). In 1995, the average length of service for prison wardens was 2.83 years. The warden with the greatest longevity in 1995 was William Fauver of New Jersey. Warden Fauver had been on the job for 17.1 years. Other wardens with considerable longevity were Sam Lewis of Arizona with 10.3 years of service, followed by Chase Riveland of Washington with 9 years (Camp and Camp, 1995a:68). These warden's salaries averaged $81,106. In general, wardens' salaries averaged $49,087 in 1995, with a low of $27,492 and a high of $123,100 (Camp and Camp, 1995a:68–69).

Of the 1,359 wardens, superintendents, or prison managers reported by alternative sources in 1994, 86 percent were male (1,127), and 229 (16.8 percent) were black. Table 8.3 shows the distribution according to gender and race/ethnicity of wardens and superintendents of adult correctional systems (Maguire and Pastore, 1996:92).

Some insight into the backgrounds of prison wardens and superintendents may be gleaned from a study of Pennsylvania wardens by Whitmore (1995). Whitmore conducted both a survey and interviews with 55 Pennsylvania prison and jail administrators. The results of his survey are shown in Tables 8.4 and 8.5.

Whitmore found that most respondents, 82 percent, had completed some college, with only 14 percent possessing advanced degrees. Most respondents (96 percent) were white. The field of undergraduate study most common to these administrators was Criminal Justice, while 42 percent of these managers had their first corrections position in security, followed by treatment (34.5 percent). The most frequent ages of these wardens, by category, were 41 to 45 (24 percent) and "over 56" (24 percent). The mean length of service of these administrators in corrections was about 17 years, with the range of service for all survey participants ranging from 3 years to 36 years (Whitmore, 1995:54–55). The administrators indicated that there performed a total of 272 tasks, with the most common being the following (Whitmore, 1995:57):

1. Managing change within the institution
2. Providing leadership for the organization
3. Managing organizational performance
4. Conducting inspections and tours
5. Managing liability exposure and risk management
6. Maintaining professional staff

Although this description is not necessarily typical of administrators in other state jurisdictions, it does give us some idea of the range of backgrounds represented as well as some of the principal duties performed by these managers.

At least some wardens influence directly the nature of prison security.

TABLE 8.3 Wardens and Superintendents of Adult Correctional Systems by Race, Ethnicity, Sex, and Jurisdiction, as of June 30, 1994

		Characteristics									
		White		Black		Hispanic/Other		Female Administrator/ Male Institution	Female Administrator/ Coed Institution	Male Administrator/ Female Institution	Male Administrator/ Coed Institution
Jurisdiction	Total	Male	Female	Male	Female	Male	Female				
Total	1,359	946	124	181	48	52	8	90	8	32	50
Alabama	40[a]	29	1	8	1	1	0	1	0	1	0
Alaska	11[b]	9	1	1	0	0	0	0	1	0	1
Arizona	45[c]	33	4	3	0	5	0	0	0	0	0
Arkansas	24	13	2	8	1	0	0	2	0	1	0
California	28	10	2	5	3	4	4	0	0	0	0
Colorado	15	12	1	2	0	0	0	1	0	1	1
Connecticut	23	13	6	1	1	2	0	5	0	0	0
Delaware	7	6	0	0	1	0	0	1	0	1	2
District of Columbia	9	3	0	4	2	0	0	0	2	0	1
Florida	137	105	9	17	6	0	0	13	0	3	0
Georgia	76	52	7	12	5	0	0	9	0	3	4
Hawaii	8[d]	3	0	0	0	4	1	0	1	1	2
Idaho	10	6	4	0	0	0	0	2	0	0	0
Illinois	40	26	1	6	5	2	0	3	1	0	2
Indiana	29	20	5	4	0	0	0	3	0	2	0
Iowa	8	6	1	1	0	0	0	0	0	0	1
Kansas	9	7	1	1	0	0	0	0	1	0	2
Kentucky	11	8	1	2	0	0	0	0	0	0	0
Louisiana	14	11	0	2	1	0	0	0	0	1	1
Maine	6	6	0	0	0	0	0	0	0	0	2
Maryland	12	7	1	4	0	0	0	1	0	1	0
Massachusetts	22	14	6	2	0	0	0	1	1	0	1
Michigan	31	16	5	5	3	2	0	6	0	0	0
Minnesota	10	8	1	1	0	0	0	0	0	0	1
Mississippi	3	3	0	0	0	0	0	0	0	0	1
Missouri	17	15	1	0	1	0	0	0	1	1	3
Montana	3	3	0	0	0	0	0	0	0	1	0
Nebraska	11	9	2	0	0	0	0	2	0	2	2

(table continues)

TABLE 8.3 (continued)

		Characteristics									
		White		Black		Hispanic/Other		Female Administrator/ Male Institution	Female Administrator/ Coed Institution	Male Administrator/ Female Institution	Male Administrator/ Coed Institution
Jurisdiction	Total	Male	Female	Male	Female	Male	Female				
Nevada	8	4	1	2	0	1	0	1	0	1	0
New Hampshire	3	2	1	0	0	0	0	0	0	0	1
New Jersey	14	8	1	5	0	0	0	0	0	0	0
New Mexico	6	4	1	0	0	1	0	1	0	0	0
New York	66	46	3	10	4	3	0	3	0	2	1
North Carolina	89	61	7	20	0	0	1	3	0	0	0
North Dakota	5	5	0	0	0	0	0	0	0	0	5
Ohio	26	13	5	5	3	0	0	6	0	1	1
Oklahoma	22	11	4	4	1	2	0	3	0	1	1
Oregon	8	6	1	1	0	0	0	0	0	0	1
Pennsylvania	22	19	0	2	1	0	0	0	0	1	1
Rhode Island	5	4	1	0	0	0	0	0	0	0	0
South Carolina	30	21	2	6	1	0	0	2	0	1	1
South Dakota	9	9	0	0	0	0	0	0	0	1	4
Tennessee	19	17	1	1	0	0	0	0	0	0	2
Texas	123	77	11	15	4	16	0	9	0	2	0
Utah	29	29[e]	NA	NA	NA	NA	NA	NA	NA	NA	NA
Vermont	8	7	1	0	0	0	0	1	0	0	1
Virginia	37	27	2	7	1	0	0	2	0	0	0
Washington	14	7	4	0	1	2	0	4	0	0	0
West Virginia	8	8	0	0	0	0	0	0	0	0	4
Wisconsin	24	17	6	1	0	0	0	5	0	1	0
Wyoming	5	4	1	0	0	0	0	0	0	1	0
Federal Bureau of Prisons	120	87	9	13	2	7	2	0	0	0	0

[a] Includes wardens of work release facilities.
[b] Data as of June 30, 1992.
[c] Includes wardens, deputy wardens, and superintendents.
[d] Data as of June 30, 1993.
[e] Detailed breakdowns unavailable at time of publication.

Source: American Correctional Association, *1996 Directory of Juvenile and Adult Correctional Departments, Institutions, Agencies and Paroling Authorities* (Lanham, MD: American Correctional Association, 1996), p. xlvi. In Maguire and Pastore (1996:92).

TABLE 8.4 Demographics of Survey Respondents (N = 54)

Characteristic	Superintendents	Wardens	Total	Percentage
Gender				
Male	14	39	53	98.15
Female	0	1	1	1.85
Age (years)				
26–30	0	1	1	1.85
31–35	0	2	2	3.70
36–40	0	7	7	12.96
41–45	4	9	13	24.07
46–50	6	5	11	20.37
51–55	0	7	7	12.96
over 56	4	9	13	24.07
Race				
African American	1	1	2	3.37
Caucasian	13	39	52	96.30

Source: Robert C. Whitmore, "Tasks and Duties of Superintendents and Wardens in Pennsylvania." *American Jails*, 1995:54.

TABLE 8.5 Education and First Position in Corrections of Survey Respondents

Characteristic	Superintendents	Wardens	Total	Percentage
Education (N = 55)				
High school	0	10	10	18.18
Some college	4	11	15	27.27
Associate degree	2	2	4	7.27
Bachelor's degree	1	12	13	23.64
Master's degree	5	5	10	18.18
Doctorate	2	1	3	5.45
Undergraduate study (N = 35)				
Criminal justice	3	14	17	48.57
Psychology	3	3	6	17.14
Business	3	1	4	11.43
Education	1	1	2	5.71
History	2	0	2	5.71
Health care	0	1	1	2.86
Prelaw	0	1	1	2.86
Sociology	1	0	1	2.86
Theology	0	1	1	2.86
First position in corrections (N = 55)				
Security	4	19	23	41.82
Administration	2	17	19	34.54
Treatment	6	5	11	20.00
Business	1	0	1	1.82
Education	1	0	1	1.82

Source: Whitmore, 1995:54.

For example, at the Calipatria State Prison in California, Warden K.W. Prunty has established an electrified perimeter to deter prison escapes. The electrified fence carries 4,000 volts and 650 milliamperes. Seventy milliamperes is sufficient to kill someone. This lethal fence surrounds numerous buildings and 3,900 inmates who are being held in maximum- and medium-security custody. Some inmate rights advocates are disturbed by the presence of the fence and suggest that it is tantamount to administering the death penalty. In response, Warden Prunty says that "The fence doesn't get distracted, it doesn't look away for a moment, and it doesn't get tired. We already had a lethal perimeter (referring to armed correctional officers in guard towers). This is simply a way to keep that same level of security while saving money."

PRISON PRIVATIZATION

About 20 percent of all U.S. prisons were under court order in 1996 to reduce their inmate populations. Furthermore, 10 percent of all U.S. jails were under similar sanctions (Blakely and Bumphus, 1996:49). The problem of jail and prison overcrowding, in epidemic proportions, has given rise to the *privatization* of jails and prisons. Privatization of jails and prisons is the financing and/or operation of jails, prisons, and other correction institutions by private, for-profit organizations (Blakely and Bumphus, 1996).

Privatization is not a new phenomenon—private business enterprises have been contracting with prisons and jails on a regular basis for several decades for the provision of various goods, services, and prison work programs. Private enterprise operations in corrections have been particularly noticeable in the juvenile justice system, where minimum-security detention facilities are often privately organized and managed. While no state prison system was privately operated in the late 1980s, at least 21 states have either established privately operated prisons or have promoted enabling legislation for their creation (Blakely and Bumphus, 1996:49). These states include Alaska, Arizona, Arkansas, California, Florida, Indiana, Kansas, Kentucky, Louisiana, Montana, Minnesota, Nebraska, Nevada, New Hampshire, New Mexico, North Dakota, Oklahoma, Tennessee, Texas, Utah, and West Virginia.

The primary arguments advanced by those in the private sector interested in gaining control of jails and prisons are that (1) jail and prison operations can be run more smoothly and effectively by private enterprise than by government agencies; (2) government agencies rely on the sluggish actions of legislatures and other political bodies for appropriations and approval before implementing new policies or engaging in new prison or jail construction; (3) private enterprise can furnish the same quality of services currently provided by governments, and these services can be furnished at lower cost to governments; (4) prisons and jails can be operated on a for-profit basis, with prisoner labor functioning to defray program operating costs and managerial expenses; and (5) the private sector is in a more advantageous position to negotiate with other private enterprises in the community to furnish necessary goods, services, and programs for offenders (Durham, 1994; Thomas, 1991a).

Opponents of privatization raise legal, moral, and ethical issues. Among these issues are (1) the accountability of private enterprise officials to government for conduct relating to prisoner management and discipline; (2) the ideological conflict between the power of the state to sanction offenders and the ability and/or authority of private enterprise to do so; (3) the potential for exploitation of prison labor by private interests, and (4) the potential for greatly expanding the present level of incarceration of society's offenders (Durham, 1994). Unfortunately, little empirical evidence currently exists to support the arguments of either the proponents or opponents of privatization (Durham, 1994).

Some of the major private organizations that have offered serious proposals to state and local governments for the possible management and operation of their prison systems are the Corrections Corporation of America, Behavioral Systems Southwest, Buckingham Security Limited, and the American Corrections Corporation (Bowditch and Everett, 1987:442). These organizations bid regularly on government proposals to construct and operate new prisons in different jurisdictions. Those contracts awarded thus far have been for the management of small, low-security facilities such as the Silverdale work farm in Hamilton County, Tennessee, and Bay County, Florida (Bowditch and Everett, 1987:442).

A survey of 21 states in which privatization is either being used for prison operations or in which enabling legislation is being proposed has shown that these states vary regarding (1) private contractor qualifications for operating corrections systems; (2) the services, both traditional and treatment, to be provided to correctional operations by private contractors; and (3) the types of correctional sanctions that should be relegated to private contractors or retained by public agencies.

SELECTED ISSUES ON PRIVATIZATION

Five major issues of privatization of jails and prisons are investigated in this section. These are (1) the professionalization of administration; (2) public accountability: who monitors the monitors?; (3) prison labor and prisons run for profit: the case of UNICOR; (4) public reactions to privatization; and (5) political considerations.

The Professionalization of Administration

Because there are no statutory prohibitions that would rule out the appointment of private administrators for prisons or jails in any jurisdiction, the question is, who would do the better job—someone appointed by the governor or some independent correctional body or someone hired by private enterprise? Many prison administrators have backgrounds unrelated to corrections. A majority have no previous experience as prison correctional officers or as correctional officers in any capacity. A majority have business or social science backgrounds, most are educated with at least a bachelor's degree, and most have some managerial experience. Thus, considerable private sector involvement in prison management currently exists, despite the objections of critics to private sector management of these institutions (Ammons, Campbell, and Somoza, 1992).

The question in the minds of some critics is, "Should the Ford Motor Company operate San Quentin?" Will private enterprise do less well in the management of prisons and jails than public appointees who currently hold these top administrative posts? Presently, managers of prisons and jails are being criticized by various sources because of policies they have implemented and the administrative styles with which they have chosen to run their institutions (Durham, 1994). It is unlikely that the encroachment of private enterprise into prison or jail management on a large scale would serious undermine the current state of professionalism among those holding these top warden, superintendent, or managerial posts.

Public Accountability: Who Monitors the Monitors?

For many opponents of privatization, the issue of accountability is their most serious legal and policy concern. Their argument is that the state is solely vested with the right to sanction offenders, that the imprisonment of offenders is inherently and exclusively a governmental function (Colson et al., 1989). Furthermore, if private enterprise imposes criminal sanctions, including the death penalty, and disciplines inmates for rule infractions, inmates may allege successfully that their civil rights have been, and are being, infringed by these private interests (Pellicciotti, 1987). The legal bases for this civil rights claim are (1) whether privately operated prisons and jails are "state" agencies and are therefore liable under 42 USC Section 1983 of the Civil Rights Act, and (2) whether private operation of prisons and jails is inherently constitutional (Field, 1987). These claims have been settled by the U.S. Supreme Court as the result of lawsuits filed by inmates.

In the case of *Medina v. O'Neill* (1984), 16 inmates of a privately operated Houston Immigration and Naturalization Service facility had been confined in a 12-by-20-foot cell designed to hold six inmates. They sued the private corporation as well as the Immigration and Naturalization Service, alleging that these conditions and the nature of their control by a private organization violated their civil rights. Tort claims arising from the injury and death of inmates due to the inexperience of private security correctional officers in the facility with firearms were also made in the same suit. The U.S. Supreme Court rejected the inmate claims and ruled that the private facility was an agent of the state (Robins, 1986:26). Furthermore, the Supreme Court went on to note that state action always exists when the state delegates to private parties a power traditionally and exclusively reserved to the state. Thus, they resolved the issue of whether private enterprises can perform public functions:Yes, they can.

The issue of whether a privately operated correctional facility is a violation of one's constitutional rights was addressed in the case of *Milonas v. Williams* (1982). This case was the result of allegations by several former students of a school for youths with behavioral problems. The school had used a behavior modification program to alter their behavior, and they believed that this program was a violation of the Eighth Amendment right protecting citizens from "cruel and inhuman punishment" (Robins, 1986:27). The Tenth Circuit Court of Appeals ruled in the facility's favor and held under the "close-nexus" test that there was sufficient "close-nexus" between the state and the facility that the action of the latter may be fairly treated as that of the state itself (Robins, 1986:27).

It is reasonably clear that the courts view private enterprises as extensions of state authority to sanction offenders (Levinson, 1984:46). This is consistent with the "agency" doctrine, by which the private facility is an agent of the government, in much the same way as employees are agents of their employers. For instance, if a Safeway Market truck driver injures another party in an automobile accident while on a food delivery mission for the market, the market is liable for the truck driver's action if a lawsuit is filed by the injured motorist.

Prison Labor and Prisons for Profit: The Case of UNICOR

The use of prison labor for profit dates back several centuries. Great Britain exploited prison labor, not only for state benefit, but for private enterprise as well. Currently, for-profit prisoner enterprises are found in both prisons and jails (Lilly and Knepper, 1993). One of the more successful federal enterprises is **UNICOR,** a profitable, government-owned corporation that sells many prisoner-made goods and products to federal agencies and employs thousands of federal prisoners (Saylor and Gaes, 1991). UNICOR is the trade name for **Federal Prison Industries** (U.S. General Accounting Office, 1985a).

Private for-profit prison industries also are operated in many states (McGlone and Mayer, 1987:32–33). The Ohio Department of Rehabilitation and Correction has established a plan for "productive prisons" whereby inmates engage in profitable employment. Through this program, employee-inmates become qualified for jobs in the private sector, and prison officials assist them in job placements (McGlone and Mayer, 1987:33). Some of the work includes carpentry, computer programming, drafting, and electronics.

While some critics view prisoner labor as state exploitation of inmates, others see this labor as significantly reducing inmate idleness (Thomas, 1991a, 1991b). Furthermore, not all inmate labor is performed behind prison walls. In Oklahoma City, Oklahoma, the Howard Johnson Company has established a satellite reservations center for its hotels and motels (Ewing,

1985). Several inmates from the nearby Mabel Bassett Correctional Center have been used to work as reservationists and receptionists in this center.

When inmates perform work for UNICOR, they learn many useful tasks that can get them jobs when they are subsequently released. The U.S. Bureau of Prisons operates a Post-Release Employment Project (PREP), which is designed to equip inmates with various useful vocational and educational skills. Studies of PREP participants show that they are better adjusted than other parolees, both in and out of prison; they have fewer misconduct reports; and they are rated as having much higher levels of personal responsibility (Saylor and Gaes, 1991).

The problem of product quality has been raised by some opponents to prison labor. Is the work of prisoners comparable to product quality of major corporations? Yes. Studies comparing product quality of private corporations and prison-operated industrial and business ventures have shown that prisoner-made goods and other products are comparable in quality to similar items manufactured by the private sector (Grieser, 1989; U.S. General Accounting Office, 1985a). Some myths about UNICOR have existed for several decades but have been debunked in recent years. One popular myth is that prison-made goods cost less than goods made in the private sector; thus, prison-made goods are unfair competition. In reality, prison-made goods cost more than comparable products in the private sector. Another myth is that prison industries have monopolized much of the economic market from private firms. In reality, prison-made goods make up about .16 percent of the total production of goods in the United States (Grieser, 1989).

Public Reactions to Privatization

Unquestionably, one of the most looming obstacles to overcome for the privatization movement is public reluctance to see private enterprise intrusion into correctional operations (Logan, 1990). In recent years, however, public acceptance of privately operated facilities has been increasing (Lilly and Knepper, 1993). Cullen (1986:13–14) observes that public acceptance of prison and jail privatization is furthered by factors such as the strong incentive among private interests to make prisons and rehabilitation work and the lower cost of prison operations compared with typically high, cost-ineffective government expenditures. At the same time, Cullen says that the public may be opposed to privatization because of the potential such operations have for abuses, such as using unethical therapies to achieve program objectives (e.g., the extensive use of prescription drugs to control prisoner behavior) and the possibility that the quality of services would not necessarily improve. However, some critics say that public opposition is rooted in the age-old philosophy, justified or unjustified, that the state, not private enterprise, should sanction its offenders and assume all incarcerative responsibilities. However, private management is delegated power to act on behalf of the state. But legal acceptance is different from public acceptance. Public opposition to privatization remains fairly strong (Bowditch and Everett, 1987).

Political Considerations

The political considerations associated with prison and jail privatization center around the control factor (Saxton, 1988). Who should be vested with the control of prisoners? Many public officials believe that the privatization of prisons and jails will deprive them of prisoner control (Logan, 1990). But proponents of privatization say they can provide more client-specific services more effectively than public agencies (Logan, 1990). Therefore, any loss of control over inmates would be offset by improvements in program quality and delivery services (Durham, 1991). Yet other observers say that prison and jail privatization research is still in its infancy and that empirical tests are needed to test the effectiveness of private enterprise intervention and control in the correctional role (Shichor, 1995).

KEY TERMS

Authoritarian model
Bureaucratic-lawful model
Bureaucracy
Centralization
Coercive power
Decentralization
Expert power
Federal Prison Industries
Human relations model
Inmate-control model
Legitimate power
Participation hypothesis
Power clusters
Referent power
Reward power
Shared-powers model
Total quality management (TQM)
UNICOR

QUESTIONS FOR REVIEW

1. What is meant by privatization of prisons and jails?
2. How does impersonality influence the attainment of organizational goals in correctional settings? How does the human relations model modify impersonality?
3. Which managerial model best typifies that used by top prison and jail administrators?
4. What is the difference between the authoritarian model and the inmate-control model?
5. What legal opposition is associated with prison and jail privatization?
6. What two court cases have addressed civil rights, tort, and other constitutional issues on the matter of liability when inmates are injured or harmed by private corrections programs?

7. What is the basis for court decisions, relating to privately operated prisons and other correctional programs, in which inmate allegations have been rejected? What is meant by "agency"?
8. Are prison industries profitable? What trends are apparent in prison privatization?
9. What is the nature of public opposition to the privatization of prisons and jails?
10. What are some of the characteristics of prison and jail administrators? Do most prison administrators have previous correctional experience?
11. What general differences and similarities exist between contemporary administrators of prisons and jails and those who would likely occupy these posts if privatization of prisons and jails were to occur on a large scale?
12. What is the issue of accountability relating to prison privatization?

SUGGESTED READINGS

Alexander, Jack, and James Austin. *Handbook for Evaluating Objective Prison Classification Systems.* Washington, DC: U.S. National Institute of Corrections, 1992.

American Correctional Association. *Classification: A Tool for Managing Today's Offenders.* Laurel, MD: American Correctional Association, 1993.

American Correctional Association. *Standards for the Administration of Correctional Agencies* (2nd ed.). Laurel, MD: American Correctional Association, 1993.

Cangemi, Joseph P., and Casimir J. Kowalski. *Andersonville Prison: Lessons in Organizational Failure.* Lanham, MD: University Press of America, 1992.

Klofas, John, Stan Stojkovic, and David Kalinich. *Criminal Justice Organizations: Administration and Management* (2nd ed.). Belmont, CA: Wadsworth Publishing Company, 1995.

Silverman, Ira, and Manuel Vega. *Corrections: A Comprehensive View.* St. Paul, MN: West Publishing Company, 1996.

9

Jailhouse Lawyers and Inmate Rights

CHAPTER OUTLINE

OVERVIEW

- An inmate from Laos in the Iowa State Penitentiary corresponded regularly with his parents. His letters were written in Lao and prison officials could not understand them. Thus, they established a regulation requiring that all incoming and outgoing mail must be in English. The inmate sued the Iowa Department of Corrections, alleging his First Amendment right of free speech was being abridged. [*Thongvanh v. Thalacker,* C.A.8 (Iowa), 17 F.3rd 256 (1994)]
- Carved hair designs, wearing sunglasses and stocking caps, and growing long fingernails and hair are not permitted in the Wisconsin Department of Corrections. The rationale given by prison officials was that such styles were evidence of gang-related activity and thus prohibited. Prisoners filed suit to force officials to allow them to carve their hair, wear sunglasses and stocking caps, and grow their hair and fingernails long. [*Betts v. McCaughtry,* W.D.Wis., 827 F.Supp. 1400 (1992)]
- A cross-dressing male inmate wore female attire and make-up in the Illinois State Penitentiary. He filed suit when the prison officials prevented him from cross-dressing. Further, the inmate alleged that the prison commissary did not stock female clothing or make-up, thus depriving him of the opportunity of making himself attractive to other inmates. [*Star v. Gramley,* C.D.Ill., 815 F.Supp. 276, (1993)]
- A female inmate of the Missouri State Penitentiary filed suit against prison officials when they denied her the right to mail a letter to her brother, wherein she said of a female correctional officer, "There's a beetle-eyed bitch back here who enjoys reading people's mail . . . she [the officer] was hoping to read a letter talking dirty s--- so she could go in the bathroom and masturbate." The court allowed the letter sent to the inmate's brother since it did not implicate security concerns or violate the decorum of the prison environment. [*Loggins v. Delo,* C.A.8 (Mo.), 999 F.2d 364 (1993)]
- A New York appellate court ruled that it did not constitute a First Amendment violation of an inmate's free speech when he was disciplined for using the word "s---" in expressing his anger and frustration toward a corrections officer through a window at a New York penitentiary. [*Harry v. Smith,* 561 N.Y.S.2d 374, 148 Misc.2d 629 (1990)]
- An Arizona penitentiary inmate received an electronic typewriter from his mother. Prison officials seized the typewriter as being against prison policy. The inmate sued to recover and use his typewriter. The court decided in favor

of the prison, holding that the prison directive did not violate the inmate's free speech rights. [*Sands v. Lewis,* C.A.9(Ariz.), 878 F.2d 1188 (1989)]

- A Wyoming inmate filed suit against the Wyoming Department of Corrections because penitentiary officials allowed an AIDS-infected inmate into the general population without segregating him. Further, the AIDS test results were not disclosed to the general inmate population. The suit alleged cruel and unusual punishment. The inmate lost the suit. [*Goss v. Sullivan,* D.Wyo., 839 F.Supp. 1532 (1993)]
- A California inmate fell in love with a female visitor. They agreed to have a baby and the inmate requested that prison officials preserve a sample of his sperm so that the woman could be artificially inseminated. The prison refused and the inmate filed a lawsuit, alleging cruel and unusual punishment and "unnecessary and wanton infliction of pain" as prohibited by the Eighth Amendment. The inmate lost the suit. [*Anderson v. Vasquez,* N.D.Cal., 827 F.Supp. 617 (1992)]

We are in the midst of an **inmate litigation explosion** (Champion, 1988b). In 1962, federal prisoners filed 1,500 suits alleging various complaints against prison administrators and staff. By 1995, the annual number of federal prisoner filings had increased to 63,550 (Maguire and Pastore, 1996:517). In 1971, inmates of state prisons filed over 12,000 petitions or suits alleging rights violations by prison staff. By 1995, the annual number of state prisoner filings had increased to 54,599 (Maguire and Pastore, 1996:517).

This chapter examines some of the rights inmates have acquired in the past few decades. In the 1950s and 1960s, the authoritarian regimes of federal and state prisons, as well as similar administrative modes in city and county jails, were largely unchallenged. Those raising questions about inmate rights then did so in the midst of an unaccepting and insensitive public. Judges received petitions from prison and jail inmates unenthusiastically, and the presumption was almost always that prison and jail administrators had neither violated the law nor infringed the rights of any inmate. Legally untrained and uneducated prisoners found this presumption difficult to overcome. Some writers have said that during the 1960s, a **prisoners' rights movement** was established (Jacobs, 1980:431). This movement was not highly organized and well-coordinated, but it gathered enough momentum over the next 20 years to deluge the courts by large numbers of increasingly sophisticated inmate filings. This dramatic upsurge in lawsuits has been labeled by correctional experts and others as the "inmate litigation explosion."

Described also are the constitutional bases for inmate litigation, including several Amendments that have frequently been cited in court actions by prisoners. The First, Fourth, Eighth, and Fourteenth Amendments are particularly relevant here. As inmates became more sophisticated and educated in the ways of the law, a new term was coined to describe certain, legally knowledgeable inmates who provide legal advice to their companions or help themselves—the jailhouse lawyer. The role of jailhouse lawyers is also explored.

Court actions by inmates have been prompted by several continuing problems related to the nature of prison and jail management and operation. These problems have led to the identification of several key issues that stimulate much of the inmate litigation. In recent years, all prison systems have instituted administrative procedures whereby prisoners can file grievances and complaints about the general nature of their confinement. In some prisons and jails, inmate committees have been formed to perform similar functions. These administrative and inmate grievance mechanisms are examined in this chapter. The present level of litigation by inmates has not gone unnoticed by the public, the courts, and prison and jail administrators. Attempts by officials and courts to "head off" legal actions by prisoners have directly or indirectly resulted in significant changes in prison and jail management and operation (Palmer, 1997). Each year correctional personnel are better trained and educated, and more stringent selection requirements are reducing the number of inmate actions resulting from allegations of mistreatment by officers. Some trends in inmate litigation are also described.

WHAT ARE "JAILHOUSE LAWYERS"?

There are jailhouse lawyers and there are jailhouse lawyers. Those who file "nuisance" suits such as the case of *In re Green* (1981) do a disservice to all other inmates of prisons and jails who file legitimate grievances and raise important constitutional issues. **Jailhouse lawyers** are inmates who have acquired some degree of legal expertise and assist both themselves and others in filing petitions and suits against their institutions. Jailhouse lawyers and lawyering have, and will continue to have, a tremendous impact on reforming jails and prisons (Milovanovic, 1988). The efforts of many jailhouse lawyers are a form of primitive rebellion against the system. They are exiled and powerless. However, they have several ways of resisting either the control or the conditions imposed upon them by their state keepers (Milovanovic and Thomas, 1989).

Considerable informal legal schooling frequently occurs within penitentiaries. The schooling is of all types. Prisonization imparts improved criminal skills for those desiring to acquire greater criminal expertise. Other types of schooling pertain to the law and how appeals can be filed. Jailhouse lawyers are self-taught and well-schooled in the finer points of inmate appeals. They may file appeals on their own behalf or on the behalf of other inmates who lack legal knowledge (Davidson, 1995).

Perhaps the most famous jailhouse lawyer was Caryl Chessman, author of *Cell 2455, Death Row.* Chessman was arrested and charged on January 23, 1948, with 18 counts of robbery and rape stemming from a series of incidents occurring in the Hollywood hills area of Los Angeles, a remote region known as "lover's lane." Tagged by the press as the "Red Light Bandit," Chessman was subsequently convicted and sentenced to death in the San Quentin gas chamber. Before he was executed on May 2,

1960, he had filed 39 appeals and had his execution stayed or delayed eight times. Thus, he avoided execution for almost 12 years while he fought his court battles. He acquired an extensive legal library and became a legal expert of sorts on the appeals process and on finding legal loopholes. Historical accounts suggest that Chessman was convicted largely on the basis of circumstantial evidence, and that because he conducted his own defense in a highly inflammatory and arrogant manner, the jury was unsympathetic to his arguments, however persuasive. But the circumstantial evidence against Chessman was sufficiently persuasive to jurors.

Another death row inmate who eventually sprung himself out of death row in 1965 was Jerry Rosenberg (Bello, 1982). Rosenberg, a fourth-grade dropout who left his middle-class Brooklyn family for an abortive career in organized crime, was on death row for killing a police officer. Claiming he was innocent of the police officer's murder, Rosenberg began an intensive study of the law. Eventually, he convinced Governor Rockefeller to commute his death sentence to life imprisonment. Over the next three years (1965–1968), Rosenberg acquired a law degree by correspondence while at Attica State Prison and was subsequently recognized as the nation's foremost jailhouse lawyer (Bello, 1982).

THE CONSTITUTIONAL BASIS FOR INMATE RIGHTS

In some respects, the question of prisoner rights is similar to the problems of other minorities in America (Palmer, 1997). Prisoners have not always enjoyed the protection of the U.S. Constitution and Bill of Rights. Their struggle to be recognized as human beings who are entitled to the same rights as those possessed by other U.S. citizens has been a long and difficult one. In 1871, for example, a Virginia judge declared that "prisoners have no more rights than slaves" (Palmer, 1997:141). While this declaration was harsh, it nevertheless reflected public sentiment that imprisonment is, and should be regarded as, a punishment, and the loss of certain rights is a significant element of that punishment (*Ruffin v. Commonwealth,* 1871).

It was not considered unusual to view prisoners as "guinea pigs" for a variety of scientific medical and social experiments. Some U.S. prisoners were used to determine the physical effects of various gases and other wartime products during World War I. In May 1980, experimental drug research was being conducted on inmates of several prisons, including the Michigan State Prison at Jackson. The National Commission for the Protection of Human Subjects of Biomedical and Behavioral Research has made numerous recommendations, including a ban on nontherapeutic experimental drug research on prisoners. The U.S. Food and Drug Administration has sought to implement some of these recommendations and to extend to prisoners the right to participate in such experiments on the bases of informed consent and voluntariness (Schroeder, 1983). In addition, until the early 1940s, some state prisons sterilized certain inmates, believing that their criminality was hereditary.

As recently as 1970, the U.S. Supreme Court declared that the Arkansas state prison system was guilty of committing numerous barbaric acts against inmates, including a variety of corporal punishments (*Holt v. Sarver,* 1970). Inmate compliance with prison rules was obtained by different painful and inhumane methods such as shoving needles under inmates' fingernails, starvation, flogging, and a special device called the Tucker telephone. The **Tucker telephone** (named after the Tucker, Arkansas, Prison Farm) was a crank-type apparatus, an electrical generator taken from an old-style crank telephone. Inmates were strapped to a table in the Tucker Hospital where physicians and correctional officers fastened electrodes to their penis, testicles, and toes. Turning the hand-crank on the telephone device caused its electrical generator to send a charge into the prisoner's body inflicting unbearable shocks. So-called "long-distance calls" were made for especially unruly prisoners, and more than one prisoner emerged from this torture with irreparable testicle damage and psychological disorders (Murton and Hyams, 1976).

For many years, Arkansas inmates had complained about the atrocities and inhumane treatment they received while in prison. However, officials were inclined to be skeptical about these complaints. In 1967, for instance, an Arkansas state representative, Lloyd Sadler, declared that he didn't believe that "stuff," because "ninety-five percent of the complaints of convicts are lies." Another Arkansas official, State Senator Knox Nelson, claimed that same year that Arkansas had "the best prison system in the United States" (Murton and Hyams, 1976). Under a new administration, the governor appointed Thomas O. Murton, a former professor of criminology at Southern Illinois University, as the new administrator of Arkansas's prison system in 1966. Murton was charged with the responsibility of "reforming" the old prison system. His early efforts at reform uncovered some of the atrocities that prisoners had complained of years earlier. Because Murton's discoveries and new policies were believed to be potentially embarrassing to Arkansas, he was relieved of his administrative responsibilities in 1968. The governor claimed that he had been "a poor administrator." But his intervention had uncovered what came to be known as the **Arkansas prison scandal,** and the *Holt v. Sarver* decision in 1970 concluded the scandal.

Prisons are designed to incarcerate those who have violated the law. Jails fulfill this basic purpose as well, although we have seen that jails house other types of inmates besides law violators. Thus, prisons and jails have been established generally to incapacitate, control, and monitor criminals. These facilities perform other functions, including punishment, discipline, and to some extent, rehabilitation. Because prisons and jails are low-priority items in local, state, and federal budgetary allocations and because many of them are old and dilapidated, large numbers of penal facilities in the United States are considered deplorable by critics. Hundreds of prisons and jails are currently under court order to improve their physical plants and other facilities so that minimal health and safety standards can be attained (Hall, 1987). In addition, large numbers of penal institutions are currently operating according to minimally acceptable health and safety standards. Although no court has ever declared that prisons and jails must be comfortable, numerous inmate suits have been prompted from a variety of deprivations relating to these minimal standards.

Furthermore, it is the responsibility of prison and jail officials to operate orderly systems and to ensure that inmates comply with policies and rules. Because of the inherently coercive nature of prison and jail settings, differences of opinion and disagreements between prisoners and prison staff over the polices, rules, and conditions of confinement are inevitable. Prison and jail staff must actively seek to control the flow of contraband, because inmate access to various forms of contraband is potentially disruptive and might pose safety problems for other inmates. Prison and jail regulations exist to authorize routine official body and cell searches for the purpose of discovering and seizing any illegal materials. X-rays and searches of body cavities have yielded drugs, weapons, and other materials potentially injurious to prison staff or other inmates. **Shakedowns,** by which a thorough search is conducted of an inmate's cell, also uncover illicit materials that are considered disruptive to prison or jail discipline.

Because of the coercive nature of an inmate's confinement and the tight discipline that must be maintained by prison or jail officials, inmates suffer deprivations, indignities, and other forms of treatment alien to their lives outside of institutional settings. Therefore, prisons and jails are prime sites for inmate grievances and legal action. It is difficult to achieve a balance between the responsibilities of prison and jail officials to maintain orderly premises and a reasonable social system that ensures acceptable inmate conduct on the one hand and sees that inmate constitutional rights are fully observed on the other.

The Arkansas prison scandal is one extreme, representing extensive corporal cruelty to prisoners. Inhumane conditions of confinement, in which prisoners were forced to sit for many days in their own excrement, naked, in solitary confinement and on starvation diets, and being tortured from time to time by the Tucker telephone and other devices represents one of the worst cases against prison administrations. The other extreme is the case of *In re Green* (1981). Green was a prison inmate who filed between 600 and 700 lawsuits on behalf of himself and other inmates during the 1970s. The courts consistently found his suits to be "frivolous, irresponsible, and unmeritorious," and one court even suggested that Green hoped to force his own release from custody by swamping the court with these frivolous suits (Knight and Early, 1986:15). Large numbers of frivolous filings by inmates damage their credibility in the courts of any jurisdiction. All lawsuits, including those that are dismissed, consume valuable court time.

For many years after the judicial declaration that prisoners were "slaves of the state" in *Ruffin v. Commonwealth* (1871), inmates of jails and prisons were treated as second-class citizens and given little or no standing in U.S. courts. The *Ruffin* case led to the "hands-off" doctrine practiced by U.S. courts during the next 70 years. The courts consistently refused to intervene in the management and operation of prison affairs. Prison and jail authorities determined penal policies and prescribed the means whereby these policies would be implemented. However, the first major breakthrough separating the past from the present occurred in 1941 in the case of *Ex parte Hull*.

In 1941, prison and jail officials carefully screened all outgoing inmate mail, including legal documents and petitions addressed to state or federal courts. Inmate petitions to the court for virtually any grievance or complaint, founded or unfounded, were often conveniently trashed by prison officials who claimed that these petitions were improperly prepared and thus ineligible for court action. Prison and jail policies permitted the disposal of such materials. In *Ex parte Hull* (1941), the U.S. Supreme Court declared that no state or its officers may abridge or impair a prisoner's right to have access to federal courts. The court, not prison or jail officials, would determine whether petitions were properly prepared. While the original *Hull* decision pertained to a particular class of legal petitions, it was eventually extended to include categorical access to the courts (Palmer, 1997:44, 100). Despite the *Hull* ruling, courts have continued to take a hands-off attitude toward lawsuits filed by prisoners in later years.

Inmates have continuously challenged the legality of their confinement under writs of *habeas corpus*. A *writ of habeas corpus* is a document that commands authorities to show cause why an inmate should be confined in either a prison or jail. It is a Latin term meaning "produce the body" or "you should have the body." While many inmate *habeas corpus* petitions are rejected by the courts, they nevertheless represent one means by which an inmate can seek relief from confinement. The *Hull* case involved a ***habeas corpus* petition.** In 1944, another important case was decided that extended *habeas corpus* relief to include the "conditions of confinement" in addition to confinement itself. This was the case of *Coffin v. Reichard* (1944).

The *Coffin* case is significant because it is the first instance that a federal appellate court declared that prisoners do not lose their civil rights when entering confinement (Coles, 1987:48–49). The **hands-off doctrine** was based on two rationales: (1) that correctional facilities were managed by the executive and that under the "separation of powers" doctrine the judiciary should not interfere with that management, and (2) that judges were not experts in correctional administration, and therefore should not interfere with the experts who ran such facilities (Coles, 1987:49–50).

Currently, *habeas corpus* petitions challenge (1) the fact of confinement, (2) the nature of confinement, and (3) the length of confinement. However, the U.S. Supreme Court has determined that these writs shall *only* be used after inmates have exhausted their state remedies. Thus, state prisoners planning to file *habeas corpus* writs in federal district courts must first demonstrate that they have pursued their grievances in state courts. Otherwise, district judges will direct these suits to appropriate state courts for action. However, federal prisoners may file *habeas corpus* petitions directly in federal district courts.

An inmate challenge about the nature of confinement within the context of the federal *habeas corpus* statute must allege that by virtue of confinement, the prisoner is deprived of some right to which he or she is entitled despite the confinement, and that the deprivation of this right makes the imprisonment more burdensome (Palmer, 1997). *Habeas corpus* relief might be sought by state or federal prisoners being incarcerated in a local jail that has contracted with the state or federal government to house a portion of prison overflow to ease overcrowding. Compared with prisons, jail facilities are particularly inadequate. State and federal prisoners rightfully feel deprived of various vocational and educational programs and other benefits otherwise available to them if they were housed in long-term prison settings.

While there are many suits filed by inmates annually, a large number of these suits are dismissed. The two most frequently used methods that courts employ to dismiss these suits are (1) motions to dismiss and (2) motions for summary judgments (Collins, 1986:65). **Motions to dismiss** are usually granted when the plaintiff or inmate has simply failed to "state a claim upon which relief can be granted." In brief, the court has read the petition and decided that no basis exists for the suit. **Motions for summary judgments** are granted in cases in which prison officials offer their version of events to be considered together with the views and arguments of the prisoner. Thus, the court considers both sides of the complaint in motions for summary judgment, but it hears only the facts as outlined by the inmate in a motion to dismiss (Collins, 1986:65). Several Amendments to the U.S. Constitution form the basis for many lawsuits against federal, state, and local penal institutions and their agents. These include the First, Fourth, Eighth, and Fourteenth Amendments.

The First Amendment

The First Amendment states that Congress shall make no law respecting an establishment of religion, or prohibiting the free exercise thereof; or abridging the freedom of speech, or of the press; or the right of the people peaceably to assemble, and to petition the government for a redress of grievances. This Amendment has sparked numerous lawsuits by prisoners, in part because it involves the transmittal of communications with others outside of prison as well as the receipt of communications from others. Several of the scenarios at the beginning of this chapter involved First Amendment rights challenges.

Furthermore, the First Amendment specifies that a prisoner's religious beliefs will be respected, so long as those beliefs do not violate existing laws and do not interfere with or pose a threat to prison discipline and operations. Regarding the censorship of an inmate's mail, censorship is justified to the extent that the letter "jeopardizes security, order, or rehabilitation, and the regulations may be only as broad as is necessary to meet those goals. However, officials may not censor mail simply to eliminate unflattering opinions, factually inaccurate statements, or inflammatory racial, political, or religious views" (Bronstein, 1980:30; *Procunier v. Martinez,* 1974).

Prior to the *Procunier* holding, virtually every piece of inmate mail was inspected, both leaving and entering these institutions. The judgments of officials determined whether the mail would be forwarded. Many of these communications were between inmates and their attorneys. A separate case focused upon the nature of privileged communications between attorneys and their inmate-clients. This was the case of *Wolff v. McDonnell* (1974).

The *Wolff* case dealt solely with the question of whether letters determined or found to be from attorneys may be opened by prison authorities in the presence of the inmate or whether such mail must be delivered unopened if normal detection techniques fail to indicate contraband. The U.S. Supreme Court did not add a great deal of clarity to this issue in their decision. The Court indicated that attorneys must clearly identify themselves by placing their names and addresses in plain view on envelopes and that the letters should show that they came from lawyers. In any case, prison authorities may inspect and read any document leaving and entering the institution in an effort to determine whether inmates are abusing their rights by communicating about "restricted matters" (Bronstein, 1980:29–30). Despite the *Wolff* ruling, there are continuing challenges by inmates of mail policies of various prison systems (*Avery v. Powell,* 1992; *Bressman v. Farrier,* 1993; *Martyr v. Bachik,* 1991).

The courts have been more restrictive about communications between prisoners within and between different penal institutions. Policies in many prisons and jails prohibit written communications between inmates in different institutions. Thus, if a California state prisoner in San Quentin wishes to correspond with a federal prisoner in Marion, Illinois, prison rules that prohibit such exchanges are in effect. The courts have continually upheld the right of prison officials to restrict or deny such correspondence between prisoners as potentially disruptive of prison discipline, without violating their free speech rights (*Bryson v. Iowa Dist. Court, Iowa,* 1994). However, sometimes prison officials may be asked to defend why and how they believed such communications threatened the security of their prisons and presented a "clear and present danger" to prison discipline (*Turner v. Safley,* 1987). Unsatisfactory explanations to the court by prison officials may result in such censorship being determined a violation of the inmate's constitutional right to free expression.

The freedom of worship issue is also the subject of numerous prisoner-initiated lawsuits. The courts have been reluctant to make decisions that restrict inmate opportunities to worship the religion of their choice, despite the fact that some religions are questionably "religious." Thus, prisoners may request permission to attend regular religious services. They might grow beards or long hair in compliance with certain religious beliefs or standards. They may request visits from chaplains or other church officials representing their religious beliefs. In short, there is an endless string of religion-related requests generated by prisoners. Compliance with these requests often involves special custody transfers of prisoners from one area of a prison to another or some other special transportational provision. To what extent are such special religious-related arrangements potentially disruptive to prison discipline?

The courts have generally held that inmates of jails and prisons should enjoy the right to freedom of religion, but that right is subject to restrictions (*Cooper v. Pate,* 1967; *Inmates, Washington County Jail v. England,* 1980). Sometimes, the near impossibility of furnishing certain materials to prisoners to practice their religion outweighs the prisoner's religious rights. For example, prisoners belonging to the Muslim faith requested special diets consisting of organic fruits, juices, vegetables, meats, raw milk, distilled water, and other items. This special diet was so costly to administer compared with the other foods served most prisoners that the court ruled in favor of the government by denying the inmate access to the special diet (*Udey v. Kastner,* 1986). In a similar case involving a Muslim inmate, the Arkansas Department of Corrections provided sack lunches to prisoners that consisted in part of bologna sandwiches. Again, the court ruled that constitutional right of freedom of religion was not violated because of inmate claims that bologna contained pork, which was forbidden by the Muslim faith (*Tisdale v. Dobbs,* 1986).

Native American inmates in various prisons have sued prison officials and departments of corrections for rights pertaining to possession of religious artifacts used in religious rituals. In Missouri, for example, the Department of Corrections prohibited ceremonial pipes, medicine bags, eagle claws, and altar stones because of increased security risks. The courts declared that such prohibitions did not violate Native American inmate religious rights under the First Amendment (*Bettis v. Delo,* 1994). However, other jurisdictions have permitted certain Native American religious items such as ceremonial pipes (*Sample v. Borg,* 1987).

For more conventional religious practices, such as Catholicism, inmates have been denied the use of crucifixes and rosaries. Wisconsin and Oregon officials have outlawed such religious items as contrary to prison safety because of their possible use as weapons (*Escobar v. Landwehr,* 1993; *McClafin v. Pearce,* 1990).

The matter of hair growth and beards as a religion-related issue has been bothersome to prison officials. In past years, prison and jail officials have claimed that permitting prisoners to grow their hair below their shoulders and to grow long beards would disrupt prison discipline because this would impair an official's ability to identify inmates easily. A case involving an Orthodox Jewish inmate's belief that he refrain from shaving, trimming, or cutting his facial hair was opposed by prison officials on several grounds, including safety, search, and identification problems posed by the lengthy beard. The court ruled in the inmate's favor, however, arguing that prison officials could take new photographs of the prisoner with long facial hair, that the prisoner could wear special protective facial gear when working around dangerous machinery or food, and that contraband could be detected in beards in a variety of ways that would not require trimming them (*Friedman v. State of Arizona,* 1990). In another case, a prisoner who had not cut his hair for 20 years because of religious beliefs was not required to comply with a New York State Department of Correctional Services directive (*People v. Lewis,* 1986). However, in other cases, the use of marijuana or other illegal substances in order to complete certain religious services obviously has been prohibited. In one case, incense used by Muslim inmates was banned because its odor could be used to mask the smell of marijuana. Further, the odor might be offensive to other non-Muslim inmates (*Munir v. Scott,* 1992).

The Fourth Amendment

The Fourth Amendment states that the right of the people to be secure in their persons, houses, papers, and effects, against unreasonable searches and seizures, shall not be violated, and no Warrants shall issue, but upon probable cause, supported by Oath or affirmation, and particularly describing the place to be searched, and the persons or things to be seized. Prison officials contend that the right to privacy ends whenever an inmate enters a prison or jail (Bronstein, 1980:35). Although searches are necessary to discover contraband and other materials that are either illegal or potentially injurious to inmates, including weapons and other items, some experts disagree and contend that interfering with a prisoner's right to privacy counters any possibility for rehabilitation (Schaar, 1985). The Fourth Amendment provision relating to "search and seizure" is quite apparent in prison and jail settings, where searches and seizures of contraband are routinely conducted. Even those not yet convicted of crimes or awaiting trial in jail settings are subjected to searches and seizures for security purposes. This is understandable. But for prisoners, violations of their privacy are sometimes regarded as discriminatory and evidences of administrative harassment.

One of the first things inmates learn when incarcerated is that prisoners do not enjoy the same rights of privacy as do ordinary citizens in their homes or offices (*United States v. Dawson,* 1975). For example, random shakedowns of cells are permitted in either jails or prisons, without prefacing such searches with a search warrant or probable cause (*Hudson v. Palmer,* 1984; *United States v. Cohen,* 1986; *United States v. Mills,* 1983). Although prison correctional officers do not need probable cause or a search warrant to conduct searches of prisoner cells, prisoners can retain the reasonable expectation that their personal effects will not be wantonly destroyed as a result of the search (*Clifton v. Robinson,* 1980).

Searches and seizures have also included visitors to prisons and jails as well as correctional officers and other institutional staff. Visitors may attempt to smuggle contraband to inmates either in their clothing or body cavities. Searches are sometimes prompted if a reasonable suspicion exists that smuggling of some sort is occurring. Of course, there are almost always disagreements between visitors and prison staff about what constitutes reasonable suspicion. Ordinarily, visitors may be subject to a "pat down" or general frisk in order to determine whether they are concealing contraband. **Strip searches** or "bend and spreads" are degrading and, under certain circumstances, unconstitutional.

In 1985, a 68-year-old mother of an inmate was strip searched in an Arkansas prison on the basis of an informant's tip that she was smuggling drugs to her son (*Smothers v. Gibson,* 1985). It was considered extraordinary by the court that the strip search was conducted one hour after she had begun the visit with her son. Furthermore, she had visited her son every week for the past eight years without incident, and she had been strip searched seven times during this interval without discovery of contraband. The court ruled in the woman's favor that the search was unreasonable (Collins, 1986:60–61).

In a similar case, a woman was subjected to a strip search when visiting her brother. The matron touched her breasts and buttocks and used a flashlight for a **body cavity search.** No contraband was found nor was there ever any suspicion that she was attempting to smuggle anything to her brother (Collins, 1986:60). The search was determined by the court to be unreasonable and in violation of the Fourth Amendment, and the woman was awarded $177,040 in punitive damages (*Blackburn v. Snow,* 1985).

Prison personnel are also subjected to searches from time to time, as they sometimes convey contraband to inmates in exchange for money or other favors. In a sense, they relinquish certain rights to privacy, such as the right against searches and seizures without warrant or probable cause, when they enter prison or jail settings (*Gettleman v. Warner,* 1974). However, the courts have held prison officials to a higher standard when conducting searches of prison staff.

In the New York State Department of Corrections, a handbook provided officers of prisons and jails warned that random strip searches may be conducted. When an officer was subjected to a strip search, including a visual body cavity inspection, he challenged this search on constitutional grounds. The court upheld his claim and ruled that although the state had provided a warning and notice about the possibility of such searches, it was insufficient within the context of the Fourth Amendment. In any case, the court held that body cavity searches of prison staff required a search warrant issued upon probable cause by a judicial officer (*Security and Law Enforcement Employees District Council #82 v. Carey,* 1984). Of course, searches of employee vehicles that are accessible to inmates are permitted as are patdowns and frisks of employees when reasonable suspicion exists (Collins, 1986:60–61).

The Eighth Amendment

The Eighth Amendment says that excessive bail shall not be required, nor excessive fines imposed, nor cruel and unusual punishments inflicted. The **cruel and unusual punishment** provision of this Amendment is most frequently cited by prisoners who challenge the conditions under which they are incarcerated and how they are treated by prison staff. Prison overcrowding, exposure to AIDS or attacks by other prisoners, double-bunking, strip searches, heat or temperature of cells, visitation rights, and adequacy of medical care are only a few of the many issues falling within the scope of the Eighth Amendment that may pertain to cruel and unusual punishment.

Under the Eighth Amendment, prisoners have exhausted practically every conceivable complaint about being incarcerated. They have sought court relief because of a state prison's "failure" to provide prisoners access to vocational or educational training, the "failure" of the prison to provide Spanish-speaking prisoners with courses in Spanish, assignment by prison staff of inmates to work camp details, "failure" of prison officials to make it possible for inmates to hear their favorite television programs during the day, "failure" of prison officials to allow inmates to exercise in any manner they see fit, and placing inmates in solitary confinement for punitive purposes where they lack companionship, intellectual stimulation, and are inactive. Prisoners have also raised issues of prison hygiene and fire safety regulations, the presence of insects in dining areas, plumbing, lighting, and even the location of the prison in relation to the prisoner's family. Most of these complaints have been held by courts to be without merit and not in violation of the cruel and unusual punishment provisions of the Eighth Amendment. This does mean that all prisoner complaints alleging such violations end in dismissals. Deliberate indifference by prison officials to prisoner needs when prisoners are in need of medical treatment and the wanton infliction of pain violates a prisoner's Eighth Amendment rights (*Estelle v. Gamble,* 1976).

Prison and jail overcrowding has already been highlighted in previous chapters as a major correctional issue. There are limits reached by prison and jail populations when overcrowding does become cruel and unusual within the provisions of the Eighth Amendment. Many prisons and jails are currently under court order to reduce their populations so that overcrowding will no longer be problematic and violate inmate rights.

Some court decisions relating to prison and jail overcrowding have been favorable for prisoners. In the case of female pretrial detainees in a California women's detention facility, for example, it was determined that the degree of physical insecurity and psychological stress suffered by inmates as the result of noise, lack of privacy, and shortage of space constituted cruel and unusual punishment (*Fisher v. Winter,* 1983). And in an Oklahoma prison, inmates were forced to sleep in garages, barbershops, libraries, and stairwells, and they were also placed in dormitories without any toilet or shower facilities. These conditions were determined by the court to be in violation of the Eighth Amendment (*Battle v. Anderson,* 1977). Ordinarily, the rated capacities of prisons and jails are used as standards for determining whether they are overcrowded. In another case, a female inmate in an Alaska prison claimed that her Eighth Amendment right against cruel and unusual punishment was violated when she was placed in an all-male wing of the prison. However, the court considered the *evolving standards of decency* test in determining whether her Eighth Amendment rights were seriously infringed in view of the overcrowding at that particular institution (*Galvan v. Carothers,* 1994).

Two landmark cases that have been cited by correctional experts as setbacks for inmates relate to conditions of crowding in prisons and jails. The first case, *Bell v. Wolfish* (1979), is considered by several experts to be a significant setback to the prisoners' rights movement (Coles, 1987:50). This case involved the minimum-security Metropolitan Correctional Center in New York City, a facility operated by the U.S. Bureau of Prisons and designed to accommodate 449 federal prisoners, including many pretrial detainees. It was constructed in 1975 and was considered architecturally progressive and modern, generally a comfortable facility.

Originally, the facility was designed to house inmates in individual cells. But soon, the capacity of the facility was exceeded by inmate overpopulation. Inmates soon were obligated to share their cells with other inmates. This double-bunking and other issues related to overcrowding eventually led to a class-action suit against the facility by several of the pretrial detainees and prisoners. A lower court ruled in favor of the prisoners, holding that "compelling necessity" had not been demonstrated by prison officials in their handling of the overcrowding situation. But the U.S. Supreme Court overturned the lower court and said that the "intent" of prison officials should decide whether double-bunking was intended as "punishment" or a simple deprivation because of necessity. Because no "intent" to punish pretrial detainees could be demonstrated, there was no punishment. Hence, the Eighth Amendment was not violated. The suit by the pretrial detainees and prisoners was lost.

The second case is *Rhodes v. Chapman,* an Ohio matter decided in 1981. In this instance, the single issue of double-bunking was raised and alleged to be cruel and unusual punishment prohibited by the Eighth and Fourteenth Amendments. Kelly Chapman and Richard Jaworski were two inmates of the Southern Ohio Correctional Facility and were housed in the same cell. They contended that double-celling violated their constitutional rights. Furthermore, in support of their claim, they cited the facts that their confinement was long-term and not short-term as was the case in *Bell,* that physical and mental injury would be sustained through such close contact and limited space for movement, and that the Ohio facility was housing 38 percent more inmates than its design capacity specified.

The U.S. Supreme Court ruled that double-celling in this long-term prison facility was neither cruel and unusual punishment nor unconstitutional per se. The court based its holding on the "totality of circumstances" associated with Chapman's and Jaworski's confinement. The cruel and unusual provisions of the Eighth Amendment must be construed in a "flexible and dynamic" manner. Thus, when all factors were considered, no evidence existed that Ohio authorities were wantonly inflicting pain on these or other inmates. These conditions, considered in their totality, did not constitute serious need deprivations. Double-celling, made necessary by the unanticipated increase in prisoners in the facility, did not result in food deprivations, a decrease in the quality of medical care, or a decrease in sanitation standards (Palmer, 1997). The long-term consequences of the *Bell* and *Chapman* cases are the subjects of controversy among correctional experts and scholars (Palmer, 1997).

The Fourteenth Amendment

The relevant portion of the Fourteenth Amendment for inmates is that "no state shall make or enforce any law which shall abridge the privileges or immunities of citizens of the United States; nor shall any State deprive any person of life, liberty, or property, without due process of law; nor deny to any person within its jurisdiction the equal protection of the laws." The "due process" and "equal protection" clauses have resulted in numerous legal challenges by inmates of jails and prisons. Anytime inmates perceive or feel that other inmates are receiving special treatment or privileges, the Fourteenth Amendment is cited as the basis for these grievances. Any discriminatory action by penal authorities against prisoners because of their gender, race, socioeconomic status, ethnicity, or religion would be grounds for Fourteenth Amendment action.

Prisoner classifications according to minimum-security, medium-security, and maximum-security designations are frequently challenged, because they usually result in widely disparate privileges for those in different security categories. Also challenged under the Fourteenth Amendment are denial of participation in various programs such as furloughs and work release, exercise and yard privileges, and conjugal visits with spouses.

Female prisoners often do not receive the same sorts of benefits extended to male prisoners. Prisons for male offenders are designed primarily for male offenders, with little thought given to provisions for female inmates. Services and vocational/educational programs are aimed primarily at male inmates, while female prisoners find these same programs totally unsuitable for their interests. In 1979, however, it was held that state prison authorities must provide women inmates with treatment and facilities that are "substantially equivalent" to those provided men inmates (*Glover v. Johnson,* 1979).

Another Fourteenth Amendment issue pertains to equal protection under the law through access to courts. In a 1977 landmark case in North Carolina, the U.S. Supreme Court declared that adequate law libraries in prisons are one constitutionally acceptable method for ensuring meaningful access to courts. However, the court did not rule out other forms of access such as legal aid clinics, assistance from volunteer attorneys or law students, or some other constitutionally acceptable and equivalent plan (*Bounds v. Smith,* 1977).

Law Libraries and Other Forms of Legal Assistance. Jails and prisons are required to provide modest legal materials and aid to inmates.

Most courts do not specify the nature of this legal aid or material. Each case is judged on its own merits. Some prisons hire lawyers to work with inmates as they prepare appeals and other legal documents. Some prisons have extensive law libraries, xeroxing services, and other legal amenities. However, providing *any* form of legal aid, whether it be books or actual attorney assistance, is costly for any department of corrections (Vogel, 1995a:158).

As technology has transformed our processing of information, the solution to providing legal assistance to prisoners through computers is becoming increasingly common. West Publishing Company has converted the *Supreme Court Reporter* and *U.S. Code Annotated* to CD-ROM formats, with modest updating costs and services. Most regional reporters are available on CD-ROM as well as through West and other companies.

While this particular format is not the same as actual books in library stacks, it is a more economical format for prison systems with scarce resources. The estimated cost of a recommended law book collection for a prison is about $40,000, with a yearly upkeep cost of about $5,000 (Vogel, 1995a:158). For a fraction of this cost, CD-ROMs from West and other companies can be obtained by prisons and maintained for modest update fees annually. Further, CD-ROMs cannot be tampered with in the sense that pages cannot be torn out or destroyed. If the CD itself is damaged, it can be replaced at a nominal charge by the company producing it.

CD-ROM information can be downloaded to floppy disks on computers, and information can be printed with conventional printers. With such computer access, inmates may be granted greater freedom to locate and use relevant materials for their appeals. Vogel (1995a:160) says that information retrieval through CD-ROMs is more rapid than conventional search methods with actual books in libraries. Additionally, on-line services are also available so that inmates can access other law libraries besides the volumes provided by West on CD. Using computers also saves considerable space when compared with the thousands of yards taken up by numerous law volumes.

Situations can be avoided such as occurred in the case of *Vandelft v. Moses* (1994). Vandelft was a prisoner housed in a segregation unit for disciplinary reasons. He was denied access to the prison's law library and could not check out hardbound books. He could only obtain copies of legal cases if he could provide prison staff with the exact citation. He filed suit against the prison, alleging an actual injury as the result of his denial of access to the law library. The court ruled in favor of prison officials, because Vandelft could not specify how he was actually injured by these rules and regulations. Furthermore, Vandelft could not effectively challenge the prison disciplinary infraction leading to his segregative confinement. With computerized library services, it is likely that this and other prison systems might provide more liberal access to prisoners, even those in administrative segregation for disciplinary infractions.

The *actual injury* rule applies if an inmate has no access to legal materials, as opposed to *limited access* to legal materials (Collins and Hagar,

1995:26). Inmates must show proof of harm in suits in which rights infringements are alleged that involve access to legal materials or law libraries. The standard is difficult for inmates to meet, even in cases in which law libraries or legal materials are nonexistent in a prison or jail facility (*Hause v. Vaught,* 1993; *Strickler v. Waters,* 1993). Even where inmates are confined for several days without access to legal materials, they must prove some harm as the result of this inaccessibility to legal materials (*Housely v. Dodson,* 1994) (Collins and Hagar, 1995:26).

State and Federal Statutes

From time to time, state and federal statutes relating to prisoners and the nature of their confinement come into conflict. Significant constitutional issues may be involved. If a state has a law that deprives any inmate of equal protection under U.S. laws or of the right to due process, that law may be challenged as unconstitutional. The successfulness of a suit by an inmate in either a state or federal court does not mean that conditions leading to court action will automatically change, however. There is a considerable lag between court declarations and policy changes, if any policy changes occur at all. Many inmate victories are empty ones, because institutional changes may be strictly forms of tokenism, paying lip service to U.S. Supreme Court decisions. The responsibility for implementing changes in accordance with court guidelines and decisions usually rests with wardens and superintendents. The law is often unclear about the nature of how these court declarations are enforced. In addition, the law permits changes to be made gradually or in stages. Thus, overnight modifications of prison or jail policies are unrealistic and seldom occur.

Sometimes there are circumstances that make it difficult for jails and prisons to comply with what the court says. If adequate law libraries are to be made available for prisoner use, there must be space to locate such library facilities. If this space is lacking, it is difficult for the institution to comply with court demands. In some cases, the exigencies of the situation have caused courts to be less strict with the smaller jails and prisons that lack the necessary space or personnel.

Flagrant conflicts between federal and state statutes attract more court attention, however. Despite the fact that *Ex parte Hull* extended to all jail and prison inmates access to the courts as early as 1941, this was an instance in which states were slow to comply with what the court said. In 1969, for example, the case of *Johnson v. Avery* brought matters to a head by forcing the issue of inmate court access. The case occurred in Tennessee and involved a prisoner, Johnson, who was serving a life sentence. Johnson studied the law diligently, and on numerous occasions helped other inmates to prepare legal documents such as *habeas corpus* petitions, usually for a small fee or other reward.

Tennessee had a statute prohibiting providing legal aid from one prisoner to another. The statute read in part that "no inmate will advise, assist or otherwise contract to aid another, either with or without a fee, to prepare writs or other legal matters . . . inmates are forbidden to set themselves up as practitioners for the purpose . . . of writing writs." Thus, Johnson was violating a Tennessee law, but he was also assisting other prisoners, many of whom were illiterate and could not prepare petitions themselves, in accessing the courts under the 1941 U.S. Supreme Court declaration. As a punishment for his legal assistance to other prisoners, Tennessee authorities placed Johnson in solitary confinement for a year. Eventually, his case was heard by the U.S. Supreme Court. The Court ruled that neither Tennessee nor any other state could prohibit the exercise of legal strategies by inmates, either on their own behalf or on the behalf of other prisoners, as means of accessing the courts. All states would be obligated to comply with this ruling unless they could demonstrate that prisoners had access to some alternative and equivalent form of legal assistance for those seeking postconviction relief. **Postconviction relief** is an attempt by prisoners to obtain some satisfaction for a grievance. This may be a challenge about the nature of their confinement, their initial conviction, or a grievance about some other matter. Thus, the Supreme Court ushered in the "new age in jailhouse lawyering" (Jacobs, 1980:436).

THE JAILHOUSE LAWYER AND THE NATURE OF CIVIL REMEDIES

As we have seen, jailhouse lawyers do not curry the favor of prison or jail officials, and sometimes, officials seek revenge through withholding privileges or denying other ordinary prisoner benefits. Sometimes, retaliatory action takes other forms. In *Johnson v. Avery* (1969), Johnson suffered the punishment and deprivations associated with solitary confinement for nearly a year before the U.S. Supreme Court intervened. Some of the rules Johnson had violated involved furnishing other inmates with telephone numbers of attorneys they might contact for legal help or contacting a public defender on behalf of another inmate.

An illustration of the sluggishness with which various states comply with U.S. Supreme Court decisions is the Texas Department of Corrections and the case of *Novak v. Beto* (1972). At the time the *Johnson* decision was entered, all other state jurisdictions in addition to Tennessee were obligated to revise their correctional regulations to provide some form of *acceptable legal assistance* to prisoners. This acceptable legal assistance might be providing inmates with access to attorneys or to law libraries or both. Of course, other forms of legal assistance would be acceptable as well, provided that they were roughly the equivalent of these types. The Texas Department of Corrections had a prohibition similar to the one in Tennessee voided by the U.S. Supreme Court. But Texas officials maintained that they provided inmates with significant legal aid and that this assistance brought them into compliance with the spirit of the *Johnson* decision.

The U.S. Supreme Court disagreed. While it did not accuse Texas officials of deliberate deception, it did inquire about how many of the 12,000 Texas prisoners at the time wanted legal assistance and how many were actually receiving it. The Court said that it could not be certain from the record of court proceedings whether Texas officials had *not* provided adequate inmate legal assistance, but they could also not ascertain whether Texas officials had provided it either. Therefore, the U.S. Supreme Court obligated Texas officials to show by clear and convincing evidence and in specific terms what the need was for legal assistance on *habeas corpus* matters in the Texas Department of Corrections and to demonstrate that Texas was reasonably satisfying that need.

This Texas case gave many of those unfamiliar with the Texas Department of Corrections an apparent example of institutionalized foot-dragging. For example, Dr. George Beto, director of the Texas Department of Corrections during the period 1962 to 1972, declared that the reason he did not want some inmates setting themselves up as lawyers for other inmates was that "[those inmates] could develop unconscionable control over other inmates" [emphasis mine]. Beto declared that he would "live in mortal fear of a convict-run prison." Subsequently, the issue in Texas was resolved, and jailhouse lawyers in Texas prisons are currently permitted to assist their fellow inmates without interference from prison authorities.

Sixteen years later in 1988, Beto was a professor of criminology at Sam Houston State University in Huntsville, Texas. In a telephone interview with this author, Beto explained some of the reasons for his comments and actions while director of the Texas Department of Corrections. Beto explained that the U.S. Supreme Court had made it fairly clear in the case of *Johnson v. Avery* (1969) that state prisoners were entitled to some form of legal assistance or its equivalent. At the time of the *Novak v. Beto* (1972) case, Beto had retained three full-time attorneys for the Texas Department of Corrections. Their sole responsibility was to handle inmate complaints and serve as legal advisors and inmate attorneys.

Beto noted that many inmate grievances were unrelated to general prison conditions or poor treatment by correctional officers and others. Rather, many prisoners had child adoption matters to contest with their estranged wives or inheritance questions to be resolved. In an attempt to comply with U.S. Supreme Court admonitions, Beto hired an additional seven full-time attorneys to deal with inmate legal issues and problems and to represent them in various complaints. Money allocated for correctional purposes was never an issue. Also, prison overcrowding in the Texas Department of Corrections was not problematic. The U.S. Supreme Court decision hinged mainly on the interpretation it made of Texas's attempt to provide "acceptable" legal assistance or some reasonable alternative.

Beto was concerned that some prisoners who acquired legal knowledge would use this information for their own personal gain. The image of the altruistic "jailhouse lawyer" doing only what was right to assist other inmates was not a true picture of how inmate legal assistance was being dispensed. Rather, the legal aid provided by some inmates for others, regardless of its quality, was used primarily as a means of controlling other inmates. It was an instrument whereby the inmate pecking order could be strengthened. In fact, some inmates profited from the advice they provided their fellow prisoners. Thus, Beto was interested in preventing an inmate-dominated and exploitative legal system rather than prolonging Texas compliance with U.S. Supreme Court orders for provisions of acceptable legal assistance to prisoners.

Avenues for Civil Remedies

There are three basic avenues whereby jail and prison inmates can petition the courts concerning civil wrongs. The most widely used avenue is 42 U.S.C., Section 1983 (1997), which holds that "every person who, under color of any statute, ordinance, regulation, custom, or usage, of any State or Territory, subjects, or causes to be subjected, any citizen of the United States or other person within the jurisdiction thereof to the deprivation of any rights, privileges, or immunities secured by the Constitution and laws, shall be liable to the party injured in an action at law, suit in equity, or other proper proceeding for redress" (Palmer, 1997). These actions are known as **Section 1983 actions.**

A second avenue is through 28 U.S.C., Section 2674 (1997), known as the **Federal Tort Claims Act of 1946.** This Act provides that "the United States shall be liable, respecting the provisions of this title relating to tort claims, in the same manner and to the same extent as a private individual under like circumstances, but shall not be liable for interest prior to judgment for punitive damages." The U.S. Supreme Court decided in 1963 that inmates of federal prisons could file petitions against prison administrators and correctional officers under the Federal Tort Claims Act in the case of *United States v. Muniz* (1963). Until this Supreme Court action, prison officials enjoyed sovereign immunity from suits by prisoners alleging damages or injuries through administrative negligence. Currently, officials have qualified immunity, excepting them from suits under this section, alleging that "any claim arising out of assault, battery, false imprisonment, false arrest, malicious prosecution, abuse of process, libel, slander, misrepresentation, deceit, or interference with contract rights" (28 U.S.C. Sec. 2680, 1997).

Like a *habeas corpus* action, Section 1983 actions may challenge the conditions of confinement, but the fact and length of incarceration are not within this section's purview (*Preiser v. Rodriguez,* 1973). In order for prisoners to effectively challenge their imprisonment in court, they must file a *habeas corpus* petition under the Federal Habeas Corpus Statute (28 U.S.C., Section 2241, U.S. Code (1997). In recent years, *habeas corpus* petitions filed by prisoners have declined appreciably, while the number of Section 1983 petitions has systematically increased. Since state courts have concurrent jurisdiction with federal courts in deciding cases based entirely upon federal claims, state or federal prison inmates may choose either court for their litigation.

Table 9.1 shows the numbers of petitions filed by state and federal prison inmates from 1977 through 1995 (Maguire and Pastore, 1996:517). These figures do not include inmate filings in state courts.

Civil Rights Petitions. Federal prisoners filed 483 civil rights (42 U.S.C. Section 1983) petitions in 1977, and these filings escalated to 510 in 1995. For state prisoners, 7,752 civil rights petitions were filed in 1977 in U.S. district courts, while these petitions increased to 40,569 in 1995.

***Habeas Corpus* Actions.** *Habeas corpus* petitions made up 1,745 for prison inmates in 1977, while the number of federal inmate *habeas corpus* filings decreased to 1,343 in 1995. For state inmates, however, *habeas corpus* petitions rose from 6,866 filed in 1977 to 13,632 filings in 1995.

Total petitions filed by federal inmates in 1977 were 19,537, while state prison inmates filed 14,846 petitions that same year. By 1995, 63,550 petitions were filed in federal courts by federal prisoners, while state prisoners filed 54,599 petitions (Maguire and Pastore, 1996:517). Thus, in 1995, federal district courts processed 118,149 petitions by state and federal prison inmates. This is only a fraction of state court filings, however. Most of these inmate petitions have been considered frivolous and a waste of court time (Maahs and del Carmen, 1996:53).

The Prison Litigation Reform Act of 1995

In 1995 Congress enacted the **Prison Litigation Reform Act of 1995** (PLRA), which was designed to decrease the sheer numbers of state and federal filings of inmate lawsuits in federal courts. Among other things, the PLRA was geared to prevent multiple suit filings by the same prisoners in cases in which the suits were determined to be frivolous.

Prior to the PLRA, inmates who could not afford the filing fees for their lawsuits could rely upon the government to pay these fees for them. Further, there was no limit regarding the number of times a particular issue could be litigated by filing different lawsuits. Following the Act's passage, the PLRA pertained to all federal, state, or local prisons; jails; and detention centers.

Note that the PLRA does not apply to state claims raised by inmates in state courts. However, the PLRA does pertain to federal claims raised in state courts. Section 804 of the PLRA is particularly important, because it causes inmates to be accountable for their own filing fees. If prisoners cannot afford the filing fees for their suits against prisons, then provisions are made for deducting filing fee costs from their prison earnings on a monthly basis. Because inmates earn very little in prisons, this provision hurts them in their own pocketbooks. Thus, they will be prevented from purchasing certain goods in prison commissaries if their money is taken to cover the fees involved in their frivolous litigation.

Section 804 of the PLRA further provides that courts may dismiss prisoner-filed suits on grounds including frivolousness, maliciousness, fail-

TABLE 9.1 Petitions Filed in U.S. District Courts by Federal and State Prisoners by Type of Petition, 1977–1995

		Petitions by Federal Prisoners					Petitions by State Prisoners				
	Total	Total	Motions to Vacate Sentence	Habeas Corpus	Mandamus, etc.	Civil Rights	Total	Motions to Vacate Sentence	Habeas Corpus	Mandamus, etc.	Civil Rights
1977	19,537	4,691	1,921	1,745	542	483	14,846	NA	6,866	228	7,752
1978	21,924	4,955	1,924	1,851	544	636	16,969	NA	7,033	206	9,730
1979	23,001	4,499	1,907	1,664	340	588	18,502	NA	7,123	184	11,195
1980	23,287	3,713	1,322	1,465	323	603	19,574	NA	7,031	146	12,397
1981	27,711	4,104	1,248	1,680	342	834	23,607	NA	7,790	178	15,639
1982	29,303	4,328	1,186	1,927	381	834	24,975	NA	8,059	175	16,741
1983	30,775	4,354	1,311	1,914	339	790	26,421	NA	8,532	202	17,687
1984	31,107	4,526	1,427	1,905	372	822	26,581	NA	8,349	198	18,034
1985	33,468	6,262	1,527	3,405	373	957	27,206	NA	8,534	181	18,491
1986	33,765	4,432	1,556	1,679	427	770	29,333	0	9,045	216	20,072
1987	37,316	4,519	1,669	1,812	313	725	32,797	7	9,542	276	22,972
1988	38,839	5,130	2,071	1,867	330	862	33,709	0	9,880	270	23,559
1989	41,481	5,577	2,526	1,818	315	918	35,904	0	10,554	311	25,039
1990	42,630	6,611	2,970	1,967	525	1,149	36,019	0	10,823	353	24,843
1991	42,462	6,817	3,328	2,112	378	999	35,645	0	10,331	268	25,046
1992	48,423	6,997	3,983	1,507	597	910	41,426	0	11,299	481	29,646
1993	53,451	8,456	5,379	1,467	695	915	44,995	0	11,587	390	33,018
1994	57,940	7,700	4,628	1,441	491	1,140	50,240	0	11,918	397	37,925
1995	63,550	8,951	5,988	1,343	510	1,110	54,599	0	13,632	398	40,569
Percent change 1995 over 1994	9.7%	16.2%	29.4%	–6.8%	3.9%	–2.6%	8.7%	X	14.4%	(a)	7.0%

[a] Less than 0.5 percent.

Source: Administrative Office of the United States Courts. *Annual Report of the Director, 1985,* p. 149; *1986,* p. 176; *1995,* p. 139 (Washington, DC: Administrative Office of the United States Courts); and Administrative Office of the United States Courts, *Annual Report of the Director, 1987,* p. 179; *1988,* p. 182; *1989,* p. 178; *1990,* p. 138; *1991,* p. 191; 1992, p. 179; *1993,* p. A1-55; *1994,* Table C-2 (Washington, DC: USGPO). Table adapted by SOURCEBOOK staff. In Maguire and Pastore (1996:517).

Box 9.1 The Prison Litigation Reform Act Summarized

(Commerce—Justice—State Appropriations Bill Version)

Section 801. Title

"Prison Litigation Reform Act of 1995"

Section 8.2 Appropriate Remedies for Prison Conditions

(Amends 18 U.S.C.§3626)

Limits on "prospective relief" (injunctive relief and consent decrees) (§ (a)(1)(A)):

- Cannot be entered unless there is a finding of a federal violation;
- Order must be narrowly drawn, extend no further than necessary to correct the federal violation, and be the least intrusive remedy;
- "Substantial weight" to any adverse impact on public safety or operation of a criminal justice system;
- Cannot violate local or state law—limited exceptions (§(a)(1)(B); BUT: Court can't order prison construction or new taxes (§(a)(1)(C)).
- Preliminary injunctions—90-day time limit (§(a)(2)).

Additional Limitations on Population Caps (§(a)(3)):

- Court must first order a "less intrusive" remedy with "reasonable time" to comply;
- In federal court: can only be ordered by three-judge panel;
- Crowding must be the "primary cause" of the federal violation and there is no other remedy that will cure violation;
- Intervention for state or local officials (prosecutors, corrections, appropriators);

Termination of Injunctions and Consent Decrees (§(b)):

- Party entitled to termination, upon motion, if injunction/consent decree is more than two years old (pre-PLRA orders terminable two years after enactment: (§(b)(1));
- Party or intervenor entitled to immediate termination where court did enter findings in accordance with PLRA (§(2)); BUT: No termination if injunctive relief still necessary to correct current or ongoing violation (§(3)).
- Parties may still seek modification/termination under existing law (§(4)).

Settlements (§(c)):

- Consent decrees must comply with PLRA requirements (§(c)(1));
- "private settlement agreements" (agreement provisions not court enforceable) not subject to PLRA (§(c)(2));

State Law Remedies (§(d)):

- PLRA limitations do not apply to state law claims raised in state court [Note: PLRA will apply to federal claims raised in state court].

Procedure on Motion to Modify or Terminate (§(e)):

- Injunctive relief is automatically stayed if court does not timely rule on the motion. Time limits: PLRA motions 30 days; all other motions 180 days.

Special Masters (§(f)):

- Appointment: person must be "disinterested and objective" and give "due regard to the public safety"; selected from lists submitted by parties; parties may appeal appointment order; court must review appointment every six months;
- Limited Powers and Duties; can only make proposed findings of fact based upon the record; no ex parte communications or findings; may assist in remedial plans;
- Compensation: Same rate as court appointed counsel, paid by federal funds;
- Termination of appointment; may be removed at any time, but not later than termination of relief.

Definitions (§(g)): Make Clear That PLRA Limitations:

1. Apply to any injunctive order based upon consent or acquiesce;
2. Apply to all prisoner (adult and juveniles) claims except habeas; and
3. Apply to federal, state or local prisons, jails and detention centers.

PLRA Application: fully retroactive; applies to orders entered before enactment date.

Section 803. Amendments to CRIPA

- For actions by United States (on behalf of prisoners), requires Attorney General to personally sign complaints, certifications, and intervention motion;
- For suits by prisoners:
  - Must exhaust administrative remedies (even if procedures are not certified);
  - Court on own motion may dismiss civil rights action on four grounds (frivolous, malicious, fails to state claims, defendant immune);
  - Attorneys fees (under Civil Rights Act)

    Only awarded if "directly incurred" in proving "actual" federal violation, or remedial matters [This eliminates fees for related, but unsuccessful, claims, fees for voluntary actions in response to lawsuit (known as the "catalyst" theory of recovery); and fees for ancillary litigation.];

    Cannot proportionally exceed relief obtained (but later refers to 150 percent of judgment limitation);

    First 25 percent of monetary judgment shall be applied to attorney's fees;

    Maximum hourly rate 150 percent of rate for court appointed attorneys.
  - No recovery for mental/emotional injury w/o prior showing of physical injury;
  - Pretrial hearings may be conducted by telephone or video;
  - Defendant may waive the right to reply, Court may order reply, but can't grant relief w/o first requiring reply.

Section 804. In Forma Pauperis Proceedings

- Establishes a partial filing fee system;
- Prisoner must submit certified copy of prison account;
- Court must assess full filing fee;
- Court must collect initial partial filing payment (when funds exist, 20 percent of the greater of average monthly deposits or average monthly balance);

continued

- After initial partial payment, prisoner shall make monthly payments whenever account amount exceeds $10;

BUT: Prisoner cannot be prevented from bringing action on basis that he has no assets.

- Court may appoint counsel for any person [this would also apply to indigent defendants, such as crime victims or witnesses];
- Court may dismiss on four grounds (frivolous, malicious, fails to state a claim, immunity);
- Bankruptcy exception-fees not dischargeable in bankruptcy;
- Prisoner shall be required to pay full amount of any costs assessed;
- Successive claims—if three or more actions dismissed on grounds of frivolous, malicious, fails to state a claim, prisoner cannot bring an IFP action unless imminent danger of serious physical injury.

Section 805. Judicial Screening

- Court must screen prisoner claims against government or government officials;
- Must identify cognizable claims or dismiss (if frivolous, malicious, fails to state claims, or immunity).

Section 806. Federal Tort Claims

- Prisoner can't bring action against U.S. (or employee) for mental/emotional injury w/o prior showing of physical injury.

Section 807. Payment of Damage Award in Satisfaction of Pending Restitution Orders

- Any damage award to prisoner in civil rights action must first satisfy any outstanding restitution orders; remainder then goes to the prisoner.

Section 808. Notice to Crime Victims of Pending Damage Award

- Prior to payment of compensatory damages, crime victims must be notified of pending payment.

Section 809. Revocation of Federal Good Time Credit

- Good time credit can be revoked where prisoner brings civil action—
  —for a malicious purpose;
  —to harass defendant;
  —false testimony or false evidence by prisoner

Section 810 Severability

Sarah B. Vandenbraak
Chief Counsel, Pennsylvania
Department of Corrections

Source: American Jails, 1996:104–105.

ure to state a claim upon which relief can be granted, and immunity. Further, filing fees are not dischargable through inmate bankruptcy proceedings. Another provision of Section 804 is that if three or more actions are dismissed on frivolous or malicious grounds, then the prisoner cannot bring an *in forma pauperis* action (claiming indigence) unless it is clearly demonstrated that there is imminent danger or serious physical injury.

Section 805 of the PLRA provides for judicial screenings of inmate suit filings. Prisoners are prevented under Section 806 from bringing tort actions against the United States government or its employees for mental or emotional injuries unless they can demonstrate actual physical injury. Furthermore, any monetary damages awarded to successful inmates must be paid first as restitution to one's victims or to any outstanding restitution orders, and then the remainder goes to the prisoner. And last but not least, Section 809 provides that good-time credit can be revoked in cases in which prisoners bring civil actions for malicious purposes, or for purposes of harassment, or if they give false testimony or present false evidence. Thus, the PLRA is a general deterrent to much of the previously filed inmate litigation. If these sanctions are enforced, it is likely that in future years the sheer amount of inmate litigation will decline. (Call, 1995b; Maahs and del Carmen, 1996).

PRISONER RIGHTS AND SELECTED LITIGATION ISSUES

Thus far, we have examined the U.S. Constitution and selected Amendments that are frequently the grounds of inmate lawsuits against prison staff and administration. In this section, several issues that pertain to each of these Amendments have been selected. This coverage is not intended to be comprehensive. Rather, it seeks to highlight briefly some of the types of cases that reach federal and state courts of appeals. Some of these issues are significant enough to reach the U.S. Supreme Court where they become landmark cases in corrections. These issues include (1) racism, due process, and equal protection; (2) the right to rehabilitation; (3) misclassification problems and program eligibility; (4) cell searches and seizures of contraband; (5) cruel and unusual punishment; (6) double-bunking, overcrowding, and a right to privacy; (7) plain negligence, intentional neglect, and deliberate indifference; and (8) the death penalty: the why's, who's, and how's of its administration.

Racism, Due Process, and Equal Protection

Because nearly half the prison population is black and a majority of that same population is nonwhite, considerable legal action is prompted by alleged racism within the correctional system. It is not a phenomenon particularly related to corrections. Sentencing disparities, plea bargain arrangements, and arrests seem closely connected with racial and ethnic factors (Hanson and Daley, 1995; Palmer, 1997). It is not surprising, therefore, that these same disparities carry over into corrections and influence in various ways the nature and circumstances of prisoner confinement.

Successful legal action by inmates in cases in which racism is alleged is difficult to sustain in court. Many inmate petitions alleging discrimination or racism are categorically rejected as lacking merit or are dismissed out of hand by federal and state judges. For instance, many incarcerated Black Muslims deluged the courts with petitions alleging that they were denied racial and religious equality during the 1960s (Jacobs, 1980:434). According to Jacobs (1980:434), there were 66 reported federal court decisions pertaining to Black Muslims between 1961 and 1978. Despite the successes achieved by these actions, the Muslims experienced a fairly high failure or rejection rate in the suits they filed. But they emerged in the 1970s as the best organized prisoner aggregate, and they demonstrated for other prisoners the fruits of organized protest and the influence of solidarity in legal actions (Jacobs, 1980:435). We have seen that not all actions alleging discrimination involve racial or ethnic factors. Some discrimination suits pertain to women and their equal protection under the law. Thus, the U.S. Supreme Court has stated that female prisoners are entitled to facilities and programs comparable to those enjoyed by male inmates, with the primary exceptions being when the implementation of these comparable programs causes hardships for prison administration (Sharbaro and Keller, 1995).

The Right to Rehabilitation

Unless otherwise specified by particular state jurisdictions, prisoners do not have an absolute right to be rehabilitated (Knight, 1992). Thus, if parolees commit new crimes, the state is immune from suits in which it is alleged that the prison system failed to rehabilitate a given offender properly. Most prisons provide various educational and vocational services, however. Thus, if certain inmates wish to improve their skills or obtain counseling or other forms of personal assistance, such assistance can usually be provided in most prison systems. Service delivery for mental health care within prison settings has received much attention in the last several decades. It is increasingly important for prison officials to see to the mental health needs of certain types of offenders with psychological problems (Marra, Shively, and Minaker, 1989).

Female inmates are particularly affected, because their facilities typically are smaller and less well equipped than men's institutions. Although we will examine female inmates more extensively in Chapter 13, for the present it is sufficient to note that even when courts recognize equal protection claims raised by female inmates, identical treatment for men and women is not mandated, and separate can be equal (Knight, 1992).

Misclassification Problems and Program Eligibility

There is a tendency in most prison systems in the United States to overclassify offenders. That is, instead of classifying an offender as minimum-security, he or she is classified as medium- or maximum-security for purposes of supervision and custody. The higher the level of custody, usually the fewer the amenities enjoyed. In addition to these restrictions, prisoners may not be eligible for certain types of programs designed for low-risk offenders. Some programs bar medium-security and maximum-security inmates, because the programs involve fewer restrictions and greater access to prison areas that are otherwise off-limits to those classified at higher security levels (Champion, 1994).

Cell Searches and Seizures of Contraband

Inmates of jails and prisons have little standing in court when the issue of searches and seizures is raised (Ellis, 1986; Palmer, 1997). It has been determined that prisoners can have absolutely no expectation of privacy when they enter prisons and jails (*Bell v. Wolfish,* 1979; *Hudson v. Palmer,* 1984). However, correctional officers are encouraged to exercise caution so that an inmate's personal effects, as distinguished from legitimate contraband, will not be damaged in the process of their search. Otherwise, tort liability may attach, and correctional officers may be sued for damages sustained to prisoner personal property.

Jail inmates and those incarcerated in prisons are subject to strip searches, including examinations of their body cavities, for purposes of discovering contraband. Again, no warrant is necessary for such searches, despite the psychological and physical discomforts such searches may cause prisoners. Also, if reasonable suspicion exists, searches may be conducted of correctional officers and visitors, under limited conditions. It has been determined, however, that searches of correctional officer body cavities require warrants based upon probable cause and authorized by a judicial officer (*Security and Law Enforcement Employees District Council #82 v. Carey,* 1984).

Cruel and Unusual Punishment

The question of what constitutes cruel and unusual punishment within the context of the Eighth Amendment is highly subjective. The U.S. Supreme Court and lower federal and state courts have had to wrestle with this question for many decades. However, the U.S. Supreme Court has chosen never to define explicitly what this phrase means (Knight and Early, 1986:59). When correctional officers or other prison staff have used force against inmates to induce compliance to prison rules and regulations, some prisoners have labeled this force cruel and unusual. Prison and jail overcrowding have also been labeled as cruel and unusual, although as we have seen, it takes considerable overcrowding in any institutional setting before the U.S. Supreme Court will take notice and intervene to limit or prevent it.

Virtually every type of corporal punishment has been banned in prisons and jails. The infamous "Red Hannah" whipping post used in Delaware was eventually prohibited as a sanctioning device in prisons. Other similar lashing punishments also have been banned in other jurisdictions. Sometimes, noncorporal punishments such as placement in solitary confinement have caused prisoners to complain that this is cruel and unusual. Physical separation from others and the lack of communication are psychologically painful, but the courts find little merit in prisoner complaints that this punishment form is cruel and unusual per se.

If the punishment is excessive in relation to the crime committed, the courts will probably agree that the test for cruel and unusual punishment under the Eighth Amendment is met. In the case of *Enmund v. Florida* (1982), Enmund and another defendant were convicted of first-degree murder by a Florida court and sentenced to death. However, evidence produced at the trial showed that Enmund was only incidentally related to the murders, since he was only a passenger in the getaway vehicle. Under Florida law, however, the "felony murder" statute prescribed the death penalty for anyone involved in the perpetration of a felony in which anyone is killed, despite the fact that there may be no premeditation or intent to cause one's death. The U.S. Supreme Court decided in favor of Enmund that his sentence of death was disproportionate to his involvement in the crime. Simply put, the death penalty was too severe a punishment.

However, in another case, an habitual offender named Rummel with two previous felony convictions (both fraud cases) in Texas was convicted of a third felony, theft by false pretenses in the amount of $120.00. Rummel was sentenced to life imprisonment for his third felony conviction under the Texas statute. In his case, the U.S. Supreme Court determined that the mandatory penalty of life imprisonment for habitual offenders was constitutional and not disproportionate to the crime committed (*Rummel v. Estelle,* 1980). Suffice it to say that cruel and unusual punishment is an elusive concept, and that the U.S. Supreme Court has not yet dealt with the term adequately. Seemingly, injustices occur against some inmates and not against others for essentially the same or similar infractions, although the courts strive, under *stare decisis,* to be uniform in the application of judicial precedents.

Double-Bunking, Overcrowding, and the Right to Privacy

The issue of **double-bunking** (placing more than one person in a cell designed to accommodate only one person) has already been partially decided by *Rhodes v. Chapman* (1981) and earlier in *Bell v. Wolfish* (1979) (Coles, 1987). In the *Bell* case, the new Metropolitan Correctional Center in New York City was the target of prisoner complaints. Specifically, numerous pretrial detainees objected to the crowding in their cells as well as other matters that included cell searches, strip searches, and mail censorship. Successes achieved by prisoners in lower courts in the *Bell* case were overturned by the U.S. Supreme Court, which held that the crowding was inadvertent and not a deliberate act of punishment by jail authorities. The fact that the Metropolitan Correctional Center was considered a short-term confinement facility may have influenced their decision. However, a similar ruling was handed down by the U.S. Supreme Court for a long-term facility in the *Rhodes v. Chapman* case. It determined that 32 square feet (a 4-by-8-foot cell shared by two inmates) was not sufficiently small to constitute cruel and unusual punishment within the context of the Eighth Amendment. When is a jail or prison overcrowded? This is subject to judicial interpretation. Some courts use the rated capacity/actual capacity ratio as a means of determining the seriousness of overcrowding. Other courts inspect the premises and determine whether overcrowding exists on a purely subjective basis (Wener and Keys, 1988).

Furthermore, there is no constitutional right to privacy for inmates of jails and prisons (Coles, 1987; Schaar, 1985). The premises of facilities designed to confine and control prisoners, regardless of their status, are subject to search by authorities. If contraband, meaning any illegal goods, is found in their possession or on their premises, such contraband is subject to seizure. Of course, we know that correctional officers and other officers are expected to exercise some degree of care in handling an inmate's personal effects.

Plain Negligence, Intentional Neglect, and Deliberate Indifference

Because jail and prison overcrowding, inmate violence, and substandard health and safety conditions seem to characterize many U.S. penal facilities, it is often difficult for judges to distinguish between the administrative actions of these facilities that are primarily the function of these conditions and those actions that are deliberately intended to cause prisoners physical or psychological harm (Cole and Call, 1992). Thus, if a prisoner is sexually assaulted by another prisoner in a cell that contains four inmates but is designed to accommodate only two, is this assault the fault of the prison administrator or simply the result of unanticipated overcrowding, something over which the administrator exerts little or no control (Hunt et al., 1993)?

Negligence generally refers to a duty of one person to another, to act as a reasonable person might be expected to act, or the failure to act when action is appropriate. Legally, negligence is the failure to exercise reasonable care toward another (Black, 1990:1033–1034). There are different kinds of negligence as well as different degrees of negligence. State and federal governments may be liable if their prison correctional officers fail to perform according to certain standards of training. Under theories of **negligent training** (an officer is simply improperly trained or untrained),

negligent assignment (an officer is assigned a position for which he or she is unqualified), **negligent entrustment** (administrators fail to monitor those officers entrusted with items they are unfamiliar with using, such as giving firearms to prison correctional officers without first exposing them to firearms training), or **negligent retention** (those officers determined to be unfit for their jobs are kept in those jobs anyway), inmates may have grounds to sue the government or their administrative representatives (del Carmen, 1986:160–172).

Degrees of negligence include slight, ordinary, and gross, although the courts regard these as significant degrees of care rather than degrees of negligence (Black, 1990:1033–1034). However, gross negligence includes willful, wanton, and reckless negligence, where acts are performed that are totally unreasonable and without regard for the consequences. The standard for establishing negligence of officials or officers is a civil one, the "preponderance of evidence" standard. Thus, whether the plaintiff (usually the inmate) or the defendant (usually administrators of a prison or jail or their agents—correctional officers or other officers) prevails is contingent upon whether the preponderance of evidence is in the plaintiff's favor or the defendant's favor. These cases become "judgment calls" by either judges or juries, provided the cases reach trial. And, as we have seen, few inmate cases reach the trial stage because of motions to dismiss or because of summary judgments granted.

It is generally conceded that if the government is negligent or if any agent or agency of the government is negligent in its treatment of prisoners, liability is incurred and damages may be sought by inmates for relief. But establishing negligence is difficult. Consider the following cases. An inmate was placed in a District of Columbia prison in a cell with another inmate who had active tuberculosis (*Sypert v. United States,* 1983). The plaintiff sued the government and administrators, alleging negligence, because he was placed in a cell with a tubercular inmate, and subsequent skin tests showed the presence of tubercle bacilli in his body. However, because he never developed active tuberculosis, the court ruled that he had suffered no physical injury and dismissed the case against the government.

In another case, an Oregon prison inmate was stabbed with a knife by another inmate (*Walker v. United States,* 1977). The injured inmate sued Oregon officials, alleging that they were negligent in the enforcement of prison rules regarding the search for contraband knives and other dangerous weapons potentially hazardous to other inmates. However, the preponderance of evidence presented in court by the injured inmate failed to show that either the correctional officers or other correctional officials were negligent.

Two cases involving administrative knowledge of gang warfare and violence and prisoner safety are also of interest here (Hunt et al., 1993). In one case, a prisoner alleged administrative negligence in the classification of the prisoner to a higher level of security and interaction with more dangerous prisoners. The inmate was subsequently killed by other violent inmates and his relatives brought suit against the administrator of corrections (*Quinones v. Nettleship,* 1985). Questions were raised and affidavits presented by other inmates about general jail safety conditions, about where the correctional officers were or could have been positioned, and what steps were taken by administrators to protect other inmates from gang warfare. Again, administrative blame was not established by a preponderance of the evidence.

A Texas case involved an inmate being held in the Dallas County Jail. He had testified briefly against another inmate, held in the same jail, that the other inmate had told him he had possessed and transported another's stolen automobile. Through local newspapers distributed among other prisoners at the jail, inmates soon learned of the plaintiff's testimony. They subjected him to a severe beating, and he subsequently sued the U.S. government and jail employees, alleging that they failed to foresee the tortious and criminal acts that would occur as the result of his court testimony. The court ruled that the government had no duty to foresee such acts and absolved jail officials of blame in the incident (*Hackett v. United States,* 1978). In many cases, severe overcrowding problems create serious security problems for inmates in need of protection from other prisoners (Salive, Smith, and Brewer, 1990; Semanchik, 1990).

Many authorities agree that inmates are at a considerable disadvantage in the suits they file. Whenever they "win," it is difficult to determine the substance of their victory. Jail and prison officials may engage in subtle reprisals. These reprisals may involve civil rights violations or deliberate torts, but as we have seen, even seemingly flagrant tortious cases are difficult to prove, especially using the preponderance of evidence standard. And when property claims are awarded prisoners, these amounts are often token damages and very small (Hunzeker and Conger, 1985).

The Death Penalty: The Why's, Who's, and How's of Its Administration

Perhaps the most controversial of all prisoner issues is **capital punishment** and the imposition of the death penalty. The following discussion is not intended as a philosophical critique or examination of capital punishment. More extensive theoretical discussions of the pros and cons of the death penalty are found elsewhere (Gewerth and Dorne, 1991; Sellin, 1980). Rather, the discussion is designed to highlight some of the stronger arguments for and against capital punishment. Further, some indication is provided of the frequency of its use in the United States during the last several decades. Prisoners who have been convicted of capital crimes and sentenced to death contend that the death penalty is cruel and unusual punishment. As such, they claim that it violates their Eighth Amendment rights and should not be applied. Attorneys for these defendants argue similarly that while their clients should be punished, they should be punished by means other than capital punishment.

Death Row Inmates. The death penalty has almost always been used in the United States as a punishment for those committing capital or extremely serious offenses. Not all states have death penalty provisions, however. In 1996, 38 states and the federal government had death penalty statutes and inmates on death row (Maguire and Pastore, 1996:604). Table 9.2 shows the 3,122 prisoners under sentence of death and on **death row** as of April 30, 1996, according to their race or ethnicity (Maguire and Pastore, 1996:604).

California leads all states with 444 death row inmates, followed by Texas with 394, and Florida with 351. Several states with death penalty statutes did not have any inmates on death rows by the end of April 1996. These included Kansas, New Hampshire, New York, and Wyoming.

Characteristics of Death Row Inmates. Table 9.3 shows a profile of death row inmates by year-end 1994 (Maguire and Pastore, 1996:604). Most death row inmates are male (98.6 percent), while about 41 percent are black. About half of all death row inmates were never married, and about 24 percent were widowed, divorced, or separated. Almost 70 percent had previous felony convictions. About 52 percent of these death row inmates had less than a high school education, while over 50 percent were between the ages of 20 and 39. Less than 1 percent of all death row inmates were under age 20 (Maguire and Pastore, 1996:604).

Numbers of Executions Since 1930. Between 1930 and year-end 1994, there were 4,116 executions in the United States. Table 9.4 shows a distribution of these executions by state. Table 9.4 also shows numbers of executions carried out by individual states since 1977. (In 1972, capital punishment was suspended temporarily while the courts determined an appropriate procedure to follow in death penalty cases [*Furman v. Georgia,* 1972]). In 1976, capital punishment resumed following the case of *Gregg v. Georgia* (1976). The first execution since the *Gregg* case was carried out in 1977. Between 1977 and year-end 1994, there were 257 executions. Texas, Florida, Virginia, and Louisiana led all states in the numbers of offenders executed between 1977 and 1994. Figure 9.1 shows graphically the trend in U.S. executions from 1930–1994.

Time Lapse Between Sentences of Death and Execution of Sentences. There is a considerable time interval between the time that prisoners are sentenced to death and when they are ultimately executed. The average amount of time lapsing between sentences of death and carrying out these sentences is 97 months, or about 8 years. The reason for this 8-year interval is that there are numerous appeals filed by death row inmates. Appeals often result in stays of execution until the appeals can be decided. In most instances, the death sentences eventually are imposed, after all appeals have been exhausted. However, in some cases, executives may commute death sentences to life-without-parole sentences. Table 9.5

TABLE 9.2 **Prisoners Under Sentence of Death by Race, Ethnicity, and Jurisdiction, on April 30, 1996**

		Race, Ethnicity					
Jurisdiction	Total	White	Black	Hispanic	Native American	Asian	Unknown
United States[a]	3,122	1,493	1,272	236	50	22	49
Federal statutes	8	2	5	1	0	0	0
U.S. military	8	1	6	0	0	1	0
Alabama	144	79	56	1	0	1	7
Arizona	121	80	16	21	4	0	0
Arkansas	37	20	15	1	1	0	0
California	444	179	158	61	13	7	26
Colorado	4	2	1	1	0	0	0
Connecticut	5	3	2	0	0	0	0
Delaware	11	5	6	0	0	0	0
Florida	351	192	122	35	1	1	0
Georgia	108	61	46	0	0	0	1
Idaho	19	18	0	1	0	0	0
Illinois	164	54	104	5	0	0	1
Indiana	50	32	17	1	0	0	0
Kansas	0	X	X	X	X	X	X
Kentucky	28	21	7	0	0	0	0
Louisiana	53	13	33	5	0	0	2
Maryland	17	3	14	0	0	0	0
Mississippi	54	21	32	0	0	0	1
Missouri	92	49	38	1	1	1	2
Montana	6	5	0	0	1	0	0
Nebraska	10	7	2	0	1	0	0
Nevada	85	41	33	10	0	1	0
New Hampshire	0	X	X	X	X	X	X
New Jersey	14	6	7	1	0	0	0
New Mexico	3	1	0	2	0	0	0
New York	0	X	X	X	X	X	X
North Carolina	154	73	74	1	4	0	2
Ohio	150	70	74	3	2	0	1
Oklahoma	119	68	34	1	13	3	0
Oregon	22	19	1	1	1	0	0
Pennsylvania	200	62	124	12	0	2	0
South Carolina	71	33	37	0	1	0	0
South Dakota	2	2	0	0	0	0	0
Tennessee	102	66	32	1	2	1	0
Texas	394	165	147	68	5	3	6
Utah	10	7	2	1	0	0	0
Virginia	54	26	27	1	0	0	0
Washington	13	10	2	0	0	1	0
Wyoming	0	X	X	X	X	X	X

Note: The NAACP Legal Defense and Educational Fund, Inc. periodically collects data on persons on death row. As of April 30, 1996, 38 states, the federal government, and the United States military had capital punishment laws; 34 states, the federal government, and the United States military had at least 1 prisoner under sentence of death. Between January 1, 1973 and April 30, 1996, an estimated 1,529 convictions or sentences have been reversed or vacated on grounds other than constitutional. Between January 1, 1973 and May 30, 1990, an estimated 558 death sentences have been vacated as unconstitutional.

[a] Detail will not add to total because prisoners sentenced to death in more than one state are listed in the respective state totals, but each is counted only once at the national level.

Source: Table constructed by SOURCEBOOK staff from data provided by the NAACP Legal Defense and Educational Fund, Inc. In Maguire and Pastore (1996:604).

TABLE 9.3 Prisoners Under Sentence of Death by Demographic Characteristics, Prior Felony Conviction History, and Legal Status, United States, on December 31, 1994

Total number	2,890
Sex	
Male	98.6%
Female	1.4
Race	
White	56.9
Black	41.4
Other	1.7
Ethnicity	
Hispanic	8.4
Non-Hispanic	91.6
Age[a]	
17 years or younger	(b)
18 to 19 years	0.7
20 to 24 years	9.0
25 to 29 years	16.6
30 to 34 years	23.1
35 to 39 years	20.9
40 to 44 years	12.4
45 to 49 years	9.9
50 to 54 years	4.1
55 to 59 years	1.7
60 years and older	1.6
Education	
Grade 8 or less	15.3
Grades 9 to 11	37.1
High school graduate/GED	37.4
Any college	10.2
Marital status	
Married	26.6
Divorced or separated	21.3
Widowed	2.5
Never married	49.6
Prior felony conviction history	
Prior felony convictions	67.1
No prior felony convictions	32.9
Legal status at time of capital offense	
Charges pending	6.8
Probation	9.8
Parole	20.2
Prison escapee	1.6
Prison inmate	2.4
Other status	1.2
None	58.0

Note: Thirty-seven states and the federal government had death penalty statutes in effect on Dec. 31, 1994. Data on ethnicity were not reported for 237 prisoners; education, 381 prisoners; marital status, 228 prisoners; prior felony conviction history, 191 prisoners; legal status at time of capital offense, 325 prisoners.
[a] The youngest person under sentence of death was a white male in Nevada born in January 1977 and sentenced to death in November 1994. Their oldest person under sentence of death was a white male in Arizona born in September 1915 and sentenced to death in June 1983.
[b] Less than 0.05 percent.

Source: U.S. Department of Justice, Bureau of Justice Statistics, *Capital Punishment 1994,* Bulletin NCJ-158023 (Washington, DC: U.S. Department of Justice, February 1996), p. 8, Tables 6 and 7; p. 9, Table 8. Table adapted by SOURCEBOOK staff. In Maguire and Pastore (1996:604).

TABLE 9.4 Number of Persons Executed, by Jurisdiction, 1930–1994

State	Number Executed	
	Since 1930	Since 1977
United States total	4,116	257
Georgia	384	18
Texas	382	85
New York	329	
California	294	2
North Carolina	269	6
Florida	203	33
Ohio	172	
South Carolina	166	4
Mississippi	158	4
Louisiana	154	21
Pennsylvania	152	
Alabama	145	10
Arkansas	127	9
Virginia	116	24
Kentucky	103	
Tennessee	93	
Illinois	92	2
New Jersey	74	
Missouri	73	11
Maryland	69	1
Oklahoma	63	3
Washington	49	2
Colorado	47	
Indiana	44	3
Arizona	41	3
District of Columbia	40	
West Virginia	40	
Nevada	34	5
Federal system	33	
Massachusetts	27	
Connecticut	21	
Oregon	19	
Iowa	18	
Utah	17	4
Delaware	16	4
Kansas	15	
New Mexico	8	
Wyoming	8	1
Montana	6	
Nebraska	5	1
Idaho	4	1
Vermont	4	
New Hampshire	1	
South Dakota	1	
Alaska	0	
Hawaii	0	
Maine	0	
Michigan	0	
Minnesota	0	
North Dakota	0	
Rhode Island	0	
Wisconsin	0	

Source: Stephen and Snell (1996:10).

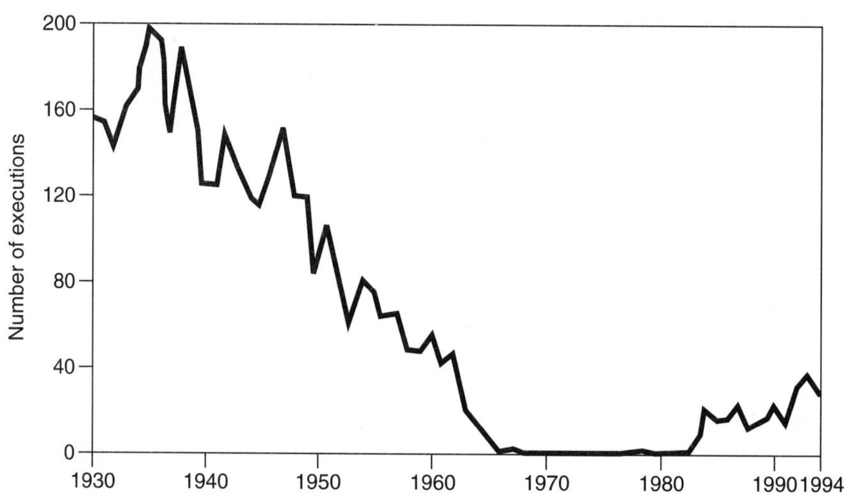

FIGURE 9.1 Persons executed, 1930–1994 (*Source:* Stephen and Snell 1996:2)

TABLE 9.5 Time Under Sentence of Death and Execution, by Race, 1977–1994

Year of Execution	Number Executed			Average Elapsed Time from Sentence to Execution		
	All Races[a]	White	Black	All Races[a]	White	Black
Total	257	156	99	97 months	92 months	106 months
1977–1983	11	9	2	51 months	49 months	58 months
1984	21	13	8	74	76	71
1985	18	11	7	71	65	80
1986	18	11	7	87	78	102
1987	25	13	12	86	78	96
1988	11	6	5	80	72	89
1989	16	8	8	95	78	112
1990	23	16	7	95	97	91
1991	14	7	7	116	124	107
1992	31	19	11	114	104	135
1993	38	23	14	113	112	121
1994	31	20	11	122	117	132

Note: Average time was calculated from the most recent sentencing date. Some numbers have been revised from those previously reported.

[a] Includes Native Americans.

Source: Stephan and Snell (1996:10).

TABLE 9.6 **Status of the Death Penalty, December 31, 1994**

Executions During 1994		Number of Prisoners Under Sentence of Death		Jurisdictions Without a Death Penalty
Texas	14	Texas	394	Alaska
Arkansas	5	California	381	District of Columbia
Virginia	2	Florida	342	Hawaii
Delaware	1	Pennsylvania	182	Iowa
Florida	1	Illinois	155	Maine
Georgia	1	Ohio	140	Massachusetts
Idaho	1	Alabama	135	Michigan
Illinois	1	Oklahoma	129	Minnesota
Indiana	1	Arizona	121	New York
Maryland	1	North Carolina	111	North Dakota
Nebraska	1	Tennessee	100	Rhode Island
North Carolina	1	Georgia	96	Vermont
Washington	1	23 other jurisdictions	604	West Virginia
				Wisconsin
Total	31	Total	2,890	

Source: Stephan and Snell (1996:1).

shows the time intervals between death sentences and actual executions from 1977 through 1994. The status of the death penalty in various states is shown in Table 9.6.

Methods of Execution Used by the States and Federal Government. There are five different execution methods used by the states and federal government. The most frequent method of execution is by lethal injection. Twenty-seven states and the federal government prescribe lethal injection for executing their prisoners. Twelve states use electrocution, seven states use gas chambers, four states use hanging, and one state, Utah, uses a firing squad. Many states offer prisoners the choice of lethal injection or one of the other execution methods. Table 9.7 shows the method of execution used by the different states and federal government.

Minimum Age Authorized for Capital Punishment. In 1996, 14 states had a minimum age of 18 for administering the death penalty, while other states had lower or unspecified ages. The minimum age for executing someone has previously been set at 16 in the cases of *Wilkins v. Missouri* (1989) and *Stanford v. Kentucky* (1989). Thus, it is unconstitutional to execute someone who committed capital murder before they reach 16 years of age. States with lower execution ages are obligated to follow the *Wilkins* and *Stanford* standard despite their statutes. Table 9.8 shows the minimum ages used by the states and federal government for executing those convicted of capital murder.

While the death penalty itself has never been held to be cruel and unusual punishment in violation of the Eighth Amendment nor has it ever been officially abolished, several U.S. Supreme Court decisions have interpreted the

TABLE 9.7 Method of Execution, by State, 1994

Lethal Injection	Electrocution	Lethal Gas	Hanging	Firing Squad
Arizona[a,b]	Alabama	Arizona[a]	Delaware[a,c]	Utah[a]
Arkansas[a,d]	Arkansas[a,d]	California[a]	Montana[a]	
California[a]	Connecticut	Maryland[a,e]	New Hampshire[a,f]	
Colorado	Florida	Mississippi[a,g]	Washington[a]	
Delaware[a,c]	Georgia	Missouri[a]		
Idaho	Indiana	North Carolina[a]		
Illinois	Kentucky	Wyoming[a,h]		
Kansas	Nebraska			
Louisiana	Ohio[a]			
Maryland[a,e]	South Carolina			
Mississippi[a,g]	Tennessee			
Missouri[a]	Virginia			
Montana[a]				
Nevada				
New Hampshire[a,f]				
New Jersey				
New Mexico				
North Carolina[a]				
Ohio[a]				
Oklahoma				
Oregon				
Pennsylvania				
South Dakota				
Texas				
Utah[a]				
Washington[a]				
Wyoming[a]				

Note: The method of execution of federal prisoners is lethal injection, pursuant to 28 CFR, Part 26. For offenses under the Violent Crime Control and Law Enforcement Act of 1994, the method is that of the state in which the conviction took place, pursuant to 18 USC 3596.

[a] Authorizes 2 methods of execution.

[b] Arizona authorizes lethal injection for persons whose capital sentence was received after November 15, 1992; for those sentenced before that date, the condemned may select lethal injection or lethal gas.

[c] Delaware authorizes lethal injection for those whose capital offense occurred after June 13, 1986; for those whose offense occurred before that date, the condemned may select lethal injection or hanging.

[d] Arkansas authorizes lethal injection for those whose capital offense occurred after July 4, 1983; for those whose offense occurred before that date, the condemned may select lethal injection or electrocution.

[e] Maryland authorizes lethal injection for those whose capital offense occurred after March 25, 1994 and also for those whose offense occurred before that date, unless within 60 days from that date, the condemned selected lethal gas.

[f] New Hampshire authorizes hanging only if lethal injection cannot be given.

[g] Mississippi authorizes lethal injection for those convicted after July 14, 1984 and lethal gas for those convicted prior to that date.

[h] Wyoming authorizes lethal gas if lethal injection is ever held to be unconstitutional.

Source: Stephan and Snell (1996:5).

TABLE 9.8 Minimum Age Authorized for Capital Punishment, 1994

Age Less than 18	Age 18	None Specified
Alabama (16)	California	Arizona
Arkansas (14)[a]	Colorado	Idaho
Delaware (16)	Connecticut[d]	Montana
Georgia (17)	Federal system	Louisiana
Indiana (16)	Illinois	Pennsylvania
Kentucky (16)	Kansas	South Carolina
Mississippi (16)[b]	Maryland	South Dakota[e]
Missouri (16)	Nebraska	Utah
Nevada (16)	New Jersey	
New Hampshire (17)	New Mexico	
North Carolina (17)[c]	Ohio	
Oklahoma (16)	Oregon	
Texas (17)	Tennessee	
Virginia (15)	Washington	
Wyoming (16)		
Florida (16)		

Note: Reporting by states reflects interpretations by state attorney general offices and may differ from previously reported ages.

[a] See Arkansas Code Ann.9-27-318(b)(1)(Repl. 1991).

[b] Minimum age defined by status is 13, but effective age is 16 based on an interpretation of U.S. Supreme Court decisions by the state attorney general's office.

[c] Age required is 17 unless the murderer was incarcerated for murder when a subsequent murder occurred; the age then may be 14.

[d] See Conn. Gen. Stat. 53a-46a(g)(1).

[e] Juveniles may be transferred to adult court. Age may be a mitigating circumstance. No one under age 10 can commit a crime.

Source: Stephan and Snell (1996:5).

method whereby it is imposed by judges and juries to be cruel and unusual or otherwise unconstitutional.

The first significant U.S. Supreme Court case in the 1960s that led to the death penalty being suspended for nearly a 10-year period was *Witherspoon v. Illinois* (1968). In the Witherspoon case, the prosecution had effectively excluded all persons from the jury that were opposed to the death penalty. Thus, when Witherspoon was convicted and sentenced to death, it was by a so-called **death-qualified jury.** The U.S. Supreme Court overturned the decision, however, and ruled that it was unconstitutional to exclude persons from the jury simply because they opposed the death penalty.

Three years later, the U.S. Supreme Court heard the case of *McGautha v. California* (1971). McGautha was convicted of murder by a California jury. The judge instructed the jury to decide whether McGautha should receive life imprisonment or the death penalty. Ultimately the U.S. Supreme Court ruled that it is unconstitutional for juries to have the "power of life or death" in a capital case.

Box 9.2 How They Do Things in Afghanistan

The Case of Ghulam Mahmad

It happened in Taliban, Afghanistan. Mohammed Alif was a money-changer. He lived in a middle-class neighborhood in Micrayon. One evening, three persons broke into his home and robbed him of $300. In the process, they gunned down his pregnant wife. When police officers made their arrest, they had Ghulam Mahmad in custody. Mahmad confessed and implicated a second man and a teenage girl. The teenage girl was released, because under Afghanistan law, teenagers cannot be tried for crimes.

With Mahmad in custody, justice was swift. Mahmad was convicted and sentenced to death by an Afghanistan court. His victim was given the opportunity of executing him personally. On Wednesday, December 18, 1996, Ghulam Mahmad was led to a public square in Taliban, a city with over 100,000 people. His victim, Mohammed Alif, was given an automatic rifle and he knelt and took aim at Mahmad. A burst of gunfire ripped through Mahmad's body. Then, Alif approached the body while Mahmad was on the ground, writhing in pain, mortally wounded. A second burst of gunfire from Alif finished off the murderer. A crowd watched and cheered Alif as he killed his victimizer in the public square. That's how things are done in Afghanistan. The other assailant was still at large and being sought by police. If he is caught, he will suffer the same fate as Mahmad.

In Afghanistan, murderers are executed, usually by a firing squad. In this case, the victim's husband, Alif, wanted to do it. For adulterers, death is accomplished by stoning. Thieves have their hands amputated. One hundred lashes are given to those who engage in illicit sex. These and other types of punishments are set forth under Islamic law. The Afghanistan Information Ministry spokesman, Mohammed Alam, said "We want to impose total peace and security." In this case, they did. Moments after Alif shot and killed Mahmad, he told a radio source, "I won't be satisfied until the remaining man in the case is captured."

Source: Adapted from Associated Press, "Taliban Justice Includes Public Execution." *Minot (N.D.) Daily News,* December 19, 1996:A7.

In 1972, a landmark death penalty case was decided by the U.S. Supreme Court. This was *Furman v. Georgia* (1972). For many years, Georgia and several other Southern states had used the death penalty with considerable frequency in cases such as rape and robbery. The unusual situation in Georgia was that the death penalty was being selectively applied primarily to blacks and not to whites convicted of the same offenses. This discriminatory application of the death penalty was eventually challenged. In a significant ruling, the U.S. Supreme Court declared that the death penalty was being arbitrarily applied in Georgia, and therefore it was held to be cruel and unusual punishment.

The *Furman* case caused a suspension of the death penalty in virtually every state for a four-year period, while various state courts examined their own methods for applying it. But in 1976, another Georgia case, *Gregg v. Georgia* (1976), prompted the U.S. Supreme Court to say that the death penalty is not cruel and unusual punishment per se. Furthermore, the Court acknowledged the constitutionality of the **bifurcated trial,** a two-stage proceeding in which guilt is established in one stage and the penalty decided in the other. Today, the bifurcated trial is mandatory in all capital cases in which the death penalty is requested by the prosecution. The second stage of this proceeding permits the jury to consider any especially aggravating or mitigating circumstances that might influence their decision as to whether the death penalty ought to be applied. Figure 9.2 shows graphically the increased use of the death penalty in the United States following the *Gregg* decision. It shows the death penalty pattern for the states and federal government from 1954 to 1994. Table 9.9 shows the regional, state, and federal distribution of those under sentence of death for the years 1993 to 1994 by race.

Also in the 1976 to 1977 period, three other cases were decided by the U.S. Supreme Court that changed drastically the types of crimes for which the death penalty is suitable. In *Woodson v. North Carolina* (1976), a North Carolina statute called for the mandatory imposition of the death penalty in any premeditated, first-degree murder case. Because the mandatory nature of imposing this penalty ruled out considering aggravating or mitigating circumstances, it was held to be unconstitutional. Similarly, in Louisiana, a statute existed that called for the mandatory imposition of the death penalty if a convicted offender killed a police officer in the line of duty. Again, the U.S. Supreme Court declared this statute unconstitutional on grounds similar to those in the case of *Woodson.*

FIGURE 9.2 Persons under sentence of death, 1954–1994.
(*Source:* Stephan and Snell 1996:11)

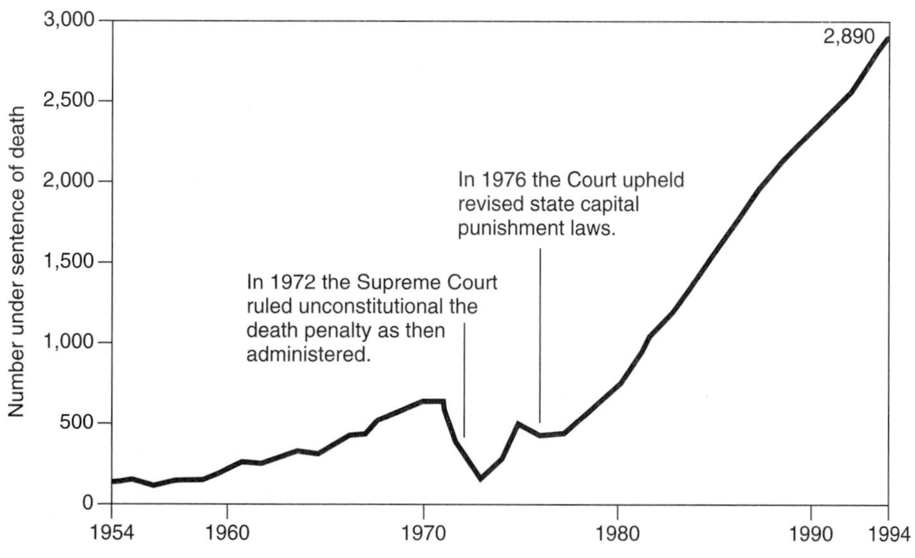

TABLE 9.9 Prisoners Under Sentence of Death, by Region, State, and Race, 1993 and 1994

Region and State	Prisoners Under Sentence of Death, December 31, 1993			Received Under Sentence of Death			Removed from Death Row (Excluding Execution)[a]			Executed			Prisoners Under Sentence of Death, December 31, 1994		
	Total[b]	White	Black	Total[b]	White	Black	Total[b]	White	Black	Total[b]	White	Black	Total[b]	White	Black
U.S. total	2,729	1,577	1,111	304	160	136	112	72	39	31	20	11	2,890	1,645	1,197
Federal[c]	6	3	3	0	0	0	0	0	0	0	0	0	6	3	3
State	2,723	1,574	1,108	304	160	136	112	72	39	31	20	11	2,884	1,642	1,194
Northeast	180	68	107	24	7	15	9	3	6	0	0	0	195	72	116
Connecticut	5	3	2	0	0	0	1	1	0	0	0	0	4	2	2
New Hampshire	0	0	0	0	0	0	0	0	0	0	0	0	0	0	0
New Jersey	7	4	3	3	0	3	1	0	1	0	0	0	9	4	5
Pennsylvania	168	61	102	21	7	12	7	2	5	0	0	0	182	66	109
Midwest	420	207	211	36	19	17	11	8	3	3	1	2	442	217	223
Illinois	151	57	94	11	5	6	6	4	2	1	1	0	155	57	98
Indiana	47	31	16	2	1	1	1	1	0	1	0	1	47	31	16
Missouri	80	47	33	9	5	4	1	1	0	0	0	0	88	51	37
Nebraska	11	7	3	1	1	0	1	1	0	1	0	1	10	7	2
Ohio	129	63	65	13	7	6	2	1	1	0	0	0	140	69	70
South Dakota	2	2	0	0	0	0	0	0	0	0	0	0	2	2	0
South	1,512	882	610	195	103	89	71	46	24	26	17	9	1,610	922	666
Alabama	120	64	54	24	13	11	9	3	6	0	0	0	135	74	59
Arkansas	33	20	13	8	5	3	0	0	0	5	4	1	36	21	15
Delaware	15	7	8	0	0	0	0	0	0	1	0	1	14	7	7
Florida	325	208	117	39	23	16	21	16	5	1	1	0	342	214	128
Georgia	96	48	48	6	6	0	5	1	4	1	0	1	96	53	43
Kentucky	29	22	7	4	4	0	4	3	1	0	0	0	29	23	6
Louisiana	43	14	29	6	3	3	2	1	1	0	0	0	47	16	31
Maryland	14	3	11	0	0	0	0	0	0	1	1	0	13	2	11
Mississippi	50	20	30	5	2	3	5	2	3	0	0	0	50	20	30
North Carolina	99	55	42	27	11	15	14	10	3	1	1	0	111	55	54
Oklahoma	122	80	33	12	4	7	5	5	0	0	0	0	129	79	40
South Carolina	52	28	24	7	3	4	0	0	0	0	0	0	59	31	28
Tennessee	99	67	30	4	2	2	3	3	0	0	0	0	100	66	32
Texas	366	221	140	43	25	17	1	1	0	14	10	4	394	235	153
Virginia	49	25	24	10	2	8	2	1	1	2	0	2	55	26	29

West	611	417	180	49	31	15	21	15	6	2	2	0	637	431	189
Arizona	117	100	14	10	5	2	6	5	1	0	0	0	121	100	15
California	363	217	138	22	11	11	4	2	2	0	0	0	381	226	147
Colorado	3	3	0	0	0	0	0	0	0	0	0	0	3	3	0
Idaho	21	21	0	0	0	0	1	1	0	1	1	0	19	19	0
Montana	8	6	0	0	0	0	0	0	0	0	0	0	8	6	0
Nevada	64	41	23	8	7	1	6	3	3	0	0	0	66	45	21
New Mexico	1	1	0	1	1	0	0	0	0	0	0	0	2	2	0
Oregon	13	12	0	6	5	1	2	2	0	0	0	0	17	15	1
Utah	11	9	2	0	0	0	1	1	0	0	0	0	10	8	2
Washington	10	7	3	2	2	0	1	1	0	1	1	0	10	7	3
Wyoming	0	0	0	0	0	0	0	0	0	0	0	0	0	0	0

Note: States not listed and the District of Columbia did not authorize the death penalty as of December 31, 1993. Some figures shown for year-end 1993 are revised from those reported in *Capital Punishment 1993* (NCJ-150042). The revised figures include 27 inmates who were either reported late to the National Prisoner Statistics Program or were not in custody of state correctional authorities on December 31, 1993 (12 in Texas; 5 in Arizona; 3 in Florida; 2 each in Georgia and Illinois; and 1 each in California, North Carolina, and Tennessee) and exclude 19 inmates who were relieved of the death sentence on or before December 31, 1993 (3 each in Illinois and Texas; 2 each in Florida, Georgia, and Louisiana; and 1 each in California, Idaho, Kentucky, Maryland, Nevada, North Carolina, and South Carolina).

[a] Includes 8 deaths from natural causes (3 in Florida, 2 in Arizona, and 1 each in California, Illinois, and Pennsylvania), 3 suicides (1 each in Alabama, California, and Florida), and 1 inmate shot to death by a correctional officer (California).

[b] Totals include persons of other races.

[c] Excludes persons held under Armed Forces jurisdiction with a military death sentence for murder.

Source: Stephan and Snell (1996: 8–9).

In 1977, the case of *Coker v. Georgia* (1977) was decided by the U.S. Supreme Court. Coker had been convicted of rape and was sentenced to death. His appeal was eventually heard by the Supreme Court in which a ruling was issued to the effect that the death penalty as a punishment for rape cases is too harsh or excessive. As noted earlier, the application of the death penalty in the United States is a highly controversial and emotionally charged issue. The primary reasons for applying the death penalty, according to its advocates, include (1) deterrence, (2) retribution, (3) justice, and (4) elimination (Cook and Slawson, 1993; Keve, 1992).

Does the death penalty deter people from murdering others? Although there are mixed findings on this issue (Durham, 1994), the overwhelming evidence suggests that the death penalty is not an effective deterrent (Baldus, Woodworth, and Pulaski, 1990). During those years when the death penalty was temporarily suspended while different states examined their capital punishment statutes, no significant changes in the rate of homicide were observed, either nationally or in selected states (Keil and Vito, 1990).

Alternatives to the death penalty are considered in all jurisdictions. Some proposals include segregation of murderers from others in solitary confinement. Snellenburg (1986) has proposed that those convicted of capital crimes be sentenced to solitary confinement for life, without possibility of commutation or parole. However, some authorities might contend that such prolonged isolation is cruel and unusual and violative of the Eighth Amendment. Although the U.S. Supreme Court attempted to correct the administration of the death penalty, in those states that use it, so that racial discrimination would be eliminated, evidence suggests that some discrimination according to racial, ethnic, and gender factors continues (Keil and Vito, 1990).

Women and the Death Penalty. Women particularly are least likely to be sentenced to death in the United States. By year-end 1994 there were 41 women on death row. Of these, 27 women were white and 14 were black.* They were distributed by state as follows:

State	Total	White	Black
	41	27	14
California	6	4	2
Alabama	5	3	2
Illinois	5	2	3
Florida	4	3	1
Oklahoma	4	3	1
Pennsylvania	4	1	3
Texas	4	3	1
Missouri	2	2	0

* James J. Stephan and Tracy L. Snell. *Capital Punishment 1994.* Washington, DC: U.S. Department of Justice, 1996:7.

North Carolina	2	2	0
Arizona	1	1	0
Idaho	1	1	0
Mississippi	1	1	0
Nevada	1	0	0
Tennessee	1	1	0

It is unlikely that the death penalty will be abolished in the United States in the near future, although groups such as the American Civil Liberties Union and many professional organizations oppose it. No doubt the Supreme Court will continue to issue opinions that will narrow the circumstances under which it can be applied (Amnesty International, 1994; Baldus et al., 1990).

INMATE GRIEVANCE PROCEDURES

Although it is not a prerequisite for inmates to exhaust all state remedies before filing a Section 1983 petition in federal courts, there is an exception provided under Title 42, Section 1997, whereby a federal judge may refer inmate lawsuits back to the state correctional systems where they originated, if a U.S. Department of Justice-certified grievance procedure exists. Virginia was the first state to establish a certified inmate grievance procedure in 1982. The administrative procedures for inmate grievances must satisfy certain minimum standards, including the provision that inmates and employees perform advisory roles, that maximum time limits are established for written replies to grievances, that priority processing of grievances is made on an emergency basis where undue delay might result in inmate harm, and that an independent review is made of the disposition of grievances by a person or persons not under the direct supervision or control of the correctional facility (Toch, 1995b). Thus, the number of inmate petitions filed in federal courts will be affected by the presence or absence of certified administrative grievance procedures as internal remedies.

The most frequent constitutional rights violations cited in civil petitions filed by prisoners under Section 1983 are the "cruel and unusual" punishment provisions of the Eighth Amendment (*Hutto v. Finney,* 1978; *Pugh v. Locke,* 1976; *Reynolds v. Sheriff, City of Richmond,* 1983), the unreasonable search and seizure provisions of the Fourth Amendment (*Burnette v. Phelps,* 1985; *Cook v. City of New York,* 1984; *Gardner v. Johnson, 1977; Hanrahan v. Lane,* 1984; *Smith v. Montgomery County, MD,* 1986), and the due process and equal protection under the law provisions of the Fourteenth Amendment (*Owens v. Brierley,* 1971; *Martinez Rodriguez v. Jimenez,* 1976). Other violations upon which inmate petitions are based include, but are not limited to, freedom of speech, privacy, and religious practices.

Inmate Disciplinary Councils

An intervening factor influencing inmate litigation in the courts has been the large-scale establishment of alternative dispute resolution mechanisms for prisoner grievances. These mechanisms include inmate grievance procedures, ombudsmen, mediation, inmate councils, legal assistance, and external review bodies (Ducker, 1984; Toch, 1995b). These mechanisms were stimulated largely by the 1967 President's Commission on Law Enforcement and the Administration of Justice. Although some state corrections facilities had internal prisoner grievance mechanisms, many prisons lacked such systems (Cole, Hanson, and Silbert, 1984; Turner, 1985). By 1982, all 50 states had created inmate grievance systems. Thus, court caseloads were eased as internal prison committees and administrative personnel responded positively to inmate grievances as an alternative to filing petitions with the court alleging civil rights violations. However, in recent years these internal alternative dispute mechanisms have not functioned as originally anticipated to reduce the sheer numbers of inmate petition filings.

Administrative Review of Inmate Grievances

Some misunderstanding exists on the functions and origins of inmate councils that hear prisoner grievances. Some writers have erroneously concluded that inmate councils are somehow evidence of participatory management. Participatory management implies that inmates would have a "say" in the governance of prisons. This is not so. Rather, inmate councils function as buffers between the administration and prisoners. They are also designed to resolve petty disputes among inmates.

Tom Murton, a former administrator with the Arkansas prison system, has said that some persons have claimed that inmate government exists, that it is corrupting, and that it is a dysfunctional modality for prison management (Murton, 1976). Murton indicates that in most participatory models in which inmate councils are used, the prisoners have not been given any sort of real power in the sense that they can make decisions affecting their lives. He says that with a few notable exceptions, inmate councils have "just grown." They have come into existence in response to crises, to aid in communications, or just because it seemed like a good thing to do at the time. He says that there are some obvious positive effects resulting from involving the participants in their own destiny. Inmates can sanction other inmates and provide the means of addressing various minor grievances that otherwise might result in court action.

In virtually every prison in which inmate councils exist to resolve petty disputes, administrative overview or review is conducted. This is to ensure that prisoners do not exploit other inmates with abuses of discretion. Administrative review is fundamental to operating inmate councils in

Florida prisons as well as in other jurisdictions (Lay, 1986; Toch, 1995a; Turner, 1985).

KEY TERMS

Arkansas prison scandal
Bifurcated trial
Body cavity searches
Capital punishment (death penalty)
Cruel and unusual punishment
Death-qualified jury
Death row
Double-bunking
Federal Tort Claims Act of 1946
Habeas corpus petition
Hands-off doctrine
Inmate litigation explosion
Jailhouse lawyer
Motion for summary judgment
Motion to dismiss
Negligence
Negligent assignment
Negligent entrustment
Negligent retention
Negligent training
Postconviction relief
Prisoners' rights movement
Prison Litigation Reform Act of 1995
Section 1983 actions
Shakedowns
Strip search
Tucker telephone

QUESTIONS FOR REVIEW

1. What is meant by the "bifurcated trial"? Under what conditions is it used? What are some of the guarantees of the First Amendment?
2. What are three civil avenues for filing petitions with the court alleging grievances against prison or jail administration and staff?
3. Is the death penalty cruel and unusual punishment in the opinion of the U.S. Supreme Court? What are three major cases involving the death penalty?
4. Why did states suspend the death penalty in the late 1960s? What U.S. Supreme Court decisions were influential in causing states to reevaluate their death penalty statutes and the form in which the death penalty was administered?
5. What decision led to a resumption of the death penalty?
6. Is the death penalty administered in a discriminatory fashion? In what sense might it be considered discriminatory?
7. What theories of negligence might be used by inmates in lawsuits against prison or jail administrators and staff?
8. What administratively operated or inmate-operated grievance procedures exist within prisons and jails throughout the United States whereby prisoners can air grievances?
9. What are some of the rights prisoners have on the search and seizure of contraband?

10. May prison and jail correctional officers seize any material possessions of prisoners, regardless of whether they constitute contraband?
11. What is meant by double-bunking or double-celling? Is it constitutional? What key cases may be cited regarding this issue?
12. What is a jailhouse lawyer? What decisions have been made by the U.S. Supreme Court condoning or approving jailhouse lawyers or some other form of legal aid for prisoners?
13. What major cases gave prisoners access to federal and state courts?
14. What is the hands-off doctrine? Is this doctrine still in effect?
15. What is a *habeas corpus* petition? What two conditions may it challenge?
16. What is a shakedown? What is a strip search? Who may be strip searched and under what conditions?

SUGGESTED READINGS

Cabana, Donald A. *Death at Midnight:The Confessions of An Executioner.* Boston: Northeastern University Press, 1996.

Johnson, Robert. *Hard Time: Understanding and Reforming the Prison* (2nd ed.) Belmont, CA: Wadsworth Publishing Company, 1995.

Mello, Michael. *Against the Death Penalty: The Relentless Dissents of Justices Brennan and Marshall.* Boston: Northeastern University Press, 1996.

Palmer, John W. *Constitutional Rights of Prisoners* (5th ed.). Cincinnati, OH: Anderson Publishing Company, 1997.

10

Parole, Parole Programs, and Effectiveness

CHAPTER OUTLINE

OVERVIEW

- You are a parole board member. It is your job to evaluate inmates who are eligible for early release and to decide whether an inmate should be granted parole. Seated before you is a murderer. He killed his wife during a family argument. He was an accountant and held down a very stressful job with the Internal Revenue Service. Otherwise, his record is impeccable. He has been a model prisoner for the past 13 years. His original sentence was 25 years. He has done considerable work for other prisoners and has taught some basic accounting classes to inmates through the Continuing Education Department at a nearby university. The man is now eligible to be released. You consider the seriousness of what he has done. No matter how many years he endures behind bars, his wife can never be brought back. What should you do as a parole board member? Should you parole this murderer, who will probably never murder again, or should you vote to keep him behind bars for more years?
- You are a parole board member. Seated before you is a woman who participated in a highly publicized triple murder 20 years ago. She was a part of a cult, a family of six others, who believed that they should commit human sacrifice to show their purity. She still maintains contact with other members of her "family" through correspondence. She murdered a pregnant woman and her fetus. She also stabbed to death an elderly businessman and his wife in an especially cruel manner. There is evidence that the woman she stabbed was made to beg for her life before other members of the "family" strangled and stabbed her to death. The woman, who has a very pleasant personality and appears friendly and outgoing, pleads with you and other members of the parole board to look at her life since she has been incarcerated. She obtained her G.E.D. She joined Alcoholics Anonymous. She has taken 10 years of counseling and psychological therapy. She is a member of an inmate council to hear inmate grievances. She is otherwise a model prisoner. However, friends and relatives of her victims speak out against her. They do not want this woman—the woman who slaughtered their loved ones—released. Should you

vote for her early release or should you vote to keep her behind bars for more years?

Parole decision making is not an easy task. Members of parole boards must make early-release decisions almost daily. There is great diversity among inmates. Even those convicted of the same types of crime vary greatly in their characteristics. Some inmates are more amenable to reform and rehabilitation than others. It is not an easy job to determine which ones should be granted parole and which ones should not.

This chapter is about parole and how it originated in the United States. In addition, the underlying philosophy of parole is examined, together with some of the objectives it seeks to achieve. A pivotal role in the parole process is played by parole boards. These boards are reviewed and their functions discussed. One question parole boards must attempt to answer is whether the offender will be successful in the community if early release from prison is granted. This prediction is influenced by several social, psychological, and background factors that also are examined. Those who are responsible for parolee supervision are parole officers. These officers are frequently given large offender **caseloads,** and their tasks are varied and complex. Because of the extensive demands on those performing parole officer roles, they must be carefully selected and recruited for this work. There is high turnover among parole officers, accompanied by stresses and burnout associated with overwhelming responsibilities and pressures. Some reasons for turnover and stress are investigated.

Because parole is a conditional release, it is the responsibility of parole officers to ensure offender compliance with parole program conditions. Various infractions may result in parole revocation, where offenders may lose their freedom in the community and be returned to prison. But parolees have legal rights, and they are all entitled to hearings before their parole is revoked. The process of parole revocation is explored.

PAROLE DEFINED

Parole is the conditional release of a prisoner from incarceration (either from prison or jail) under supervision after a portion of the sentence has been served. Thus, the major distinguishing feature between probation and parole is that **parolees** have served some time incarcerated in either jail or prison, whereas probationers have avoided incarceration, with limited exceptions. Some common characteristics shared by both parolees and probationers are that (1) they have committed crimes; (2) they have been convicted of crimes; (3) they are under the supervision or control of probation or parole officers; and (4) they are subject to one or more similar conditions accompanying their probation or parole programs. Some general differences are that, in general, parolees have committed more serious offenses than probationers, and parolees have been incarcerated for a portion of their sentences whereas probationers are not generally incarcerated after their convictions for crimes. Furthermore, parolees may have *more* stringent conditions (e.g., curfew, participation in drug or alcohol rehabilitation, counseling, halfway house participation, more face-to-face contacts with their parole officers [POs]) accompanying their parole programs compared with probationers.

The Jurisdictional Difference Between Probation and Parole

Probation is governed by the sentencing judge. When probationers face revocation for violating one or more rules or conditions of their probation programs, judges decide whether to revoke these programs. In contrast, parolees are sentenced to indeterminate prison terms. Thus, their early-release eligibility is set by legislatures, and a **parole board** determines whether they should be released conditionally. When parolees violate one or more terms of their parole programs, parole boards hear their cases and decide whether to revoke their programs. In sum, judges oversee probationers; parole boards oversee parolees.

THE HISTORY OF PAROLE IN THE UNITED STATES

Parole is not unique to the United States. It has European origins, although we are not exactly sure who should have the credit for inventing it. Early release of offenders from prison for various reasons, especially reform and rehabilitation, was seen in sixteenth-century France and Spain, although Great Britain and Wales also used it to some extent at about the same time (Waite, 1993). Because a majority of the colonists in America originated from England and Wales, these countries have been most influential on the subsequent establishment of parole systems in the United States.

After the Revolutionary War, Great Britain directed many prisoners to be transported to remote islands near Australia. Two of these islands were Norfolk and Van Diemen's Land. In 1836, the lieutenant governor of Van Diemen's Land appointed Alexander Maconochie (1787–1860), a former naval officer, as his private secretary. Four years later, Maconochie was appointed superintendent of a penal colony located on Norfolk Island. Maconochie observed the extensive use of corporal punishment when he initially assumed his new duties. Very much a penal reformer, Maconochie wrote criticisms of the system he administered, and he directed these criticisms to the British Parliament and penal officials. These criticisms quickly made Maconochie unpopular with his administrators, and he was relieved of his superintendent duties at Norfolk in 1844 and returned to England.

Marks of Commendation

Maconochie was transferred to various nonadministrative posts for the next several years. Eventually, he was appointed on a trial basis to the new governorship or superintendency of Birmingham Borough Prison. Again, he was dismissed from this job after less than two years for what his superiors regarded as excessive leniency in his penal policies. During his involvement with various penal systems, Maconochie consistently pushed for more humane treatment of prisoners. He firmly believed that offenders should be rehabilitated. Furthermore, he suggested an incentive system whereby prisoners could earn early release for good behavior. While he was head of Birmingham Borough Prison, he established a system whereby prisoners could accumulate **marks of commendation** for good work performed and for complying with prison rules. Thus, Maconochie pioneered what later came to be known as the good-time credits that are used today in U.S. prisons.

Marks of commendation resulted in the early release of prisoners. Early release was earned according to the following principles established by Maconochie:

1. Early release should not be computed on the amount of time served, but rather, upon the amount of work completed.
2. Prisoners can earn marks by hard work, better conduct, and industrious working habits. Prisoner release was determined on the basis of the number of marks accumulated.
3. Prisoners must earn everything they receive. Food and other indulgences were charged against the marks they had acquired.
4. Prisoners should work in small groups; the entire group would be held accountable for the conduct of individual members.
5. Prisoners would move through various stages of progressively less discipline; eventually, they would be given more rights in their own labor, to prepare them for release to society (Barnes and Teeters, 1959:419).

Maconochie used his judgment and authority to sanction administrative releases for the more well-behaved prisoners. These administrative early releases granted by Maconochie to prisoners, who were otherwise working productively for various British economic enterprises, were not acceptable to the government, and they were chiefly responsible for his early dismissal. However, before his dismissal from these prison posts, Maconochie demonstrated both the success and potential of early release. Selectively applied, it functioned as an incentive for prisoners to comply with prison rules and policies. Furthermore, it fostered order within the prison system. Fighting and other forms of prisoner misconduct operated against an inmate's early release, and most convicts were eager to be freed at the earliest possible opportunity. Maconochie created an informal version of what later came to be known as *indeterminate sentencing,* although an Irishman, Sir Walter Crofton, formally introduced the concept more than a decade after Maconochie had first used it. Maconochie's persistence finally paid off in 1853, when the British Parliament passed the **English Penal Servitude Act.** This Act authorized the establishment of rehabilitative programs for inmates, and banishment was gradually eliminated. In England, at least, Maconochie is considered the "father of parole."

Tickets-of-Leave and the Irish System

Impressed with the reforms Maconochie had instituted in British penal policies, Sir Walter Crofton, an Irish reformer and director of Ireland's prison system, gradually established the Irish system. The **Irish system** was a multistage process by which inmates could earn early release from prison. Also called the *indeterminate system* (the forerunner to indeterminate sentencing in the United States), the Irish system consisted of solitary confinement and hard labor for two years, congregate labor (comparable to what was later used at the Auburn State Penitentiary in New York) for an "indeterminate period," limited work on outside jobs (comparable to our present version of work furloughs), and finally, early conditional release through tickets-of-leave. **Tickets-of-leave** were authorizations for conditional early release from prison. Violating one or more conditions of the early release resulted in revocation of these leaves and return to prison. Those granted tickets-of-leave were expected to submit regular reports of their progress while free. Tickets-of-leave are acknowledged as the first use of parole.

The American Connection

Gaylord Hubbell, the Sing Sing, New York, prison warden, traveled to Ireland in 1863 to discuss penal reforms and prisoner rehabilitation with Crofton and to become more acquainted with the Irish system. Although massive prison policy changes were beyond the authority of Hubbell, he was nevertheless influential in bringing about eventual changes in New York sentencing and parole policies. When the National Prison Association (later the American Correctional Association) convened for the first time in Cincinnati, Ohio, in 1870, Hubbell, together with Crofton, promoted the Irish system strongly to those in attendance. The membership set forth a Declaration of Principles including indeterminate sentencing and an elaborate offender classification system. Crofton was most influential in the development of these principles and the resulting classification system. This classification system is illustrated in Table 10.1.

Although many corrections officials in the United States were impressed with what the National Prison Association had accomplished and recommended, it was not until 1876 that Elmira Reformatory actually established a workable good-time credit system for inmates comparable to the ones suggested and used by Maconochie and Crofton. Zebulon Brockway, the first superintendent of Elmira, was impressed with the good-time credit system, and he successfully incorporated the system for Elmira inmates. In fact, the example set by the Elmira Reformatory led to the passage of the first indeterminate sentencing law in the United States. Other states eventually adopted similar sentencing systems, and by the 1950s, every state and the federal system had indeterminate sentencing (Smykla, 1981).

TABLE 10.1 Mark System Developed by Sir Walter Crofton

Class and Number of Marks to be Gained for Admission to the Intermediate Prisons for Different Sentences[a]	Sentences of Penal Servitude (Years)	Shortest Periods of Imprisonment: In Ordinary Prisons		Shortest Periods of Imprisonment: Shortest Period of Detention in Intermediate Prisons		Periods of Remission on License
		Years	Months	Years	Months	
Class 1st $\frac{108}{90}$	3	2	2	0	4	The periods remitted on License will be proportionate to the length of sentences, and will depend upon the fitness of each Convict for release after a careful consideration has been given to his case by the Government.
			2–	–6		
Class 6 A, or 6 months in A class	4	2	10	0	5	
			3–	–3		
Class 14 A, or 14 months in A class	5	3	6	0	6	
			4–	–0		
Class 17 A, or 17 months in A class	6	3	9	0	9	
			4–	–6		
Class 20 A, or 20 months in A class	7	4	0	1	3	
			5–	–3		
Class 28 A, or 28 months in A class	8	4	8	1	4	
			6–	–0		
Class 44 A, or 44 months in A class	10	6	0	1	6	
			7–	–6		
Class 59 A, or 59 months in A class	12	7	3	1	9	
			9–	–0		
Class 68 A, or 68 months in A class	15	8	0	2	0	
			10–	–0		

[a] The earliest possible periods of removal to Intermediate Prisons apply only to those of the most unexceptionable character, and no remission of the full sentence will take place unless the Prisoner has qualified himself by carefully measured good conduct for passing the periods in the Intermediate Prisons prescribed by the Rules; and any delay in this qualification will have the effect of postponing his admission into the Intermediate Prisons, and thereby deferring to the same extent the remission of a portion of his sentence.

Source: Mary Carpenter, *Reformatory Prison Discipline as Developed by the Rt. Hon. Sir Walter Crofton in the Irish Convict Prison* (Montclair, N.J.: Patterson-Smith, 1967, reprint of 1872 ed.).

An informal version of parole had been used by U.S. prisons, both federal and state, much earlier than 1876. During George Washington's administration, the U.S. prison system was designed so that all offenders had to serve their sentences in their entirety. Prison overcrowding quickly occurred, and administrative decisions had to be made. Wardens frequently authorized discretionary releases of certain prisoners to make room for more serious offenders, even though there was no statutory basis for their actions. Some states were so hard-pressed to find space for the growing offender population that they passed good-time laws.

The first state to pass a good-time law was New York in 1817 (Bottomley, 1990). This law authorized officials to commute inmate sentences to shorter lengths. Thus, early release on the basis of an inmate's good behavior occurred in the United States many decades before the official action taken at Elmira Reformatory (Levine, Musheno, and Palumbo, 1986). The distinction is that in 1817, early release through the accumulation of good-time credits resulted in an official pardon by the governor or other authority. **Pardons** are unconditional releases, and released inmates are no longer accountable to prison authorities or parole officers. Therefore, it was not counted as parole in the formal sense, although prisoners benefited from it similarly.

The Official Introduction of Parole

The Massachusetts State Legislature acted to implement parole officially into its prison system in 1884 (Shane-DuBow, Brown, and Olsen, 1985:6). It is significant that Massachusetts was also the first state to establish probation six years earlier in 1878. By 1900, 20 states had passed parole statutes, and by 1944, all states had established parole systems for prisoners. The U.S. Board of Parole was created by congressional action in 1930, although the federal groundwork for this board had been established in 1925. Until the mid-1970s, parole was used by every state as a back-door solution to the problem of prison overcrowding as well as a way to reintegrate prisoners into their communities. The rehabilitative ideal had been promoted in the mid-1800s, and it dominated American corrections for the next century.

Rehabilitation gradually fell into disfavor with the public for various reasons, however. Parolees exhibited high recidivism rates. Recidivism among parolees is variable in part according to different types of programs, the intensity of their supervision, the jurisdiction, the length of the follow-up period, and how recidivism is defined. No standards exist for what is meant by high recidivism, and recidivism may not necessarily mean the commission of new crimes by parolees. If new convictions for crimes are used, then recidivism among parolees has been as low as 6 percent and as high as 75 to 80 percent, depending upon the particular study cited (Champion, 1996). If recidivism is simply defined as "return to prison," the reason may be revocation of parole because of a parole program rule violation unrelated to new crimes such as consumption of alcohol, violation of curfew, or missing work. An analysis of the literature suggests that 30 percent or less is an informal acceptable recidivism figure for parolees, although not everyone agrees (Champion, 1996).

A second reason for the decline of rehabilitation was political. Rehabilitation was not a sufficiently "tough" measure for dealing with criminals. Some governors gained in political popularity by advocating punitive correctional themes and criticizing the liberal policies of their opponents. Despite the rehabilitative programs, including vocational, educational, and technical training provided in prison settings, and despite all of the psychological and social counseling, drug and alcohol therapy, and medical treatment provided by prisons and prison staff, recidivism among ex-offenders soured the public on rehabilitation. Many offenders were not being rehabilitated. Instead, they were taking advantage of the system, exploiting it to their own ends (Walker, 1989).

Federal and State Abolition of Parole. Maine took the first step and abolished parole outright in 1976. Several other states greatly modified or abolished parole in later years. In 1984, the Comprehensive Crime Control Act was passed by Congress. This Act prescribed that parole should be abolished for federal prisoners commencing November 1992. Postrelease supervision was substituted for parole by the federal government in 1993 (Camp and Camp, 1995a:11). Among the states, 10 had abolished parole by 1995. These include (year abolished in parentheses) Arizona (1994); Delaware (1990); Florida (1983); Kansas (1993); Maine (1976); Minnesota (1980); North Carolina (1994); Oregon (1989); Virginia (1995); and Washington (1984) (Camp and Camp, 1995a:11).

Many states have retained provisions for indeterminate sentencing. Furthermore, Maine and other states that have abolished parole have also acted to provide alternative means whereby prisoners can earn early release. For example, Maine has enacted provisions to expand good-time credits earned by prisoners that will reduce time served in Maine prisons by as much as 20 percent. The estimated savings to the state are $48 million, the cost associated with adding nearly 250 new beds to accommodate growing numbers of inmates (Ehrenkrantz Group, 1984).

This is a good example of what may result from a get-tough policy relating to criminals. Getting tough by abolishing parole creates staggering prison overcrowding problems. Thus, Maine officials had to step back, reassess the implications of their 1976 parole abolition, and perhaps decide that their original action had unintended or unanticipated consequences. It is no coincidence that these more lenient good-time provisions were enacted by the Maine Legislature in 1983, seven years after their get-tough parole abolition occurred and prison overcrowding became problematic. If the original intent of Maine officials was to deter crime by eliminating the possibility of parole, then their action was ineffective. Crime in Maine continues to increase. If their original intent was to ensure that prisoners served the full terms of their sentences, then Maine has withdrawn from this position as well, given that the more liberal good-time policy drastically shortens the amount of time served by prisoners.

THE PHILOSOPHY AND GOALS OF PAROLE

The original philosophy of parole was rehabilitation. Alexander Maconochie, Sir Walter Crofton, Gaylord Hubbell, Zebulon Brockway, and other penal reformers and officials were unanimous in their belief that prisoners could be rehabilitated. In some respects resembling the carrot-stick analogy, parole was used originally as an incentive for prisoners to learn to get along with others, to behave, and eventually to return to their communities. It was a reward for good behavior. But beyond that, it was an incentive to undertake various work tasks, to learn new skills, and to become more productive.

In later years, other philosophies emerged. Some of these philosophies had nothing to do with prisoner rehabilitation. Rather, certain civil rights groups were interested in eliminating sentencing disparities according to gender, race, ethnicity, and socioeconomic status. Therefore, attacking the length of incarceration through parole reforms seemed a useful strategy for reducing or eliminating inequities in the system. Another point of view concerned the discrepancy between an inmate's sentence of incarceration and the nature of the crime committed. To what extent do discrepancies exist to the point at which punishment is more severe than the crime itself? Thus, those interested in just deserts have regarded parole as a means of curbing inequities in sentencing, whereby discrepancies between crime and punishment can be rectified. The major aims and philosophy of parole are summarized by the following:

1. Parole serves as a means whereby prisoners can be rehabilitated. Confinement in prison is punishment. But few inmates are rehabilitated by confinement alone. Even those who work at various jobs through prison industries sometimes fail to acquire useful skills that will make them employable when they eventually are released. Parole permits ex-convicts to support their families, to participate in counseling or therapeutic programs, and otherwise take the necessary steps to make positive improvements.

2. Parole makes it possible for inmates to reintegrate into society. Prison is a form of life alien to most citizens. Those who have been in prison for several years often find the transition to community life traumatic. Early release through parole may permit ex-convicts to make a gradual transition back to normal life and reenter their communities without incurring psychological or social traumas.

3. Parole is an incentive for inmates to comply with prison rules and behavior. Good behavior while in custody may increase inmate chances for early release. This functions as an incentive to obey the rules and to maintain prison discipline and orderliness.

4. Parole reduces prison overcrowding. Parole is a back-end solution to prison overcrowding. It functions as an administrative safety valve to control overcrowding. In recent years, however, various jurisdictions have acted to restrict or eliminate entirely the conditions under which parole may be granted (U.S. Sentencing Commission, 1987).

5. Parole acts as a deterrent to further crime, since parolees are often placed in conditional programs with some degree of supervision by parole officers. Those programs with higher degrees of control over parolees make it increasingly difficult for parolees to commit new crimes. New monitoring systems exist that permit parole officers to conduct location checks to verify if offenders are where they should be at different times.

6. Parole directly or indirectly protects the public through the degree of control it provides over individual parolees by parole officers. Parole is a means whereby parole officers can and do conduct visits to parolee residences and workplaces to verify their whereabouts and conduct. Thus, the likelihood for parolees deviating and harming others is decreased. If parole officers detect program violations or receive reports of parolee wrongdoing, their recommendations may result in parole revocations for the violators. Parole revocations are formal proceedings and are discussed later in this chapter.

7. Parole helps to reduce sentencing disparities according to race, ethnicity, gender, and socioeconomic status. Those inmates who have committed similar crimes but who have been sentenced to drastically different terms of confinement in prison can have their sentences adjusted by parole boards. Early-release decisions are designed, in part, to remedy sentencing inequities that may have been imposed earlier in the criminal justice process. The sentencing disparities may not have been deliberate, but paroling authorities can take into account inmate conduct and their conviction offense when deciding to grant or withhold early release. Of course, parole board decisions are sometimes inequitable as well.

8. Parole makes it possible for equity to occur between the punishment and nature of crime. Just as parole boards may act to remedy sentencing inequities, they may also function to adjust sentence lengths in relation to the seriousness of the crime committed. Parole boards may also reflect public sentiment. Two inmates serving terms for first-degree murder may be treated differently by the same parole board if one inmate has killed a popular figure. Sirhan Sirhan, convicted murderer of Robert Kennedy, has been denied parole on several occasions by the California Board of Prison Terms, while others committing essentially the same act of first-degree murder have been granted early release. Thus, despite attempts by paroling authorities to be equitable, political factors are obviously influential in their decision making.

9. Parole is also a continuation of punishment, since most parole is conditional, supervised, and subject to revocation. Many parolees are assigned to temporary residences while they work at various occupations during daytime hours. Failure to comply with residence rules may result in a parole revocation hearing. In short, parolees do not enjoy the full range of privileges available to other citizens. In many jurisdictions, parolees may not vote in political elections, they may not possess or own firearms, and they may be denied particular kinds of jobs (e.g., security work or law enforcement positions) because of their backgrounds.

THE FUNCTIONS OF PAROLE

The functions of parole are probably best understood when couched in terms of manifest and latent functions. **Manifest functions** are intended or recognized, apparent to all. **Latent functions** are also important, but they are hidden and less transparent. Two important manifest functions of parole are (1) to reintegrate parolees into society, and (2) to control and/or deter crime. Three latent functions of parole are (1) to ease prison and jail overcrowding, (2) to remedy sentencing disparities, and (3) to protect the public.

Offender Reintegration

Parole provides a means whereby an offender may make a smooth transition from prison life to living in a community with some degree of freedom under supervision (Calder, 1993).

Crime Deterrence and Control

Some persons believe that keeping an offender imprisoned too long will increase an inmate's antagonism toward society and result in the commission of new and more serious offenses (Travis, 1985:130). Early release from prison, under appropriate supervision, implies an agreement of trust between the state and offender (Metchik, 1992b).

Decreased Prison and Jail Overcrowding

Parole is considered a back-end solution to prison and jail overcrowding. Without parole, our already overcrowded prisons and jails would become even more overcrowded, many reaching unconstitutionally safe or approved levels (Petersilia and Turner, 1992). More than a few experts are concerned, however, that to reduce prison and jail overcrowding, the wrong types of offenders will be released short of serving their full sentences. Supposedly, parole boards are in place, in part, to screen the more dangerous parole applicants and to prevent their early release. But, in reality, it doesn't always turn out this way.

Compensation for Sentencing Disparities

In many early-release cases, inmates are released in part to rectify previous sentencing inequities. In a case in which an inmate has been given an unusually harsh sentence compared with other inmates who have committed similar offenses and who have been paroled, parole boards can act to correct these disparities. Some disparities in sentencing have been minimized through determinate sentencing in selected jurisdictions (Holmes et al., 1993; Steffensmeier, Kramer, and Streifel, 1993).

Public Safety and Protection

Can we predict with 100 percent accuracy those offenders who will or will not reoffend at the time of their early-release hearings? No. In fact, predicting future dangerousness is one of the most difficult decisions to make in the criminal justice system (Champion, 1994; Gottfredson and Gottfredson, 1988:251–252). However, parole boards do their best to protect society by authorizing the release only of those most likely to succeed. These parole-eligible inmates usually file a parole plan indicating that they have a job waiting on the outside and enough other support to suggest that they will be stable and law abiding.

PAROLEES IN THE UNITED STATES

Numbers of Parolees Under Supervision. By 1995, 5.3 million persons were under some form of correctional supervision in the United States. Of these, 700,000 or about 13.7 percent were on parole (Department of Justice, 1996:1). This represents a 218 percent increase in the parolee population between 1980 and 1995 (Department of Justice, 1996:7). The parole population grew in the United States by 36.6 percent between 1990 and 1995 (Department of Justice, 1996:7). Table 10.2 shows the number of state and federal offenders on parole, according to both state and U.S. region.

Methods of Release from Prison. Releases of large numbers of inmates on parole are the result of many factors. Some of these factors are prison overcrowding and good behavior of prisoners while confined. Also, prisons are attempting to manage their scarce space to accommodate the most dangerous offenders. Another major contributing factor is court-ordered prison population reductions because of health and safety regulations and cruel and unusual punishment conditions associated with some

BOX 10.1 The "College Terrace Rapist" and "Good Time"

The Case of Melvin Carter

In the early 1980s, Melvin Carter was arrested and eventually confessed to more than 100 rapes on three California college campuses. Dubbed the "College Terrace Rapist," he was permitted to plead "no contest" to 23 counts of rape, assault, burglary, and attempted burglary and was sentenced to 25 years in prison in 1982. Will he serve all 25 years? No. In fact, California authorities had to release Melvin Carter in September 1994 after he had served only 12 years of his 25-year sentence. What happened?

California is one of many states that use good-time credit, which is credit applied to the maximum sentence one receives. Many states allow inmates to accrue 15 or even 30 days per month for every month of prison time they serve. The public regards this time as "time off for good behavior." And to some extent, that is true. Good-time credit dates back to the early 1800s, and it was, and continues to be, used to induce prison inmates to behave well while confined.

When Carter was released by the California Department of Corrections, no town in California wanted him. He was ultimately assigned to reside in Alturas, a town of 10,000 persons. Most citizens of Alturas protested Carter's presence there. Governor Pete Wilson promised the people of Alturas that Carter would be confined to a restricted area at a nearby prison camp.

The Bureau of Justice Statistics has reported that just 3 percent of all felony arrests result in trials and that 97 percent are either dismissed or plea bargained, whereby defendants are encouraged to enter guilty pleas in exchange for reduced charges against them. For violent crimes such as murder and manslaughter, about 23 percent of these cases result in trial, while less than 5 percent of all property crimes are tried in courts. Only about 11 percent of all rape cases ever go to trial.

In Melvin Carter's case, Carter had served more than 12 years of his 25-year sentence. Therefore, at the rate of accruing 30 days per month against his maximum sentence for good-time credit, 1994 was about the point that his time served matched his time off. California is not alone in providing good-time credits for inmates. Most states provide such credit. In fact, 30 days off for every 30 days served is not the most liberal standard. In some jurisdictions, a state will allow its inmates to accrue 2½ months of credit for every 30 days served—that's right—for every 30 days served, inmates get 75 days off of their original sentences.

Prosecutors often are blamed for being too lenient on defendants accused of crimes. Plea bargaining is attacked, since it almost always results in a sentence less severe than one resulting from a jury conviction.

Are judges and prosecutors too lenient? Where would you draw the line regarding good-time credit and how much inmates should receive? What would happen if inmates were forced to serve their entire sentences? How would we manage the inmate population growth from such a policy, considering that it would take at least five times as much jail and prison space as we have presently to incarcerate all of those in need of incarceration?

Source: Adapted from Alice Vachss, "How to Keep Dangerous Criminals Behind Bars." *Parade,* September 25, 1994:4–5.

TABLE 10.2 Adults on Parole, 1995

Region and Jurisdiction	Beginning Parole Population, 1/1/95	During 1995 Entries	During 1995 Exits	Ending Parole Population, 12/31/95	Percent Change in Parole Population During 1995	Number on Parole on 12/31/95 per 100,000 Adult Residents
U.S. total	690,371	411,369	391,298	700,174	1.4	361
Federal[a,b,c]	61,430	29,491	22,552	59,136	—	30
State	628,941	381,878	368,746	641,038	1.9	330
Northeast	173,882	77,451	67,082	184,122	5.9	474
Connecticut	1,146	1,934	1,847	1,233	7.6	50
Maine[c]	40	1	2	41	2.5	4
Massachusetts[c]	4,755	3,727	3,702	4,639	–2.4	100
New Hampshire[c]	835	702	762	785	–6.0	92
New Jersey	41,802	17,198	11,589	47,411	13.4	793
New York	53,832	27,158	25,422	55,568	3.2	409
Pennsylvania	70,355	25,814	22,935	73,234	4.1	799
Rhode Island	525	597	529	593	13.0	79
Vermont	592	320	294	618	4.4	141
Midwest	82,478	62,155	56,698	87,364	5.9	192
Illinois	26,695	22,706	19,860	29,541	10.7	339
Indiana	3,409	5,310	5,120	3,599	5.6	83
Iowa	3,696	1,665	1,826	3,535	–4.4	167
Kansas	6,291	3,741	3,938	6,094	–3.1	325
Michigan	12,846	9,078	8,062	13,862	7.9	197
Minnesota	1,904	2,581	2,368	2,117	11.2	63
Missouri[c]	12,592	5,352	5,278	13,023	3.4	330
Nebraska	771	718	828	661	–14.3	55
North Dakota	94	209	189	114	21.3	24
Ohio	6,453	5,332	5,203	6,582	2.0	79
South Dakota	662	590	564	688	3.9	132
Wisconsin[c]	7,065	4,873	3,462	7,548	6.8	200
South	253,731	101,722	111,741	243,309	–4.1	358
Alabama	7,235	1,525	1,525	7,235	0	228
Arkansas	5,224	4,108	4,477	4,855	–7.1	265
Delaware	1,029	40	259	810	–21.3	150
District of Columbia	6,574	2,702	2,580	6,696	1.9	1,523
Florida[c]	20,573	3,769	9,649	13,746	–33.2	127
Georgia[c]	17,505	10,862	9,479	19,434	11.0	368
Kentucky	4,380	3,256	3,379	4,257	–2.8	147
Louisiana	17,112	9,793	7,877	19,028	11.2	613
Maryland	14,795	11,921	10,968	15,748	6.4	418
Mississippi[c]	1,519	840	847	1,510	–.6	78
North Carolina	20,159	11,530	13,188	18,501	–8.2	343
Oklahoma	2,604	661	909	2,356	–9.5	98
South Carolina	6,077	1,522	1,702	5,897	–3.0	216
Tennessee	9,353	3,357	3,859	8,851	–5.4	224
Texas	108,563	24,425	29,899	103,089	–5.0	774
Virginia	9,649	10,766	10,227	10,188	5.6	204
West Virginia	1,380	645	917	1,108	–19.7	79
West	118,850	140,550	133,225	126,243	6.2	303
Alaska	412	439	392	459	11.4	111

(table continues)

TABLE 10.2 (continued)

Region and Jurisdiction	Beginning Parole Population, 1/1/95	During 1995 Entries	During 1995 Exits	Ending Parole Population, 12/31/95	Percent Change in Parole Population During 1995	Number on Parole on 12/31/95 per 100,000 Adult Residents
Arizona	4,351	5,693	5,935	4,109	–5.6	136
California	85,082	118,948	112,223	91,807	7.9	403
Colorado	2,463	3,021	2,460	3,024	22.8	109
Hawaii	1,650	668	629	1,689	2.4	192
Idaho[c]	931	539	676	862	–7.4	106
Montana	710	431	386	755	6.3	119
Nevada	3,529	1,787	1,856	3,460	–2.0	306
New Mexico	1,078	815	775	1,118	3.7	94
Oregon	14,264	6,160	5,405	15,019	5.3	641
Utah	2,417	1,818	1,504	2,731	13.0	214
Washington	1,650	75	850	875	–47.0	22
Wyoming	313	156	134	335	7.0	97

Note: Counts are subject to revision.

[a] Defined as persons received for probation supervision upon release from prison. Includes supervised release, parole, military parole, special parole, and mandatory release.

[b] The decrease resulted from a review of the statistical database by the Administrative Office of the U.S. Courts, which identified and closed cases that had been coded incorrectly.

[c] Because of nonresponse or incomplete data, the population on December 31, 1995, does not equal the population on January 1, 1995, plus entries, minus exits.

Source: Department of Justice (1996:6).

prison facilities that have been unable to comply with federally mandated guidelines under which inmates may be confined. No court has ever declared that prison must be "comfortable." However, some prisons are notoriously ill-equipped to safely house their inmates. Some of the older prisons in the United States are rat-infested, roach-ridden structures without proper heat or ventilation in winter or summer months. Coupled with chronic overcrowding, some of these institutions are simply inhumane. This is where courts draw the line and require minimal conditions under which human beings can be held in confinement.

These release-through-parole figures are somewhat misleading, however. They suggest that granting parole under the discretionary authority of parole boards is *increasing* while just the opposite is true. Sentencing reforms have modified greatly the methods of releasing state and federal prisoners in recent years. New presumptive sentencing guidelines and determinate sentencing schemes will probably modify inmate release profiles over the coming years.

State prison releases by discretionary parole board decisions in 1977 accounted for 72 percent of all releasees. By 1990, this figure had dropped to 40.5 percent, reflecting the diminished role of parole boards through sentencing reforms (Jankowski, 1991:5). However, during the same 1977 to 1990 period, the number of supervised mandatory releases rose from 5.9

TABLE 10.3 Number of Adults Under Community Supervision or Incarcerated, 1980–1995

Year	Total Estimated Correctional Population	Community Supervision: Probation	Community Supervision: Parole	Incarcerated[a]	Percent of U.S. Adults Under Supervision
1980	1,840,400	1,118,097	220,438	501,886	1.1
1985	3,011,500	1,968,712	300,203	742,579	1.7
1990	4,348,000	2,670,234	531,407	1,146,401	2.3
1991	4,535,600	2,728,472	590,442	1,216,664	2.4
1992	4,762,600	2,811,611	658,601	1,292,347	2.5
1993	4,944,000	2,903,061	676,100	1,364,881	2.6
1994	5,147,100	2,981,400	690,371	1,475,329	2.7
1995[b]	5,357,800	3,090,626	700,174	1,567,000	2.8
Percent change					
1994–1995	4%	4%	1%	6%	
1980–1995	191%	176%	218%	212%	
Annual average change					
1990–1995	4%	3%	6%	6%	
1980–1995	7%	7%	8%	8%	

Note: Counts for probation, prison, and parole are for December 31 of each year. Jail counts are for June 30. Because some persons may have multiple statuses, the sum of the number of persons incarcerated or under community supervision overestimates the total correctional population. Percent of adults under supervision was computed using the U.S. adult resident population on July 1 of each year.

[a] The incarcerated population count consists of inmates in the custody of jail and prison authorities.

[b] Incarcerated total was estimated and rounded to the nearest 1,000.

Source: Department of Justice (1996:7).

percent to 29.6 percent (Jankowski, 1991:5). Table 10.3 shows the number of adults under community supervision or incarcerated from 1980 through 1995 (Department of Justice, 1996:7).

Profiles of Parolees. The characteristics of persons under some form of community supervision, including both probationers and parolees, are shown in Table 10.4.

About 54 percent of these parolees for 1995 were violent offenders, while about 26 percent were property offenders. Drug offenders accounted for another 21 percent, while public order and "other" accounted for another 7 percent. About 94 percent had been incarcerated for periods longer than one year. About 90 percent of all parolees were men, while 50 percent were black. Those of Hispanic origin accounted for 21 percent of all parolees. Seventy-nine percent of all parolees had active supervision status. Note in Table 10.4 that about 6 percent of these parolees have absconded, meaning that they have fled the jurisdiction and their whereabouts are presently unknown. About 4 percent of all parolees in 1995 were under the supervision of parole agencies in other states. For example, if certain Alabama parolees wanted to move to Delaware to be closer to their

TABLE 10.4 Characteristics of Persons Under Community Supervision, 1995

	Probation	Parole
Number of persons supervised	3,090,626	700,174
Sex		
Male	79%	90%
Female	21%	10%
Race		
White	64%	50%
Black	34%	49%
Other	2%	1%
Hispanic origin		
Hispanic	14%	21%
Non-Hispanic	86%	79%
Supervision status		
Active	78%	78%
Inactive	8%	11%
Absconded	10%	6%
Out-of-state	2%	4%
Other	2%	[a]
Type of offense		
Felony	54%	—
Misdemeanor	26%	—
Driving while intoxicated	17%	—
Other infractions	3%	—
Sentenced to Incarceration		
More than 1 year	...	94%
1 year or less	...	6%

Note: Percentages based on reported data only. Detail may not add to total because of rounding.

[a] Less than 0.05%.

—Not reported

. . . Not applicable

Source: Department of Justice (1996:8).

families or other relatives and friends, arrangements would be made with some Delaware parole agency for their continued supervision.

Changing Parolees for Supervision. Of all states with parole programs, 29 states charged parolees supervisory fees in 1995 (Camp and Camp, 1995d:60). The average supervision fee was $24.14. Idaho had the highest parole supervision fees assessed parolees at $50 per month, while Tennessee had the lowest parole supervision fee of $5 per month (Camp and Camp, 1995d:60).

Successful Parolees

A profile of those who successfully completed their parole is shown in Table 10.5. Table 10.5 shows that 216,710 parolees were discharged from parole in 1992 (Maguire and Pastore, 1996:587). About 49 percent of all discharges

TABLE 10.5 **Parole Discharges in 29 States by Method of Parole Discharge, Sex, Race, and Hispanic Origin, United States, 1992**[a]

Method of Parole Discharge	All Discharges	Sex		Race[b]			
		Male	Female	White	Black	Other[c]	Hispanic[d]
Number of discharges	216,710	196,884	17,096	96,811	98,682	1,589	38,766
All methods	100%	100%	100%	100%	100%	100%	100%
Successful completion	49.3	49.2	57.8	50.7	48.6	55.6	41.8
Absconder	1.0	1.0	1.1	0.9	1.2	0.6	0.7
Return to jail or prison[e]	47.8	47.9	39.7	46.5	48.4	42.4	55.8
Transfer	0.2	0.2	0.2	0.2	0.2	0.4	0.1
Death	1.1	1.2	0.7	1.0	1.1	0.8	1.2
Other	0.6	0.6	0.5	0.7	0.5	0.2	0.4

[a] Detail may not add to total because of rounding.
[b] Includes persons of Hispanic origin.
[c] Includes American Indians, Alaska Natives, Asians, and Pacific Islanders.
[d] Includes persons of all races.
[e] Includes those returned to prison with a new sentence, technical parole violators, and those returned pending parole revocation or a new charge.

Source: U.S. Department of Justice, Bureau of Justice Statistics, *National Corrections Reporting Program, 1992,* NCJ-145862 (Washington, DC: U.S. Department of Justice, 1994), p. 67. In Maguire and Pastore (1996:597).

were successful completions of parole programs. Nearly 48 percent of all parolees were returned to prison. About 2 percent either died or absconded while on parole (Maguire and Pastore, 1996:587). The average amount of time spent on parole was 20.5 months (Camp and Camp, 1995d:55). Tennessee parolees spent the most time on parole, averaging about 58 months, while the shortest parole lengths occurred in Arizona (6 months) (Camp and Camp, 1995d:55). Some more recent figures indicate that within 39 reporting jurisdictions in 1994, there were 184,565 parole revocation hearings conducted (Camp and Camp, 1995d:55). About a third (62,052) were revoked because of new crimes committed.

Unsuccessful Parolees

Table 10.6 shows the numbers of sentenced prisoners who had their parole revoked in 1994 (Maguire and Pastore, 1996:595). There were 73,685 parole revocations in 1994. About half of these revocations resulted in new sentences and return to prison, while the remainder involved changes in one's parole program. One change that usually occurs when one's parole program is revoked is that one's supervision is intensified. That is, instead of reporting once a month to one's parole officer, a parolee might have as many as five face-to-face visits with his or her parole officer weekly or monthly. The intensiveness of one's supervision is contingent upon the amount of available supervisory staff in any given parole agency.

TABLE 10.6 Sentenced Prisoners Admitted to State and Federal Institutions for Violation of Parole or Other Conditional Release (by Whether New Sentence Was Imposed, Sex, Region, and Jurisdiction, 1994)

Region and Jurisdiction	Total	Parole Violators					Other Conditional Release Violators				
			New Sentence		No New Sentence			New Sentence		No New Sentence	
		Total	Male	Female	Male	Female	Total	Male	Female	Male	Female
United States, total	170,974	73,685	36,998	2,551	31,878	2,258	97,289	29,053	2,048	60,845	5,343
Federal	3,146	1,859	NA	NA	1,750	109	1,287	NA	NA	1,214	73
State	167,828	71,826	36,998	2,551	30,128	2,149	96,002	29,053	2,048	59,631	5,270
Northeast	17,365	12,726	985	47	10,975	719	4,639	327	30	4,105	177
Connecticut[a]	709	235	3	0	224	8	474	10	3	404	57
Maine	268	4	0	0	4	0	264	77	3	175	9
Massachusetts[b,c]	1,155	1,070	100	0	907	63	85	75	10	NA	NA
New Hampshire	261	261	NA	NA	249	12	NA	NA	NA	NA	NA
New Jersey	3,922	3,912	414	17	3,232	249	10	NA	NA	10	0
New York	6,548	5,796	X	X	5,463	333	752	X	X	745	7
Pennsylvania	4,171	1,233	393	25	767	48	2,938	111	9	2,715	103
Rhode Island[a]	246	130	45	4	79	2	116	54	5	56	1
Vermont[a]	85	85	30	1	50	4	NA	NA	NA	NA	NA
Midwest	21,477	13,809	4,331	199	8,669	610	7,668	4,246	161	2,979	282
Illinois[b]	4,452	NA	NA	NA	NA	NA	4,452	3,749	121	548	34
Indiana	594	594	204	9	359	22	NA	NA	NA	NA	NA
Iowa[b]	996	705	403	36	240	26	291	163	23	101	4
Kansas	2,078	1,705	270	11	1,322	102	373	49	7	281	36
Michigan[b]	3,315	3,315	1,150	72	1,943	150	0	0	0	0	0
Minnesota	926	NA	NA	NA	NA	NA	926	135	5	733	53
Missouri	2,996	2,566	538	27	1,865	136	430	79	2	339	10
Nebraska	368	368	NA	NA	325	43	0	0	0	0	0
North Dakota	81	30	NA	NA	28	2	51	NA	NA	47	4
Ohio	4,094	3,217	1,424	25	1,684	84	877	NA	NA	740	137
South Dakota	189	133	4	0	119	10	56	3	2	50	1
Wisconsin	1,388	1,176	338	19	784	35	212	68	1	140	3

South	57,000	39,374	30,473	2,214	6,201	486	17,626	8,049	570	8,271	736
Alabama	1,856	1,410	128	8	1,195	79	446	414	32	NA	NA
Arkansas	999	742	393	2	309	38	257	86	1	154	16
Delaware[a]	194	49	48	1	NA	NA	145	133	12	NA	NA
District of Columbia[a]	2,370	2,082	1,400	85	597	NA	288	216	NA	72	NA
Florida[b]	7,423	136	18	1	111	6	7,287	2,142	159	4,652	334
Georgia[b]	3,851	3,851	3,392	162	267	30	NA	NA	NA	NA	NA
Kentucky	1,686	1,471	113	6	1,241	111	215	17	1	170	27
Louisiana	5,873	670	349	25	275	21	5,203	2,038	138	2,703	324
Maryland[c]	1,672	1,666	884	48	696	38	6	0	0	6	0
Mississippi	152	133	54	4	67	8	19	19	0	0	0
North Carolina	5,426	5,426	5,051	375	NA	NA	NA	NA	NA	NA	NA
Oklahoma[c]	225	225	139	23	54	9	NA	NA	NA	NA	NA
South Carolina	2,246	1,466	476	22	895	73	780	317	16	422	25
Tennessee[c]	2,970	2,096	1,959	137	NA	NA	874	802	72	NA	NA
Texas	18,209	16,459	15,241	1,218	NA	NA	1,750	1,620	130	NA	NA
Virginia	1,756	1,400	781	96	451	72	356	245	9	92	10
West Virginia	92	92	47	1	43	1	0	0	0	0	0
West	71,986	5,917	1,209	91	4,283	334	66,069	16,431	1,287	44,276	4,075
Arizona[b]	1,856	424	63	8	311	42	1,432	278	13	990	151
California[b]	62,776	NA	NA	NA	NA	NA	62,776	15,875	1,245	41,871	3,785
Colorado[c]	1,071	930	155	14	709	52	141	47	2	85	7
Hawaii[a,c]	845	389	78	6	283	22	456	158	21	246	31
Idaho	447	224	8	0	209	7	223	68	6	129	20
Montana	116	116	10	2	100	4	X	X	X	X	X
Nevada	612	612	NA	NA	569	43	NA	NA	NA	X	X
New Mexico	1,054	657	NA	NA	619	38	397	NA	NA	382	15
Oregon	1,367	1,367	669	46	590	62	0	0	0	0	0
Utah	1,093	1,093	213	15	805	60	0	0	0	0	0
Washington	700	56	7	0	47	2	644	5	0	573	66
Wyoming	49	49	6	0	41	2	0	0	0	0	0

[a] Figures include both jail and prison inmates; jails and prisons are combined in one system.
[b] Data are custody rather than jurisdiction counts.
[c] Some or all release categories are estimated.

Source: U.S. Department of Justice, Bureau of Justice Statistics, *Correctional Populations in the United States, 1994,* NCJ-160091 (Washington, DC: U.S. Department of Justice, 1996), Table 5.16. In Maguire and Pastore (1996:595).

Cases That Parole Boards Must Review. Any prisoner sentenced under an indeterminate sentencing system must be considered for parole by a parole board from time to time. The timeliness of these early-release hearings is ordinarily governed by statute. In California, for instance, there is a three-year interval between parole hearings for more serious offenders serving lengthy terms. Jurisdictions vary from six months to five years or more in terms of how often parole boards must convene to hear a parole-eligible inmate's argument for early release.

Cases That Parole Boards Do Not Have to Review. Prisoners who are sentenced to life without parole or the death penalty are not entitled to a hearing before any parole board. This does not mean that some of these life-without-parole or death row inmates will *never* have their cases heard by some future parole board, however. During the early 1970s, for instance, the U.S. Supreme Court heard the case of *Furman v. Georgia* (1972) and declared that the death penalty, as it was presently being applied in Georgia, was cruel and unusual punishment. One compelling argument was that Georgia was executing large numbers of blacks who had committed noncapital offenses such as robbery and rape, while white offenders convicted of the same crimes were normally receiving sentences of 10 or 15 years. California was among several states electing to *suspend* their application of the death penalty *temporarily,* until such time as an appropriate procedure for administering the death penalty could be fashioned by their state legislature. Charles Manson, a notorious murderer, had been sentenced to death in the late 1960s by a California court. Some of his cohorts, including Patricia Krenwinkle and Leslie Van Houton, were likewise under sentences of death. Therefore, California authorities commuted the sentences of Charles Manson and Leslie Van Houton to life imprisonment. This meant that each would be eligible for parole at some future date and would not face execution. Since the early 1980s, these notorious murderers have faced parole boards periodically, only to have their parole denied. It is unlikely that Manson or Van Houton will ever be paroled, although they are entitled to parole hearings every three years. There has been sufficient prosecutorial and victim input in their parole hearings that their parole chances are slight. Sirhan Sirhan is another notorious inmate who was convicted of the assassination of Robert Kennedy in 1968. It is unlikely that he will ever be paroled, although the California Parole Board meets regularly to consider his early-release application. Public sentiment is so strong that the more notorious the case, the less likely one's parole chances, even if the offender is a model inmate.

The case of Danny Harold Rolling is another case parole boards will not have to review. Rolling was a drifter who killed five University of Florida students in Gainesville in 1990. Rolling was convicted of their murders in early 1994. There were numerous aggravating circumstances and only a few questionable mitigating ones. Rolling had stabbed his victims repeatedly, bound them with duct tape, raped and mutilated them, and decapitated one victim. Persuasive evidence indicates that he tortured his victims prior to killing them in a brutal manner. Is there any way to murder victims kindly? In March 1994, a second-phase jury decision recommended the death penalty for Rolling. Barring any compelling appeals, which are unlikely, Rolling will eventually be executed by Florida authorities. Daniel Harold Rolling will *never* kill any other community residents.

Parole Boards and the Get-Tough Movement. Most states had changed their sentencing provisions by 1988 (Champion, 1994). In many instances, these changes in sentencing provisions significantly limited the discretionary authority of parole boards to grant prisoners early release. This was part of the get-tough-on-crime movement among several states. An example of the effects of the get-tough policy occurred in Pennsylvania where reductions in sentence commutations dropped from 128 in 1977 to 2 in 1981. More recent examples of the get-tough movement are President Bill Clinton's "three-strikes-and-you're-out" anticrime legislation, stiffer penalties for more serious offenses, and greater certainty of punishment through mandatory prison terms for particular crimes. Habitual offender statutes are also evidence of the get-tough movement. These statutes carry life-without-parole terms. However, few states currently use their habitual offender statutes on any consistent basis.

Metchik (1992a:1) says that given today's era of judicial decision-making guidelines and determinate sentencing systems, the future prospects for parole at the federal and state levels are increasingly unclear. In fact, says Metchik, many empirical studies of the importance of severity instrumentation, relied upon by parole boards in making their early-release decisions, show that offense severity evaluations and other retributive judgments often are negatively correlated with risk assessment. This means that relying on risk assessment scores that indicate that certain offenders pose greater risk than others may generate just the opposite outcomes. Metchik doesn't say that we should use these risk assessment instruments as negative predictors, but he does raise an important issue about the reliability of these instruments and perhaps that we ought to consider their value conservatively. Other researchers have found a variety of factors that relate to one's success chances if paroled (Bodapati and Marquart, 1992). Many of these factors are not included on risk assessment instruments or are not available to parole boards on any consistent basis.

In addition, increasing numbers of parole-eligible inmates are elderly. There appears to be an inverse relation between age and criminality, although we can certainly find adequate numbers of dangerous elderly offenders today. Considered as an aggregate, however, the growing population of parole-eligible elderly offenders is such that risk-needs assessment instruments may be very misleading on whether certain of these offenders ought to be supervised intensively while on parole. Hall (1992) recommends better client management methods, so that the elderly offenders on parole are not unduly sanctioned and unreasonably supervised to the extent that such supervision is cost ineffective.

Parole Board Composition and Diversity

There is considerable diversity among parole boards in the United States. No graduate school in the United States offers a degree in parole board membership. Thus, it is difficult if not impossible to generalize about all parole boards, the decisions they make, and the reasons for those decisions. Table 10.7 shows the size, composition, and functions of most parole boards in the United States.

Functions of Parole Boards

The actions of parole boards in a majority of jurisdictions are influenced by a philosophy promoting accountability, punishment, reintegration, and rehabilitation. Not every parole board in the United States has identical functions. However, a listing of functions is possible by comparing the goals and philosophical statements of various boards. The major functions of parole boards are

1. To evaluate prison inmates who are eligible for parole and act on their application to approve or deny parole
2. To convene to determine whether a parolee's parole should be revoked on the basis of alleged parole violations
3. To evaluate juveniles to determine their eligibility for release from detention
4. To grant pardons or commutations of sentences to prisoners, where mitigating circumstances or new information is presented that was not considered at trial
5. To make provisions for the supervision of adult offenders placed on parole; to establish supervisory agencies and select parole officers to monitor offender behavior
6. To provide investigative and supervisory services to smaller jurisdictions within the state
7. To grant reprieves in death sentence cases and to commute death penalties
8. To restore full civil and political rights to parolees and others on conditional release including probationers
9. To review disparate sentences and make recommendations to the governor for clemency
10. To review the pardons and executive clemency decisions made by the governor

TABLE 10.7 **Parole Board Size and Nature of Parole Board Appointments in the United States, 1994**

State	Size of Parole Board	Means of Appointment	Functions
Alabama	3	Governor	Paroles adults, provides adult probation services
Alaska	5	Governor	Paroles adults
Arizona	7	Governor	Paroles adults, reviews executive clemency decisions
Arkansas	7	Governor	Paroles adults
California	8	Governor	Paroles adults, reviews disparate sentencing, considers parole for lifers
Colorado	7	Governor	Paroles adults
Connecticut	11	Governor	Paroles adults
Delaware	5	Governor	Paroles adults
District of Columbia	5	Mayor	Paroles adults and juveniles
Florida	7	Governor	Paroles adults
Georgia	5	Autonomous	Paroles adults, grants reprieves, pardons, commutations
Hawaii	3	Governor	Paroles adults
Idaho	5	Board of Correction	Paroles adults
Illinois	12	Governor	Paroles adults
Indiana	5	Governor	Paroles adults, reviews clemency applications for those serving life sentences
Iowa	5	Governor	Paroles adults
Kansas	5	Governor	Paroles adults, reviews clemency applications
Kentucky	7	Governor	Paroles adults
Louisiana	7	Governor	Paroles adults
Maine	5	Governor	Paroles adults[a]
Maryland	7	Secretary of Department of Public Safety	Paroles adults, reviews clemency applications
Massachusetts	8	Governor	Paroles adults
Michigan	10	Department of Corrections	Paroles adults
Minnesota	3	Commissioner of Corrections	Paroles adults[b]
Mississippi	5	Governor	Paroles adults
Missouri	5	Governor	Paroles adults
Montana	3	Governor	Paroles adults[c]
Nebraska	5	Governor	Paroles adults
Nevada	6	Governor	Paroles adults
New Hampshire	5	Governor	Paroles adults
New Jersey	9	Governor	Paroles adults and juveniles
New Mexico	4	Governor	Paroles adults, reviews clemency applications
New York	19	Governor	Paroles adults
North Carolina	5	Governor	Paroles adults
North Dakota	3	Governor	Paroles adults
Ohio	9	Governor	Paroles adults

(table continues)

TABLE 10.7 (continued)

State	Size of Parole Board	Means of Appointment	Functions
Oklahoma	5	Governor	Paroles adults, reviews pardons
Oregon	4	Governor	Paroles adults
Pennsylvania	5	Governor	Paroles adults
Rhode Island	6	Governor	Paroles adults
South Carolina	7	Governor	Paroles adults
South Dakota	6	Governor	Paroles adults
Tennessee	7	Governor	Paroles adults
Texas	18	Board of Criminal Justice	Paroles adults
Utah	5	Governor	Paroles adults, reviews pardons
Vermont	5	Governor	Paroles adults
Virginia	5	Governor	Paroles adults
Washington	5	Governor	Paroles adults, fixes minimum terms
West Virginia	3	Governor	Paroles adults
Wisconsin	5	Governor	Paroles adults
Wyoming	7	Governor	Paroles adults

[a] Maine has abolished parole; the Maine Parole Board meets only to hear parole requests from pre-1976 inmates.

[b] Minnesota abolished the Corrections Board in 1982; since then, the Office of Adult Release makes recommendations concerning parole for applicants, with the exception of those serving life sentences; a special advisory panel advises the Commissioner regarding life sentence inmates who apply for parole.

[c] Montana has a Board of Pardons that is attached administratively to the Corrections Division but is autonomous in its authority to parole adults.

Source: Adapted from American Correctional Association, *ACA Directory, 1994.* Laurel, MD: American Correctional Association, 1994.

Most parole boards make parole decisions *exclusively.* In a limited number of jurisdictions, additional functions are performed, either according to statute or at the pleasure of the governor. In a limited number of jurisdictions, the paroling authority is vested in agencies independent of the governor. Parole boards may evolve their own standards, subject to legislative approval.

The Connecticut Parole Board (1974) has several standards that govern each early-release decision:

1. The nature and circumstances of inmate offenses and their current attitudes toward them
2. The inmate's prior record and parole adjustment if paroled previously
3. The inmate's attitude toward family members, the victim, and authority in general
4. The institutional adjustment of inmates, including their participation in vocational/educational programs while incarcerated
5. Inmate's employment history and work skills
6. Inmate's physical, mental, and emotional condition as determined from interviews and other diagnostic information available

7. Inmate's insight into the causes of his or her own criminal behavior in the past
8. Inmate's personal efforts to find solutions to personal problems such as alcoholism, drug dependency, and need for educational training or developing special skills
9. The adequacy of the inmate's parole plan, including planned place of residence, social acquaintances, and employment program

Virtually every parole board establishes criteria such as those developed by Connecticut. Sometimes psychiatric reports or examinations are used. Presentence investigation reports are used as well. These reports are often used to assist board members in making the best early-release decisions. Finally, victim testimony is solicited for many parole hearings. Parsonage (1992) indicates that several states currently permit victim participation in parole board consideration for specific inmates. Victims may offer either written or oral testimony at these parole hearings, and parole boards weigh such written or oral testimony accordingly.

Parole Board Decision Making and Inmate Control

A key factor influencing prison overcrowding is parole board decision making. It is exerting a tremendous impact on how corrections professionals do their jobs. Dramatic increases in parole supervision have been observed, and the number of parole release and revocation hearings has grown markedly over the years (Burke, 1987:74). It has been suggested by some corrections experts that parole boards should focus on at least five major areas, including the following (Burke, 1987:78):

1. *Policy making.* How does policy making differ from individual decision making? How does it relate to individual discretion? What steps are involved? Who must participate? How can policy be made operational?
2. *Management.* What management needs exist? How can board and staff roles for management be clarified?
3. *Roles of research.* How can research be used to inform policy making and decision making? What role must policy makers play in developing risk instruments? How can parole decision makers communicate effectively with technical staff?
4. *Criminal justice system issues.* How can the critical overlaps between parole and other agencies be identified? What are viable mechanisms for cooperation? How do other agencies' policies and practices influence workload?
5. *Strategies.* What are effective strategies for handling and building effective working relationships with the various public interests that are of importance to parole?

Parole boards must balance carefully the decision to release an inmate who might be truly rehabilitated and reintegrated into his or her community with the decision to release an offender who might inflict further harm upon the community. They must resolve, or attempt to resolve, this dilemma in the context of satisfying consistent and impartial standards expected by both prisoners and public alike. If two persons in the same jurisdiction are convicted of identical crimes under similar circumstances and sentenced by the same judge to identical terms, and if a parole board decides to grant early release of one prisoner before the other, a disparity exists that ought to be explained.

When offenders become eligible for parole, this does not mean parole will automatically be granted by the parole board. Parole boards have considerable discretionary power, and in many jurisdictions, they have absolute discretion over an inmate's early release potential. In fact, when federal courts have been petitioned to intervene and challenge parole board actions, the decisions of parole boards have prevailed (*Tarlton v. Clark,* 1971). Although we have already examined parole boards, their composition, and their functions, it is helpful to review briefly some of the more important factors influencing parole board decision making. In deciding whether or not to grant parole for given inmates, the following factors are considered (Dietz, 1985:32):

1. The commission of serious disciplinary infractions while confined
2. The nature and pattern of previous convictions
3. The adjustment to previous probation, parole, and/or incarceration
4. The facts and circumstances of the offense
5. The aggravating and mitigating factors surrounding the offense
6. Participation in institutional programs that might have led to the improvement of problems diagnosed at admission or during incarceration
7. Documented changes in attitude toward self or others
8. Documentation of personal goals and strengths or motivation for law-abiding behavior
9. Parole plans
10. Inmate statements suggesting the likelihood that the inmate will not commit future offenses
11. Court statements about the reasons for the sentence (e.g., the presentence investigation report)

If parole boards decide favorably and grant an inmate parole, it is usually conditional and subject to compliance with various rules and regulations. If the parole board reacts unfavorably and denies the inmate parole, usually one or more reasons are provided by the board for the action taken.

Most parole boards rely on past behaviors of inmates while confined to indicate how they *might* behave if paroled. Parole-release policies that use an inmate's "good behavior" while confined as a crucial factor in determining their early release are in for a rude awakening. Evidence suggests that good behavior while incarcerated does not necessarily mean that an inmate will successfully adapt to the community and be law-abiding following a favorable early-release decision (Haesler, 1992; Metchik, 1992a, 1992b).

Another indicator of parolee success is whether offenders have had vocational and/or academic training. A study of 760 parolees showed that they were largely successful, particularly if they had sought and retained employment while on parole (Anderson, Schumacker, and Anderson, 1991). Those whose parole programs were revoked tended to have less vocational and educational involvement than those who were more successful.

Parole Board Orientations

Decisions made by parole boards are increasingly standardized and professional (Runda, Rhine, and Wetter, 1994). Generally, they can be classified into six general categories, each manifesting a particular value system: (1) the jurist, (2) the sanctioner, (3) the treater, (4) the controller, (5) the citizen, and (6) the regulator (Gottfredson and Gottfredson, 1988:231–233). The *jurist value system* sees parole decisions as a natural part of criminal justice where fairness and equity predominate. Emphasized are an inmate's rights, and parole board members strive to be sensitive to due process. The *sanctioner value system* equates the seriousness of the offense with the amount of time served. In some respects, this is closely connected with the "just deserts" philosophy (Rhine, Smith, and Jackson, 1991).

The *treater value system* is rehabilitative in orientation, and decisions are made in the context of what might most benefit the offender if parole is granted. Thus, participation in various educational or vocational programs, therapy or encounter groups, restitution, and other types of conditions might accompany one's early release. The *controller value system* emphasizes the functions of parole supervision and monitoring. The conditions are established that increase the degree of control over the offender. Perhaps electronic monitoring or house arrest might be a part of one's parole program. In any case, the controller value system sees offender incapacitation or severe restrictions of freedom while on parole as desirable. The controller value system is most concerned with the risk posed to the public by an offender's early release.

The *citizen value system* is concerned with appealing to public interests and seeing that community expectations are met by making appropriate early-release decisions. How will the public react to releasing certain offenders short of serving their full terms? Will public good be served by such decisions? Finally, the *regulator value system* is directed toward inmate reactions to parole board decisions. How will current inmates react to those decisions in view of their own circumstances? Will the parole supervision system be undermined or enhanced as the result of parole-board decision making (Langston, 1988a, 1988b)?

Objective Parole Board Criteria. Objective parole criteria have been compared with determinate sentencing policies, whereas traditional parole criteria have been equated with indeterminate sentencing systems (Langston, 1990; Lombardi and Lombardi, 1986:86). Among the advantages of objective parole criteria are the following (Lombardi and Lombardi, 1986: 86–87):

1. Inmates know their presumptive release dates within several months of their incarceration.
2. The paroling authority is bound or obligated to meet the presumptive release date.
3. The paroling authority uses scores consisting of an inmate's criminal history and offense severity to determine time ranges for parole release.
4. The paroling authority uses a composite group score representing criminal histories of similar offenders to predict parole success.

Salient Factor Scores and Risk Assessments

A weighting system for parole prognosis was developed by Ernest W. Burgess of the University of Chicago in 1928 (Glaser, 1987:256). However, the development of more contemporary objective parole decision-making guidelines can be traced to the pioneering work of Don Gottfredson and Leslie Wilkins, leaders of the Parole Decision-Making Project in the early 1970s (Goldkamp, 1987:106). At that time, the National Council on Crime and Delinquency and the United States Parole Commission (originally the United States Board of Parole) were interested in parole decision making and solicited the assistance of social scientists to examine various criteria involved in early-release decisions (Goldkamp, 1987:106).

The Salient Factor Score 81 (SFS 81). The **Salient Factor Score** (SFS) was designed to help parole board members make fair parole decisions. Any departures by parole boards from these guidelines were to be accompanied by written rationales outlining the reasons for such departures. At the federal level, the salient factor score was made up of seven criteria, and these were refined in 1976. This was referred to as **SFS 76.** In August 1981, the salient factor scoring instrument underwent further revision and a new, six-factor predictive device, **SFS 81,** was constructed (Hoffman, 1983). A comparison of the revised SFS 81 with its previous counterpart (SFS 76) was made according to validity, stability, simplicity, scoring reliability, and certain ethical concerns. Both instruments appeared to have similar predictive characteristics, although the revised device possesses greater scoring reliability (Hoffman, 1983). Of even greater significance is that SFS 81 places considerable weight on the extent and recency of an offender's criminal history (Hoffman, 1983). Up to seven points can be earned by having no prior convictions or adjudications (adult or juvenile), no prior commitments of more than 30 days, and being 26 years of age or older at the time of the current offense (with certain exceptions). Figure 10.1 shows the six-item federal Salient Factor Score instrument, SFS 81.

Salient Factor Score Index

1. Prior convictions/adjudications (adult or juvenile):
   - None (3 points)
   - One (2 points)
   - Two or three (1 point)
   - Four or more (0 points)
2. Prior commitments of more than 30 days (adult or juvenile):
   - None (2 points)
   - One or two (1 point)
   - Three or more (0 points)
3. Age at current offense/prior commitments:
   - 25 years of age or older (2 points)
   - 20–25 years of age (1 point)
   - 19 years of age or younger (0 points)
4. Recent commitment/free period (three years):
   - No prior commitment of more than 30 days (adult or juvenile) or released to the community from last such commitment at least three years prior to the commencement of the current offense (1 point)
   - Otherwise (0 points)
5. Probation/parole/confinement/escape status violator this time:
   - Neither on probation, parole, confinement, or escape status at the time of the current offense, nor committed as a probation, parole, confinement, or escape status violator this time (1 point)
   - Otherwise (0 points)
6. Heroin/opiate dependence:
   - No history of heroin/opiate dependence (1 point)
   - Otherwise (0 points)

Total score = ___________

FIGURE 10.1 Salient Factor Score Index, SFS 81. (*Source:* U.S. Parole Commission, *Rules and Procedures Manual.* Washington, DC: U.S. Parole Commission, 1985.)

Classification systems, such as the SFS 81 instrument, are simply models. These models are assigned names such as the National Institute of Corrections Prison Classification Model or the Iowa Risk Assessment Model (Hoffman, 1994; Rans, 1984:50). Some authorities have outlined some important and desirable characteristics of such predictive models. These include the following (Rans, 1984:50):

1. The model should be predictively valid.
2. The model should reflect reality.
3. The model should be designed for a dynamic system and not remain fixed over time.

4. The model should serve practical purposes.
5. The model should not be a substitute for good thinking and responsible judgment.
6. The model should be both qualitative and quantitative.

Scores on the SFS 81 can range from "0" to "10". The following evaluative designations accompany various score ranges:

Raw Score	Parole Prognosis
0–3	Poor
4–5	Fair
6–7	Good
8–10	Very Good

The paroling authority next consults a table of offense characteristics consisting of categories varying in offense severity. Adult ranges in numbers of months served are provided for each category and are cross-tabulated with the four-category parole prognosis shown. Thus, a parole board can theoretically apply a consistent set of standards to prisoners committing similar offenses. When the board departs from these standards, especially when parole is possible for an offender but denied, a written rationale is provided for both the prisoner and appellate authorities.

TYPES OF PAROLE

There are several types of parole programs available to parolees. Virtually every one of these programs involves a fair amount of contact with one or more community agencies. Some are administered through community corrections programs (Fulton, 1995). These programs include (1) prerelease, (2) standard parole with conditions, (3) intensive supervised parole, (4) furloughs, (5) shock parole/shock probation, (6) work release/study release, and (7) halfway houses.

Prerelease Action

Prerelease may be either conditional or unconditional. **Conditional releases** are further subdivided into (1) parole board release, (2) mandatory parole, and (3) other conditional. **Unconditional releases** are divided according to (1) expiration, (2) commutation/pardon, and (3) other unconditional (Minor-Harper and Innes, 1987). The greatest number of conditional releases occur through parole board action, whereas early-release decisions are made according to parole board discretion (Deschenes, Turner, and Petersilia, 1995). Mandatory parole releases involve those inmates who have served their sentences *less* the good-time credits they have accumulated (Gray and Wren, 1992). Thus, these releases are determined by calculating the original sentence less any good behavior credits inmates acquired while in prison. These mandatory releases accounted for about a third of all conditional releases (Quigley and VanGheem, 1992). The remainder, other conditional, are probation and court-ordered releases. Some of these include inmates in overcrowded prisons, where court-ordered prison population reductions are implemented (Phelan, Brown, and Friel, 1992).

Unconditional releases comprise those whose prison terms have expired. These are *statutory releases,* since the maximum time prescribed by law for the offense has been served in its entirety. A small portion of these offenders have their sentences commuted through pardons or other administrative action (Quigley and VanGheem, 1992). Again, some of the unconditional releases in the "other unconditional" category result from court-ordered prison population reductions. Overall, about 75 percent of all those paroled complete their parole terms successfully (Minor-Harper and Innes, 1987).

Standard Parole with Conditions

On the average, parole accounts for about 41 percent of all time served for all offender categories. The average length of time spent on parole is 20.5 months (Camp and Camp, 1995d:54–55). Those offenses drawing the longest parole lengths include murder (38 months), kidnapping (26 months), rape (26 months), and robbery (25 months). Those offenses drawing the shortest parole lengths pertain to public order (13 percent), stolen property (15 percent), and larceny/theft (15 percent) (Maguire, Pastore, and Flanagan, 1993). Violent offenders serve substantially longer paroles than property offenders. Violent offenders require more intensive and longer parole supervision to refrain from recidivating when released. Regardless of whether parolees are violent or are property offenders, they are subject to certain standard parole conditions.

Standard Parole Conditions. Most parole agreements contain the following generic information:

1. The defendant shall not leave the judicial district or other specified geographical area without the permission of the court or parole officer.
2. The defendant shall report to the parole officer as directed by the court or parole officer and shall submit a truthful and complete written report within the first five days of each month.
3. The defendant shall answer truthfully all inquiries by the parole officer and follow the instructions of the parole officer.
4. The defendant shall support his dependents and meet other family responsibilities.
5. The defendant shall work regularly at a lawful occupation unless excused by the parole officer for schooling, training, or other acceptable reasons.

6. The defendant shall notify the parole officer within 72 hours of any change in residence or employment.
7. The defendant shall refrain from excessive use of alcohol and shall not purchase, possess, use, distribute, or administer any narcotic or other controlled substance, or any paraphernalia related to such substances, except as prescribed by a physician.
8. The defendant shall not frequent places where controlled substances are illegally sold, used, distributed, or administered, or other places specified by the court.
9. The defendant shall not associate with any persons engaged in criminal activity and shall not associate with any person convicted of a felony, unless granted permission to do so by the parole officer.
10. The defendant shall permit a parole officer to visit him or her at any time at home or elsewhere and shall permit confiscation of any contraband observed in plain view by the PO.
11. The defendant shall notify the parole officer within 72 hours of being arrested or questioned by a law enforcement officer.
12. The defendant shall not enter into any agreement to act as an informer or a special agent of a law enforcement agency without the permission of the court.
13. As directed by the parole officer, the defendant shall notify third parties of risks that may be occasioned by the defendant's criminal record or personal history or characteristics, and shall permit the probation officer to make such notifications and to confirm the defendant's compliance with such notification requirement.

Parole agreements are contracts between the offender and the state. The parole officer is usually responsible for ensuring offender compliance with the conditions set forth in the contract. In the event one or more conditions of the agreement are not complied with by the parolee, the discretionary power of the parole officer is invoked. The parole officer may choose to overlook the violation, depending upon its seriousness. Or the officer may decide under the circumstances to recommend parole revocation. In some jurisdictions, the discretionary power of these officers is severely limited by judges, by parole boards, or by statute.

Intensive Supervised Parole

Parolees are subject to the same behavioral requirements as probationers who are managed in intensive supervision programs. The New Jersey Intensive Supervision Program is made up of inmates who have served at least three or four months of their prison terms (Pearson, 1987:86). In fact, the term *shock parole* has been applied to this and similar programs because an inmate is shocked with what it is like to be incarcerated.

The use of house arrest, electronic monitoring, and a host of other programs may be a part of one's conditional early release from prison. The level of monitoring will vary according to the risk posed by the offender. But as has been seen time and time again, it is very difficult to predict accurately one's risk to the public or general dangerousness.

AN OVERVIEW OF ALTERNATIVE PAROLE PROGRAMS

Furloughs

Furloughs are authorized, unescorted leaves from confinement granted for specific purposes and for designated time periods, usually from 24 to 72 hours, although they may be as long as several weeks or as short as a few hours (McCarthy and McCarthy, 1997). The overall aim of furlough programs as a form of temporary release is to assist the offender in becoming reintegrated into society. In 1918, Mississippi was the first state to use furloughs on a limited basis for low-risk, minimum-security prison inmates who had served at least two or more years of their sentences and were regarded as good security risks (McCarthy and McCarthy, 1997). Since then, about half the states and the Federal Bureau of Prisons have established furlough programs.

Work/Study Release

Another type of temporary release program is work release. **Work release** (also called work furlough, day parole, day pass, and community work) refers to any program that provides for the labor of jail or prison inmates in the community under limited supervision and pays inmates the prevailing wage (McCarthy and McCarthy, 1997). Sometimes, work release and furlough are used interchangeably, referring to similar activities, such as an inmate's participation in an educational program not ordinarily available to prison inmates. These are **study release** programs and are directly connected to an inmate's improvement and plans for employment when paroled.

Although work release was unofficially condoned in the United States in 1906 when Vermont sheriffs assigned inmates to limited community work, this type of temporary release was actually an integral feature of Alexander Maconochie's plan for prison improvement in the 1840s and 1850s (McCarthy and McCarthy, 1997). The first formal establishment of work release by any state occurred in Wisconsin when the **Huber Law** was passed in 1913. By 1993 work/study release programs were operating in at least 43 states involving approximately 21,000 inmates (*Corrections Compendium,* 1993b:5). One of the primary worries of persons administering work/study release programs is that offenders may abscond. Typically, absconders account for less than 2 percent of all program participants in most work/study release programs (Camp and Camp, 1995d; New York State Department of Correctional Services, 1992).

Shock Probation and Parole

Shock probation or shock parole refers to planned sentences by judges who order offenders imprisoned for statutory incarceration periods related to their conviction offenses (New York State Department of Correctional Services Division of Parole, 1994). However, after 30, 60, 90, or even 120 days of incarceration, offenders are taken out of jail or prison and resentenced to probation, provided they behaved well while incarcerated. The *shock* factor relates to the shock of being imprisoned initially. Theoretically, this trauma will be so profound that inmates will not want to return to prison later. Therefore, a strong deterrent factor is associated with these terms. Ohio introduced the first shock probation law in 1965. Two thirds of all states have adopted similar laws in recent years. In 1995, 35 state jurisdictions and the Federal Bureau of Prisons operated shock probation or parole programs (Camp and Camp, 1995d:32). About 7,000 convicted offenders participated in these programs (American Correctional Association, 1996a:xviii–xxix).

Halfway Houses

Halfway houses are either publicly or privately operated facilities staffed by professionals, paraprofessionals, and volunteers. They are designed to assist parolees in making the transition from prison to the community. They provide food, clothing, temporary living quarters, employment assistance, and limited counseling. Again, if the parolee has been confined for a long period, the transition can be difficult, possibly even traumatic (Tonry and Hamilton, 1995).

Two thirds of the states have halfway houses for parolees. Although the precise origin of halfway houses is unknown, some experts say evidence of halfway houses existed during the Middle Ages as a part of Christian charity (McCarthy and McCarthy, 1997). The Salvation Army was associated with halfway house operations in the United States in the early 1900s, although there were shelters such as the Philadelphia House of Industry in existence to serve the various needs of parolees as early as 1889 (McCarthy and McCarthy, 1997). Much earlier in 1817, some reformist groups lobbied for halfway houses as a means of solving prison overcrowding problems. At that time, these proposals were rejected because of the belief that prisoners would contaminate one another if they lived together in common quarters (McCarthy and McCarthy, 1997). Temporary facilities for released prisoners also were established in New York City as early as 1845. The Quakers operated the Isaac T. Hopper Home for those released from prison. And in 1864, the Temporary Asylum for Disadvantaged Female Prisoners was established in New York City (McCarthy and McCarthy, 1997).

Although progress in the development of halfway houses in the United States has been slow, the Prisoner Rehabilitation Act was passed by Congress in 1965. This Act authorized the creation of community-based residences for both adults and juveniles (J. Wilson, 1985). In 1995 there were about 18,000 clients involved in halfway programs in the United States (American Correctional Association, 1996a:xxviii–xxix).

PREDICTING DANGEROUSNESS AND PUBLIC RISK

Factors Associated with Dangerousness and Risk

Several factors influence a parole board's decision to grant early release for one inmate and deny it to another. Do inmates have a sound plan for surviving in the community if parole is granted? What sort of record do inmates have while in custody? Have they complied with prison rules and regulations? Do they have any record of disciplinary infractions? Have they participated in various programs aimed at self-improvement? Have they undergone counseling, therapy, or treatment for any condition that contributed initially to their conviction offense? Do they have dangerous propensities? Are they psychologically disturbed or antisocial? These are complex questions, and psychiatrists on the parole board may be helpful in evaluating a prospective parolee's chances for success on the outside.

Psychiatrists' opinions and predictions about an inmate's future dangerousness are also used, although these opinions and predictions may not be any better than anyone else's opinions. In some research, more than 40 percent of psychiatrists' predictions about offender dangerousness have been erroneous (Sepejak, Webster, and Menzies, 1984).

Parole board members in Kansas have reported that the primary variables considered before granting early release to any inmate include (1) the parole plan, (2) recidivism risk, (3) physical health, (4) time served, (5) institutional behavior, (6) program use, (7) substance abuse, and (8) mental health (Bonham, Janeksela, and Bardo, 1986). Kansas authorities found that the age of prisoners at the parole hearing, the class of their original felony conviction, and their history of alcohol use were related strongly to their successfulness on parole. Kansas is not unlike other states in that these factors may be generalized to other parole board decision making.

Some Prediction Problems

Some of the problems associated with predictions of public risk and dangerousness have already been discussed. Among the problems cited was included inadequate instrumentation (Champion, 1994; Gottfredson and Gottfredson, 1988). Investigators such as Goldkamp (1987) have been critical of the use of prediction instruments in such areas as bail decision making.

Gottfredson (1987) suggests that several factors influence the accuracy of predictions of dangerousness, including measurement reliability and validity, sample representativeness, and cross validation with various offender groups. Accordingly, the inaccuracy of such measures leads to

BOX 10.2 How Good Are Halfway Houses?

The Case of Scott Stewart and 180 Degrees, Inc.

It's never supposed to happen like this. A parole board releases inmates short of serving their full terms. These releases are risks for both the parole board and the parolee. There are no guarantees that parolees will obey the law once they are free within their communities. However, parole boards are able to forecast with some accuracy which parole-eligible inmates will be most successful while on parole.

One way of increasing the chances of a parolee's success while on parole is to obligate parolees to stay in halfway houses when released. Halfway houses are homes in the community in which recently released inmates may ease themselves back into their communities from the rigid regimentation of prison life. Halfway houses are transitional centers. They are designed to provide counseling, job placement assistance, and other aids to facilitate parolee community reintegration.

In Hennepin County, Minnesota, a halfway house known as 180 Degrees, Inc. has been operating for many years. Halfway house residents have been fairly successful at adapting to the change to ordinary community life. 180 Degrees, Inc. has made a strong contribution to the rehabilitation of numerous ex-cons. Scott Stewart was an exception.

Scott Stewart was a twice-convicted sex offender. He was serving a lengthy sentence in the Minnesota State Penitentiary. The Minnesota Parole Board heard his application for an early release and granted it on July 4, 1991, subject to his being assigned to 180 Degrees, Inc. in St. Paul. His instructions from the Minnesota Parole Board were to report to the halfway house the same day he was released. However, when he exited the prison, no one from 180 Degrees, Inc. was there to pick him up and transport him to the halfway house for continued supervision. Five days later, Stewart kidnapped, raped, and murdered Melissa Johnson, a 23-year-old St. Cloud University student.

The Johnson family was outraged and filed suit against 180 Degrees, Inc. After a protracted legal battle, the Minnesota Supreme Court ruled that 180 Degrees, Inc. could not be held liable for Stewart's subsequent actions following his parole. The halfway house, 180 Degrees, Inc., had not previously entered into any agreement with the state to meet and transport Stewart to their St. Paul premises. The Johnsons alleged that the halfway house *was* responsible, since it had failed to assign someone to take him to the halfway house and had not taken prompt action when he failed to show up. Because of Stewart's prior record of past escapes and previous violent sexual offenses, the Johnsons argued that the 180 Degrees, Inc. halfway house should be held liable in their wrongful death action. The Minnesota Supreme Court settled the case by ruling in favor of the halfway house. The Minnesota Justices said that the halfway house was not liable, because Stewart never checked in.

Should halfway houses be held liable for the actions of their clients? How much responsibility should the state bear whenever dangerous offenders are released without supervision? Should persons such as Stewart be paroled or should they be compelled to serve their full terms?

Source: Adapted from Associated Press, "Court Rules Halfway House Not Liable in Rape, Murder Case." *Minot (N.D.) Daily News,* August 30, 1996:B3.

questions of a moral and ethical nature when these instruments are actually applied in the real world (Clear and Gallagher, 1985). Determining prisoners' life chances by a scale score from an instrument whose validity is questionable is problematic. The question becomes one of devising priorities among those eligible for early release.

A key ethical problem with using prediction devices such as the Salient Factor Score Index is that misclassifications occur with disturbing frequency. Even though a scale score says an inmate will probably be dangerous and should not be released, the inmate may not have been dangerous (Webster et al., 1994). On the other hand, the scale score may show that the inmate probably will not be dangerous, but the reverse may prove true. Both of these misclassifications and erroneous predictions present problems (Klein, 1987). First, those predicted to be dangerous who turn out not to be so are deprived of liberty they deserve. The parole board may be criticized for overpenalizing certain inmates because of their past records. Second, those predicted to be low risk and nonviolent and who actually commit new violent acts when released cause blame to be directed at parole boards for making poor early-release decisions (Joo, 1993).

The false positive and false negative dilemma arises, and this dilemma is never fully resolvable. False positives are those inmates predicted to be dangerous who turn out not to be, whereas false negatives are predicted to be harmless and turn out to be dangerous. An injustice is committed against one aggregate of offenders (prolonged detention of the false positives), whereas an injustice is perpetrated against society (the release into society of the false negatives). Judges encounter the same problem as they consider incarcerating certain offenders and not others in cases in which both offenders have committed identical crimes under similar circumstances.

MEASURING PAROLE EFFECTIVENESS THROUGH RECIDIVISM

The success of parole board decision making is frequently measured by the degree of recidivism among parolees. Descriptive information about recidivist parolees is abundant, although there is considerable inconsistency about which characteristics seem most associated with recidivism. Complicating the picture is the fact that many measures of recidivism are used, and each of these measures refers to a different conceptual phenomenon. For example, recidivism is commonly measured by rearrests, reconvictions, parole revocations, parole violations not resulting in revocation, and return to prison. Maltz (1984) has identified at least 14 different meanings of the term *recidivism.* Therefore, when recidivism figures are examined in relation to parolees, we must understand what type of recidivism we are examining.

The most frequently cited predictors of an inmate's chances for success on the outside appear to be age and prior record (Harer, 1994). Thus, these factors are given proportionate weight in Hoffman's Salient Factor

Score Index and other similar scales. Hoffman (1994) believes that the SFS 81 risk instrument adequately separates prisoners into categories having significantly different probabilities of recidivism. He based this conclusion on his study of more than 6,000 federal inmates during the period 1978 to 1987. Of course, recidivism rates among parolees are also contingent, in part, upon the type of parole programs they are assigned to as a component of their conditional release (Hoffman, 1994). In recent years, there has been a trend toward establishing community-based corrections programs, many involving close supervision of offenders, either probationers or parolees. Intensive supervised probation for probationers, house arrest or home incarceration, electronic monitoring, and other community-based programs are currently operating in many communities throughout the United States (McCarthy and McCarthy, 1997). For parolees, several transitional programs are in place in most states.

Recidivism Defined

Recidivism is reoffending following a conviction for an earlier crime. Not all reoffending involves commissions of new crimes. Whereas there are at least 14 different definitions of recidivism (Maltz, 1984), four of the more common definitions are (1) rearrest, (2) reconviction, (3) revocation of parole or probation, and (4) reincarceration.

Rearrests. By definition, *any* probationer or parolee has already been convicted of one or more crimes. When these persons are arrested again while on probation or parole, these rearrests are sometimes counted as recidivism. It doesn't make any difference whether these arrestees are later released because police lack sufficient evidence to detain them. The fact is that a mere arrest is indicative of recidivism. The major problem with using rearrests as measures of recidivism is that arrestees may not have engaged in any illegal behavior. For example, if a former child sexual abuser is on parole and lives on Sixth Avenue in Long Beach, California, and if a child is sexually abused by an unknown person on Sixth Avenue, then police may suspect the former child sexual abuser. This suspicion is the pretext used for making an arrest. After they have arrested the former child sexual abuser, the abused child may say that the arrestee is not the man who abused him or her. Police then will release the parolee without filing any charges. Thus, use of rearrest to measure recidivism is a poor indication of actual new crime committed by probationers or parolees. Better recidivism measures exist.

Reconviction. The best indicator of recidivism is conviction for a new offense following a conviction for a previous offense. When probationers and parolees commit new crimes and are convicted, these convictions are used to measure their rates of recidivism (Harer, 1994). Reconvictions are considered the most significant indicators of recidivism because new crimes are involved. If a probation or parole program is going to be evaluated properly, then reconvictions are perhaps the best criteria to use in such program evaluations. Using any other indicator may lead to false conclusions about a program's effectiveness. If 30 percent of all parolees are revoked for technical program violations, for instance, this may mean that the program may be successful at curbing new crime offending, but also more successful at detecting technical violations. This event occurs when parolees are supervised more closely by parole officers. Parole officers who make more frequent visits to parolee residences are going to discover more program infractions (e.g., curfew violations, failed drug/alcohol checks) than in cases in which less frequent visits are made. It would be silly to trash a parole program simply because a large number of parolees violate curfew by five minutes or test positive for alcohol on one occasion. Yet, some experts have condemned certain parole programs because of these events.

Revocations of Parole or Probation. Another way of measuring recidivism is to count the number of **parole** (or probation) **revocations.** A study of 1994 parolees and probationers showed that there were 170,974 violators (Maguire and Pastore, 1996:595). However, only half of these offenders were given new sentences involving incarceration. The rest simply had their parole or probation programs changed to reflect more intensive supervision. Again, we encounter the problem of counting a simple revocation as though it involved a conviction for a new offense. This may not be the case. Indeed, in at least half of the revocation cases from 1994, about 90,000 offenders had mere technical violations. This is not intended to demean technical violations or diminish their importance; however, violating curfew is not the same as robbing a grocery store or killing or raping an innocent victim. We must examine the *reasons* for the revocations in order to determine whether new offenses are involved.

Return to prison or jail does not always specify the reason for the return. New crimes and new convictions for those crimes certainly account for some of these returns. But it would be misleading to conclude that parole programs are not effective because substantial numbers of parole clientele return to prison. Again, the reason for returning a parolee to prison must be given. If new crimes are involved, then this is a more serious scenario than if technical program violations are involved; although some persons contend that if parolees violate technical program requirements, they are but a short step from committing serious crimes. This thinking suggests that there is automatic escalation associated with committing parole program infractions. No researchers have found that automatic escalation occurs from mere technical program violations to serious crime.

Reincarceration. Being placed back into jail or prison following one's parole means either that a new crime has been committed or that a program violation or infraction was committed. This meaning of recidivism suffers from weaknesses associated with parole revocation and rearrest. We do not know whether new crimes are involved. Nevertheless, parole program effectiveness has been assessed in various studies by using reincarceration as a measure of program recidivism and failure.

THE PROBATION/PAROLE REVOCATION PROCESS

A Virginia judge proclaimed in *Ruffin v. Commonwealth* (1871) that prisoners have "no more rights than slaves" (Bronstein, 1980:20). This pronouncement was most harsh and led to a milder expression that "conditions in prisons were off-limits to judicial scrutiny." In short, prisoners were left to the mercy of their keepers (Bronstein, 1980:20). Subsequently, inmate rights have changed substantially. However, it was not until the late 1960s that due process under the Fourteenth Amendment was extended by the U.S. Supreme Court to include revocation of the respective statuses of parolees and probationers. The most significant cases influencing probation or parole revocation or any probation or parole revocation proceeding occurred in the early 1970s. These were *Mempa v. Rhay* (1967), *Morrissey v. Brewer* (1972), and *Gagnon v. Scarpelli* (1973).

Landmark Probation and Parole Revocation Cases

***Mempa v. Rhay* (1967).** The first case involved a probation revocation rather than a parole revocation, although the decision eventually influenced parole proceedings significantly. Jerry Mempa was convicted of "joyriding" in a stolen vehicle on June 17, 1959. He was placed on probation for two years by a Spokane, Washington, judge. Several months later, on September 15, 1959, Mempa was involved in a burglary. The county prosecutor in Spokane moved to have Mempa's probation revoked. Mempa admitted participating in the burglary. At his probation revocation hearing, the sole testimony about his involvement in the burglary came from his probation officer. Mempa was not represented by counsel, was not asked if he wanted counsel, and was not given an opportunity to offer statements in his own behalf. Furthermore, there was no cross-examination of the probation officer about his statements. The court revoked Mempa's probation and sentenced him to 10 years in the Washington State Penitentiary.

Six years later in 1965, Mempa filed a writ of *habeas corpus,* alleging that he had been denied a right to counsel at the revocation hearing. The Washington Supreme Court denied his petition, but the U.S. Supreme Court elected to hear it on appeal. The U.S. Supreme Court overturned the Washington decision and ruled in Mempa's favor. Specifically, the U.S. Supreme Court said Mempa was entitled to an attorney but was denied one. While the Court did not question Washington authority to defer sentencing in the probation matter, it said that any indigent (including Mempa) is entitled at every stage of a criminal proceeding to be represented by court-appointed counsel in cases in which "substantial rights of a criminal accused may be affected." Thus, the U.S. Supreme Court considered a probation revocation hearing to be a "critical stage" that falls within the due process provisions of the Fourteenth Amendment. In subsequent years, several courts also applied this decision to parole revocation hearings.

***Morrissey v. Brewer* (1972).** The first landmark case involving the constitutional rights of parolees was *Morrissey v. Brewer* (1972). In 1967, John Morrissey was convicted by an Iowa court for "falsely drawing checks" and sentenced to not more than seven years in the Iowa State Prison. He was eventually paroled from prison in June 1968. However, seven months later, his parole officer learned that while on parole, Morrissey had bought a car under an assumed name and operated it without permission, obtained credit cards under a false name, and gave false information to an insurance company when he was involved in a minor automobile accident. In addition, Morrissey had given his parole officer a false address for his residence.

The parole officer interviewed Morrissey and filed a report recommending that parole be revoked. The reasons given by the officer were that Morrissey admitted buying the car and obtaining false I.D., as well as obtaining credit under false pretenses. He also admitted being involved in the auto accident. Morrissey claimed he "was sick," and that this condition prevented him from maintaining continuous contact with his parole officer. The parole officer claimed that Morrissey's parole should be revoked because Morrissey had a habit of "continually violating the rules." The parole board revoked Morrissey's parole, and he was returned to the Iowa State Prison to serve the remainder of his sentence. Morrissey was not represented by counsel at the revocation proceeding. Furthermore, he was not given the opportunity to cross-examine witnesses against him, he was not advised in writing of the charges against him, no disclosure of the evidence against him was provided, and reasons for the revocation were not given. Morrissey also was not permitted to offer evidence in his own behalf or give personal testimony.

Morrissey's appeal to the Iowa Supreme Court was rejected, but the U.S. Supreme Court heard his appeal. While the Court did not address directly the question of whether Morrissey should have had court-appointed counsel, it did make a landmark decision in his case. It overturned the Iowa Parole Board action and established a two-stage proceeding for determining whether parole ought to be revoked. The first or preliminary hearing is held at the time of arrest and detention, at which time it is determined whether probable cause exists that the parolee actually committed the alleged parole violation. The second hearing is more involved and establishes the guilt of the parolee relating to the violations. This proceeding must extend to the parolee certain minimum due process rights, such as the following:

1. The right of the parolee to have written notice of the alleged violations of parole conditions
2. The right to have disclosed to the parolee any evidence of the alleged violation
3. The right of the parolee to be heard in person and to present exculpatory evidence as well as witnesses in his or her behalf

4. The right of the parolee to confront and cross-examine adverse witnesses, unless cause exists why they should not be cross-examined
5. The right to a judgment by a neutral and detached body, such as the parole board itself
6. The right to a written statement of the reasons for the parole revocation

The *Morrissey* case is significant because it sets forth minimum due process rights for all parolees, creating a two-stage proceeding whereby the alleged infractions of parole conditions can be examined and a full hearing conducted to determine the most appropriate disposition of the offender.

***Gagnon v. Scarpelli* (1973).** Since the matter of representation by counsel was not addressed directly in Morrissey's case, and since it had been the subject of previous U.S. Supreme Court action in the case of Jerry Mempa, it was only a matter of time that the U.S. Supreme Court made a decision about a parolee's right to court-appointed counsel in a parole revocation proceeding. This decision was rendered by the U. S. Supreme Court in the case of *Gagnon v. Scarpelli* (1973), a year after the *Morrissey* ruling.

In July 1965, Gerald Scarpelli pled guilty to a charge of robbery in a Wisconsin court. He was sentenced to 15 years in prison. But the judge suspended this sentence on August 5, 1965, and placed Scarpelli on probation for a period of seven years. The next day, August 6, Scarpelli was arrested and charged with burglary. His probation was revoked without a hearing, and he was placed in the Wisconsin State Reformatory to serve his 15-year term. About three years later, Scarpelli was paroled. Shortly before his parole, he filed a *habeas corpus* petition, alleging that his probation revocation was invoked without a hearing and without benefit of counsel. This constituted a denial of due process. Following his parole, the U.S. Supreme Court acted on his original *habeas corpus* petition and ruled in his favor. Specifically, the U.S. Supreme Court said that Scarpelli was denied his right to due process because no revocation hearing was held, and he was not represented by court-appointed counsel within the indigent claim. In effect, the Court, referring to *Morrissey v. Brewer* (1972), said that "a probation revocation, like parole revocation, is not a stage of a criminal prosecution, but does result in loss of liberty . . . We hold that a probationer, like a parolee, is entitled to a preliminary hearing and a final revocation hearing in the conditions specified in *Morrissey v. Brewer.*"

The significance of this case is that it equated probation with parole as well as the respective revocation proceedings. While the Court did not say that all parolees and probationers have a right to representation by counsel in all probation and parole revocation proceedings, it did say that counsel should be provided in cases in which the probationer or parolee makes a timely claim contesting the allegations. While no constitutional basis exists for providing counsel in all probation or parole revocation proceedings, subsequent probation and parole revocation hearings usually involve defense counsel if legitimately requested. The U.S. Supreme Court declaration has been liberally interpreted in subsequent cases.

Other Cases

***Bearden v. Georgia* (1983).** Other more recent cases of interest involving parolees and probationers and whether to revoke their respective programs are *Bearden v. Georgia* (1983) and *Black v. Romano* (1985). In the *Bearden* case, Bearden's probation was revoked by Georgia authorities because he failed to pay a fine and make restitution to his victim as required by the court. He claimed he was indigent, but the court rejected his claim as a valid explanation for his conduct. The U.S. Supreme Court disagreed. It ruled that probation may not be revoked in the case of indigent probationers who have failed to pay their fines or make restitution. They further suggested alternatives, such as community service, for restitution and punishments that were more compatible with the abilities and economic resources of indigent probationers. In short, the probationer should not be penalized when a reasonable effort has been made to pay court-ordered fines and restitution.

***Black v. Romano* (1985).** In the *Black v. Romano* (1985) case, a probationer had his probation revoked by the sentencing judge because of alleged program violations. The defendant had left the scene of an automobile accident, a felony in the jurisdiction in which the alleged offense occurred. The judge gave reasons for the revocation decision, but did not indicate that he had considered any option other than incarceration. The U.S. Supreme Court ruled that judges generally are not obligated to consider alternatives to incarceration before they revoke an offender's probation and place him in jail or prison. Clearly, probationers and parolees have obtained substantial rights in recent years. U.S. Supreme Court decisions have provided them with several important constitutional rights that invalidate the arbitrary and capricious revocation of their probation or parole programs by judges or parole boards. The two-stage hearing is extremely important to probationers and parolees in that it permits ample airing of the allegations against offender, cross-examinations by counsel, and testimony from individual offenders.

***United States v. Bachsian* (1993).** Offender indigence does not automatically entitle parolees to immunity from restitution orders. In a 1993 case, *United States v. Bachsian* (1993), Bachsian was convicted of theft. He was required to pay restitution for the merchandise still in his possession under the Victim Witness Protection Act. Bachsian claimed, however, that he was indigent and unable to make restitution. The 9th Circuit Court of Appeals declared in Bachsian's case said that it was *not* improper to impose restitution orders on an offender at the time of sentencing, even if the offender was unable to pay restitution then. In this instance, records indicated that Bachsian was considered by the court as having a future ability to pay, based on a presentence investigation report. Eventually, Bachsian would become financially able and in a position to make restitution to his victim. His restitution orders were upheld. Also, bankruptcy does not discharge an offender's obligation to make restitution, although the amount and rate of restitution payments may be affected (*Baker v. State,* 1993; *State v. Hayes,* 1993).

THE RIGHTS OF PROBATIONERS AND PAROLEES

There has been continuing interest in the rights of probationers and parolees (South Carolina Department of Probation, Parole and Pardon Services, 1993). Various courts in different jurisdictions, including the U.S. Supreme Court, have set forth landmark decisions that influence either positively or negatively the lives of those in probation or parole programs (Bodapati and Marquart, 1992; Petersilia and Turner, 1992; Vigdal and Stadler, 1994:44).

Probationer and Parolee Rights Generally

Pardons. Whenever governors pardon someone who may or may not be on probation or parole, the effect of these pardons is different, depending upon the jurisdiction. Generally, a pardon is tantamount to absolution for a crime previously committed. Someone has been convicted of the crime, and the intent of a pardon is to terminate whatever punishment has been imposed. In *United States v. Noonan* (1990), for instance, Gregory Noonan was convicted and sentenced in 1969 for "failing to submit to induction into the armed forces." President Jimmy Carter granted a pardon to Noonan on January 21, 1977, wherein Carter declared a "full, complete and unconditional pardon" to persons convicted during the Vietnam War for refusing induction. Noonan sought to have his record of the original conviction *expunged.* An expungement order has the effect of wiping one's slate clean, as though the crime and the conviction had never occurred. Noonan believed that his conviction, which remained on his record, adversely affected his employment chances. Thus, he sought to expunge his record because of the pardon he had received from Carter. However, the Third Circuit Court of Appeals, a federal appellate court, refused to grant him this request. The court declared that "a pardon does not blot out guilt nor does it restore the offender to a state of innocence in the eye of the law." In Noonan's case, the presidential pardon was effective in removing the punishment, but it did not expunge his criminal record.

In some appellate courts, a different position has been taken regarding the influence of a pardon on one's criminal record. For instance, the Indiana Court of Appeals declared in the case of *State v. Bergman* (1990) that a pardon *does* expunge one's criminal record. The governor of Indiana had pardoned a convict, Berman, for a crime he had previously committed. Bergman sought to have his record expunged in much the same way as Noonan. The Indiana Court of Appeals declared that pardons "block out the very existence of the offender's guilt, so that, in the eye(s) of the law, he is thereafter as innocent as if he had never committed the offense." Subsequent state court decisions have concurred with both Pennsylvania and Indiana.

Probationer or Parolee Program Conditions. When probationers or parolees are subject to having their programs revoked by respective authorities, what is the nature of evidence that can be used against them to support their program revocation? What are their rights concerning parole officer searches of their premises? What about the program conditions they have been obligated to follow? What about parole board recognition of and obligation to follow minimum-sentence provisions from sentencing judges?

1. *Conditions of probation/parole, including victim restitution payments, are legitimate; however, there are situations in which offenders may or may not be able to pay restitution declared by the court.* In the case of *Bearden v. Georgia* (1983), we saw that an inability to pay restitution cannot entitle judges to automatically revoke one's probation program. In Bearden's case, the judge had not examined other options in lieu of the restitution order. More recent cases have upheld *Bearden,* and some interesting spins have been added. For instance, a Florida man, Moore, was convicted of purchasing a stolen truck (*Moore v. State,* 1993). The original truck's owner, the victim, claimed that there were tools worth $500 in the truck when it was stolen by the one who sold the truck to Moore. Nevertheless, the judge imposed a sentence of probation, with a restitution condition that Moore repay the victim $500 for the loss of the tools. A Florida Court of Appeals set aside this condition, since it did not show that the loss was caused by Moore's action, nor that there was a significant relation between the loss and the crime of purchasing a stolen vehicle.

Judicial Actions and Rights. Judges often impose various sentences that differ from those provided or recommended by statute. Sometimes these sentences contain special conditions of probation that involve victim compensation, community service, or participation in group or individual therapy. Following are some of the liberties taken by judges in sentencing decisions and/or departures and a discussion of whether these liberties are valid.

2. *Judges who impose probation in lieu of mandatory sentences for particular offenses may have their probation judgments declared invalid.* In a New York case, a plea bargain was worked out between the state and a defendant named Hipp (*People v. Hipp,* 1993). Hipp was determined by the court to be addicted to gambling. The nature of the conviction offense and the gambling addiction compel the Court under mandatory sentencing to prescribe a jail term as well as accompanying therapy for the addiction. In this instance, the judge simply accepted a plea agreement, accepting the defendant's guilty plea in exchange for a term of probation. The New York

Court of Appeals overruled the judge in this case, indicating that New York statutes do not authorize a trial court to ignore clearly expressed and unequivocal mandatory sentencing provisions of the New York Penal Law. However, in Florida, a judge imposed probation on an offender convicted under an Habitual Offender Statute (*McKnight v. State,* 1993). McKnight was convicted of being a habitual felony offender. Ordinarily, this conviction carries a mandatory life-without-parole penalty. However, the judge in McKnight's case imposed probation. Although the Florida Court of Appeals did not like the judge's decision, it upheld it anyway, supporting the general principle of *judicial discretion.*

3. *Defendants can refuse probation if the court imposes probation as a sentence.* Cannon (*Cannon v. State,* 1993) was convicted of criminally negligent homicide after entering a guilty plea. However, in open court, after probation was imposed, Cannon refused the probation and demanded to be incarcerated instead. The judge insisted that the probation sentence be accepted by Cannon. Cannon appealed. The Alabama Court of Appeals upheld Cannon's right to refuse probation, and he was remanded to prison instead. This is not as bad as it sounds, however. Cannon had been incarcerated for some time prior to his criminally negligent homicide conviction. By accepting probation, Cannon would have been obligated to adhere to certain restrictive conditions for a period of time far in excess of the time remaining to be served. In effect, he had only a few more months to serve of his original sentence, counting the many months he had been behind bars before his trial and conviction. Thus, a probation sentence in Cannon's case would have involved a longer term of conditional freedom rather than the number of months remaining before his unconditional release from prison. The court said that "Our holding merely recognizes a convict's right to reject the trial court's offer of probation if he or she deems it to be more *onerous* than a prison sentence."

4. *Judges may revoke one's probation program or supervised release and impose a new sentence that the offender must serve the remainder of the term in confinement.* A federal probationer, Levi, was under supervised release (*United States v. Levi,* 1993). During his first 11 months of supervised release, Levi committed one or more probation violations. The Judge revoked his probation and declared that he must spend the remaining 13 months incarcerated. The 8th Circuit Court of Appeals upheld the judge's action, since the 13-month imprisonment was within the 2-year sentence of probation originally imposed by the same judge.

Sometimes parole officers obligate their probationer-clients to conform to rules outside of those specified in probation orders. In the eyes of Texas law, at least, such orders or conditions are unconstitutional. In the case of *Lemon v. State* (1993), Lemon, a probationer convicted of misappropriation of property, was required by a judge to perform community service at the orders or discretion of his probation officer. The Texas Court of Appeals reversed this condition of his probation, since the nature of community service had not been articulated by the judge. It is improper for correctional officers to determine the nature of one's community service to be performed under a sentence of probation with conditions.

Parole Board Actions and Rights. Parole boards have considerable discretionary powers. They may deny parole or grant it. They may revoke one's parole and return the offender to prison, or they may continue the offender's parole program, with additional supervision and other conditions. Below are some of the actions parole boards may take and how parolees are impacted.

5. *Inmates who become eligible for parole are not automatically entitled to parole.* Parole boards have considerable discretion whether to grant or deny parole to any inmate. Short of serving their full sentences or completing a portion of their term less any applicable good-time credit, inmates are not automatically entitled to be paroled. In the case of *Williams v. Puckett* (1993), a Mississippi man convicted of armed robbery and forgery was sentenced to a mandatory sentence of 10 years plus a 5-year term for the forgery conviction. In Mississippi, inmates become eligible for parole after serving 10 years of terms imposed in excess of 10 years, by statute. However, since the armed robbery conviction involved a mandatory prison term of 10 years, this meant that the entire sentence of 10 years must be served. Thus, according to Mississippi law, the inmate must serve at least one fourth of the five-year term for the forgery conviction before *actual* parole eligibility occurred. Even then, the Mississippi Parole Board would not be obligated to automatically grant early release.

6. *Parole boards do not have to recognize minimum-sentence provisions from sentencing judges when considering an inmate's parole eligibility.* In another case, this time in Oregon, an inmate became eligible for parole after serving his minimum sentence, under a determinate minimum-maximum sentence originally imposed by a judge (*Carroll v. Board of Parole,* 1993). The Oregon Parole Board is vested with the power to override any minimum-sentence provision that might otherwise provide a means whereby an offender might be paroled automatically. In this case, the inmate had been convicted of murder and had served the minimum sentence prescribed by law. However, the Parole Board voted to override the minimum sentence and to continue the inmate's incarceration, given the seriousness of the crime and other factors. The inmate contested this Parole Board action, but the Oregon Court of Appeals upheld the Parole Board action as legitimate, since a unanimous vote was required to override the minimum sentence and the Parole Board had voted unanimously.

7. *Inmates who have been paroled and who subsequently commit a new violent act while on parole may have their parole programs revoked and may be returned to prison to serve the remaining sentence in its entirety.* In New York, a parolee, Richardson, committed a new violent felony while on parole. The Parole Board revoked his parole and returned him to prison without further parole consideration, despite the fact that he had not, as yet, been tried and convicted on the new violent offense charge (*Richardson v. New York State Executive Department,* 1993).

KEY TERMS

Caseloads
Conditional release
English Penal Servitude Act
Furloughs
Huber law
Irish system
Latent functions
Manifest functions
Marks of commendation
Pardon
Parole
Parole boards
Parolee
Parole revocation
Salient Factor Score (SFS 76, SFS 81)
Tickets-of-leave
Unconditional release
Work/study release

QUESTIONS FOR REVIEW

1. Identify three important cases associated with probationer and parolee rights. What is the significance of the cases you have cited?
2. Where did parole originate? Who are some important historical figures in the development of parole in the United States? What were their respective contributions?
3. What are tickets-of-leave? How were they allocated?
4. What is the nature of control parole exerts over inmates in prison?
5. What are good-time credits? When were they initially used in the United States? Are they still used in prisons in the United States?
6. What are some important functions of parole?
7. Differentiate between conditional and unconditional release for inmates. What are some significant variations of conditional release?
8. What are some important functions performed by parole boards? What criteria do they usually employ when reaching decisions about individual inmates?
9. What is the Salient Factor Score Index? Is there any apparent bias associated with this index?
10. Identify some of the major problems associated with trying to predict an offender's future dangerousness and then making a decision whether to parole the offender.
11. Differentiate between furloughs and work release. Briefly discuss the origin of each in the United States. Are these programs successful?

12. In what respect is shock probation a misnomer? Why does shock incarceration appear to be a more acceptable term?
13. Is there any consistency among states about the minimum criteria for selecting parole officers? What are some parole officer functions?
14. What are the selection effect and the early release effect?

SUGGESTED READINGS

American Correctional Association. *Improved Media Relations: A Handbook for Corrections.* Laurel, MD: American Correctional Association, 1993.

Castello, Anthony, Rick Garnett, and Vincent Schiraldi. *Parole Violators in California: A Waste of Money, a Waste of Time.* San Francisco: Center on Juvenile and Criminal Justice, 1991.

Rhine, Edward E., William R. Smith, and Ronald W. Jackson. *Paroling Authorities: Recent History and Current Practice.* Laurel, MD: American Correctional Association, 1991.

11

Community Corrections: Types, Goals, and Functions

CHAPTER OUTLINE

OVERVIEW

During the late 1970s, several states established correctional programs within various communities. These programs were designed to supervise offenders who had either not been sentenced to jail or prison or who had been released from prison or jail and were on parole. A primary objective of these programs was to find alternative means of managing offenders apart from institutionalizing them. Incarcerating offenders is expensive. If less costly and safe community supervision methods could be created, then both the government and the public would benefit from such programs.

This chapter describes the origins of community corrections. Beginning with a discussion of community corrections acts, the chapter examines both the history and philosophy of community programs. The functions and goals of community corrections are described. Key elements of community corrections are listed, together with a rationale for the creation of such programs.

Since the late 1970s, community corrections burgeoned. Diverse forms of community corrections exist today. Some persons refer to such programs as *intermediate punishments,* because they represent a degree of offender control somewhere between standard probation and incarceration. Whatever their label, they have been established as control and supervision alternatives to incarcerating both probationers and parolees. Some of these programs are probationer-centered, while other community programs are parolee-centered.

Two types of corrections programs operating within the community are home confinement and electronic monitoring. Home confinement is described, including its history, goals, and functions. Several issues about home confinement as a punishment are raised and discussed. Home confinement clients are profiled. Electronic monitoring is presented, including its functions and goals. Described are different types of electronic monitoring systems. Several issues concerning electronic monitoring are presented, including the ethics of such monitoring, its constitutionality, and whether it functions as a deterrent and preserves public safety.

Furlough programs and work/study release programs are also described. These programs enable parole-eligible inmates to have brief leaves from their prisons to be with their families or to study or work at some productive job. Halfway houses, transitional residences for those recently released from prisons, are also discussed. Other sanctions, such as day fines, community service, restitution, and victim compensation, are defined and explained as conditional provisions often associated with postrelease community programs. The chapter concludes with an examination of several important issues about community corrections.

THE COMMUNITY CORRECTIONS ACT

A **community corrections act** is the enabling medium by which jurisdictions establish local community corrections agencies, facilities, and programs. It generally is a statewide mechanism through which funds are granted to local units of government to plan, develop, and deliver correctional sanctions and services at the local level. The overall purpose of this mechanism is to provide local sentencing options in lieu of imprisonment in state institutions (McManus and Barclay, 1994:12).

Community corrections acts in various states are designed to make it possible to divert certain prison-bound offenders into local-, city-, or county-level programs through which they can receive treatment and assistance rather than imprisonment (Harris, Jones, and Funke, 1990). For instance, Kansas implemented a community corrections act in 1978. This act was designed to provide alternatives to both incarceration and new prison construction by encouraging local communities to provide appropriate community sanctions for adult and juvenile offenders. Kansas community corrections currently uses a variety of programs as part of its community corrections, including home confinement, day reporting centers, halfway houses, electronic monitoring, and intensive supervised probation and parole (Townsend, 1991:26–27).

There were 20,000 offenders in Ohio community corrections programs in 1993 (Ortega and Hardin, 1993:15). Nonviolent clients who had participated in both residential and nonresidential placement options were targeted. Ortega and Hardin say these placement options included work release and halfway house programs, intensive supervised probation, day reporting centers, home confinement, community service, and standard probation. Urinalyses of clients, as well as other forms of behavioral monitoring, were conducted.

The following eight common elements are essential to the success of community corrections acts:

1. Prison/jail-bound offenders are targeted rather than adding additional punishments to those who would have otherwise remained in the community.
2. Financial subsidies are provided to local government and community agencies.
3. A performance factor is implemented to ensure that funds are used for the act's specific goals.

4. Local advisory boards in each local community assess local needs, propose improvements in the local criminal justice system, and educate the general public about the benefits of alternative punishments.
5. Advisory boards submit annual criminal justice plans to the local government.
6. There is a formula for allocating funds.
7. Local communities participate voluntarily and may withdraw at any time.
8. There are restrictions on funding high-cost capital projects as well as straight probation services.

COMMUNITY CORRECTIONS PROGRAMS

Community-based programs vary in size and scope among communities, but they tend to have in common the following characteristics:

1. One or more large homes or buildings located within the residential section of the community with space to accommodate between 20 and 30 residents are within walking distance of work settings and social services.
2. A professional and paraprofessional staff is "on call" for medical, social, or psychological emergencies.
3. A system is in place for heightening staff accountability to the court concerning offender progress.
4. Community-based program administrators have the authority to oversee offender behaviors and enforce compliance with their probation conditions.
5. These programs have job referral and placement services by which paraprofessionals or others act as liaisons with various community agencies and organizations to facilitate offender job placement.
6. Administrators of these programs are available on-premises on a 24-hour basis for emergency situations and spontaneous assistance for offenders who may need help.

GOALS OF COMMUNITY CORRECTIONS

The goals of community corrections programs include (1) facilitating offender reintegration, (2) fostering offender rehabilitation, (3) providing an alternative range of offender punishments, and (4) heightening offender accountability.

Facilitating Offender Reintegration

Although the major aims of community corrections have been strongly linked with diversion, advocacy, and reintegration, Lawrence (1990, 1991) says that the emphasis upon reintegration has been replaced in recent years by an emphasis on offender control, surveillance, and monitoring. Benekos (1990) concurs with Lawrence, although Benekos says that the new emphasis is upon punitive-restrictive restraint rather than therapeutic-integrative considerations.

Fostering Offender Rehabilitation

Community-based corrections programs assist first-time nonviolent offenders. Through probation, diversion, halfway houses, and parole, community-based programs are thought to have considerable success in rehabilitating offenders. The importance of job development and assistance in job placement is underscored by the fact that those without jobs or who are underemployed tend to recidivate and cause programs to be less effective. Between July 1, 1988, and June 30, 1989, for example, English and Mande (1991) studied 1,796 male and female offenders who were terminated from the residential component of community corrections programs. They found that about half of all community corrections clients studied were returned to prison within a few months. These cases were classified as failures. A follow-up study of those who failed in their community programs disclosed that most clients were younger, non–high school graduates with extensive criminal histories and employment problems.

Providing an Alternative Range of Offender Punishments

Some programs for youthful adults include boot camp–like atmospheres such as the Georgia Special Alternative Incarceration Program (SAI). In Georgia, the SAI program is a special condition of probation. Judges sentence offenders to 90 days in prison in a regime of manual labor, rigorous physical conditioning, and military-like discipline. The second phase consists of less structured, postconfinement community supervision. An examination of participants across the years from 1983 to 1990 showed that clients had a recidivism rate of about 41 percent (Flowers, Carr, and Ruback, 1991). Higher recidivism rates of 50 percent and 62 percent were observed for standard probationers and traditional incarcerated inmates.

Heightening Offender Accountability

A national survey of privately operated community corrections agencies conducted by the International Association of Residential and Community Alternatives (IARCA) has found that the following programs are currently offered to offender-clients: intensive supervision, house arrest, electronic monitoring, day fines, community services, day/evening reporting, and community residential centers (Huskey and Lurigio, 1992).

FUNCTIONS OF COMMUNITY CORRECTIONS

Community corrections has the following functions: (1) monitoring and supervising clients, (2) providing employment assistance, (3) alleviating prison and jail overcrowding, (4) providing vocational and educational training, and (6) ensuring public safety.

Monitoring and Supervising Clients

One program is the Florida Community Control Program (FCCP). FCCP also seeks to provide a milieu of accountability for offender-clients. The FCCP was established in 1983 and serves 40,000 clients (Wagner and Baird, 1993:1). Supervision of Florida offenders placed in this program is intense. Offenders must have a minimum of 28 supervisory contacts per month. Supervising officers have caseloads of between 20 and 25 offenders. These caseloads are very low compared with standard probation or parole supervision. Besides close offender supervision, the FCCP employs home confinement. Offenders are regularly screened for drug and alcohol use and are monitored to ensure their payment of victim compensation, restitution, and/or community service. Offenders also pay supervision fees to offset some of the program costs. FCCP costs per day average $6.49, while jail and prison costs per day per offender are $19.52 and $39.05, respectively. Recidivism is less than 20 percent for FCCP clients (Wagner and Baird, 1993:4).

Providing Employment Assistance

One objective of community corrections is to provide offender-clients with job assistance. Often, these clients do not know how to fill out simple job application forms. One successful employment assistance program tailored for female offenders was established in Pennsylvania in 1974 (Arnold, 1992). Known as **The Program for Female Offenders, Inc.,** the program was guided by two goals: reforming female offenders and creating economically independent women. The program started with a job placement service. Training centers were eventually created and operated by different counties on a nonprofit basis. Training center offerings have included remedial math instruction, English instruction, and clerical classes such as word processing, data entry, and telecommunications skill training. Psychological counseling has also been provided for those women with various types of problems.

Alleviating Jail and Prison Overcrowding

Community-based corrections functions to alleviate jail and prison populations (Corrigan, 1990; English and Mande, 1991). One short-term benefit is reducing jail and prison populations by diverting a substantial number of offenders to community-based supervision. A long-term benefit is that offenders in community-based programs tend to have lower rates of recidivism than paroled offenders who have served time in prison.

Providing Vocational and Educational Training

Community corrections agencies help offender-clients in many useful ways. Many of these agencies provide education services for offenders with language deficiencies or who have dropped out of school previously. Many offenders do not know how to fill out job placement forms or applications. Community corrections staff offers assistance in this regard. In addition, offender-clients may participate in study release through local schools.

A task force in Arizona investigated the literacy level of Arizonans and found that more than 400,000 were functionally illiterate. Another 500,000 did not have a high school diploma. About 60 percent of Arizona's prison inmates had a sixth-grade reading level (O'Connell and Power, 1992). Seeking to remedy this situation, Arizona implemented L.E.A.R.N. (Literacy, Education, and Reading Network) labs to remedy learning and educational deficiencies among its probationers and inmates. One purpose of this program is to raise the educational and reading level of offender-clients so that they will be more competitive in the workplace. The L.E.A.R.N. program has been successful in accomplishing these objectives.

Ensuring Public Safety

Crime control is a major concern for community corrections administrators (Byrne and Taxman, 1994). An obvious concern of community residents is safety, given that recently convicted felons are roaming their neighborhoods more or less freely and in relatively large numbers (Johnson et al., 1994). The public safety factor was the subject of a study of community corrections in Kansas. Harris, Jones, and Funke (1990) investigated various participating Kansas counties over time during the 1980s. They compared incarcerated felons with community corrections clients and those placed on standard probation. Interestingly, these researchers found few significant differences in recidivism rates between inmates and program clients. In fact, they indicate that at least a 50 percent false-positive rate would have been incurred had these offenders been incarcerated initially. In short, at least 50 percent of the prison-bound offenders did not recidivate after placement in community corrections programs. Further, the offenses committed by community corrections clients tended to be less serious than their conviction offenses.

TYPES OF COMMUNITY CORRECTIONS PROGRAMS

Electronic Monitoring

Electronic monitoring is primarily designed for low-risk, petty offenders, particularly misdemeanants and first-offender felons, and appears to be an increasingly attractive alternative to incarceration in prison or jail (Mainprize, 1992). Several manufacturers, such as GOSSlink, BI Incorporated, and Controlec, Inc., produce tamper-resistant wrist and ankle bracelets that emit electronic signals that are often connected to telephone devices and are relayed to central computers in police stations or probation departments.

Electronic Monitoring Defined. **Electronic monitoring** is the use of telemetry devices to verify that offenders are at specified locations during particular times (Brown and Elrod, 1995). Electronic devices such as wristlets or anklets are fastened to offenders and must not be removed by them during the course of their sentence. The sanction for tampering with an offender's telemetry device is strong, consisting of revocation of privileges and return to prison or jail (Bellassai and Toborg, 1990; McCarthy, 1987a). In 1987, only 800 offenders were under some type of electronic monitoring program in the United States. By 1992, that figure had greatly increased and was estimated to be approximately 70,000 (Lilly, 1992:500).

Goals of Electronic Monitoring Programs. The first commercial use of electronic monitoring devices occurred in 1964 as an alternative to incarcerating mental patients and certain parolees (Gable, 1986). In subsequent years, electronic monitoring was extended to include monitoring office work, employee testing for security clearances, and many other applications (Sluder, Garner, and Cannon, 1995). The feasibility of using electronic devices to monitor probationers was investigated by various researchers during the 1960s and 1970s, although New Mexico officially sanctioned its use for criminal offenders in 1983 (Rasmussen and Benson, 1994).

New Mexico Second Judicial District Judge Jack Love implemented a pilot project in 1983 to electronically monitor persons convicted of drunk driving and various white collar offenses. The New Mexico Supreme Court examined the program and approved it subject to the voluntary consent and participation of offenders as a condition of their probation and as long as their privacy, dignity, and families were protected (Rasmussen and Benson, 1994). Offenders were required to wear anklets or wristlets that emitted electronic signals that could be intercepted by probation officers conducting surveillance operations.

Following the New Mexico experiment, other jurisdictions commenced using a variety of electronic monitoring systems for supervising parolees, probationers, inmates of jails and prisons, and pretrial releasees (Sluder et al., 1995). Both praised and condemned by criminal justice practitioners, electronic monitoring seems to be the most promising cost-effective solution to the problems of prison overcrowding and the management of probation officer caseloads (Corbett and Marx, 1991; Quinn and Holman, 1991). Until the advent of electronic monitoring devices, the idea of confining convicted offenders to their homes as a punishment was simply unworkable, unless a jurisdiction was willing to pay for the continuous monitoring services of a probation officer. In 1983, an electronic device was used to monitor low-risk offenders in New Mexico (Schmidt and Curtis, 1987). In the next few years, experiments with electronic monitoring devices were tried in Florida, California, and Kentucky (Tonry and Hamilton, 1995).

Types of Electronic Monitoring Systems. There are four basic categories of electronic monitoring equipment used for surveillance of offenders. These include (1) **continuous signaling devices** that emit a continuous signal that can be intercepted by telephonic communication from a central dialing location such as a probation office or police station, (2) **programmed contact devices,** by which telephonic contact is made at random times with the offender, whose voice is verified electronically by computer, (3) **cellular telephone devices,** which are transmitters worn by offenders and which transmit a signal that can be intercepted by local area monitors, and (4) **continuous signaling transmitters,** which are also transmitters worn by offenders and emit continuous signals that may be intercepted by probation officers with portable receiving units. Probation officers only need to drive by an offender's home to verify the offender's presence during random hours thus eliminating the need for face-to-face contact (Schmidt, 1986).

All electronic devices used for offender surveillance are considered tamper-resistant, although some claim to be tamper-proof. In any case, the penalty for attempting to remove or successfully removing these devices while on probation is revocation of probation and incarceration in a prison or jail. Therefore, the possible penalty is ordinarily sufficient to deter offenders tampering with the monitoring equipment (Corbett and Marx, 1994).

Between May 1985 and December 1986, electronic monitoring was used together with home incarceration for managing 35 offenders convicted of nonviolent offenses in Kenton County, Kentucky. These offenses included drunk driving, violation of child support orders, and chronic misdemeanants. The experiment was timely since Kenton County was one of several Kentucky jurisdictions ordered by the court during that time period to reduce the jail population and alleviate overcrowding. Although these researchers acknowledged the study had several methodological flaws as well as a small sample size, they were able to demonstrate the cost savings and effectiveness of electronic monitoring for the offender/clients during the term of the investigation. It is important to recognize that the initial or direct costs of purchasing electronic monitoring equipment represented a significant expenditure. Despite this expenditure, the program more than paid for itself during the study period, however.

The total cost of establishing and operating the program of home confinement with electronic monitoring, including hardware, software, postage, telephone, computer training, probation officer salaries, and travel reimbursement was $42,568. This is significant since the comparable cost of maintaining the 35 offender/clients in the Kenton County Jail during the 1985 to 1986 study period would have been $44,720. Therefore, within 18 months, the program had paid for itself. Continuing to operate the program for new offenders beyond December 1986 would mean even greater savings for jail officials and county residents, since the initial equipment expenditures and investments had already been made and defrayed. Thus, by the end of 1987, Kenton County savings would increase to more than $30,000, compared with the costs of jailing the same offenders placed on electronic monitoring during the same time period. These figures are based on an average daily incarceration fee per inmate of $26 contrasted with $3 or $4 per day per offender using the electronic monitoring system (Lilly, Ball, and Wright, 1987).

The Ethics of Electronic Monitoring. One criticism of electronic monitoring is the potential for the ultimate political control of the public. Is electronic monitoring ethical? Currently, the Internal Revenue Service, FBI, and other agencies maintain electronic files and other information about millions of citizens. The use of electronic monitoring conjures up frightening pictures of George Orwell's *1984* and "Big Brother" images. If criminal offenders are electronically tracked into their own homes, what is in store for the law-abiding public-at-large from an inventive government? Ball, Huff, and Lilly (1988:39) have asked "Does house arrest represent 'progress' as a genuine alternative to the harsh conditions of jail and prison? Is it a promising policy that must be given careful scrutiny because of certain latent dangers of going awry? Or are we witnessing a general decline of privacy and personal autonomy and a movement toward a society characterized by a passive and docile citizenry and devoted to maximum security through technological power?"

One response to these questions is to address the fundamental purpose or intent of electronic monitoring. Is electronic monitoring intentionally designed to snoop on private citizens? No. Is electronic monitoring intentionally designed to invade one's privacy? No. Is electronic monitoring intentionally designed to assist correctional officers in verifying an offender's whereabouts? Yes. Is electronic monitoring capable of detecting program violations in lieu of direct parole officer supervision? Yes. (See Smykla and Selke, 1995.)

Perhaps the ethical issue becomes more relevant or focused if we theoretically project what the limits of electronic monitoring might be in some future context. Some critics might be justified, therefore, in contending that if we use electronic monitoring for a limited purpose today (e.g., to verify an offender's whereabouts), what other uses might be made of electronic monitoring in future years (e.g., intruding into bedrooms to detect criminal sexual acts or other possible criminal behaviors)? Presently, electronic monitoring equipment is placed in convenient areas such as kitchens or living rooms. Video-capable electronic monitoring equipment is also presently limited to verifying one's identity and whether drug or alcohol program violations have occurred. No one has suggested that cameras be placed in one's bedroom or bathroom to be activated at the whim of an equipment operator. If there is an issue to be raised here, then it would be the *reasonableness* issue (Tonry and Hamilton, 1995).

Strengths and Weaknesses of Electronic Monitoring. Some of the pros and cons of electronic monitoring are summarized as follows (Tonry and Hamilton, 1995; Smykla and Selke, 1995):

Pros

1. Offenders are helped to avoid criminogenic atmosphere of prisons or jails and helped to reintegrate into their communities (e.g., avoids labeling as criminals).
2. Offenders are permitted to retain jobs and support families.
3. Probation officers are assisted in their monitoring activities, and potential exists for easing their caseload responsibilities.
4. Judges and other officials are given considerable flexibility in sentencing offenders (e.g., persons in halfway houses or on work release).
5. It provides more potential to reduce recidivism rates than do existing probationary alternatives.
6. It is potentially useful for decreasing jail and prison populations (Goss, 1989, 1990).
7. It is more cost-effective than incarceration.
8. Pretrial release monitoring is allowed, as are special treatment cases such as substance abusers, the mentally retarded, women who are pregnant, and juveniles.

Cons

1. Some potential exists for race, ethnic, or socioeconomic bias by requiring offenders to have telephones or to pay for expensive monitoring equipment and/or fees.
2. Public safety may be compromised through the failure of these programs to guarantee that offenders will go straight and not endanger citizens by committing new offenses while free in the community.
3. Electronic monitoring may be too coercive, and it may be unrealistic for officials to expect full offender compliance with such a stringent system.
4. Little consistent information exists about the impact of electronic monitoring on recidivism rates compared with other probationary alternatives.
5. Persons frequently selected for participation are persons who probably don't need to be monitored anyway.
6. Technological problems exist, making electronic monitoring somewhat unreliable.
7. Electronic monitoring may result in widening the net by being prescribed for offenders who otherwise would receive less costly standard probation.

8. It raises right to privacy, civil liberties, and other constitutional issues such as Fourth Amendment search and seizure concerns.
9. Much of the public interprets this option as going easy on offenders and perceives electronic monitoring as a nonpunitive alternative.
10. The costs of electronic monitoring may be more than published estimates.

The Constitutionality of Electronic Monitoring. Certain legal issues about electronic monitoring are presently unresolved to everyone's satisfaction, although the constitutionality of electronic monitoring has never been successfully challenged (Tonry and Hamilton, 1995). Many of the same legal arguments that are raised to question the constitutionality of home confinement also are raised about the current applications of electronic monitoring. However, most, if not all, offenders who are placed in electronic monitoring programs agree to abide by all electronic monitoring program conditions. The consensual nature of offender participation in such programs undermines virtually all challenges they may raise about whether such program conditions are constitutional (Corbett and Marx, 1994). If we consider the restrictive nature of jail or prison confinement and the high degree of control exerted over offenders by jail and prison officers, electronic monitoring actually imposes fewer restrictive conditions by comparison. Nevertheless, reasonable searches and seizures of one's residence without warrant are permitted by correctional officers in much the same way that correctional officers might conduct warrantless searches of one's cell in a jail or prison setting.

One of the better discussions of the constitutional issues raised in conjunction with electronic monitoring programs is by del Carmen and Vaughn (1986:62–63). These authors describe the landmark case of *Olmstead v. United States* (1928), which held that a wiretap executed without an accompanying trespass into a person's home was not a Fourth Amendment violation. Two subsequent cases upheld the use of "bugging" devices by police officers to eavesdrop on conversations of crime suspects. In *Goldman v. United States* (1942), police officers eavesdropped with a bugging device through an adjoining wall of the offices of suspected criminals. In the case of *On Lee v. United States* (1952), a government informant entered the subject's laundry and wore a concealed microphone to record their subsequent conversation. In this instance, however, *On Lee* gave the informant permission to enter the premises, and thus the trespass was lawful. The issue of trespass was rendered irrelevant in the case of *Katz v. United States* (1967), however. In that case, a public telephone booth was wired with a microphone by police officers so that they could monitor conversations of a criminal suspect named Katz. The U.S. Supreme Court excluded the conversations by Katz recorded by police, since they violated the defendant's reasonable expectation of privacy. Further, no warrant had ever been issued to authorize the surveillance.

Another constitutional issue raised pertains to the Fifth Amendment right against self-incrimination (Gross, 1992). Some offender-clients have alleged that the fact of electronic monitoring is self-incriminating, since clients must disclose to correctional officers information about themselves at random times. This information may be adverse for these clients, in that their probation program may be revoked. The courts have held, however, that technical program violations that result in probation revocation do not fall within the Fifth Amendment self-incrimination provision. The nature of incrimination must be considered. In electronic monitoring cases, these involve *physical incrimination* rather than *testimonial incrimination* (del Carmen and Vaughn, 1986:66). Physical incrimination is not protected as a Fifth Amendment right.

Most, if not all, of these constitutional questions are undermined by the fact that one's participation in either electronic monitoring or home confinement is *voluntary*. Offenders are not forced into home confinement, and they are not compelled to wear anklets or wristlets if there are other sentencing options that may be exercised. In view of this voluntariness, therefore, it is peculiar that some of these program volunteers have sought relief in court for alleged infringements of their constitutional rights. Supposedly, these offender-clients sign rights waivers, submitting themselves to random visits and searches of their premises by their supervising parole officers. Del Carmen and Vaughn (1986:69) suggest that the constitutionality of electronic monitoring will likely be upheld in future legal cases involving probationers or parolees, primarily based on the concept of *diminished rights*.

Punishment versus Rehabilitation and Reintegration. Another criticism is that home confinement and electronic monitoring are not really punishments at all, because offenders are not assigned "hard time" behind jail or prison walls. However, scattered personalized reports from offenders themselves suggest that home confinement and/or electronic monitoring are possibly more intimidating and restrictive than any jail or prison. One offender sentenced to house arrest reported the intense frustration experienced by not being able to do something as simple as taking his child for a walk to get an ice cream cone at the corner market (Petersilia, 1986c). The average length of time offenders are placed on electronic monitoring is about 80 days, according to the *NIJ Reports* (*Corrections Compendium,* 1991a:14). Thus, critics might claim that less than three months is insufficient time to accomplish any significant reintegration or rehabilitation.

Public Safety and Electronic Monitoring. Arguably, if offenders are placed on electronic monitoring and/or under house arrest, they are relatively free to commit new crimes of their own volition. They are not incapacitated; therefore, they pose possible risks to public safety. However, the criteria used for including offenders in electronic monitoring programs are rather restrictive. For example, the Nevada County Probation Department uses electronic monitoring with home confinement as a means of providing an alternative incarceration site besides jail. Participants are eligible for electronic monitoring if they meet the following criteria (Lattimer, Curran, and Tepper, 1992):

1. Participants must be assessed as low-risk offenders.
2. Participants must exhibit good conduct while in jail.
3. They must be physically and mentally capable of caring for themselves or to be in circumstances in which another person can provide their needed care.
4. Participants must have a verifiable local address as well as a telephone and electricity at their home location.
5. They must have no less than 10 days and no more than 90 days to serve in jail.
6. Participants must pay an administrative fee of $10 per day while being monitored.
7. Participants cannot have any holds or warrants from other jurisdictions while in the program.
8. Participants must wear an electronic anklet and have a field monitoring device placed in their home.
9. Participants must have the support and cooperation of family members.
10. Participants must seek and maintain employment while in the program.
11. Participants must participate in any specified rehabilitative programs while in the program.
12. Participant *must volunteer to participate in the program* [italics added].

Electronic Monitoring and Deterrence. Despite these technological innovations, however, technology can be beaten (Corbett and Marx, 1994). Parole officers have found that some offenders have installed call forwarding systems so that when the computers dial their telephone numbers, they may seem to be in the required location when, in fact, they are in another location several miles from their residences. Also, some offenders have devised tape-recorded messages so that electronic voice verifications are deceived about their actual whereabouts (Swanson and Ward, 1993). Some offenders convert their homes into a criminal base of operations, conducting fencing operations, fraud, illegal drug exchanges, and other criminal activity without attracting suspicion from the correctional officers who supervise them.

In Houston, Texas, for instance, a 17-year-old was placed on electronic monitoring while on pretrial release on a robbery charge. The youth thereby remained free from a juvenile detention center. While on electronic monitoring, the youth allegedly "slipped free" from an electronic ankle bracelet and killed a restaurant employee during another robbery. The Harris County Juvenile Detention Center personnel responsible for placing the youth on electronic monitoring stated that they did not view this killing as a "failure" of electronic monitoring. Journalists misinterpreted the electronic monitoring as some sort of behavior control device, which it isn't. Whether the youth slipped free of the device or did not slip free of it would have failed to prevent the murder in any case, since electronic monitoring does not control behavior to that degree (*Associated Press,* 1993:A2). Perhaps the Houston officials in charge of the electronic monitoring program could have exercised better judgment in allowing a teenage robbery suspect and potentially dangerous felon to be eligible for the electronic monitoring program initially.

Privatization and Net Widening. Electronic monitoring is susceptible to *privatization* by outside interests. Companies that manufacture electronic monitoring equipment and the wristlets and anklets worn by offenders already are involved to a degree in the implementation and operation of home confinement programs in various jurisdictions. They train probation officers and others in the use of monitoring equipment, and they offer instruction to police departments and probation agencies on related matters of offender control. Thus, it is conceivably a short step to complete involvement by private interests in this growing nonincarcerative alternative.

One additional concern is the potential home confinement and electronic monitoring have for net widening (Mainprize, 1992). Some officials have said that judges and others may use these options increasingly for larger numbers of offenders who would otherwise be diverted to standard probation involving minimal contact with probation officers. In order for home confinement and electronic monitoring to be maximally effective at reducing jail and prison overcrowding and to not result in the feared net widening, only jail- or prison-bound offenders should be considered for participation in these programs (Rogers and Jolin, 1989).

Home Confinement or House Arrest

Home Confinement or House Arrest Defined. House arrest or **home confinement (incarceration)** is an intermediate punishment consisting of confining offenders to their residences for mandatory incarceration during evening hours, after a specified curfew, and on weekends (Burns, 1992). Home confinement was used to punish St. Paul the Apostle, who was detained under house arrest in biblical times. During the 1600s, Galileo, the astronomer, was made to live the remaining eight years of his life under house arrest. In 1917, Czar Nicholas II of Russia was detained under house arrest until his death. (Meachum, 1986:102). And during Czar Nicholas II's reign, Lenin was placed under house arrest for a limited period.

The first city to use house arrest was St. Louis in 1971. Although St. Louis officials originally limited its use to juvenile offenders, house arrest became widespread during the next 15 years as an alternative to incarceration for adults as well as for juveniles in many jurisdictions including Washington, DC; Baltimore; Newport News; San Jose; and Louisville (Ball et al., 1988:34).

Florida was the first state to adopt home confinement as a statewide intermediate punishment through its Correctional Reform Act of 1983 (Rackmill, 1994). As originally conceived by this Act, Florida's community control house arrest is not an intensive supervision program. Offenders are confined to their own homes, instead of prison, where they are allowed to serve their sentences (Flynn, 1986:64). The cost of home confinement is only $2.86 per day compared with nearly $30 per day for imprisonment. Florida statutes define community control as "a form of intensive supervised custody in the community, including surveillance on weekends and holidays, administered by officers with restricted caseloads . . . an individualized program in which the freedom of an offender is restricted within the community, home, or noninstitutional residential placement and specific sanctions imposed and enforced." Community control officers work irregular hours and at nights to help ensure that offenders stay in their homes except while working at paid employment to support themselves and dependents (Flynn, 1986:64–66).

Goals of Home Confinement. The goals of home confinement programs include the following:

1. To continue one's punishment while permitting offenders to be confined to their personal residences
2. To enable offenders freedom to hold jobs and earn a living while caring for their families and/or making restitution to victims
3. To reduce jail and prison overcrowding
4. To provide a means for ostracism while ensuring public safety
5. To reduce the costs of offender supervision
6. To foster rehabilitation and reintegration by maintaining one's controlled presence within the community

Petersilia (1988b:2–4) has described several advantages and disadvantages of home confinement or house arrest. Among the advantages she notes are the following: (1) it is cost-effective; (2) it has social benefits; (3) it is responsive to local citizen and offender needs; and (4) it is easily implemented and is timely in view of jail and prison overcrowding. Some of the more important disadvantages of home confinement include: (1) house arrest may actually widen the net of social control; (2) it may narrow the net of social control by not being a sufficiently severe sentence; (3) it focuses primarily upon offender surveillance; (4) it is intrusive and possibly illegal; (5) race and class bias may enter into participant selection; and (6) it may compromise public safety. Some of these advantages and disadvantages are later addressed at length as issues concerning home confinement where electronic monitoring is also used.

Community controllees or offenders in Florida eligible for the house arrest program include low-risk, prison-bound criminals. They are expected to comply with the following program requirements (Flynn, 1986:66–68):

1. Contribute from 150 to 200 hours of free labor to various public service projects during periods ranging from six months to one year
2. Pay a monthly maintenance fee of $30 to $50 to help defray program operating costs and officer salaries
3. Compile and maintain daily logs accounting for their activities; these logs are reviewed regularly by officers for accuracy and honesty
4. Pay restitution to crime victims from a portion of salaries earned through employment
5. Remain gainfully employed to support themselves and their dependents

6. Participate in vocational/technical or other educational courses or seminars that are individualized to each offender's needs
7. Observe a nightly curfew and remain confined to their premises during late evening hours and on weekends, with the exception of court-approved absences for health-related reasons or other purposes
8. Submit to monitoring by officials 28 times per month either at home or at work
9. Maintain court-required contacts with neighbors, friends, landlords, spouses, teachers, police, and/or creditors

By 1996, more than 23,000 offenders were under house arrest and supervision by probation officers in the United States (American Correctional Association, 1996a:xxviii–xxix). House arrest is a growing sentencing option, especially for low-risk first-offenders. In Florida alone, there were over 10,000 home confinement clients in 1991 (Blomberg, Bales, and Reed, 1993).

Early Uses of Home Confinement. A good idea of home confinement client characteristics may be gleaned from published research on the types of offenders who are deemed eligible for home confinement participation. Actually, two types of offender aggregates should be included in this description. One consists of probationers sentenced to home confinement, whereas the other consists of inmates who are released into home confinement programs. For the probationer aggregate, the following characteristics have been identified:

1. Clients tend to be first-offenders.
2. Clients tend to be nonviolent and/or have been convicted of nonviolent property offenses.
3. Clients tend to be those with fairly strong family ties and are married and live with their spouses in structured living arrangement.
4. Clients do not have drug or alcohol dependencies.
5. Clients have jobs or good prospects of becoming employed and maintaining their employment over time.
6. Clients tend to have higher amounts of education and vocational skills.
7. Clients tend to be older, age 30 and over.

For parolees, the following characteristics have been identified:

1. Clients tend to be older, over 30.
2. Offenders have low-risk scores indicating nonviolence and low public risk.
3. Clients have jobs or arrangements for full-time employment.
4. Clients have fewer prior convictions.
5. Clients have stable home environments.
6. Clients do not have drug or alcohol dependencies.
7. Clients have clean records relating to institutional behavior.

Home Confinement Issues. Issues include the following: (1) home confinement not seen as much of a punishment; (2) the constitutionality of home confinement; (3) public safety versus offender needs for community reintegration; and (4) home confinement not seen as much of a crime deterrent.

Punishment versus Rehabilitation and Reintegration. One of the most frequently leveled criticisms of home confinement is that it does not appear to be much of a punishment. The public sees offenders confined to their homes and considers this "incarceration" more of a luxury than "just deserts." However, some of the experiences of those who have been sentenced to home confinement for a period of weeks or months, either involuntarily or voluntarily, suggest that home confinement is very much a punishment (Byrne, Lurigio, and Petersilia, 1992). Home confinement is one of several sanctions collectively described as **smart sentencing.**

One reason for regarding home confinement as something less than a true punishment compared with institutional incarceration is that the courts do not often equate time served at home with time served in prison (Durham, 1994; Rackmill, 1994). In 1990 an Illinois defendant, Ramos, was placed at his parent's home for a period of weeks under house arrest while awaiting trial for an alleged crime. He was not permitted to leave the premises except for work or medical care. Subsequently, he was convicted of the crime and requested the court to apply the time he spent at home toward the time he would have to serve in prison. The court denied his request, holding that his confinement at home did not amount to custody (*People v. Ramos,* 1990). Subsequent court decisions have been consistent with the *Ramos* ruling. Several federal cases have held that the amount of time offenders spend in house arrest cannot be counted against jail or prison time to be served (*United States v. Zackular,* 1991; *United States v. Insley,* 1991; *United States v. Arch John Drummond,* 1992; *United States v. Edwards,* 1992; and *United States v. Wickman,* 1992).

Also, when offenders leave their residences without permission while under house arrest, they are not guilty of escape from prison; rather, they are guilty of a technical program violation. Lubus, a convicted Connecticut offender, was sentenced to house arrest. At some point, he failed to report to his supervising probation officer. The officer claimed this was the equivalent of an "escape" and sought to have him prosecuted as an escapee. The Connecticut Supreme Court disagreed, indicating that unauthorized departures from community residences are not the same as unauthorized departures from halfway houses, mental health facilities and hospitals, and failures to return from furloughs or work release (*State v. Lubus,* 1990).

Public Safety. In any community corrections program, corrections staff consider as paramount the need for public safety. This is why great care is taken to restrict the eligibility requirements of those who become involved in home confinement programs. If offenders are first-timers without prior records, and if their conviction offenses are nonviolent, they are considered for inclusion. An absence of a prior record is no guarantee that an offender will automatically qualify, however. Furthermore, the public is not the only concern. Often, families of home confinement clients may have strong reservations about having these persons in their midst. The client's presence may create more problems for the family than are resolved for the client (Quinn and Holman, 1991).

Crime Control and Deterrence. Does home confinement function as a crime deterrent? No. It isn't supposed to function as a crime deterrent (Maxfield and Baumer, 1990). Being confined in a prison or jail does not deter some incarcerated offenders from exploiting and victimizing other inmates. Why should we regard home confinement differently? The primary function of house arrest is to enable correctional officers to maintain a high degree of supervisory control over an offender's whereabouts. No house arrest program can claim that house arrest deters crime from occurring.

Furlough Programs

Furloughs are authorized, unescorted leaves from confinement granted for specific purposes and for designated time periods (Marlette, 1988; McCarthy and McCarthy, 1997). Nationwide, more than 230,960 furloughs were granted in 1990 from 40 U.S. prison systems. This was an increase of 15 percent over the estimated 200,000 furloughs granted in 1987 and 35 percent more than the 170,000 granted in 1988 for all systems (Su Davis, 1991:10). Abscondence rates are quite low, about one half of 1 percent (Smith and Sabatino, 1989; 1990). Furloughs may be granted to prisoners for periods ranging from 24 hours to several weeks and are similar to leaves enjoyed by military personnel. In 1996, the number of furloughees was 6,500 (American Correctional Association, 1996a:xxvii–xxix).

Furloughs originated in 1918 in Mississippi. By 1970, about half the states had furlough programs (Marley, 1973). In those days, prisoners who had completed two or more years of their original sentences were considered eligible for furloughs. These furloughs usually involved conjugal visits with families or Christmas holiday activities for brief, 10-day periods. These furloughs were believed valuable for preparing offenders for permanent reentry into their respective communities once parole had been granted. In 1990, 46 states and the federal government had furlough programs (Su Davis, 1991:10).

Furloughs have many of the same characteristics as work release programs. Furloughs are only used about a third as often as work release, however. The length of the temporary release varies according to the jurisdiction. Most furlough programs tend to range from 24 to 72 hours throughout the United States, although some programs may provide inmates with two weeks or more of freedom for special activities (McCarthy and McCarthy, 1997).

The Goals of Furlough Programs. Offenders are given a high degree of trust by prison officials and are permitted leaves to visit their homes and families. Interestingly, such furloughs are beneficial to both prisoners and to their families, because they permit family members to get used to the presence of the offender after a long incarcerative absence. Sometimes, prisoners may participate in educational programs (like study release) outside of prison. They can arrange for employment once paroled, or they can participate in vocational training for short periods.

Furloughs also provide officials with an opportunity to evaluate offenders and to determine how they adapt to living with others in their community. Thus, the furlough is a type of test to determine, with some predictability, the likelihood that inmates will conform to society's rules if they are eventually released through parole. For some prisoners, furloughs function as incentives to conform to prison rules and regulations, because only prisoners who have demonstrated that they can control their behaviors in prison will be considered by officials for temporary releases. Usually, though not always, prisoners selected for participation in furlough programs are nearing the end of their sentences and will eventually be paroled or released anyway. They are good risks because the likelihood they will abscond while on a furlough is quite remote. A survey of furlough programs taken in 1988 showed that all 52 U.S. systems had some form of temporary release program and that they were generally problem-free. Virtually all considered furloughs helpful in preparing inmates for release and improving institutional morale (Marlette, 1990:6).

The Functions of Furlough Programs. Furloughs are intended to accomplish (1) offender rehabilitation and reintegration, (2) the development of self-esteem and self-worth, (3) the provision of vocational/educational programs, and (4) assistance to parole boards in determining when inmates are ready to be released.

Offender Rehabilitation and Reintegration. As has been observed with other temporary release programs, for example, work release, the manifest intent of furloughs is to provide offenders with outside experiences to enable them to become accustomed to living with others in the community apart from the highly regulated life in prison or jail settings. Indications are that in most instances, furloughs fulfill this objective.

Increasing Self-Esteem and Self-Worth. In addition, furloughs seem to instill within inmates greater feelings of self-esteem and self-worth. The element of trust plays an important role in enabling those granted furloughs to acquire trust for those who place trust in them.

Vocational/Educational Programs. If inmates wish to take courses in typing, art, automobile repair, or in philosophically oriented offerings in the social sciences or related areas, furloughs permit them to do so.

Assistance to Parole Boards. A key function of furloughs as tests of inmate behavior is to inform parole boards which inmates are most eligible to be released and which are most likely to be successful while on parole (Milling, 1978).

Weaknesses and Strengths of Furlough Programs. Not all states have furlough programs. One reason is that under certain types of sentencing systems, temporary release of any sort is not permitted. Those offenders sentenced to mandatory prison terms cannot be released before serving their entire sentences, less the good-time credits they may have acquired during the initial incarceration period. Under an indeterminate sentencing scheme, there is considerable latitude for paroling authorities to grant furloughs or work releases to those inmates who have shown they can conform their conduct to the institutional rules (Harer and Eichenlaub, 1992).

In recent years, however, sentencing reforms have been undertaken at the federal level and in virtually every state (Jolin and Stipak, 1992). A general shift has been observed toward determinate and presumptive sentencing schemes that permit little variation from whatever sentences have been imposed by judges. Thus, it is difficult, if not impossible, because of statutory prohibitions in some jurisdictions, to operate furlough or work release programs (Su Davis, 1991).

Because of both diminished resources and an unenthusiastic response from the public and corrections officials both to furlough programs and other temporary release options, these alternatives are less prevalent than they were in past years. States such as Arkansas and North Carolina continue to offer furloughs in relatively large numbers to deserving inmates, but the administrative costs have surpassed the general benefits derived from such programs.

The successfulness of furlough programs is demonstrated by the relatively low recidivism rates in certain jurisdictions using such programs on a limited basis. In 1977, for example, the Oahu Community Correctional Center, Corrections Division, Department of Social Services and Housing, implemented a furlough program for selected offenders. Officials kept track of offender progress on furloughs during a six-year period. By December 1983, they had permitted 98 inmates to participate in the furlough program. Of these, nearly 70 percent of the offenders successfully complied with furlough rules and completed their program. These authorities regard their success rate of 68 percent as highly favorable for future adult correctional programs, despite the fact that most of the failures were convicted of new offenses while on furloughs (Uriell, 1984).

Work/Study Release Programs

What is work/study release? The growth of work release among state correctional departments has been substantial. For instance, in 1996, New York led all states with 6,200 inmates involved in work/study release programs. Other states with large numbers of work releasees include Florida (2,149), California (1,040), Alabama (1,750), and North Carolina (1,200). There were about 24,000 work releasees in 1996 (American Correctional Association, 1996a:xxvii–xxix).

The first use of work release in the United States was in Vermont in 1906 where sheriffs, acting on their own authority, assigned inmates to work outside jail walls in the community (*Corrections Compendium,* 1993b). Legislation-authorized work release was first introduced in Wisconsin in 1913, and by 1975, all states and the federal system had initiated some form of a work release program (*Corrections Compendium,* 1993b). At that time, county sheriffs issued passes to certain low-risk inmates to work in the community during daytime hours, but they were obligated to return to jail at a particular curfew period. Work release is also known as **day pass, day parole, temporary furlough,** and **work** or **education furlough** (Marlette, 1990).

Work release was not formally adopted on a statewide basis until 1913, when Senator Huber of Wisconsin successfully secured the passage of a bill that permitted Wisconsin correctional institutions to grant temporary releases to low-risk misdemeanants (Wisconsin Department of Health and Social Services, 1978). Like the furlough system, work release was not popular and only sluggishly adopted on a large scale as an alternative to incarceration in the 1960s and 1970s. By the early 1980s, almost all states had work release programs. An inspection of professional literature cataloged by the National Institute of Justice shows early descriptive and investigative articles about work release in the mid-1960s. The frequency of such articles increased gradually throughout the 1980s and 1990s. If the accumulation of research and investigations of work release programs in the justice literature is any indication of the growing popularity of this type of preparole program, then it is quite popular.

Some work release is labeled "study release," because specific high school or college courses or other curricula are taken by eligible inmates. Prisons lacking educational facilities or programs sometimes use study release to supplement their existing resources, and only minimum-security offenders are permitted entry into such programs (Marlette, 1990). Many work release and study release programs are closely connected with community-based supervisory services for ex-offenders, both probationers and parolees. One long-range advantage of work release is that it makes available employment opportunities to offenders who become acquainted with employers in the private sector while temporarily unconfined. For example, many Massachusetts work releasees have found employment in the private sector as the result of work release experiences (Marlette, 1990).

The Goals of Work/Study Release. The goals of work/study release programs are to

1. Reintegrate the offender into the community.
2. Give the offender an opportunity to learn and/or practice new skills.

3. Provide offenders with the means to make restitution to victims of crimes.
4. Give offenders a chance to help support themselves and their families.
5. Help authorities to more effectively predict the likelihood of offender success if paroled.
6. Foster improvements in self-images or self-concepts through working in a nonincarcerative environment and assuming full responsibility for one's conduct.

Before offenders can be eligible for work release, they must meet the following criteria statutorily imposed by the state (McCarthy and McCarthy, 1997):

1. Inmates must have served a minimum of 10 percent of their sentences.
2. Inmates must have attained minimum custody by the date they are to begin participating in work release.
3. Inmates must not have had an escape within six months of the approval.
4. Inmates must not have had a major infraction of prison rules within three months of approval.
5. If inmates are serving a sentence for a serious sexual or assaultive crime or have such a history, the approving authority for minimum custody is the director's review committee.

Weaknesses and Strengths of Work/Study Release Programs. Whether work release is successful may be gauged according to individual parolee successes such as low recidivism rates and parole revocations. Or the successfulness of work release may be couched in the context of how much people benefit from inmate labor. Are victims compensated for their financial losses? Are the families of work releasees recipients of supporting funds? Does inmate participation in work release foster self-esteem and help prisoners become reintegrated into their communities?

Generally, work release programs have been successful when one or more of these standards have been applied. These programs tend to have low recidivism rates compared with standard parole recidivism figures (McCarthy and McCarthy, 1997). However, some programs such as those operated in North Carolina and Florida have found little difference, if any, in recidivism among work releasees and other parolees (McCarthy and McCarthy, 1997).

One way states have of incorporating more inmates into continuous work projects and programs is to sponsor such work programs themselves. For instance, in Minnesota there is a project known as State Use Industries (SUI). State Use Industries is an organization authorized under Minnesota statutes to use inmate labor for the manufacture of goods, services, and merchandise to be sold to the state and to public agencies or private charitable or educational organizations. The SUI program provides work experiences that replicate nonprison work environments as well as job training and apprenticeship programs. A placement service under the auspices of SUI is available to all former inmates employed by SUI (St. Paul Police

Department, 1991). In the St. Paul SUI program, postrelease employment was obtained by 58 of 65 inmates. During the period of the study, 75 percent worked at least half the time, while former inmates were employed in a variety of semiskilled, service, and white-collar occupations and professions. Their pay averaged $5.95 per hour. Another project, Project CARE (Cooperative Assistance and Resources for Employment), provides for job skills training and placement services to ex-offenders. During the report period, 707 offenders were referred to Project CARE. Of these, 328 requested services from the organization and 177 were placed in jobs. Many of these Project CARE clients were placed in lower-skill occupations, while some were placed in skilled or white-collar jobs. Their pay averaged $4.39 per hour. Many of the other offenders secured and maintained jobs through self-placement (St. Paul Police Department, 1991).

Halfway Houses

Halfway houses are transitional residences for inmates who are released from prison (McBurney, 1989). Ordinarily, these homes offer temporary housing, food, and clothing for parolees recently released from prison. Their assignment to one of these homes may be mandatory for a short period. In many jurisdictions, these homes offer services to offenders on a voluntary basis. They assist greatly in helping former inmates make the transition from rigid prison life to community living. In 1996, there were over 15,000 clients in public or private halfway houses in the United States (American Correctional Association, 1996a:xxviii–xxix).

The Origin of the Halfway House. The halfway house concept probably originated in England during the early 1800s. But the first formal recommendation for the creation of a halfway house in the United States occurred in 1817 in Pennsylvania (McCarthy and McCarthy, 1997). A Pennsylvania prison riot had stirred the legislature to think of various prison reforms including housing provisions for ex-convicts who were often poor and could not find employment or adequate housing. But these proposals were never implemented, because the public feared **criminal contamination,** and that if ex-offenders lived together, they would spread their criminality like a disease (McCarthy and McCarthy, 1997).

Sponsorship of halfway houses for the next 150 years stemmed primarily from private and/or religious sources. In 1845, the Quakers opened the **Isaac T. Hopper Home** in New York City, followed by the Temporary Asylum for Disadvantaged Female Prisoners established in Boston in 1864 by a reformist group (G. Wilson, 1985:153). In 1889, the House of Industry was opened in Philadelphia, and in 1896, Hope House was established in New York City by Maud and Ballington Booth. Receiving considerable financial support from a missionary religious society called the Volunteers of America, the Booths were able in future years to open additional **Hope Houses** or **Hope Halls** in Chicago, San Francisco, and New Orleans (G. Wilson, 1985:153).

State and federal governments during the 1800s and early 1900s continued to work toward the creation of halfway houses apart from those established in the private sector, however. In 1917, the Massachusetts Prison Commission recommended the establishment of houses to accommodate recently released offenders who were indigent (G. Wilson, 1985:152). But this plan was rejected. Eventually in the 1960s, Attorney General Robert F. Kennedy recommended government sponsorship and funding for halfway house programs. In 1965, the Prisoner Rehabilitation Act was passed that authorized the establishment of community-based residential centers for both juvenile and adult prerelease offenders (G. Wilson, 1985:154).

One of the most significant events to spark the growth of state-operated halfway houses was the creation of the **International Halfway House Association** (IHHA) in Chicago in 1964. Although many of the halfway house programs continued to be privately operated after the formation of the IHHA, the growth in the numbers of halfway houses was phenomenal during the next decade. For instance, from 1966 to 1982, the number of halfway houses operating in the United States and Canada rose from 40 to 1,800 (G. Wilson, 1985:154). These figures are probably lower than the actual number of halfway houses in existence during those time periods, since these numbers were based on affiliation with the IHHA and the American Correctional Association. Other researchers have reported as many as 2,300 halfway house facilities with over 100,000 beds existing in 1981 (Gatz and Murray, 1981).

Halfway House Variations. Because there are so many different government-sponsored and private agencies claiming to be halfway houses, it is impossible to devise a consistent definition of one that fits all jurisdictions. There is extensive variation in the level of custody for clients, ranging from providing simple shelter on a voluntary basis to mandatory confinement with curfew. There are also many different services provided by halfway houses. These might include alcohol- or drug-related rehabilitation facilities with some hospitalization on premises, minimal or extensive counseling services, and/or employment assistance (McCarthy and McCarthy, 1997). In addition, halfway house programs are designed for offenders ranging from probationers and prereleasees to parolees and others assigned to community service with special conditions.

In 1973, Dreyfous House in New Orleans was established for emotionally disturbed youths. Strong community opposition to Dreyfous House resulted in its termination in 1975, however (Slotnick, 1976). In San Mateo, California, the El Camino House was established for ex-mental patients (Richmond, 1970). The El Camino House has a two-fold program thrust—a performance-oriented culture for residents within the halfway house, and the use of existing housing in the community to create post-halfway house living accommodations with built-in provisions for follow-up. These programs serve the overall program goal of assisting severely disturbed psychiatric patients in their adjustment to the community by preparing them socially and emotionally for more independent living (Richmond, 1970). Other halfway houses include the Ralph W. Alvis House, the Bridge Home for Young Men, the Denton House, Fellowship House, Fresh Start, Inc., the Helping Hand Halfway Home, Inc., Talbert House, and Vander Meulen House.

Halfway-Out and Halfway-In Houses. At least two versions of halfway houses have been identified (Travis, 1985). First, **halfway-out houses** are facilities designed to serve the immediate needs of parolees from those established to accommodate probationers in the community. Second, **halfway-in houses** provide services catering to those probationers in need of limited or somewhat restricted confinement apart from complete freedom of movement in the community (McCarthy and McCarthy, 1997).

Travis (1985) adds that halfway-in houses, designed for probationers, are deliberately intended to create *uncomfortable atmospheres* for them. Halfway-in houses structure the lives of probationers in various ways, mostly by making them comply with various program requirements (e.g., curfew, random drug and alcohol checks, and other technical details). This is because probation is actually a punishment and must necessarily contain certain elements of punishment. In contrast, halfway-out houses, for parolees, are designed to provide homelike and supportive environments aimed at aiding the offender's readjustment to society. Like halfway-in houses, these homes also continue punishment through the high degree of supervision or offender control exerted by halfway-out house staff. But because their clientele are parolees and have served substantial time behind bars, their functions are more therapeutic, rehabilitative, and reintegrative rather than punishment-centered.

The Functions of Halfway Houses. The major functions of halfway houses overlap with some of those associated with other programs for parolees. These include (1) parolee rehabilitation and reintegration into the community; (2) provisions for food and shelter; (3) job placement, vocational guidance, and employment assistance; (4) client-specific treatments; (5) alleviating jail and prison overcrowding; (6) supplementing supervisory functions of probation and parole agencies; and (7) monitoring probationers, work/study releasees, and others with special program conditions.

Parolee Rehabilitation and Reintegration into the Community. The major function of halfway houses is to facilitate offender reintegration into the community. This is accomplished, in part, by providing necessities and making various services accessible to offenders. The administrative personnel of halfway houses as well as the professional and paraprofessional staff members help offenders with specific problems they might have, such as alcohol or drug dependencies.

Provisions for Food and Shelter. Some parolees have acquired savings from their work in prison industries, while other parolees have no

BOX 11.1 What Goes On in a Halfway House?

The Case of the Mandan Halfway House and Irene Leingang

Halfway houses are supposed to help parolees. They should provide parolees with job placement services, supervision, and counseling, among other things. At the Mandan Halfway House in Mandan, North Dakota, parolees receive these services and more, thanks to the assistance of a veteran teacher, 62-year-old Irene Leingang.

Irene Leingang has taught in various schools for 28 years. She is a former sister of Annunciation Priory and an aspiring writer of children's books. In her spare time, she assists parolee-clients at the Mandan Halfway House. One of her clients is Tony Cooley, who has spent nearly 10 years in jails and prisons in various states. On August 28, 1996, he was released from Stutsman County Jail in North Dakota and paroled to the halfway house in Mandan.

Cooley, who has had few breaks in life, passed much of his prison time writing poetry and stories. He shared some of his work with Leingang. Leingang thought there was promise in Cooley's writing and she encouraged him to do more. Cooley, who also plays the guitar and writes songs, responded enthusiastically with Leingang's assistance. Iliad Press plans to publish some of his work, including the "Plowman Ministries" and "Poet's Review." Cooley has also written three songs and has completed music to accompany at least four of his original poems.

Leingang says, "I am not his mother. While Tony Cooley was in prison, he was cynical, but he is less so now. It's a process of letting go, then it will surface." Leingang picked up Cooley when he was released from prison, and she also plans to drive him to Kansas later where he can reunite with his family. She considers Cooley to be a spiritual child and a friend.

Leingang grew up in and around Mandan, graduating from Mandan High School in 1952. She entered the Annunciation Priory convent when she was 22. Although she never wanted to be a nun, she said that she is grateful for the Benedictines. "God loved me through those nuns. They gave me self-esteem and made me a teacher." Leingang lives as she was taught, teaching more unfortunate persons such as Tony Cooley.

Is this extraordinary assistance something you would expect to find in the average community halfway house? Are there any drawbacks for staff such as Leingang becoming too close to halfway house clients? What kinds of services do you think halfway houses should provide new parolees?

Source: Adapted from the Associated Press, "Teacher Guides Writer's Creativity." *Minot (N.D.) Daily News,* September 13, 1996:B4.

operating capital. Thus, halfway houses furnish offenders with a place to stay and regular meals while they hunt for new occupations and participate in self-help programs.

Job Placement, Vocational Guidance, and Employment Assistance. Almost every halfway house assists offenders by furnishing them with job leads and by negotiating contacts between them and prospective employers.

Client-Specific Treatments. Those offenders with special needs or problems (e.g., ex-sex offenders, drug addicts or alcoholics, or mentally retarded clients) benefit from halfway houses by being permitted the freedom to take advantage of special treatment programs.

Alleviating Jail and Prison Overcrowding. Any program that provides a safety valve for prison or jail populations helps alleviate overcrowding problems. Thus, halfway houses alleviate jail and prison overcrowding in that some probationers are "diverted" to them, whereas certain inmates may be paroled to them for brief periods as transitional phases.

Supplementing Supervisory Functions of Probation and Parole Agencies. One latent function of halfway houses is to exercise some degree of supervision and control over both probationers and parolees. These supervisory functions are ordinarily performed by probation or parole officers. However, when some inmates are released to halfway houses, halfway house staff assume a high degree of responsibility for client conduct (Donnelly and Forschner, 1987).

Monitoring Probationers, Work/Study Releasees, and Others with Special Program Conditions. Offender benefits accruing to halfway house residents include food, clothing, and shelter as well as employment opportunities that serve to defray the costs of maintaining these homes (McCarthy and McCarthy, 1997). Costs of operating a majority of these halfway houses range from $15 to $25 per day per resident, with the state accounting for about 75 percent of the funding and city/county monies providing the remainder (G. Wilson, 1985:158–159).

Weaknesses and Strengths of Halfway House Programs. Some of the major strengths and weaknesses of halfway house programs have been summarized by Carlson et al. (1977):

1. Halfway houses are effective in preventing criminal behavior in the community as alternatives that involve community release.
2. The placement of halfway houses in communities neither increases nor decreases property values.
3. Halfway houses assist their clients in locating employment but not necessarily maintaining it.
4. Halfway houses are able to provide for the basic needs of their clients as well as other forms of release.
5. At full capacity, halfway houses cost no more, and probably less, than incarceration, although they cost more than straight parole or outright release from correctional systems.

Community Residential Centers and Day Reporting/Treatment Programs

Closely related to halfway houses are community residential centers and day reporting/treatment programs. **Community residential centers** are transitional agencies located in neighborhoods in which offenders may obtain employment counseling, food and shelter, and limited supervision pertaining to one or more conditions of probation or parole. Day reporting/treatment programs are an integral part of community residential centers. The Alaska Department of Corrections, for instance, operates several community residential centers as relatively open facilities located in neighborhoods. These centers rely heavily on community resources to provide most of the services required by offenders, including offender detention and/or supervision on behalf of the Department of Corrections (Alaska Department of Corrections, 1990). Alaska centers are designed to provide individuality for a variety of offender needs, including employment, housing, and counseling services. The diversity of clientele served by Alaska community residential centers includes furloughees, parolees, probationers, misdemeanants, and offenders who are under court orders to pay restitution or victim compensation. Citizen involvement is solicited through volunteer work.

Day Reporting Centers

As their name indicates, day treatment centers are operated primarily during daytime hours for the purpose of providing diverse services to offenders and their families. Day reporting is defined as a highly structured nonresidential program utilizing supervision, sanctions, and services coordinated from a central focus (Curtin, 1990:8). Offenders live at home and report to these centers regularly and daily (Diggs and Pieper, 1994:9).

Williams (1990:4) says that day reporting centers are like "invisible jails," or halfway houses without the houses. In a way, they are jails on an "outpatient" basis. Actually, they are a hybrid of intensive probation supervision, house arrest, and early release. Many participants serve out their last few weeks or months of jail still in the government's custody, but technically on their own—living at home, perhaps working at a regular job in the community (Williams, 1990:4). Certain guidelines for operating day reporting centers have been established. An editorial in the *Corrections Compendium* (1990b:14) indicates the following day reporting program suggestions:

1. Sign a contract with participants spelling out expectations about home, work, schooling, financial matters, drug tests, counseling, community service, and restitution.
2. Notify the police department in the offender's hometown.
3. Set a curfew; 9:00 P.M. is frequent.
4. Require an advance copy of the participant's daily itinerary points.

5. Perform spot checks of the participant's home, job, other itinerary points.
6. Institute proper urinalysis procedures—this is crucial; twice a week is typical.
7. Schedule telephone checks more heavily on Thursday, Friday, and Saturday nights.
8. Establish services—addiction education, parenting, and transition skills are popular topics.

Fines

An integral part of sentencing in an increasing number of cases is the use of **fines** (Gordon and Glaser, 1991). The use of fines as sanctions can be traced to preindustrialized and nonWestern societies (Davis and Lurigio, 1992:25; Winterfield and Hillsman, 1993:1). Estimates suggest that over 14 million persons are arrested each year in the United States, and that a significant portion of these receive fines upon conviction (McDonald, Greene, and Worzella, 1992:1). Ordinarily, state and federal criminal statutes provide for various incarcerative lengths upon conviction. Additionally, various fines are imposed as "and/or" conditions exercised at the discretion of sentencing judges. For instance, if law enforcement officers were to violate one's civil rights by the unlawful use of physical force or excessive force in making an arrest, they might be subject to penalties, including confinement in a state penitentiary for up to five years and a fine of "not more than" $10,000. This means that if these law enforcement officers are convicted of violating one's civil rights, the judge can sentence them to prison for up to five years and impose a fine of $10,000. This would be within the judge's discretionary powers.

Types of Fines and Fine Collection Problems. Different types of "fine" scenarios have been described. These include (1) fines plus jail or prison terms, (2) fines plus probation, (3) fines plus suspended jail or prison terms, (4) fines or jail alternatives ($30 or 30 days), (5) fines alone, partially suspended, and (6) fines alone (Hillsman, Sichel, and Mahoney, 1984:12). The arguments for and against the use of fines as sanctions have also been clearly delineated. For instance, McDonald, Greene, and Worzella (1992:1) say that (1) fines are logically suited for punishment because they are unambiguously punitive; (2) many offenders are poor and cannot afford fines; (3) because the poor cannot afford fines as easily as the rich, there is obvious discrimination in fine imposition; (4) someone else may pay the fine other than the offender; (5) often, fine payments are enforceable because of offender absconding; (6) courts lack sufficient enforcement capability; and (7) fines may actually *increase crime* so that the poor can get enough money to pay previously imposed fines [italics added]. The problems of fine collection are such that less than half of the fines imposed are ever collected in most U.S. courts (McDonald et al., 1992). Billions of dollars are involved in fine nonpayment. In New York City, for instance, a sampled jurisdiction disclosed that the fine payment rate upon conviction was 19 percent. In another nearby jurisdiction, the fine payment rate at conviction was only 14 percent (Parent, 1990).

OTHER COMMUNITY PROGRAMS

Community Service Orders and Options

Under the Victim and Witness Protection Act of 1982 (18 U.S.C. Sec. 3579-3580, 1997), restitution to victims was incorporated as an option in addition to incarceration at the federal level. One flaw of the act was that it left unspecified when restitution orders were to be imposed. Thus, judges could impose restitution orders at the time of sentencing, or parole boards could make restitution a provisional requirement for an inmate's early release (Fletcher, 1984).

Community service is different from restitution in that usually, though not always, offenders perform services for the state or community. The nature of community service to be performed is discretionary with the sentencing judge or paroling authority (Maher and Dufour, 1987). In some jurisdictions, prisoners must perform a specified number of hours of community service such as lawn maintenance, plumbing and other similar repairs, or services that fit their particular skills (Carter, Cocks, and Glaser, 1987). The philosophy underlying community service is more aligned with retribution than rehabilitation. Few judges in any jurisdiction offer community service sentences as alternatives to imprisonment, however (Immarigeon, 1986).

Community service orders are symbolic restitution, involving redress for victims, less severe sanctions for offenders, offender rehabilitation, reduction of demands on the criminal justice system, and a reduction of the need for vengeance in a society, or a combination of these factors. Community service orders are found in many different countries and benefit the community directly (Sapers, 1990). Furthermore, in cases in which convicted offenders are indigent or unemployed, community service is a way of paying their fines and court costs. Donnelly (1980) summarizes some of the chief benefits of community service: (1) the community benefits because some form of restitution is paid; (2) offenders benefit because they are given an opportunity to rejoin their communities in law-abiding responsible roles; and (3) the courts benefit because sentencing alternatives are provided. Typically, offenders sentenced to community service should be individually placed where their skills and interests can be maximized for community benefit. Usually, between 50 and 200 hours of community service are required for any particular convicted offender (Byrne et al., 1992).

Community service is considered a punishment and is court-imposed (Galaway, 1988). Many types of projects are undertaken by offenders as community service. Usually, these projects are supervised by correctional officers or other officials, although reports are sometimes solicited from private individuals such as company managers or supervisors. A portion of offender earnings is allocated to victims as well as to the state or local public or private agencies overseeing the community services provided.

Restitution to victims may be through periodic payments from offender earnings while on work release, probation, or parole. Sometimes, restitution takes nonmonetary forms, in cases in which offenders rebuild or restore property destroyed earlier by their crimes. But the restitution ordered by the court or specified by parole boards often only covers partially the losses suffered by crime victims.

Restitution Programs

An increasingly important feature of probation programs is restitution (Staples, 1986). **Restitution** is the practice of requiring offenders to compensate crime victims for damages offenders may have inflicted (adapted from Davis and Lurigio, 1992:25). Several models of restitution have been described, including the following:

1. The **financial/community service model.** This model stresses the offender's financial accountability and community service to pay for damages inflicted upon victims and to defray a portion of the expenses of court prosecutions. It is becoming more commonplace for probationers and divertees to be ordered to pay some restitution to victims *and* to perform some type of community service. Community service may involve cleanup activities in municipal parks, painting projects involving graffiti removal, cutting courthouse lawns, or any other constructive project that can benefit the community (McDonald, 1986). These community service sentences are imposed by judges. Probation officers are largely responsible for overseeing the efforts of convicted offenders in fulfilling their community service obligations. These sentencing provisions are commonly called community service orders.

2. The **victim/offender mediation model.** This model focuses upon victim-offender reconciliation. Alternative dispute resolution is used as a mediating ground for resolving differences or disputes between victims and perpetrators (Patel and Soderlund, 1994). Usually, third-party arbiters, such as judges, lawyers, or public appointees, can meet with offenders and their victims and work out mutually satisfactory arrangements whereby victims can be compensated for their losses or injuries.

3. The **victim/reparations model.** This model stresses that offenders should compensate their victims directly for their offenses. Many states have provisions that provide **reparations** or financial payments to victims under a *Crime Victims Reparations Act.* The Act establishes a state-financed program of reparations to persons who suffer personal injury and to dependents

BOX 11.2 Conviction of Offender Doesn't Stop Victim's Parents

The Case of Polly Klaas

On October 1, 1993, Polly Klaas, a 12-year-old girl, was abducted one evening from her home during a slumber party with her girlfriends in Petaluma, California. Her body was later found and a man, Richard Allen Davis, was charged with her murder. Davis was subsequently convicted and sentenced to death on August 5, 1996. Upon being convicted by a jury, Davis turned to the jury and court audience in general and made an obscene gesture, showing absolutely no remorse. Davis had been convicted of other felonies prior to murdering Polly Klaas. The defense attorney, Lorena Chandler, said that "there's just been enough pain," attempting to persuade the jury away from imposing the death penalty. Marc Klaas, Polly Klaas's father, thought otherwise.

Davis, 42, was portrayed by his defense as a man who was so damaged by his environment that he could not help but make damaged choices in life. They said his mother was distant, once held his hand over a flame, and all but abandoned him after a bitter divorce from his father. The deceased father was described as physically abusive and neglectful, once punching the boy's jaw so hard that he broke or dislocated it.

Marc Klaas was more than a little upset over the fact that an ex-convict had murdered his daughter. He questioned the system that had freed Davis and failed to supervise him properly. During the two months that Polly was missing and her body was found, Klaas and others formed the Polly Klaas Foundation, an organization devoted to finding missing children. In 1994, Marc Klaas established the Marc Klaas Foundation for Children. He has continued to lobby in California for greater control over convicted violent offenders such as Davis. He has been critical of California's "three-strikes-and-you're-out" law, since he feels that it is too harsh on petty offenders and a waste of taxpayers' money.

Currently, many states have implemented sentencing reforms as part of a general get-tough philosophy. The intent of such reforms is to deter those intent on recidivating by promising life-without-parole sentences for repeat offenses. While the pace of new prison construction has not kept pace with the increased incarceration of offenders under these sentencing reforms, it has not lessened the resolve of Klaas and others who believe that the United States needs to deal more effectively with persons like Davis.

Should *all* offenders be incarcerated for life, if they have been convicted of three or more felonies? Should we reserve prison space only for the most violent offenders? What should we do with less serious offenders, such as burglars and thieves?

Source: Adapted from Curtis Rist and Laird Harrison (1996). "No Surrender: As A Jury Recommends Death for Daughter Polly's Killer, Marc Klaas Carries on His Fight for Kids." *People,* August 19, 1996:91–95; Michelle Locke (1996). "Davis Sentenced to Death in Klaas Murder." *Minot (N.D.) Daily News,* August 6, 1996:A1.

of persons killed as the result of certain criminal conduct. In many jurisdictions, a specially constituted board determines, independent of court adjudication, the existence of a crime, the damages caused, and other elements necessary for reparation. Reparations cover such economic losses as medical expenses, rehabilitative and occupational retraining expenses, loss of earnings, and the cost of actual substitute services (Patel and Soderland, 1994).

SELECTED ISSUES IN COMMUNITY CORRECTIONS

Beyond this debate about the philosophical ends of punishment and community-based program goals, there are several other controversial issues that remain unresolved. These issues pertain to (1) the NIMBY syndrome, (2) punishment versus rehabilitation and reintegration, (3) offender needs and public safety, (4) services delivery, and (5) coping with special-needs offenders.

The NIMBY ("Not In My Back Yard") Syndrome

When community corrections agencies are proposed for different communities, the problem of where to locate these facilities arises. Community officials may desire community corrections programs in theory, anticipating that the community will acquire additional external resources from state or federal funding agencies. Community corrections organizations will provide new jobs for the community. Certain community businesses will anticipate additional revenue from these corrections agencies. However, the matter of locating these facilities becomes a sensitive one. This has become a major issue in many communities and persists today as the **NIMBY syndrome** (Benzvy-Miller, 1990). No one seems to want a halfway house or community corrections agency next door or across the street (Schiff, 1990).

Punishment versus Rehabilitation and Reintegration

The true aims of community-based correctional programs are punishment- and rehabilitation-centered, although there is some disagreement over these stated objectives among the experts (Schiff, 1990). It is unsettling for some citizens to know that 1 percent of California's population is on probation and that one's next door neighbor might be a convicted felon involved in a community-based probation program, for example (Petersilia, 1985b). But the advantages and strengths of community-based programs need to be considered together with their disadvantages and weaknesses.

Some societal reintegration occurs as one of community-based corrections' key goals (Lauen, 1984), although some critics say we are moving toward operations that have deterrence and control as priorities (Holman and Quinn, 1989). Some researchers have examined regular U.S. population growth and compared these figures with the concurrent growth of prison populations. Between 1970 and 1985, the U.S. prison population grew by more than 60 percent, while the U.S. population increased about 10 percent (Lawrence, 1985:108). Thus, some persons have concluded erroneously that the impact of community corrections on prison populations has been negligible (Martinson, 1974).

Offender Needs and Public Safety

A continuing issue in community corrections is public safety from dangerous offenders. Neighborhoods don't like the idea that convicted felons are roaming freely among residents. Some of this fear is overcome through the inclusion of low-risk inmates for community placement. For example, in January 1989, inmate work crews were put to the task of renovating Lake Murray State Park in Ardmore, Oklahoma. Ten inmates lived, ate, and slept in buildings on the park grounds. They were supervised by five correctional officers from the Lexington Assessment and Reception Center, about 75 miles south of Ardmore. Subsequent inmate work crews expanded the scope of their original renovation activities by doing additional building renovation, trail and bridge construction and improvement, and picnic table fabrication and placement. Some inmates performed routine maintenance functions. The general public soon learned about what the inmates had accomplished and were more receptive to the idea of permitting ex-convicts into their communities (Lawrence, 1992).

Services Delivery

Services delivery can be improved to the extent that the goals for specific offenders are individualized (Dickey, 1989). In Grant County, Wisconsin, parole officers identify through interviews various offender needs, such as economic and/or social stresses in coping with life. Some offender-clients have family problems or problems living in their communities. Certain problems can be targeted for treatment with proper parole officer-client interactions (Dickey, 1989). Certain innovative programs in other states are responsive to particular community resources that exist.

Special-Needs Offenders

Community-based corrections will invariably have to deal with and make provisions for special-needs offenders. Special-needs offenders include physically, mentally, psychologically, or socially impaired or handicapped offenders who require extraordinary care and supervision. Major problems have been identified for special-needs offenders, including lack of access to adequate mental health services, inadequate information and training among court and corrections personnel, and insufficient interagency coordination and cooperation (Illinois Office of the Governor, 1988).

It may not be possible for community corrections to provide the degree of protection needed for persons who are disabled. Mentally ill persons may not be able to function normally in their communities. Some offenders who are mentally impaired may require constant monitoring and supervision, primarily for their own protection. It may be necessary for entire Departments of Correction to examine the problems of special-needs offenders in greater detail.

KEY TERMS

Cellular telephone device
Community corrections act
Community residential centers
Community service orders
Continuous signaling device
Continuous signaling transmitter
Criminal contamination
Day pass
Day parole
Education furlough
Electronic monitoring
Financial/community service model
Fines
Halfway-in houses
Halfway-out houses
Home confinement
Home incarceration
Hope Houses
House arrest
International Halfway House Association
Isaac T. Hopper Home
NIMBY syndrome
Program for Female Offenders, Inc.
Programmed contact device
Reparations
Restitution
Smart sentencing
Temporary furloughs
Victim/offender mediation model
Victim/reparations model
Work furloughs

QUESTIONS FOR REVIEW

1. What is meant by intermediate punishments? What are several types of intermediate punishments?
2. What is meant by net widening in connection with the use of certain intermediate punishments such as electronic monitoring or house arrest?
3. What are four kinds of electronic monitoring systems? Is the presence of the probation officer required when any of these devices is used to monitor offender behavior?
4. What is a community-based correctional program? How does it differ from intensive supervised probation?
5. What are some general program requirements associated with offender behavior where the offender has been assigned to intensive supervised probation?
6. Compare and contrast the Massachusetts and Oregon models of Intensive Supervised Probation.

7. What are some of the social and legal issues raised in connection with house arrest and electronic monitoring?
8. Describe an electronic monitoring program and the resulting cost difference compared with incarceration.
9. Why is it difficult to evaluate whether house arrest and electronic monitoring have eased prison and jail overcrowding?
10. What are some potential liabilities of paraprofessionals, volunteers, and regular probation officers who work in community-based correctional programs?

SUGGESTED READINGS

Brody, Ralph. *Effectively Managing Human Service Organizations.* Thousand Oaks, CA: Sage, 1993.

McShane, Marilyn D. and Wesley Krause. *Community Corrections.* New York: Macmillan Publishing Company, 1993.

Pace, Denny F. *Community Relations Concepts* (3rd. ed.). Placerville, CA: Copperhead Publishing Company, 1993.

Shilton, Mary K., with Sandy Pearce and John Madlor. *Community Corrections Acts for State and Local Partnerships: A Technical Assistance Guide.* Laurel, MD: American Correctional Association, 1992.

12

Correctional Officer Selection and Training

CHAPTER OUTLINE

OVERVIEW

An estimated 5.1 million adults were under some form of correctional supervision by 1995. Local jails held about 484,000 adults, while nearly 3 million adults were on probation, and 690,000 were on parole (U.S. Department of Justice, 1996:1). About 992,000 men and women were confined in prisons by 1995. Supervising these offenders were 182,000 correctional officers (Camp and Camp, 1995a:71). For the 690,000 parolees, there were about 17,300 parole officers. For the 3 million probationers, there were 26,800 probation officers (Camp and Camp, 1995d:9, 38).

Caseloads, or the number of probationers and parolees supervised by probation or parole officers, averaged 117 probationers per officer and 84 parolees per parole officer (Camp and Camp, 1995d:21, 50). The highest probationer caseloads were in California and Rhode Island, with 400 and 310 clients per officer, and the highest parolee caseloads occurred in Alabama and the District of Columbia, with 178 and 159 parolees per parole officer respectively (Camp and Camp, 1995d:21, 50).

This chapter is about the persons who work with prison and jail inmates, probationers and parolees. How are these persons selected and trained? What are the requirements for their eligibility to perform corrections, probation, or parole work? How long do they stay in their positions? How much turnover occurs in this work activity?

The chapter begins by distinguishing between correctional officers who work in jails and prisons and those who work with probationers and parolees. For brevity, we will abbreviate probation and parole officers as POs. The methods of selecting those working in institutional corrections and community probation and parole agencies will be described. The next part of the chapter describes the education and training of correctional officers. Assessment centers are described. The recruitment of women and minorities into correctional officer roles is increasing. Some explanations for this phenomenon will be presented. PO caseloads and their variations are described. Because correctional work is stressful for most persons performing these roles, stress and burnout are examined. The chapter concludes with an examination of auxiliary personnel who work in institutional and community corrections. These are paraprofessionals and volunteers. Several issues relating to the use of paraprofessionals and volunteers are presented.

CORRECTIONS OFFICERS AND PROBATION/PAROLE OFFICERS: A DISTINCTION

What should probation and parole officers be called? Technically, probation and parole officers are also correctional officers, because part of their responsibilities include the rehabilitation and reintegration of offenders. This is generally considered an integral part of corrections. Labeling probation and parole officers corrections officers also makes sense because most probation and parole departments in the United States are under the general administrative rubric of Department of Corrections. In addition, it has become customary to refer to *officers* in prisons and jails as *correctional officers* (Philliber, 1987:9–10). The American Jail Association and the American Correctional Association have both made official statements to the effect that the term *guard* is outmoded, since it no longer reflects the skills and training required to perform correctional officer work. Furthermore, this labeling Tower of Babel is complicated and perpetuated by official state and federal reports that lump all correctional personnel (probation officers, parole officers, jail officers, prison officers, correctional officers, secretaries, jail and prison administrators, paralegals who work in jails and prisons, volunteers, and paraprofessionals who work in community corrections) into one general category (National Manpower Survey, 1978:8).

Correctional officers are prison or jail staff and their supervisors who manage inmates, whereas probation and parole officers supervise and manage probationers and parolees in a variety of offender aftercare programs (American Correctional Association, 1996a:xlii–xliii). Since the departments of correction in many states select correctional officers as well as prison staff and conduct training programs for all of their correctional personnel, similar criteria are often used for selecting correctional officers and POs.

The number of personnel working in the area of adult and juvenile corrections has steadily increased. In 1996 there were over 390,000 personnel in corrections for both adults and juveniles. This is an increase of 26 percent over the 309,000 personnel reported in 1992, and a 37 percent increase over the 285,000 reported in 1988 (American Correctional Association, 1994:xlii–xliii; *Corrections Compendium,* 1990b:14; *Corrections Compendium,* 1993a:4). These figures include probation and parole officers as well as their administrative staffs. These officers make up about 25 percent of all correctional personnel. Probation officers supervise probationers, while parole officers supervise parolees.

In many jurisdictions, probation and parole officers supervise *both* types of offenders interchangeably (American Correctional Association, 1994:xii–xiii). In many states, probation and parole officers are combined in official reports of statistical information to organizations such as the American Correctional Association. Within the adult category, states such as Alabama, Florida, Virginia, Washington, and Wyoming report total numbers of probation and parole aftercare personnel and do not distinguish between them. In this and other chapters, probation and parole officers will be treated as a single category, or POs, while continuing to recognize that some jurisdictions make sharp distinctions between these officers according to the types of offender clientele supervised.

THE SELECTION AND TRAINING OF CORRECTIONAL OFFICERS

Correctional facilities run smoothly largely because of the professional and forward-thinking attitudes and actions of the correctional officers employed (Barrington, 1987:116). Of course, the administrative component plays a significant role in outlining the mission and goals of corrections facilities, and this clarity, in turn, generates the degree of enthusiasm necessary for individuals to maximize their work performance.

The traditional approach to training in most jurisdictions involves classifying recruits into several categories, subjecting each group to limited specialized training, and then moving along to the next recruit group. It is expected that recruits will learn general job responsibilities, procedures for carrying out these responsibilities, practical skills for task performance, and something about the expectations of supervisors (Lewis, 1986:12). But many recruits leave these training sessions untrained. Some experts recommend the inclusion of veteran correctional officers as resource persons to answer specific questions about correctional role performance and expectations.

Numbers of Correctional Officers in the United States. In 1996 there were 181,489 correctional officers, a 64 percent increase over the 117,000 correctional personnel reported in 1985 and a 17 percent increase between 1994 and 1996 (*Corrections Compendium,* 1996a:12–13). In 1995, there were approximately 15,000 new positions in corrections. In 1996, however, there was a substantial decline in new hires for correctional officers, an addition of only 7,390 positions (*Corrections Compendium,* 1996a:12). Figure 12.1 shows the distribution of these officers according to race and gender in most states where information was furnished.

Figure 12.1 indicates that 67 percent of all correctional officers are white, and about 18 percent are female (Camp and Camp, 1995a:70). There is an underrepresentation of minority corrections officers to manage an offender population that is 50 percent black. Only about 33 percent of the correctional officers are nonwhite.

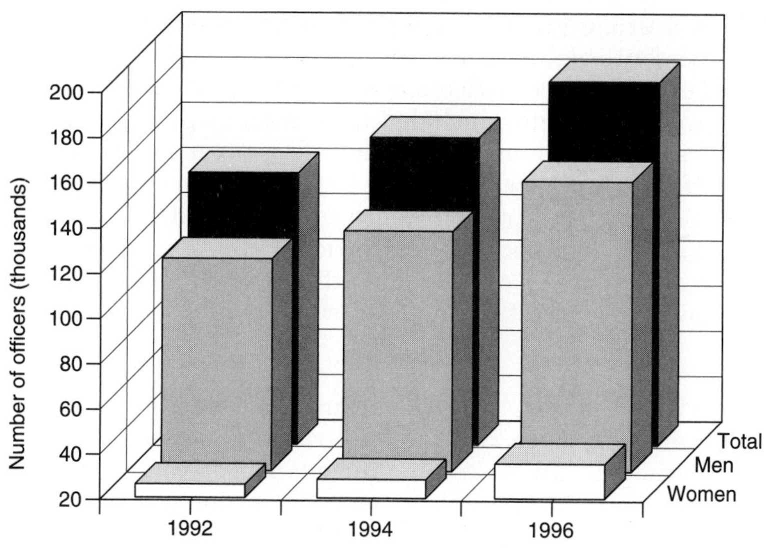

FIGURE 12.1 Correctional officers in U.S. systems (*Source: Corrections Compendium,* 21:13)

Education. Those aspiring to be correctional officers must possess either a high school diploma or G.E.D. in 78 percent of the U.S. jurisdictions. Two percent require a diploma from a two-year community college, 2 percent require a minimum of 15 college credits, and at least 12 percent have no specific educational requirements.

Obtaining more education is often equated with becoming more professional. Some experts have questioned whether more education makes better officers, however (Burke, Rizzo, and O'Rear, 1992:174). Generally, more education for officers was instrumental in gaining managerial positions. Thus, those officers who aspire to middle-level or upper-level management in prison settings would probably benefit from acquiring an advanced degree. Some officers have reported that having a higher level of education helps them to understand inmate culture better and to resolve inmate-officer conflicts more effectively (Burke et al., 1992). However, some experts say that top-level prison managers ought to seek additional educational training together with their correctional staff. This will underscore the importance of training as well as improve the image of correctional officers in their respective institutions (Carter, 1991:17).

Entry Requirements and Salaries. Most jurisdictions require prospective officers to be between 18 and 21 years of age, to have a high school diploma or its equivalent, and to have no felony convictions. More than a few jurisdictions require written and oral examinations, physical fitness assessments, and mental assessments (*Corrections Compendium,* 1996a:13).

Average annual salaries in 1996 for new officers range from $17,297 to

$41,736 and average $26,122 for all U.S. jurisdictions. These salaries are about 14 percent higher than the salaries reported in 1994 (Wees, 1996b:14). For experienced officers, salaries ranged in 1996 from $26,500 to $44,491. Standard benefits included a retirement plan, annual and sick leave, insurance programs, and deferred compensation. Officers also received uniform allowances, longevity pay, tuition assistance, and optional insurance packages and other incentives (Wees, 1996b:14). Tables 12.1, 12.2, and 12.3 show respectively correctional officer programs, screening, and training; numbers of correctional officers working in U.S. and Canadian systems; and correctional officer work requirements, salaries, and benefits.

Preservice Training. In 1996, training hours for most correctional officer applicants averaged 221, whereas training programs ranged from 17 days in Colorado to 16 weeks in Michigan (*Corrections Compendium,* 1996a:13). However, considerable in-service training was observed in most jurisdictions. Preemployment screenings were also conducted for illegal drug use through drug-testing of some kind. Psychological tests and screening were administered and performed in 39 percent of all jurisdictions. The average probationary period was 8.9 months, with the shortest being six months and the longest being 13 months (Camp and Camp, 1995a:77).

Assessment Centers

One method of selecting correctional personnel is the use of assessment centers (Page, 1995). Assessment centers are not panaceas for solving the correctional officer recruitment problem. And, they are not cookbook methods for staff selections. Rather, **assessment centers,** originally devised during World War II by the Office of Strategic Services, are rigorous identification and evaluation mechanisms lasting as long as one week that are geared to test thorough selected relevant attributes of prospective officers. Staffed by psychologists, veteran correctional officers, and prison administrators, these centers subject prospective candidates to grueling exercises that test general mental ability; oral, written, and human relations skills; creativity; self-sufficiency; realism of expectations; tolerance of uncertainty; organization, planning, and energy; decision-making ability; and interest ranges (Carini, 1986). Assessment centers also assist in the selection of managerial personnel for correctional institutions and police departments (Pynes and Bernardin, 1992). A popular format used by various jurisdictions is one established by the New York City Police Department during the 1970s. The following skills areas were identified (Pelfrey, 1986:67):

1. *Problem-solving dimensions* (problem analysis—ability to grasp the source, nature, and key dimensions of a problem; judgment—recognition of the significant factors to arrive at sound and practical decisions)

TABLE 12.1 Officer Programs, Screening, and Training

System	Officer Support Programs	Screening		Pre-Service Training					Graduation Rates	
		Type	When Tested	Hours	Cost	Length	No. of Staff	Curriculum Topics	% Pass	% Fail
U.S. Systems										
Alabama	EAP (officer-initiated); 16 hrs annual training; professional seminars held by various agencies, associations, universities.	Psych Drug Background	Pre-employ Pre-employ Ongoing Pre-employ	400 (4/95)	$1,006 (operations	10 weeks	12	Administrative/personnel; ethics & professional; communication; inmate management; officer safety/fitness; medical/mental health; legal issues; security; conflict & crisis management; correctional operations.	N/A	N/A
Alaska	40 hrs annual training.	Psych Background	Pre-employ Pre-employ	240	N/A	6 weeks	5 (academy)	Correctional Officer Recruit Training Program accredited by AK Police Standards Council consisting of at least 200 hrs security procedures, custody & supervision; use of force, firearms, other weapons & restraints; communication skills, report writing, & record keeping; emergency procedures, CPR & first aid; legal issues.	100%	N/A
Arizona	*No response*									
Arkansas	EAP by self-admission or referral; 40 hrs annual training; in-service training.	Psych Background	Pre-employ Pre-employ	240	$1,700	6 weeks	6	Self defense, crisis management, chemical agents, report writing, professionalism, first aid, basic life support (CPR), substance abuse awareness, narcotics & dangerous drugs, sexual harassment, special inmate population, radio communications, race relations, inmate mental health, security devices/procedures, communicable disease, inmate programs.	N/A	N/A
California	Data not available									

(table continues)

TABLE 12.1 (continued)

		Screening		Pre-Service Training					Graduation Rates	
System	Officer Support Programs	Type	When Tested	Hours	Cost	Length	No. of Staff	Curriculum Topics	% Pass	% Fail
Colorado	EAP program; 40 hrs annual training; in-service training in approx. 25–30 areas.	Psych Drug Background	Pre-employ Pre-employ Ongoing Pre-employ	120	$32	17 days	9 (+4 admin. support)	Department & correctional history; harassment; tours; legal issues; correctional philosophy/mission; professionalism; diversity; inmate lifestyles & vocabulary; hostage survival; offender management; contraband; communicable disease; first aid; key control; communications; corr. services; report writing; drug and alcohol, mental health; tool control; communication; towers & perimeters; gangs; fire safety; hazardous materials; use of force; searches; restraints & transport; pressure point control tactics.	96%	4%
Connecticut	"Time Out for You" programs, EAP, Health fairs; 40 hrs annual training; voluntary training based on needs assessment.	Drug Background	Pre-employ Pre-employ	240	N/A	13 weeks	23	Classification; health services; inmate programs; behavior management; site sensitization; security skills; dormitory supervision; report writing; professionalism; prison environment; cultural issues; critical incident care; EAP; cross-gender supervision; legal issues; hostage survival; disciplinary procedures; radio procedures; first aid, communicable disease; security risk groups; gender issues; community services; emergency procedures; transport; addiction services, other.	98.5%	1% (male)

Delaware	STEP Program (State Troubled Employee Program) is a confidential volunteer referral service; Post-Trauma Program; approx. 20 hrs annual training; related volunteer training.	Drug Background	Pre-employ Ongoing Pre-employ	257	$1,500 (approx.	7 weeks	29	Security; IPC, defense tactics, physical training, weapons; inmate behavior; staff manipulation.	97% (M) 95% (F)	2% (M) 2% (F)
District of Columbia	EAP; 40 hrs annual training.	Drug	Pre-employ	240	$1,669 (DS-5) $1,850 (DS-6)	6 weeks	N/A	N/A	100% (M) 99% (F)	0% (M) 0% (F)
Florida	EAP; Post-Trauma staff support program; min. 40 hrs annual training; voluntary training.	Drug Background	Pre-employ Pre-employ	411 minimum pre-service training hours. Services provided by community colleges and voc/tech schools. Cost, length, etc. varies by institution.						
Georgia	EAP; referral to state agencies; 20–40 hrs annual training.	Drug Background	Pre-employ Ongoing Pre-employ	160	$3,500	6 weeks	10	Intro to corr; stress awareness; ethics; CPR/first aid; fire safety; emergency response; use of force/tactics; legal issues; rules, grievance, disciplinary procedures; classification; contraband/searches; key, tool & weapon control; supervision; report writing.	91% (M) 84% (F)	9% (M) 15% (F)
Hawaii	*No response*									
Idaho	EAP; 40 hrs annual training.	Drug Background	Pre-employ Pre-employ	320 OJT	N/A	8 weeks (approx)	No designated staff	N/A	N/A	N/A
Illinois	*No response*									
Indiana	*No response*									
Iowa	EAP; 40 hrs annual training; security & counseling staff offered advanced training.	Psych Drug Background	Pre-employ Pre-employ Pre-employ	144	$363	4 weeks	4	Interpersonal communication skills; transport procedures; searches; report writing; riot control; personal safety; weapons; diversity.	99%	1%

(table continues)

TABLE 12.1 (continued)

System	Officer Support Programs	Screening		Pre-Service Training					Graduation Rates	
		Type	When Tested	Hours	Cost	Length	No. of Staff	Curriculum Topics	% Pass	% Fail
Kansas	EAP; 160 hrs annual training	Drug Background	Pre-employ Pre-employ	40	N/A	N/A	N/A	N/A	N/A	N/A
Kentucky	EAP; gym facilities; 40 hrs annual training; multiple options for voluntary training.	N/A	N/A	120	$150	3 weeks	14	Criminal justice system; community corrections; criminal behavior; inmate profile, classification, discipline, grievance; legal issues; violence; hostage situations; fire safety; diversity; sexual harassment; substance abuse; searching; mental health; suicide prevention; communication; crisis intervention; personal protection; tool/key control; report writing, use of force & firearms; transport; restraining devices; security skills.	100%	Less than 1%
Louisana	EAP; 40 hrs annual training, voluntary training calendar.	Drug Background	Pre-employ Ongoing Pre-employ	120	N/A	3 weeks	8	Rules & procedures; accreditation/standards; functions of corr. services; legal aspects; first aid/CPR; communicable disease; security, custody & control; inmate lifestyles; communication; inmate supervision; officer survival; discipline; report writing; contraband & searches; use of force/defense; suicide prevention; hostage situations; stress management; drug-free workplace; anatomy of a set-up.	72% (M) 19% (F)	8% (M) 1% (F)
Maine	EAP; annual & voluntary training based on need.	Drug Background	Pre-employ Pre-employ	80	N/A	N/A	Rotating groups	N/A	10%	1%
Maryland	EAP; 18 hrs annual training.	Drug Background	Pre-employ Pre-employ	160	$4,200	25 days	10	Administrative procedures; introduction to corrections; supervision; relations and treatment; security; custody and control; discipline.	N/A	N/A

Massachusetts	Training academy offers stress-related training, other programs; 40 hrs (min) annual training; voluntary training.	Psych Drug Background	Pre-employ Pre-employ Pre-employ	255	$4,300	7 weeks	3	Employee rules & regulations; report writing; disciplinary procedures; use of force; fire safety; key & tool control; first aid/CPR; inmate accountability; firearms; restraint; self defense; communication skills; physical training; military movements.	99%	1%
Michigan	Training services & employee service program; 40 hrs annual training; voluntary training.	Drug Background	Pre-employ Pre-employ	640	N/A	16 weeks	10	Custody & security; prisoner management; self-defense; weapons; disturbance control; report writing; communication skills.	N/A	N/A
Minnesota	EAP; 40 hrs annual training; voluntary training in first aid, self-defense.	Drug Background	Pre-employ Pre-employ	200–360	$862– $1,207	N/A	9	Inmate management; crisis intervention; suicide prevention; hostage situations; avoiding setups; corr. policies & legal issues; diversity; inmate lifestyles; communications; crime scene preservation; inmate gangs.	98% (M) 99% (F)	2% (M) 1% (F)
Mississippi	Stress management; annual training; in-service training.	Background	Pre-employ	200	$2,080	4 weeks	19	Management; firearms certification; leadership; team building; report writing; first aid/CPR; other.	54% (M) 39% (F)	5% (M) 3% (F)
Missouri	EAP; assignment rotation; 40+ hrs annual training; voluntary (in-service) training.	Background	Pre-employ	216	$750	N/A	16 (academy) 17 (institution) 200 (part-time)	Basic custody; security issues; diversity; communication; use of force; legal issues; firearms; defense tactics; CPR; SFA; special needs; street management; cross-gender issues; policies & procedures; staff-inmate relations; NVCI; riots & hostages; set-ups; treatment; communicable disease; searches; department overview; restraints; chemicals; contraband; gangs.	95%	1%

(table continues)

TABLE 12.1 (continued)

System	Officer Support Programs	Screening: Type	Screening: When Tested	Pre-Service Training: Hours	Cost	Length	No. of Staff	Curriculum Topics	Graduation Rates: % Pass	% Fail
Montana	*No response*									
Nebraska	EAP; 40 hrs annual training; voluntary training.	Background (plus reference, fingerprint)	Pre-employ	160	$3,632	4 weeks	4 training spec. plus 3 admin.	Personnel issues; corr. orientation; C.Q.I.; use of force; communication; report writing; discrimination & harassment; communicable disease; security; recognizing critical behavior; emergency procedures; safety & sanitation; driving; weapons; CPR/First aid; inmate rules; crime scene/evidence; legal issues; hostages; con-games; searches; religion; substance abuse; chemical agents; P.P.C.T.; restraints & transport; survivair & forced cell moves.	99%	1%
Nevada	Stress management & awareness in basic courses plus First Line Supervision & Basic Organizational management courses; 24 hrs annual training.	Drug Background	Pre-employ Pre-employ	160	N/A	N/A	5	N/A	99.9%	.1%
New Hampshire	*No response*									
New Jersey	Employee advisory service; annual training; specialized training available if needed.	Psych Drug Background	Pre-employ Ongoing Pre-employ Ongoing Pre-employ	60–80 at institution (10 weeks at academy)	N/A	2 weeks agency training; 10 weeks academy training	30	Physical; administrative rules/regulations; psychology; drug and identification plus Correction Officers Training Academy.	N/A	N/A

New Mexico	40 hrs annual training; voluntary training through human resource development division.	Psych Drug Background	Pre-employ Pre-employ Ongoing Pre-employ	280	$3,981	7 weeks	9 regular instructors; 13 trainers	Criminal justice/corr./department orientation; fitness; security & offender supervision; policies & procedures; professionalism; offender/staff relations; communication; report writing; diversity; legal issues; classification/management/special needs; key & tool control; use of force; fire safety; first aid/CPR; transport; restraints; hostage situations; suicide prevention; gangs; stress management; infectious disease; courtroom demeanor; harassment/EEO; driving; leadership.	88% (M) 46% (F)	1% (M) 0% (F)
New York	EAP; 40 hrs annual training; voluntary training.	Psych Drug Background	Pre-employ Pre-employ Pre-employ	280	$8,054	7 weeks	37 (perm & temp)	Orientation & emergency response; security procedures; communications; firearms; legal procedures; supervision; abnormal inmate behavior.	99% (M) 95% (F)	1% (M) 5% (F)
North Carolina	State EAP; 18 hrs annual training; voluntary training (with tuition assist. & educational leave).	Psych Drug Background	Pre-employ Pre-employ Pre-employ	160	$273 (academy) $427 (offsite if needed)	N/A	35 (basic training)	Firearms; self-defense; life support; communication; chemical agents; emergency operations; inmate behavior/supervision; transport; report writing; harassment; role of correctional witness.	98% +	less than 1%
North Dakota	EAP & Critical Incident Stress Debriefing Team; 40 hrs annual training.	Background	Pre-employ	80	$750	N/A	2	Security related; sexual harassment; firearms; use of force; con games; report writing; employee handbook; overview, on-the-job training.	98% (M) 100% (F)	2% (M) 0% (F)

(table continues)

TABLE 12.1 (continued)

System	Officer Support Programs	Screening		Pre-Service Training					Graduation Rates	
		Type	When Tested	Hours	Cost	Length	No. of Staff	Curriculum Topics	% Pass	% Fail
Ohio	EAP; 40 hrs annual training; voluntary (in-service) training.	Psych Drug Background	Pre-employ Pre-employ Pre-employ	280	$47.17/ day	N/A	51	Interpersonal communications; diversity; security; administrative regulations; policies & procedures; searches (cell & body); self-defense; weapons training & certification; EEO issues; personal issues.	99.8%	.2%
Oklahoma	EAP; 40 hrs annual training; voluntary training.	Background	Pre-employ	320	$1,100 (approx)	6 weeks (academy) 2 weeks (facility)	39	N/A	81% (M) 19% (F)	N/A
Oregon	"Handling Stress" part of orientation, reinforced during annual in-service; EAP; 40 hrs annual training; voluntary training.	Drug Background	Pre-employ Pre-employ	320	$10,000 (approx)	8 weeks	7	N/A	99% (M) 100% (F)	1% (M)
Pennsylvania	Stress management (pre-service), in-service stress management offered every 3 years; 40 hrs annual training; voluntary training.	Psych Drug Background	Pre-employ Pre-employ Pre-employ	320 (160 basic plus 160 orientation)	$1,500	4 weeks formal, 4 weeks orientation	13 full time plus 5 with 1 year limited term	Defensive tactics; weapons; chemical munitions; CERT; EBID; emergency preparedness; fire emergency; hostage rescue/negot; HIV/AIDS; communications; conflict management; report writing; first aid; stress management; suicide prevention; supervisory development; team building.	75.3% (M) 24.7% (F)	20% (M) 80% (F)[a]
Rhode Island	Department stress unit; counseling included in medical benefits; 40 hrs annual training; voluntary training.	Psych Drug Background	Pre-employ Pre-employ Pre-employ	320	$7,500	N/A	8	Security procedures; supervision of inmates; suicide signs & precautions; use of force; report writing; inmate rules & regulations; inmate rights; fire & emergency procedures; safety procedures; firearms; key control; interpersonal relations & communications; lifestyles of inmates; first aid/CPR; fitness; defense tactics.	N/A	N/A

South Carolina	EAP; 40 hrs annual training.	Background	Pre-employ	200	$3,428	N/A	37	Varied security and non-security areas.	69.3% (M) 30.7% (F)	N/A
South Dakota	Critical Incident Stress Debriefing; individual counseling; 40 hrs annual training; voluntary training.	Drug Background	Pre-employ Pre-employ	120	$100 (plus staff salaries & OT Pay)	5 weeks	3	Basic security; staff/inmate relations; searches & transports; non-violent crisis intervention.	99% (M) 100% (F)	1% (M) 0% (F)
Tennessee	EAP; 40 hrs annual training; voluntary training offered by state & state vendors.	Psych Drug Background	Academy Academy Pre-employ	120	N/A	3 weeks at academy	96	Employee survival; violence in the workplace; Employee Assistance Program; security threat groups; how to manage your boss; ADA; harassment; inmate manipulation; time management; stress reduction techniques.	70%	30%
Texas	EAP; 40 hrs annual training; voluntary training.	Background	Pre-employ	240	N/A	6 weeks	7	Self defense; firearms; chemical agents; CPR/first aid; fitness; non-violent crisis intervention; use of force standards; ethics; interpersonal skills; public relations; inspections; safety.	N/A	N/A
Utah	*No response*									
Vermont	EAP; 40+ hrs annual training; voluntary training stipend.	N/A	N/A	240	$3,000	N/A	5	Legal; CPR/first aid; suicide prevention; non-abusive physical & psychological intervention; bloodborne/airborne pathogens; team-building; baton; fire safety; professionalism; corr. theory into practice; diversity; mission; classification; field training; applied learning.	N/A	N/A
Virginia	*No response*									

(table continues)

TABLE 12.1 (continued)

System	Officer Support Programs	Screening		Pre-Service Training					Graduation Rates	
		Type	When Tested	Hours	Cost	Length	No. of Staff	Curriculum Topics	% Pass	% Fail
Washington	Employee Advisory Service; 30 hrs annual training; voluntary training.	Background	Pre-employ	160	DOC does not provide pre-service training.					
West Virginia	40 hrs annual training.	Psych Background	Ongoing Pre-employ	140	N/A	N/A	6	Corr. officer duties; firearms; riot & disturbance; counseling inmates; HIV/AIDS training; personal combat training, etc.	99.5% (M) 98% (F)	.5% (M) 2% (F)
Wisconsin	Critical Incident Stress Debriefing Program; EAP; 20 hrs annual training; voluntary training.	Background	Pre-employ	280	N/A	7 weeks (5 wks classroom, 2 wks OJT)	6 (director, 4 training staff, program assistant)	Admin; chemical agents; civil rights; communication; con games; contraband; decision making; supervision; disturbance situations; weapons; emergency procedures; EAP; fire safety; first aid/CPR; fitness; key & tool control; legal issues; OJT; evidence/crime scene; subject control; professionalism; communications; report writing; restraints/transport; safety; searches; harassment; stress management; suicide prevention; unions; uniforms; visiting.	92% (M) 84% (F)	5% (M) 4.5% (F)
Wyoming	In-house counseling & stress sessions; 80–160 hrs annual training.	Background	Pre-employ	No pre-service training provided. Annual training of 80–160 hrs.			2	Elements of penology; harassment; security expectations; ethics; staff-inmate relations; supervision; types of inmates; custody, security & control; safety; disturbances; suicides; searches; hostage situations; treatment; discipline; restraints; transport; emergency procedures; use of force; weapons; control tactics.	N/A	N/A

Federal Bureau of Prisons	Each facility has a local EAP staffed by psychologists who are available if the need arises; 40 hrs annual training; voluntary training.	Psych Drug Background	Pre-employ Pre-employ Pre-employ	177	$1,000	5 weeks	Minimum 88[b]	Physical activities; weapons handling & qualifying; fundamentals of correctional law; use of force; correctional supervision; writing skills assessment; interpersonal communications; sexuality in prisons; suicide prevention; hostage situations; inmate/workforce diversity; inmate profiles; computer security; wellness; stress management; inmate drug & alcohol.	71.2% (M) 28.8% (F)	.5% (M) 1.6% (F)
Canadian Systems										
Alberta	*No response*									
British Columbia	*No response*									
Monitoba	*No response*									
New Brunswick	*No response*									
Newfoundland	EAP & division Stress Management Team; annual training; voluntary training/workshops.	Psych Background	Pre-employ Pre-employ	4 semesters	$2,250/ per semester	2 years	N/A	Post-secondary coursework (no details available)	N/A	N/A
Northwest Territory	*No response*									
Nova Scotia	EAP; attendance management program (light or modified duties); voluntary training.	Background	Pre-employ	10 months (community college) plus 6 wks (in-house)	N/A	N/A	2 full time plus 30 part time	Interpersonal relationships; conflict & conflict crisis intervention; inmate supervision; security concepts; procedures & drills; suicide intervention; verbal crisis intervention; emergency/crisis situations (crime scene, suicides, cell extractions/insertions, contingency plans, inmate programs, etc.).	N/A	N/A

(table continues)

TABLE 12.1 (continued)

System	Officer Support Programs	Screening		Pre-Service Training					Graduation Rates	
		Type	When Tested	Hours	Cost	Length	No. of Staff	Curriculum Topics	% Pass	% Fail
Ontario	EAP; Attendance Enhancement Program; Employee Counseling Service.	Background	Pre-employ	Current correctional officer training involves a 4 phase program intended to take place during first year on the job. After hire, recruit has orientation training at the facility level (approx. 3 weeks), followed by 15-day formal classroom training, 20 weeks on-the-job training and a final 10-day classroom training phase. The ministry will shortly be implementing the findings of a major staff training and recruitment review.						
Prince Edward Island	EAP; CISD (in-service); private counseling; addiction counseling; Critical Incident Stress Debriefing, Operational Debriefing; Stress Mapping; annual training; voluntary training.	Psych Background	Pre-employ Pre-employ	90	Training at candidates' own cost	12 days	8–10	Non-violent crisis intervention; infection control; WHMIS; suicide prevention; CPR/first aid/emergency situations; conflict resolution; racism awareness; sexual assault awareness; chemical dependency; family violence; case management process.	N/A	N/A
Quebec	Stress management course; operational debriefing; post-traumatic debriefing; annual training; voluntary training.	Background	Pre-employ	160	N/A	N/A	10–30 at each facility	Role of detention and the officer's place in the governmental environment; employee functions; work teams; inmate profiles; probation; information systems; special events; surveillance & control; urgent measures; crisis situations and suicide prevention; drugs; infectious disease; physical intervention; stress.	N/A	N/A
Saskatchewan	*No response*									
Yukon Territory	EAP; Temporary "reassignment"; annual & on-the-job training (probationary); voluntary training.	Security check with RCMP, medical & reference checks on initial hiring.		Orientation training (8 days), which includes restraint training & non-violent crisis intervention, upon employment. Thereafter, 6 months of on-the-job training. Must successfully participate in training to pass mandatory 6 month probation period.						
Correctional Service of Canada	EAP; referral to community sources; info sessions on personal health; Critical Incident Debriefing; access to nursing services; 4–6 days annual training; voluntary training.	N/A	N/A	440	$11,000	N/A	41	Security; substance abuse; case management; law, policy & regulations; offender programs; interpersonal skills; special needs offenders.	91% (M) 93% (F)	2% (M) 1% (F)

[a] Five people.

[b] Each institution has at least one Employee Development Manager and/or Specialist. There are approximately 58 staff at our training academy, Glynco, GA. They served 3,558 new employees during FY95.

Source: Correctional Compendium (1996a: 23:29).

TABLE 12.2 Correctional Officers

System	C.O. Total	Percent			Males in Female Facilities	Females in Male Facilities	Officer Inmate Ratio	Annual Turnover Rate	Recruitment Problems
		Men	Women	Minority					
U.S. Systems									
Alabama	2,291	78%	22%	59%	1%	19%	1 to 10	11%	Funding shortages, etc.
Alaska	727	83%	17%	25%	N/A	N/A	N/A	11% (1995)	None
Arizona	*No response*								
Arkansas	1,919	77%	23%	54%	31.3%	17.8%	1 to 5	38% (corr. officer)	None
California	18,280	81%	19%	45%	N/A	N/A	1 to 6	N/A	N/A
Colorado	1,957 1,125 (C.O. I, entry-level)	80%	20%	27.5%	3.8%	70%	1 to 24	7.5%	Yes—attributed to large no. of positions to be filled, recent turnaround in economy creating jobs in all sectors.
Connecticut	4,007	84%	16%	36%	6%	68%	1 to 3.7	2%	None
Delaware	988	86%	14%	43%	28%	varies[a]	1 to 4	7.7% (c.o.) 5.3% (other)	None—recruitment efforts match vacancy levels.
District of Columbia	2,391	70%	30%	N/A	N/A	N/A	1 to 3.83	9%	Yes—low salary/high cost of living; competition; reduced applicant pool; privatization.
Florida	10,301	72%	28%	31% (approx)	51%	26%	1 to 6	16.19%	Yes—low salaries; local jails pay more; more inmates; expanded number of prisons.
Georgia	8,338	78%	22%	48.5% (approx)	6.6%	19.3%	1 to 4	21%	Yes—salary/location of jobs are two largest factors.
Hawaii	*No response*								
Idaho	483	84.5%	15.5%	9%	7.2% (total staff)	87% (total staff)	1 to 18	15.01% (13.43% security turnover)	None
Illinois	*No response*								
Indiana	*No response*								
Iowa	1,155	83%	17%	5.9% (approx)	2.7%	16%	1 to 5	9.51%	None—great deal of interest in Iowa's corr. system, many criminal justice programs.
Kansas	1,404	85%	15%	12%	71%	14.4%	1 to 5	21%	None

(table continues)

TABLE 12.2 (continued)

System	C.O. Total	Percent Men	Percent Women	Percent Minority	Males in Female Facilities	Females in Male Facilities	Officer Inmate Ratio	Annual Turnover Rate	Recruitment Problems
Kentucky	1,448	82%	18%	5% (approx)	2%	17%	1 to 7	24%	None
Louisana	3,858	78%	22%	38% (black)	4%	19%	3 to 5	23%	Yes—lack of qualified applicants recently in the industrial area of the state.
Maine	407	N/A	N/A	N/A	N/A	N/A	1 to 3.6	9%	None
Maryland	4,558	77%	23%	49.2%	1%	85%	1 to 5	10%	None—approx. 3,000 eligible candidates from which to select applicants.
Massachusetts	3,346	89.6%	10.4%	13%	6.3%	13%	1 to 3	3%	None—all new hires are from civil service exam lists.
Michigan	7,962	79%	21%	20.3%	2.6%	91.3%	N/A	4.5%	Yes—difficulty recruiting female, minority employees.
Minnesota	1,592	73.8%	26.2%	10% (approx)	1.2%	88%	1 to 3.17	5.8%	None
Mississippi	1.887	53%	47%	84.4%	11.5%	4.8%	1 to 7	N/A	None—agency has had outstanding success in recruitment efforts to staff new facilities.
Missouri	3,361	82.9%	17.1%	7%	52%	15.9%	1 to 5.75	15–20%	Yes—turnover and current job market impact ability to fill all positions.
Montana	*No response*								
Nebraska	635[b]	82%	18%	13%	29.7% (custody staff)	14.9% (custody staff)	1 to 4.81[d]	13.7% (1995)	Yes—unemployment in Neb. at an all time low. No. of applicants has recently increased, however.
Nevada	999	83.8%	16.2%	16.3%	1.6%	11.2%	1 to 3.8	12.5%	Yes—in some rural areas.
New Hampshire	*No response*								
New Jersey	4,824	85%	15%	49%	3%	81%	1 to 3.77	5.5%	None
New Mexico	1,181	93%	7%	70%	N/A[c]	100%	1 to 4	17.63%	Yes—for certain locations due to cost of living.
New York	18,500	92%	8%	13.7%	4%	70%	1 to 3.5	3.1%	None
North Carolina	6,490	82%	18%	41%	N/A	N/A	1 to 4	12% (4/95–3/96)	None
North Dakota	105	90%	10%	3%	20%	15%	1 to 4.5	3%	None
Ohio	6,647	62%	38%	22%	18%	15%	1 to 6.7	5.1%	None—generally have far more applicants available to hire than needed.

Oklahoma	1,957 (1/1/96)	84.9%	15.1%	21%	.05%	74%	1 to 7	9.18%	None
Oregon	1,251	82.6%	17.3%	12.3%	.04%	87%	1 to 6	10.6%	Varies
Pennsylvania	6,512	92.4%	7.6%	9.7%	33.4%	4.3%	1 to 5	3.22% (1995)	None—recruitment through state civil service exam.
Rhode Island	978[d]	89.98%	10.02%	10.53%	4.91%	3.58%	1 to 3.11	5%	No training classes conducted since 1991.
South Carolina	2,869	69.15%	30.84%	69% (approx)	14.28%	27.44%	1 to 6.8	26.4%	Yes—lack of pool of applicants for high turnover/low paying jobs.
South Dakota	285	80%	20%	5.6%	31% (co-ed)	52% (co-ed)	1 to 7	30% (approx)	None
Tennessee	2,656	76.6%	23.4%	23.5%	3.25%	3.64%	1 to 5	17.5% (all) 24% (officers)	Yes—low unemployment, high proportion of unemployed w/felony convictions, lack of GEDs in unemployed, low starting salary compared to county/federal officers.
Texas	23,673	71%	29%	40.8%	3%	77%	1 to 5	11%	None, except for isolated area in NW corner of state.
Utah	*No response*								
Vermont	407	89.1%	10.9%	Not tracked	N/A—no separate female facility.		1 to 3	11.5%	None
Virginia	*No response*								
Washington	2,129	79.6%	20.4%	16.6%	5%	86%	N/A	7.2%	None—hundreds of eligible candidates on statewide register.
West Virginia	607	90%	10%	1%	30%	20%	1 to 3	10%	None
Wisconsin	2,782	82.67%	17.33%	7.36%	2%	79%	N/A	7.28%	Yes—difficult to keep pace with demand for officers because of growth.
Wyoming	189	83%	17%	28%	79%	21%	1 to 5.9	22%	Some difficulty w/local recruitment.
Federal Bureau of Prisons	12,028 (on 3/30/96)	88.4%	11.6%	36.6%	4.26%	65.92%	N/A	6.6% (all 1995) 6.2% (c.o. 1995)	None—estimate approximately 10,000 qualified applicants currently on Correctional Officer Register at the entry level (GS-5/GS-6).

(table continues)

TABLE 12.2 (continued)

System	C.O. Total	Percent			Males in Female Facilities	Females in Male Facilities	Officer Inmate Ratio	Annual Turnover Rate	Recruitment Problems
		Men	Women	Minority					
Canadian Systems									
Alberta	*No response*								
British Columbia	*No response*								
Manitoba	*No response*								
New Brunswick	*No response*								
Newfoundland	166	89.7%	10.3%	N/A	40%	7%	1 to 1.9	2%–5%	None
Northwest Territory	*No response*								
Nova Scotia	188	93%	7%	N/A	10% (work hours)	5% (work hours)	1 to 2.7	N/A	None—typically more applicants than needed.
Ontario	3,893	76%	24%	N/A	13%	63%	1 to 2.1	10.2% (1995)	None—increasing job loss in economy; community college programs provide continuous supply of qualified recruits.
Prince Edward Island	63	87%	13%	N/A	N/A	100%	N/A	1% (approx)	None
Quebec	1,339	81%	19%	N/A	15%	15%	1 to 1.38	5%	None, except for rural areas.
Saskatchewan	*No response*								
Yukon Territory	55	64%	36%	N/A	N/A—facilities are co-ed.		1 to 20[e] 1 to 4[f]	9%[e]11%[f]	None—sufficient number of individuals w/necessary qualifications in Yukon.
Correctional Service of Canada	5,182	80%	20%	N/A	9.3%	16.3%	1 to 1.37	3.3% (permanent & term officers)	N/A

[a] Ranges from 3%–9% in smaller institutions and 11%–16% at larger institutions.
[b] Statistics for correctional officers include all custody staff, officer, corporal, sergeant, lieutenant, captain and major.
[c] The women's facility is privately operated.
[d] Includes captains, lieutenants, line officers, training academy staff, stewards, nurses, records & ID/bail.
[e] Whitehorse Correctional Centre
[f] Teslin Community Correctional Centre

Source: Corrections Compendium (1996a:15–17).

TABLE 12.3 Requirements, Salaries, and Benefits

System	Entry Requirements	How Often Met or Exceeded?	Annual Salary		New Hires		Benefits	Unions
			Starting	Average	1995	1996		
U.S. Systems								
Alabama	High school or GED; driver's license; physical exam; drug test; 21 years old; physically fit; no felonies; U.S. citizen; honorable military.	Large no. of young officers, former military, most with no education beyond high school.	$1,485.25/mo.	31,408	0	0	Full retirement @ 25 yrs; health ins.; subsistence pay.	Alabama Highway Maintenance Local 1370
Alaska	21 years old; high school, GED or equiv; U.S. citizen or resident alien with intent to become citizen; no felonies; valid AK driver's license.	Generally met by new recruits.	$2,631/mo.	N/A	0	Unk	Health ins.; retirement; promotional opportunities.	AK State Employees Association
Arizona	*No response*							
Arkansas	High school or equivalent.	Requirements generally met.	$17,293 (CO-I)	$20,800/yr	N/A	N/A	Retirement—vested at 10 years.	None
California	High school or equiv.; 21 years old; physically & mentally fit; no felonies; drug test.	Requirements generally met.	$2,001/mo.	$2,355–$3,835/mo.	N/A	N/A	N/A	N/A
Colorado	60 sem. hours of college course work, 30 related; 21 years old; CO resident; physically fit. Possible: drug test; CO driver's license.	Requirements generally exceeded due to poor economy.	$1,982/mo.	$2,529–$3,735/mo.	50 positions added FY 95–96.		Retirement; 401K; health/dent/life ins.	CO not a collective bargaining state, but individuals may join.
Connecticut	18 years old; high school or equiv.; permanent employment contingent on successful completion of medical/physical exam and drug screen.	Based on current employment pool, candidates exceed basic requirements.	$25,192 ($27,991 after training)	$30,880 (avg. base salary, step 4)	0	0	Group medical & life ins. + accidental death/disability; 20 years retirement regardless of age; shift differential; tuition reimbursement; meal allowances; EAP; career counseling.	American Federation of State, City & Municipal Employees (AFSCME)
Delaware	High school or equivalent; 21 years old; valid driver's license.	Most new officers meet the minimum requirements.	$20,553 +$1,200 Hazard Duty annually	$25,900	N/A	98	Life/health/dental ins.; pension plan; blood bank; EAP.	Delaware Correctional Officer's Assoc.; AFSCME Local 247

(table continues)

TABLE 12.3 (continued)

System	Entry Requirement	How Often Met or Exceeded?	Annual Salary		New Hires		Benefits	Unions
			Starting	Average	1995	1996		
District Of Columbia	Driver's license; written test; interview; medical/psych exam; complete training; background check/drug screen; possible lie detector.	Requirements generally met.	$21,707 (DS-5)	$30,729	N/A	80	Retirement; personal, annual & sick leave; comp time; life ins.; paid portion of health insurance.	Fraternal Order of Police
Florida	19 years old; U.S. citizen; high school or equiv.; good moral character; complete basic training; no felonies or misdemeanor involving perjury or false statement.	Requirements generally met.	$18,109	$19,110	1,502 (FY 94–95)	2,207 (FY 95–96)	13 vacation/13 sick days 1st year; incentive pay to $130/mo.; full retirement; health/life ins. (subsidized); pre-tax medical, child care benefits; supplemental ins.; tuition waiver at most college/univ.	Florida Police Benevolent Assoc.
Georgia	18 years old; High school or GED; U.S. Citizen; no felonies.	Requirements generally met.	$17,652	$21,306	2,927	876	Health/life ins.; deferred comp; dental plan; retirement; direct deposit; annual, family & sick leave.	State Employees Union
Hawaii	*No response*							
Idaho	18 years old; complete and sign "Qualifications Statement/Willingness Application."	Requirements generally met.	$6.72/hr (1st 8 wks.)	$21,715 ($10.44/hr.)	36	0	Mandatory retirement; health/life ins.; deferred comp/401K; comp time; annual & sick leave; EAP.	Idaho Service Employees Union
Illinois	*No response*							
Indiana	*No response*							
Iowa	High school or GED; psych & observational test; background check; medical test.	Approximately 1/2 exceed education requirements.	$24,980	$27,310	N/A	N/A	Early retirement; health ins.; deferred compensation.	AFSCME
Kansas	High school or GED; 21 years old; no felonies; valid driver's license; drug screen.	Not eligible for employment unless minimums are met.	$17,868	N/A	N/A	23	Full retirement (age 55); 12 vacation/12 sick days per year.	AFSCME and Kansas Assoc. of Public Employees
Kentucky	21 years old; high school or GED; no felonies.	Requirements generally met.	$16,260 (1st 6 months).	$21,138	N/A	N/A	Uniforms; group life/health ins.; vacation & sick leave; educational assistance; hazardous duty retirement; 401K.	None

Louisiana	18 years old; valid driver's license; felony or felony indictment disqualified until relief from disabilities imposed by state/fed laws granted.	Requirements generally met.	$1,228/mo.	$1,734/mo.	N/A	30	1/2 insurance paid by state; annual and sick leave; retirement & cafeteria plan.	AFSCME
Maine	High school or equiv.	Requirements generally met.	$17,722	$19,427 (est.)	0	0	State paid health, life, dental ins.	AFSCME
Maryland	21 years old; high school or GED; U.S. citizen or resident alien; physical; training academy; 24 hour call; telephone; substance abuse test; background check; firearms test; interview; valid driver's license; 70% on written exam.	Bulk of applicants meet requirements; no statistics kept on number who exceed requirements.	$22,004	$32,460	76	219	Vacation, personal & sick leave; 20 year retirement; deferred comp (401K, 457, 403B); subsidized health ins.; pharmacy; vision.	Maryland Correction Employee Assn (MCEA); AFSCME; Maryland Correctional Union (MCU); Teamsters
Massachusetts	19 years old; high school, GED or 3 yrs military; no felonies; no misdemeanor w/time served; U.S. citizen.	Requirements generally exceeded. Some have college degrees.	$540.65/wk	$37,015.16	106	N/A	Education incentive; longevity pay; shift differential; roll call pay; clothing allowance; 20 year retirement.	Mass. Correction Officers Federation Union
Michigan	High school or GED; corrections certificate or 15 (sem) or 23 (term) credits in corrections or related, or any bachelor's; agility & drug test.	Most applicants exceed requirements, tend to have more education than required.	$11.04/hr	N/A	800	977	Medical, dental, vision; retirement; 401K; vacation & sick leave.	Michigan Corrections Organization
Minnesota	Pass video, reading comprehension, interview tests; physical & drug screen.	Requirements generally met.	$23,114	$30,673	50 (est)	50 (est)	Health & life ins.; retirement; vacation & sick leave.	AFSCME
Mississippi	High school; 21 years old; valid driver's license; no criminal record.	Barring occasional exceptions, requirements generally met.	$16,237.92	N/A	325	500	Health ins.; retirement; personal & major medical leave.	None

(table continues)

TABLE 12.3 (continued)

System	Entry Requirements	How Often Met or Exceeded?	Annual Salary		New Hires		Benefits	Unions
			Starting	Average	1995	1996		
Missouri	2 years work experience; high school (extended work experience may substitute on year-by-year basis).	Most exceed requirements & a few have college and/or degrees.	$1,543/mo.	$1,634–$1800 month.	71.25 FTE	336 FTE	All federal & state benefits & requirements; retirement; long-term disability; health & life ins.; worker's comp; unemployment; shared leave; annual & sick leave, other leave benefits.	AFSCME
Montana	*No response*							
Nebraska	Ability to perform required duties; valid driver's license; training program.	Many officers exceed requirements with extra experience or bachelor's.	$1,691/mo.	$22,388.78	32	45.66 FTE	Life & health ins.; leave time; retirement; EAP; holidays; tuition assistance; worker's comp.	National Assoc. of Public Employees
Nevada	21 years old; 2 years work experience (any type).	Requirements generally exceeded.	$25,618	$26,689	149	25	Public Emp. Retirement System (w/survivor benefits); life, health, dental ins.	None
New Hampshire	*No response*							
New Jersey	18 years old; U.S. citizen; proof of eligibility; medical & psychological examinations; training program; driver's license.	Requirements generally met.	$31,805	N/A	1997: 250		Dental & eye care plan; temp disability; deferred comp; vacation, personal & sick days; holidays; health ins.; uniform allowance; tuition refund.	State Policemen's Benevolent Association
New Mexico	U.S. citizen; 18 years old; high school or equiv.; no felonies.	Very few officers exceed requirements.	$16,118	$19,173	N/A	N/A	N/A	New Mexico State Labor Coalition
New York	21 years old; High school or GED.	Many recruits over 21 w/post-secondary education.	$22,500	$35,000	N/A	N/A	Health ins.; dental & vision care; retirement; uniform allowance.	Council 82
North Carolina	High school or equivalent; eligible for criminal justice certification.	Requirements generally met.	$19,645	N/A	N/A	N/A	Annual, civil, military, parental & sick leave; holidays; premium, longevity & OT pay; comprehensive major medical; worker's comp; retirement; group dental; prepaid legal services; 401K.	None

North Dakota	2 years college with emphasis in criminal justice or 3 years related work experience.	Requirements generally met.	$1,283/mo.	$1,720/mo.	N/A	0	Annual & sick leave; retirement; health ins.; optional life & flex plans; EAP.	None
Ohio	High school or GED; driver's license; psych & written test; physical agility test; interview; background investigation; drug test.	Majority of recruits meet requirements. Many recent recruits w/some college or assoc. degree.	$23,878	$27,082	452	375	Retirement; health ins.; shift & roll call; uniform allowance; deferred comp; dental, vision & group life after 1 year.	OCSEA-AFSCME Local 11 & AFL-CIO
Oklahoma	21 years old; 30 sem hours of college or high school or GED; completion of training.	N/A	$1,077.66/mo.	$19,800.24	185	0	Health, dental, life, disability ins.; worker's comp; retirement.	None
Oregon	21 years old; U.S. citizen; High school or GED; no felonies; fitness requirement.	Candidates unable to meet or exceed requirements are not hired.	$2,050/mo. (varies w/union contract)	$2,250/mo. (varies w/union contract)	25	300	Medical & dental ins.; enhanced retirement; vacation, holiday & sick leave; min. life ins.; uniforms. Also: additional life, accidental death/dismemberment; deferred comp.	Oregon Public Employees Union; AFSCME
Pennsylvania	21 years old; U.S. citizen; high school or equivalent combination of experience & training.	Candidates meet conditions as established by civil service testing program.	$20,426	$31,724.03	N/A	N/A	Stress pay; uniform allowance; civil, parental & military leave; life ins.; retirement; deferred comp; health & medical coverage, other.	AFSCME, Council 13
Rhode Island	18 years old; high school or GED; pre-screening process including criminal records check.	Requirements generally exceeded. Most applicants over 18, some with 2/4 year degree or credits toward degree.	$25,808	$41,736	N/A	40	Medical; dental; vacation, personal & sick leave; paid holidays; shift differential.	Rhode Island Brotherhood of Correctional Officers
South Carolina	21 years old; high school or GED; no DUI conviction last 5 years; no sentence of $1,000 or 1 year in jail; no conviction of crimes of moral turpitude.	Requirements generally met. Most have no prior experience.	$15,310	$17,297	200	200	Medical; retirement; 401K; holidays; sick & annual leave.	None

(table continues)

TABLE 12.3 (continued)

System	Entry Requirements	How Often Met or Exceeded?	Annual Salary		New Hires		Benefits	Unions
			Starting	Average	1995	1996		
South Dakota	High school or GED plus 1 year work experience or equivalent combination of related education & experience.	Requirements are generally met.	$7.70/hr	$19,000	N/A	N/A	Vacation & sick leave; retirement; medical ins.; life ins.	United Steel Workers
Tennessee	18 years old; high school or equivalent.	Requirements generally exceeded (recruiting from military bases common).	$14,688	N/A	669	N/A	Health, dental ins.; retirement; annual, sick leave; worker's comp; EAP; deferred comp; tuition assistance; longevity pay.	None
Texas	U.S. citizen or resident alien; 18 years old; high school or GED; not active military or on probation; no pending charges or warrants; 15 years since end of felony sentence; no Class A misdemeanor last 12 mo. or Class B last 6 mo.; no DUI or DWI last 2 yrs; perform essential functions; pre-employment test.	Requirements generally exceeded. Approx. 1/2 of new officers have more than high school diploma.	$16,524	N/A—career ladder	5,400	250	Uniforms & laundering furnished; group life & health ins.; meals while on duty; annual & sick leave; holidays; retirement.	Texas State Employees Union; AFSCME
Utah	*No response*							
Vermont	High school & 2 years any full time work experience.	Requirements generally exceeded; college degrees in many cases.	$20,000	$27,000 (with overtime)	0	0	Retirement; annual & sick leave; tuition reimbursement (50%); retirement.	Vermont State Employees' Assoc.
Virginia	*No response*							
Washington	N/A	Requirements generally met.	$23,280	N/A	N/A	N/A	Vacation, sick leave; medical, dental & life ins.; long-term disability; retirement; deferred comp.	Washington Public Employees Assoc.
West Virginia	High school or equiv.; physical agility test; criminal background check; written & personal interview; psychological test; 18 years old.	Requirements generally met.	$16,110	$19,500	N/A	30–40	Health ins.; retirement.	None

Wisconsin	18 years old; valid WI driver's license; civil service exam; able to bear firearms (no convicted felons).	Because of large number hired, applicants generally meet but do not exceed requirements.	$9.11/hr	N/A	500	350	Retirement; income, health & life ins.; accidental death; reimbursement; deferred comp; long-term care supplement major medical, dent.	Wisconsin State Employee Union—Security & Public Safety; AFSCME
Wyoming	High school or equivalent; able to complete all training.	Requirements generally met.	$1,391/mo.	$17,556.48	19	3	100% retirement; vacation & sick leave; 100% paid medical, dental, life; holiday bonus pay.	None
Federal Bureau of Prisons	Under age 37[a]; 9 semester hours graduate study in Criminology, Criminal Justice or related (GS-6) or 4 year course of study leading to bachelor's (GS-5).[b]	New appointees must meet requirements and most exceed them.	$23,915 (1995)[c]	$30,577 (as of 3/30/96)	1,335	320	Retirement; thrift savings plan; life ins.; annual & sick leave; public safety benefit for correctional officers killed in the line of duty.	Council of Prison Locals; American Federation of Government Employees
Canadian Systems								
Alberta	*No response*							
British Columbia	*No response*							
Manitoba	*No response*							
New Brunswick	*No response*							
Newfoundland	Canadian citizen; 19 years old; high school; mental & physical health certification; 2 year training program.	Officers generally meet requirement; however, increasing number exceed education requirement.	$23,945	$38,701	N/A	N/A	Uniforms; annual leave; holidays; pension plan; group insurance.	Newfoundland Assoc. of Public Employees
Northwest Territory	*No response*							
Nova Scotia	Grade 12; B.A. in sociology or psychology w/criminology certificate or 10-month correctional officers program.	Requirements generally exceeded; most new hires have the CO program and a degree.	$13.24/hr.	$31,900	0	0	Medical, dental, LTD, life ins.; pension plan; general illness; short-term illness; vacation; training, bereavement leave; maternity leave; parental leave.	Nova Scotia Government Employees' Union

(table continues)

TABLE 12.3 (continued)

System	Entry Requirements	How Often Met or Exceeded?	Annual Salary		New Hires		Benefits	Unions
			Starting	Average	1995	1996		
Ontario	Grade 12 or letter of equivalency; eligible to work in Canada; related post-secondary credentials, related work experience, volunteer work and employment history considered.	As the job market has grown increasingly higher due to the economic climate, more applicants exceed requirements.	$17.39/hr	$44,491.20	0	0	100% Health, hospital, life, short term sickness ins.; worker's comp; hearing & vision care; income protection; pension.	Ontario Public Service Employees Union
Prince Edward Island	Undergraduate degree in Human Services or diploma from recognized correctional program offered by community college.	Requirements generally met.	$24,500	$26,500	0 0	0	Pension plan; blue cross (medical, dental & optical); long-term disability; worker's comp.	Union of Public Sector Employees
Quebec	High school & 2 years post-secondary study; satisfy conditions of employment required by Police Act (LRQ, c.p. - 13), including medical exam.	Requirements generally exceeded.	$36,087	$40,600	0	0	Training; retirement after 32 years of service; meals & uniforms furnished; salary assurance (2 years).	Syndicat Des Agents De La Paix En Services Correctionnels du Quebec
Saskatchewan	*No response*							
Yukon Territory	Coursework in criminology, corrections, social science or related; ability to perform duties; cross-cultural awareness; first aid and CPR certification and valid driver's license.	Requirements generally met.	$40,056	$43,088	0	0	Vacation & sick leave; dental/medical coverage; pension plan; death benefit ins.; worker's comp; shift premiums; paid meals during shift, etc.	Public Service Alliance of Canada
Correctional Service of Canada	N/A	N/A	$14,609	$29,321 42,369	0	0	Vacation, family, maternity & sick leave; full pension at age 50 with 25 years service; health ins.	Public Service Alliance of Canada; Union of Solicitor General Employees

[a] Unless previously employed in federal civilian law enforcement position covered by special civil service retirement provisions.
[b] May substitute 1 year full-time specialized experience in correctional environment, law enforcement or mental health (GS-6) or 3 years general experience counseling, teaching, supervising, managing, instructing, persuasive sales, etc. (GS-5).
[c] According to "Fiscal Year-End 1995–2000 Workforce Forecast" report (March 29, 1995).

Source: Corrections Compendium (1996a:18–22).

2. *Communication dimensions* (dialogue skills—effectiveness of discussion in person-to-person or small group interactions; writing skills—expression of ideas in writing with facility)
3. *Emotional and motivational dimensions* (reactions to pressure—functioning in a controlled, effective manner under stress; keeping one's head; drive—amount of directed and sustained energy brought to bear in accomplishing objectives)
4. *Interpersonal dimensions* (insight into others—the ability to proceed giving due consideration to the needs and feelings of others; leadership—the direction of behavior of others toward the achievement of common goals by charisma, insights, or the assertion of will)
5. *Administrative dimensions* (planning—forward thinking, anticipating situations and problems, and preparation in advance to cope with these problems; commitment to excellence—determination that the task will be well-done, the achievement of high standards)

The Florida Assessment Center. In Dade County, Florida, the Department of Corrections and Rehabilitation was one of the first agencies to establish an assessment center to select entry-level officers (Stinchcomb, 1985:120). While this is not a new concept, the use of these centers in corrections recruitment and training is somewhat innovative. The Florida Assessment Center moves beyond traditional selection mechanisms such as the use of paper-pencil measures and standard personality, interests, and aptitude/IQ tests or inventories by examining a candidate's potential on the basis of the full scope of the job (Stinchcomb, 1985:122). A previously established job task analysis is made of the different correctional chores to be performed by the applicants. The following skills associated with corrections work of any kind have been identified:

1. The ability to understand and implement policies and procedures
2. The ability to be aware of all elements in a given situation and to use sensitivity to others and good judgment in dealing with the situation
3. The ability to communicate effectively

THE RECRUITMENT OF WOMEN IN CORRECTIONAL WORK

Women have had a particularly difficult time entering the correctional field. Until 1972, the practice of hiring men for correctional positions and excluding women for the same posts was unquestioned in most jurisdictions (Zimmer, 1986:1). However, throughout the 1980s and 1990s, increasing numbers of women have entered fields traditionally identified with men. Among the obstacles women have had to overcome, especially in correctional work, are resentments and opposition from administrative personnel and male correctional employees (Jurik, 1985). In-depth interviews with a sample of male and female correctional officers reveal that some of the barriers women encounter are informal organizational resistance and the lack of administrative support in hiring, training, and on-the-job experiences. Many male correctional officers retain traditional and stereotypical views that females cannot perform the prison guard role effectively. However, objective research investigations have shown that women tend to perform as well as men.

For instance, Walters (1993a) investigated 178 male correctional officers in four state prisons. He surveyed their attitudes toward female officers and toward corrections in general. Walters found that males tended to regard their female counterparts as competent and able to perform correctional work satisfactorily. Male officers with pro-woman attitudes stressed the quality of the working relationship they had with female officers, job satisfaction, custody orientation, educational level, and prison type. In some related research, Walters (1993b) found that a survey of 229 correctional officers yielded generally positive attitudes toward female correctional officers. Thus, it seems that at least in the jurisdictions studied by Walters, rank-and-file male attitudes toward female correctional officers are changing—and for the better.

Opposition to women as correctional officers stems from other sources in addition to administrators and male correctional personnel. Some male prisoners object to being supervised by females. They consider the female officer-male prisoner scenario an invasion of their right to privacy (Alpert and Crouch, 1991). Some court support exists for these inmate objections. In *Bowling v. Enomoto* (1981) and *Hudson v. Goodlander* (1980), lawsuits were filed by prison inmates alleging their constitutional right to privacy was violated as the result of females being posted to positions where they could view male inmates completely unclothed. In both cases, the court upheld the inmates' right to privacy and held that prisoners have a right to limited privacy in that they should be free from unrestricted observations of their genitals and bodily functions by prison officials of the opposite sex (Zimmer, 1986:7).

However, various courts have approved opposite-sex pat-down searches of male inmates by female correctional officers. For instance, inmates at the Nebraska State Penitentiary brought suit alleging that their right to privacy was violated when prison officials promulgated a rule permitting female officers to conduct pat-down searches of them. The court declared that such opposite-sex pat-down searches of male inmates by female correctional officers was not an unreasonable regulation based on security and equal employment considerations (*Timm v. Gunter,* 1990). The courts have drawn the line on opposite-sex strip searches, however. Generally, female correctional officers are prohibited from conducting strip searches of male prisoners (*Kennedy v. New York State Department of Correctional Services,* 1990).

Female correctional officers suffered a legal setback when the U.S. Supreme Court upheld an appeal by the Alabama Supreme Court that contended that women in maximum-security prisons present a risk to prison security. U.S. Supreme Court Justices decided in favor of Alabama and relied on the assumption that the mere presence of women in maximum-security prisons decreases prison security (Zimmer, 1986:6). However, these decisions have not deterred women from seeking employment in prison settings as correctional officers. While sex stereotyping continues, evidence suggests that it is lessening annually. More women are being selected for correctional officer positions, and gradually, salary discrepancies are being eliminated (Kerle, 1985). In 1995, about 18 percent of all correctional officers in U.S. jurisdictions were female (Camp and Camp, 1995a:70–71). And women are entering administrative posts as well. In 1996, 185 wardens and superintendents of prisons for adults were women, accounting for about 15 percent of all administrators (American Correctional Association, 1996a:xlvi).

Sexual Harassment Issues. In most jurisdictions, correctional officers are subjected to mandatory courses and issues dealing with sexual harassment and management strategies for different-sex supervision of male and female prison inmates (Bergsmann, 1991). Discrimination because of gender includes sexual harassment, which means unwelcome sexual advances, requests for sexual favors, and other verbal or physical conduct or communication of a sexual nature when

- Submission to such conduct or communication is made a term or condition either explicitly or implicitly to obtain employment, public accommodations or public services, education, or housing
- Submission to or rejection of such conduct or communication by an individual is used as a factor in decisions that affect such individual's employment, public accommodations or public services, education, or housing
- Such conduct or communication has the purpose or effect of substantially interfering with an individual's employment, public accommodations or public services, education, or housing, or creating an intimidating, hostile, or offensive employment (Brown and Van Ochten, 1990:64)

Female-Male Officer Differences in Job Satisfaction and Other Work-Related Factors. Reviews of the literature about women working as correctional officers suggest that women regard prisons as more stressful than their male officer counterparts (Wright and Saylor, 1991:505). Female officers tended to feel less safe than reports from male officers working in prison settings. Wright and Saylor (1991) mailed 8,099 surveys to about one half of all employees working in 46 federal prisons. In all, 3,325 usable surveys were returned, with a response rate of 41 percent. The survey administered was the *Prison Social Climate Survey,* which sought information about numerous job dimensions and factors. Generally, female and male officers reported similar job satisfaction levels. Women did not differ from men on the quality of supervision they received. Furthermore, women working in women's prisons do not have more positive work experiences than women working in men's prisons. Minority women also reported no significant differences in work experiences when compared with white female officers.

THE ORGANIZATION AND OPERATION OF PROBATION AND PAROLE PROGRAMS

Probation and parole departments in various states are administered by different agencies. Although most states have departments of corrections that supervise both incarcerated and nonincarcerated offenders, these tasks are sometimes overseen in other jurisdictions by departments of human services, departments of youth services, or some other umbrella agency that may or may not have the expertise to service these clients adequately.

During the 1980s and 1990s, a growing concern has been the professionalization of all correctional personnel (Sieh, 1990). When the President's Commission on Law Enforcement and Administration of Justice made its recommendations in 1967, in most jurisdictions there were few standards in place to guide administrators in their selection of new recruits. Thus, it was not unusual for critics of corrections to frequently make unfavorable remarks about, and unflattering characterizations of, those who manage criminals and oversee their behaviors.

Criticisms of Probation and Parole Programs

Officials believed in the early years of correctional reforms that the treatment or medical model was sound, and that rehabilitation on a large scale was possible for both incarcerated and nonincarcerated offenders. Rehabilitation was projected as the direct result of proper therapeutic programs and treatments. Educational and vocational-technical programs were coupled with group and individual counseling in prisons and jails. Offenders sentenced to probation were slotted for involvement in various training courses and assigned to programs designed to improve their self-concept, skills, and marketability as jobholders and breadwinners.

Criticisms of correctional personnel generally have centered on the inadequacy of their training, lack of experience, and poor educational background. Because of their similarities to corrections officers who perform inmate management chores, PO characteristics have implications for the quality of services delivered by probation and parole agencies. If it is true that a majority of POs enter this work with little or no training, that they lack the enthusiasm and energy to perform their jobs efficiently and effectively, and that they lack basic educational skills for dealing with offender-clients, then it may be that these factors significantly influence the quality of services delivered to offenders (Bishop, 1993:13–14). If probation and parole officers cannot cope effectively with the demands of their jobs because of their own limited resources and experiences, then suggested reforms involving their professionalization would be justified. Often underemphasized are people skills and the ability to cope with human problems, or those abilities required if officer effectiveness is to be improved (*Georgia*

Parole Review, 1990:174–176). Following are some of the major criticisms of probation and parole programs and personnel:

1. Until the early 1980s, only one state required a college education of probation or parole officer applicants, and some states had as their only prerequisite the ability to read and write, presumably for the purpose of completing PSI reports.
2. Past selection procedures for probation and parole officers have focused upon physical attributes and security considerations.
3. Probation and parole officer training has often been based upon the military model used for police training.
4. Probation and parole programs have historically been fragmented and independent of other criminal justice organizations and agencies.
5. The general field of corrections has lacked the professionalization associated with established fields with specialized bodies of knowledge.
6. Most jurisdictions have lacked licensing mechanisms whereby officers can become certified through proper in-service training and education.

Probation/Parole Officers: A Profile

Interacting with ex-offenders, visiting their homes or workplaces, and generally overseeing their behavior while on probation or parole is a stressful experience. The dangerousness associated with PO work is well-documented, and each day exposes most POs to risks similar to those encountered by police officers (Cullen et al., 1985). Of course, offenders are obliged to comply with probation or parole program requirements, whatever they might be, and to be responsive and accessible whenever POs wish to contact them.

The primary control mechanism operating to moderate offender behavior is the probation or parole revocation power possessed by POs. Although their recommendations for a parole or probation revocation are not binding on any body convened to hear allegations of violations against an offender, it is their report that initially triggers a revocation proceeding. An unfavorable report about an offender may involve a technical violation or a serious crime allegation. POs often overlook minor supervision violations, in part because they do not judge such violations to be serious, and also because they do not wish to prepare the extensive paperwork that is a preliminary requirement for a formal probation/parole revocation hearing. Despite the leverage POs have over their offender-clients, the possibility of violent confrontation ending with injury or death and of hostility from the public-at-large make PO work increasingly stressful and demanding.

Characteristics of Probation and Parole Officers. Who are probation and parole officers? What are their characteristics? Although little comprehensive information about POs exists, surveys have been conducted in recent years that depict the characteristics of those performing various

PO roles. These surveys indicate a gradual move toward greater PO professionalization. One indication of greater professionalization of POs has been the movement toward accreditation and the establishment of accreditation programs through the American Correctional Association (ACA) and the American Probation and Parole Association (APPA).

The *Corrections Compendium* (1990b) conducted a survey of parole officers in 1990, and the American Correctional Association (ACA) solicited information from its probation and parole officer membership in 1994. Whereas the responses may not necessarily be typical of *all* correctional personnel in the United States, the ACA boasts a membership of about a third of all correctional personnel nationwide. Over 10,000 ACA members responded and provided information about their age, educational level, and other pertinent information about their positions. Table 12.4 summarizes selected socioeconomic and job-related characteristics for these responding POs.

Most POs are male, white, possess bachelor's degrees, and have 9 to 12 years' experience. The length of employment for these POs is longer than the period suggested by others who note a high amount of turnover among POs. It may be that those belonging to the American Correctional Association are perhaps more committed to their work as evidenced through their membership in this voluntary professional association. Average PO annual salaries in 1994 ranged from $12,768 to $41,215. These salaries are slightly higher than those reported by Shirley Davis (1990) for POs surveyed in 1990 ($12,768–$34,560). In 1995 the average entry salaries for POs was $24,082, whereas the average maximum salary was $40,039 (Camp and Camp, 1995d:44–45). The actual salary range for POs in 1995 was from $15,948 (Tennessee) to $58,236 (California).

Table 12.4 Summary Characteristics for Probation and Parole Officers in the United States

	Percentage/Median	
Characteristic	*American Correctional Association*	*Corrections Compendium*
Age	34	36
Gender		
Male	64.4%	74.6%
Female	35.6%	25.4%
Educational Level	B.S.	B.S.
Length of experience	9–11 yrs	11–12 yrs
Average annual salary	$16,135–$41,215	$12,768–$34,560
Cultural background		
Caucasian	82.4%	80.2%
Black	9.6%	12.3%
Hispanic	4.1%	5.0%
Other	3.9%	2.5%

Source: "Survey I: Fourteen State Systems Reduce Correctional Officer Positions." *Corrections Compendium,* 17:7–20, 1990; *Corrections Today* "Survey" 1994.

The larger proportion of women in the *Corrections Compendium* survey is actually larger than the proportion of women in corrections generally. In 1995, 30.7 percent of all POs were women (Camp and Camp, 1995d:40). However, those pursuing PO careers have voiced the opinion that they must constantly prove themselves to their male coworkers (Walters, 1993a, 1993b). This greater aggressiveness among female POs *may* manifest itself in part through more frequent professional associations and memberships such as the ACA or APPA.

Most POs in the sample studied have a bachelor's degree as the median educational level attained. However, a majority of state systems, 29, require the bachelor's degree as the minimum educational level for entry-level parole officer positions. In many states, however, the general entry-level requirements for PO positions are less stringent. In 1990, sixteen jurisdictions required a bachelor's degree or "equivalent experience" (Su Davis, 1990b:7).

What Do POs Do? Although there have been definite gains in the selection, recruitment, and professionalization of POs, little has occurred simultaneously to cause them to change their attitudes about their work roles and relationships with offender-clients. The highest labor turnover among POs usually occurs during the early years of their employment (Camp and Camp, 1995d). Those anticipating changing careers will probably avoid these professional memberships, because they may perceive that the programs offer little or nothing of value for their advancement in other professions.

POs perform diverse functions (Ring, 1989:43–48). At least 23 different functions are associated with PO work. These include supervision, surveillance, investigating cases, assisting in rehabilitation, development and discussion of probation conditions, counseling, visiting homes and working with clients, making arrests, making referrals, writing PSI reports, keeping records, performing court duties, collecting fines, supervising restitution, serving warrants, maintaining contracts with courts, recommending sentences, developing community service programs, assisting law enforcement officers and agencies, assisting courts in transferring cases, enforcing criminal laws, locating employment for clients, and initiating program revocations (Burton, Latessa, and Barker, 1992: 277–280).

THE SELECTION REQUIREMENTS FOR PROBATION/PAROLE OFFICERS

Minimum educational requirements of those entering the correctional field in 1990 continued to be fairly low. About 78 percent of the jurisdictions required the G.E.D. or a high school diploma for an entry-level PO position, while 4 percent required either a community college (two years) diploma or

15 credit hours of college work. Because of the emphasis upon professionalization, it is surprising that 12 percent of the jurisdictions had no educational requirements as the minimum for entry-level PO positions (Su Davis, 1990b).

The examination processes for PO recruitment used in most jurisdictions for 1991 have been described by the American Correctional Association. Over 80 percent of the programs required a written examination, and only about 20 percent subjected recruits to psychological screening. The Minnesota Multiphasic Personality Inventory and Inwald Personality Inventory appear to be those most popularly applied, when any are used. Very few programs included physical examinations, medical checks, or FBI inquiries. Several programs had no formal testing or examination procedures with which to screen correctional officer candidates (American Correctional Association, 1991).

These programs place considerable emphasis on the legal liabilities of POs and other types of corrections officers. They also stress the cultivation of skills in the management and supervision of offender-clients. Programs are also offered for managing stress, crisis intervention and hostage negotiations, proposal and report writing, legal issues training, managing community corrections facilities, dealing with the mentally ill offender, and suicide prevention.

Currently most agencies require bachelor's degrees or equivalent experience, with an emphasis on a social science major. At least two states lack strenuous entry requirements. For instance, Minnesota requires applicants to pass a basic reading comprehension examination and a structured oral interview. In Nevada, POs must possess a high school diploma and have four years of experience, although the type of experience is unspecified. Nevada does offer prospective recruits the option of possessing a bachelor's degree in lieu of the four years of experience, however.

The Use of Firearms in Probation and Parole Work

Because the idea of POs carrying firearms is fairly new, not a great deal has been written about it. It is also too early to evaluate the long-range implications of PO firearms use in the field (Velt and Smith, 1993:17–20). More probation and parole officer training programs are featuring topics related to PO safety, especially in view of the shift from the medical model toward more proactive, client-control officer orientations (A. Smith, 1991b:38–39). Few professionals in criminology and criminal justice question that each generation of probationers and parolees includes more dangerous offenders (Lindner, 1992a). Largely because it is impossible at present to incarcerate everyone convicted of crimes, the use of probation and parole as front-end and back-end solutions to jail and prison overcrowding is increasing. Also increasing are reports of victimization from POs working with probationers and parolees in dangerous neighborhoods (Blauner and Migliore, 1992:21–23). It is *not* necessarily the case that probationer-clients or

BOX 12.1 Rapes by Correctional Officers

The Case of the "Long Island Lolita"

It happened at the Albion Correctional Facility in Buffalo, New York. In 1992, Amy Fisher, a teenager, was in love with Joey Buttafuoco, a businessman. Buttafuoco was married at the time. Fisher went to Buttafuoco's home when only Buttafuoco's wife was present. Fisher shot and seriously wounded Buttafuoco's wife in the head. Fisher was eventually convicted of attempted murder. She became known as the "Long Island Lolita" because of the notoriety the case was given by the media. She was ordered to serve a 5- to 15-year sentence.

While at the Albion Correctional Facility, Fisher had sex with several correctional officers. A convicted drug dealer and friend of Amy Fisher, Lillian "Lucky" Nieves, 38, told authorities later that the Albion facility was driving Fisher crazy, and that Fisher wanted to be transferred to another prison. Fisher believed that she would never be paroled while at Albion. In order to get transferred, Nieves said, Fisher decided to have sex with several correctional officers and then allege that she had been raped by them. Nieves said that all of the sex Fisher had with the officers was consensual.

In order to bolster her story about the alleged rapes by correctional officers, Fisher collected their semen following intercourse. She planned to present their semen later in court as evidence against them. "Lucky" Nieves added that she thought that Fisher also wanted to be closer to home than Albion. Neives said that Fisher is a manipulative liar who has been promiscuous with other female inmates.

If the allegations by Fisher are true, what should be the sanctions imposed against the correctional officers involved? Even if the sexual intercourse was consensual, is this proper conduct for correctional officers? What do situations like this say about men guarding women or women guarding men? What do you think?

Source: Adapted from the Associated Press, "Inmate Says Amy Fisher Willingly Had Sex with a Prison Guard." *Minot (N.D.) Daily News,* October 22, 1996:A2.

parolee-clients are becoming more aggressive or violent toward their PO supervisors, although there have been reports of escalating client violence against their supervising POs. The fact is that POs are obligated to conduct face-to-face visits with their clients, and that in many instances, these face-to-face visits involve potentially dangerous situations and/or scenarios (Lindner, 1992c). However, some evidence suggests that in the future there will be a decline in home visits as a standard PO function (Lindner, 1991:115).

Danger in Probation and Parole Work. Probation and parole work is hazardous and stressful (Holgate and Clegg, 1991). Among other things, probation and parole officers are authorized to conduct warrantless searches of their clients' premises at any time. Sudden intrusions into the apartments or homes of clients may be unwelcomed, and dangerous incidents may be created that jeopardize the lives of POs (Rackmill, 1993). A summary of the results of a nationwide survey conducted by the Federal Probation and Pretrial Officers Association in 1993 is shown below (Bigger, 1993:14–15). Increasing numbers of POs are frightened by the prospect of working in high-crime areas where their lives are in danger (Lindner and Bonn, 1996:22–23). The following types of assaults or attempted assaults against officers nationwide since 1980 were listed by the survey (Bigger, 1993:15):

Murders or attempted murders	16
Rapes or attempted rapes	7
Other sexual assaults or attempted sexual assaults	100
Shot and wounded or attempted shot and wounded	32
Uses or attempted use of blunt instrument or projectile	60
Slashed or stabbed or attempted slashed or stabbed	28
Car used as weapon or attempted use of car as weapon	12
Punched, kicked, choked, or other use of body/attempted	1,396
Use or attempted use of caustic substance	3
Use or attempted use of incendiary device	9
Abducted or attempted abduction and held hostage	3
Attempted or actual unspecified assaults	944
Total	2,610

Use of Firearms by POs Is Debatable. Should POs arm themselves during their visits with clients? When POs are surveyed, they are often evenly divided 50–50 on the question. Researchers conducting a study of 159 POs attending a state probation training academy in 1990 asked these officers their opinions about whether they should carry firearms during their visits with clients. The question "Should POs be given the legal option to carry a firearm while working?" was asked of these 159 POs. More than 59 percent of the officers believed that they should be permitted to carry a firearm on the job.

Jurisdictions vary in their opinions about firearms use during PO work. In California, for example, the Parole Division adopted a firearms policy in 1979 (Sluder, Shearer, and Potts, 1991:3–5). Many officers, as well as the public, believed that PO firearms possession and display during PO-client confrontations would lead to numerous shooting incidents, even deaths of officers and/or clients. During the next 12 years, however, there were a reported 7 unholsterings per month among California POs, and only one incident was reported of a gun being fired. *No* agents were killed or seriously injured during this period. The California Parole Division averaged 800 armed agents during this period, ranging from 250 in 1979 to 1,500 in 1990, with an average of 7,000 arrests per year (Smith, 1991a). One explanation for this record is that POs are taught to deal with increasingly dangerous offenders and to use various behavior modification techniques in their client encounters (Remington and Remington, 1987; Smith, 1991a).

Some of those opposed to POs carrying firearms believe that this could escalate a situation between a PO and an armed client to the point where injuries or deaths could occur. However, other professionals claim that changing offender populations have become increasingly dangerous and violent clientele (Schuman and Holden, 1989:7–8). A fundamental issue at the center of this controversy is the amount and type of training POs who will carry these firearms receive (Paparozzi and Bass, 1990:8–9). Some states (e.g., Florida) have authorized their POs to use firearms in 1992 (*Corrections Compendium,* 1992b, 1992c).

Negligent Training, Job Performance, and Retention. POs are increasingly liable for their actions taken in relation to their clients. Numbers of lawsuits filed against POs are becoming more commonplace. Many of these lawsuits are frivolous, but they consume much time and cause many job prospects to turn away from PO work (Jones and del Carmen, 1992). There are three basic forms of immunity: (1) **absolute immunity,** meaning that those acting on behalf of the state can suffer no liability while performing their state tasks (e.g., judges, prosecutors, and legislators); (2) **qualified immunity,** such as that enjoyed by probation officers if they are performing their tasks *in good faith;* and (3) **quasi-judicial immunity,** which generally refers to PO preparation of PSI reports at judicial request (Jones and del Carmen, 1992:36–37). In the general case, POs enjoy only qualified immunity, meaning that they are immune only when their actions were taken in good faith. However, there is some evidence that the rules are changing with regard to the types of defenses available to POs, although the limits of immunity continue to be vague and undefined. Jones and del Carmen (1992) have clarified at least two different conditions that seem to favor POs in the performance of their tasks and in the immunity that they derive from such conditions:

1. Probation officers are considered officers of the court and perform a valuable court function, namely the preparation of PSI reports.
2. Probation officers perform work intimately associated with court process, such as sentencing offenders.

Jones and del Carmen (1992) believe that it is unlikely that POs will ever be extended absolute immunity to *all* of their work functions. Subsequently, del Carmen and Pilant (1994:14–15) have described judicial immunity and qualified immunity as two types of immunity that are generally available to public officials, including POs. Judicial liability is like the absolute immunity described earlier. Judges *must* perform their functions and make decisions that may be favorable or unfavorable to defendants. Lawsuits filed against judges are almost always routinely dismissed without trial on their merits. Parole boards also possess such judicial immunity in most cases. In contrast, qualified immunity ensues only if officials, including POs, did not violate some client's constitutional rights according to what a reasonable person would have known (del Carmen and Pilant, 1994:14).

Liability Issues Associated with PO Work. A summary of some of the key liability issues related to PO work follows.

1. Some information about a probation/parole officer's clients is subject to public disclosure and some information is not.
2. Probation/parole officers have a duty to protect the public; their work in this regard may subject them to lawsuits.
3. Probation/parole officer use of firearms may create hazards for both POs and their clients.
4. Probation/parole officers may supervise their clients in a negligent manner.
5. Probation/parole officer PSI report preparation may result in liability.
6. Liabilities against probation/parole officers and/or their agencies may ensue because of negligent training, negligent retention, and deliberate indifference to client needs.

This listing describes the major situations in which POs incur potential problems from lawsuits. Jones and del Carmen (1992:36) and Sluder and del Carmen (1990:3–4) suggest at least three different types of defenses used by POs when performing their work. These defenses are not perfect, but they do make it difficult for plaintiffs to prevail under a variety of scenarios:

1. POs were acting in good faith while performing the PO role.
2. POs have official immunity, since they are working for and on behalf of the state, which enjoys sovereign immunity.
3. POs may not have a "special relationship" with their clients, thus absolving them of possible liability if their clients commit future offenses that result in injuries or deaths to themselves or others.

PROBATION/PAROLE OFFICER CASELOADS

The caseload of a probation or parole officer is considered by many authorities to affect the quality of supervision POs can provide their clients. **Caseloads** refer to the number of offender-clients supervised by POs. Caseloads vary among jurisdictions (Su Davis, 1990b:16). Seemingly, the larger the caseload, the poorer the quality of supervision and other services. Intensive probation supervision (IPS), for instance, is based on the premise that low offender caseloads maximize the attention POs can give their clients, including counseling, employment, social, and psychological assistance. The success of such IPS programs suggests that lower caseloads contribute to lower recidivism rates among parolees and probationers.

Ideal Caseloads

No one knows the ideal caseload. Actual caseloads of POs vary greatly, ranging from a low of 5 or 10 clients to a high of 400 clients (Su Davis, 1990b:7). After evaluating caseloads of POs in a variety of jurisdictions, Gottfredson and Gottfredson (1988:182) have concluded that "it may be said with assurance . . . that (1) no optimal caseload size has been demonstrated, and (2) no clear evidence of reduced recidivism, simply by reduced caseload size, has been found." This declaration applies mainly to standard probation/parole supervision, and it is not intended to reflect on the quality of recent ISP programs established in many jurisdictions. Because the composition of parolees and probationers varies among jurisdictions, it is difficult to develop clear-cut conclusions about the influence of supervision on recidivism and the delivery of program services. An arbitrary caseload figure based upon current caseload sizes among state jurisdictions would be about 30 clients per PO, perhaps closest to an ideal caseload size.

Changing Caseloads and Officer Effectiveness

Can Smaller PO Caseloads Increase PO Effectiveness? The *frequency* of contacts between POs and their clients is sometimes less important than the *quality* of these contacts. Frequent face-to-face contacts help POs determine whether clients are observing curfew rules and are staying away from drugs and other illegal substances. POs can make a significant difference in the lives of their clients to the extent that they can connect clients with prospective employers or assist clients when filling out job application forms.

A classic study of the effectiveness of probation was the San Francisco Project, an investigation of the federal probation system in the 1960s (Banks et al., 1977). Probationers were assigned to POs with varying caseloads. Some POs had caseloads of 20 offenders, and other POs had caseloads of 40 offenders. The ideal level of supervision was considered 40 clients, whereas 20 probationers as a caseload was considered intensive. The San Francisco Project showed *no differences* in probation supervision effectiveness when the intensity of supervision was increased. Greater offender monitoring through the lower caseload assignments merely made it possible for officers to spot more technical violations committed by probationers.

However, some offenders benefited immeasurably by POs who were able to spend more time with them. Some POs are good listeners and function as emotional outlets for offenders with special problems. The primary benefit to probationers from greater contact with their POs was the more personalized attention they received. No substantial impact was made on client recidivism, however.

One explanation for these nonsignificant findings is that there is not a great deal of difference between 20 and 40 clients as a PO caseload. In many jurisdictions, these respective caseloads are considered *close supervision,* where POs can see their clients monthly. In those jurisdictions where POs have 400 or more clients, such as in California, we might expect significant differences in recidivism rates in cases where POs supervise 400 clients as opposed to those jurisdictions where POs supervise only 40 or fewer clients.

Caseload Assignment Models

Various caseload assignment schemes for POs have been described (Carlson and Parks, 1979). These include (1) the conventional model, (2) the numbers game model, (3) the conventional model with geographic considerations, and (4) the specialized caseloads.

1. *The Conventional Model.* The **conventional model** involves the random assignment of probationers or parolees to POs. The conventional model is the one used most frequently in probation and parole agencies throughout the United States. The major drawback is that POs must be extremely flexible in their management options, because of the diversity of clientele they must supervise.

2. *The Numbers Game Model.* The **numbers game model** involves dividing the total number of clients by the number of POs. If there are 1,000 offenders and 20 POs, 1,000÷20 = 50 offenders per PO. For offenders who require some continuing contact with an agency but not a high degree of intervention, *group reporting* seems to be an economical way of supervising these offenders. Group reporting is conducted in Anoka County, Minnesota, through the Community Corrections Department (Soma, 1994).

3. *The Conventional Model with Geographic Considerations.* The **conventional model with geographic considerations** is applied on the basis of the travel time required for POs to meet with their offender-clients regularly. Those POs who supervise offenders in predominantly rural regions are given lighter caseloads so that they have the time to make reasonable numbers of contacts with offenders on a monthly or weekly basis.

4. *The Specialized Caseloads Model.* The **specialized caseload model** takes advantage of the unique skills and knowledge relative to drug or alcohol dependencies of some POs. Others have had extensive training and education to better serve certain offender-clients who may be retarded or mentally ill (Leonardi and Frew, 1991). Some POs by virtue of their training may be assigned to more dangerous offenders and can manage dangerous offenders more effectively than can fresh new PO recruits. In some respects, this amounts to *client-specific planning,* in which individualization of cases is stressed (Yeager, 1992:537–544). Interviews with ex-offenders and clients in New York found that their interactions with parole officers were particularly useful in helping them to avoid contacts with gangs and other criminal influences for the duration of their parole programs (Duggan, 1993). They credited parole officer support and assistance in enabling them to lead productive and law-abiding lives.

Correctional Officer Stress and Burnout

Correctional Officer Stress. Stress is a nonspecific response to a perceived threat to an individual's well-being or self-esteem (Selye, 1976). These stress responses are not specific, and each person reacts differently to the same stress-triggering situation. People react differently to stress, with somatic complaints of aches and pains, whereas others may exhibit irritability, loss of attention span, or fatigue (Cornelius, 1994). What is stressful for one person may not be stressful to another. Several factors, including one's previous experiences with the event, constitutional factors, and personality may function to mediate the stress and one's reaction to the event (Holgate and Clegg, 1991).

Some stress is good. A moderate amount of stress enhances the learning and creative processes, whereas too little stress may induce boredom or apathy (Whitehead, 1989). We don't know for sure, however, how much stress is too much. We do know that correctional officers have twice the national average divorce rate. They also have the highest heart attack rates among all types of state employees, including police officers (Moracco, 1985:22). These statistics appear to result directly from the stressful aspects of corrections work.

However, Patterson (1992) found that 4,500 police, correctional officers, and POs exhibited a *curvilinear relationship* between perceived stress and time on the job. This might be interpreted as follows: considerable stress exists among many of these officers in their early years on the job, followed by a decline in stress. Eventually, this stress increases as on-the-job experience increases.

Sources of Stress. Stress among correctional officers and other professionals emanates from several sources. Stress researchers have targeted the following as the chief sources of stress among POs: (1) job dissatisfaction; (2) role conflict; (3) role ambiguity; (4) officer-client interactions; (5) excessive paperwork and performance pressures; (6) low self-esteem and public image; and (7) job risks and liabilities (Stohr et al., 1994; Walters, 1993a, 1993b).

1. *Job dissatisfaction.* Job dissatisfaction is somewhat unwieldy, as it occurs as the result of a variety of factors (Gray and Wren, 1992). Specific reasons for dissatisfaction among correctional officers have been identified by Cheek and Nouri (1980) and include the following:

a. Lack of clear guidelines for job performance
b. Institutional policies not being clearly communicated to all staff members
c. Crisis situations
d. Conflicting orders from supervisors
e. Having to do things against your better judgment
f. Having your supervisor give you things to do that conflict with other things you have to do
g. Not being treated as a professional
h. Low morale of other officers
i. Lack of training
j. Officers not being quickly informed about policy changes
k. Criticism from supervisor in front of clients
l. Poor physical conditions and equipment
m. Having too little authority to carry out assigned responsibilities
n. Not being kept well-informed by the immediate supervisor
o. Not having adequate sharing of information among all officers
p. Not receiving adequate pay
q. Not having a chance to develop new talents
r. Feelings of pressure from having to please too many bosses
s. Lack of opportunity to participate in decision making

2. *Role conflict.* Mills (1990:3–6) summarizes many of the feelings of correctional officers who sense the frustrations of **role conflict:** "Nobody said it would be like this"; "Why do you think they call them cons?"; "If there is a problem, see the probation officer"; "How am I doing so far?"; "I never took this job to get rich"; and "Will this ever end?" Mills (1990:7) says that for the correctional officer, it is important to maintain a freshness and enthusiasm toward the career.

3. *Role ambiguity.* Closely related to role conflict is role ambiguity. **Role ambiguity** occurs whenever correctional officers have inadequate or even conflicting information about their work roles, the scope and responsibilities of the job, and the ethics of certain unwritten practices that are commonplace among many correctional officers (Brown, 1987:20; Wehmhoefer, 1993:8–9). On-the-job training can do much to clarify one's work role, however (Stohr, Stohr-Gilmore and Lovrich, 1990).

4. *High correctional officer risks and liabilities.* Some risk is inherent when working with dangerous inmates (Brown, 1994; Johnson and Jones, 1994). Many inmates were convicted of aggravated assault, murder, rape, or some other type of violent crime and may pose a degree of risk to the personal safety of correctional officers.

Burnout. Burnout is one result of stress. Maslach (1982b:30–31) has identified at least 15 different connotations of the term:

1. A syndrome of emotional exhaustion, depersonalization, and reduced personal accomplishment that can occur among individuals who do "people work" of some kind.
2. A progressive loss of idealism, energy, and purpose experienced by people in the helping professions as a result of the conditions of their work.
3. A state of physical, emotional, and mental exhaustion marked by physical depletion and chronic fatigue, feelings of helplessness and hopelessness, and the development of a negative self-concept and negative attitudes toward work, life, and other people.
4. A syndrome of inappropriate attitudes toward clients and self, often associated with uncomfortable physical and emotional symptoms.
5. A state of exhaustion, irritability, and fatigue that markedly decreases the worker's effectiveness and capability.
6. To deplete oneself. To exhaust one's physical and mental resources. To wear oneself out by excessively striving to reach some unrealistic expectations imposed by oneself or by the values of society.
7. To wear oneself out doing what one has to do. An inability to cope adequately with the stresses of work or personal life.
8. A malaise of the spirit. A loss of will. An inability to mobilize interests and capabilities.
9. To become debilitated, weakened, because of extreme demands on one's physical and/or mental energy.
10. An accumulation of intense negative feelings that is so debilitating that a person withdraws from the situation in which those feelings are generated.
11. A pervasive mood of anxiety giving way to depression and despair.
12. A process in which a professional's attitudes and behavior change in negative ways in response to job strain.
13. An inadequate coping mechanism used consistently by an individual to reduce stress.
14. A condition produced by working too hard for too long in a high-pressure environment.
15. A debilitating psychological condition resulting from work-related frustrations, which results in lower employee productivity and morale.

The importance of burnout is that it signifies a reduction in the quality or effectiveness of an officer's job performance (Patterson, 1992). Debilitating reductions in effectiveness are often accompanied by higher recidivism rates among probationers and parolees, more legal problems and case filings from officer-inmate interactions, and greater labor turnover among correctional officers (Stinchcomb, 1986:22).

Some variables, such as gender, age, amount and type of education, length of job-related experience, self-esteem, marital status, and the degree of autonomy and job satisfaction, function as intervening ones (Virginia Department of Corrections, 1987). The social support system is made up of others who perform similar tasks as well as the frequency of contact with these people for the purpose of sharing the frustrations of work. These factors form a mosaic from which stress stems. Stress is manifested by physiological, psychological, and/or emotional indicators. Burnout may result. One important consequence of burnout may be labor turnover.

Correctional Officers and Labor Turnover. Burnout and stress occur among correctional officers, especially during the first year of their duties. Turnover rates are as high as 38 percent in some jurisdictions, such as Arkansas, during the first year of an officer's employment. Some experts recommend the use of more experienced correctional officers as mentors for new recruits (T. Wright, 1993). Between 1990 and 1995, turnover among correctional officers ranged from a low of 9.6 percent in 1991 to a high of 14.6 percent in 1990. In 1995 the turnover was 11.6 percent, meaning that on the average, about 11.6 percent of all correctional officers left corrections work and entered other professions or positions (Camp and Camp, 1995a:77).

Recruiting the right kinds of personnel to perform correctional officer roles is designed to identify those most able to handle the stresses and strains accompanying the job. The concern about occupational stress has been rising steadily in recent years (Olekalns, 1985). Virtually all occupations and professions have varying degrees of associated stress. Probation and parole work is not immune from stress and burnout. Whitehead and Gunn (1988:143) studied 400 probation and parole officers in various states and found that they tended to offer more negative than positive comments about their work.

Alleviating Stress and Burnout. Many authorities believe that probation and parole organizations and agencies are at fault in creating dangerously high stress and burnout levels among correctional officers and other correctional employees (Huckabee, 1992). Some experts say that it is virtually impossible to prevent burnout among POs, regardless of their coping strategies and mechanisms, and that it is possible for the organization to implement changes to minimize it (R. Thomas, 1988). If organizational heads will recognize what causes stress and burnout, they have a better than even chance of dealing with it effectively (Wright and Sweeney, 1990).

One strategy for alleviating stress and burnout is to permit correctional officers greater input into organizational decision making, such as using their knowledge of prison culture to establish more secure inmate policies and correctional officer safety (Unsinger and More, 1990). This is often accomplished through participative management. **Participative management** is the philosophy of organizational administration by which substantial input is solicited from the work staff and used for decision making purposes where one's work might be affected. Thus, subordinates' opinions become crucial to organizational decision making as lower-level participants are given a greater voice in how the organization is operated or administered (Champion, 1975; Shirley Davis, 1990).

Greater employee involvement in the decision-making process relating to offender treatment and supervision is stressed by participative management (Cushman and Sechrest, 1992). Generally, a lack of participation in decision making is a key source of stress and burnout (Shirley Davis, 1990). Correctional officers often say that their supervisors focus only on the negative aspects of work performed. Interviews with correctional officers in a study conducted in 1984 showed that many officers believed that they were either not recognized by their superiors or only given attention "when something goes wrong" (Stinchcomb, 1986:22). When supervisors provide criticisms only for work improperly done and leave work of good quality unnoticed, the morale of personnel suffers greatly (Brown, 1987).

Supervisors are regarded as pivotal in most organizations for reducing employee stress. Shapiro (1982) indicates some ways by which supervisors can reduce stress levels of correctional officers:

1. Leadership that provides support, structure, and information
2. Communication that is timely, appropriate, and accurate
3. An environment that is efficient and orderly
4. Rules and policies that are explicit
5. Workers who have freedom to be self-sufficient and make their own decisions
6. Room for staff creativity and innovation
7. Support and nurturing from supervisory staff
8. Manageable job pressure
9. Peer networks of friendship and support among staff

Probation/Parole Officer Labor Turnover

PO work is often not what new recruits had in mind when they began working for probation or parole agencies. New PO recruits think that PO work frequently involves meaningful interactions with offenders who want to be helped, and POs must provide counseling and assistance to offenders. They believe they must supervise offender progress and influence the course of an offender's program. They believe they will have minimal paperwork and spend most of their time in helping capacities. However, most POs spend a great deal of their time preparing PSIs, performing routine checks of their clients' premises and workplaces, and furnish courts with periodic up-dated information about offender progress. One's writing skills seem more highly valued than one's interpersonal skills. This is a major disenchantment for many new PO recruits.

Many POs leave their positions during their first few years. They report that they considered the work temporary, as a position to be held while they seek better-paying jobs in the private sector (Philliber, 1987). Since the educational requirements are not particularly demanding, probation and parole work is fairly easy to obtain. Holding a job with some degree of responsibility is considered an asset on one's vita or resume, especially for those looking forward to working in other professions after they have acquired work experience in a related field.

VOLUNTEERS IN COMMUNITY CORRECTIONS

There is little information about volunteers in correctional work. Winter (1993:22) says that **volunteers** are people helping people. Margaret A. Moore, Deputy Commissioner assigned to the Central Region of the Pennsylvania Department of Corrections, has given some breadth to Winter's definition by noting that "volunteers are integral to correctional programming . . . *they are hardworking, dedicated individuals who fill in the gaps for correctional agencies and provide much-needed services that victims, inmates, parolees, probationers and their families might otherwise not receive because of limited funding for programs*" (Moore, 1993:8, italics added).

Thus, a **corrections volunteer** is any unpaid person who performs auxiliary, supplemental, augmentative, or any other work or services for any law enforcement, court, or corrections agency. Corrections volunteers vary greatly in their characteristics and abilities, in their ages, and in their functions. For instance, Girl Scouts, ages 12 to 16, work closely with female inmates and their children at the Maryland Correctional Institution for Women in Jessup, Maryland (Moses, 1993:132). Girl Scouts play with the daughters of female inmates during twice monthly Girl Scout troop meetings. Troop projects are planned as well as future activities, where female inmates and their daughters may become involved and experience more intimate bonding not ordinarily possible under penal conditions (Codelia and Willis, 1989:168–170).

What Do Corrections Volunteers Do? Some volunteers are retired school teachers who work with jail and prison inmates to assist them in various kinds of literacy programs (Tracy, 1993:102). The Gray Panthers, an organization of elderly volunteers, provide various services and programs specifically targeting older inmates (Lehman, 1993:84). Some volunteers, such as septuagenarian Brigitte Cooke in Huntington, Pennsylvania, work with death row inmates or those serving life sentences. Her services include spiritual guidance, support, and compassion (Love, 1993:76–78).

How Many Correctional Volunteers Are There? A Gallup Poll conducted in 1989 revealed that an estimated 98.4 million Americans volunteered an average of four hours per week. Between 1987 and 1989, the number of adult volunteers increased by 23 percent. The use of volunteer services in criminal justice settings is at best uneven (Winter, 1993:20). A 1987 estimate by Wayne Lucas suggests that between 300,000 and 500,000 citizen volunteers were involved in community corrections in approximately 2,000 to 3,000 jurisdictions (Lucas, 1987:63). In subsequent years, the literature suggests that the number of correctional volunteers has dramatically increased (American Correctional Association, 1992a; Bayse, 1993; Hawk et al., 1993). For instance, in the Alston Wilkes Society, a nonprofit agency that assists offenders, former offenders, and their families in South Carolina, boasts a volunteer component of at least 5,000 persons

(Walker, 1993:94). Approximately 3,000 volunteers work in various capacities with the Pennsylvania Department of Corrections (Lehman, 1993:84). The Federal Bureau of Prisons uses at least 4,000 volunteers in different ways for institutional and community corrections services.

Examples of Correctional Volunteer Work

One volunteer program is presently underway in 19 Connecticut prisons. At the Brooklyn, Connecticut, Community Correctional Center, several female volunteers work daily with groups of 11 or 12 female inmates in producing quilts. Fabric is cut, and six sewing machines are used to produce brightly decorated quilts that are subsequently distributed to children and families of female inmates. The program is known as ABC, which stands for At-Risk Babies Crib (Wheeler, 1993:136). This project started in August 1992. It was patterned after programs in 39 other states.

Another volunteer program designed for working with female offenders, both in prison and in community-based programs, is called *The Program for Female Offenders.* This program provides for volunteers who visit the Allegheny County, Pennsylvania, Jail three times a week and the State Correctional Institution at Muncy on a less frequent but regular basis (Arnold, 1993:120). Incarcerated women are assisted by volunteers who help them adjust to prison life. Certain family and legal problems may be dealt with, using the volunteers as intermediaries. For those women who have been recently released, the agency operates a training center, two residential facilities, and a day treatment program. All of these facilities are located in Pittsburgh (Arnold, 1993:120).

Arnold (1993:120–122) notes that volunteers deserve special recognition for the unpaid services they perform, including the following functions:

1. Serving as tutors at the skill training center and handling most GED preparation;
2. Providing transportation to parenting sessions at their residential centers;
3. Teaching women hobby skills such as knitting, sewing, and dressmaking;
4. Teaching computer and job search skills at the skill training center; and
5. Providing gifts for women and their children every Christmas.

Often, these tasks lead to friendships between volunteers and inmate/clients. Arnold also advises that it is important to place volunteers in positions where they will feel safe and comfortable. She suggests the following guidelines (1993:122):

1. Don't take offenders home or lend them money.
2. Don't share your troubles with offenders.
3. Learn to listen effectively.
4. Don't try to solve offenders' problems.
5. Don't make judgments.

6. Report irregular behavior to the agency staff. This is not being disloyal.
7. Don't provide drugs or alcohol to offenders.
8. Don't always expect to be appreciated.
9. Do have empathy and patience.
10. Do care.

Criticisms of Volunteers in Community Correctional Work

Volunteer Naiveté. Unusual situations arise from time to time where inmates and other types of offenders might harm volunteers or be harmed by the very volunteers trying to help them. One problem that is cited frequently by critics of correctional volunteerism is volunteer naiveté. John Kramer, a professor of sociology at Pennsylvania State University, says that sometimes volunteers are asked to serve as mediators between inmates and their spouses or to contact inmates' attorneys. Whenever these volunteers attempt to do things that they are not trained to do (e.g., marriage counseling), their well-intentioned, do-gooding may go awry and prison staff may regard them as a "pain" (Rose, 1988:218).

Volunteers Should Not Make Long-Term Commitments with Clients. Because of the voluntary, unpaid nature of volunteer work, many volunteers may be in correctional settings for brief periods, tire of their activities, and leave.

Volunteers Should Not Work Independently. Some volunteers in the Missouri Division of Probation and Parole were reluctant to work independently with individual probationers and parolees. Thus, a regular PO would be required to monitor or supervise volunteer-client relations. This necessitated a considerable and unnecessary expenditure of valuable time on the part of the supervising PO, who was often overworked with heavy caseloads and numerous other required duties.

Volunteers Lack Experience. A chief concern of POs in the Missouri Division of Probation and Parole was that volunteers lacked general knowledge about the specific rules and policies of the Division. Some volunteers did not know how to handle unusual developing scenarios between themselves and particularly troublesome clients (Lucas, 1987:72). If offenders were violating program rules, volunteers experienced difficulty reporting them for these infractions. Volunteers were thus more easily manipulated than regular POs.

Information-Sharing with Volunteers Is Limited. A dim view is taken of disclosing confidential information about offender-clients to volunteers. Most volunteers are not credentialed. They do not carry badges and other formal documentation to initiate formal client inquiries. They may use the information they obtain in ways that harm clients rather than help them.

Volunteers Threaten Job Security. If volunteers supplement the work performed by full-time staff, then some of the full-time staff may not be needed in the future years.

Volunteers Are Unpaid and Less Motivated. Unpaid personnel who work with corrections agencies on a voluntary basis are under no special obligation to adhere to specific working hours or schedules.

Volunteers Contribute to Criminal Activity. A local pastor regularly brought church members into the prison for worship services together with inmates (Bayse, 1993:16). He allowed a woman from a nearby church to join the group one Sunday at the last moment. The pastor did not know that the woman was wearing *two dresses and a wig.* When she excused herself to go to the bathroom, an inmate discreetly followed her and outfitted himself in her extra dress and wig. Dressed as a woman, he returned with her to the church group and left with them when they exited the prison. He was apprehended a few days later.

Programs that use volunteers may attract persons who may endanger specific types of clientele, such as children. Pedophiles and child sexual abusers may volunteer to work in community corrections programs where young children are involved. If these child molesters are allowed to work around children, considerable harm might result to the children involved. Interviews with prospective volunteers who want to work with children are not foolproof.

Ogburn (1993:66) suggests the following safeguards to screen volunteers:

1. Evaluate the need for volunteers.
2. Develop goals and job descriptions for volunteers.
3. Involve staff together with volunteers as teams.
4. Actively recruit volunteers more selectively.
5. Educate volunteers about inmates and how volunteers might be manipulated.
6. Explain security needs to volunteers.
7. Give volunteers the big picture of where they fit in and how they can best fulfill the organizational mission.
8. Evaluate program effectiveness.
9. Recognize your volunteers' contributions.

Bayse (1993:48–50) adds that volunteers should observe the following rules and regulations:

1. Use appropriate language. Don't pick up inmate slang or vulgarity. Using language that isn't a part of your style can label you a phoney.
2. Do not volunteer if you are a relative or visitor of an inmate in that institution.

3. Do not engage in political activities during the time voluntary services are being performed.
4. Do not bring contraband into prison. If you are not sure what is contraband, ask the staff. People who bring in contraband are subject to permanent expulsion and/or arrest.
5. Do not bring anything into or out of a facility for an inmate at any time, no matter how innocent or trivial it may seem, unless the written permission of the superintendent is given. Volunteers should adopt a policy of saying no to any request by an inmate to bring in cigarettes, money, magazines, or letters. If in doubt, ask a staff member.
6. Keep everything in the open. Do not say or do anything with an inmate you would be embarrassed to share with your peers or supervisors.
7. Do not give up if you failed at your first try. Try again.
8. Don't overidentify. Be a friend, but let inmates carry their own problems. Be supportive without becoming like the inmates in viewpoint or attitude.
9. Do not take anything, including letters, in or out of a correctional facility without permission. Respect the confidentiality of records and other privileged information.
10. Do not bring unauthorized visitors or guests with you to the institution. They will be refused admission.
11. Do not give out your address or telephone number. If asked, you might say, "I'm sorry, but I was told that it was against the rules to do that."
12. Do not correspond with inmates in the facility in which you volunteer or accept collect telephone calls from them at your place of residence.
13. Be aware that the use of, or being under the influence of, alcohol or drugs while on institution grounds is prohibited.
14. Don't impose your values and beliefs on inmates. Do not let others impose a lower set of values on you.
15. Don't discuss the criminal justice system, the courts, inconsistency in sentencing or related topics. Although everyone is entitled to his or her own opinion, what volunteers say can have serious repercussions in the dorms or with staff.
16. Ask for help. If you are uncertain about what to do or say, be honest. It is always best to tell the inmate that you will have to seek assistance from your supervisor. Inmates don't expect you to have all the answers.
17. Know your personal and professional goals. Be firm, fair, and consistent.
18. If you have done something inappropriate, tell your coordinator regardless of what happened. It is far better to be reprimanded than to become a criminal.

The Legal Liabilities of Volunteers and Agencies Using Them

Lawsuits against agencies because of volunteer conduct are not infrequent. They are diverse and may include negligence in training, hiring, assignment, supervision, entrustment, and retention (Williams, Callaghan, and Scheier, 1974). Officers may be liable to third parties for injuries caused by offenders or by program volunteers, and liability to offenders may occur because of unauthorized or inappropriate record disclosures, injuries in job performance, and offender physical injuries caused by volunteers (del Carmen and Trook-White, 1986).

Volunteers may incur liability as the result of (1) improper record disclosures, (2) injuries inflicted on clients in job performance, and (3) injuries sustained while on the job. Some volunteers obtain liability insurance as a hedge against potential lawsuits for any wrongful acts that they might commit (del Carmen and Trook-White, 1986).

PARAPROFESSIONALS IN COMMUNITY CORRECTIONS PROGRAMS

A corrections **paraprofessional** is someone who possesses some formal training in a given correctional area, is salaried, works specified hours, has formal duties and responsibilities, is accountable to higher-level supervisors for work quality, and has limited immunity under the theory of agency. Agency is the special relation between an employer and an employee whereby the employee acts as an agent of the employer and is able to make decisions and to take actions on the employer's behalf (Black, 1990:62). Black (1990:1112) also defines a paraprofessional as "one who assists a professional person though not a member of the profession himself."

Training of Paraprofessionals

Paraprofessionals perform valuable services for professionals working in the same correctional endeavors (Gaudin, 1993; McCarthy and McCarthy, 1997). It is difficult to profile the education and training of all paraprofessionals as an aggregate. Rather, specific categories of paraprofessionals are more easily described. Third-year law school students may "clerk" for attorneys as paraprofessionals, since they have acquired sufficient legal expertise to look up cases and brief them for use in courtroom arguments.

Paraprofessionals who are responsible for maintaining surveillance with various juveniles involved in a home detention program in Tuscaloosa, Alabama, in 1977 have been described by Smykla and Selke. These youth workers are authorized to send juveniles directly to secure confinement when they fail to meet program requirements. These rules include regular school attendance, curfew, restraint in the use of drugs or alcohol, avoidance of companions or places that might lead to trouble, and notification of parents or workers as to their whereabouts at all times when not in school, at home, or at work (Smykla and Selke, 1982). Responsibilities of paraprofessionals in this program included regular one-on-one, face-to-face visits with each juvenile daily, together with personal or telephonic contacts with parents, teachers, and/or employers.

Criticisms of Paraprofessionals

Because paraprofessionals are hired employees of various corrections agencies, their liability coverage is very similar to that of volunteers. Organizations using both volunteers and paraprofessionals are subject to lawsuits in the event that an action by a paraprofessional or volunteer results in damages to inmates or offender-clients. These damages may be monetary, physical, or intangible, such as psychological harm. Title 42, Section 1983 of the U.S. Code (1997) outlines various types of civil rights violations that might be used as bases for lawsuits. The bases for different lawsuits by offender-clients are allegations of negligence and include the following (Barrineau, 1994:55–58):

1. Negligent hiring (e.g., organization failed to "weed out" unqualified employees who inflicted harm subsequently on an inmate or probationer/parolee)
2. Negligent assignment (e.g., employee without firearms training is assigned to guard prisoners with a firearm; firearm discharges, wounding or killing an inmate)
3. Negligent retention (e.g., an employee with a known history of poor work and inefficiency is retained; subsequently, work of poor quality performed by that employee causes harm to an inmate or offender-client)
4. Negligent entrustment (e.g., employee may be given confidential records and may inadvertently furnish information to others that may be harmful to inmates or offender-clients)
5. Negligent direction (e.g., directions may be given to employees that are not consistent with their job description or work assignment; this may result in harm to inmates or offender-clients)
6. Negligent supervision (e.g., employee may supervise prisoners such that inmate problems are overlooked, causing serious harm and further injury or death to inmate or offender-client)

Minimizing lawsuits against paraprofessionals and other employees of correctional agencies can be accomplished through more adequate training. Barrineau (1994:84) lists several criteria:

1. The training was necessary as validated by a task analysis.
2. The persons conducting the training were, in fact, qualified to conduct such training.
3. The training did, in fact, take place and was properly conducted and documented.
4. The training was state-of-the-art and up-to-date.
5. Adequate measures of mastery of the subject matter can be documented.
6. Those who did not satisfactorily "learn" in the training session have received additional training and now have mastery of the subject matter.
7. Close supervision exists to monitor and continually evaluate the trainee's progress.

KEY TERMS

Absolute immunity
Assessment centers
Burnout
Caseload
Conventional model
Conventional model with geographic considerations
Correctional officer
Corrections volunteers
Numbers game model
Paraprofessionals
Participative management
Qualified immunity
Quasi-judicial immunity
Role ambiguity
Role conflict
Specialized caseloads model
Stress
Volunteers

QUESTIONS FOR REVIEW

1. What is stress? What are some manifestations of stress?
2. What is burnout? What are some common meanings of burnout? What causes burnout and how can it be dealt with effectively?
3. How does education relate to burnout and stress? What can organizational administrators do to alleviate the stresses and accompanying burnout associated with PO work?
4. What are various common sources of stress? What is it about the PO role that triggers unusually high stress levels?
5. What is the source and nature of role conflict associated with the officer-client relation?
6. What are some of the mitigating factors that can alleviate burnout and stress?
7. What seems to account for comparatively high levels of labor turnover in corrections work in relation to other occupations or professions? How do many correctional officers perceive their work and what reasons do they cite for leaving it?
8. Is there an ideal caseload for a PO? How are caseloads determined?
9. Identify and describe four types of caseload assignment methods.
10. How does the size of caseload relate to a PO's effectiveness?
11. What are some of the dilemmas associated with the PO role? Why is role conflict an inherent part of this role?

SUGGESTED READINGS

Bayse, Daniel J. *Helping Hands: A Handbook for Volunteers in Prisons and Jails.* Laurel, MD: American Correctional Association, 1993.

Corrections Today. Entire issue deals with volunteers in various dimensions of corrections. Volume 55 (August). Laurel, MD: American Correctional Association, 1993.

Morris, Norval, and Michael Tonry. *Between Prison and Probation: Intermediate Punishments in a Rational Sentencing System.* Chicago: University of Chicago Press, 1990.

Palmer, Ted. *The Re-Emergence of Correctional Intervention: Developments Through the 1980s and Prospects for the Future.* Thousand Oaks, CA: Sage, 1992.

13

Women and Corrections

CHAPTER OUTLINE

OVERVIEW

This chapter is about female offenders and the correctional institutions that house them. Typically, this area has been neglected by criminal justice analysts and correctional experts, and these women have increasingly been referred to as the **forgotten offenders** (Fletcher, Shaver, and Moon, 1993). One major reason for this neglect is the fact that women accounted for only about 10.2 percent of all jail inmates in 1995, whereas they accounted for only 7.4 percent and 6 percent of the federal and state prison populations respectively that same year (Gilliard and Beck, 1996:6, 10). The average daily population of women in U.S. jails in 1995 was 455,098; there were 7,398 and 61,146 federal and state female prisoners.

Because their numbers are so small, female inmates have not been given sufficient attention by state legislatures. The development of prisons and jails for women in the United States has been slow. Most prisons and jails have been designed almost exclusively for male offenders. Provisions for women, including separate accommodations, bathing facilities, and different recreational, vocational, and educational opportunities have been slowly implemented by administrators of co-correctional institutions. And in many co-correctional institutions, programs and facilities for women are limited compared with programs and facilities for their male counterparts.

Men are incarcerated more than 20 times as often as women, although women account for about 25 percent of all arrests for index crimes (Maguire and Pastore, 1996). In recent years, however, crime trends have shown increasing numbers of female arrests and incarcerations, although these numbers continue to be small in relation to proportionate numbers of arrests and incarcerations of male offenders. This does not necessarily mean that there is a new female crime wave, or that women are necessarily committing more crime than they have committed proportionately in past years. It may mean, for instance, that police are changing their attitudes about how women should be treated (Ortega and Burnett, 1987:158–159). It may also be the result of the women's movement, by which women's ideologies have been transformed and greater opportunities now exist for them to commit more crime. And, it might also mean that a growing proportion of women in the U.S. population is giving the appearance of more crime among women (Ortega and Burnett, 1987:158). Whatever the explanation, increased numbers of female arrests and incarcerations have drawn public attention to the plight of prisons for women and to the differential treatment women receive in co-correctional institutions. These and other related issues will be examined here.

This chapter discusses the history and evolution of women's prisons in the United States. Some selected characteristics of female prisoners will be described as well as some of the classification problems officials have encountered in devising appropriate programs for females. Similar to prisons for men, women's prisons have a distinct subculture apart from that imposed by administrative policies and rules. This subculture is examined as well. Administrators of prisons for women or those co-correctional prisons with separate facilities and programs for women must create and maintain useful, rehabilitative, educational, and vocational programs that can benefit women when they are released and seek employment. Many women admitted to prisons and jails are also mothers. Judges and others are hesitant in separating mothers from their children, and some prison accommodations permit prolonged mother-child interactions. Also, many women enter prison pregnant and require prenatal and postnatal care. Some of the administrative efforts to cater to the special needs of female offenders are described.

Large numbers of women are diverted from the criminal justice system or receive probation. Probation often means assignment to some form of intermediate punishment, including intensive supervised probation, possibly electronic monitoring or home confinement. Some of these options available to women are examined. Finally, an evaluation of corrections for women is made. Are women re-offending at a rate similar to their male counterparts? Is there any evidence that the prison or jail experience does anything to deter women from becoming recidivists? These questions also are examined.

THE HISTORY OF WOMEN'S PRISONS IN THE UNITED STATES

Rachel Welch didn't know it at the time, but her unfortunate plight at the Auburn, New York, prison in 1826 did much to advance women's correctional reforms throughout the United States. Welch was a prisoner at the Auburn State Prison. She and many other women like her were herded into a large attic room in the prison where they were confined without benefit of recreation or even limited freedom for 24 hours a day. Food was sent up once from the kitchen daily, and "slops" were removed once a day as well (Rafter, 1983a:135). One of the Auburn State Prison correctional officers raped Welch, impregnated her, and, after learning that she was five months' pregnant, flogged her so severely that she died soon afterward from the wounds. A committee investigated her death, and although the facts about what had occurred were unclear and inconsistent testimony was presented, the condition of women at Auburn was publicly revealed (Hunter, 1984). Several religious and philanthropic organizations intervened and pressed for various reforms that would improve significantly the conditions under which women were housed.

It is ironic that the death of a female inmate occurred in a "modern prison" touted for its correctional accomplishments and farsightedness in prisoner planning. It will be remembered that Auburn introduced the congregate system whereby prisoners could work and socialize daily for recreational, dining, and labor purposes, and that during evening hours, prisoners were kept isolated from one another in solitary cells. That is, these innovations were exclusively for men. Even at the "modern" Walnut Street Jail where separate quarters for women and men had been suggested several decades earlier, conditions had degenerated by the 1820s such that women at the Walnut Street facility were no better off than the women at Auburn.

The conditions for women at Auburn and other similar institutions were criticized initially by religious and philanthropic organizations not because of their substandard and deplorable living accommodations. Rather, these common living areas were considered conducive to moral degeneration and widespread promiscuity. Male correctional officers had virtually unlimited social and sexual access to all incarcerated females. While increasingly segregated celling accommodations were gradually introduced for female inmates, male correctional officers continued to carry the keys to their individual cells. Thus, as Rafter suggests, segregation of female prisoners from male prisoners was not a foolproof method of birth control (Rafter, 1983a:136–137).

The first major prison for women was established in 1835 in New York, a few years after the organization of the **Magdalen Society** (1830), a women's prison reform-oriented movement. The facility was called the Mount Pleasant Female Prison (Rafter, 1983a:138). Rafter (1983a:138–139) says this facility was important for at least three reasons:

1. Mount Pleasant was the first and only penal institution for women before the great era of prison construction starting in the late 1800s.
2. Mount Pleasant was managed initially by women and significant internal operational and administrative improvements were made, thus increasing the quality of life for incarcerated women.
3. Mount Pleasant was an almost exclusively custodial facility providing a place for New York's female prisoners; New York simply ran out of other places to house its female convicts.

In fact, the Mount Pleasant Female Prison typified a prevalent model for women's prisons during the 1790 to 1870 period: the custodial model. Rafter (1983a) has divided the historical evolution of prisons for women into three general categories, paralleling particular penal developments and innovations and different treatment-therapeutic emphases for each period. These models and their characteristics as outlined by Rafter are shown below:

Model	Time Period	Features*
Custodial Model	1790–1870	Confinement, containment, discipline and uniformity
Reformatory Model	1870–1935	Reformation, reintegration, skill acquisition, moral and social improvement.
Campus Model	1935–present	Diffuse goals, skill acquisition including cosmetology, reform, parenting, office skills, arts, crafts

Divisions such as those proposed by Rafter are not necessarily universally recognized "stages" of women's penal developments. Prison administrators did not meet collectively in 1935 and say, "We are now entering the 'campus model' era of female correctional reforms and will discontinue the 'custodial model.'" A few U.S. prisons for women today continue to reflect predominantly custodial and reformatory policies, although the dominant correctional theme for women has shifted dramatically in the last half century.

Rather, these models are useful constructs that help us conceptualize and understand the emphasis of specific programs and objectives of women's prisons during particular time periods. Frequently, these developments coincide with the correctional thinking of the period. When we attempt to explain why women and men were treated or mistreated in certain ways while incarcerated, the explanation is almost always related to the dominant correctional philosophy of the period.

The mother of corrections for women in the United States was a Quaker Englishwoman, **Elizabeth Gurney Fry.** She traveled extensively, advocating prison reforms for women. On the basis of her experiences with women's prisons in Europe and elsewhere, she published an important work, *Observations in Visiting, Superintendence and Government of Female Prisons* in 1827. Her work was widely acclaimed by other prison reformers. Influenced by John Howard, another prominent prison reformer, she continued her reformist efforts until her death in 1845. She encouraged separate facilities for women, religious and secular education, improved classification systems for female prisoners, and rehabilitative and reintegrative programs emphasizing the learning of practical skills.

When Fry was conducting her personal visits to correctional facilities throughout the world, the custodial model was dominant. Little thought was given by prison officials to the rehabilitation of female offenders. Coin-

* Adapted from Rafter, 1983a.

cidentally in the year of Fry's death, the Women's Prison Association was established. This philanthropic organization led to the sponsorship of the Hopper Home, a halfway house for female ex-convicts. Hopper Home, in New York City, is considered the oldest halfway house for female offenders (Feinman, 1986:36). Attempts by matrons at prisons such as Sing Sing in New York to incorporate Fry's ideas met with resistance from other prison administrators, and the custodial model was continued until the early 1870s.

It will be remembered that the National Prison Association (later the American Correctional Association) met in Cincinnati in 1870 to consider proposals from various correctional experts about new ways of treating prisoners, both male and female. The meeting was attended by prison reformers, superintendents of prisons, wardens, theorists, criminologists, academicians, and humanitarians who believed that the prisons of the future ought to emphasize reform, reintegration, and rehabilitation. The Irishman Walter Crofton was present, as was Zebulon Brockway, the first superintendent of Elmira Reformatory in 1876. Interestingly, a major prison for women based upon the principles of the new reform era was created in Indiana in 1873, three years prior to the construction of the Elmira facility (Freedman, 1981). One major difference between the Indiana Women's Prison and the Mount Pleasant Female Prison was the fact that the Indiana institution was established as a reformatory facility, not just a custodial one. Thus, using the general schema proposed by Rafter, U.S. prisons for women, although few in number, entered the reformatory period. Table 13.1 shows state and federal correctional institutions for women from 1873 through 1973. Table 13.2 shows subsequent women's prisons constructed in various states and the Federal Bureau of Prisons.

Table 13.1 shows several interesting things. First, between 1913 and 1934, 19 women's prisons were built for various states and the federal government. Yet, for a similar two-decade period following 1934, only seven women's prisons were constructed. Many of the prisons for women during the 1913 to 1934 period were constructed during the height of Prohibition. This extensive construction may have been prompted by the influx of large numbers of male offenders into state and federal prison facilities because of liquor law violations or bootlegging. We know that during the Prohibition Era, prison overcrowding at the state and federal levels was extensive, and female prison construction might have been one way of alleviating certain logistical problems such as accommodating increased numbers of female bootleggers or their companions in the same prison settings.

In any case, the construction of women's prisons during the 1920s and 1930s did much to alleviate the problems of prison administrators who were seeking solutions to the co-correctional arrangements they were increasingly obligated to provide (Rafter, 1990). These new construction programs were not necessarily accompanied by new correctional innovations, however. In fact, many of the programs commenced in the late 1800s in women's reformatories were continued on a large-scale basis. Today, the

TABLE 13.1 State and Federal Correctional Institutions for Women, by Date of Opening

Date of Opening	State	Name at Opening
1873	Indiana	Women's Prison
1877	Massachusetts	Reformatory Prison for Women
1887	New York	House of Refuge for Women, Hudson
1893	New York	House of Refuge for Women, Albion
1902	New York	Reformatory Prison for Women Bedford Hills
1913	New Jersey	State Reformatory for Women
1916	Maine	Reformatory for Women
1916	Ohio	Reformatory for Women
1917	Kansas	State Industrial Farm for Women
1917	Michigan	State Training School for Women
1918	Connecticut	State Farm for Women
1918	Iowa	Women's Reformatory
1920	Arkansas	State Farm for Women
1920	California	Industrial Farm for Women
1920	Minnesota	State Reformatory for Women
1920	Nebraska	State Reformatory for Women
1920	Pennsylvania	State Industrial Home for Women
1921	Wisconsin	Industrial Home for Women
1927	United States	Industrial Institution for Women (now Federal Reformatory for Women)
1929	Delware	Correctional Institution for Women
1930	Connecticut	Correctional Institution for Women
1930	Illinois	State Reformatory for Women
1932	Virginia	State Industrial Farm for Women
1934	North Carolina	Correctional Center for Women
1936	California	California Institution for Women
1938	Kentucky	Correctional Institution for Women
1938	South Carolina	Harbison Correctional Institution for Women
1940	Maryland	Correctional Institution for Women
1942	Alabama	Julia Tutwiler Prison for Women
1948	West Virginia	State Prison for Women
1954	Puerto Rico	Industrial School for Women
1957	Georgia	Rehabilitation Center for Women
1960	Missouri	State Correctional Center for Women
1961	Louisiana	Correctional Institute for Women
1963	Ohio	Women's Correctional Institution
1964	Nevada	Women's Correctional Center
1965	Oregon	Women's Correctional Center
1966	Tennessee	Prison for Women
1968	Colorado	Women's Correctional Institute
1970	Washington	Purdy Treatment Center for Women
1973	Oklahoma	Women's Treatment Facility
1973	South Carolina	Women's Correctional Center

Source: Adapted from *Their Sisters' Keepers,* by E. Freedman, pp. 144–145. Copyright © 1981 by the University of Michigan. Reprinted by permission of the University of Michigan Press.

TABLE 13.2 Women's Prison Construction 1973–1995

Tucker Unit for Women (1983) Arkansas
Northern California Women's Facility (1987) California
Pueblo Minimum Center (1994) Colorado
Janet S. York Correctional Institution (1994) Connecticut
Jefferson Correctional Institution (1990) Florida
Metro Correctional Institution (1980) Georgia
Pulaski Correctional Institution (1994) Georgia
Washington Correctional Institution (1994) Georgia
Metro Transitional Center (1980) Georgia
Pocatello Women's Correctional Center (1994) Idaho
Indiana Women's Prison (1973) Indiana
Rockville Training Center (1995) Indiana
Iowa Correctional Institution for Women (1982) Iowa
Crane Women's Facility (1985) Michigan
Scott Correctional Facility (1986) Michigan
Minnesota Correctional Facility (1986) Minnesota
Central Mississippi Correctional Facility (1986) Mississippi
Chillicothe Correctional Center (1981) Missouri
Women's Correctional Center (1982) Montana
New Mexico Women's Correctional Facility (1989) New Mexico
Black Mountain Correctional Center for Women (1986) North Carolina
Fountain Correctional Center for Women (1984) North Carolina
Neuse Correctional Institution (1994) North Carolina
Raleigh Correctional Center for Women (1988) North Carolina
Wilmington Residential Facility for Women (1986) North Carolina
Mabel Bassett Correctional Center (1974) Oklahoma
State Correctional Institution at Cambridge Springs (1992) Pennsylvania
Women's Division (1978) Rhode Island
Leath Correctional Institution-Women (1991) South Carolina
Lois M. DeBerry Special Needs Facility (1992) Tennessee
Gatesville Unit (1980) Texas
Hilltop Unit (1980) Texas
Hobby Unit (1989) Texas
Mountain View Unit (1975) Texas
Neal Unit (1995) Texas
Lockhart (1994) Texas
Plane Facility (1995) Texas
Burnet Unit (1995) Texas
Women's Correctional Facility (1988) Utah
Brunswick Work Center (1995) Virginia
Pocahontas Correctional Unit (1995) Virginia
Wyoming Women's Center (1977) Wyoming
Federal Prison Camp (1988) Federal Bureau of Prisons, Texas

vast majority of female offenders are housed in prisons modeled after these early reformatories. Either intentionally or unintentionally, these prison programs continue to perpetuate a degree of structurally induced sexism (Ross and Fabiano, 1985).

But such massive prison construction for women during that time period had its drawbacks. Many of these prisons are still being used today (Florida Joint Legislative Management Committee, 1995). Thus, like many of the prisons for men, they are outdated, unhealthy, substandard, and inadequate for meeting the diverse needs of today's female prisoners (Culliver, 1993). Furthermore, prison conditions for women have been challenged with extensive litigation in recent years (Knight, 1992). It seems that prisons for women have bred their own jailhouse lawyers (Palmer, 1997; Quinlan et al., 1992). This should not be taken to mean that no improvements have occurred in prisons for women. On the contrary. Many contemporary facilities are designed to make available a wide variety of vocational and educational programs for women that depart from stereotypical trades or occupations. In 1984, the American Correctional Association adopted a national correctional policy applicable to female offenders that has been influential in prompting legislators and others to ensure that needed reforms in female facilities are implemented. However, many female inmates are mothers, and women's prisons typically lack facilities that can accommodate inmate mothers and the special problems they create (Clark, 1995).

Subsequent to 1973, there were at least 44 new women's prisons constructed in the United States, as shown in Table 13.2. This figure does not include contemplated construction of additional women's prisons in various jurisdictions. Interestingly, this subsequent growth of women's prisons (1973–1995) has produced more prisons for women than all prisons for women combined for the years 1873 to 1973.

ACA Guidelines for Women's Prison Construction and Programming. A guiding principle of the ACA guidelines and recommendations is the parity of services for male and female offenders. These services include traditional programs for pregnant women, child and family services, programs to establish homes and sound family relations and maintain family ties. Additionally, nontraditional programs have been recommended, including career counseling, nontraditional vocational training, social and economic assertiveness, and a full range of diversion, probation, and parole services (Florida Joint Legislative Management Committee, 1995). Evidence of the campus model is not only found in new women's prison construction, but in the layout and arrangement of women's quarters and work accommodations (Carp and David, 1991). The Mississippi State Penitentiary at Parchman has constructed a new women's facility on 17,000 acres originally designed to house male inmates in different levels of close custody. Four residential facilities for women were constructed, each with a capacity for housing 50 inmates. Besides a typical dayroom, counseling offices, and other critical prison elements, four living units have been provided specifically for mother/child visitations. These are apartment-like units that parallel closely real-life living conditions on the outside (Maxey, 1986:141–142).

Although there have been significant improvements in the quality of life in women's prisons, gaps in how female prisoners are accommodated are apparent among the states (Fuller, 1993). Some experts say that while women have won several important legal battles in court on prison improvements, these improvements either have not been implemented or have been implemented very slowly (Benekos and Merlo, 1992). In some states, such as Hawaii, a 775 percent increase in women prisoners was reported between 1975 and 1987, with few accompanying improvements in either housing or social services (Chesney-Lind, 1987). However, several jurisdictions including Massachusetts are making significant progress at instituting and maintaining innovative programs that seek to reintegrate females into society and reestablish their familial associations (Rocheleau, 1987a, 1987b).

CHARACTERISTICS OF FEMALE OFFENDERS

How Many Female Federal and State Prison Inmates Are There? What are female prisoners like in the United States? Other than gender, do they differ from their male counterparts by committing less violent offenses? Are they younger? Are there more black than white females behind bars? This section describes some of the characteristics of incarcerated state and federal female offenders. Table 13.3 shows the number of women under the jurisdiction of state or federal correctional authorities, year-end 1995 (Gilliard and Beck, 1996:6). As can be seen from Table 13.3, women make up only a small percentage of these prison populations. Only 7,398 female inmates were institutionalized by the Federal Bureau of Prisons in 1995 (7.4 percent), whereas 61,146 female inmates were incarcerated in state prison systems that same year (6.9 percent) (Gilliard and Beck, 1996:6).

What are the Characteristics of Female Prison Inmates? Table 13.4 (see p. 522) shows the characteristics of female inmates for the comparison periods of 1986 and 1991 (Snell and Morton, 1994:2). Table 13.4 shows that about half of all female inmates in prison in 1991 were between 25 and 34 years of age, with nearly half (45 percent) never married. About 53 percent were unemployed at the time they were arrested. Nearly half (46 percent) were black and 14 percent were Hispanic. White female inmates made up about 36 percent of the female prison population. Over 60 percent had not completed high school. Interestingly, these proportions have changed very little between 1986 and 1991.

Female prison inmates are profiled according to their conviction offenses in Table 13.4. Females were incarcerated most frequently in 1991 for violent offenses (32.2 percent) and drug offenses (32.8 percent). There were significantly fewer female property offenders incarcerated between 1986 and 1991. In 1986, 41.2 percent of all female inmates were convicted of property crimes, while this proportion dropped to 28.7 percent in 1991. However, females incarcerated for violent offending dropped from 40.7 percent in 1986 to 32.2 percent in 1991. A third significant finding is that the proportion of women incarcerated for drug offenses rose from 12 percent in 1986 to 32.8 percent in 1991. These figures suggest that incarcerated women are increasingly drug offenders, and that the proportions of incarcerated female violent and property offenders are dramatically declining, at least between the years 1986 and 1991. To some extent, at least, this dispels the idea that

TABLE 13.3 Women Under the Jurisdiction of State or Federal Correctional Authorities, Year-End 1995

Region and Jurisdiction	Number of Female Inmates	Percent of All Inmates	Percent Change in Female Inmate Population, 1994–1995	Prison Incarceration Rate, 1995[a]
U.S. total	68,544	6.1%	6.5%	47
Federal	7,398	7.4%	3.6%	4
State	61,146	6.0	6.9	43
Northeast	8,397	5.2%	3.3%	29
Connecticut	975	6.6	–2.4	34
Maine	46	3.2	–4.2	6
Massachusetts	657	5.7	–6.9	13
New Hampshire	107	5.3	–2.7	18
New Jersey	1,307	4.8	11.9	32
New York	3,615	5.3	1.1	39
Pennsylvania	1,501	4.6	13.5	24
Rhode Island	157	5.4	4.7	10
Vermont[b]	32	—	—	6
Midwest	10,852	5.6%	9.7%	34
Illinois	2,196	5.8	21.1	36
Indiana	892	5.5	8.0	30
Iowa	425	7.2	21.1	29
Kansas	449	6.4	30.5	34
Michigan	1,842	4.5	–8.9	37
Minnesota	223	4.6	–5.9	9
Missouri	1,174	6.1	12.7	43
Nebraska	194	6.2	10.2	21
North Dakota	29	4.8	81.3	8
Ohio	2,793	6.3	9.3	49
South Dakota	133	7.1	29.1	35
Wisconsin	502	4.5	21.8	18
South	27,471	6.0%	4.2%	55
Alabama	1,295	6.3	6.7	56
Arkansas	544	5.8	–6.2	42
Delaware	357	7.4	26.6	44
Dist. of Col.	487	5.0	–29.1	133
Florida	3,660	5.7	19.3	49
Georgia	2,036	5.9	1.2	54
Kentucky	734	6.1	15.2	37
Louisiana	1,464	5.8	13.1	62
Maryland	1,079	5.0	3.9	38
Mississippi	827	6.4	27.6	55
North Carolina	1,709	5.8	44.5	41
Oklahoma	1,815	10.0	12.9	108
South Carolina	1,045	5.3	2.3	51
Tennessee	637	4.2	8.5	23
Texas	7,935	6.2	–10.2	77
Virginia	1,718	6.2	9.8	50
West Virginia	129	5.1	41.8	13
West	14,426	6.7%	12.5%	45
Alaska	232	6.6	6.4	40
Arizona	1,432	6.7	12.5	60
California[c]	9,082	6.7	—	52

TABLE 13.3 (continued)

Region and Jurisdiction	Number of Female Inmates	Percent of All Inmates	Percent Change in Female Inmate Population, 1994–1995	Prison Incarceration Rate, 1995[a]
Colorado	713	6.4	6.4	37
Hawaii	312	8.8	21.4	39
Idaho	212	6.4	23.3	35
Montana	65	3.6	–30.1	15
Nevada	565	7.2	28.1	70
New Mexico	297	7.1	55.5	27
Oregon	465	5.9	22.7	18
Utah	161	4.7	22.9	16
Washington	793	6.8	13.6	29
Wyoming	97	6.9	18.3	40

—Not calculated.
[a] The number of female prisoners with a sentence of more than 1 year per 100,000 female residents on December 31, 1995.
[b] Custody-only counts were reported for the first time in 1995.
[c] Jurisdiction counts were reported for the first time in 1995.
Source: Gilliard and Beck (1996:6).

there has been a prominent escalation of female violent offending during the 1980s and early 1990s.

CLASSIFICATION OF FEMALE OFFENDERS

The question of how sophisticated the measures designed to classify female offenders as to risk, either for proper placement in a prison or jail or for selective incapacitation, is presently unanswerable (Quay and Love, 1989). This is because 90 percent or more of the studies of selective incapacitation, risk predictions, and screening decisions for determining the appropriate level of custody have simply excluded women from consideration. This exclusion is not necessarily deliberate or sexist. Rather, it is probably because there are so few women in prisons and jails that most researchers have not bothered to devise classification schemes or prediction devices for them.

When prediction devices have been devised, they have usually been tailor-made for male offender audiences and then tested to see whether they work for females (Hunter, 1984). For instance, in 1983, the Missouri Department of Corrections evaluated the reliability and validity of the Initial Classification Analysis, a device for determining the treatment plan and institutional assignments (level of custody based on risk or dangerousness) for male inmates. Inmate records were inspected, tests were administered, and interviews were conducted with the nearly 10,000 male inmates in Missouri prisons. Medical and health needs, educational needs, work skills, and proximity to residence/family ties were considered in these

TABLE 13.4 Characteristics of State Prison Inmates, by Sex, 1991 and 1986

	Percent of Female Inmates		Percent of Male Inmates	
Characteristic	1991	1986	1991	1986
Race/Hispanic origin				
White non-Hispanic	36.2	39.7	35.4	39.5
Black non-Hispanic	46.0	46.0	45.5	45.2
Hispanic	14.2	11.7	16.8	12.7
Other[a]	3.6	2.5	2.3	2.5
Age				
17 or younger	.1	.2	.7	.5
18–24	16.3	22.3	21.6	26.9
25–34	50.4	50.5	45.5	45.5
35–44	25.5	19.6	22.6	19.4
45–54	6.1	5.5	6.6	5.2
55 or older	1.7	1.8	3.2	2.5
Median age	31 years	29 years	30 years	29 years
Marital status				
Married	17.3	20.1	18.1	20.4
Widowed	5.9	6.7	1.6	1.6
Divorced	19.1	20.5	18.4	18.0
Separated	12.5	11.0	5.9	5.8
Never married	45.1	41.7	55.9	54.3
Education[b]				
8th grade or less	16.0	16.5	19.6	20.9
Some high school	45.8	49.7	46.2	50.6
High school graduate	22.7	19.1	21.9	17.7
Some college or more	15.5	14.8	12.3	10.8
Prearrest employment				
Employed	46.7	47.1	68.5	70.1
Full time	35.7	37.1	56.5	58.4
Part time	11.0	10.0	12.0	11.7
Unemployed	53.3	52.9	31.5	30.0
Looking	19.2	22.0	16.2	17.8
Not looking	34.1	30.9	15.3	12.2
Number of inmates	38,796	19,812	672,847	430,604

Note: In 1991, data were missing on marital status for 1.1% of cases, on education for 0.8%, and on prearrest employment for 0.7%. In 1986, data were missing for race and Hispanic origin for 0.4% of cases, on marital status for 0.1%, on education for 0.4%, and on prearrest employment for 0.5%.

[a] Includes Asians, Pacific Islanders, American Indians, Alaska Natives, and other racial groups.

[b] Based on highest grade completed.

Source: Snell and Morton (1994:2).

evaluations. Subsequently, institutional assignments were made. The following year, 120 female inmates processed at the Missouri Diagnostic Center were given the Initial Classification Analysis instrument and assigned to various Missouri penal facilities on the basis of their scores. The results disclosed that the instrument was "a reliable and objective instrument" for security classifications of female inmates (Robins et al., 1986). Missouri is not alone in this practice.

It might be expected that those states with large female offender populations will be at the vanguard in the development of classification instruments. Yet in states such as California (which leads all states in the absolute number of female inmates), the state of the art on classification and prediction is at best uncertain for all offenders, male or female (Baird and Austin, 1986; Petersilia and Turner, 1987).

Finally, recidivism figures exhibit a male bias. Those types of offenders most likely to recidivate are labeled "persistent felony offenders." Most of these are males. In Wisconsin, for example, a comparison was made between female and male ex-convicts on their rate of recidivism during a two-year period following parole. Female offenders recidivated only 18 percent compared with 32 percent for males. Furthermore, their crimes were nonviolent, passive, and low risk (e.g., forgery, theft, fraud) compared with male recidivists, who tended to commit violent crimes (e.g., robbery, assault, rape, and murder) (Wisconsin Department of Health and Social Services, 1989). Therefore, little incentive exists for administrators to create elaborate schemes to differentiate female offenders from one another for assignments to various custody levels (Knight, 1992).

DeCostanzo and Scholes (1988:108) have examined the needs of female offenders in prison settings. They note that "despite correctional policymakers' growing awareness concerning female offenders, 5 percent of a state's total inmate population is comprised of women who are handicapped, substance abusers, parents, the unskilled, and elderly. Each subgroup requires a unique response to its characteristics and needs. The challenges before us are complicated." Since many women's prisons in the United States are in desperate need of improvements unrelated to specific programs and plans that cater to special female offender problems, it may be expecting too much of most jurisdictions to establish fully equitable accommodations for all inmates within a short time period (Morash, Haarr, and Rucker, 1994).

Another problem that complicates the parity issue is that in most jurisdictions the female offender population changes fairly rapidly. While increasing numbers of females are incarcerated, the duration of their incarceration is shorter, on the average, compared with male offenders. This statement also holds for parolees and the length of male and female parole programs (Minor-Harper and Innes, 1987). With more rapid turnovers in the types of female inmates in state and federal prisons, inmate needs change as well. Again, it is difficult for state prisons to plan for every contingency for both the male and female incarcerated populations (DeCostanzo and Scholes, 1988:106). Thus, classification devices may only be effective for short-term assessments and placements (Hunter, 1984). Greater reliance upon the private sector in selected areas may be in order if these women's facilities are to offer a range of programs and services commensurate with those currently offered in all-male prison settings.

FEMALE CRIME TRENDS

Moyer and Giles (1993) note that there were 12,000 women in prison in 1979, 32,700 in 1988, and 43,000 in 1992. Most are single mothers who are the sole support of their dependent children (Bloom, 1993; Radosh, 1988). Thus, there are compelling needs to preserve the mother-child bonds while women are confined. The first part of this chapter examines female probationers and parolees. This includes a description of the various kinds of programs established to meet the needs of female offenders, including women with dependent children.

FEMALE PROBATIONERS: A PROFILE

In 1992, females accounted for 15 percent of all probationers and 8.3 percent of all parolees (Maguire, Pastore, and Flanagan, 1993:570, 661). Table 13.5 shows the distribution of conviction offenses for women on probation for 1992, while Table 13.6 shows the percentage distribution of females, by conviction offense, paroled for the same year.

Table 13.5 shows that for 1992, 15 percent of all probationers in the United States were women. Women comprised 9 percent of all probationers convicted of violent offenses. It is clear from Table 13.5 that women were most represented proportionately in various property offense categories, such as fraud (42 percent) and larceny (21 percent). Overall, women made up 18 percent of all probationers convicted of property offenses. Reading between the lines, this figure suggests that on the average, women are sentenced to probation more often than men. But this is likely attributable to the fact that male and female offenders have different offending patterns. Males are involved to a greater degree in violent offending, while females are involved to a greater degree in property offending. Another explanation

TABLE 13.5 Percentage of Female Offenders on Probation for Selected Offense Categories, 1992

Offense	Percentage Female
All Offenses	15
Violent Offenses	9
Murder	15
Rape	3
Robbery	7
Assault	11
Property Offenses	18
Burglary	5
Larceny	21
Fraud	42
Drug Offenses	15
Other	14

Source: Maguire, Pastore, and Flanagan, 1993:570.

TABLE 13.6 Conviction Offenses for Women on Parole in 34 States, 1992

Offense	Percentage[a]
All Offenses	8.3
Violent Offenses	16.1
Murder	3.8
Rape	0.2
Robbery	6.8
Assault	4.3
Property Offenses	40.3
Burglary	6.4
Larceny	16.6
Fraud	14.3
Drug Offenses	37.1
Other	2.0

[a] Percent does not equal 100% because of selected offenses; not all offenses included.

Source: Maguire, Pastore, and Flanagan; (1993:661).

for these sentencing differences is that judges have tended to be more paternalistic toward female offenders in the past. In recent years, however, presumptive or guidelines-based sentencing schemes used by different states and the federal government have caused male-female sentencing differentials to narrow. Generally, the rate of female offending and incarceration has increased both dramatically and systematically since the early 1980s (Nesbitt, 1992:6). This does not necessarily mean that there is a "new breed" or a more dangerous female offender in society—rather, more women are being subject to less lenient treatment by a more equitable criminal justice system (Erez, 1988). Some experts have labeled this phenomenon *gender parity* (Steffensmeier and Streifel, 1989).

Regarding parole, women tended to be distributed in ways similar to their conviction patterns. For instance, only 8.3 percent of all parolees in 1992 were women. This proportion is similar to the proportionate distribution of women incarcerated in federal and state prisons. With a few exceptions, female parolee distributions by conviction offense were similar to their original conviction offense patterns. For instance, 16.1 percent of all female parolees had been convicted for violent offenses. Also, 40.3 percent of all female parolees were property offenders. This is approximately the same percentage for women convicted of property offenses. Over 37 percent of all female parolees had prior convictions for drug offenses. A similar figure accounts for the proportion of convictions for women involving drug offenses. Another interesting observation is that the female "failure rate" while on parole is approximately the same as it is for male parolees, about 61.5 percent (Maguire, Pastore, and Flanagan, 1993:662). Men have a slightly lower "success rate"—36.3 percent compared with 37.3 percent for female parolees.

In 1992, the American Correctional Association formulated a National

Correctional Policy on Female Offender Services (Nesbitt, 1992:7). This policy is as follows:

> *Introduction:* Correctional systems must develop service delivery systems for accused and adjudicated female offenders that are comparable to those provided to males. Additional services must also be provided to meet the unique needs of the female offender population.
>
> *Statement:* Correctional systems must be guided by the principle of parity. Female offenders must receive the equivalent range of services available to other offenders, including opportunities for individualized programming and services that recognize the unique needs of this population. The services should:
>
> A. Assure access to a range of alternatives to incarceration, including pretrial and posttrial diversion, probation, restitution, treatment for substance abuse, halfway houses, and parole services.
>
> B. Provide acceptable conditions of confinement, including appropriately trained staff and sound operating procedures that address this population's needs in such areas as clothing, personal property, hygiene, exercise, recreation, and visitation with children and family.
>
> C. Provide access to a full range of work and programs designed to expand economic and social roles of women, with emphasis on education; career counseling and exploration of non-traditional as well as traditional vocational training; relevant life skills, including parenting and social and economic assertiveness; and prerelease and work/education release programs.
>
> D. Facilitate the maintenance and strengthening of family ties, particularly those between parent and child.
>
> E. Deliver appropriate programs and services, including medical, dental, and mental health programs, services to pregnant women, substance abuse programs, child and family services, and provide access to legal services.
>
> F. Provide access to release programs that include aid in establishing homes, economic stability, and sound family relationships.

Criticisms of Women's Prisons and Community Programs. A Minnesota study highlights some of the continuing problems associated with women's prisons and community-based treatment services. Hokanson (1986) gathered information about female inmates from 87 county correctional facilities and 31 jails. She found that the typical female offender was young, either single, divorced, or separated; educated at a level approximating the general population; lacking in work skills and dependent upon public assistance; overrepresentative of minority groups; and having a high probability of physical and/or sexual abuse victimization and a history of substance abuse. Similar observations have been made about women offenders by others (Carp and Schade, 1992:152).

It is generally acknowledged that women's prisons and programming for women in community-based correctional programs have not compared favorably with programs and facilities for men (Florida Joint Legislative Management Committee, 1995; Morash, Haarr, and Rucker, 1994). For instance, programs for female offenders have been poorer in quality, quantity, variability, and availability in both the United States and Canada

(Muraskin, 1990; Smith et al., 1994). Despite these inequities, courts generally declare that men and women in prisons do *not* have to be treated equally, and that *separate* can be *equal* when men's and women's prisons are compared (Knight, 1992). There are exceptions, however.

In 1979, the case of *Glover v. Johnson* (1979) involved the Michigan Department of Corrections and the issue of equal programming for female inmates. A class action suit was filed on behalf of all Michigan female prison inmates to the effect that their constitutional rights were violated because they were being denied educational and vocational rehabilitation opportunities that were then being provided to male inmates only. Among other things, the Michigan Department of Corrections was ordered to provide the following to its incarcerated women: (1) two-year college programming; (2) paralegal training and access to attorneys to remedy past inadequacies in law library facilities; (3) a revised inmate wage policy to ensure that female inmates were provided equal wages; (4) access to programming at camps previously available only to male inmates; (5) enhanced vocational offerings; (6) apprenticeship opportunities; and (7) prison industries that previously existed only at men's facilities (American Correctional Association, 1993c:32). Several similar cases in other jurisdictions have been settled without court action (Connecticut, California, Wisconsin, and Idaho).

The *Glover* case is like the tip of an iceberg when it comes to disclosing various problems associated with women's prisons and other corrections institutions for women. The following are criticisms that have been leveled against women's correctional facilities in the last few decades (Knight, 1992). Some of these criticisms have been remedied in selected jurisdictions.

1. *No adequate classification system exists for female prisoners* (Culliver, 1993:407). Women from widely different backgrounds with diverse criminal histories are celled with one another in most women's prisons. This is conducive to greater criminalization during the incarceration period. Furthermore, most women's prisons have only medium-security custody, rather than a wider variety of custody levels to accommodate female offenders of differing seriousness and dangerousness (Pollock-Byrne, 1990:84–85). Better classification methods should be devised.
2. *Most women's prisons are remotely located.* Thus, many female prisoners are deprived of immediate contact with out-of-prison educational or vocational services that might be available through study or work release.
3. *Women who give birth to babies while incarcerated are deprived of valuable parent–child contact.* Some experts contend that this is a serious deprivation for newborn infants (Culliver, 1993:406; Pollock-Byrne, 1990:35; Ryan and Grassano, 1992:184).
4. *Women have less extensive vocational and educational programming in the prison setting.*
5. *Women have less access to legal services.* In the past, law libraries in women's facilities were lacking or nonexistent; recent remedies have included provisions for either legal services or more adequate libraries in women's institutions.

6. *Women have special medical needs.* Women's prisons do not adequately provide for meeting these needs.
7. *Mental health treatment services and programs for women are inferior to those provided for men in men's facilities.*
8. *Training programs that are provided women do not permit them to live independently and earn decent livings when released on parole* (Culliver, 1993:407; Klausner, 1991).

Because of the rather unique role of women as caregivers for their children, many corrections professionals rule the imprisonment of women differently than the imprisonment of men (Clark, 1995). For various reasons, female imprisonment is opposed on moral, ethical, and religious grounds. Legally, these arguments are often unconvincing. In an attempt to at least address some of the unique problems confronting female offenders when they are incarcerated or when they participate in community-based programs, some experts have advocated the following as recommendations (Culliver, 1993:409–410):

1. Institute training programs that would enable imprisoned women to become literate.
2. Provide female offenders with programs that do not center on traditional gender roles—programs that will lead to more economic independence and self-sufficiency.
3. Establish programs that would engender more positive self-esteem for imprisoned women and enhance their assertiveness and communication and interpersonal skills.
4. Establish more programs that would allow imprisoned mothers to interact more with their children and help them overcome feelings of guilt and shame for having deserted their children. In addition, visitation areas for mothers and children should be altered to minimize the effect of a prison-type environment.
5. An alternative to mother-and-child interaction behind prison bars would be to allow imprisoned mothers to spend more time with their children outside of the prison.
6. Provide imprisoned mothers with training to improve parenting skills.
7. Establish more programs to treat drug-addicted female offenders.
8. Establish a community partnership program to provide imprisoned women with employment opportunities.
9. Establish a better classification system for incarcerated women—one that would not permit the less-hardened offender to be juxtaposed with the hardened offender.
10. Provide in-service training (sensitivity awareness) to help staff members (wardens, correctional officers) understand the nature and needs of incarcerated women.

Other experts have recommended the establishment and provision of an environment that would allow all pregnant inmates the opportunity to rear their newborn infants for a period of one year and provide counseling on available parental services, foster care, guardianship, and other relevant activities pending their eventual release (Goodstein and MacKenzie, 1989). Some women's facilities have cottages on prison grounds where inmates with infants can accomplish some of these objectives (LeFlore and Holston, 1989).

The Program for Female Offenders, Inc. (PFO). The Program for Female Offenders was established in 1974 as the result of jail overcrowding in Allegheny County, Pennsylvania (Arnold, 1992:37). This program is a work-release facility operated as a nonprofit agency by the county. It is designed to accommodate up to 36 women and space for 6 preschool children. It was originally created to reduce jail overcrowding, but because of escalating rates of female offending and jail incarceration, the overcrowding problem persists.

When PFO was established, the Allegheny County Jail was small. Only 12 women were housed there. Nevertheless, agency founders worked out an agreement with jail authorities so that female jail prisoners could be transferred to PFO by court order. Inmate-clients would be guilty of prison breach if they left PFO without permission. While at PFO, the women would participate in training, volunteering in the community, and learning how to spend their leisure time with the help of a role modeling and parent education program for mothers and children. The program is based on freedom reached by attaining levels of responsibility (Arnold, 1992:37–38). In 1984, a much larger work-release facility was constructed in Allegheny County. Currently, over 300 women per year are served by PFO. PFO authorities reserve the right to screen potential candidates for work release. During 1992, the following companion projects were implemented in Allegheny County:

1. Good-time project at the county jail
2. Male work-release center accommodating 60 beds
3. Development of criminal justice division in county government
4. Drug treatment/work-release facility at St. Francis Health Center's Chemical Dependency Department
5. Development of a male job placement program
6. Expansion of the existing PFO Women's Center
7. Expansion of the retail theft project (Arnold, 1992:38)

The successfulness of PFO is demonstrated by its low 3.5 percent recidivism rate in the community program and only a 17 percent recidivism rate at the residential facility. Over $88,000 has been collected in rent, $27,000 in fines, and $8,000 in restitution to victims of the female offenders. For the male offenders, $106,500 has been collected in rent and $107,400 in fines and restitution. Long-range plans for PFO call for a crime prevention program, including a day care center, intervention therapy for drug-abusing families, intensive work with preschool children who are already giving evidence of impending delinquency, and a scholarship program (Arnold, 1992:40). Plans also include expanding PFO's services to more areas throughout Pennsylvania.

The Women's Activities and Learning Center (WALC) Program. The Kansas Department of Corrections has established a program for women with children that has been patterned after PATCH (Parents and Their Children) commenced by the Missouri Department of Corrections and MATCH (Mothers and Their Children) operated by the California Department of Corrections. The Kansas program is known as the Women's Activities and Learning Center or WALC. WALC was started with a grant from the U.S. Department of Education under the Women's Educational Opportunity Act and is based in Topeka (Logan, 1992:160).

The Topeka facility has a primary goal of developing and coordinating a broad range of programs, services, and classes and workshops that will increase women offenders' chances for a positive reintegration with their families and society upon release (Logan, 1992:160). A visiting area at the center accommodates visitations for female inmates and their children. Thus, women with children are given a chance to take an active part in caring for them. Mothers acquire some measure of a mother-child relationship during incarceration. They are able to fix meals for their children and have recreation with them in designated areas. Various civic and religious groups contribute their volunteer resources to assist these women. Both time and money are expended by outside agencies and personnel such as the Kiwanis, the Kansas East Conference of the United Methodist Church, and the Fraternal Order of Police (Logan, 1992:161).

One advantage of WALC is that it provides various programs and courses in useful areas such as parenting, child development, prenatal care, self-esteem, anger management, nutrition, support groups, study groups, cardiopulmonary resuscitation, personal development, and crafts. The parenting program, for instance, is a 10-week course where inmate-mothers meet once a week to discuss their various problems. To qualify for inclusion in this program, female inmates must be designated as low risk, minimum security, and have no disciplinary reports filed against them during the 90 days prior to program involvement. When the 10-week course is completed, the women are entitled to participate in a three-week retreat sponsored by the Methodist Church. The retreat includes transportation for inmates, with fishing, horseback riding, hay rides, and game-playing for mothers and their children. Volunteers and a correctional officer are present during the retreat experience. Since September 1991, more than 300 women and 500 children have participated in the WALC program, with a low rate of recidivism (Logan, 1992:161).

THE CULTURE OF WOMEN'S PRISONS

Attempts to describe the "typical" women's prison are about as productive as attempts to depict the typical men's prison. Hollywood portrayals of women's prisons carry provocative titles such as *Caged Heat* or *Women in Chains,* and they depict inmates as consisting mostly of lesbians or sex-starved ex-beauty queens who are the standard targets of lesbians (Faith, 1987). Cases such as *California v. Lovercamp* (1974) do little to change this Hollywood stereotype.

In the early 1970s, two female inmates, Lovercamp and Wynashe, were housed in the California Rehabilitation Center. They had been confined in the facility for about two months and, according to their version of events, were continually threatened into performing a variety of sex acts with a gang of lesbian inmates that appeared to dominate the institution. "F--- or fight" was the challenge continually yelled at them by the lesbian inmates who became more physical in their harassment. One afternoon, Lovercamp and Wynashe fled the minimum-security facility to avoid being sexually assaulted. They turned themselves in to correctional officers shortly after leaving the facility.

Although a lower California court later found them guilty of escape, their excuse was accepted by the California Court of Appeals which overturned their conviction in 1974. The defense of "necessity" became a viable defense to avoid assaults by other prisoners. Prison escapes are serious matters, and the California court was careful not to issue license to all inmates, male or female, to consider escape from their institutions if they felt endangered by other inmates for whatever reason. The court advised that prisoners should report threatening behaviors of other inmates to correctional officers and prison administration. In fact, Lovercamp and her companion had complained on previous occasions to officers about the threats they were receiving from the lesbians. Their escape was even more justified given that officials took no action whatsoever to safeguard them from the sexual advances of others.

Adding to depictions of female prisons as bastions of lesbianism are works such as *Women's Prison: Sex and Social Structure* by Dave Ward and Gene Kassebaum, published in 1965. Their study was concerned not only with the social behavior of female prison inmates, but with their sexual behavior as well. In fact, over half of the book is devoted to their interviews with several prisoners and their investigations of the prevalence of lesbianism among female inmates. Their study occurred at the California Institution for Women at Frontera, California. Although the sample of inmates interviewed was small, much valuable information about life in at least one women's prison was disclosed. The existence of an "inmate code" was revealed, although compared with the inmate codes existing in prisons for men, the one at Frontera was almost nonexistent and unenforceable. This was explained by Ward and Kassebaum to result from the lack of solidarity and loyalty among inmates (Ward and Kassebaum, 1965:53).

It was estimated by respondents that over 50 percent of all female inmates at Frontera were sexually involved with at least one other female inmate at least once during their incarceration. Ward and Kassebaum found this figure unremarkable, since studies by other researchers showed that lesbianism among large samples of unmarried female college graduates disclosed similar percentages of sexual encounters among one another (Ward and Kassebaum, 1965:93). They also noted the absence of other comparative works examining lesbianism in other women's prisons. In short, we have a seemingly sensationalized account of rampant lesbianism in one California women's prison, based on interviews conducted with nine women selected originally by a lesbian inmate-informant picked by Ward, Kassebaum, and the warden as well as questionnaires completed by several other inmates. But according to the authors, having opinions from an articulate, experienced yet small number of inmates was more important than a larger representative sample for hypothesis-testing purposes (Ward and Kassebaum, 1965:249–250). More recent evidence suggests that these earlier estimates of lesbianism among females in U.S. prisons have been greatly exaggerated and that inmate-lesbians make up a small hardcore portion of female offenders (Faith, 1987; Leger, 1987). However, no one knows for sure how many lesbians there are in women's prisons (Williams and Fish, 1985:220).

Incarcerated Mothers

A majority of female inmates in U.S. prisons are mothers. While this status does not shield them from sexual advances from others or prevent them from initiating such advances themselves, efforts by prison officials to maintain the family unit appear to be moderately influential for decreasing the perceived need for lesbian activity. Women in prison are much disturbed by the "convict" label to begin with, and arrangements by prison officials to ensure their prolonged and frequent contact with their infants and young children would seem to naturally discourage same-sex situations that would further mar their image if detected.

The American Civil Liberties Union (ACLU) has fought for female inmate rights involving access to their children. In one South Carolina case, a woman serving a 21-year sentence for armed robbery wished to keep her child with her in prison (Baunach, 1985:4). While there are moral, ethical, practical, and logistical problems with such long-term arrangements, suits have been filed seeking such associations (Baunach, 1985:124–125). In these cases, suggestions have been made for the creation of appropriate off-premises facilities where low-risk female offenders can reside with their children in reasonably "normal" settings. Thus, it is neither essential nor desirable that infants or young children be housed in cell areas with their mothers. The ACLU has other types of living accommodations in mind when advancing such legal actions against prison administrators and state prison systems.

Furthermore, some states such as Massachusetts have permitted parent-child living arrangements in special quarters (Rocheleau, 1987b). Significantly, the **Visiting Cottage Program** in Lancaster, Massachusetts, is available only to eligible female inmates, and eligibility is determined by compliance with prison rules. Although the subject has not been investigated extensively, there is some indication that inmate-mothers derive positive therapy from the anticipation of resuming parenthood when eventually released. The maintenance of inmate-child ties seems to foster greater compliance with prison rules, since these offenders wish to gain early release from a favorable parole decision. Showing responsibility in caring for one's child while in prison is one way of demonstrating that a successful life may be led on the outside if released.

Excellent portrayals of female inmate culture exist in the professional literature (Hewitt, 1996). Kathryn Watterson's *Women in Prison: Inside the Concrete Womb,* provides an excellent and in-depth description of what goes on inside women's prisons (Watterson, 1996). Again, depending upon the source, different pictures emerge describing female interactions and life behind prison walls. A majority of jurisdictions have only a single female facility to house these prisoners (Nadel, 1996). Many of these institutions do not make distinctions between female inmates other than to separate those in need of immediate medical attention from the others. For violent female prisoners, however, solitary confinement in one form or another is an option in many women's institutions.

The Square, the Cool, and the Life

In some women's prisons, inmates have developed a jargon to depict the particular lifestyle chosen by an inmate for the duration of her incarceration (Heffernan, 1985:228). Because incarcerated women often experience severe shock and a period of painful adjustment after being separated from their families, friends, and children, they seek to establish temporary social relations with other inmates. In addition, they have given up many creature comforts that were associated with their identity on the outside—jewelry, certain expensive clothing, and other items (Williams and Fish, 1985:215). Sometimes they establish quasi-families consisting of other inmates who play various familial roles. A new inmate may be asked to join a "family" as the daughter or mother. In some instances, other roles may emerge stemming from these lesbian relations. Occasionally, these unisex unions are considered binding on all parties for the period of incarceration (Williams and Fish, 1985:216–217). These interactions replace temporarily those relationships on the outside that women associated with stability, security, and love.

"Getting by" or "making it" in prison requires certain adaptations. Inmate terminology in some prisons has divided women into three categories: **squares, cools,** and **lifes.** Squares are considered "noncriminal." These are often first-offenders who have been convicted of petty offenses. They identify with the establishment and don't fit in with other inmates who may be professional thieves, forgers, or drug users. The cools generally consist of women with prior records who attempt to get by with rule infractions and obtain fringe benefits within the system without getting caught.

The life type is the habitual offender who engages in deviant behavior with little regard for the punitive consequences (Heffernan, 1985:228–230). These designations imply three types of goal-seeking behavior and goals that lead to the formation of social networks of those inmates with similar interests (Weisheit and Mahan, 1988:74).

One problem in applying this argot to all women's prisons is that there is less continuity among female inmates who usually spend time in only one prison, while many male inmates serve additional terms for other crimes in different prisons (Kruttschnitt, 1981). Therefore, male inmates share more of their prison culture in a greater variety of prison settings. Women's sentences are generally shorter, the facilities are smaller, there is apparently greater selfishness and less loyalty, and many offenders prefer to operate independent of others. Female inmates are slow to form unions, and inmate gangs don't exist on the same scale that they exist in male facilities. This retards the development of female inmate culture, at least to the degree, sophistication, and organization of male inmate cultures in state and federal prison settings. The low rate of female recidivism, except for a small offender hardcore, further interferes with perpetuating an identifiable female inmate subculture.

ADMINISTRATION OF WOMEN'S PRISONS

While some prison administrators would probably argue the point, women's prisons are generally easier to administer than prisons for men. First, they are less organizationally complex, since significantly fewer services and programs ordinarily are available to female inmates than are found in men's prisons. Second, the number of women in any prison is small. Thus, monitoring or supervising fewer offenders involves fewer staff and less coordination between them than is required with the larger staff in male institutions. And third, although some female inmates are dangerous in any prison setting, most women prisoners are low-risk offenders (Benekos and Merlo, 1992; Fuller, 1993). Although women in prison have engaged in riots, their "rioting" record is quite low, again when contrasted with the rioting frequency of their male inmate counterparts. There is little unity or organization among female inmates in most prisons, and collective action is not observed with any consistent frequency (Culliver, 1993).

Many of the facilities designed for women throughout the United States are located in remote rural areas (Fuller, 1993). The decision to locate many women's prisons in remote regions was based originally on the idea that women needed privacy and seclusion where they could think and reflect and thereby become rehabilitated (Culliver, 1993; Fuller, 1993). Another reason was that these remote locations "removed them from corruption" (Feinman, 1986:48–49). Actually, this decision has operated to their disadvantage for several reasons. First, the spatial distance between themselves and family or close friends makes visits difficult and infrequent. As Mann (1984:203) observes, "since most of their [the inmates'] families are poor, family members cannot afford the trips to visit them." Of course, even when women's prisons are located in urban areas of their respective jurisdictions, it is likely that families of inmates will still have to travel great distances to see them. Additionally, most states and the Federal Bureau of Prisons have only one all-female facility to serve their needs, and women of all security levels are housed in that same institution (Feinman, 1986:49). In short, female offenders are assigned to the "nearest" female prison, which may be 300 miles or more from where they were convicted.

Another limitation of the isolation of these prisons is that it is difficult to attract and retain qualified personnel to administer and operate these facilities (Quinlan et al., 1992; U.S. Federal Bureau of Prisons, 1991). Prison staff usually is recruited from among interested applicants living in those areas in which women's institutions are located. Often, the prison correctional officers recruited may not be as qualified for their jobs as correctional officers in urban areas, where prison officials have access to a higher-quality workforce (Mann, 1984:204–205). It should be noted that this is largely an inference drawn by critics of the women's prisons that are in remote areas. There are few, if any, studies directly comparing female prison correctional officer quality according to the urban-rural distinction.

A third significant disadvantage is that, compared with men's prisons located predominantly in urban areas, women's prisons are not easily accessible to vocational, educational, technical, or other services that nearby communities might otherwise be able to provide (Florida Joint Legislative Management Committee, 1995). This makes it difficult for women to take advantage of nearby programs on either a furlough or work release basis, since the distance between the prison and the services is too great for the limited time allocated to furloughs or work releases.

In part because of the attention drawn to women's prisons by the media and by the nature of lawsuits successfully filed by female inmates, prison administrators and superintendents have been compelled by the courts and others to work toward establishing programs for women similar to those already established for men (Wheeler et al., 1987). For example, it was found that in Kentucky and Michigan, recreational programs in women's institutions were either underfunded or nonexistent (Hunter, 1984:134). These and other states have raised the defense that the cost of implementing programs in women's prisons equivalent to those of men would be prohibitive. These arguments have been systematically rejected by the courts (Hunter, 1984).

Besides identifying women's needs and creating programs to meet those needs, prison administrators must work within extremely narrow budgets. Legislators and others are inclined to allocate funds in relation to the proportionate numbers of female offenders that must be accommodated in their prisons. Thus, if their entire prison population consists of 3 percent female offenders, the women's prison budget within which the administrator must work is usually 3 percent of all correctional expenditures. In future years, court-ordered improvements in women's facilities will no doubt result in larger appropriations (Ryan, 1984). Another administrative headache pertains to the placement of growing numbers of female offenders. Like male prisons, female facilities are faced with increased amounts of overcrowding. Although the extent of overcrowding in women's prisons has not reached epidemic proportions, in some jurisdictions indications are that such overcrowding has resulted in a diminished quality of services available, including poorer medical care, counseling, and program staffing (Immarigeon and Chesney-Lind, 1992).

The implementation of administrative policies in state prison systems sometimes results in unusual and humorous outcomes. For example, one state prison system issued an "approved"

> Christmas present list to distribute to the families of inmates. This list was to be stringently observed and enforced throughout all prisons in the system. Included on the "approved" gift list were jock straps or athletic supporters for men, although no provisions were made for women's underwear or panties. One superintendent of the women's institution in that state pointed out to the administration that jock straps were not a "big item" in her institution (Hunter, 1984:132).

SELECTED ISSUES IN WOMEN'S PRISONS

Some Comparisons of Women's and Men's Prisons

Prisons for men tend to have a greater range of vocational and educational training programs and services. They are more centrally located to urban areas, whereas women's prisons are more remotely located. Men's prisons tend to be larger and have more amenities, such a weight rooms, jogging areas, and other sports facilities. The law libraries of men's facilities tend to be better equipped, although substantial improvements in female facilities toward greater parity with men's institutions on various forms of legal assistance and materials have been made (Palmer, 1997).

Women tend to commit rule infractions more frequently than men, but the punishments meted out to women seem more severe than the punishments for men for the same types of infractions (McClellan, 1994). For instance, a comparison of Texas prisons for men and women revealed that such infractions as "cursing" were meticulously enforced in women's prisons but routinely ignored in men's prisons. Thus, it was concluded that gender-specific rule enforcement was being practiced within the same prison system (McClellan, 1994). Texas policymakers were in the process of making significant changes in the nature and enforcement of these policies for both men's and women's prisons for future years.

The "Equal Protection" Clause Applied to Incarcerated Females

Are female inmates treated equally compared with their male counterparts? The research says that they are not treated equally. In fact, as we have already seen, there are disciplinary differentials attributable to one's gender, at least in several Texas prisons. Female offenders are sanctioned, and sanctioned more severely, for less serious types of infractions, such as swearing, compared with their male inmate counterparts, who also swear extensively, but without any consequence.

Vocational and educational needs for women are not being met as well in women's institutions compared with similar programming in men's institutions (Florida Joint Legislative Management Committee, 1995). Even where there are attempts to provide programming on the same level as men, the programming is often inconsistent with the real needs of women (Pollock-Byrne, 1990). The remoteness of women's prisons from major urban areas makes it more difficult for family members to visit them when compared with male inmates (Benekos and Merlo, 1993; Fuller, 1993).

Women's prisons seem every bit as overcrowded as men's facilities. Some investigators have observed that a large proportion of incarcerated women are there for less serious crimes than male offenders. Thus, these experts argue, there may be an argument for releasing more female offenders from prison to make space for more serious types of offenders (Immarigeon and Chesney-Lind, 1992). Greater rates of incarceration for women have often been the result of policy changes in state jurisdictions rather than any new female crime wave. It would seem that we have not moved very far from the way women were treated during the period of 1865 to 1935. Persistent neglect characterized the women's prisons of that period, and the same can be said for many of the facilities for women today (Rafter, 1990).

Rehabilitative Services for Women

Some attempts have been made by prison officials in different jurisdictions to meet certain needs of their female offenders. Many female inmates enter prison pregnant or having just had infants. As noted above, the Massachusetts Department of Corrections has made available to women a wide variety of programs that enable them to have lengthy visits with their children under a Visiting Cottage Program. This program permits women to visit with their children overnight in special, on-premises cottages established by Massachusetts prison officials. The visits from children have been found quite therapeutic in assisting women to make the transition from incarceration to freedom and to lead reasonably normal lives (Rocheleau, 1987a). Another facility that is attempting to change the image of at least some female residents is the Bedford Hills, New York, Reformatory Prison for Women constructed in 1902. For certain inmates with young children, Bedford officials have created a special top-floor area in an old brick building

BOX 13.1 Female Chain Gangs?

The Case of Sheriff Joe Arpaio, Phoenix, Arizona

Did I understand that correctly? Is it true that female inmates of the Maricopa County Jail are chained together in leg irons in groups of five and placed along roadsides to pick up trash and pull weeds on a "chain gang"? Yes, it is true.

In September 1996, Sheriff Joe Arpaio of the Maricopa County Sheriff's Department created a female chain gang to work at odd jobs about the community. Sheriff Arpaio, known as the toughest sheriff in the nation, has already established himself as a law enforcement maverick by creating "tent cities" for housing his overflow of inmates from the county jail. Arpaio has also established male chain gangs as a means of punishing offenders.

One female chain gang member, Rebecca Lopez, was in jail for violating parole relating to a drunk driving conviction. Lopez says that "Jail life is boring. It's dehumanizing. But this chain gang isn't so bad. At least it gets you back into the outside world for a couple of hours a day." Another jail inmate, Ernestine White, 33, said "I'll do anything to get out of jail. I just started serving an eight-month jail sentence for solicitation. I want to get out. I have a year-old daughter I can't even hug and kiss anymore."

When Arpaio took office in 1993, he was one of the first county sheriffs to ban coffee, smoking, "girlie" magazines, and R-rated movies from his jail. He has made headlines for making inmates wear pink underwear, primarily so they won't steal it, he says. When asked about the female chain gang, Sheriff Arpaio said that "I don't believe in discrimination in my jail system. Crime knows no gender and neither should punishment."

Some observers label what Arpaio is doing as a "stunt." We don't think so. It seems to be getting the message across to Phoenix residents. Don't commit crime in Phoenix, or the chain gang may be where you wind up. As the female inmates work along roadsides each day, passersby in cars honk their horns and hoot. Arpaio defends his system of justice by noting that "I don't want them in the desert chopping rocks. I want them out in the open where everybody can see them and show people that this could happen to them if they commit a crime. This might get publicity, but it is not a stunt. I'm doing what I was elected to do—get tough on crime. I want inmates to hate jail so much they'll never come back. That's why I'm known as America's toughest sheriff."

About 50 female prisoners in the Maricopa County Jail must remain in their cells for 23 hours a day for disciplinary reasons. They will work six days a week for a month on the chain gang detail as a means of escaping the 23-hour daily lockup.

Do you think chain gangs are an appropriate form of punishment? Are criminals "shamed" by such tactics? Are chain gangs cruel and unusual under constitutional guidelines? How do you react to Sheriff Joe Arpaio's actions? Should he be applauded or voted out of office in the next election?

Source: Adapted from Associated Press, "'It Was All a Big Show': Get Tough Sheriff Puts Women to Work on Chain Gang." *Minot (N.D.) Daily News,* September 20, 1996:A7.

that functions as a "home" for both mother and child. Twenty-one cots and cribs are placed side by side, where these inmate-mothers receive parenting courses and are served by a resident pediatric nurse (Creighton, 1988:23).

If there is anything typical about women's prisons, it is that they are small. Populations of 500 or more females in one prison are considered large. A survey of female institutions in the United States showed that by the end of 1984, only 12 women's prisons had populations in excess of 500 (Nesbitt, 1986:80). Organizationally, smaller prisons are somewhat easier to manage and control. Administrators have fewer inmate problems because of fewer inmates. But there are drawbacks to small inmate populations. One of the major drawbacks is that smaller penal facilities receive less funding priority by state legislatures. Furthermore, it is more difficult for administrators of small institutions to justify the same range of vocational, educational, and technical programs found in large men's prisons (Nesbitt, 1986:80).

New York's Prison Nursery/Children's Center. At the Bedford Hills, New York, Correctional Facility, a 750-woman maximum-security prison constructed in 1933, a Children's Center was established in 1989 to 1990. Since 1930, New York legislation provided for women in prison to keep their babies. Presently, New York is the only state that maintains a prison nursery (Roulet, 1993:4).

Authorities at Bedford Hills believe that it is important for women to maintain strong ties with their families during incarceration. Furthermore, they believe that women will have a greater chance at reintegration and lower recidivism as the opportunity for familial interaction increases. Further, there is a positive impact on babies, since they can remain with and be nurtured by their mothers. In 1993, there were two state nurseries. Besides the one at Bedford Hills, another was opened at Taconic. This is a smaller facility, also located in Bedford Hills, housing about 400 female offenders.

Roulet (1993:4) says that not all women incarcerated at Bedford Hills are eligible to participate in the prison nursery program. A woman's criminal background, past parenting performance, disciplinary record, and educational needs are examined and assessed before they are accepted. Women who are selected are expected to make the best use of their time by developing their mothering skills and caring for their infants. They are also expected to participate in various self-help programs of a vocational and educational nature (Roulet, 1993:4). The center's main program goal is to help women preserve and strengthen family ties and to receive visits from their children as often as possible in a warm, nurturing atmosphere. They are kept closely informed of their children's physical, educational, intellectual, and emotional well-being while they are separated. Through the various classes and programs offered at Bedford Hills, women acquire a better understanding of their roles as parents and are able to reinforce their feelings of self-worth (Roulet, 1993:5).

Inmates at Bedford Hills also participate in a Parent's Center. The primary concerns and components of the Parent's Center include the following (Roulet, 1993:5–6):

1. Bilingual parenting (allows women to learn English while exploring issues of mothers and children; provides a bilingual parenting class)
2. Child development associate course (the CDA is a national accreditation program that prepares candidates to teach in accredited nursery schools anywhere in the country)
3. Children's advocate office (trained advocates meet with inmate mothers individually to address all child-related problems)
4. Children's library (caregivers help mothers to select age-appropriate books; occasionally films and special storytime sessions are arranged)
5. Choices and changes courses (this class helps inmates to develop self-awareness and to learn the process of decision-making and accountability to improve parenting)
6. Foster care committee (the committee helps women learn their legal rights and responsibilities as incarcerated women; the committee helps mothers with letter writing, direct services, monthly group meetings; provides handbooks, support groups, etc.)
7. Holiday activities (the center provides holiday activities, as directed by inmate staff members)
8. Infant day care center (cares for the babies of nursery mothers who are programmed into school or work assignments; provides 'hands-on' experience for CDA interns)
9. Mental hygiene program (inmate staff become 'parents' for other less fortunate inmate parents; it is considered to be useful and relaxing therapy for these women)
10. Mother's group (a certified social worker conducts group sessions for women who have children and want an opportunity to discuss their relationships; it also provides the services of a family therapist)
11. Nursery aides (inmate staff member works with nursery coordinators; she sews clothes for nursery babies and helps with inventory and distribution of clothes)
12. The overnight program (volunteer host parents in the community take in nursery children for a day and overnight once a month)
13. Parenting program (covers parenting from the prenatal stages to adulthood through the use of educational classes and films)
14. Prenatal center (women receive parenting classes, address their drug problems, learn sewing, crocheting, and other handiwork)
15. Records and teaching material (inmate staff member collects information on the history of the nursery program, new materials or studies on children, education, imprisoned women, drugs and their effects on children; these archival resources are used by staff and facility college students)
16. Summer program (older children spend a week during the summer with volunteer host families who live near the nursery; each day the children are brought to visit their mothers for a few hours)
17. Study corner (mothers tape-record themselves reading a children's story, which is then sent to their child)

18. Sponsor a baby (churches, temples, and other groups provide necessities for inmate mothers and babies when they leave prison and the nursery and also for families of inmates not eligible for the nursery program who are unexpectedly burdened with an infant)
19. Transportation clinic (provides transportation for children of inmates to visit their mothers at the nursery and children's center)
20. Toy library (mothers select games, crafts, and toys for their children's visit; some can be taken home; others are returned to the library)

Roulet (1993:6) says that women whose babies are born while incarcerated may keep them at Bedford for up to one year. Babies are delivered in a hospital outside of prison, and the mother and infant live in the nursery for as long as the child remains. If it is likely that the mother will be paroled by the time the infant is 18 months old, then the infant may remain with the mother with special permission until that date. It is important to keep mothers and children together as much as possible while at Bedford Hills. The child's welfare is of utmost concern to authorities (Roulet, 1993:6). Such bonding is considered significant at reducing rates of recidivism among paroled Bedford Hills women. Parenting programs for female inmates have been implemented in many other state jurisdictions, attesting to the importance of this theme for corrections officials throughout the United States and abroad (Mott, 1989; Stevens et al., 1993).

Changing Policies, Programs, and Services for Female Offenders. In 1992, *Corrections Compendium* published the results of a survey of 85 state-operated women's facilities in 46 states (S. Davis, 1992b). Approximately 31,000 women were housed in these facilities at a cost of $1.5 million annually. Serious health problems were related to pregnancies, AIDS, substance abuse, and mental health (Justice Education Center, Inc. 1993). When this survey was conducted, all facilities had on-site medical staff available. Not all facilities had gynecological/obstetrical services, however. Only 68 percent of all facilities offered prenatal/postpartum services and none of the responding institutions allowed newborn infants to remain with their mothers. In the most recent 12-month period, 1,445 babies were born to inmates (S. Davis, 1992b:7).

Su Davis (1992b:7) says that more women are being convicted of drug offenses annually. Three-fourths of all women inmates were in need of substance abuse treatment, although only 28 percent of all incarcerated women had conviction offenses involving drugs. Most offenders had dropped out of high school or had not received the GED. Most had been unable to hold a job for longer than six months. Presently, most of the surveyed institutions offer vocational and educational courses for these women. Two thirds offer college courses and 70 have prerelease programs. Most facilities have institutional work assignments, and about half have parenting programs.

Between 1987 and 1992, policy changes have been implemented in over half of the facilities surveyed (Su Davis, 1992b:8). These policy changes involve increased opportunities for women to work and/or participate in vocational and educational programming originally available only to male inmates. Major changes have occurred in classification, visitation, and housing. Clothing policy changes have also been effected. Many of these changes have been occasioned by the parity issue, with women's facilities being brought more in line with men's facilities. In most instances, this has meant improved services delivery to women's prisons. In some instances, however, deprivations have resulted.

Although as a matter of right, female inmates are entitled to the same legal considerations as male prisoners (e.g., access to legal services, law libraries), historically, women's prisons have been largely ignored by the criminal justice system (Knight, 1992) Female jailhouse lawyers emerged during the 1970s and 1980s to obtain numerous concessions from prison administrators, the courts, and legislatures (Wheeler et al., 1987). A push is underway to establish a full range of programs and services for female inmates that most male or predominantly male institutions have. There is no question that presently, programs for female offenders are poorer in quantity, quality, variability, and availability than those for male offenders (Carp and David, 1991; Immarigeon and Chesney-Lind, 1992).

One disturbing feature of many rehabilitative programs offered to women in prison is that they often reflect stereotypical views of what women "should" do when released (Benekos and Merlo, 1993). Thus, courses are offered to make female inmates better "homemakers," "seamstresses," clerk-typists, and mothers (Florida Joint Legislative Management Committee, 1995). Since many women in prison currently lack a high school education (15 percent have not completed elementary school), many remedial educational courses are offered to them so that they may complete their GEDs or achieve high school diplomas. Advanced courses are also available, either directly or through correspondence, whereby women may obtain college credits, even college degrees. Ironically, those academic courses most frequently offered to women emphasize preparation for the usual stereotypical roles, including family life education, child development, personal grooming, textiles and clothing, and consumer education (Mann, 1984:215). Comparatively few courses are available in electronic engineering, computer programming, business, law, or medicine. Even if a woman wanted to prepare for a professional career or a particular occupation of a nontraditional nature when paroled or released, she would be unable to do so on the basis of what courses she had taken while incarcerated.

The Federal Bureau of Prisons has operated an exclusively female correctional facility at Alderson, West Virginia. This institution was opened in 1927, and by 1985 it was accommodating over 700 federal female prisoners (Weisheit and Mahan, 1988:66). Despite the fact that the federal government has initiated large-scale prison industries programs to assist inmates in learning new vocational skills and acquiring other types of training, only 200 females from Alderson were working in these industries by 1985. Most of these women were working in a garment factory performing sewing work, while a few other female prisoners were working in graphic design in a decal shop (Weisheit and Mahan, 1988:66–67). Thus, the leading federal female correctional institution is perpetuating traditional, stereotypical work roles for its women inmates. This same situation is mirrored in most states as well, where female inmates are offered a limited array of courses, including cosmetology, clerical work, and food services (Culliver, 1993).

Mann (1984:216) suggests the following six reasons for the lack of vocational and educational programs for women prisoners, despite recent prison reforms and legal milestones:

1. Women make up such a small proportion of the prison population so that extensive programming is cost-prohibitive.
2. Women prisoners are less of a threat to society than males; therefore, they do not require equivalent financial expenditures to fund such programs.
3. Training costs for women prisoners are too high compared with their male counterparts.
4. When programs are offered, few women participate voluntarily.
5. Women's prisons are isolated and inaccessible to many services, thus making service delivery difficult or impossible.
6. Society's traditional view of women as wage-earners is secondary to their roles as mothers and housewives.

It is insufficient to simply expand the number of services available to female inmates. Proper planning must occur, by which the special needs of certain offenders are anticipated and met with adequate services and programs (Benekos and Merlo, 1993). One matter that is infrequently considered when designing curricula for women's prisons is whether the skill, vocation, or education is realistic in view of the criminal record the women have acquired. Many states have licensing laws and policies associated with certain kinds of jobs that prohibit hiring those with criminal records or those who have served time in prison or jail. Minnesota, for instance, has worked to establish an Office of Planning for Women Offenders. This office is particularly geared to serve the needs of minority women who are overrepresented in these settings and frequently lack basic skills to obtain jobs when they are eventually released. The overall goal of this office is to better serve the needs of those women housed in Minnesota's prisons, the 87 county correctional facilities, and the 31 jails (Hokanson, 1986).

The matter of proper health care for incarcerated women has already been resolved by the U.S. Supreme Court. Deliberate indifference to the medical needs of prisoners was determined to be "cruel and unusual" punishment and in violation of the Eighth Amendment in *Estelle v. Gamble* (1976). But women often require special health care, and they have gynecological needs including pap smears and assistance with menstrual problems, obstetrical help, and other medical services (e.g., breast cancer examinations, biopsies) that may not be immediately available. Again, this is because the facilities are remote and access to quality services is lacking when needed on an emergency basis. Often, these prisons cannot afford to maintain on-premises medical help to cope with anything other than minor health problems and injuries (Feinman, 1986:56–57).

Those women with drug or alcohol dependencies or who may be mentally ill are at a disadvantage as well. Estimates vary, although it is reasonable to assume that from 10 to 15 percent of all incarcerated females have some form of mental illness or are psychologically disturbed. Over a third are incarcerated who have drug- or alcohol-related problems. Many of these inmates should be hospitalized and treated with professional medical and/or psychiatric services rather than imprisoned (Moon et al., 1994). Yet, an unknown number of psychologically disturbed female inmates receive minimal and superficial treatment equivalent to that received by the average person in a community health clinic. In some jurisdictions, at least, women's treatment centers rely heavily on the use of tranquilizers to placate inmates instead of more costly but necessary psychotherapy and counseling. The counseling these women do receive, whenever it is available, is of questionable quality (Pollock-Byrne, 1990). These insufficient treatment methods often aggravate rather than alleviate mental problems or chemical dependencies (Moon et al., 1994; Pollock-Byrne, 1990). Many states are establishing oversight committees intended to rectify many of these inequities between men's and women's prisons, however (Oregon Governor's Task Force on Corrections Planning, 1990).

Boot Camps for Women? At the Eddie Warrior Correctional Center in Oklahoma, a program known as the Female Offender Regimented Treatment Program (FORT) has been established (Russell, Nicholson, and Buigas, 1990). FORT was established for several purposes. First, officials observed how effective comparable boot camps were for youthful offenders, and they envisioned a similar program that might be workable for certain types of female offenders. The result was FORT.

FORT consists of a substantial substance abuse treatment component; classes in parenting, decision making, and moral development; educational opportunities; and discipline. Periodic assessments were made of women in terms of their psychopathology; ego strength and self-esteem; educational achievement; behaviors and characteristics associated with substance abuse; and perceived benefits and satisfaction with the program. Regimented drills supplemented the educational and vocational activities with favorable results. Indications are that female participants have acquired sufficient self-esteem and discipline to make a better adjustment to community living once they are paroled. Investigators also indicate that participants like the program and what it has done for them (Russell et al., 1990).

Domestic Violence Prevention Programs

Family violence among probationers and parolees is fairly high. Often, familial disruptions contribute to criminal acts originally committed. Family violence is not only high among offender-clients, but it has also received national recognition as a major social problem (Dickstein and Nadelson, 1989). A contemporary approach to family violence stresses violence prevention before it occurs (Lees and DeCostanzo, 1994; Stratton, 1988).

In 1988, a consortium of U.S. federal agencies asked the National Academy of Sciences to assess the understanding of family violence and the implications of that understanding for developing preventive interventions (Reiss and Roth, 1993). Violence was defined as behaviors by individuals that intentionally threaten, attempt, or inflict physical harm on others. Four recommendations were forthcoming:

1. Sustained problem-solving initiatives should be undertaken on interventions related to biological and psychosocial development of individuals' propensity for violent behavior, modifying crime-prone settings and situations, and intervening to reduce public and domestic violence.
2. High priority should be given to modifying and expanding statistical information systems on violent behavior.
3. New research is needed on instrumental effects of weapons, risk factors, and comparative development sequences.
4. A new, multicommunity program of developmental studies of aggressive, violent, and antisocial behaviors should be launched to improve both causal understanding and preventive interventions (Reiss and Roth, 1993).

One of the first problems for correctional officers is to detect spouse abuse and family violence (Ford and Regoli, 1993). This is often discovered during face-to-face visits with offender-clients and their families. However, many victims of family violence are unwilling to report such abuse to correctional officers at any time. This is a prevalent phenomenon observed by experts investigating family violence (Saunders and Azar, 1989). Saunders and Azar (1989:486–491) indicate the following measures to be taken in many family violence cases:

1. Crisis lines are established for victims as well as offenders.
2. Shelters are provided for victims.
3. Victims or offenders are removed from the family setting.

Family abuse victims often need legal aid, medical treatment, psychological counseling, and job readiness preparation. For sexually abused women and children, several treatment models exist that emphasize or promote child advocacy. These programs are also concerned with restructuring the legal system and developing procedures for reducing the trauma to young children, developing psychiatric and family systems orientation, and engaging in behavior modification designed to assist offenders. Some of these techniques are considered coercive, since they force offenders to enter specific treatment programs (Saunders and Azar, 1989:502–504). One program is the Child Sexual Abuse Treatment Program (SCATP). This program involves individual counseling for all family members of offender-clients, including mother-daughter counseling, marital counseling, father-daughter counseling, and group counseling, where such counseling is based on the principles of humanistic psychotherapy; self-help groups are also provided (Saunders and Azar, 1989:504). Volunteer men's collectives, social services agencies, and women's shelters are also effective in changing offender behaviors. Because probationers and parolees are under the immediate jurisdiction of either the courts or parole boards, their participation in different kinds of intervention programs and therapies can be incorporated into their probation or parole programs as an important component and requirement. Continued familial abuses of any kind can be grounds for probation or parole revocation if detected.

Special Programs and Services for Female Offenders

A growing problem among the female offender population is AIDS (Marcus and Bibace, 1993). Many incarcerated women know very little about AIDS or how it is transmitted. They do not know the signs of AIDS or whether they should seek medical attention for an AIDS diagnosis (Kuhns and Heide, 1992). Thus, some prisons for women are instituting programs to assist inmates in their understanding of AIDS and its contagiousness (Marcus and Bibace, 1993).

Other incarcerated women have substance abuse problems that must be addressed while they are confined. Otherwise, they will leave prisons untreated and resume their drug or alcohol dependencies once again within their communities. In Oklahoma, a study was conducted of 547 female prisoners and the extent of drug use among them (Moon et al., 1994). Female drug users tended to be older than other inmates and had longer criminal histories. Those with drug dependencies tended to have histories of child abuse. White female drug users differed from black female drug users in that black drug users had lower levels of self-esteem and had multiple drug use from more extensive involvement with the criminal justice system. White drug users reported higher levels of drug use. White offenders had less multiple drug use. Thus, programs were recommended to meet the needs of those with histories of childhood abuse and chronic offending. Counseling sessions were recommended for high drug users (Moon et al., 1994).

Increasingly, designers of women's prisons are planning for areas where counseling and other women's services can be conducted (Flanagan, 1995). Programming needs of women are directed toward more productive activities to make these women more competitive in the job market once they are released (Carp and David, 1991). Thus, there is a gradual movement away from those kinds of activities traditionally associated with women's societal roles (Florida Joint Legislative Management Committee, 1995).

CO-CORRECTIONS: ONE LOGICAL AND CONTROVERSIAL SOLUTION TO A COMPLEX PROBLEM

The segregation of prisoners according to their gender dates back several centuries to the Walnut Street Jail, and later, to the Auburn Penitentiary in New York. Reasons given then included the improvement of inmate morality, a reduction in inmate promiscuity, and greater privacy for both sexes. In recent years, however, prisoners, both male and female, have expressed interest in co-correctional or co-ed prisons (Feinman, 1986:64–65; Rafter, 1990). Advocates of co-correctional prisons have used as their support the Fourteenth Amendment equal protection clause as well as U.S. Supreme Court decisions declaring the "separate, but equal" doctrine to be null and void as applicable to education, employment, public utilities, and other areas.

Co-correctional prisons are those where men and women prisoners live, supervised by female and male staff, and participate in all activities together, although, unlike in Denmark and other countries, inmates may not share the same quarters or have sexual encounters. Co-correctional prisons are not prisons that merely house male and female offenders somewhere in separate facilities on the prison grounds such as in Utah and Tennessee. In traditional prison settings such as these where specific areas are assigned females, no interaction occurs between them. In co-correctional prisons, there *is* interaction, even though it may be limited to recreational periods and certain educational, counseling, or vocational programs (Mahan, 1986).

The first co-correctional prison in the United States was the Federal Correctional Institution in Fort Worth, Texas, opened in 1971 by the U.S. Bureau of Prisons (Smykla, 1978). Among the states, the Massachusetts Correctional Institution at Framingham is generally regarded as the first state co-correctional facility (Carter, Glaser, and Wilkins, 1985:237). While the objectives of co-correctional prisons vary, generally these objectives include the following (Feinman, 1986:65–66):

1. Permitting a more normal contact between male and female inmates as a means of alleviating the tension of gender isolation
2. Permitting mutual access to prison services ordinarily offered to male or to female inmates
3. Permitting male and female inmates opportunities to engage in social exchange, thus helping to ease the transition back into the community when eventually paroled
4. Permitting more cost-effective program operations and access to more services (Feinman, 1986:65–66)

The ratio of male to female inmates is recommended to be 50-50 (Mahan, 1986:134). When women outnumber men or vice versa, realistic integration is made increasingly difficult. When women are in the minority (and they usually are in most prisons), they feel conspicuous, and they tend to be treated as a minority group by their male counterparts (Mahan, 1986:134). Also, jealousies among the dominant sex may arise because of greater competition for social encounters and more intimate relationships. The smallest effective proportion of women in a co-correctional prison has been recommended as 40 percent. Furthermore, keeping such facilities small means more effective monitoring and supervision by correctional officers and other staff.

A major public misconception about co-correctional prisons is that there is unchecked promiscuity, shared quarters by male and female inmates, and numerous illegitimate births (Halford, 1984). This is quite removed from what actually occurs. The Kansas Correctional Institution at Lansing provides a good example of the reality of a co-correctional prison. Formerly the Kansas Correctional Institution for Women, the traditional female prison in Kansas, it was changed in September 1980, with the introduction of 27 male inmates from the Kansas State Prison (Halford, 1984:44). Those male inmates transferred were low-risk offenders who had been employed earlier on a limited work-release basis. Thus, not all male prisoners were considered for integration in the new co-correctional facility.

While there were initial resentments on the part of both male and female inmates (i.e., some males felt they had been "demoted" by being transferred to a prison for women), these were gradually resolved. The Kansas institution is an example of a very positive experience in co-correctional imprisonment. Some of the success measures used by evaluators of the project included greater staff enthusiasm, considerable support from the Kansas Department of Corrections, positive media coverage, and observation of privacy rights of both sexes, and parolees found it easier to gain employment when released. Also, compared with 1979, there was a 40 percent reduction in the number of violent discipline charges, a 73 percent reduction in the number of general discipline charges, and a 42 percent reduction in the number of grievances filed by inmates (Halford, 1984:54).

There have been some minor problems encountered by Kansas prison authorities in that institution, but these are relatively minor considering the nature of the inmate population. Only 4 pregnancies occurred during the first 33 months of the co-correctional operation. On the positive side according to officials, homosexuality decreased considerably. However, there were a few incidents among male prisoners fighting for the attentions of certain female inmates. As expected, the general public objections to the Kansas co-correctional facility are that there is widespread promiscuity (not true) and that officials are not being "tough enough" with inmates (Halford, 1984:54).

Actually, the nature of inmate interaction in virtually every co-correctional facility today is structured and fairly closely supervised. Some researchers have found that inmates feel too closely monitored, however, compared with unisex prison settings. This causes a degree of tension and anxiety (Mahan, 1986:136). Furthermore, the "look but don't touch" aspect of these settings acts to aggravate sexual frustrations for both male and female inmates. But reports have largely been positive about inmate opportunities to talk to those of the opposite sex. The preoccupation of these inmates is not exclusively sexual (Mahan, 1986:138). One inmate said, "It gives you an opportunity to have 'woman' conversations . . . verbalize frailties and inner fears . . . vent hurt and anger . . . I don't have to act hardened . . . Weakness won't cause me to be devoured here . . . The primitive law of prison isn't in operation here" (Mahan, 1986:138).

Some opponents of co-correctional institutions believe that women need to be physically separated from men for a time in order to regain their self-respect and identities. Also, the "look but don't touch" rule of these institutions may actually encourage homosexual relationships rather than discourage them. Finally, these institutions are considered exploitative by some authorities. Women become or continue to be sexual objects of men (Smykla, 1980:262–272).

Men Guarding Women and Women Guarding Men. A closely related issue is whether men should be placed in correctional officer positions in all-female institutions, and whether female correctional officers should be placed in all-male institutions. The question is academic at this point, since both types of scenarios are being played out in prisons throughout the United States. In 1995, 45 agencies were surveyed. It was found that 25,623 female corrections officers were working in male institutions, while 4,037 male correctional officers were working in female institutions (Camp and Camp, 1995a:73). Reported in 1986 as a "major breakthrough" in the hiring of female correctional officers in men's institutions, this matter is now fairly commonplace (Zimmer, 1986).

INTERMEDIATE PUNISHMENTS FOR WOMEN

The same range of intermediate punishments exists for women as it does for men. In fact, arrest and incarceration figures suggest that proportionately more women than men are either diverted from the criminal justice system altogether or sentenced to nonincarcerative intermediate punishments. One reason is that the nature of offending among women is such that a greater proportion of them are considered low risk and nonviolent (Weisheit and Mahan, 1988:55). These intermediate punishments may include fines, conditions for restitution and victim compensation, community service, or some other alternative provision. Even those women who are incarcerated stand a better chance of being paroled or serving shorter sentences than men. Parole criteria in many states include the requirements that offenders must be in minimum custody within six months of their anticipated parole, that they committed no assaultive offense, that they had not attempted escape, and that they did not engage in major rule infractions within three months of the scheduled parole date (McCarthy and McCarthy, 1997).

Intermediate punishments include intensive supervised probation, community-based correctional programs, home confinement, and electronic monitoring. More women than men, for instance, tend to be placed under house arrest in those areas where home confinement programs are available. For those offenders who are first-offenders or low risk and considered nondangerous, they may be placed in a diversion program or sentenced to probation. Women are generally considered good risks for such programs, because their success rates are much higher than for men (Norland and Mann, 1984). And when women do commit rule infractions, these are usually technical violations and noncrime related (Norland and Mann, 1984). Women in prison may be granted furloughs, work release, or parole, where they will be subject to varying levels of supervision by parole officers (Minnesota Department of Corrections, 1984). This section briefly examines the use of diversion and probation, community-based supervision, and intensive supervised parole for female offenders.

Diversion and Probation

There are comparatively few diversion programs offered to female offenders. Immarigeon (1987b) says that because of the relatively small number of female offenders compared with male offenders, the need simply hasn't existed in most jurisdictions to devise programs to accommodate those few female offenders. Of the few diversion programs that presently exist in the United States, three have achieved some visibility. These include the Women's Self-Help Center's Justice Outreach Program in St. Louis, the Community Services for Women in Boston, and the Elizabeth Fry Center in San Francisco. Each of these programs also provides assistance to female probationers. Thus, they are not exclusively diversion programs.

While now there may be few diversionary programs operating that are gender-specific, there are many other diversion programs that are available to both males and females. The Monroe County, New York, Pretrial Diversion Program is one of the more successful. Started in the mid-1970s as an alternative to a formal prosecution, the Monroe diversion program has been extensively evaluated over the years. Findings from these evaluations show that about 80 percent of the participants complete the program successfully, and only a small proportion are ever rearrested or convicted of new offenses (McCarthy and McCarthy, 1997). Actually, women are better candidates for diversion programs than men. They tend to commit less violent offenses, are more responsive to supervision by probation officers and others, and have better records for completing these programs. If they are mothers, they often are able to continue their parenting with assistance from various community agencies. These relations with agencies are frequently mandated by their diversion programs. Thus, they receive valuable information and education that they might not have received if imprisoned.

It is presently unknown how many female divertees have characteristics similar to female inmates. Some structural features of programs such as California's statutory diversion operate to exclude those who have been charged with drug violations or who have a previous history of drug offenses. Since a fairly large proportion of female prison inmates were convicted of drug-related offenses, many of these persons probably were automatically excluded from participating in the diversion program initially. Also operating against women is the fact that diversion programs often require financial stability through gainful employment. If female arrestees share many of the same characteristics as female prison inmates (e.g., young, unemployed or underemployed, uneducated), then these factors may discourage prosecutors from considering many female offenders for diversion programs. But since diversion information either is not made public or is difficult to access by investigators, no figures are available to show whether these factors actually make a difference in diversion-granting decisions.

The major benefits of diversion for females, especially those who are mothers, are that they may maintain contact with their families and children and may receive treatment for their mental problems or drug/alcohol dependencies. They may also participate in educational programs that will lead to better-paying jobs or to the acquisition of valuable work skills, and their self-image is enhanced. Probation for women is also a desirable option, but it means that they have been convicted of a crime. In the case of divertees, there are usually no convictions, since the case is withdrawn from prosecution. Their clean record enhances their opportunities for seeking employment and performing work requiring no prior criminal convictions.

Because of overcrowding in most prisons and jails, and because women tend to commit less serious offenses than men, their chances for being sentenced to probation are greater. Annual arrest, conviction, and incarceration figures for men and women support this. Furthermore, available evidence suggests that women are better probation risks, commit fewer violations of their probation conditions, and are less likely than men to be charged with technical violations even when they do commit them. Researchers say some reasons for this include certain paternalistic dispositions of probation officers, such that they resist reporting women in order to preserve their family stability (Norland and Mann, 1984). Also, factors unrelated to probation program violations such as excessive paperwork and prison overcrowding cause some probation officers to hesitate reporting *any* offender, unless the offense or violation is quite serious (Norland and Mann, 1984).

By year-end 1995, 20 percent of the adult probation population consisted of women (Camp and Camp, 1995d:18). Probation officers report, however, that supervising women may be troublesome. According to some probation officers, women take up an inordinate amount of their time with trivial or minor matters, emotional problems, or upsetting familial situations that require intensive counseling. Probation officers generally prefer to maintain amiable, yet superficial, contacts with their clients, and these types of associations are easily established with male probationers. However, female probationers often form relationships of emotional dependency and rely increasingly on probation officers as their counselors and crying towels (Norland and Mann, 1984).

A successful probation program has been described in Bexar County,

Texas, where an intensive supervision program was instituted in 1981 by the Adult Probation Department (Williams et al., 1982). Interestingly, this program tended to favor the inclusion of low-risk nonviolent female offenders and the systematic exclusion of more serious male offenders. A profile of participants showed that a majority were female, young, white, unmarried, possessing lower educational backgrounds, and having sporadic work histories. These are precisely the sorts of characteristics possessed by female prison inmates. The program has been somewhat successful in that 60 percent of all probationers (consisting mostly of women) have been "diverted" from prison. Some amount of net widening might be found in the Bexar County project. Although no authoritative figures are available, it would be interesting to know how many of these low-risk nonviolent females could have been diverted from the system entirely and not convicted.

Under the new federal sentencing guidelines, probation may be used with decreasing frequency, at least in the federal system. More sentences involving incarceration, although for shorter periods, are being imposed on most offenders convicted of federal crimes. It is too early to tell whether these new guidelines will have any discernible impact on the rate that women are placed on probation in the federal system. While some authorities feel that these guideline changes may result in greater equity and fairness in sentencing offenders, these changes may be disadvantageous to female offenders who have been granted probation more frequently than males in past years (McCarthy and McCarthy, 1997).

In many diversion and probation programs, one or more conditions of these programs may be the payment of fines, some amount of restitution or victim compensation, and/or community service orders. It has been found that community service has been used only infrequently as a condition of either probation or diversion. Furthermore, it is seldom used in the case of female offenders (Griffiths and Patenaude, 1990). In addition, fines and other penalties are imposed with less frequency for convicted female offenders than male offenders. While no precise figures are available, it would appear that restitution or victim compensation orders are disproportionately assigned to male offenders. Since women tend to commit a greater proportion of property and nonviolent offenses, it may be that there is less victim injury associated with female criminality. This would account for the disproportionate use of fines or victim compensation among male and female offenders.

Intensive Supervised Parole

About 11 percent of the population of parolees in 1995 were female (Camp and Camp, 1995d:34). Many female parolees are assigned to live in halfway houses before being completely free to live on their own resources in the community. A halfway house for female offenders has been operated successfully for many years in Long Beach, California, where recidivism rates have been extremely low (Dowell, Klein, and Krichmar, 1985). These halfway houses are considered by most program officials to be helpful at giving female clients an "edge" in their successful return to society.

Although it is not known how many public and private halfway houses are operated exclusively for women, there are several thousand halfway houses throughout the United States operated with varying degrees of organization and sophistication. Co-ed halfway houses exist, but there is some evidence to indicate that many communities view these houses unfavorably (McCarthy and McCarthy, 1997). Generally, females do better on parole than males (McCarthy and McCarthy, 1997). Not only do they comply with parole program requirements more consistently, their absconding rates also are negligible. Absconding is minimized through effective risk/needs prediction instruments, but these instruments are often heavily biased toward male offender characteristics. Thus, attempting to predict accurately whether female parolees will abscond is a near-impossible task for parole officers and others. Ordinarily, less than 5 percent of all probationers and parolees ever abscond during any given year (Camp and Camp, 1995a, 1995d).

One very important factor associated with female parolee recidivism is whether the ex-offender is either employed or receives unemployment compensation while looking for work. A study of recidivism among female ex-offenders, the Transitional Aid Research Project, was conducted in the late 1970s. It showed that women who recidivated did so because of economic necessity, whereas those with jobs or who were receiving unemployment compensation tended not to recidivate (Jurik, 1983). This finding contradicts what criminologists tend to believe about why women recidivate generally. A common belief is that they recidivate because of sexual or emotional reasons rather than economic ones. At least this study shows that economic factors are more important. An increasing number of jurisdictions are offering employment services to ex-offenders. A large number of female releasees from correctional facilities in San Diego, Chicago, and Boston were studied in the early 1980s to determine whether these special follow-up services were of value in decreasing recidivism. The results were largely favorable, again showing that employment tended to decrease recidivism among these females significantly. Thus, there is additional support for the work of Jurik (1983) who also found the economic variable influential.

KEY TERMS

Campus model
Co-correctional prisons
Cools
Custodial model
Forgotten offenders
Elizabeth Gurney Fry
Lifes
Magdalen Society
Reformatory model
Squares
Visiting Cottage Program

QUESTIONS FOR REVIEW

1. What is a co-correctional prison? How does a co-correctional prison differ from a prison that houses both male and female offenders?
2. What provisions do some states make for female inmates who are mothers?
3. What was the historical significance of Rachel Welch?
4. When was the first prison for women in the United States established? During what period did most of the construction of women's prisons occur?
5. What types of models exist that portray different stages in the development of prisons for women?
6. What are some of the reasons for establishing co-correctional prisons? Are all correctional officials pleased with co-correctional prisons? What are some objections cited?
7. Describe female offenders. Is the amount of crime among women increasing? Is there a "new wave" of female criminals in the United States?
8. In what ways are women favored by the criminal justice system in the way they are sentenced and processed?
9. How sophisticated are the classification schemes devised to separate female offenders when incarcerated? What are some general problems with these classification schemes that make them less applicable to females than to males?
10. Is there a unique female prison culture? How extensive is lesbianism among female prisoners in state and federal institutions?
11. Do female inmates enjoy the same constitutional rights as male inmates?
12. Why were prisons for women originally located in remote, rural areas? What types of problems have these remote locations caused female inmates in recent years?
13. What are some of the more popular intermediate punishments for women? How do women fare compared with men in successfully completing their probation or parole programs? What are some of the reasons that account for this?
14. How will the new U.S. sentencing guidelines act to the disadvantage of the female offender?

SUGGESTED READINGS

American Correctional Association. *Female Offenders: Meeting Needs of a Neglected Population.* Laurel, MD: American Correctional Association, 1993.

Burke, Carol. *Vision Narratives of Women in Prison.* Knoxville, TN: University of Tennessee Press, 1992.

Culliver, Concetta C. (ed.). *Female Criminality: The State of the Art.* New York: Garland Publishing Company, 1993.

Immarigeon, Russ, and Meda Chesney-Lind. *Women's Prisons: Overcrowded and Overused.* San Francisco: National Council on Crime and Delinquency, 1992.

Klausner, Marian L. *Opening Doors for Change: Alternatives to Incarceration—A Report on Alternative Sentencing for Women.* Boston: Social Justice for Women, 1991.

Morton, Joann B. (ed.). *Change, Challenge & Choices: Women's Role in Modern Corrections.* Laurel, MD: American Correctional Association, 1991.

Watterson, Kathryn. *Women in Prison: Inside the Concrete Womb* (rev. ed.). Boston: Northeastern University Press, 1996.

14

Juvenile Corrections

CHAPTER OUTLINE

OVERVIEW

- There is a video arcade game called "Centipede." The objective is to crush all enemies, some of whom evolve from "mushrooms." Thus, the more mushrooms killed, the longer the game can be played and the higher the score. For gangs on the streets of South Central Los Angeles, more deadly games are played daily. There is extensive rivalry between gangs over the ownership of turf, which may be two or three city blocks in a run-down neighborhood. For every neighborhood resident, the sound of nearby gunfire is routine, a common environmental sound, like wind blowing or birds chirping. One day, a cruising carload of Crips, a Los Angeles gang, was out looking for Bloods, a rival gang. Crip colors are blue, and the carload of Crips sported blue checkered bandannas, shirts, and jackets. Bloods wore red. The Crips were searching for "red." They saw some red in a crowd of teens waiting to enter a movie theater. Shotguns and semiautomatic weapons protruded from the Crip car, and gunfire erupted. In the aftermath, there were 12 dead or wounded teenagers lying in front of the theater. It turned out that none of them, even those wearing red shirts or jackets, was affiliated with the Bloods gang. One Crip gang member quipped later, "Well, so we took out a couple of mushrooms. So what? Big deal!" To gang members, life is cheap in L.A. It was just another day.
- In Tacoma, Washington, four girls, ranging in age from 13 to 16, were on their lunch hour at a high school. Deciding that they needed some money, they paid a visit to an 85-year-old lady who lived nearby. The lady held Bible classes for neighborhood children and had provided them with occasional gifts or small amounts of money. The four girls armed themselves with a hammer and some knives. They gained entry to the old woman's home easily, since two of them knew her from the bible classes they had taken. When the old woman turned her back for a moment, the girl with the hammer hit the woman in the back of the head, causing her to fall to the floor unconscious. The other three girls pounced on the old woman with their knives thrashing. Later, when the old woman's dead body was discovered, it was determined that she had been stabbed 53 times and had sustained at least 6 fatal hits to the head with a hammer. The community was stunned when incriminating evidence was found that linked one of the girls, a 14-year-old, to the old woman's murder. A locket belonging to one of the girls was inadvertently left at the crime scene, obscured by the blood. The 14-year-old girl incriminated the other three, and eventually confessions were obtained. The girls got $15 from the old woman's

purse, later spending the money at a local Taco Bell. They showed no remorse as they were brought into court to hear the charges against them.

- In Florida, a local group of teenagers defined themselves as a vampire cult. They performed Satanic rituals, cut one another, and drank blood. One evening they decided that the parents of one of the girls in the cult should be sacrificed. They went to the home and slayed the parents, performing various rituals with the parents' bodies and blood. Eventually, they were arrested. The juvenile court decided to send them to criminal court to be tried as adults. The most serious punishment for premeditated murder in Florida is the death penalty.

Are these scenarios exceptional? Do they typify only occasional events? Or are these youths only the tip of an iceberg of a pattern of pervasive juvenile violence? In the United States today, juvenile violence is escalating at a disturbing rate. Not only are *more* youths committing violent offenses annually, but these violent acts are being committed by younger and younger juveniles. Drive-by shootings involving youths under age 10 are commonplace. Advocates of change want the age lowered for transferring juveniles to criminal courts for more serious prosecutions and punishments. Juvenile court reformers want harsher punishments meted out to those who commit heinous acts against innocent citizens. The "mushrooms" are striking back, wanting to retake their streets and neighborhoods. If juvenile delinquency cannot be prevented, then it can be punished more severely whenever it is encountered. Some experts believe that this is where juvenile corrections can do the most good, by incapacitating and punishing more chronic, persistent violent youths.

This chapter is about corrections for juveniles. Until the mid-1960s, juveniles had few legal rights in courts. Their affairs were administered by civil authorities, usually family or domestic courts, chancery courts, or other exclusively civil agencies. In recent years, however, significant advancements have been made in juvenile corrections, with substantial improvements in juvenile case dispositions. This chapter does not deal with the causes of delinquency. Rather, it focuses on the processing of youthful offenders. First, a brief history of juvenile corrections in the United States is presented. Several goals of juvenile corrections are outlined, together with the types of offenses normally included within delinquency designation. Selected characteristics of juvenile offenders are discussed, together with some significant developments and trends pertaining to juvenile correctional processing.

An overview of the juvenile justice system is presented, and each stage of this process is treated. The intent of many juvenile courts is to divert juveniles away from the system so that they will not develop self-definitions of delinquency. For some juvenile offenders, however, greater discipline and harsher treatment are required, including detention in secure facilities. These facilities and programs are described and assessed. Finally, several key issues in juvenile corrections are presented, including proposals for modifying the sorts of offenses that qualify for the delinquency label. One issue of interest is the privatization of juvenile corrections. Like its adult counterpart, juvenile corrections is susceptible to management by private interests. In fact, juvenile corrections is an area where privatization has been most noticeable. The issue of capital punishment for juveniles is also treated briefly. This is especially important since the U.S. Supreme Court has recently determined that the death penalty may not be administered to any juvenile under the age of 16 at the time a capital crime was committed (*Stanford v. Kentucky,* 1989; *Thompson v. Oklahoma,* 1988; *Wilkins v. Missouri,* 1989).

THE HISTORY OF JUVENILE CORRECTIONS

Juvenile delinquency is any act committed by a juvenile which, if committed by an adult, would be a crime (Champion and Mays, 1991). Since a civil disposition is made about juvenile offenders whenever they commit felonies or misdemeanors, their acts are classified as "offenses" rather than as "crimes." A majority of states define age 18 as the upper limit for juvenile court jurisdiction. The remaining states use age 17 as the upper limit (8 states) or age 16 as the upper limit (4 states). While the lower age limit for juvenile court jurisdiction varies among states, age 10 is cited most frequently as the minimum age for this jurisdiction. Children under age 7 are generally presumed incapable of formulating criminal intent and in most jurisdictions are subject to the jurisdiction of civil agencies such as departments of social welfare or child and family services.

During the 1800s and early 1900s, juvenile matters in the United States were handled by a variety of civil courts and nonlegal institutions such as welfare agencies. The doctrine under which juveniles were managed and processed was called *parens patriae,* which means "parent of the country" (Black, 1990:1114). Historically, this term was a part of English common law during the medieval period, and it meant that juvenile matters were within the purview of the king and his agents, usually chancellors and other officials in various regions. Figuratively, the king was the "father of the country" and assumed responsibility for all juveniles. Through the centuries this term was accepted by most jurisdictions. It eventually carried over into U.S. juvenile matters and influenced significantly the discretion exercised over juveniles by adult courts and other institutions.

Early efforts to deal with juvenile offenders in the United States led to the establishment of the first public reformatory, the **New York House of Refuge,** organized in New York City in 1825 by the Society for the Prevention of Pauperism (Hess and Clement, 1993). The manifest goals of this house of refuge were to provide poor, abused, or orphaned youths with food, clothing, and lodging, although in return, hard work, discipline, and study were expected. Since there was little centralized organization to these houses of refuge, it is difficult to determine the impact these facilities exerted on delinquency in any city area (Rogers and Mays, 1987:426).

Charles Loring Brace set up a New York Children's Aid Society in

1953 that functioned primarily as a placement service for parentless children (Mennel, 1983:199). The term juvenile delinquency was seldom used during the early 1800s, because public authorities stressed parental control of children and regarded youthful misbehaviors as a lack of discipline rather than as something to be dealt with more formally (Mennel, 1983:198). Many early institutions designed to care for and reform juveniles were operated under private, charitable, and religious sponsorship. The Civil War was followed by the Reconstruction Period and vast industrialization. The war had left many families fatherless, and in the years that followed, many of these families gravitated to urban areas seeking employment in factories and shops. Many children were exploited by so-called "sweat shops" in the absence of child labor laws, and a large number of them roamed the streets unattended while their parents worked long hours at various jobs. **Children's tribunals** were created in different states including Massachusetts and New York to deal with youths charged with committing crimes. The first statute authorizing such a tribunal to deal with juvenile matters was passed in Massachusetts in 1874 (Hahn, 1984). A similar statute was passed in New York in 1892.

Jane Addams established and operated Hull House in 1889, a settlement home for children of immigrant families in Chicago. This home was financed by charitable organizations and philanthropists, and it existed to provide children with activities to alleviate boredom and monotony while their parents were at work. Many children without parents were accommodated by Addams. Teaching children morality, ethics, and certain religious precepts were integral features of correctional thought in Addams's day. The influence of Cesare Beccaria, the father of classical criminology, was apparent. Beccaria, an Italian criminologist, wrote in 1764 that the purposes of punishment were to deter others from committing crimes. Furthermore, the punishment should fit the crime. This theorizing was combined with humanitarianism, especially for youthful offenders (Springer, 1987:8–11).

The Colorado legislature passed the **Compulsory School Act** in 1899 to prevent truancy among juveniles. This Act included those youths who were habitually absent from school, who wandered about the streets during school hours, and who had no obvious business or occupation. These youths were labeled "juvenile disorderly persons." Since the Act was aimed primarily at truancy, it is not considered a juvenile court act in a technical sense. The Illinois legislature created the first juvenile court act on July 1, 1899. It was called **An Act to Regulate the Treatment and Control of Dependent, Neglected and Delinquent Children.** Between 1899 and 1909, 20 states had passed similar legislation for the establishment of juvenile courts. By 1945, *all* states had juvenile court systems. However, these systems varied greatly among jurisdictions, and the responsibility for deciding juvenile dispositions rested with a variety of courts.

The first census of juvenile offenders in public institutions occurred in 1880 and was conducted by the U.S. Bureau of Census. This report disclosed that there were 11,468 juvenile offenders in institutions in the

United States. That figure had more than doubled by 1904, and by 1980, there were 59,414 juveniles in various public detention facilities throughout the United States (Cahalan, 1986:104).

TYPES OF JUVENILE OFFENDERS

Just as their adult counterparts vary according to the nature and seriousness of the offenses they commit, there is an exceptional array of offenses committed by juveniles. There are *violent* and *property* or *nonviolent* juvenile offenders. Female juveniles commit basically different kinds of offenses than male juveniles, and it appears that both male and female delinquency rates are increasing (Heide, 1992; Matthews, Matthews, and Speltz, 1989). For instance, a greater proportion of female juvenile offenders tend to engage in shoplifting and sex offenses including prostitution (Matthews et al., 1989). However, some persons believe that these differences are greatly exaggerated. Some analysts suggest that a *new* female delinquent is emerging as one outcome of the Women's Movement, but others say this is more a function of the law and order phase we have entered in law enforcement (Curran, 1984). Whatever the trends in juvenile delinquency happen to be and the rationales advanced to explain them, there are two broad categories of juvenile offenders: (1) status offenders, and (2) juvenile delinquents.

Status Offenders

Status offenders are juveniles who commit offenses that, if committed by adults, would not be considered crimes. Examples of status offenses include truancy, running away from home, and violating curfew. These offenses are considered illegal for juveniles. However, if adults enroll in courses at school and do not attend them, they are not considered truant. If adults run away from home, they are not criminals. If adults walk the streets after certain hours in particular communities, they are not arrested. In short, the *status* of being under 18 or 17 or 16, depending on the jurisdiction, places the juvenile in a special category as a status offender (Black, 1990).

Juvenile Delinquents

There are some major differences between delinquent acts and status offenses. Status offenses are not as serious as delinquent offenses. However, for many decades, more than a few states have lumped status offenses and delinquent offenses together into a single category and have processed offenders similarly through the juvenile courts. This means that at least in some state jurisdictions, juveniles are adjudicated as either delinquent offenders or status offenders by juvenile court judges and placed in the same programs or custodial facilities.

In predominantly rural states, such as North Dakota, Montana,

Nebraska, and South Dakota, for instance, both status offenders and delinquent offenders often are incarcerated in industrial schools for more or less lengthy terms. At Mandan, North Dakota, an industrial school is operated as a secure facility for both male and female juveniles. Both status and delinquent offenders are confined at the Mandan Industrial School for periods ranging from 3 to 27 months. In many other states, however, status offenders are not confined with delinquent offenders. Rather, they are managed or supervised by one or more community agencies.

The Juvenile Justice and Delinquency Prevention Act of 1974. In 1974, the **Juvenile Justice and Delinquency Prevention Act,** which encouraged the states to deal differently with their juvenile status offenders, was passed. The act made available monies to various states and individual communities to create community-based treatment programs as an alternative to institutionalizing juveniles in secure detention such as a reform or industrial school. Also, the act encouraged states to divert status offenders away from the juvenile justice system entirely, so that their problems could be dealt with more adequately in nonthreatening settings by various community agencies (Richeson and Klofas, 1990). This has been referred to as the *jail removal initiative,* because it aims to prevent juveniles from being held in jails for virtually *any* length of time (E. Johnson, 1990). A third aim of the act was to provide monies to explore ways of preventing delinquency and to create various projects with this primary objective. Although no states are obligated to comply with the provisions of this act, most jurisdictions have made efforts to remove juvenile status offenders from the juvenile justice system and to process them differently. In addition, programs in different parts of the United States have been established for the purpose of preventing delinquency or for diverting youths to various community-based services (E. Johnson, 1990; Roy, 1995).

CHINS

A third category of juveniles is within the jurisdiction of juvenile courts. This category is neither status nor delinquent offenders. **CHINS** are Children In Need of Supervision. Youths who have been abandoned by their parents, who have inadequate supervision by parents, who are unmanageable or incorrigible, or who have social or psychological problems that interfere with traditional family living, may be placed in foster homes, group homes, or some other out-of-home placement where they can receive special services. These services may include group or individual counseling. In Alabama, for example, juvenile law has been changed to transfer the jurisdiction over youths who are beyond parental control to the Department of Pensions and Security (Lewis, 1980). Prior to this change in juvenile law, these youths were combined with delinquent offenders and processed through juvenile courts. Such youths accounted for about 33 percent of all juvenile court cases (Lewis, 1977). After the January 1977 law, these CHINS could be diverted to more productive and beneficial community programs, where both parents

BOX 14.1 Punishments Linking Parents with Offending Children

The Case of the Shackled Mother and Daughter

Deborah Harter, 38, and her daughter, Tonya Kline, were ordered shackled together by a Summerville, South Carolina judge in late December 1995. It seems that the daughter, Tonya, was a chronic runaway. Runaway behavior is not a crime, but it is a status offense for juveniles. Tonya's runaway behavior was eventually reported to the juvenile court and the juvenile court judge ordered Tonya's mother, Deborah Harter, to keep Tonya on a tether chain whenever Tonya ventured outside of the home. The mother failed to keep Tonya tethered, and a new juvenile court appearance was ordered.

On December 21, 1995, Family Court Judge Wayne Creech ordered Tonya and her mother shackled together with handcuffs and a chain. The punishment was imposed because of the mother's failure to maintain control over her daughter. The judge cited Deborah Harter with contempt of court for her failure to keep hold of the chain linking her with her daughter. Harter denied that she ever let go of the chain. "She didn't let go at all," Harter said. "It's just not fair. I think they have tortured me enough." Judge Creech said that if Deborah Harter lets her daughter run away again, Deborah will face 30 days in jail for contempt of court. Tonya had run away to New Hampshire earlier in 1995.

Are such punishments constitutional? Should parents be required to be shackled to their errant offspring? Does punishing the parent deter juvenile runaway behavior?

Source: Associated Press, "Mother Shackled to Her Daughter Charged with Violating a Court Order." *Minot (N.D.) Daily News,* December 22, 1995:A2.

and children can participate in various forms of therapy and self-help training (Lewis, 1977, 1980).

SOME CHARACTERISTICS OF DELINQUENT OFFENDERS

The *Uniform Crime Reports* compiled by the FBI annually shows distributions of selected offenses according to age, gender, and several other categories. Table 14.1 shows the total juvenile arrests for 1994. Table 14.1 shows that those under age 18 accounted for 18.6 percent of all arrests during 1994, up from 16.8 percent of all arrests reported in 1987 (Maguire and Pastore, 1996:404–405). However, "peaks" for different types of offenses are achieved for most juvenile offenders. For example, property crime (theft, burglary) arrests peak at about age 16 for most juveniles, while violent crime arrests peak at about age 18. Thus, in later years, the frequency of arrests drops off drastically for advancing age categories. An inspection of

TABLE 14.1 Arrests: By Offense Charged and Age, United States, 1994 (10,654 agencies; 1994 estimated population 207,624,000)

Offense Charged	Total All Ages	Ages Under 15	Ages Under 18	Ages 18 and Older	Under 10	10 to 12	13 to 14	15	16	17	18	19
Total	11,877,188	780,979	2,209,675	9,667,513	37,130	176,289	567,560	428,697	489,089	510,640	520,831	505,122
Percent[a]	100.0%	6.6	18.6	81.4	0.3	1.5	4.8	3.6	4.1	4.3	4.4	4.3
Murder and nonnegligent manslaughter	18,497	379	3,102	15,395	3	31	345	535	912	1,276	1,418	1,418
Forcible rape	29,791	1,863	4,859	24,932	103	442	1,318	892	993	1,111	1,217	1,158
Robbery	146,979	13,543	47,094	99,885	245	2,478	10,820	10,008	11,753	11,790	10,653	8,701
Aggravated assault	449,716	23,190	70,030	379,686	1,043	5,261	16,886	13,219	15,993	17,628	17,857	17,030
Burglary	319,926	47,481	115,681	204,245	3,135	11,833	32,513	22,232	23,413	22,555	20,223	15,889
Larceny-theft	1,236,311	185,811	412,349	823,962	9,145	51,765	124,901	76,459	77,418	72,661	62,806	49,702
Motor vehicle theft	166,260	21,867	73,265	92,995	206	2,592	19,069	17,986	18,087	15,325	11,698	8,718
Arson	16,764	6,289	9,268	7,496	1,153	2,041	3,095	1,224	964	791	531	488
Violent crime[b]	644,983	38,975	125,085	519,898	1,394	8,212	29,369	24,654	29,651	31,805	31,145	28,307
Percent[a]	100.0%	6.0	19.4	80.6	0.2	1.3	4.6	3.8	4.6	4.9	4.8	4.4
Property crime[c]	1,739,261	261,448	610,563	1,128,698	13,639	68,231	179,578	117,901	119,882	111,332	95,258	74,797
Percent[a]	100.0%	15.0	35.1	64.9	0.8	3.9	10.3	6.8	6.9	6.4	5.5	4.3
Total Crime Index[d]	2,384,244	300,423	735,648	1,648,596	15,033	76,443	208,947	142,555	149,533	143,137	126,403	103,104
Percent[a]	100.0%	12.6	30.9	69.1	0.6	3.2	8.8	6.0	6.3	6.0	5.3	4.3
Other assaults	991,881	72,514	171,642	820,239	3,731	18,961	49,822	32,005	33,602	33,521	31,173	31,652
Forgery and counterfeiting	93,003	927	7,013	85,990	33	184	710	981	2,057	3,048	4,199	4,512
Fraud	330,752	4,409	18,594	312,158	127	657	3,625	4,082	4,120	5,983	8,969	11,896
Embezzlement	11,614	92	803	10,811	8	22	62	60	211	440	574	631
Stolen property; buying, receiving, possessing	134,930	10,751	36,218	98,712	240	1,890	86,621	7,376	8,714	9,377	9,690	8,078
Vandalism	259,579	60,250	122,085	137,494	6,074	17,782	36,394	21,415	21,381	19,039	13,965	11,017
Weapons; carrying, possessing, etc.	213,494	16,661	52,200	161,294	611	3,424	12,626	9,963	12,199	13,337	14,213	12,554
Prostitution and commercialized vice	86,818	120	1,013	85,805	10	18	92	129	289	475	1,317	1,900
Sex offenses (except forcible rape and prostitution)	81,887	7,506	14,418	67,469	658	2,081	4,767	2,442	2,230	2,240	2,205	2,183
Drug abuse violations	1,118,346	21,830	131,220	987,126	266	2,281	19,283	24,103	36,747	48,540	60,142	57,786
Gambling	15,845	242	1,493	14,352	2	24	216	299	423	529	531	537
Offenses against family and children	92,133	1,475	4,234	87,899	98	293	1,084	815	978	966	2,009	2,207
Driving under the influence	1,079,533	329	10,573	1,068,960	117	24	188	534	2,708	7,002	15,769	22,312
Liquor laws	424,452	10,083	94,030	330,422	153	832	9,098	14,001	27,520	42,426	60,029	59,868
Drunkenness	571,420	2,065	14,778	556,642	120	197	1,748	2,298	3,606	6,809	12,831	14,090
Disorderly conduct	601,002	48,868	137,328	463,674	1,741	10,752	36,375	27,057	30,178	31,225	30,639	27,148
Vagrancy	21,413	925	3,657	17,756	19	154	752	773	946	1,013	1,072	860
All other offenses (except traffic)	3,046,100	99,318	343,669	2,702,431	5,396	20,348	73,574	61,382	81,918	101,051	124,694	132,388
Suspicion	11,395	551	1,712	9,683	39	128	384	396	385	380	407	399
Curfew and loitering law violations	105,888	31,609	105,888	X	537	4,552	26,520	24,667	28,098	21,514	X	X
Runaways	201,459	90,031	201,459	X	2,117	15,242	72,672	51,634	41,246	18,548	X	X

[a] Because of rounding, percents may not add to total.
[b] Violent crimes are offenses of murder and nonnegligent manslaughter, forcible rape, robbery, and aggravated assault.
[c] Property crimes are offenses of burglary, larceny-theft, motor vehicle theft, and arson.
[d] Includes arson.

Source: U.S. Department of Justice, Federal Bureau of Investigation, *Crime in the United States, 1994* (Washington, DC: USGPO, 1995), pp. 227, 228. In Maguire and Pastore (1996: 404–405).

20	21	22	23	24	25 to 29	30 to 34	35 to 39	40 to 44	45 to 49	50 to 54	55 to 59	60 to 64	65 and Older
459,948	433,449	419,027	420,909	406,399	1,761,357	1,713,145	1,298,615	796,890	433,908	227,419	120,448	70,677	79,369
3.9	3.6	3.5	3.5	3.4	14.8	14.4	10.9	6.7	3.7	1.9	1.0	0.6	0.7
1,215	1,097	938	803	706	2,538	1,847	1,342	856	533	271	164	113	136
1,156	1,065	990	1,107	1,001	4,674	4,617	3,382	2,023	1,120	621	334	216	251
6,808	5,946	5,398	5,130	4,740	19,712	15,823	9,621	4,432	1,745	658	255	118	145
16,115	16,485	16,315	16,741	16,195	72,265	70,262	52,262	31,176	17,003	8,763	4,920	2,862	3,435
11,818	10,234	9,497	9,258	8,385	38,079	35,507	24,140	12,426	5,180	2,017	805	355	432
39,440	34,473	31,926	31,928	30,636	140,027	141,593	109,829	68,611	36,125	18,320	10,259	6,854	11,433
6,516	5,510	4,989	4,642	4,217	17,153	13,812	8,348	4,133	1,848	761	305	132	213
341	283	263	264	245	1,178	1,268	1,069	665	407	238	99	80	77
25,294	24,593	23,641	23,781	22,642	99,189	92,549	66,607	38,487	20,401	10,313	5,673	3,309	3,967
3.9	3.8	3.7	3.7	3.5	15.4	14.3	10.3	6.0	3.2	1.6	0.9	0.5	0.6
58,115	50,500	46,675	46,092	43,483	196,437	192,180	143,386	85,835	43,560	21,336	11,468	7,421	12,155
3.3	2.9	2.7	2.7	2.5	11.3	11.0	8.2	4.9	2.5	1.2	0.7	0.4	0.7
83,409	75,093	70,316	69,873	66,125	295,626	284,729	209,993	124,322	63,961	31,649	17,141	10,730	16,122
3.5	3.1	2.9	2.9	2.8	12.4	11.9	8.8	5.2	2.7	1.3	0.7	0.5	0.7
30,938	33,605	35,257	36,524	36,465	163,495	160,971	117,939	67,879	35,759	17,997	9,173	5,401	6,011
4,308	4,174	4,115	4,088	4,086	17,829	16,234	11,234	6,046	2,856	1,226	540	258	285
13,192	13,559	14,146	14,739	14,606	63,001	57,461	43,331	27,414	15,181	7,271	3,425	1,900	2,067
599	556	553	499	519	2,042	1,716	1,295	799	513	260	123	62	70
6,440	5,754	5,158	4,833	4,503	18,057	14,875	10,417	5,761	2,708	1,237	616	282	303
8,347	7,804	6,898	6,664	6,200	24,811	21,565	14,552	7,794	3,853	1,872	917	481	754
10,361	10,462	9,449	8,650	7,827	28,035	21,742	15,325	9,676	5,663	3,282	1,735	1,047	1,273
2,275	2,727	2,953	3,501	3,876	20,017	20,712	13,527	6,851	2,962	1,429	786	460	512
2,058	2,127	2,244	2,227	2,167	11,056	12,191	9,903	6,695	4,483	2,853	1,849	1,333	1,895
51,330	48,063	45,564	45,455	43,839	190,382	183,565	133,141	73,403	32,406	12,773	5,170	2,270	1,837
533	466	389	433	389	1,770	1,880	1,775	1,563	1,191	970	726	601	598
2,383	2,731	2,916	3,256	3,465	16,778	19,310	15,461	8,913	4,419	1,980	989	534	548
27,223	38,711	40,866	44,180	43,818	195,657	201,508	161,847	111,111	70,710	41,984	23,910	14,628	14,726
47,987	14,628	11,150	9,477	8,012	29,069	27,355	22,918	16,126	9,964	6,035	3,657	2,112	2,035
14,841	19,260	18,959	18,928	18,599	87,057	101,426	90,333	65,154	40,160	24,643	13,776	8,502	8,083
24,627	26,244	23,791	23,202	20,985	81,732	76,119	56,300	33,277	18,142	9,664	5,078	3,083	3,643
677	580	591	647	602	2,930	3,265	2,747	1,739	1,009	541	227	141	128
128,076	126,545	123,337	123,304	119,931	510,184	484,602	365,026	221,462	117,530	59,593	30,525	16,798	18,436
344	360	375	429	385	1,829	1,919	1,551	905	438	160	85	54	43
X	X	X	X	X	X	X	X	X	X	X	X	X	X
X	X	X	X	X	X	X	X	X	X	X	X	X	X

Table 14.1 shows that runaways peak at about age 13 to 14, and runaway arrests decline thereafter. Arrests for curfew violations peak at about age 13 to 14, while liquor law arrests peak at around age 18.

When arrests are made, those arrested are usually taken to the nearest jail for booking, citation, or further processing. If the arrestee is a juvenile, police will usually take the arrestee to a juvenile officer. Complicating the processing of some juvenile arrestees is the fact that they may possess false identification or fake ID's.

Presently, it is unknown how many juveniles are held in U.S. jails on any given day (Snyder, Sickmund, and Poe-Yamagata, 1996). Estimates are that about 6,725 juveniles are held in jails on an average day for short time intervals (Maguire and Pastore, 1996:549). This translates into over 2.4 million juveniles per year, assuming that each juvenile were to be jailed for one day or less. Juvenile admissions to secure facilities, such as jails or juvenile custodial institutions, appear to be increasing (Butts, 1996).

Federal guidelines from the Office of Juvenile Justice and Delinquency Prevention strongly recommend the separation of juvenile offenders by both sight and sound from adult offenders while they are in any type of jail custody. This means providing separate space and facilities in jails or lockups for both juveniles and adults. However, many jails are simply too small and unequipped for such separate confinement or accommodation. Most jurisdictions attempt to abide by these federal guidelines. But false identification, slow processing of individual cases, and jail overcrowding mean that some juveniles may not be identified as such and thus may not be separated from adults when they are initially brought to jails. When these juveniles eventually are identified and separated, they are sent to the **juvenile justice system** for further processing.

THE JUVENILE JUSTICE SYSTEM

The juvenile justice system varies in sophistication, organization, and application among jurisdictions. No single diagram or model typifies the "average" juvenile justice system. However, there are sufficient similarities among the systems of different states to generalize on the subject of juvenile processing and dispositional alternatives. Figure 14.1 shows a diagram of the juvenile justice system. The following discussion covers briefly the significant stages of juvenile case processing.

Juvenile Court Jurisdiction

Cases heard and decided by juvenile courts are considered within the jurisdiction of these courts. Although states vary regarding the upper age limit for juvenile court jurisdiction, the maximum age for the majority of states is 18. The lower age limit varies among states as well, with several states using the age of 7 as a minimum cutoff. This minimum follows early English common law precedent, where those under age 7 are presumed inca-

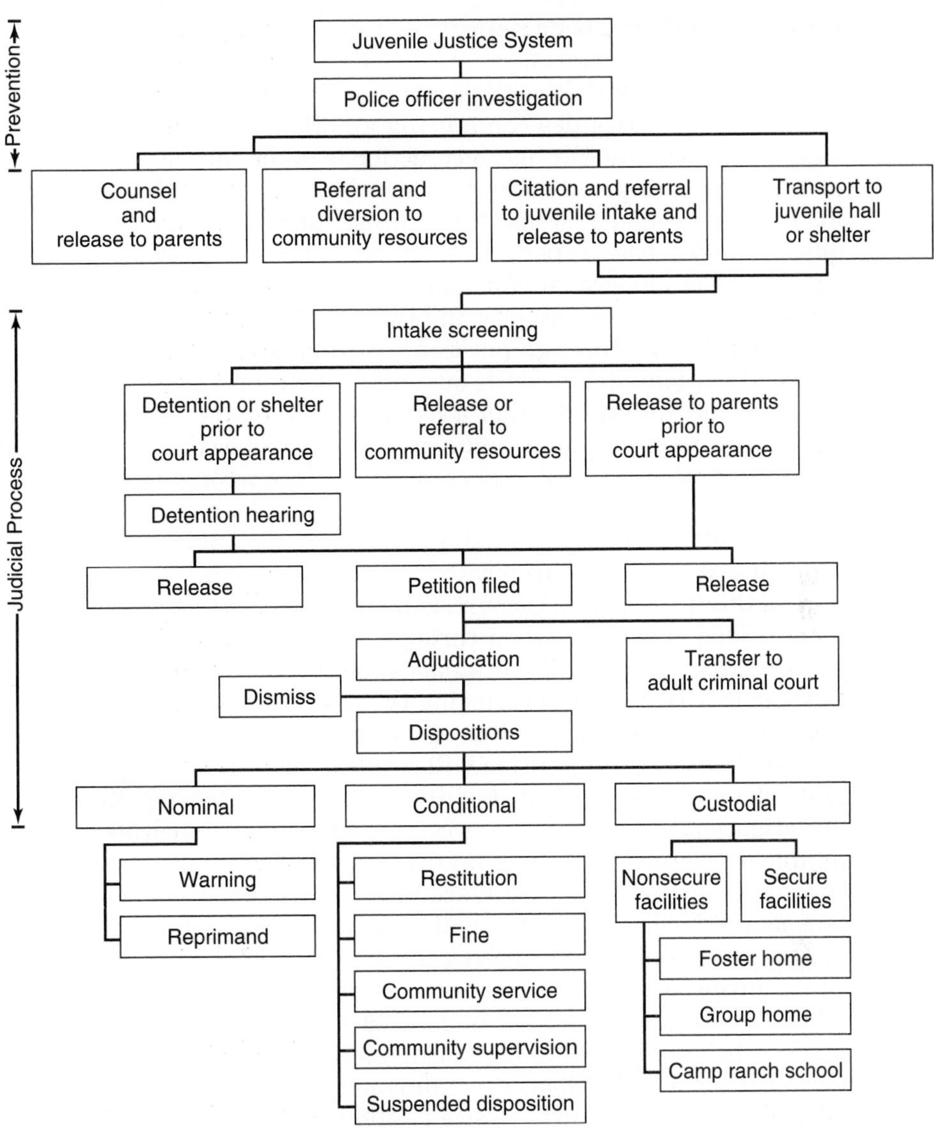

FIGURE 14.1 Procedures of the juvenile justice system. (*Source:* National Advisory Committee on Criminal Justice Standards and Goals, Task Force on Juvenile Justice and Delinquency Prevention, *Report of the Task Force on Juvenile Justice and Delinquency Prevention* [Washington, DC: U.S. Government Printing Office, 1976], p. 9, by permission of the U.S. Department of Justice.)

pable of formulating criminal intent, are not held responsible for their actions, and must be supervised by agencies other than juvenile courts. Wisconsin, for example, has set the minimum age for juvenile court jurisdiction at 12, while other states set the minimum age at 10 (Rogers and Mays, 1987:349–350). Again, no single minimum age typifies the age jurisdiction of all juvenile courts in the United States.

Police Actions or Other Reports

Juvenile contact with juvenile court most often occurs whenever police officers encounter juveniles committing an offense or behaving in suspicious ways on city streets. For instance, action is taken by police who may observe juveniles breaking and entering, vandalizing automobiles or homes, joyriding in stolen vehicles, soliciting for prostitution, or committing other delinquent offenses. Also, reports by neighbors of child abuse by a juvenile's parents, obvious neglect, and/or abandonment will also lead police or social services agents to investigate and intervene. Schools are another source of juvenile referrals through petitions. **Referrals** are either formal or informal notifications delivered to juvenile courts and/or court officers that a juvenile has committed either a status or delinquent offense or is a CHINS. **Petitions** are formal documents prepared by police officers, school officials, parents, or other interested persons that allege wrongdoing, misconduct, or a lack of supervision/control, and that result in having a juvenile's case brought to the attention of the juvenile court (Black, 1990:1145–1146). Thus, if a juvenile is chronically truant from school, the school principal may petition the juvenile court to hear the allegation that the juvenile is truant. This is accomplished through the filing of a petition. If a juvenile assaults another juvenile or steals something of value, a petition may be filed against that juvenile alleging the assault or theft. An investigation of the allegations will be conducted. Depending on the sophistication of the jurisdiction, this intervention will result in juveniles being taken to a juvenile hall or another juvenile facility for further processing, to jail for further investigation, or perhaps to a community agency such as child welfare, human services, or child and family services.

Whether juveniles are placed in detention centers temporarily or in jails again depends upon the elaborateness of arrangements and facilities in the jurisdiction (Thornberry, Tolnay, and Flanagan, 1991). In larger cities, juvenile detention centers are temporary shelters supervised by adults where juveniles may be housed and provided with food and other necessities while parents or guardians are notified. These detention centers also serve as temporary confinement facilities for juveniles who are alleged to have committed serious offenses and who must await further processing by the juvenile court. Reasons for detention include the absence of other forms of juvenile care in the particular community, the threat of the juvenile to the safety of others, the juvenile's protection, and the assurance that the juvenile will appear at a later juvenile court hearing (Schwartz and Hsieh, 1994). The length of detention varies from an hour in emergency holdover cases to two years, depending on the nature of the detention facility (Schwartz and Hsieh, 1994).

Therefore, police or other authorities may take the following preliminary actions:

1. They may counsel juveniles and release them to the custody of their parents or guardians.

BOX 14.2 Juvenile Curfews

The Case of Untamed Teens

In 1994, 85,000 youths were arrested for curfew violations or loitering. Over half (52 percent) were 15 to 16 years of age; 19 percent were 17; 24 percent were 13 to 14 years old; and only 5 percent were 12 years of age or younger. Of the 85,000 curfew violators, 18 percent were white, and 79 percent were black. Between 1984 and 1994, the arrest rate for such violations escalated by 260 percent. Experts with the Office of Juvenile Justice and Delinquency Programs say that by the year, 2010, this rate will have doubled again.

President Bill Clinton proposed a national curfew for juveniles in 1996, with the clear indication that such a curfew would deter youths from committing violent crimes, which occur mostly during evening hours. There is a seemingly sound basis for such reasoning. More than 2,800 juveniles committed homicides in 1994, three times as many as in 1984. Thirty percent of these youths didn't know the people they killed, usually in drive-by shootings. However, experts say that only about 17 percent of all youth-related violent crimes occur during curfew-proposed hours, 11:00 P.M. to 6:00 A.M. Rather, 22 percent of these violent youth-related offenses occur between 2:00 P.M. and 6:00 P.M. Furthermore, about 20 percent of such violence occurs during times when youths are supposed to be in school. Thus, there is another problem—truancy—that must be addressed in addition to the time element.

Officials with the Office of Juvenile Justice and Delinquency Programs estimate that youths under age 18 commit the bulk of violent crimes today, such as murder, forcible rape, aggravated assault, and armed robbery. The trend projected by these experts for youths age 10 to 17 is for a 145 percent increase in murder, a 66 percent increase for forcible rape, a 58 percent increase for robbery, and a 129 percent increase for aggravated assault. They say that each generation of juvenile offenders is more violent and vicious than their predecessors.

A tiny portion of the youth population today has no conscience, and this wilding fraction has managed to terrorize everyone. In large cities today it is commonplace for schools to require entering students to pass through metal detectors. Numerous weapons, including firearms and knives, are confiscated during these inspections.

It has been suggested that we shouldn't ask police officers to waste time checking juvenile I.D. cards. Rather, we need cops to spend their time rounding up bad guys—Baretta-toting 12-year-olds in baggy pants and backwards baseball caps. They should not have to waste time shuttling waifs to midnight basketball or other social services, according to some observers. One note is that "old-fashioned curfews used to work for one simple reason: parents enforced them." The ominous prediction is that the *real crime wave is about to begin.* And there is no way of containing it by simply telling youths that they have to stay indoors.

Should cities impose curfews on youths? What should be these curfews? Are curfews the cure for youth violence? What should the penalties be for those who violate curfews? How would you deal with escalating juvenile violence?

Source: Adapted from Tony Snow, "Curfews Won't Tame Teens." *USA Today,* June 3, 1996:13A.

2. They may refer and divert the juvenile to the care and responsibility of community resources.
3. They may cite the juvenile, refer the juvenile to juvenile intake for further processing, and release the juvenile to the temporary custody of parents or guardians.
4. They may transport the juvenile to a jail, a juvenile hall, or to a detention center for further processing.

Intake

Juveniles placed in detention centers, juvenile halls, jails, or community agencies are subsequently screened or evaluated by an intake officer. **Intake officers** are usually juvenile probation officers under the administration of the probation department of the community or county. It is the responsibility of intake officers to examine closely each juvenile's case and to make a professional determination of what further action should be taken. On the basis of the seriousness of the offense(s) alleged, the apparent responsibility of the parents, and/or the manifest needs of the juvenile, the intake officer will take one of the following actions:

1. Intake officers will warn the juvenile and/or parents/guardians and release the juvenile to the parents' custody. This releases the juvenile from further involvement with the juvenile justice system.
2. Intake officers will release the juvenile to the custody of parents or guardians, but the officer will schedule a future juvenile court appearance at which the juvenile's attendance is required.
3. Intake officers will refer and remand the juvenile to the care and supervision of some appropriate community agency or institution for particular care and treatment. This transfer of responsibility shifts the decision for releasing the juvenile to agency officials. They determine later on the basis of their own evaluations whether further juvenile justice action is warranted or whether the juvenile should be released to parents or guardians.
4. Intake officers will cause the juvenile to be detained in a detention facility or shelter to await a detention hearing, will file a petition to have the juvenile court determine the ultimate disposition of the juvenile, or both.

Juvenile Court

All juvenile courts are *civil* bodies. This means that juveniles cannot acquire a criminal record directly from juvenile court actions, where the actions remain confined to juvenile courts. In most jurisdictions, juveniles are brought to the attention of juvenile courts through filing petitions. In the case of petitions directed to juvenile court, these are applications for the court to consider whether the juvenile is delinquent, neglected, dependent, or otherwise in need of a special disposition or care. These petitions may be filed by anyone, including the police who may allege serious or nonserious juvenile misconduct (misdemeanors, felonies, runaway behavior), school officials who may allege truancy or incorrigibility, parents who may allege unruliness or unmanageability, neighbors who may allege child sexual abuse, neglect, or mistreatment, or intake officers who wish official court action of some type to be taken (Skibinski, 1992).

The actual juvenile court proceeding is quasi-adversarial, with a juvenile court prosecutor bringing specific charges against the juvenile. If the juvenile or juvenile's parents/guardians choose, they may be represented by counsel to defend against the charges alleged. Action on the petition by the juvenile judge may be a ruling that the juvenile is, indeed, delinquent. Or the ruling may result in a dismissal of charges. The particular action taken by a juvenile judge is an adjudication of charges brought against the juvenile. An **adjudication** is a formal court judgment or determination. Thus, a juvenile court judge may believe the facts alleged in the petition and adjudicate the juvenile a delinquent or status offender. Or the judge may determine that the facts are not sustained as set forth in the petition. Therefore, the juvenile is adjudicated nondelinquent and is subsequently freed from the juvenile justice system. Sometimes juvenile court proceedings are called **adjudicatory proceedings.** Thus, a juvenile may be adjudicated delinquent; adjudicated dependent, neglected or abused; adjudicated a status offender; or some other type of adjudication. If a juvenile court judge adjudicates a youth as either a delinquent or status offender, then the case will be **disposed.** Several types of **dispositions** are available to judges. These are the equivalent of sentences meted out in criminal courts. But in juvenile courts, these are not called sentences; rather, these actions are called dispositions. These dispositions include: (1) nominal, (2) conditional, or (3) custodial.

Nominal Dispositions. **Nominal dispositions** consist of verbal warnings or reprimands by the judge, and these warnings normally result in the juvenile's return to the custody of parents or guardians.

Conditional Dispositions. **Conditional dispositions** vary among jurisdictions. But the usual conditional dispositions imposed by juvenile court judges include one or more of the following: fines or restitution to victims, some form of community service, some form of community supervision, such as probation under the administrative authority of juvenile probation officers, or a suspension of one or more of these conditions once they have been imposed as the sentence.

Custodial Dispositions. The **custodial disposition** has several different forms. Youths may be placed in some type of custody for a period of time. The custody may be secure or nonsecure. Secure custody might be an industrial school or reform school. These are the equivalent of prisons or jails for adults. In the case of nonsecure custody, the juvenile may be assigned a foster home if the juvenile's parents are judged irresponsible or inadequate. Or the juvenile may be placed in a group home, a camp ranch, or school, where supervision and restrictions are minimal. Together with the conditional option, these custodial options make up juvenile corrections. Before we examine these correctional options, however, some of the more important constitutional rights of juveniles are described.

Juvenile Rights

Under the ***parens patriae*** doctrine, many different kinds of courts assumed responsibility for juveniles until the early 1960s. Juvenile judges and other court officials overseeing juvenile matters functioned on the basis of ***in loco parentis,*** meaning literally "in the place of parents," and they made important decisions about juvenile dispositions. These decisions were largely unquestioned and unchallenged. However, in recent years the U.S. Supreme Court has vested juveniles with several important constitutional rights. At the same time, juvenile courts have been forced to acknowledge these rights under the constitution and make decisions consistent with them. When juveniles are arrested by police today for theft or some other offense, certain constitutional rights automatically attach or become relevant. Police must advise juvenile arrestees of their right to an attorney and to refrain from further questioning, if they so desire. The juvenile court trial has become an adversarial proceeding much like criminal court for adults. The path toward obtaining these rights has been long and arduous. Several important landmark juvenile cases have made these rights possible.

***Kent v. United States* (1966).** This was the first important landmark juvenile case heard by the U.S. Supreme Court. Morris Kent was a 16-year-old residing in the District of Columbia. He was arrested by police and charged with rape, burglary, and robbery. When police first arrested Kent, they interrogated him extensively about the offenses. He was not told that he could remain silent. Under the circumstances, this was a right he did not yet have. He was also denied access to an attorney. This was another right he did not yet have. Under a lengthy interrogation, Kent confessed to the crimes. The juvenile judge in his case, on his own authority, transferred Kent to criminal court jurisdiction where Kent could be prosecuted as an adult for the crimes alleged. No hearing was held regarding the transfer and no reasons were given by the judge to explain it. But the implications for Kent were devastating. As a juvenile, if adjudicated as delinquent on any of the charges, Kent faced incarceration in a reform school until age 21, whereupon he would be released. As an adult tried on those same charges, Kent faced the maximum sentence of death penalty under District of Columbia statutes.

In criminal court, the jury found him guilty of the crimes alleged. However, the jury also found him to be insane when the rape was committed. Thus, he was sentenced to a mental institution to be treated until sane. At that time, he would face a 30- to 90-year incarceration for the previous conviction offenses. Kent's attorney appealed to the U.S. Supreme Court. The Supreme Court overturned his conviction. The *Kent* case is significant because of *why* his conviction was overturned. First, the U.S. Supreme

Court said, Kent was denied a hearing before he was transferred to criminal court by the juvenile judge. Second, they said, he was denied access to an attorney during his interrogation by police and then later at the proceeding when a decision was made about his transfer to criminal court. Third, his attorney should have been permitted access to all reports and records relating to the transfer decision. And fourth, the judge should have furnished Kent's attorney and parents with a statement outlining the reasons for the transfer.

***In re Gault* (1967).** In 1967, the U.S. Supreme Court decided the case of *In re Gault,* perhaps the most important of all landmark juvenile cases. Gerald Gault was a 15-year-old who was arrested in 1964 in Gila County, Arizona, for making an obscene telephone call to a female neighbor, Mrs. Cook. Gault's parents were both working at the time and neither was notified of his arrest. Gault was interrogated extensively and detained overnight in a local juvenile detention center. Later, a petition was filed by a juvenile probation officer alleging his delinquency, although the grounds were not specified in the petition. The juvenile judge ordered a hearing several days later. The hearing was held, no witnesses were called, no one was sworn to testify, and on the basis of the limited factual information available, the judge sentenced Gault to the Arizona Industrial School (a prison for juveniles) until he reached 21 years of age. This amounted to a six-year sentence for allegedly making an obscene telephone call. Had an adult been convicted of the same offense, the maximum penalty imposed would have been up to a $50 fine and/or a two-month jail term.

Gault's parents obtained an attorney, and eventually through appeals, the U.S. Supreme Court heard and decided the case in 1967. The bases for Gault's appeal involved several alleged constitutional rights violations that are extended to adults. Gault's appeal alleged that he was not notified of the specific charges against him, he was not apprised of his right to counsel, he was not permitted to confront and cross-examine witnesses against him such as Mrs. Cook or the probation officer, he was not advised of his right against self-incrimination, and he was denied the right to a transcript of the proceedings against him as well as an appellate review of his case.

The U.S. Supreme Court said that Arizona was in error in denying Gault several significant rights. In their landmark decision, they established the following rights for juveniles:

1. The right to an attorney
2. The right to be notified of charges
3. The right to confront and cross-examine witnesses
4. The right against self-incrimination.

Although Gault's attorney complained that a transcript was not made available of the proceedings, and an appellate review provision was not prescribed according to Arizona statutes, the U.S. Supreme Court did not take action on these two points. They concluded that since they struck down Arizona's other action against Gault, the appellate review criticism was irrelevant. Furthermore, although the Supreme Court said it is not necessary for juvenile courts to furnish transcripts of their proceedings, they indicated that it would be necessary in the future for juvenile courts to bear the responsibility for reconstructing all significant events if challenged by juvenile defendants. This would mean that juvenile judges would be subject to cross-examination by defense counsel at later hearings as well as other burdensome actions. Within a few months of the *Gault* decision, the Arizona legislature issued new statutes providing for full juvenile appellate reviews, with a strong recommendation to juvenile court judges that transcripts be maintained of all proceedings before these courts.

***In re Winship* (1970).** Two other landmark cases involving juveniles occurred in 1970 and 1971. *In re Winship* (1970) involved a 12-year-old New York juvenile, Samuel Winship, who was arrested for stealing $100 from a woman's handbag. The juvenile judge found Winship guilty of the charge, adjudicated him delinquent, and sentenced him to a New York juvenile training school for 18 months. The standard of evidence used in Winship's case was "the preponderance of evidence," a standard typically associated with civil case dispositions and tort actions.

Winship's case was appealed on the grounds that the criminal court standard of "proof beyond a reasonable doubt" should have been used in his case rather than the civil standard. New York authorities contended that because juvenile court actions are civil in nature, the "preponderance of evidence" standard was acceptable. However, the U.S. Supreme Court overturned the verdict in Winship's case, concluding that where substantial loss of freedom may occur (such as confinement for 18 months in a juvenile training school), a more stringent standard is necessary to protect juveniles. Thus, the criminal court "proof beyond a reasonable doubt" standard has been mandated for juvenile courts in all cases where loss of freedom is a possible penalty.

***McKeiver v. Pennsylvania* (1971).** In 1971, another important decision was rendered by the U.S. Supreme Court. In *McKeiver v. Pennsylvania* (1971), Joseph McKeiver, a 16-year-old, was charged with robbery, receiving stolen goods, and larceny. His attorney requested a trial by jury but was denied one by the juvenile judge. Ordinarily in criminal cases, if the possible incarcerative penalty for offenses alleged is six months or more, the defendant may request and be entitled to a jury trial. The U.S. Supreme Court decided in *Duncan v. Louisiana* (1968) that a jury trial was mandatory if requested by a defendant in cases in which "serious offenses" were alleged. Many states interpreted this decision to mean felony charges against criminal defendants rather than misdemeanor charges. However, the "six months or more" standard was made explicit in *Baldwin v. New York* (1970). Now, any criminal defendant who may suffer incarceration of six months or more if convicted of either felony or misdemeanor charges is entitled to a jury trial in any state, if requested.

The attorney for McKeiver believed the charges would conceivably result in McKeiver's detention in a juvenile facility for a lengthy period, probably well beyond the six-month standard established by *Baldwin,* and no doubt this possibility influenced McKeiver's subsequent appeal. But the U.S. Supreme Court rejected the appeal and declared that juveniles do not have a right to a jury trial. They gave many reasons for their decision in McKeiver's case, but their decision was influenced largely by the fear that a juvenile right to jury trials would greatly transform the juvenile court into largely an adversarial system. This would effectively undermine any rehabilitative potential the juvenile court could invoke within the remaining parts of the *parens patriae* authority it possessed. Thus, the U.S. Supreme Court left juvenile court judges with the authority to grant juveniles jury trials only if the judge wished to grant them. In short, whether a juvenile receives a jury trial is a purely discretionary decision on the part of the juvenile judge.

Decisions About Waivers or Transfers to Criminal Courts

Historically, juvenile courts have sought to insulate juvenile offenders from the trappings of adult courts in an effort to minimize the possible criminogenic effects of labeling resulting from exposure to criminal-like case processing. Informally handled juvenile cases are common, and diversion is used extensively to decrease one's contact with the juvenile justice system. The use of probation is considerable, even where serious offenses have been committed or alleged. But during the last few decades, the public has become increasingly concerned with the apparent leniency of the courts in dealing with adult criminals as well as juveniles (Champion, 1992). The rehabilitation model of corrections has gradually been replaced by a more punitive, just deserts rationale that seeks to adjust the punishment to fit the crime committed. One result of this philosophical shift has been the implementation of large-scale sentencing reforms at the state and federal levels.

As the amount of violent crime committed by juveniles has increased, public disenchantment with juvenile case processing has also intensified. Between 1975 and 1988, the rate of juvenile violence remained fairly constant. However, between 1988 and 1994, the amount of juvenile violence soared (Snyder, Sickmund, and Poe-Yamagata, 1996:14). Figure 14.2 shows arrests for juveniles ages 10 to 17 involving violent crime between 1975 and 1994. In 1975, there were about 300 arrests per 100,000 juveniles ages 10 to 17 compared with over 500 arrests per 100,000 juveniles in 1994. This abrupt upward shift in juvenile violence caused many persons to rethink existing juvenile justice policies and how juvenile offenders ought to be treated.

The result has been a noticeable policy shift toward the criminal court processing of more serious juvenile offenders and the adoption of a more punitive philosophy regarding juvenile sanctions generally (Feld, 1995).

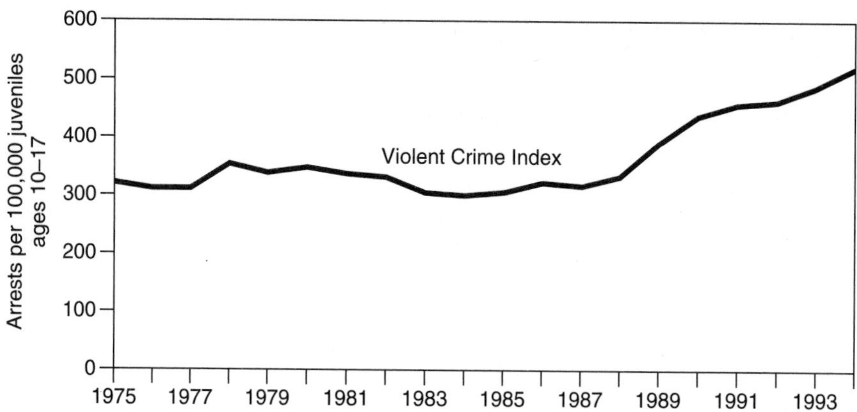

FIGURE 14.2 Violent crime juvenile arrest rates, 1975–1993. (*Note:* 1993 and 1994 arrest rates were estimated by the National Center for Juvenile Justice by using data presented in *Crime in the United States* reports and population data from the U.S. Bureau of the Census. *Data sources:* FBI. [1994]. *Age-specific arrest rates and race-specific arrest rates for selected offenses 1965–1992.* [1994]. *Crime in the United States 1993.* [1995]. *Crime in the United States 1994.* Bureau of the Census [1995]. *Resident Population of States 1992–1994]* [machine-readable data file] and *Current Population Reports, series P-25.*)

There is greater use of criminal courts for punishing youthful offenders (Lieb, Fish, and Crosby, 1994). Juveniles are sent from juvenile courts to criminal courts through actions known as waivers, transfers, or certifications. **Waivers** or **transfers** refer to relocating jurisdiction over juveniles from juvenile courts to criminal courts. Thus, juvenile court jurisdiction over particular juveniles is waived or transferred to criminal court judges. Once a juvenile's case has been transferred or waived to criminal courts, then the juvenile is processed as though he were an adult. For all practical purposes, all juveniles transferred to criminal courts are considered adults for the purpose of imposing criminal court penalties, including life without parole and capital punishment.

Certification is the process of declaring a juvenile to be an adult for the purpose of a criminal prosecution. In Utah, for instance, juveniles who have committed serious offenses may be certified as adults and sent to criminal courts for processing as though they were adult offenders. For all practical purposes, the objectives of certification, waivers, or transfers are identical. Juveniles charged with serious offenses are considered adults so that criminal courts may impose harsher punishments if these persons are subsequently convicted of crimes.

It should be noted that although there has been a substantial increase in the rate of juvenile violence, the proportionate number of violent juveniles is relatively small. For instance, in 1994, less than one-half of 1 percent of all juveniles in the United States ages 10 to 17 were arrested for a violent crime (Snyder et al., 1996:14). Looking at the total picture, about 6 percent

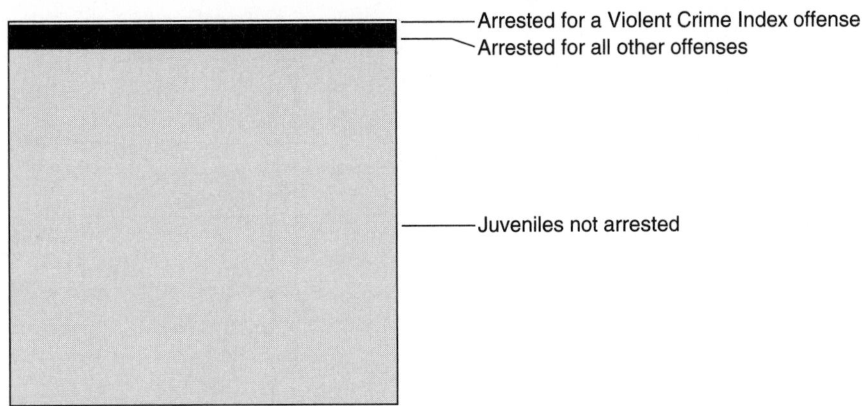

FIGURE 14.3 Proportion of juveniles arrested for violent offenses in 1994. (*Note:* This analysis is based on the assumption that (1) the average arrested juvenile is arrested 1.5 times per year and (2) the average juvenile arrested for a violent crime is arrested for 1.2 violent crimes per year. *Source:* FBI. [1995]. *Crime in the United States 1994.*)

of all juveniles were arrested in 1994. Of these, about 7 percent were arrested for violent crimes (e.g., murder and nonnegligent manslaughter, forcible rape, robbery, and aggravated assault). Figure 14.3 shows the proportion of juveniles arrested for violent crimes relative to all U.S. juveniles.

Over half of all states have implemented juvenile justice reforms resulting in greater use of waivers (Florida Advisory Council on Intergovernmental Relations, 1994; Forst, 1995). For instance, between 1988 and 1992, waivers increased in the United States by 68 percent (Sickmund, 1994). However, for some states such as New Mexico, the use of waivers is somewhat rare. Between 1981 and 1990, for instance, New Mexico juvenile courts transferred only 49 juveniles out of 18,994 cases processed (Mays and Houghtalin, 1992). But New Mexico authorities were using these waivers as they were intended—to transfer only the most serious cases to criminal courts for processing (Houghtalin and Mays, 1991).

Many juveniles do not want to have their cases transferred from juvenile courts to criminal courts (Sickmund, 1994). They may want to contest these waiver actions by juvenile court judges or prosecutors. Juveniles in all jurisdictions are entitled to a waiver or transfer hearing and the right to an attorney at such a hearing. They may present evidence in their own behalf for the purpose of defeating waivers contemplated against them. Although juveniles and their attorneys may formally oppose waivers or certification, the ultimate discretion to transfer juveniles to criminal courts rests exclusively with juvenile court judges. It is rare that transfer hearings result in favorable rulings for juveniles (Champion and Mays, 1991). Essentially, if the juvenile court wants a particular juvenile transferred to criminal court, there is little or nothing juveniles or their attorneys can do to prevent such transfers or waivers. Figure 14.4 shows the juvenile court

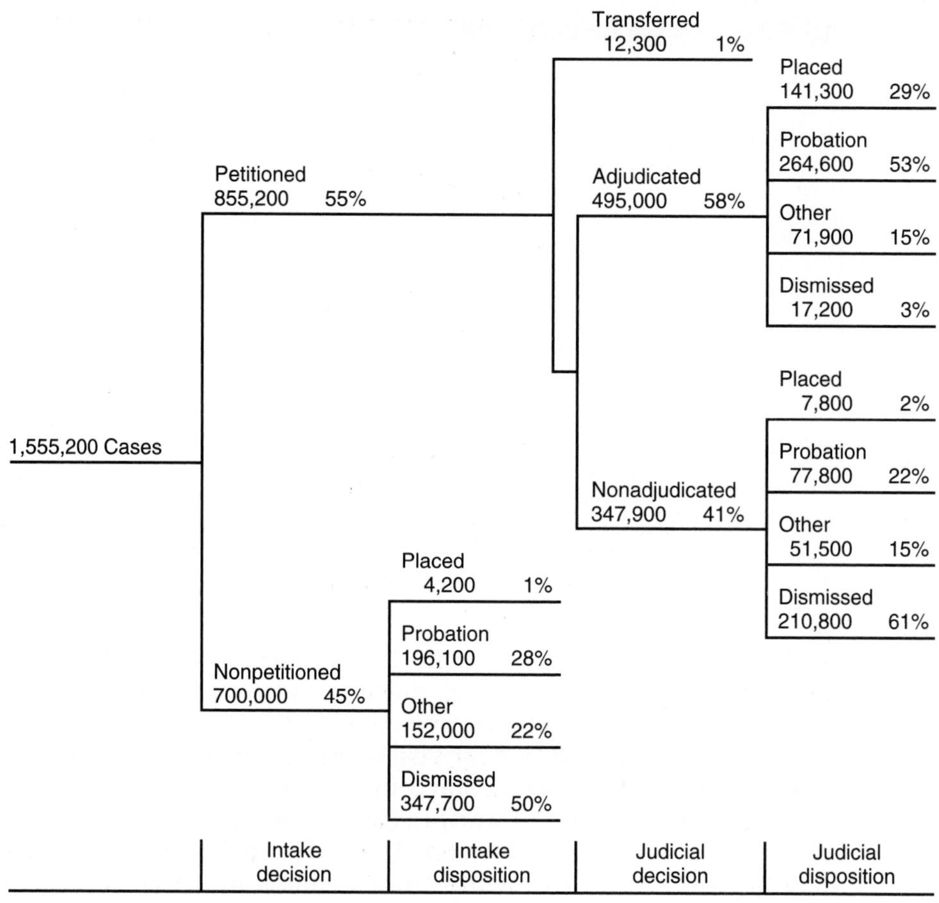

FIGURE 14.4 Juvenile court processing of delinquency cases, 1994. (*Source:* Butts, 1996:6)

processing of 1,555,200 cases in 1994. Of particular interest is the relatively small number of juveniles actually transferred to criminal courts through waivers, transfers, or certifications. Less than 1 percent (12,300) of all processed juveniles were actually waived to criminal courts in 1994 (Butts, 1996:6).

It is expected that those juveniles who are transferred to criminal courts are the most serious (and violent) juveniles. However, Figure 14.5 shows numbers of cases transferred to criminal court between 1985 and 1994 for all juveniles processed.

Until 1992, property offenders accounted for a majority of all juveniles transferred to criminal court. Violent (person offense) juvenile offenders accounted for about 33 percent of all transferred juveniles in 1985, although in 1994, violent juvenile offenders made up about 43 percent of all youths transferred to criminal courts (Butts, 1996:7). However, property

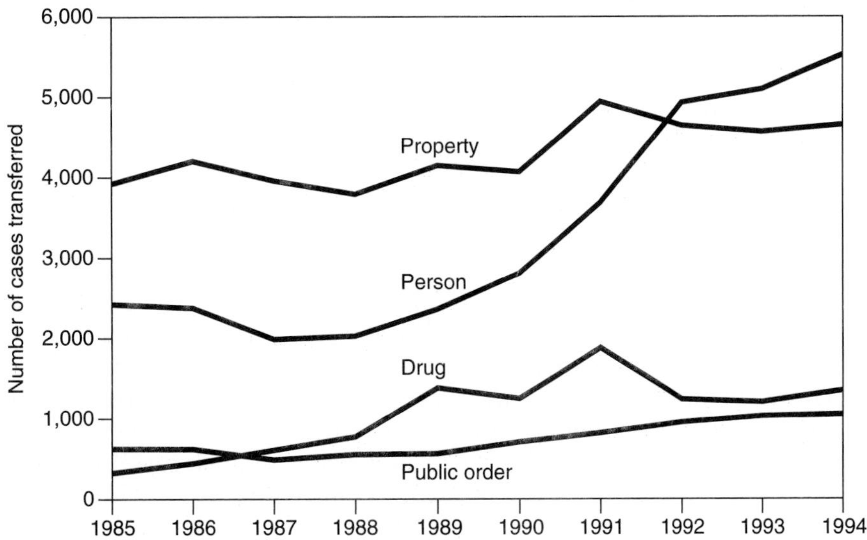

FIGURE 14.5 Delinquency cases transferred to criminal court, 1985–1994. (*Source:* Snyder, Sickmund, and Poe-Yamagata, 1996:7)

offenders continued to make up a substantial number (37 percent) of all juveniles transferred. About 8 percent of all youths transferred to criminal courts in 1994 involved public order offending (e.g., disturbing the peace, drunk and disorderly), while 10 percent involved drug offending. Clearly, property and public order offenders have not been the *intended* targets of transfers, although many juvenile court judges continue to send these less serious offenders to criminal courts. Often, when prosecutors in criminal courts review case files of transferred juveniles to determine which cases should or should not be prosecuted, they will often drop the less serious cases and decline to prosecute juveniles charged with public order or property offenses.

Frankly, prosecutors prefer more serious cases that merit prosecution. Although it is beyond the scope of this book to examine all of the possible reasons for juvenile court judges would send less serious juveniles to criminal courts for processing, some juvenile court judges have said that they want to rid their courts of troublesome teenagers who are chronic property or public order offenders. Literally, these judges want these less serious juveniles out of their courtrooms. Thus, they are passing the buck to criminal courts where these cases are routinely dismissed, downgraded, or ignored.

Juvenile Exploitation of Juvenile Court Leniency. Some experts claim that most juveniles who commit serious offenses know that there is a small likelihood that they will be confined in either a juvenile industrial school or adult prison following their arrest and adjudication as delinquents. Most often juvenile court judges impose probation on these juveniles, even repeat serious juvenile offenders. Thus, it is suggested that at least some juveniles use their status as juveniles to great advantage in violating the law. Their subsequent lenient treatment from juvenile court judges strengthens their resolve to recidivate, despite the increased chances of secure confinement, even if they are apprehended again in the same jurisdiction (Nimick, Szymanski, and Snyder, 1986).

To some extent, judicial leniency toward juveniles is supported by public opinion. In 1992, for instance, telephone interviews with 681 adult householders in Georgia were directed toward determining views about whether juvenile murderers should be tried as adults (Stalans and Henry, 1994). About 76 percent of all respondents preferred juvenile court as the better place to hear these cases, when first-time offenders were involved. The respondents were divided over whether juveniles with prior records of violent offending should be tried in adult courts rather than in juvenile courts, however. About 48 percent believed that such juveniles should have their cases heard in juvenile courts. Their thinking was influenced by the belief that juvenile courts would make decisions more on the basis of the best interests of youths rather than due process considerations.

One reaction to this apparent juvenile court leniency where serious crimes are involved has been that many state legislatures have authorized the automatic transfer of serious young offenders from the juvenile court to the criminal court in order that more severe punishments can be imposed (Sagatun, McCollum, and Edwards, 1985). This is particularly true in cases where the death penalty can be applied, a sentence that is well-beyond the purview of juvenile judges (Streib, 1983). However, some evidence suggests that transfers of juveniles to the jurisdiction of adult criminal courts do not automatically result in more serious punishments. In fact, some authorities suggest that just the opposite results are frequently observed or reported (Champion and Mays, 1991).

Further, some experts believe that automatic transfers of juveniles to criminal courts in those jurisdictions with automatic transfer provisions are overly simplistic and do not take into account mitigating factors, such as previous child abuse or other background problems (Podkopacz, 1994; Stalans and Henry, 1994; Virginia Commission on Youth, 1994).

GOALS OF JUVENILE CORRECTIONS

The goals of juvenile corrections are similar to those for adult offenders. These include (1) rehabilitation and reintegration, (2) deterrence, (3) isolation and control, (4) prevention, and (5) punishment or retribution. In some respects, these goals are contradictory (Thornton, Voigt, and Doerner, 1987:350–351). For instance, there are those who stress delinquency prevention through keeping juveniles away from the juvenile justice system through diversion and warnings. However, an equally vocal aggregate says that the juvenile justice system is too lenient with offenders and must "get tough" with them through more certain and stringent penalties for the

BOX 14.3 Transfers of Juveniles to Criminal Court on the Increase

The Case of Greater Punishments for Juvenile Murderers

It happened in Devils Lake, North Dakota. A convenience store clerk, Donald Jerome, 31, was gunned down early one morning as he tended the store. Four youths entered the Superpumper convenience store at about 3:30 A.M. and shot Jerome once in the head with a shotgun as they robbed the place.

The alleged gunman, Marlon Comes, is 15 years old. His accomplices were Wayne Greywater, 16, and Adrian Alex, 17, from Fort Totten, a nearby Indian reservation. A fourth youth was an unidentified 17-year-old male. The first three youths were transferred to criminal court for further processing as adults. The fourth youth remained to be tried in juvenile court as a juvenile delinquent. In a fairly quick juvenile court action, the unidentified youth was ordered to serve one year at Mandan, the North Dakota Youth Correctional Center for juveniles.

Under North Dakota law, if a juvenile court finds probable cause that a juvenile who is 14 or older has committed murder or attempted murder, that juvenile is automatically tried in adult court and his or her name becomes public. Ramsey County State's Attorney Lonnie Olson said that the youths who were transferred did not fight the transfer. Ordinarily, the youths are entitled to a hearing as to whether the transfer should be undertaken. Because of the confidential nature of juvenile court records, it is unknown whether the youths who were transferred to criminal court have records of offenses while juveniles.

At what age should youths be subject to transfer to criminal court? Does being transferred necessarily mean that a more severe type of punishment will be imposed? Should juvenile records of those transferred to criminal court automatically be made available for the information of trial judges and prosecutors?

Source: Adapted from Associated Press, "Teens Moved to Adult Court." *Minot (N.D.) Daily News,* January 4, 1996:A1.

offenses they commit (Garrett, 1985). And a middle ground is attempted by some juvenile correctional programs that stress "discipline" for punishing as well as rehabilitating.

Rehabilitation and Reintegration

Increasingly, community-based publicly and privately operated correctional programs for juveniles have a strong rehabilitative orientation (Woodward and English, 1993). Some rehabilitative and reintegrative programs stress internalizing responsibilities for one's actions, while other programs attempt to inculcate youths with social and motor skills (Barton and Butts, 1990; Krisberg et al., 1989). A few programs are oriented toward diagnosing and treating emotionally disturbed youths through alternative medical and social therapies (Krisberg et al., 1989). A Teaching-Family Treatment Model used in 125 group homes throughout the United States currently contains elements such as (1) teaching delinquent youths communication skills, daily living skills, survival skills, educational advancement and study skills, and career skills; (2) breaking such skills into specific behaviorally defined components; (3) assuring that the delinquents practice the skills in the problem setting; (4) assessing each youth's skill needs; (5) developing individualized teaching plans; and (6) teaching to the individual skill deficits (Weber and Burke, 1986).

Deterrence

Does the certainty and severity of punishment deter juveniles from committing various offenses? Yes and no. According to correctional critic Robert Martinson who has said "nothing works," no program has been shown to be 100 percent effective in deterring juveniles from committing delinquent acts or recidivating (Martinson, 1974). However, other researchers suggest that significant deterrent elements of juvenile correctional programs include clearly stated rules and formal sanctions, anticriminal modeling and reinforcement, and a high degree of empathy and trust between the juvenile client and staff (Barton and Butts, 1990; Woodward and English, 1993). Traditional counseling, institutionalization, and diversion are considered largely ineffective, according to other investigators (Pabon, 1985). The "peaks" in the amount of different kinds of crime for different youthful age groups suggest that many juveniles appear to "grow out of" the propensity to commit offenses as they become older. Thus, a "natural" intervention occurs apart from any particular program designed to deter (Krisberg et al., 1989).

Isolation and Control

Isolation of juvenile offenders is achieved through apprehension and detention, although the average length of long-term youth confinement in public facilities was 9.8 months in 1995 (Camp and Camp, 1995c:16–17). Juvenile offender behaviors may be monitored or supervised to a limited degree by juvenile probation officers, but compared with adult offenders, their recidivism chances are about the same (Roy, 1995). In fact, some investigators say there may be a "self-fulfilling prophecy" phenomenon occurring whenever youths are detained for any lengthy period. When serious youths were subjected to preventive detention by a New York City Family Court, for instance, they were more likely to be adjudicated as delinquent by judges in subsequent hearings compared with nondetained youths (McCarthy, 1987b). When youths are placed in custodial settings such as reformatories, the emphasis of the facility is more on control than rehabilitation. Thus, control for the sake of control may be self-defeating as a long-range delinquency prevention strategy (Glick and Goldstein, 1995).

Prevention

The influence of juvenile corrections upon delinquency prevention is currently uncertain (Schwartz and Hsieh, 1994). Delinquency prevention is a function of many factors, including preschool programs such as the 1962 Perry Preschool Project in Ypsilanti, Michigan (Berrueta-Clement et al., 1984). Nearly 70 percent of the children who participated in the program had no future reported offenses as juveniles, and only 16 percent were ever arrested for delinquent acts. However, about half of the nonparticipants in the same school had future reported offenses as juveniles and 25 percent were subsequently arrested for delinquency. Evidence from other early intervention programs suggests similar successes (Syracuse/Onondaga County Youth Bureau, 1984).

One of the key elements in many of the contemporary delinquency prevention programs is accountability. Accountability can be incorporated as a program element in the form of restitution, community service, or victim compensation in some form (Bazemore, 1991; Hudson and Gallaway, 1989). Restitution by itself may be insufficient to bring about long-term change in delinquent behaviors, however. Therefore, many current intensive supervision programs for juveniles and others include victim-offender contact, group and individual counseling, and educational and vocational support (Barton and Butts, 1990; Krisberg et al., 1989).

Punishment and Retribution

As we have seen, one major impact of the get tough on crime policy adopted by many jurisdictions is that the juvenile justice system seems to be diverting a larger portion of its serious offenders to criminal courts where they may conceivably receive harsher punishments. Whether this outcome occurs is questionable in view of recent research. Despite the influence of the justice model on juvenile court dispositions of youthful offenders, there appears to be a highly visible and vocal public that expresses opposite views. This element believes that rehabilitative and reintegrative efforts ought to be stressed rather than more punitive aims in juvenile correctional programs.

JUVENILE CORRECTIONAL ALTERNATIVES

Juvenile judges have several options from which to choose when deciding specific cases. They may adjudicate youths as delinquent and take no further action other than to record the event. Thus, if the juvenile appears again before the same judge, harsher measures may be taken in sentencing. Or the judge may divert juveniles to particular community agencies for special treatment. Juveniles with psychological problems or who are emotionally disturbed, sex offenders, or those with drug and/or alcohol dependencies may be targeted for special community treatments. Judges may also impose certain conditions as punishments such as fines, restitution, or some form of community service. The more drastic alternatives are varying degrees of custodial sentences, ranging from the placement of juveniles in foster homes, camps, ranches, reform schools, or industrial schools. These nonsecure and secure forms of placement and/or detention are usually reserved for the most serious offenders.

Diversion

Diversion is the temporary directing of youths from the juvenile justice system, where they can remain with their families or guardians, attend school, and be subject to limited supervision on a regular basis by a juvenile probation officer. It is claimed by some authorities that diversion of offenders should be aimed at the client population that would otherwise have received formal dispositions if diversion had not occurred (Osgood, 1983). This client population consists of youths who have committed delinquent acts and not simply status offenses. However, some critics say that status offenders "escalate" to more serious offenses if left "untreated" by the system. Therefore, intervention of some sort is necessary to prevent this escalation of offense seriousness. But other studies provide support for the idea that status offenders do not necessarily progress to more serious offenses. Sometimes, their apparent involvement in more serious offenses is a function of the same acts being labeled differently by police (Fuller and Norton, 1993). Divertees, regardless of whether they are status offenders or those who have committed delinquent acts, have some amount of recidivism in any event. And some of these divertees do progress to more serious offenses (Kenney, Pate, and Hamilton, 1990).

Diversion has certain logistical benefits. First, it decreases the caseload of juvenile court prosecutors by shuffling less serious cases to probation departments. This, of course, increases the supervisory responsibilities of probation departments. Another advantage of diversion for juvenile justice is that it does appear to reduce recidivism in those jurisdictions where it has been used (Fuller and Norton, 1993; Roy, 1995). On the negative side, claims that diversion has "widened the net" by including some youths who otherwise would have received "wristslaps" or warnings seem justified (Fuller and Norton, 1993). Much of this net widening occurs through changes in police discretion and relabeling of juvenile behaviors as more serious, however (Kenney et al., 1990).

Deferred Prosecution. In 1933, a New York lawyer, Conrad Printzlien, was an assistant U.S. Attorney in the Eastern District of New York. Subsequently, Printzlien accepted an appointment as a U.S. Probation Officer in the same district (Rackmill, 1996:8). With a growing clientele of youthful offenders, Printzlien saw firsthand how prosecution and conviction both labeled youths and destroyed their lives with the stigma of criminality. Noting that many of these youths were first-offenders, Printzlien helped to establish the *Brooklyn Plan,* a deferred prosecution program for youthful offenders in New York. The Brooklyn Plan operated from 1936 to 1946 following district court approval. **Deferred prosecution** is temporarily halting proceedings against defendants while they are subjected to a program with particular behavioral requirements for a short period. Over 250 juvenile offenders were deferred under this program during its operation, with only two youths violating their program requirements.

Similar to diversion, deferred prosecution under the Brooklyn Plan involved examining defendants' records on a case-by-case basis and determining which offenders were most likely to benefit from deferred prosecution. If an offender showed promise of being rehabilitated, then he would be freed on his own recognizance for a short period, perhaps three to six months, under the supervision of his parents and probation officer. Both parents and probation officers would furnish the court a written evaluation of a youth's progress following the deferred prosecution period. If youths did not reoffend during this period and behaved in a law-abiding manner in other respects, then prosecutions against them were terminated. Thus, some youths were able to avoid the adverse labeling effects of a criminal prosecution (Rackmill, 1996:8–9). During the course of the Brooklyn Plan, the length of the supervision program ranged up to two years for some offenders. The plan was also implemented in later years in other federal jurisdictions. Some states adopted the plan as well, with favorable results. Indications are that the use of diversion and deferred prosecution, for some youths at least, enabled them to recover their lives and pursue law-abiding lives as adults.

Supervised Probation

Placing a juvenile on probation as the result of an adjudicatory hearing is one of the juvenile judge's conditional options. Like probation for adult offenders, *juvenile probation is a sentence of supervised conditional release for a specified period.* Juvenile probation officers oversee each offender's progress through visits to homes or schools or employment sites. The juvenile judge retains control over the juvenile and may revoke probation if one or more conditions of it are violated. For all practical purposes, juvenile probationers are not in the same class as adult probationers. Therefore, if their probation is revoked by the juvenile judge, they have no right to a hearing in the matter. At least the U.S. Supreme Court failed to address or clarify the rights of juveniles in probation or parole revocation hearings when these same issues were resolved for adults. They are simply informed by the judge of a new sentence and new conditions.

In 1995, there were 105,582 juveniles in correctional programs in the U.S. (Camp and Camp, 1995c:1). About 50,600 youths were either on probation or parole. About 51,900 juveniles were in some type of public or private confinement facility (Camp and Camp, 1995c:1). Males accounted for 91.6 percent of those in residential (secure confinement) programs and about 86.5 percent of those in nonresidential programs. Black juveniles comprised

47.2 percent of all supervised youths in 1995, with whites accounting for 33.5 percent, and Hispanics accounting for 14 percent (Camp and Camp, 1995c:9). During 1995, there were 75,511 admissions to juvenile facilities or state supervision, with 4,601 parole violators and 4,665 probation violators (Camp and Camp, 1995c:11).

Conditions of probation may include supervision by juvenile probation officers or no supervision. Conditions may include restitution, if financial loss was suffered by one or more victims in cases of vandalism, property damage, or physical injury. Fines may be imposed. Or the judge may specify some form of community service. All of these conditions individually or in any combination may be a part of a juvenile's probation program. Violation of one or more conditions may result in probation revocation. Probation officers are usually the link between juvenile offenders and the courts regarding compliance with these conditions.

In jurisdictions such as Rhode Island, probation is sometimes considered a **therapeutic intervention.** Departing from traditional probation, where a probation officer might make periodic visits or inspections of the juvenile's premises and conduct checks with school officials, probation as therapy considers the **probation counselor** the "good parent the child never had" (Sweet, 1988:90). Intervention in the Rhode Island program occurs through five distinct steps:

1. *Case review.* The probation counselor must interpret the behavior of the juvenile, review the case thoroughly, conduct interviews with both the juvenile and parents, and possibly discuss the juvenile's problems with other professionals.
2. *Self-awareness.* The probation counselor needs to inspect his own reactions to adolescents and determine whether biases exist that may influence the relationship and rapport he establishes between himself and the juvenile.
3. *Development of a relationship.* The probation counselor must establish an accepting relationship between himself and the juvenile, where confidence and trust are prevalent. Respect for the juvenile's feelings must be demonstrated.
4. *The critical incident.* The testing phase of the relationship occurs when the juvenile "tests" the honesty or consistency of the counselor. The juvenile examines carefully the response given by the counselor to the "critical incident."
5. *Follow through.* If the counselor "passes the test," he will no doubt encounter other tests. But he has gained the respect and rapport with the juvenile by which new levels of progress can be achieved. In short, this involves a type of parenting that the parents originally failed to accomplish (Sweet, 1988:90). This is considered "action therapy" and appears to work well, especially for those youths with family difficulties.

An increasingly important feature of probation programs is **restitution** (Roy, 1995). Several models of restitution have been described and include the following (Schneider, 1985):

1. The *financial/community service model,* which stresses the offender's financial accountability and community service to pay for damages

2. The *victim/offender mediation model,* which focuses upon victim-offender reconciliation
3. The *victim/reparations model,* with which juveniles compensate their victims directly for their offenses

The potential significance of restitution, coupled with probation, is that it suggests a reduction in recidivism among juvenile offenders. Roy (1995) has described a juvenile victim restitution program in Lake County, Indiana. Two groups of juveniles were identified: 113 juveniles designated as the *restitution group* and 148 youths designated as *probation only.* Juvenile clients were selected from the program during 1989 and 1990. These juveniles were tracked through 1992 and compared on several salient variables, including gender, substance abuse history, prior offense history, age at first offense, and detention history. Roy found that restitution was a valuable intervention primarily for those youths considered first-offenders. Recidivism rates were lowest for first-offenders, regardless of whether they were involved in either probation with restitution or probation only. Similar findings have been observed in other programs (U.S. General Accounting Office, 1995). One caution suggested by some researchers is that net widening should be avoided. Some juveniles might be included in restitution programs simply because the programs are in place. If the programs did not exist, then these offenders would likely receive probation and not recidivate. For them, involvement in a restitution program simply because the program exists would not be particularly productive as a rehabilitative tool (Fuller and Norton, 1993).

Prescribing the right type of probation aftercare for juveniles is difficult. However, descriptions of those juveniles with chronic recidivism patterns reveal that the following factors are important predictors (Baird, 1985:36):

1. Age at first adjudication
2. Prior criminal behavior (a combined measure of the number and severity of priors)
3. Number of prior commitments to juvenile facilities
4. Drug/chemical abuse
5. Alcohol abuse
6. Family relationships (parental control)
7. School problems
8. Peer relationships

Probation supervision can be gauged according to the following standards, depending on the size of the probation department and prevailing juvenile probationer caseloads (Baird, 1985:38):

Regular Supervision

1. Four face-to-face contacts per month with youth
2. Two face-to-face contacts per month with parents

3. One face-to-face contact per month with placement staff
4. One contact with school officials

Intensive Supervision

1. Six face-to-face contacts per month with youth
2. Three face-to-face contacts per month with parents
3. One face-to-face contact per month with placement staff
4. Two contacts with school officials

Alternative Care Cases

1. One face-to-face contact per month with youth
2. Four contacts with agency staff (one must be face-to-face)
3. One contact every two months with parents

In some jurisdictions such as Prince George's County, Maryland, juvenile court judges and correctional officials have approved a unique juvenile aversion program (Mitchell and Williams, 1986:70). Sponsored and funded by the Maryland Department of Corrections, a program has been established entitled "See Our Side" or SOS. SOS is intended to "show juveniles the real side of life" (1986:70). The program was created in response to a rapid rise in the amount of violent juvenile crime in Prince George's County between 1981 and 1983. The program is presently designed to accommodate any youth between the ages of 12 and 18 who has been referred by a school, parents, or juvenile court. It is not necessarily a "last resort" before detention, but it gives participants a "shock" by exposing them to the realities of life behind bars.

SOS consists of a three-hour, four-phased program consisting of an orientation and counseling session, where jail population characteristics and environment are discussed. A second phase is a tour of a local jail facility. No sections of the jail are left out of the tour. The third phase consists of inmates discussing life behind bars with the juvenile participants. A final phase consists of written and verbal reactions to the experience. SOS officials conduct follow-up checks over the next year to determine the extent of recidivism among juveniles who participated. Interestingly, while nearly 40 percent of the youths were delinquent recidivists prior to the program, only 16 percent recidivated after program participation. SOS officials conclude that the four-phase program is doing its job and doing it well (Mitchell and Williams, 1986:71).

Confinement or Placement

The last resort for juvenile judges aside from transferring juveniles to criminal court is **confinement** or **placement,** which may be either **nonsecure** or **secure.** Nonsecure placement may involve placing the youth in a foster home if the juvenile's parents are considered unfit. Or the juvenile may be abandoned or orphaned. Foster home placement provides the youth with some semblance of a family. Other nonsecure options for juvenile judges include assignments of juveniles to group homes or camp ranches. Secure placement is placing a juvenile in a facility, such as an industrial school, where one's freedom is regulated by institution authorities. Secure-custody facilities for juveniles are the equivalent of adult prisons or penitentiaries.

One problem facing juvenile court judges is deciding *which* juveniles should be assigned to which programs (DiCataldo and Grisso, 1995; Krisberg et al., 1993). More often than not, juveniles are incarcerated in secure state facilities when they do not deserve or need such confinement (Wiebush, 1993). This problem results from *overclassification.* This is a classification problem, and the level of accuracy associated with juvenile risk prediction instruments is about as poor as adult risk prediction devices (Altschuler and Armstrong, 1994; Baird and Neuenfeldt, 1990). Nevertheless, judges attempt to make secure or nonsecure detention decisions on the basis of the following elements (Baird, 1985:34):

1. Classification based on risk of continued criminal activity and the offender's need for services
2. A case management classification system designed to help probation and parole officers develop effective case plans and select appropriate casework strategies
3. A management information system designed to enhance planning, monitoring, evaluation, and accountability
4. A work load deployment system that allows agencies to effectively and efficiently allocate their limited resources

Baird and Neuenfeldt (1990) have described a Client Management Classification System (CMCS) that provides a structured way for staff to evaluate offenders and to develop supervision strategies based upon specific offender types. The CMCS uses a structured offender interview and scoring guide to classify offenders into one of four groupings, selective intervention: casework/control, environmental structure, and limit setting. Results suggest that over 75 U.S. jurisdictions have been able to improve their supervision effectiveness over juveniles assigned to their care. Specific program evaluations have been conducted in South Carolina, Texas, and Wisconsin, indicating the successfulness of CMCS.

Juvenile Detention Centers. When juveniles are awaiting a hearing in juvenile court or have been adjudicated delinquent, they may be placed in **juvenile detention centers.** A juvenile detention center is either a short- or long-term secure placement facility to house minors who require continuous supervision. In recent years, the Office of Juvenile Justice and Delinquency Prevention has recognized that juvenile detention centers play increasingly important roles in assessing the needs of youths and providing training for their development (Roush and Jones, 1996:54). Grants have been made available to various jurisdictions for the purpose of providing more effective training for staff who work in juvenile detention and corrections facilities. For instance, a Juvenile Detention Care Giver Training Curriculum Project was instituted to provide a 40-hour training curriculum for new juvenile detention careworkers (Jones and Roush, 1995). Such curriculums are often directly connected to specific juvenile detention functions. Figure 14.6 shows job functions and effectiveness characteristics for juvenile detention centers.

Group homes may be privately or publicly operated. They require juvenile clients to observe the rights of others, participate in various vocational or educational training programs, attend school, participate in therapy or receive prescribed medical treatment, and observe curfew. Urinalyses or other tests may be conducted randomly as checks to see whether juveniles are taking drugs or consuming alcohol contrary to group home policy. If one or more program violations occur, group home officials may report these infractions to the juvenile judge who retains dispositional control over the youth. Assignment to a group home or any other type of detention is usually for a definite period.

There are numerous proponents and opponents of juvenile detention of any kind. Those favoring detention cite the disruption of one's lifestyle and separation as a positive dimension, especially when chronic offenders are treated (Parent, 1991; Sweet, 1991). For example, a youth who has been involved with a delinquent gang or a particular circle of friends who engage in frequent law violations would benefit from detention because these counterproductive associations would be interrupted or terminated. Of course, juveniles can always return to their old ways when released from detention. There is nothing the juvenile justice system can do to prevent that in any absolute sense.

However, arguments have been advanced to show that the positive effect of imprisonment on a juvenile's self-image and propensity to commit new offenses is negligible (Frazier and Bishop, 1990; Johnson et al., 1990). Thus, detention as a punishment may be the primary result, without any tangible, long-range benefits such as self-improvement or reduction in recidivism. At least there does not appear to be any substantial evidence that detention as a juvenile automatically escalates to adult crime. According to some analysts, the peak ages of juvenile criminality fall between the sixteenth and twentieth birthdays, with participation rates falling off rapidly (Greenwood, 1986c:151). Thus, detention for a fixed period may "naturally" ease the delinquency rate, at least for some of the more chronic offenders.

Outward Bound and Wilderness Programs

One productive alternative to the detention of juvenile offenders, even those considered chronic, is participation in experience programs. **Experience programs** or **wilderness programs** include a wide array of outdoor

Detention Functions: The "What" of Juvenile Detention

1. *Behavior management:* Using behavioral and developmental theories to establish clear expectations for residents' behavior and employing immediate positive and/or negative consequences as a result of direct involvement with residents.
2. *Crisis intervention:* Using skill and composure in order to prevent or minimize physical and emotional harm to residents and other staff members when handling a wide variety of crisis situations, e.g., physical violence, escapes, riots, and suicidal behaviors.
3. *Security:* Implementing the policy and procedures related to resident supervision and institutional security measures to ensure the physical presence of each resident in the facility.
4. *Safety:* Employing knowledge and skills in relation to emergency procedures, i.e., first aid, CPR, fire safety, and communicable disease, to assist the well-being of youth.
5. *Custodial care:* Assisting in the proper identification and treatment of problems relating to the physical and emotional health and well-being of detained youth through the use of knowledge and skills in basic health-related areas, e.g., medical and hygiene, adolescent sexuality, substance abuse, physical or emotional abuse, and symptoms of suicidal behavior and emotional distress.
6. *Record keeping:* Providing accurate and timely written documentation of both routine and special situations regarding residents, staff members, and program activities through the use of observation and recording skills.
7. *Program maintenance:* Implementing, teaching, creating, and supplementing the facility's daily program and activities, i.e., physical education, recreation, arts and crafts.
8. *Problem solving:* Creating an environment or institutional climate where a youth's personal, social, and emotional problems can be openly discussed, explored, and possibly resolved through staff use of effective interpersonal relationship skills, communication and consultation with clinical staff, and participation in and leadership of group discussions and activities.
9. *Organizational awareness:* Understanding, supporting, and using the philosophy, goals, values, policies, and procedures that represent the daily operations of the facility.
10. *External awareness:* Identifying and keeping up-to-date with key external issues and trends likely to affect the agency, e.g., legal, political, demographic, and philosophical trends.

Effectiveness Characteristics: The "How" of Juvenile Detention

1. *Balanced perspective:* A broad view that balances present needs and longer-term considerations.
2. *Strategic view:* Ability to collect and analyze information that forms an overall longer range view of priorities and forecasts likely needs, problems, and opportunities.
3. *Environmental sensitivity:* Awareness of broad environmental trends and their effects on your work unit.
4. *Leadership:* An ability and willingness to lead and manage others.
5. *Flexibility:* Openness to new information and tolerance for stress and ambiguity in the work situation.
6. *Action orientation:* Decisiveness, calculated risk-taking, and a drive to get things done.
7. *Results focus:* High concern for goal achievement and a tenacity in following through to the end.
8. *Communication:* Ability to express oneself clearly and authoritatively and to listen clearly to others.
9. *Interpersonal sensitivity:* Self-knowledge and awareness of impact of self on others, sensitivity to the needs and weaknesses of others, ability to empathize with the viewpoint of others.
10. *Technical competence:* Expert and up-to-date knowledge of the work methods and procedures of your work unit.

FIGURE 14.6 Job functions and effectiveness characteristics for juvenile detention centers. (*Source:* Roush and Jones, 1996:57)

programs designed to improve a juvenile's self-worth, self-concept, pride, and trust in others (Harris et al., 1993; McCarthy and McCarthy, 1997). Project **Outward Bound** is one of more than 200 programs of its type in the United States today. Outward Bound was first introduced in Colorado in 1962 with objectives emphasizing personal survival in the wilderness. Youths participated in various outdoor activities including rock climbing, solo survival, camping, and long-range hiking during a three-week period. Program officials were not concerned with equipping these juveniles with survival skills per se, but rather, they wanted to instill within the participants a feeling of self-confidence and self-assurance to cope with other types of problems in their communities.

In 1970, a similar program was commenced in Massachusetts. This program, **Homeward Bound,** is more elaborate than Outward Bound. It consists of a six-week wilderness course that increases one's physical fitness and ability to survive outdoors. Furthermore, the program includes evening instruction in subjects such as ecology, survival, and search and rescue operations (McCarthy and McCarthy, 1997). Although these programs serve limited numbers of juveniles and some authorities question their value in deterring further delinquency, some evidence suggests that these wilderness experiences generate less recidivism among participants compared with those youths who are institutionalized in industrial schools under conditions of close custody and monitoring.

SELECTED ISSUES IN JUVENILE CORRECTIONS

Juvenile corrections has been under attack from various sectors for many decades (Claggett et al., 1992). This attack comes from many quarters, and it coincides with a general attack on the criminal justice system for its apparent failure to stem the increasing wave of crime in the United States. Sentencing reforms, correctional reforms, experiments with probation and parole alternatives, and a host of other options have been attempted in an apparent effort to cure or control delinquents and criminals. The United Nations and the National Council of Juvenile and Family Court Judges adopted policy statements about the juvenile justice system that bear directly on juvenile corrections. The issues to be discussed in this final section may be better understood in the context of these statements.

Five general recommendations have been made (Dwyer and McNally, 1987, 50–51):

1. That continued individualized treatment of juveniles be continued, including the development of medical, psychiatric, and educational programs that range from least to most restrictive, according to individual need.
2. That the chronic, serious juvenile offender, while being held accountable, be retained within the jurisdiction of the juvenile court. As a resource, specialized programs and facilities need to be developed that focus on restorations rather than punishment.

3. That the disposition of juvenile court have a flexible range for restricting freedom with the primary goal focused on the restoration to full liberty rather than let the punishment fit the crime; that no case dispositions should be of a mandatory nature, but rather, they should be left to the discretion of the judge based on predetermined dispositional guidelines; that in no case should a juvenile under 18 years of age be subject to capital punishment.
4. That in situations where the juvenile court judge believes that the juvenile under consideration is nonamenable to the services of the court and based on the youth's present charges, past record in court, and his or her age and mental status, the judge may waive jurisdiction; that in all juvenile cases the court of original jurisdiction be that of the juvenile court; that the discretion to waive be left to the juvenile judge; that the proportionality of punishment would be appropriate with these cases, but the most high-risk offenders should be treated in small, but secure, facilities.
5. That policy makers, reformers, and researchers continue to strive for a greater understanding as to the causes and most desired response to juvenile crime; that research should be broad-based rather than limited to management, control, and punishment strategies.

Some of the issues noted below are affected directly by these recommendations and policy statements. While these statements are not obligatory for any jurisdiction, they do suggest opinions and positions of a relevant segment of concerned citizens—juvenile court judges and juvenile corrections personnel. These issues include (1) the deinstitutionalization of status offenses; (2) the classification of juvenile offenders; (3) the treatment of juveniles as adults; (4) violent and nonviolent juvenile offenders; and (5) capital punishment for juveniles.

The Deinstitutionalization of Status Offenses

The **deinstitutionalization** of status offenses (DSO) is the removal of youths from secure institutions and detention facilities whose only infractions are status offenses such as running away from home, incorrigibility, truancy, and curfew violations (Krause and McShane, 1994). DSO was specifically targeted as a major juvenile justice priority by Congress through the passage of the Juvenile Justice and Delinquency Prevention Act of 1974. Since 1974, many states have moved to modify their juvenile-relevant statutes to implement DSO, although the Congressional mandate was not binding on states. The major impact of DSO in various jurisdictions has been to remove from detention those juveniles charged with status offenses. Again, these are offenses that would not be considered crimes if committed by adults. However, juvenile courts continue to exercise jurisdiction over all juveniles, including status offenders. This means that although detention beyond a 24-hour period or confinement in jails is generally prohibited, it is still possible for jurisdictions to file petitions to have status offenders adjudicated as delinquent.

This is a very serious matter for affected juveniles who have not committed felonies or misdemeanors. This means, for instance, that a runaway or a curfew violator may still be labeled a juvenile delinquent according to juvenile statutes in almost every jurisdiction. Clearly, there are major differences between curfew violators, runaways, and truants and rapists, robbers, murderers, and thieves. However, they are all filtered through the same funnel and emerge with identical delinquency labels. DSO has been implemented in various jurisdictions in three different ways. First, **decarceration** may be used, where detention is prohibited, although youths may be placed in foster or group homes or on probation by the juvenile court. A second type of DSO occurs through diversion, where community-based services are used to treat juveniles for problems they may have. The juvenile court retains jurisdiction under the "dependent and neglected children" category (Bishop and Frazier, 1992). The third type of DSO is **divestiture,** where the juvenile court looses its control over status offenders and may not detain, petition, adjudicate, or place them on probation. In short, this third type of DSO results in a total loss of control by the juvenile court over the youth, since the misbehavior is a status offense (Schneider, 1984).

The implications of this third DSO option are several. Police discretion is affected indirectly, since decisions by police to charge juveniles with status offenses remove those juveniles from juvenile court jurisdiction and result in youth control by community agencies instead. Juvenile judges lose control over those status offenders, and this may be interpreted as a "power loss" which few judges like to relinquish. DSO is considered to be a "soft" measure in dealing with juvenile offenders, because the power of the court to deal with them has been withdrawn. And DSO may weaken the sanctioning powers of the state where sanctions should be invoked, since it is believed by some that a link exists between status offenders and illicit behaviors (Garbarino, Wilson, and Garbarino, 1986). Several states have implemented divestiture, including Washington and Maine. Interestingly, Washington's divestiture law widened the net, because police reacted by relabeling acts of juveniles as delinquency, whereas previously, the same offenses would have been labeled status offenses (Schneider, 1984).

A similar outcome was observed in Connecticut, where DSO occurred through removal of juveniles from secure facilities or general detention. Rather than cut down on the number of juveniles detained, Connecticut figures disclosed a rise in juvenile detentions, where the juvenile court simply substituted noninstitutional detention for institutional detention. Instead of putting status offenders in secure detention, juvenile judges began putting them in group homes or camp ranches (Logan and Rausch, 1985a). Thus, DSO did not accomplish what it was designed to accomplish, at least in the jurisdictions examined. Although the literature about recidivism among status offenders is inconsistent, sketchy, and inconclusive, at least some status offenders progress to more serious violations (Bishop and Frazier, 1992; Krause and McShane, 1994). One explanation is that they are troubled to begin with, through family adjustment problems, or personal and social difficulties. These factors influence whether delinquent acts will be committed in the future. Thus, there is some justification for recommen-

BOX 14.4 On Six-Year-Olds Who Commit Attempted Murder

The Case of the Violent Six-Year-Old

Juvenile authorities are scratching their heads over the actions of the youngest child ever to be charged with attempted murder. This is the story so far. In late April 1996, a 6-year-old boy enlisted the aid of two 8-year-old twins to help him steal a tricycle from a neighbor's house. They entered the home and took the tricycle. The adults, Mr. and Mrs. Ignacio Burmudez, were away from their home shopping. At home asleep was a month-old baby and his 18-year-old sister. The boys entered through an unlocked back door, grabbed the bike and began to flee. But the 6-year-old ringleader decided to do some damage to the sleeping infant. He entered the baby's room and beat the baby with his fists and an inch-thick stick. The beating was so fierce that the stick broke. The baby's skull was severely fractured in the unprovoked attack.

Awakened by the noise, the sister discovered her brother in his crib, bleeding. She screamed loud enough to be heard by neighbors in adjacent homes. The baby was rushed to the hospital. In the meantime, the boys were spotted trying to hide the tricycle in some bushes. Police picked them up for questioning. After determining that the two 8-year-olds had no part of the attack on the infant, police released them to the custody of their parents. The story they were told by the 6-year-old, however, was chilling.

The boy was always getting into trouble, others said who knew him. He'd steal whatever wasn't tied down. In fact, his attack of the infant was probably provoked when he attempted to enter the Burmudez home a few days earlier and Mr. Burmudez threw him out. "He entered the house with the idea of doing something. He had a large stick and I threw him out. I'd never seen him before then." The boy confessed to the attempted murder, but he showed no remorse to police.

Prosecutors say that they want the 6-year-old locked up for many years. There are no effective treatment programs for such persons, although there are various intervention methods that might assist his family in coping with what he did. Some experts have suggested out-of-home placement in foster care, while others have suggested long-term confinement in a group home. Dan Macallair, an associate director of the San Francisco-based Center on Juvenile and Criminal Justice, says that it is "ludicrous" to lock up a 6-year-old. He says the "boy should be sent home unless there is a drug or abuse problem in the household." But that's what Macallair says. There are other viewpoints. What if the child attempts to kill again? Given his "record" of violence, this is a likely forecast.

What should society do for children who kill or attempt to kill? This 6-year-old first-grade special education student obviously has problems. He already has earned the reputation of being a bully at school, threatening other kids with a big stick, stealing from them, and hitting them with his fists. He would travel up and down city streets, trying to knock other kids off of their bicycles with a large stick or by pushing them over. In other instances, he would point his stick at other kids like a gun and pretend to be shooting them. What if he actually had a gun? One of his neighbors said that he is always getting into trouble. He would sneak into neighbors' homes and steal anything that wasn't tied down, even tires. Parents would not allow their children to play with him because of his violence.

Physicians treating the one-month-old baby say that he has irreversible brain damage as the result of the beating. Prosecutors doubt that any social agency is equipped to deal with a boy as dangerous as the 6-year-old. His public defender, Leslie Blalik, wants the boy given to Child Protective Services, where he will be treated like a victim rather than a criminal. The boy needs counseling that a detention facility can't provide, he says.

What are the rights of the Bermudez family in this case? What can protect them from attacks by this same boy if he is freed? What sort of punishment and/or crime control method would be workable for this youngster, if any? What would you recommend if you had the power to decide the fate of the violent 6-year-old?

Source: Adapted from Associated Press, "So Young for Murder:Chilling Crime by Six-Year-Old Leaves Many People Shocked." *Minot (N.D.) Daily News,* April 29, 1996:A5.

dations that status offenders be subjected to some form of institutional supervision (Garbarino et al., 1986).

The Classification of Juvenile Offenders

Classification of any offender is made difficult by the fact that the state-of-the-art in predictions of risk and dangerousness is such that little future behavior can be accurately forecasted. This holds for juveniles as well as adults. We know that status offenders may or may not escalate to more serious offenses, with the prevailing sentiment favoring or implying nonescalation (DiCaltado and Grisso, 1995; Krisberg et al., 1993).

Effective classification schemes have not been devised, although we know that on the basis of descriptions of existing offender aggregates that gender, age, nature of offense, seriousness of offense, race or ethnicity, and socioeconomic status are more or less correlated (Altschuler and Armstrong, 1994; Champion, 1994). The flaws of various classification schemes are made more apparent when program "failures" are detected in large numbers. Juvenile court judges make the wrong judgements and decisions about juvenile placements. Intake officers make similar errors of classification when conducting initial screenings of juveniles. The issue of false positives and false negatives is raised here, because some youths may be unfairly penalized for what authorities believe are valid predictive criteria of future dangerousness. By the same token, some youths are underpenalized, because it is believed, wrongly, that they will not pose risks or commit serious offenses in the future, and they do (Champion, 1994).

The Treatment of Juveniles as Adults

The *intended* result of waivers is to make it possible for criminal courts to administer harsher punishments on juvenile offenders. But as we have seen, this doesn't always occur. Less than 2 percent of all juvenile offenders are transferred to criminal courts annually (Butts et al., 1996:13). Waived or transferred juveniles are *not* always those who have committed the most violent acts. Although waivers are intended to be a get-tough reaction toward serious and violent juvenile offending, the majority of those transferred to criminal court annually are nonviolent property, public order, or drug-using offenders. Let's look at how waivers for juvenile offenders have been used between 1989 and 1993.

1. *"Let's waive more juveniles to criminal court!"* OK. In 1993, 11,800 juveniles were transferred to criminal courts compared with 8,300 transferred youths in 1989. This is an increase in waiver usage of 41 percent. OK.

2. *"Let's get tough against violent juvenile offenders!"* OK. In 1993, 5,000 violent juvenile offenders were transferred to criminal courts, representing about 42 percent of all those youths transferred. In 1989, 2,300 violent juvenile offenders were transferred, about 28 percent of all transferees. Proportionately more violent juvenile offenders are being transferred to criminal courts and treated as adults. OK.

3. *"Let's reserve transfers only for the worst juvenile offenders!"* In 1993, 4,500 juvenile property offenders (38.1%) were transferred to criminal courts compared with 49.4 percent property offenders transferred in 1989. However, about 1,200 (10.1%) drug-using juveniles were transferred to criminal courts in 1993 compared with 1,400 (17%) in 1989. And in 1993, about 1,000 public order juvenile offenders (8.5%) were transferred to criminal courts compared with 600 (7.2%) public order juvenile offenders in 1989. It appears as though we are sending proportionately fewer property offenders to criminal court through waivers. But we are also sending proportionately fewer drug-using juveniles and proportionately greater numbers of public order offenders to criminal courts. Collectively, the majority (nearly 60%) of all transferred youths are property offenders, drug-users, or public order offenders of the non-violent variety.

What does this information say about the use of waivers? First, we *are* making progress by sending proportionately *more* violent juvenile offenders to criminal courts for processing. These are the most primary targets of transfers anyway, at least according to policy makers and juvenile justice experts. However, nonviolent property offenders, drug-using juveniles, and public order offenders continue to make up the majority of transferred youths. These types of offenders tend to waste valuable criminal court time. Prosecutors are not particularly interested in pursuing "disturbing the peace" cases or pursuing charges against juvenile drug users. Juveniles waived to criminal court for shoplifting, stealing cigarettes and alcohol from a burglary of a convenience store, or smoking marijuana do not generate as much prosecutorial enthusiasm as adult professional forgers, armed robbers, murderers, or career criminals. This should not be taken to mean that drug use, burglary, and disturbing the peace cases are not serious; rather, they are *not as serious* as more violent types of offending (e.g., murder, rape, aggravated assault, robbery). These less serious juvenile cases should receive the full weight of the law in juvenile courts, not criminal courts. Juvenile court judges have a variety of serious dispositional options, including several conditional intensive supervision programs, community-based treatments, and secure placement.

Because such large numbers of less serious juvenile cases are sent to criminal courts for processing, the outcomes of waivers are often just the opposite intended. About half of all transferred juvenile cases annually are either downgraded in seriousness through plea bargaining or prosecutors simply decline to prosecute them. Another 40 percent or more of the cases result in probationary sentences. Only a small fraction, less than 10 percent, of all juvenile transfers result in incarceration. And this phenomenon is repeated annually (Maguire and Flanagan, 1995).

In fact, many juveniles may even benefit from being transferred to criminal courts, where their crimes are more lightly regarded compared with those committed by recidivist adult offenders. Furthermore, juveniles also have a right to a jury trial where the penalty for their offense includes possible incarceration of more than six months. Finally, a juvenile's youthfulness functions as a mitigating factor and tends to lessen sentence severity if the juvenile is ultimately convicted.

Violent and Nonviolent Juvenile Offenders

Investigations of violent and nonviolent youthful offenders show little evidence that those who commit nonviolent offenses eventually progress to violent offenses (Altschuler and Armstrong, 1994; DiCataldo and Grisso, 1995). Furthermore, the proportion of juvenile offenders who are violent appears to be quite small in most jurisdictions throughout the United States (Butts, 1996; Snyder et al., 1996). There are mixed reactions among the public about how best to deal with violent youthful offenders (Lewis et al., 1989). The get tough on delinquency trend throughout the nation is such that many violent offenders are transferred to criminal courts for potentially harsher penalties, although we are not sure how much this is occurring (Hess and Clement, 1993; Minnesota Criminal Justice Statistical Analysis Center, 1989).

Capital Punishment for Juvenile Offenders

By the beginning of 1995, there were 2,890 prisoners on death row awaiting the penalty of death in 34 states and the federal prison system (Stephan and Snell, 1996:1). At the time of their arrest, 41 of these death row inmates were 17 years of age or younger, or about 1.7 percent of all death row inmates.

The first recorded execution of a juvenile occurred in 1642. Thomas

BOX 14.5 Drive-Bys

The Case of the Drive-By Shooters and Cherryl Tendeland

Fargo, North Dakota, was the scene of a violent drive-by shooting on November 15, 1995. Patrick Tendeland and his wife, Cherryl, were driving back to their home from a prayer meeting early that evening. Suddenly, six youths appeared in another car, which pulled parallel with the Tendeland vehicle. A 12-gauge sawed-off shotgun protruded from the window and buckshot flew though the Tendeland car. Pat was wounded by the shotgun fire and flying glass and drove away quickly, seeking medical attention. It was on his way to a nearby hospital that he realized something was wrong with his wife, Cherryl. He stopped at a convenience store to call the police, and when he did, he took a closer look at his wife. Close inspection revealed that Cherryl had been struck in the back of the head by shotgun pellets and killed instantly.

Six youths were subsequently arrested and three were charged with murder. The trigger man, or boy, was 17-year-old Barry Garcia, a member of a neighboring Minnesota gang. Through information against him provided by his gang friends, Garcia was arraigned and placed on trial in Fargo for first-degree murder in April 1996. A plea bargain resulted in Garcia's conviction and a sentence of life without parole.

No one has ever provided a motive for the shooting, other than that it was purely random, motivated by nothing more than to show one's gang friends that he could kill another human being. Pat Tendeland had few words as Garcia was placed on trial for the murder of Tendeland's wife. "My wife was murdered . . . my boys lost their mother, and a lot of people in this community lost a really good friend," said Tendeland when interviewed. He added, "I have to see the trial through. It will give me a feeling of satisfaction." However, nothing anyone can do can ever replace his loss.

How should juveniles be treated who are convicted of drive-by shootings? What types of interventions might work with such boys in school or in the community? Should the age be lowered for capital punishment to be applied in cases involving growing numbers of youthful violent offenders? Is society to blame for gang members such as Barry Garcia?

Source: Adapted from Associated Press, "Husband Deals with Anger from Wife's Death." *Minot (N.D.) Daily News,* April 14, 1996:B2.

Graunger, a 16-year-old, was convicted of bestiality. He was caught sodomizing a horse and a cow. The youngest age where the death penalty has been imposed is 10. A poorly documented case of a 10-year-old convicted murderer in Louisiana occurred in 1855. A more celebrated case, that of 10-year-old James Arcene, occurred in Arkansas in 1885. Arcene was 10 years old when he robbed and murdered his victim. He was eventually arrested at age 23 before being executed (Streib, 1987:57).

Arguments For and Against the Death Penalty for Juveniles. Those favoring the death penalty say it is "just" punishment and a form of societal revenge for the life taken or harm inflicted by the offender (Gewerth and Dorne, 1991). It is an economical way of dealing with those who will never be released from confinement (Vito et al., 1989). It may be administered "humanely" through lethal injection. It functions as a deterrent to others to refrain from committing capital crimes (Robinson and Stephens, 1992).

Opponents say it is cruel and unusual punishment (Gewerth and Dorne, 1991; Sandys and McGarrell, 1995). They claim the death penalty does not deter those who intend to take another's life. It is barbaric and uncivilized. Other countries do not impose it for any type of offense, regardless of its seriousness (Bieler, 1990). It makes no sense to kill as a means of sending messages to others not to kill (Amnesty International, 1991). Public opinion polls in the United States suggest that 75 percent or more of the citizens surveyed are in favor of the death penalty as a punishment for a capital offense, and more than 50 percent of those supporting the death penalty favor its application to older juveniles (e.g., 16 and 17 years old) who commit premeditated murder. The U.S. Supreme Court ruled in 1989 that executing juveniles ages 16 and 17 at the time they committed a capital offense did not violate the evolving standards of decency (Seis and Elbe, 1991).

For juveniles, the emotional pitch of any argument is intensified by the factor of one's age. Age functions as a mitigating factor. In any capital conviction, the convicted offender is entitled to a bifurcated trial where guilt is established first, and then the punishment is imposed in view of any prevailing mitigating or aggravating circumstances. Was the crime especially brutal? Did the victim suffer? Was the murderer senile or mentally ill? Or was the murderer a juvenile? Since age acts as a mitigating factor in cases in which the death penalty is considered for adults, there are those who say the death penalty should not be applied to juveniles under any condition.

Early English precedent and common law assumed that those under age 7 were incapable of formulating criminal intent, and thus, they were absolved from any wrongdoing. Between age 7 and age 12, a presumption exists that the child is capable of formulating criminal intent, and in every jurisdiction, the burden is borne by the prosecution for establishing beyond a reasonable doubt that the youth was capable of formulating criminal intent.

Although each case is judged on its own merits, there are always at least two sides in an issue involving the murder of one by another. The survivors of the victim demand justice, and the justice they usually seek is the death of the one who brought about the death of their own. This is a manifestation of "an eye for an eye." In many respects, it is an accurate portrayal of why the death penalty is imposed for *both* juveniles and adults. It is supposed to be a penalty that fits the crime committed. But attorneys and family members of those convicted of capital crimes cannot help but feel com-

BOX 14.6 Death Row Inmates Get Younger and Younger

The Case of the Death Row Teens

Their crimes are adult crimes. They have killed. They have committed premeditated murder. They have been convicted by a jury of their peers and sentenced to death in a bifurcated trial proceeding. Everything was done to ensure that fairness was observed. But in Texas, it still didn't prevent the juvenilization of death row.

In 1994, there were 393 inmates on death row in Texas. Of these, 12 committed murder when they were 17; 21 committed murder when they were 18; and 30 committed murder when they were 19. Experts say that among all felony arrests in the United States, the most common arrest age is 16. The next most common felony arrest age is 15.

The stories given by these youths while they await execution by lethal injection sound similar. In the case of six members of a loose-knit gang called *Black and White,* the incident began on the evening of June 24, 1993. Peter Anthony Cantu and Derrick Sean O'Brien, both 19, were gathered along a railroad trestle over a bayou drinking. They were there to initiate into their gang some new members. These included Efrain Perez, 18, Raul Villarreal, 18, and Joe Medillin, 19. A sixth member of the Black and White gang was a minor under 16. What happened next is undisputed. The gang members made Villarreal fight each of the other gang members as a part of the gang initiation.

About 11:30 P.M., the fighting stopped and the boys sat and drank. About that time, Jennifer Ertman, 14, and Elizabeth Pena, 16, were returning home from a slumber party. They took a shortcut through a field near the railroad trestle. As they passed the gang, the gang assaulted them. One gang member said that "everybody was taking turns raping them, beating them, strangling them, stomping them on their necks." Police found the girls' battered bodies four days later.

Leads were obtained from other youths when the gang members bragged about beating and killing the girls. Police brought each gang member in for questioning. Under interrogation, they confessed and were charged with the double murders. When one youth was arrested, he snarled obscenities at the camera crews sent to cover the breaking story. Testimony given at their trial showed that they divided about $40 taken from the girls, as well as some of their jewelry.

To several juvenile justice experts, such as Billie Bramlett with Sam Houston State University and Robert Lineberry, a professor at the University of Houston, "From their point of view, life is of little value. Our logic toward the criminal justice system is people are rational, but I think you're dealing with a crowd of people who are not rational by the standards of the criminal justice system." Dr. Bramlett said that "Those five young men were simply looking for an identity and proving their manhood and that's all it takes. Violence is a very powerful and effective way to get attention." Bramlett says that "The citizenry is fed up with the expense of crime, the fear of crime, the devastation of crime, and just the senseless nature of it."

Is the death penalty for these youths the most appropriate sentence? If you were related to these dead girls, how would you feel about the death penalty being imposed? What other options would the state have for punishing these boys? Do you think the boys are too young to know what they did and the seriousness of it?

Source: Adapted from Michael Graczyk, "Bad Boys Wait on Death Row." *Minot (N.D.) Daily News,* September 26, 1994:A4.

passion for their doomed relatives. Someone they love is about to lose his or her life. But hadn't they taken someone's life in the process? But does taking another life bring back the dead victim? But does taking the life of the murderer fulfill some lofty societal purpose? Should female juvenile murderers be executed? This greatly increases the sensitivity of this issue (Streib and Sametz, 1989). Although there have only been 10 female juvenile executions in the United States between 1767 and 1912, the question of executing female juveniles is an intriguing one that prompts much debate (Streib and Sametz, 1989). Regardless of whether the juveniles are male or female, the arguments over this issue are endless (Vito et al., 1989). Below are several important landmark cases involving the death penalty applied to juveniles.

***Eddings v. Oklahoma* (1982).** The *Eddings* case raised the question of whether the death penalty as applied to juveniles was "cruel and unusual" punishment under the Eighth Amendment of the U.S. Constitution. The U.S. Supreme Court avoided the issue. The Justices did *not* say it was "cruel and unusual punishment," but they also did *not* say it wasn't. What they said was that the youthfulness of the offender is a mitigating factor of great weight that must be considered. Thus, many jurisdictions were left to make their own interpretations of the high court opinion. On April 4, 1977, Monty Lee Eddings and several other companions ran away from their Missouri homes. In a car owned by Eddings's older brother, they drove, without direction or purpose, eventually reaching the Oklahoma Turnpike. Eddings had several firearms in the car, including several rifles that he had stolen from his father. At one point, Eddings lost control of the car and was stopped by an Oklahoma State Highway Patrol officer. When the officer approached the car, Eddings stuck a shotgun out of the window and killed the officer outright. When Eddings was subsequently apprehended, he was waived to criminal court on a prosecutorial motion. Efforts by Eddings and his attorney to oppose the waiver failed. In a subsequent bifurcated trial, several aggravating circumstances were introduced and alleged, while several mitigating circumstances, including Eddings's youthfulness, mental state, and potential for treatment, were considered by the trial judge. However, the judge did not consider Eddings's "unhappy upbringing and emotional disturbance" as significant mitigating factors to offset the aggravating ones. Eddings's attorney filed an appeal that eventually reached the U.S. Supreme Court. Although the Oklahoma Court of Criminal Appeals reversed the trial judge's ruling, the U.S. Supreme Court reversed the Oklahoma Court of Criminal Appeals. The reversal pivoted on whether the trial judge erred by refusing to consider the "unhappy upbringing and emotionally disturbed state" of Eddings. The trial judge had previously acknowledged the youthfulness of Eddings as a mitigating factor. The *fact* of Eddings's age, 16, was significant, precisely because the majority of Justices did not consider it as significant. Rather, they focused upon the issue of introduction of mitigating circumstances specifically outlined in Eddings's appeal. Oklahoma was now in the position of lawfully imposing the death penalty on a juvenile who was 16 years old at the time he committed murder.

Thompson v. Oklahoma **(1988).** In late 1988, the U.S. Supreme Court heard the case of William Wayne Thompson, convicted of murdering his brother-in-law on January 23, 1983. Thompson was 15 years old when the especially brutal murder occurred. Under Oklahoma law, the district attorney filed a statutory petition to have Thompson waived to criminal court where he could be tried for murder as an adult. The waiver was granted and Thompson was tried, convicted, and sentenced to death. Thompson appealed and his case was eventually reviewed by the U.S. Supreme Court, which concluded that "the Eighth and Fourteenth Amendments prohibit the execution of a person who was under 16 years of age at the time of his or her offense" (108 S.Ct. at 2700). Thompson's death sentence was overturned. Thompson's attorney had originally requested the Court to draw a line so that all those under age 18 would be exempt from the death penalty as a punishment, regardless of their crimes. The U.S. Supreme Court refused to do this.

Wilkins v. Missouri **(1989).** Wilkins was 16 when he stabbed to death a woman who was managing a convenience store. There was evidence of aggravating circumstances and torture of the woman. Wilkins was convicted of the murder after being transferred to criminal court and prosecuted as an adult. He was sentenced to death and appealed, arguing that 16 is too young an age to be executed and is therefore cruel and unusual punishment. This landmark case by the Supreme Court set a minimum age at which juveniles can be executed. If juveniles are 16 or older at the time they commit a capital crime, they can suffer execution in those jurisdictions with death penalties. Previously, a case had been decided (*Thompson v. Oklahoma* [1988]) where the Supreme Court said that someone who was 15 at the time they committed murder cannot be executed. The *Wilkins* case effectively drew this line at age 16.

Stanford v. Kentucky **(1989).** Stanford was charged with murder committed when he was 17 years old. He was transferred to criminal court to stand trial for murder as an adult. He was convicted, sentenced to death, and appealed. The appeal contended that he was too young to receive the death penalty, and that the death penalty would be cruel and unusual punishment. The Supreme Court upheld his death penalty and ruled that it is not unconstitutional to apply the death penalty to persons who are convicted of murders they committed when they were 17 years of age.

At this time the minimum age at which the death penalty can be exacted is 16. If a youth was 16 at the time he or she committed the capital offense of murder, then the state can execute the juvenile. If juveniles commit a murder before they are age 16, then the death penalty cannot be imposed. This does not mean, however, that courts are prevented from imposing life-without-parole sentences on such offenders.

THE FUTURE OF JUVENILE CORRECTIONS

The following observations can be made about the future of juvenile corrections in the United States:

1. A greater portion of juvenile corrections will be administered by private interests. A critical factor is the growing numbers of adult and juvenile offenders to manage and the slow adjustment of public correctional agencies to add staff commensurate to deal adequately with these offender increases.
2. The juvenile justice system will experience greater reforms in the area of juvenile rights commensurate with those enjoyed by adult offenders. Thus, we will likely see U.S. Supreme Court decisions extending to juveniles the right to a jury trial in cases where incarceration in secure detention facilities or even nonsecure facilities of six months or more may be imposed by juvenile judges.
3. The trend in the deinstitutionalization of status offenses will likely continue, and juvenile courts will no longer have responsibility for dealing with runaways, incorrigibles, or truants. The juvenile court will become increasingly adversarial, in many respects paralleling the adult system. Plea bargaining increasingly will occur, as prosecutors and defense attorneys negotiate the best deals for their juvenile clients.
4. The increased use of transfers of juveniles to criminal courts will continue, especially for serious offenses including rape, robbery, and murder. Already, several states, including New York and Illinois, have automatic transfer statutes that result in automatic certification of juveniles in certain offender categories to the jurisdiction of criminal courts.
5. Increased use will be made of diversion and community-based probation services as alternatives to increasingly crowded juvenile court dockets. This trend will coincide with increased privatization of corrections, especially those community-based probation agencies and services.
6. Juveniles will eventually be excluded entirely from adult facilities, including jails and lockups, even on temporary bases. Civil rights and other interest groups are attempting to see that all states remove juveniles from adult detention facilities. While this may work hardships on some isolated jurisdictions where services are not extensive, juvenile rights changes will mandate that all jurisdictions eventually comply.
7. Detention facilities for juveniles will increasingly emphasize vocational, educational, and employment-related services to assist youths in obtaining jobs when released. This will be a general shift from a custodial philosophy to one of rehabilitative and reintegrative detention on a national scale.
8. There will be greater consistency among states in future years concerning the definition of juveniles and greater systematization on their treatment and processing. The Model Penal Code devised by the American Law Institute and other organizations is an attempt to create a high degree of uniformity in laws and regulations among the states. A similar movement is underway on juvenile matters.

KEY TERMS

Act to Regulate the Treatment and Control of Dependent, Neglected and Delinquent Children
Adjudication
Adjudicatory proceedings
Brace, Charles Loring
Certifications
Children's Tribunals
CHINS
Compulsory School Act
Conditional disposition
Confinement, secure and nonsecure
Custodial disposition
Decarceration
Deferred prosecution
Deinstitutionalization
Deinstitutionalization of status offenses
Disposition, disposed
Divestiture
Experience programs
Homeward Bound
In loco parentis
Intake, intake officer
Juvenile delinquency
Juvenile delinquents
Juvenile detention centers
Juvenile Justice and Delinquency Prevention Act of 1974
Juvenile justice system
New York House of Refuge
Nominal disposition
Outward Bound
Parens patriae
Petition
Probation counselor
Referrals
Restitution
Status offenses
Therapeutic intervention
Transfers
Waivers
Wilderness programs

QUESTIONS FOR REVIEW

1. Differentiate between status offenders and those who commit delinquent acts.
2. What is meant by intake? What are some of the dispositions of a juvenile's case that can occur at the point of an intake screening?
3. What is juvenile diversion? Does it appear to be successful at curbing recidivism among juvenile offenders?
4. What are some different kinds of options to be exercised by juvenile judges in sanctioning offenders?
5. What are the forms of secure and nonsecure detention as judicial options?
6. What is meant by the deinstitutionalization of status offenses? What are some examples of states where DSO has occurred? Are police and the courts generally receptive to DSO?
7. Do all states permit the application of the death penalty for juveniles? What was the youngest juvenile to be executed in the United States? When did this occur?

8. What are some arguments favoring the death penalty for juveniles? What are some arguments opposing the death penalty for juveniles?
9. Why is it difficult to classify juvenile offenders and prescribe the appropriate sentence or treatment?
10. What are some forms of probation supervision that have been suggested? Describe them.
11. What is the rationale for the deinstitutionalization of status offenses? Is there a logical basis for distinguishing between juvenile delinquents and status offenders?
12. What is the extent of violence among juvenile offenders? Should all juveniles who commit violent offenses be confined in secure detention?
13. What are three important landmark cases involving juvenile rights? What are the rights conveyed by these decisions?
14. Do juveniles have the right to a jury trial? Under what circumstances are they entitled to a jury trial?
15. What is the means whereby a juvenile is assigned to the jurisdiction of criminal courts?
16. What is the relevance of labeling theory and the fact that diversion is used with increasing frequency? Does the deinstitutionalization of status offenses have anything to do with labeling theory?

SUGGESTED READINGS

Chesney-Lind, Meda, and Randall G. Shelden. *Girls, Delinquency and Juvenile Justice.* Belmont, CA: Wadsworth Publishing Company, 1992.

Inciardi, James A., Ruth Horowitz, and Anne E. Pottieger. *Street Kids, Street Drugs, Street Crime: An Examination of Drug Use and Serious Delinquency in Miami.* Belmont, CA: Wadsworth Publishing Company, 1993.

Miller, J. Mitchell, and Jeffrey P. Rush (eds.). *Gangs: A Criminal Justice Approach.* Cincinnati: Anderson Publishing Company, 1996.

Roberson, Cliff. *Exploring Juvenile Justice.* Placerville, CA: Copperhouse Publishing Company, 1996.

Wooden, Wayne. *Renegade Kids: Suburban Outlaws.* Placerville, CA: Copperhouse Publishing Company, 1995.

Glossary

Addams, Jane: Reformer who founded Hull House in Chicago in the late 1800s.

Adjudication: Decision by juvenile court judge on the facts alleged in a delinquency petition; comparable to a determination of guilt or innocence of a defendant in criminal court.

Adjudicatory Proceedings: Juvenile court matters are heard and resolved; judge decides guilt or innocence of juvenile or whether the facts alleged in a petition are true.

Aggravating Circumstances: Circumstances surrounding the commission of a crime that increase its seriousness; circumstances include serious injury or death to victims; unusual or cruel punishments inflicted by defendant on victims; defendant was on probation or parole when committing new crime.

AIMS (Adult Internal Management System): Self-administered questionnaire given to prison inmates to determine their psychological and emotional states.

Alternative Dispute Resolution: Removal of a criminal case from the criminal justice system temporarily and in which impartial arbiter attempts to work out an agreement between defendant and victim to their mutual satisfaction; unsatisfactory resolution places case back in system, resulting in criminal prosecution; alternative dispute resolution often results in financial compensation by defendant for property damage or physical injuries sustained by victim.

American Correctional Association: Founded in 1870 as the National Prison Association; first president was future U.S. President Rutherford B. Hayes; had 9,000 members in 1986; provides instruction and technical assistance to correctional institutions; promotes high correctional standards; provides training and publications to any interested agency.

American Prison Association: Early name given to the American Correctional Association.

Appointment on Merit: Promotion in organizations according to one's expertise and accomplishments, not on the basis of who one knows.

Arkansas Prison Scandal: Scandal in the Arkansas State Prison system uncovered by Thomas O. Murton, appointed to administer the prison system in Arkansas by the governor; scandal included exploitation of prisoners by outside businesses and torture of certain prisoners for rule infractions.

Arraignment: Formal proceeding, usually conducted by judge, by which formal charges against the defendant are stated, the defendant enters a plea (usually guilty, not guilty, nolo contendere, or guilty but mentally ill); and where a trial date is determined.

Assessment centers: Rigorous identification and evaluation mechanisms lasting as long as one week that are geared to thoroughly test selected relevant attributes of prospective corrections officers.

Auburn State Penitentiary: Penitentiary constructed in Auburn, New York, in 1816; pioneered use of "tiers" by which inmates were housed on different floors, levels, or tiers, according to their offense seriousness; introduced "congregate system," by which prisoners had opportunities to congregate with one another for work, dining, recreation; introduced stereotypical striped prison uniforms for prisoners.

Augustus, John: Father of probation in United States in 1841; considered first informal probation officer; Boston shoemaker and philanthropist; active in reforming petty offenders and alcoholics charged with crimes; assumed responsibility for them and posted their bail while attempting to reform them; considered successful.

B.A.C.I.S. (Behavior Alert Classification Identification System): Method of distinguishing between inmates according to their risk and needs; separates mentally ill jail inmates from the rest of the jail population through assessment conducted by jail officers and other personnel.

Back-Door Solution: Solution to prison or jail overcrowding problem after inmates have been incarcerated; court-ordered prison or jail population reductions through use of early release or parole, furloughs, work release, administrative release.

Bail: A surety to obtain the release of a suspect under arrest that assures the court that the defendant will appear at trial later; according to the U.S. Supreme Court, bail is only available to those "where it is proper to grant bail."

Bail Bond: Money or securities posted by a defendant to secure release from jail prior to trial; may or may not be granted by judge; a surety guaranteeing subject's appearance in court later.

Bail Bondsperson: One who is in the business of posting bail for criminal suspects; usually charges a percentage of whatever bail has been set.

Banishment: A form of punishment where an offender is ostracized from the community to a remote location; Australia and the colonies were used as places of banishment for Great Britain's dissidents, criminals, and undesirables.

Bench Trial: Adversarial proceeding in which the judge determines the guilt or innocence of the defendant after hearing the evidence.

Bentham, Jeremy (1748–1832): British hedonist; wrote *Introduction to the Principles and Morals of Legislation;* believed criminals could be deterred by minimizing pleasures derived from wrongdoing; believed punishment should be swift, certain, and painful.

Bifurcated Trial: The trial that is required in all death penalty cases; first stage determines guilt or innocence of defendant; second stage determines whether death penalty should be administered, given aggravating or mitigating circumstances.

Boot Camps: Highly regimented disciplinary programs for youthful offenders; modeled after military training camps for new recruits; these programs operate for different offenders for up to two years; objectives are to teach discipline, self-control, and to offer educational, vocational, and counseling services to disturbed youth.

Boston Children's Aid Society: Privately funded philanthropic society founded by Rufus R. Cook in 1860 that catered to orphans and other minors who did not have adequate adult supervision; used volunteers to assist juvenile offenders.

Brace, Charles Loring: Creator of New York Children's Aid Society in 1853; philanthropist and benefactor of wayward and dependent children.

Bridewell Workhouse: Jail constructed in 1557 in London to house the undesirables of the city; used inmate labor to manufacture goods for merchants and businesspersons.

Brockway, Zebulon (1827–1920): First superintendent of Elmira, New York, Reformatory; believed in rehabilitation and reformation; encouraged prisoners to become educated and to learn vocational skills.

Bureaucracy: Model of organization specifying predetermined arrangement of tasks, impersonal rules, hierarchy of authority, spheres of competence, promotion according to merit, selection by test, task specialization; invented by Max Weber (1864–1920), German sociologist.

Burnout: Term used to denote physical and/or psychological exhaustion associated with one's job; stressful aspects of job leading to poor work performance and labor turnover.

Campus Model: Model for detention of female offenders stressing skill acquisition, including cosmetology, parenting, office skills, arts and crafts.

Capital Punishment: *See* Death Penalty.

Career Criminals: Those offenders who earn their living through crime.

Caseload: The average number of parolees or probationers supervised by a parole officer or probation officer; computed differently, using numbers of clients divided by numbers of officers; assignments according to specialties such as mentally ill parolees or probationers, those with alcoholic or drug dependencies.

Cellular Telephone Devices: Electronic monitoring devices that are transmitters worn by offenders and which transmit signals that can be intercepted by local area monitors.

Centralization: Limited distribution of power among a few top staff members of an organization.

Certifications: Act of declaring a juvenile an adult for purposes of going forth with a criminal prosecution; usually reserved for serious offenses committed by juveniles; similar to a transfer or waiver. *See also* Transfers.

Charge Reduction Plea Bargaining: Type of plea bargaining by which prosecutor offers to reduce or drop certain charges in exchange for a guilty plea from defendant. *See also* Plea Bargaining.

Children's Tribunals: Informal hearings to decide juvenile cases in which offenses are alleged; used extensively in late 1880s.

Child Sexual Abuser: Adult who involves minors in all kinds of sexual activity ranging from intercourse with children to photographing them in lewd poses.

CHINS: Children in need of supervision; name given to juveniles who appear in juvenile court when it is alleged that they are in need of parental or guardian supervision.

Clark, Benjamin C.: Social reformer and philanthropist, associated with Temperance Movement; active in mid-1800s in attempting to reform alcoholics charged with crimes.

Classical School of Criminology: Promoted by Cesare Beccaria, this view advocated access to legal rights primarily as a way of controlling citizen unrest; punishment should be swift and certain; best approach to crime is prevention rather than punishment.

Classification: Inmate classification based on measures relating to one's potential dangerousness or risk posed to public; scheme to categorize offenders according to the level of custody they require while incarcerated; measures potential disruptiveness of prisoners; measures early release potential of inmates for parole consideration; based on psychological, social, and sociodemographic criteria.

Co-Corrections, Co-Correctional Prisons: Prisons in which male and female prisoners live; supervised by female and male staff and participating in all activities together; sharing same quarters is prohibited.

Coercive Power: Power form by which superior elicits compliance by subordinates through threats of punishment.

Community-Based Corrections Programs: Include intensive supervised probation; privately or publicly operated facilities that provide comprehensive support for offenders, including food, clothing, shelter, counseling, job assistance, and training.

Community Corrections Act: Statewide mechanism and enabling legislation through which funds are granted to units of government to plan, develop and deliver correctional sanctions at the local level; purpose is to provide local sentencing options in lieu of imprisonment.

Community Residential Centers: Transitional homes located in neighborhoods where offenders may obtain limited counseling, job placement services, food and shelter, and limited supervision.

Community Service Orders: Judicially imposed restitution for those convicted of committing crimes; some form of work must be performed to satisfy restitution requirements.

Compulsory School Act: Act passed in Colorado in 1899 to prevent truancy among juveniles; Act addressed juveniles who were habitually absent from school, who wandered the streets, and who had no obvious business or occupation.

Conditional Disposition: Disposition by juvenile judge authorizing payment of fines, community service, restitution, or some other penalty after an adjudication of delinquency has been made.

Conditional Diversion: Temporarily ceasing a prosecution against a criminal defendant, whereby a defendant must be law-abiding and obey conditions of a probationary type program for a period of time, usually for six months or a year; following the successful completion of this program, the charges against the defendant may be dropped or downgraded to less serious charges.

Conditional Probation: *See* Intensive Supervised Probation.

Conditional Release: *See* Parole.

Confinement (secure and nonsecure): Refers to placing a juvenile in either a foster home, out-of-home group facility, agency, or nonsecure or secure facility, such as a juvenile industrial school. *See also* Placement.

Congregate System: System pioneered at Auburn, New York, Penitentiary where prisoners were allowed to "congregate" with one another for dining, work, and recreation, but were isolated during evening hours.

Continuous Signaling Devices: Electronic monitoring devices that emit continuous signals that can be intercepted by telephonic communication from a central dialing location such as a police station or probation office.

Continuous Signaling Transmitters: Electronic monitoring systems worn by offenders that emit continuous signals that may be intercepted by probation officers with portable receiving units.

Contract Prisoners: Inmates held in jails or other incarceration facilities that are out of their own jurisdictions; Hawaiian prisoners might be housed in Texas jails, for instance, because of overcrowding; states or local jail officials contract with other jurisdictions to house a portion of their inmate overflow.

Conventional Model: Caseload assignment method for probation or parole officers by which clients are randomly assigned to officers.

Conventional Model with Geographic Considerations: Method of assigning probation/parole officer caseloads on the basis of where clients live; objective is to group clients into the geographical areas where they reside in order to decrease the amount of time spent traveling from place to place to visit clients by officers.

Cook, Rufus R.: Social reformer associated with Temperance Movement in mid-1800s; dedicated to reforming alcoholics charged with crimes.

Cools: Term used to describe female inmates by other inmates; "cools" are those females with prior records who attempt to violate prison rules and remain undetected.

Corporal Punishments: The infliction of pain on the body by any device or method; examples are flogging, dismemberment, stretching on the "rack," and mutilation.

Correctional Officer: Guard in a prison who supervises or manages inmates.

Corrections: The vast number of persons, agencies, and organizations that manage accused, convicted, or adjudicated criminal offenders and juveniles.

Corrections Volunteers: Any unpaid person who performs auxiliary, supplemental, augmentative or any other work or services for any law enforcement or corrections agency.

Court-Watchers: Private citizens who sit in courtrooms and observe judicial decision making; their purpose is to ensure that justice is done and that some defendants do not escape the full measure of the law when judges punish them.

Creaming: Selecting inmates or probationers/parolees for program involvement on the basis of their minor offending or first-offender status; selections include only those persons most likely to succeed, where in fact the program is supposed to help those most likely to fail; when program is successful, it is usually because only the most successful clients have been included in the program and the worst offenders have been excluded from the program.

Crimes Against the Person: *See* Violent crime.

Crimes Against Property: *See* Property crime.

Crime Clock: Graph used by FBI in Uniform Crime Reports showing the occurrence of specific crimes according to some time measure, such as seconds or minutes; total number of certain types of crimes annually divided by the number of days, minutes, or seconds in a year; shows frequency of occurrence of specific types of crime.

Criminal Contamination: Belief by citizens that if criminals live together in halfway houses, they will breed more criminality and infect neighborhoods with their criminal behavior.

Criminal Justice: Investigation of decision-making bodies as they pertain to the prevention, detection, and investigation of crime; the apprehension, accusation, detention, and trial of suspects; and the conviction, sentencing, incarceration, or official supervision of adjudicated defendants. Juvenile justice system is the equivalent for youthful offenders.

Criminal Justice System: Sometimes called a *process,* consisting of law enforcement, the prosecution, courts, and corrections; the system whereby offenders are processed and punished.

Crofton, Sir Walter: Established Irish System (*see* Tickets-of-Leave); Irish prison reformer; director of Ireland Prison System in mid-1800s.

Cruel and Unusual Punishment: Unspecified by U.S. Supreme Court, subjectively interpreted on case-by-case basis; prohibited by Eighth Amendment of U.S. Constitution.

Custodial Disposition: Disposition by juvenile judge following adjudication of juvenile as delinquent; includes nonsecure or secure custody; nonsecure custody may be in a foster home or community agency, farm, camp; secure custody may include detention center, industrial school, reform school.

Custodial Model: Model for housing female offenders, where main interest is confinement, containment, discipline, and uniformity.

Day Parole: *See* Furloughs.

Day Pass: *See* Furloughs.

Day Reporting Centers: Community corrections agencies that supervise probationers and parolees; may conduct drug or alcohol checks and urinalyses as well as collect fee payments for victim restitution or compensation.

Death Penalty: Capital punishment imposed in the United States and several other countries, where life of offender is taken; death penalty is carried out differently in various jurisdictions, and methods include shooting, hanging, electrocution, gassing, and lethal injection.

Death-Qualified Jury: Jury comprised of persons who can impose the death penalty despite the fact that they may be opposed to it morally; as long as their judgment to impose the death penalty is not impaired by their opposition to it, they are a death-qualified jury (*see Witherspoon v. Illinois,* 1968).

Death Row: Row of prison cells where inmates who have been sentenced to death are housed.

Decarceration: Prohibition of detention for juveniles; removal of inmates from prisons or jails.

Decentralization: Widespread distribution of power among many staff members; in prisons, limited power may be given to inmates as representatives of the larger prisoner aggregate.

Deferred Prosecution: Temporary halting of a prosecution against a defendant while he or she is subjected to a program with particular requirements for a short period. *See also* Diversion.

Deinstitutionalization: Removing juveniles from secure facilities.

Deinstitutionalization of Status Offenses: The removal of youths whose only infractions are status offenses, including running away from home, incorrigibility, truancy, and curfew violations, from secure institutions and detention facilities.

Deliberate Indifference: Attitude of prison or jail officials by which they ignore inmates with injuries or do not act as they should to prevent inmate abuse by other inmates; intentional tort.

Delinquency: Any act committed by a juvenile that would be a crime if committed by an adult. *See* Juvenile delinquency.

Delinquent Acts: Any offense committed by a juvenile that would be a crime if committed by an adult.

Design Capacity: Optimum number of inmates that architects originally intended to be housed or accommodated by jail or prison.

Detainer Warrants: Notices of criminal charges or unserved sentences pending against prisoners; usually authorized by one jurisdiction to be served on prisoners held in other jurisdictions; when prisoners serve their sentences in one jurisdiction, they are usually transferred under detainer warrants to other jurisdictions where charges are pending against them.

Detention, Secure or Nonsecure: Confinement of juvenile in foster home, group home, camp as nonsecure detention; secure detention is placement of juvenile in industrial school or reform school, similar to prisons for adults.

Determinant Sentencing: Sentencing scheme whereby judge fixes the term of an offender's incarceration, which must be served in full, less any good-time credits accumulated by offender as an inmate; parole boards are not involved in any discretionary early-release decisions.

Deterrence: Philosophy of punishment espousing that incarceration and harsh sentences will deter offenders from committing future crimes.

Disposition, Disposed: Equivalent of a sentence imposed by a judge in a criminal court; juvenile court judge imposes one of several options upon a juvenile in cases in which it is found that the facts alleged in a petition are true; options may include nominal, conditional, or custodial sanctions.

Diversion: Removing a case temporarily from the criminal justice system, during which time a defendant is required to comply with various conditions, such as attending a school for drunk drivers, undergoing counseling, performing community service, or another condition; may result in expungement of record; a pretrial alternative to prosecution; temporary and conditional removal of the prosecution of a case prior to its adjudication, usually as the result of an arrangement between the prosecutor and judge.

Diversion Programs: Any preconviction option whereby the prosecutor places an offender in either a supervised or unsupervised program for a period of time, usually six months to one year; following successful completion of diversion, offender either has record expunged or charges downgraded; helps to avoid criminal record in first-offender cases.

Divestiture: Act of juvenile court judges whereby they relinquish their jurisdiction over certain types of juvenile offenders, such as status offenders.

Double-Bunking: Practice used by jail and prison administrators whereby two or more prisoners are placed in a single cell ordinarily designed to house one offender; used as a means to alleviate overcrowding.

Drug/Alcohol-Dependent Offenders: Those with chemical dependencies, including addiction to illegal substances or drugs and alcoholic beverages.

Ducking Stool: Corporal punishment device whereby offender is placed in a chair at end of long lever and dunked in nearby pond until almost drowned; used often as a punishment for gossiping and wife beating.

Duplex Jails, Duplex Jail Model: Additions to regular jails that can accommodate juvenile offenders and keep them separate from adult offenders.

EARN-IT: *See* Victim/Offender Reconciliation Project.

Education Furlough: *See* Furloughs.

Electronic Monitoring: The use of telemetry devices to determine an offender's whereabouts at particular times.

Elmira Reformatory: First true reformatory built in 1876; first superintendent was Zebulon Brockway, a rehabilitation and reformation advocate; promoted educational training and cultivation of vocational skills; believed in prisoner reformation; questionably successful as a reformatory.

English Penal Servitude Act: Legislation passed by British Parliament in 1853 authorizing establishment of rehabilitative programs for inmates and gradually eliminating banishment as a form of punishment.

Experience Programs: Various activities for juveniles who have been adjudicated delinquent or status offenders; includes wilderness experiences and other outdoors programs where youths learn self-esteem, survival skills, self-respect, and respect toward others and authority.

Expert Power: Power form based on personal expertise or skills of superior.

Failure to Appear: The case when defendants fail to present themselves for trial or some other formal proceeding, such as arraignment or a preliminary hearing/examination.

False Negatives: Offenders who are predicted to be nonviolent or not dangerous according to various risk or dangerousness prediction devices; these offenders turn out to be dangerous or to or pose serious public risk; offenders who are predicted to be nonviolent or not dangerous but who are violent or dangerous.

False Positives: Offenders who are predicted to be dangerous or who pose serious public risk according to various prediction devices and instruments; these offenders are not dangerous and do not pose public risks; they are predicted to be dangerous but are not dangerous.

Federal Bureau of Prisons: Established in 1930 by Congress; in 1987 operated 43 correctional facilities for persons convicted of violating federal laws; operates Federal Prison Industries, a business enterprise selling manufactured goods by prisoners; functions include furnishing safe custody and a humane environment for prisoners and providing them with educational advancement, vocational training, counseling, and personal growth experiences; also contracts with 385 halfway houses for the intermediate detention of parolees.

Federal Tort Claims Act of 1946: 28 U.S.C. Section 2674; Act providing that the United States shall be liable, respecting the provisions of this title relating to tort claims, in the same manner and to the same extent as a private individual under like circumstances, but shall not be liable for interest prior to judgment for punitive damages.

Felon: One who commits a felony.

Felonies: Crimes punishable by imprisonment in prison for a term of one or more years; major crimes; any index offense.

Felony: Major crime punishable by incarceration of one year or more and/or fines; incarceration usually is in penitentiary or prison rather than jail, although jails are sometimes used to accommodate prison population overflow; FBI uses eight major felonies in *Uniform Crime Reports* for charting crime trends annually.

Financial/Community Service Model: Restitution model for juveniles that stresses the offender's financial accountability and thus community service to pay for damages.

Fines: Financial penalties optionally imposed by judges in U.S. courts for law violations; fixed fines, day fines, and standard fines used in Swedish courts for various types of offenses, depending on crime seriousness.

First-Offender: Offender who has committed one or more crimes but who has no previous criminal record.

Fixed Indeterminate Sentencing: Sentencing scheme whereby judge sentences offenders to single prison term, which for all practical purposes, is treated as the maximum sentence; parole board may determine early release date for offender. *See also* Indeterminate sentencing.

Florida Assessment Center: Established in Dade County, Florida, the purpose of this center is to train probation and parole officers for entry-level positions in probation and parole. *See also* Assessment centers.

Forgotten Offenders: Female offenders in U.S. prisons and jails.

Freedom of Information Act: Legislatively created mechanism whereby private citizens can obtain secret government files about them; some information is confidential and cannot be released to private citizens; most documented information must be disclosed to those making such requests, however.

Front-Door Solution: Solution to prison or jail overcrowding occurring at beginning of criminal justice process; includes plea bargaining resulting in diversion, probation, community service, intermediate punishment, or some other nonincarcerative alternative.

Fry, Elizabeth Gurney (1780–1845): English Quaker women's prison reformer; toured United States and other countries in early 1800s attempting to implement prison reforms; encouraged separate facilities for women, religious and secular education, improved classification systems for women, and reintegrative and rehabilitative programs.

Furloughs: Temporary release programs; authorized, unescorted leaves from confinement granted for specific purposes and for designated time periods, usually from 24 to 72 hours, although they may be as long as several weeks or as short as a few hours; first used in Mississippi in 1918.

Gaol: English term for jail.

Gender Courses: Classes conducted for jail and prison officers to sensitize them to how they can work around women in ways that will not lead to sexual harassment; classes are oriented toward respecting the work of persons of different gender.

Good-Time Credits: Credits earned by prisoners for good behavior; introduced in early 1800s by British penal authorities, including Alexander Maconochie and Sir Walter Crofton.

Great Law of Pennsylvania: Established by William Penn in 1682; law was designed to ban branding, stocks and pillories, and other forms of corporal punishment; later repealed when Penn died, and corporal punishments were restored; original intent of law was to make prison and jail conditions more humane.

Guidelines-based Sentencing: *See* Presumptive sentencing.

***Habeas Corpus* Petition:** Petition filed, usually by inmates, challenging the legitimacy of their confinement and the nature of their confinement; document that commands authorities to show cause why an inmate should be confined in either a prison or jail; means literally "you should have the body" or "produce the body"; also includes challenges to the nature of confinement.

Habitual Offender Law: Any law punishing persons more severely for having been convicted of previous crimes; often such laws carry mandatory life imprisonment penalties.

Halfway Houses: Community-based centers or homes operated either by the government or privately and that are designed to provide housing, food, clothing, job assistance, and counseling to ex-prisoners and others; publicly or privately operated facilities staffed by professionals, paraprofessionals, or volunteers; designed to assist parolees make the transition from prison to the community.

Halfway-In Houses: Halfway houses for probationers who are placed in conditional intensive supervision programs; help them adjust to new rules, regulations, and restricted freedoms.

Halfway-Out Houses: Halfway houses to assist parolees who have just been released from prison; a transitional home, whereby prisoners can learn less regimented life style compared with prison rules and rigid regulations.

Hands-Off Doctrine: Doctrine practiced by state and federal judiciary up until 1940s whereby matters pertaining to inmate rights were left up to jail and prison administrators to resolve; considered "internal" matters, where no court intervention was required or desired.

Hayes, Rutherford B.: First president of the American Correctional Association, originally called National Prison Association; later U.S. President.

Home Confinement: *See* House arrest.

Home Incarceration: *See* House arrest.

Homeward Bound: Six-week wilderness course to teach self-sufficiency, survival, self-respect, and coping skills; established in Massachusetts in 1970.

House Arrest (also known as Home Confinement, Home Incarceration): Intermediate punishment using offender's residence as the primary place of custody for a fixed term; a conditional sentence requiring offender to remain confined to residence.

Howard, John (1726–1790): Early English prison reformer; sheriff of Bedfordshire, England; influenced by other European countries such as France and lobbied for prison reforms.

Huber Law: Legislation that established first work release programs in 1913.

Hull House: Settlement home established by reformer Jane Addams; operated as a home for children of immigrant families in Chicago; financed by philanthropists; taught children religious principles, morality, and ethics.

Human Services Approach: Philosophy of some corrections officers, either in prisons or jails, whereby they regard each inmate as a human being with feelings or emotions; actions toward inmates are made in terms of how their needs can be met, apart from simply viewing inmates as objects to be guarded or confined.

I-Level Classification (Interpersonal Maturity Level Classification): Psychological assessment of convicted offenders; uses developmental and psychoanalytical theories to determine at which level or stage offenders can function and cope with interpersonal problems; the higher the I-level, the better adjusted the offender.

Implicit Plea Bargaining: Plea bargaining when defendant pleads guilty with the expectation of receiving a more lenient sentence from the judge. *See also* Plea Bargaining.

Importation Model: The idea that prison culture is brought into the prison by other inmates, depending upon their life experiences and outside cultural values.

Incapacitation (Isolation): Philosophy of corrections that espouses that offenders should suffer loss of freedom; the more serious the offense, the greater the freedom loss; belief that the function of punishment is to separate offenders from other society members and to prevent them from committing additional criminal acts.

Indentured Servants: Persons from England who paid for their passage to the American Colonies by giving up seven years of their lives as slaves to those paying for their passage.

Indeterminate Sentencing: Sentencing scheme whereby the judge, either implicitly or explicitly, sets upper and lower bounds on the time to be served in incarceration; if convicted offender is actually incarcerated, a parole board determines early release date.

Index Crimes, Index Offenses: Several crime categories used by the FBI to report crime quarterly and annually in the United States.

Initial Appearance: Appearance by suspect before a judge, magistrate, or court official after an arrest; purposes of initial appearance are to advise defendant of charges, legal rights, and to make provisions for bail.

In Loco Parentis: Means "in the place of parents" and indicates the fact that the state acts to decide what is best for a juvenile during juvenile court proceedings.

Inmate Litigation Explosion: *See* Litigation Explosion.

Intensive Supervised Probation (also Intensive Supervised Parole, Intensive Probation/Parole Supervision): No specific guidelines exist across all jurisdictions, but intensive supervised probation usually means lower caseloads for probation officers, less than 10 clients per month, regular drug tests, and other intensive supervision measures.

Intermediate Punishments: Those sanctions ranging between incarceration and standard probation on the continuum of criminal penalties.

International Halfway House Association: Public organization whose membership operates halfway houses throughout the world; established in Chicago in 1964.

Irish System: A multistage process whereby prison inmates could earn their early release from prison by acquiring tickets-of-leave.

Isaac T. Hopper Home: Halfway house established in New York City in 1845.

Jail: City or county-funded facility operated to confine offenders serving short sentences, awaiting trial, and housing prison overflow, witnesses, and others.

Jail Boot Camps: Programs similar to boot camps but operated for a wider age range of clientele; short-term programs designed to foster discipline and self-improvement and self-image. *See also* Boot camps.

Jailhouse Lawyer: Any inmate of a jail or prison who acquires sufficient legal education while incarcerated to file petitions, submit grievances, or help other inmates in their own lawsuits and legal actions against administrators or prison staff.

Jail or Prison Overcrowding: *See* Overcrowding.

Jail Removal Initiative: Under the Juvenile Justice and Delinquency Prevention Act of 1974, congressional mandate was implemented to release all juveniles from any kind of adult prison or jail after being arrested or taken into custody by police; states are not obligated to follow or adhere to this initiative.

Judicial Plea Bargaining: Plea bargaining where judge makes a specific offer to defendant in exchange for a guilty plea; *See also* Plea Bargaining.

Jurisdictions: Areas of authority, either geographical or according to type of offense, where police officers and the courts have power to make arrests and judgments against criminals; the power of the court to hear certain types of cases.

Jury: The finder of fact in determining whether a criminal defendant is guilty or not guilty; in a criminal trial, the body of persons selected to determine whether an accused is guilty.

Jury Trial: Adversarial proceeding whereby a jury, the trier of fact, decides the guilt or innocence of the defendant on the basis of the evidence presented.

Just Deserts Model: Correctional model equating punishment with the severity of the crime; based on Cesare Beccaria's ideas about punishment.

Justice Model: Correctional model that rejects rehabilitation as a correctional aim; rather, persons should be punished for their crimes, and the punishments should be commensurate with the crime seriousness; see also Just Deserts Model.

Juvenile Delinquency: Any act committed by a juvenile that, if committed by an adult, would be a crime.

Juvenile Delinquent: Any infant or youth under the age of majority who commits an offense that would be a crime if committed by an adult.

Juvenile Detention Center: Place or agency where youths are held temporarily while they await a juvenile court hearing.

Juvenile Justice and Delinquency Prevention Act of 1974: Legislation passed by Congress in 1974 encouraging states to deal differently with their juvenile offenders; promotes community-based treatment programs and discourages incarceration of juveniles in detention centers, industrial schools, or reform schools.

Juvenile Justice System: System or process whereby juvenile offenders are processed, adjudicated, and disposed of by juvenile court.

Large Jails: Jails with 250 to 999 beds.

Latent Functions: Hidden or unintended functions of an action.

Law Enforcement (Officers or Agencies): Local, state, or federal agencies and personnel who uphold the laws of their respective jurisdictions.

Legitimate Power: Power form based on belief that superior has a right to compel subordinates to follow orders.

Level of Custody: Refers to security levels that place prisoners according to their risk or dangerousness; includes minimum, medium, and maximum-security.

Lifes: Habitual female offenders in prison who engage in deviant behavior with little or no regard for punitive consequences.

Litigation Explosion: Sudden increase in inmate suits against administrators and officers in prisons and jails during late 1960s and continuing through 1980s; suits usually challenge nature and length of confinement, torts allegedly committed by administration, usually seeking monetary of other forms of relief.

Maconochie, Captain Alexander (1787–1860): Considered "father of parole"; prison reformer who held various posts in British prisons such as Norfolk and Van Diemen's Land in Australia; established good-time credits to be earned by prisoners where they could gain early release for conforming to prison rules and doing good work; credited with inventing indeterminate sentencing.

Magdelen Society: Society formed in 1830; a women's prison reform movement.

Mamertine Prison: Ancient prison constructed about 640 B.C. under the Cloaca Maxima, the main sewer of Rome, by Ancus Martius; a series of dungeons constructed to house a variety of offenders.

Management by Objectives: Organizational strategy used in early 1970s whereby administrators could cope successfully with various organizational problems; management by objectives achieved by effective goal setting and creating a system of accountability whereby one's performance can be measured over time; feedback essential from higher-ups.

Mandatory Release: Release of prisoners from prison or jail, ordered by court to secure compliance with health and safety codes and to reduce overcrowding.

Mandatory Sentencing: Sentencing system whereby judge is required to impose an incarcerative sentence of a specified length for certain crimes or for particular categories of offenders; habitual offenders or persons who use firearms during the commission of a felony may be subject to mandatory sentencing in certain jurisdictions.

Manifest Functions: Intended or known functions of an action.

Marks of Commendation: Point rewards given to inmates of the Birmingham Borough Prison by Alexander Maconochie in the 1850s.

Maximum-Security: Highest custody level observed in prisons; closed-circuit television monitoring of offenders, limited access to recreation or educational/vocational opportunities; segregated confinement of prisoners in single cells, solitary confinement; designed primarily for containment rather than rehabilitation.

Maxi-Maxi Prison: Prison such as federal penitentiary at Marion, Illinois, where offenders are confined in individual cells with limited freedom daily; confinement in individual cells may be up to 23 hours per day; continuous monitoring and supervision; no more than three prisoners per guard.

Medical or Treatment Model: Treatment model of corrections; assumes that criminal behavior is the result of psychological or biological conditions that can be treated; led to group therapy, behavior modification, and counseling of offenders as treatments.

Medium Jails: Jails with 50 to 249 beds.

Medium-Security: Most frequently observed type of prison facility; catchall term applied to prisons housing a wide variety of offenders; less freedom compared with minimum-security; limited access to educational, vocational, and therapeutic programs.

Megajails: Any jail facility that has 1,000 or more beds.

Megargee Inmate Typology: Scale devised to classify prisoners. *See also* Classification and Psychological assessment device.

Minimum–Maximum Determinate Sentencing: Judicially imposed punishment consisting of a minimum and maximum amount of time to be served by convicted offender; following minimum sentence, offender becomes eligible for parole, which is granted by a parole board, depending upon the convicted offender's eligibility.

Minimum-Security Prison: Low level of custody for supervising offenders; low-risk offenders are usually placed in minimum-security prisons; fewer guards and restrictions; often dormitory-like quality; unguarded or lightly guarded facilities.

Minnesota Multiphasic Personality Inventory: Popular measure of psychological attributes; contains over 550 true and false items that measure different personality dimensions.

Misdemeanant: Person who commits a misdemeanor.

Misdemeanor: Minor or petty crime carrying small fines and penalties; incarceration is usually less than one year, if incarceration is imposed; time served is usually served in jails rather than in prisons.

Mitigating Circumstances: Circumstances surrounding the commission of a crime that lessen its seriousness; includes very young or very old defendants; nature of participation in the offense; assisting authorities in apprehending other criminals; mental illness or insanity.

Motion for Summary Judgment: Decision by judges who have read plaintiff's version and defendant's version of events in actions filed by inmates, and decision is reached holding for the defendant, usually prison authorities.

Motion to Dismiss: Motions granted by judges when inmates who file petitions fail to state a claim upon which relief can be granted; court has read inmate claim and decided that no basis exists for suit.

Myers-Briggs Type Indicator: Method of determining correctional managers' leadership style, behaviors, and work orientations.

National Crime Victimization Survey: A semiannual compilation of crimes committed against various persons surveyed; interviews conducted with national sample of household members disclosing much unreported crime; is considered more accurate than *Uniform Crime Reports* in crime estimates in the United States.

National Prison Association: Founded in 1870; first president was future U.S. President Rutherford B. Hayes; later became American Prison Association; later became American Correctional Association. See also American Correctional Association.

Needs Assessment Device: Paper-pencil instrument used for various purposes by community and institutional corrections to determine which types of services are needed for offenders who have psychological problems or drug/alcohol dependencies.

Negligence: Tort involving a duty of one person to another, to act as a reasonable person might be expected to act, or the failure to act when the action is appropriate; failure to exercise reasonable care toward another; gross negligence includes willful, wanton, and reckless acts that have no regard for consequences and that are totally unreasonable.

Negligent Assignment: Occurs when correctional officers or probation/parole officers or other staff members are assigned to a position for which they are unqualified.

Negligent Intrustment: Occurs when administrators fail to monitor guards entrusted with items they are unfamiliar with using, such as firearms.

Negligent Retention: Occurs when officers determined to be unfit for their jobs are kept in those jobs by administrators anyway.

Negligent Training: Failure to prepare jail or prison officers for duties they must perform; failure to instruct these officers in the proper use of firearms or in transporting prisoners from one area of a prison or jail to another.

NIMBY Syndrome: Means "not in my back yard" and refers to objections citizens have about having any kind of correctional facility built in or near their neighborhoods or communities.

Nominal Disposition: Disposition by which juvenile court by which juvenile is warned or verbally reprimanded, but returned to custody of parents.

Numbers Game Model: Method of assigning probation or parole officer caseloads by which total number of clients is divided by the total number of officers and this becomes the assigned caseload.

Offender Control: The amount of supervision given to any probationer, parolee, or institutionalized prison inmate.

Operational Capacity: Total number of inmates that can be accommodated based on size of jail or prison facility's staff, programs, and other services.

Organizational Effectiveness: Measured different ways, a method of determining whether an agency is meeting its goals and fulfilling customer's or client's needs.

Outward Bound: Wilderness programs for juvenile offenders; intent of programs is to teach survival skills, coping skills, self-respect, self-esteem, and respect for others and authority.

Overcharging: Tactic by which prosecutor adds numerous serious charges against criminal defendant; intent of prosecutor is to drop more serious charges later after obtaining a guilty plea from the defendant to less serious charges.

Overcrowding: Condition that exists when prison or jail population exceeds its rated or design capacity; sometimes measured by square footage allocated per prisoner.

Overrides: Decisions by prison officials to change an inmate's risk or classification or security level from that which is indicated by some paper-pencil testing device.

Paraprofessional: Someone with some amount of formal training in a given correctional area, who is salaried, works specified hours, has specific duties and responsibilities, is accountable to higher level supervisors for work quality, and enjoys limited immunity under the theory of agency.

Pardon: Unconditional release of inmate, usually by governor or chief executive officer of jurisdiction.

Parens patriae: This doctrine, meaning "parent of the country," was established under early English common law, and meant that king or his agents assumed responsibility for matters involving juveniles; practiced in United States in most juvenile matters until mid-1960s.

Parental Banishment: Act of parents prohibiting their children from coming back to their homes after being unmanageable, incorrigible, or running away.

Parole: Conditional supervised early release from prison granted to inmates after they have served a portion of their original sentence.

Parolee: Inmate who has been released short of serving the full sentence; usually conditions apply, and inmate is supervised by parole officer for a specified time period.

Parole Boards: Boards of members, usually appointed by governor of a state or other executive, to make decisions about inmate early releases; often comprised of community representatives, teachers, corrections officials, lawyers, and law enforcement officers.

Parole Officers: Officials who supervise or manage parolees while on parole.

Parole Revocation: *See* Revocation.

Participation Hypothesis: Hypothesis that says the more subordinates participate in decision making affecting their work, the more they will like their work and comply with orders from higher-ups.

Participative Management: Involvement of clients in determining the nature of their own supervision; method of involving subordinates in decision making affecting their work.

Penitentiary: Interchangeably used with "prison" to refer to those long-term facilities in which high custody levels are observed; single-cell occupancy, where prisoners are segregated from one another during evening hours.

Penitentiary Act: Act passed by House of Commons in England in 1779; Act authorized creation of new facilities to house prisoners where they could be productive; prisoners would be well-fed, well-treated, well-clothed, and housed in safe and sanitary units; trained to perform skills.

Penn, William: Established Great Law of Pennsylvania; Quaker, penal reformer, and founder of Pennsylvania; abolished corporal punishments in favor of fines and incarceration; used gaols or jails to confine offenders.

Petition: Formal document requesting that the juvenile court hear a juvenile's case in which various offenses are alleged.

Philadelphia Society for Alleviating the Miseries of Public Prisons: Early group made up of prominent Philadelphia citizens, philanthropists, and religious reformers who believe prison conditions ought to be changed and made more humane; established in 1787; no longer exists.

Placement: Removing a juvenile from the home and remanding him or her to the custody of foster parents, group homes, camps, ranches, wilderness experiences, community corrections, or nonsecure/secure institutions.

Plea Bargaining: Preconviction agreement whereby a guilty plea is entered by the defendant in exchange for some concession or expected leniency from the prosecution; concession may be charge reduction, recommendation for leniency to judge, or promise of not making any recommendation about sentence; accounts for over 90 percent of all criminal convictions in United States annually.

Postconviction Relief: Any lawsuit filed by an inmate following a criminal conviction; intent is to appeal one or more issues to seek to overturn previous conviction.

Power: Person's ability to influence another person to carry out orders.

Power Clusters: Issue networks and vested interest groups that have a stake in correctional organizations and correctional agencies, that work in collaboration with other interest groups to bring about a particular end and ensure that their interests are protected.

Preliminary Hearing or Examination: Hearing held to establish if there is sufficient probable cause to continue a criminal prosecution against a defendant and to bring the case to trial.

Presentence Investigation: Publicly or privately conducted examination of convicted offender's background and sociodemographic information; contains interview summaries with persons who knew convicted offender; prior record and work history; educational background; purpose is to assist judges in determining most appropriate sentence for offenders.

Presentence Investigation Reports: Reports filed by probation officers, usually at the request of presiding judge; report contains information about convicted offender, the offense, victim impact statement, defendant's version of events, defendant's employment history, prior record, relatives, and social acquaintances; used both by judge and parole board to determine severity of sentence or basis for early release from prison.

Presumptive or Guidelines-Based Sentencing: Sentencing scheme using predetermined guidelines for each offense; upper, middle, and lower ranges of incarceration are established for each offense; judge selects middle range of incarceration, but judge may consider aggravating or mitigating circumstances associated with offense to increase or decrease the length of incarceration.

Pretrial Detainees: Those accused of committing crimes; suspects are arrested and held in local jails until their trial can be held.

Pretrial Diversion: *See* Diversion.

Pretrial Release: Judicially approved release of criminal defendant prior to trial, usually on a defendant's own recognizance.

Prevention: Philosophy of corrections that believes that the aim of punishment should be crime prevention.

Preventive Detention: Act of incarcerating an alleged offender, usually in a jail, until a trial can be held to determine one's guilt or innocence.

Prisons: State or federally funded and operated institutions to house convicted offenders under continuous custody on a long-term basis.

Prisoner's Rights Movement: Diffuse movement among prisoners and groups supporting rights for prisoners by which avenues are explored for means whereby prisoners can exercise their legal rights in court and challenge jail and prison administration policies; started in the late 1960s and continues, with growing numbers of petitions filed by inmates in state and federal courts annually.

Prison Litigation Reform Act of 1995: Act seeking to limit the number of lawsuits inmates may file in federal courts; intended to bar multiple filings of suits against public officials by prison inmates.

Prison Subculture: *See* Subculture.

Privatization: Refers to financing and/or operation or management of prisons, jails, and other corrections agencies by private enterprise, usually for profit; most noticeable in 1980s in juvenile programs.

Probation: Conditional release of convicted defendant into the community to avoid incarceration, under a suspended sentence, with good behavior, and generally under supervision by a probation officer.

Probation Counselor: Anyone who supervises a juvenile while the juvenile is on probation.

Probation Officers: Officials who supervise or manage probationers.

Probation Revocation: *See* Revocation.

Probationer: Convicted offender who has been granted conditional nonincarcerative release in community, usually under supervision of a probation officer, and for a specified time period.

Professionalization: Process of acquiring increased education, more in-service "hands-on" training, practical work experiences, and using higher selection standards (physical, social, and psychological) for officer or staff appointments.

Program for Female Offenders, Inc.: Community-based corrections program designed to reform female offenders and to create economically independent clients.

Programmed Contact Devices: Electronic monitoring system by which telephonic contact is made at random times with the offender with the offender's voice being verified electronically by computer.

Property Crime: Felony that is nonviolent, does not result in physical injury to victims; involves criminal acts against property including but not limited to larceny, burglary, vehicular theft.

Prosecutors: State attorneys who file charges against and prosecute alleged criminal offenders.

Prosecutorial Bluffing: Action of prosecutor who has little or no evidence against a defendant, but who nevertheless persists in offering defendant charge reduction in exchange for guilty plea to minor criminal charge; prosecutor does not expect to convict defendant if case is tried in court.

Psychological Assessment Device: Any paper-and-pencil instrument capable of disclosing one's personality characteristics, usually for purposes of institutional classification and placement.

Qualified immunity: Work performed in good faith by probation or parole officers may result in harm to clients; officers are entitled to some immunity from lawsuits as long as they performed their jobs in good faith.

Quasi-Judicial Immunity: Type of insulation from lawsuits enjoyed by probation officers who work directly for judges when preparing presentence investigation reports; officers may include erroneous information in their reports that may be harmful to probationers, but the officers enjoy some immunity within the scope of their duties under the power of the judges with whom they work.

Rabble Hypothesis: Suggested by John Irwin; theory is that persons of lower socioeconomic status are placed in jails to rid society of their presence; homeless, detached, or disreputable persons are often selected by police officers for confinement; objective is to remove these undesirables from society so that other social classes will not have to interact with them.

Rated Capacity: The number of beds or inmates assigned by a rating official to various jails or prisons.

Recidivism: The reversion of an offender to additional criminal behavior after the offender has been convicted of a prior offense, sentenced, and presumably corrected.

Reeve: County or shire officer who collected taxes and kept the peace in early England.

Referrals: Any actions taken by police officers, concerned citizens, or intake officers that alert the juvenile court that one or more juveniles has committed a serious offense or is incorrigible.

Reformatory Model: Model of custody for women stressing reformation, reintegration, skill acquisition, moral and social improvement.

Reform Model: *See* Rehabilitation Model.

Rehabilitation: Philosophy of corrections that promotes educational and vocational training for prisoners, believing these skill acquisitions will bring about prisoner reform or change; the belief that corrections can be helpful in reintegrating offenders back into society to lead productive and conforming lives.

Rehabilitation Model: Correctional model, similar to treatment or medical model, assumes offenders can be rehabilitated through meaningful work experiences, counseling, and education.

Reintegration: Punishment philosophy that promotes programs that lead offenders back into their communities; reintegrative programs include furloughs, work release, and halfway houses.

Reparations: Monetary damages awarded to victims that must be paid by criminals for any injuries suffered or property damaged.

Repeat Offender Law: *See* Habitual Offender Law.

Restitution: Conditional order by juvenile or adult courts whereby offenders must reimburse their victims for physical or property damages.

Retribution, Retributionist Philosophy: View of punishment that says offenders should be punished for purposes of revenge.

Revocation, Probation or Parole: Procedure whereby parole or probation is revoked, usually because of a program violation; requires a two-stage process to determine probable cause and punishment.

Reward Power: Power based on ability of superior to reward subordinates.

Reynolds, James Bronson: Prison reformer who established University Settlement in New York City. *See also* University Settlement and Settlement Houses.

Risk: An assessment of an offender's dangerousness, either on probation, parole, a community corrections program, or penal institution; the potential for someone to harm themselves or others; assessed with psychological instruments and counseling.

Risk-Needs Assessment: Combined items on a paper-pencil device designed to measure one's dangerousness and services required to remedy one's deficiencies, such as personality disorders, drug/alcohol dependencies, and adjustment problems.

ROBO-PO: Contemporary view of probation/parole officers who see their role as law enforcers and regulators; a move away from the traditional rehabilitation and reintegrative goals practiced by many probation/parole officers.

Rush, Dr. Benjamin (1745–1813): Quaker penal and religious reformer, physician; helped organization and operation of Walnut Street Jail for benefit of prisoners; encouraged humane treatment of inmates.

Salient Factor Score (SFS 76, SFS 81): Device used by U.S. Parole Commission and other jurisdictions to predict dangerousness of inmates and assist in early-release decisions by parole boards; uses prior record and other factors as predictors of future dangerousness.

Selective Incapacitation: The process of incarcerating certain offenders considered to be high risks, dangerous, or who have a high propensity to commit future crimes, and freeing those considered not to be dangerous or who will not pose serious public risks; controversial procedure of incarcerating offenders selectively on the basis of test scores that some offenders are likely recidivists while others are unlikely recidivists. *See also* False Positives and False Negatives.

Sentence Recommendation Plea Bargaining: Type of plea bargaining by which prosecutor suggests or recommends a particular sentence for the defendant in exchange for a guilty plea. *See also* Plea Bargaining.

Sentencing: Judicial imposition of a punishment, usually a period of months or years, offenders must serve either incarcerated or in community corrections programs following their convictions for one or more crimes.

Sentencing Disparities: Any difference in sentence imposed on different offenders who have been convicted of the same offense under similar circumstances; difference in sentencing severity is usually attributable to race, gender, ethnicity, or socioeconomic status; considered discriminatory; applied to judges in their sentencing patterns; disparities also occur in early-release decisions by parole boards.

Sentencing Hearing: Proceeding following one's conviction for a crime for which the judge imposes a sentence.

Sentencing Memorandum: Prepared by defendants following their conviction; contains their version of the events leading up to the conviction offense and an apology or acceptance of responsibility statement; attached to presentence investigation report.

Settlement Houses: Houses established during 1886 and 1900 to furnish food, clothing, and temporary lodging to wayward or disadvantaged youths; operated by charitable and religious organizations; staffed by volunteers.

Sex Offender: Individual who commits a sexual act prohibited by law; includes rapists, prostitutes, voyeurs, child sexual molestation, date rape, marital rape.

Shakedowns: Procedures by which correctional staff conduct thorough search of prison or jail cells for contraband and other illicit materials and weapons.

Sheriffs: Chief law enforcement officers of U.S. counties; derives from the word *shire,* meaning county in England, and *reeve,* meaning law enforcement officer; combining shire and reeve equals sheriff.

Shire: English equivalent to modern-day U.S. counties.

Shock Incarceration: *See* Shock Probation.

Shock Parole: *See* Shock Probation.

Shock Probation: Program first used in Ohio in 1965; planned sentences where judges order offenders imprisoned for statutory incarceration periods related to their conviction offenses; after 30, 60, 90, or 120 days of incarceration, offenders are taken out of jail or prison and "resentenced" to probation, provided that they behaved well while incarcerated; objective is to shock convicted offenders with imprisonment to deter them from committing future crime.

Small Jails: Jails with 49 or fewer beds.

Smart Sentencing: Any one of several sentencing options used by judges in lieu of incarceration; may include house arrest, electronic monitoring, or one of several different types of intensive probation supervision with conditions.

Solitary Confinement: Punishment form where prisoner is isolated in a single cell with bare necessities for survival; length of confinement varies according to seriousness of infraction committed while incarcerated.

Specialized Caseloads Model: Method of supervising parolees or probationers who have certain types of chemical or alcohol dependencies or mental illnesses; probation or parole officers who supervise these clients have special training geared to working with these types of problem offenders.

Special Needs Offenders: Criminal offenders who have problems of drug or alcohol dependencies, mental illness or retardation, handicaps; sex offenders, child sexual abusers; diffuse category of offenders committing unusual crimes or who have serious physical or psychological problems or limitations.

Special Sex Offender Sentencing Alternative Treatment: Community-based sex offender treatment program headquartered in the State of Washington, commenced in 1985.

Squares: Term to describe female inmates who are considered by other inmates to be "noncriminal"; may be first-offenders who have committed petty crimes.

Status Offense: Offense committed by juvenile which, if committed by an adult, would not be a crime; includes runaways, truancy, violation of curfew.

Street Attitudes: Describe feelings of jail or prison correctional officers who fail to do their jobs or follow their job descriptions, or who perform their duties poorly; includes those with personal prejudices toward racial or ethnic minorities.

Stress: Physical or emotional exhaustion from job pressures; real or imagined (psychosomatic) physical or psychological problems relating to job expectations and one's perceived inability to live up to those expectations.

Strip Search: Varies in thoroughness among jurisdictions, but these searches are conducted of prisoners and visitors, where these persons are asked to strip and their persons are searched; may include x-rays or visual inspection of body cavities.

Summary Offenses: Petty crimes that usually carry penalties of fines only; Great Britain uses summary offense category as least serious crime category; punishes offense by fine; magistrate decides case and jury trial is not permitted; in United States, convictions for summary offenses do not ordinarily result in criminal records; includes traffic violations, violations of city ordinances.

Superintendents: Chief executive officers of prisons or penitentiaries.

Tactical Response Teams: Also known as Correctional Emergency Response Teams and Hostage Recovery Teams, special units trained in hand-to-hand combat, firearms, and other skills designed to put down jail or prison rioting and inmate disturbances and to rescue hostages from prisons or jails.

Temporary Furloughs: *See* Furloughs.

Therapeutic Intervention: Intervention by juvenile probation officer, where officer may make visits to juvenile's home, inspect premises, check with school officials on juvenile's progress.

Tickets-of-Leave: Developed by Sir Walter Crofton, director of Ireland Prison System; multistage process by which inmates can gain early release from prison; authorizations for conditional early release from prison.

Tiers, Tier System: Innovation at Auburn State Penitentiary where prison cell blocks were built on top of one another as different floors; often, different floors segregated prisoners according to their offense seriousness.

Total Institutions: Term applied to prisons by Erving Goffman; prisons are seen as completely self-contained communities for prisoners; separate status system exists; private regulatory and enforcement personnel, inmate subculture.

Transfers: Authorization by juvenile court to change status of juvenile offender to that of an adult so that criminal court can try case and impose punishments not otherwise imposed by juvenile courts; called waivers, certifications.

Transportation: A form of banishment; temporary or permanent removal of an offender from society; used by England during the 1700s and 1800s.

Trial: An adversarial proceeding where a judicial examination and determination of facts may be made by either a judge or jury.

Unconditional Diversion: Diversion program requiring minimal or no contact with probation department; may include minimum maintenance fee paid regularly for specified period such as one year; no treatment program is indicated. *See* Diversion.

Unconditional Release: Release from prison without restrictions.

UNICOR: Profitable, government-owned corporation that sells prisoner-made goods to the public and federal agencies, and hires thousands of federal prisoners as workers or laborers.

Uniform Crime Reports: Annual compilation of crime statistics for eight major felonies and a large category of misdemeanors; compiled by the FBI on the basis of reports submitted by law enforcement agencies in cities and counties in the United States; considered an underestimate of actual amount of crime in the United States.

U.S. Parole Commission: Established in 1930, the Commission is responsible for the management and monitoring of all federal prisoners released on parole; responsible for the classification and placement of parolees and maintaining reports of their progress.

U.S. Sentencing Commission: Originating in 1984, established sentencing policies for federal criminal laws; determined sentencing guidelines currently in use; obligated to revise these laws and regulations occasionally and to determine the proper punishments for federal convictions.

University Settlement: Settlement house established in New York City in 1893 by James Bronson Reynolds; purpose of settlement was to provide job assistance and referral services to disadvantaged community residents; served as a community-based probation agency to supervise some of those placed on probation by New York courts.

Victim/Offender Reconciliation: Restitution model for juveniles that focuses on victim-offender resolutions of differences.

Victim/Offender Reconciliation Project: Form of alternative dispute resolution whereby a civil resolution is made by mutual consent between the victim and an offender; objectives are to provide restitution to victims, hold offender accountable for crime committed, and to reduce recidivism.

Victim Reparations Model: Restitution model for juveniles where juveniles compensate their victims directly for their offenses.

Victim Impact Statement: Statement by victim of crime included in a presentence investigation report prepared by probation officer; optional in most jurisdictions; may be oral statement at sentence hearing, or a written document appended to presentence investigation report, or both.

Violent Crimes: Felonies involving physical injury to one or more victims; crimes include but are not limited to homicide, aggravated assault, rape, and robbery.

Voltaire, Francois-Marie Arouet (1694–1778): French philosopher and writer who wrote about French injustices and corporal punishments.

Waivers: *See* Transfers.

Walnut Street Jail: Considered first American prison seeking to correct offenders; built in 1776 in Philadelphia, Pennsylvania; one of first penal facilities that segregated female from male offenders and children from adults; introduced solitary confinement of prisoners; separated prisoners according to their offense severity; operated on basis that inmates could perform useful services to defray the costs of confinement; operated one of first prison industry programs; inmates grew much of their own fruit through gardening.

Wardens: Chief executive officers of prisons or penitentiaries.

Warrants: Documents that direct law enforcement officers to make arrests of criminal suspects; issued by judges.

Workhouses: Early penal facilities designed to use prison labor for profit by private interests; operated in shires in mid-sixteenth century and later.

Work/Study Release: Also called work furlough, day parole, day pass, community work, study release; any program that provides for the labor of jail or prison inmates in the community under limited supervision, and where inmates are paid the prevailing wage; used first in Vermont by sheriffs in 1906.

References

Abbott, Jack Henry (1981). *In the Belly of the Beast.* New York: Random House.

Administrative Office of the U.S. Courts (1995). "United States Pretrial Services Supervision." *Federal Probation,* 59:28–35.

Advisory Commission on Intergovernmental Relations (1984). *Jails: Intergovernmental Dimensions of a Local Problem: A Commission Report.* Washington, DC: U.S. Government Printing Office.

Alaska Department of Corrections (1990). *Community Residential Center Standards.* Juneau, AK: Alaska Department of Corrections.

Alaska Governor's Task Force on Community Jails (1994). *Final Report to Governor Hickel.* Juneau, AK: Alaska Governor's Task Force on Community Jails.

Alaska Governor's Task Force on the Contract Jails Program (1993). *Report to Governor Hickel.* Juneau, AK: Alaska Governor's Task Force on the Contract Jails Program.

Alaska Governor's Task Force on the Contract Jails Program (1994). *Final Report to Governor Hickel.* Juneau, AK: Alaska Governor's Task Force on the Contract Jails Program.

Alaska Judicial Council (1992). *Resolving Disputes Locally: Alternatives for Rural Alaska . . . Executive Summary.* Anchorage, AK: Alaska Judicial Council.

Alese, John A. (1993). "Finding an Inmate Phone System That Works for You." *American Jails* 7:41–44.

Alexander, Ellen K., and Janice Harris Lord (1994). *Impact Statements: A Victim's Right to Speak.* Arlington, VA: National Victim Center.

Allen, Craig M. (1991). *Women and Men Who Sexually Abuse Children: A Comparative Analysis.* Orwell, VT: Safer Society Press.

Allen, Craig M., and Chung M. Lee (1992). "Family of Origin Structure and Intra/Extrafamilial Childhood Sexual Victimization of Male and Female Offenders." *Journal of Child Sexual Abuse,* 1:31–45.

Allen, Ron, and Tim Graves (1990). *Staff Evaluation: Commission on Jail Standards—A Staff Report to the Sunset Advisory Commission.* Austin, TX: Texas Sunset Advisory Commission.

Alpert, Geoffrey P., and Ben M. Crouch (1991). "Cross-Gender Supervision: Personal Privacy, and Institutional Security: Perceptions of Jail Inmates and Staff." *Criminal Justice and Behavior* 18:304–317.

Alschuler, Albert W. (1989). "The Selling of the Guidelines: Some Correspondence with the U.S. Sentencing Commission." In Dean J. Champion (ed.), *The U.S. Sentencing Guidelines: Implications for Criminal Justice.* New York: Praeger.

Altschuler, David M., and Troy L. Armstrong (1994). *Intensive Aftercare for High-Risk Juveniles: An Assessment.* Washington, DC: U.S. Office of Juvenile Justice and Delinquency Prevention.

American Bar Association (1994). *Just Solutions: A Program Guide to Innovative Justice System Improvements.* Chicago: American Bar Association, American Judicature Society.

American Correctional Association (1983). *The American Prison: From the Beginning . . . A Pictorial History.* College Park, MD: American Correctional Association.

American Correctional Association (1991). *Vital Statistics in Corrections.* College Park, MD: American Correctional Association.

American Correctional Association (1992a). *Correctional and Juvenile Justice Training Directory* (2nd ed.). Laurel, MD: American Correctional Association.

American Correctional Association (1992b). *Juvenile Caseworker: Resource Guide.* Laurel, MD: American Correctional Association.

American Correctional Association (1993a). *Community Partnerships in Action.* Laurel, MD: American Correctional Association.

American Correctional Association (1993b). *Gangs in Correctional Facilities: A National Assessment.* Laurel, MD: American Correctional Association.

American Correctional Association (1993c). *The State of Corrections: Proceedings of ACA Annual Conferences 1992.* Laurel, MD: American Correctional Association.

American Correctional Association (1994). *Field Officer Resource Guide.* Laurel, MD: American Correctional Association.
American Correctional Association (1995). *The State of Corrections: Proceedings of the American Correctional Association Annual Conference 1994.* Laurel, MD: American Correctional Association.
American Correctional Association (1996a). *ACA Juvenile and Adult Directory.* Laurel, MD: American Correctional Association.
American Correctional Association (1996b). "California State Supreme Court Overrules Three Strikes Law." *On the Line,* 19:1.
American Correctional Association (1996c). *Directory.* Laurel, MD: American Correctional Association.
American Correctional Association (1996d). *Juvenile and Adult Boot Camps.* Upper Marlboro, MD: American Correctional Association.
American Jail Association (1994). *Who's Who in Jail Management.* Hagerstown, MD: American Jail Association.
American Medical Association (1990). "Health Status of Detained and Incarcerated Youths." *Journal of the American Medical Association,* 203:987–991.
American Probation and Parole Association (1993). "Pros and Cons of Increasing Officer Authority to Impose or Remove Conditions of Supervision." *APPA Perspectives,* 17:31.
Ammons, David N., Richard W. Campbell, and Sandra L. Somoza (1992). *The Option of Prison Privatization: A Guide for Community Deliberations.* Athens, GA: University of Georgia, Carl Vinson Institute of Government.
Amnesty International (1991). *United States of America: The Death Penalty and Juvenile Offenders.* New York: Amnesty International.
Amnesty International (1994). *Conditions for Death Row Prisoners in H-Unit Oklahoma State Penitentiary.* New York: Amnesty International.
Anderson, David C. (1995). *Crime and the Politics of Hysteria: How the Willie Horton Story Changed American Justice.* New York: Random House.
Anderson, Dennis B., Randall E. Schumacker, and Sara L. Anderson (1991). "Releasee Characteristics and Parole Success." *Journal of Offender Rehabilitation,* 17:133–145.
Anderson, Ronald D., Dennis Gibeau, and David A. D'Amora (1995). "The Sex Offender Treatment Rating Scale: Initial Reliability Data." *Sexual Abuse: A Journal of Research and Treatment,* 7:221–227.
Arizona Department of Corrections (1991). *Offender Classification System (OCS): Classification Operating Manual.* Phoenix, AZ: Arizona Department of Corrections.
Armor, Jerry C. et al. (1989). "Amenability to Rehabilitation among Prison Inmates." *Journal of Offender Counseling, Services and Rehabilitation,* 14:137–142.
Arnold, Charlotte S. (1992). "The Program For Female Offenders, Inc.—A Community Corrections Answer to Jail Overcrowding." *American Jails,* 5:36–40.
Arnold, Charlotte S. (1993). "Respect, Recognition are Keys to Effective Volunteer Programs." *Corrections Today,* 55:118–122.
Ashworth, Andrew J. (1993). "Sentencing Reform Structures." In Michael Tonry (ed.), *Crime and Justice: A Review of Research* (Vol. 16). Chicago: University of Chicago Press.
Associated Press (1993). "Houston Police: Teen Discarded Ankle Monitor, Then Killed Restaurant Worker." *Minot (N.D.) Daily News,* December 10, 1993:A2.
Associated Press (1994). "Teens Adjust to New Life in the Wild." *Minot (N.D.) Daily News,* November 16, 1994:A7.
Associated Press (1995). "Behind Bars." *Minot (N.D.) Daily News,* August 28, 1995:A3.
Associated Press (1996). "Davis Convicted of Killing Klaas." *Minot (N.D.) Daily News,* June 19, 1996:A4.
Austin, James (1986). "Using Early Release to Relieve Prison Crowding: A Dilemma for Public Policy." *Crime and Delinquency,* 32:404–502.

Austin, James (1989). *Parole Outcomes in California: The Consequences of Determinate Sentencing, Punishment, and Incapacitation on Parole Performance.* Madison, WI: National Council on Crime and Delinquency.

Austin, James, and Luiza Chan (1989). *Evaluation of the Nevada Department of Prisons Prisoner Classification System.* San Francisco: National Council on Crime and Delinquency.

Austin, James, Michael Jones, and Melissa Bolyard (1993). *The Growing Use of Jail Boot Camps: The Current State of the Art.* Washington, DC: U.S. Department of Justice, Office of Justice Programs.

Aziz, David W. and Cheryl L. Clark (1996). "Shock Incarceration in New York." In American Correctional Association (ed.), *Juvenile and Adult Boot Camp Programs.* Upper Marlboro, MD: American Correctional Association.

Babcock, Barbara A. et al. (1993). "Symposium: The American Criminal Justice System Approaching the Year 2000." *William and Mary Law Review,* 35:1–443.

Bachman, Ronet, and Bruce M. Taylor (1994). "The Measurement of Family Violence and Rape by the Redesigned National Crime Victimization Survey." *Justice Quarterly,* 11:499–512.

Backstrand, John A., Don C. Gibbons, and Joseph F. Jones (1992). "What is in Jail? An Examination of the Rabble Hypothesis." *Crime and Delinquency,* 38:219–229.

Badillo, Herman, and Milton Haynes (1972). *A Bill of Rights: Attica and the American Prison System.* New York: Outerbridge and Lazard.

Baird, S. Christopher (1985). "Classifying Juveniles: Making the Most of an Important Management Tool." *Corrections Today,* 47:32–38.

Baird, S. Christopher, and James Austin (1986). *Current State of the Art in Prison Classification Models: A Literature Review for the California Department of Corrections.* Sacramento, CA: California Department of Corrections.

Baird, S. Christopher, and Deborah Neuenfeldt (1990). *Improving Correctional Performance Through Better Classification: The Client Management Specific System.* San Francisco: National Council on Crime and Delinquency.

Balch, Robert (1974). "The Juvenilization of the Criminal Justice System." *Federal Probation,* 38:46–50.

Baldus, David C., George Woodworth, and Charles A. Pulaski Jr. (1990). *Equal Justice and the Death Penalty: A Legal and Empirical Analysis.* Boston: Northeastern University Press.

Ball, Richard A. (1991). *Corrections in Context: Policy Options for Control of Intake, Length of Stay and System Capacity in West Virginia.* Morgantown: West Virginia University, Institute for Public Affairs.

Ball, Richard A., C. Ronald Huff, and J. Robert Lilly (1988). *House Arrest and Correctional Policy: Doing Time At Home.* Beverly Hills, CA: Sage.

Barnes, Harry E., and Negley D. Teeters (1959). *New Horizons in Criminology.* Englewood Cliffs, NJ: Prentice-Hall.

Barrington, Bob (1987). "Cor-Rec-Tions: Defining the Profession and the Roles of Staff." *Corrections Today,* 49:116–120.

Barrington, R.C. (1985). "The Development of a Computerised Major Crime Investigation System." *Police Journal,* 58:207–223.

Barton, William H., and Jeffrey A. Butts (1990). "Accommodating Innovation in a Juvenile Court." *Criminal Justice Policy Review,* 4:144–158.

Baunach, Phyllis Jo (1985). *Mothers in Prison.* New Brunswick, NJ: Transaction Books.

Bayse, D.J. (1993). *Helping Hands: A Handbook for Volunteers in Prisons and Jails.* Laurel, MD: American Correctional Association.

Bazemore, Gordon (1991). "New Concepts and Alternative Practice in Community Supervision of Juvenile Offenders: Rediscovering Work Experience." *Journal of Crime and Justice,* 14:27–52.

Bazemore, Gordon (1994). "Developing a Victim Orientation for Community Corrections: A Restorative Justice Paradigm and a Balanced Mission." *APPA Perspectives,* 18:19–24.

Beaird, Lester H. (1986). "Prison Gangs." *Corrections Today,* 48:12–22.

Beck, Jim (1990, November). "A Federal Perspective on Intermediate Sanctions." Unpublished paper presented at the annual meeting of the American Society of Criminology, Baltimore, MD.

Bedau, Hugo A. (1992). *The Case Against the Death Penalty.* Washington, DC: American Civil Liberties Union, Capital Punishment Project.

Beers, Bill, and Chris Duval (1996). "The Oregon SUMMIT Program." In American Correctional Association (ed.), *Juvenile and Adult Boot Camps.* Upper Marlboro, MD: American Correctional Association.

Beirne, Piers (ed.). (1994). *The Origins and Growth of Criminology: Essays in Intellectual History, 1760–1945.* Aldershot, UK: Dartmouth.

Bell, Gary L. (1993). "Testing of the National Crime Information Center Missing/Unidentified Persons Computer Comparison Routine." *Journal of Forensic Sciences,* 38:13–22.

Bellassai, John P., and Mary A. Toborg (1990, November). "Electronic Surveillance of Pretrial Releasees in Indianapolis." Unpublished paper presented at the annual meeting of the American Society of Criminology, Baltimore, MD.

Bello, Stephen (1982). *Doing Life: The Extraordinary Saga of America's Greatest Jailhouse Lawyer.* New York: St. Martin's Press.

Benekos, Peter J. (1990). "Beyond Reintegration: Community Corrections in a Retributive Era." *Federal Probation,* 54:52–56.

Benekos, Peter J. (1992). "Public Policy and Sentencing Reform: The Politics of Corrections." *Federal Probation,* 56:4–10.

Benekos, Peter J., and Alida V. Merlo (eds.). (1992). *Corrections: Dilemmas and Directions.* Cincinnati, OH: Anderson Publishing Company.

Benekos, Peter J., and Alida V. Merlo (1993). "Three Strikes and You're Out! The Political Sentencing Game." *Federal Probation* 59:3–9.

Benzvy-Miller, Shereen (1990). "Community Corrections and the NIMBY Syndrome." *Forum on Corrections Research,* 2:18–22.

Bergsmann, Ilene R. (1991). "ACA Women in Corrections Committee Examines Female Staff Training Needs." *Corrections Today,* 53:106–109.

Berlin, Eric P. (1993). "The Federal Sentencing Guidelines' Failure to Eliminate Sentencing Disparity: Governmental Manipulations Before Arrest." *Wisconsin Law Review,* 1:187–230.

Berrueta-Clement, John R. et al. (1984). "Preschool's Effects on Social Responsibility." In *Changed Lives: The Effects of the Perry Preschool Program on Youths Through Age 19.* Ypsilanti, MI: High/Scope Press.

Bieler, Glenn M. (1990). "Death Be Not Proud: A Note on Juvenile Capital Punishment." *New York Law School Journal of Human Rights,* 72:179–213.

Bigger, Phillip J. (1993). "Officers in Danger: Results of the Federal Probation and Pretrial Officers Association's National Study on Serious Assaults." *APPA Perspectives,* 17:14–20.

Bilchik, Shay (1996). *A Guide for Implementing Teen Court Programs.* Washington, DC: Office of Juvenile Justice and Delinquency Prevention.

Bishop, Bill (1993). "New York's Crime War: The Empire Strikes Out!" *APPA Perspectives,* 17:13–14.

Bishop, Donna M., and Charles E. Frazier (1992). "Gender Bias in Juvenile Justice Processing: Implications of the JJDP Act." *Journal of Criminal Law and Criminology,* 82:1162–1186.

Black, Henry Campbell (1990). *Black's Law Dictionary.* St. Paul, MN: West.

Blakely, Curtis R., and Vic W. Bumphus (1996). "Private Correctional Management: A Comparison of Enabling Legislation." *Federal Probation,* 60:49–53.

Blauner, Peter, and Gerry Migliore (1992). "Street Stories." *APPA Perspectives,* 16:21–23.

Blevins, L. David, Joann B. Morton, and Kimberly McCabe (1996). "Using the Michigan Alcohol Screening Test to Identify Problem Drinkers Under Federal Supervision." *Federal Probation,* 60:38–42.

Blomberg, Thomas G., William Bales, and Karen Reed (1993). "Intermediate Punishment: Redistributing or Extending Social Control?" *Crime Law and Social Change,* 19:187–201.

Bloom, Barbara (1993). "Female Offenders in the Community." *APPA Perspectives,* 17:22–23.

Blumberg, Mark et al. (1990). "Selected Articles from the Symposium on AIDS Held at Indiana University of Pennsylvania." *Criminal Justice Policy Review,* 4:288–348.

Blumstein, Alfred (1988). "Prison Populations: A System Out of Control?" In Michael Tonry and Norval Morris (eds.), *Crime and Justice: A Review of Research.* Chicago: University of Chicago Press.

Bodapati, Madhava R., and James Marquart (1992, November). "Analyzing Parole Decision Making in Texas, 1980–1990." Unpublished paper presented at the annual meeting of the American Society of Criminology, New Orleans, LA.

Bohn, Martin J., Joyce L. Carbonell, and Edwin I. Megargee (1995). "The Applicability and Utility of the MMPI-Based Offender Classification System in a Correctional Mental Health Unit." *Criminal Behaviour and Mental Health,* 5:14–33.

Boin, R. Arjen, and Menno J. Van Duin (1995). "Prison Riots as Organizational Failures: A Managerial Perspective." *Prison Journal,* 75:357–379.

Bonham, Gene, Galan Janeksela, and John Bardo (1986). "Predicting Parole Decision in Kansas via Discriminant Analysis." *Journal of Criminal Justice,* 14:123–133.

Borgman, Robert (1986). "'Don't Come Home Again': Parental Banishment of Delinquent Youths." *Child Welfare,* 65:295–304.

Bosarge, Betty (ed.). (1989). *First/Second Line Jail Supervisor's Training Manual.* Arlington, VA: National Sheriffs' Association.

Bottomley, A. Keith (1990). "Parole in Transition: A Comparative Study of Origins, Developments, and Prospects for the 1990s." In Michael Tonry and Norval Morris (eds.), *Crime and Justice: A Review of Research* (Vol. 12). Chicago: University of Chicago Press.

Bourque, Blair B., Mel Han, and Sarah M. Hill (1996). *A National Survey of Aftercare Provisions for Boot Camp Graduates.* Washington, DC: National Institute of Justice.

Bowditch, Christine, and Ronald S. Everett (1987). "Private Prisons: Problems Within the Solution." *Justice Quarterly,* 4:441–453.

Bowker, Arthur L. (1995). "Criminal History Investigations: The Key to Locking Up the Repeat Offender." *FBI Law Enforcement Bulletin,* 64:15–20.

Boyd, John S., and Thomas J. Tiefenwerth (1995). "Jail Training on the Road in Texas." *American Jails,* 9:59–60.

Brantingham, Patricia L. (1985). "Sentencing Disparity: An Analysis of Judicial Consistency." *Journal of Quantitative Criminology,* 1:281–305.

Braswell, Michael C., Reid H. Montgomery, Jr., and Lucien X. Lombardo (eds.). (1994). *Prison Violence in America* (2nd ed.). Cincinnati, OH: Anderson Publishing Company.

Brennan, Tim (1985). *Offender Classification and Jail Crowding: Examining the Connection Between Poor Classification and the Problem of Jail Crowding.* Boulder, CO: HSI, Inc.

Brien, Peter M., and Allen J. Beck (1996). *HIV in Prisons and Jails 1994.* Washington, DC: U.S. Department of Justice, Office of Justice Programs.

Brien, Peter M., and Caroline Wolf Harlow (1996). *HIV in Prisons and Jails, 1993.* Washington, DC: U.S. Department of Justice, Office of Justice Programs.

Bright, Frank (1981). "Increasing Probation and Parole Officer Job Satisfaction Through Participatory Goal Setting." In Frank Bright (ed.), *The Status of Probation and Parole?* College Park, MD: American Correctional Association.

Britt, Chester L., III, Michael R. Gottfredson, and John S. Goldkamp (1992). "Drug Testing and Pretrial Misconduct: An Experiment on the Specific Deterrent Effects of Drug Monitoring Defendants on Pretrial Release." *Journal of Research in Crime and Delinquency,* 29:62–78.

Broderick, Vincent L. et al. (1993). "Pretrial Release and Detention and Pretrial Services." *Federal Probation* 57:4–79.

Bronstein, Alvin J. (1980). "Prisoners' Rights: A History." In G. Alpert (ed.), *Legal Rights of Prisoners.* Beverly Hills, CA: Sage.

Brown, Michael P., and Preston Elrod (1995). "Electronic House Arrest: An Examination of Citizen Attitudes." *Crime and Delinquency,* 41:332–346.

Brown, Paul W. (1987). "Probation Officer Burnout: An Organizational Disease/An Organizational Cure, Part II." *Federal Probation,* 51:4–16.

Brown, Paul W. (1994). "Mental Preparedness: Probation Officers Need to Rely on More Than Luck to Ensure Safety." *Corrections Today,* 56:180–187.

Brown, Robert, Jr., and Marjorie Van Ochten (1990). "Sexual Harassment: A Vulnerable Area for Corrections." *Corrections Today,* 52:62–70.

Bryan, Darrell (1995). "Emergency Response Teams: A Prison's First Line of Defense." *Corrections Compendium,* 20:1–4.

Bryan, Darrell (1996). "For Rent: 2000 Cells, Meals Included." *Corrections Compendium,* 21:1–3.

Buchanan, Robert A., Cindie A. Unger, and Karen L. Whitlow (1988). *Disruptive Maximum Security Inmate Management Guide.* Washington, DC: U.S. National Institute of Corrections.

Buentello, Salvador, et al. (1992). "Gangs: A Growing Menace on the Streets and in Our Prisons." *Corrections Today,* 54:58–97.

Bureau of Justice Assistance (1992). *Drugs, Crime and the Justice System.* Washington, DC: U.S. Department of Justice.

Bureau of Justice Statistics (1995). *Jails and Jail Inmates 1994.* Washington, DC: U.S. Bureau of Justice Statistics.

Burke, Peggy B. (1987). *Structuring Parole Decision Making: Lessons from Technical Assistance in Nine States.* Washington, DC: Cosmos Corporation.

Burke, Tod W., Elaine Rizzo, and Charles E. O'Rear (1992). "National Survey Results: Do Officers Need College Degrees?" *Corrections Today,* 54:174–176.

Burns, Jerald C., and Gennaro F. Vito (1995). "An Impact Analysis of the Alabama Boot Camp Program." *Federal Probation,* 49:63–67.

Burns, Mark E. (1992) "Electronic Home Detention: New Sentencing Alternative Demands Uniform Standards." *Journal of Contemporary Law,* 18:75–105.

Burns, Ronald (1996). "Boot Camps: The Empirical Record." *American Jails,* 10:42–49.

Burton, Velmer S., Jr., Edward J. Latessa, and Troy Barker (1992). "The Role of Probation Officers: An Examination of Statutory Requirements." *Journal of Contemporary Criminal Justice,* 8:274–282.

Butts, Jeffrey A. (1996). *Offenders in Juvenile Court, 1994.* Washington, DC: Office of Juvenile Justice and Delinquency Prevention.

Butts, Jeffrey A. et al. (1996). *Juvenile Court Statistics 1993: Statistics Report.* Washington, DC: Office of Juvenile Justice and Delinquency Prevention.

Byrne, James M. (1986). "The Control Controversy: A Preliminary Examination of Intensive Probation Supervision Programs in the United States." *Federal Probation,* 50:4–16.

Byrne, James M. (1989). "The Effectiveness of the New Intensive Supervision Programs." *Research in Corrections,* 2:1–75.

Byrne, James M. (ed.). (1990). "Intensive Probation Supervision: An Alternative to Prison in the 1980s." *Crime and Delinquency,* 36:3–191.

Byrne, James M., and Mary Brewster (1993). "Choosing the Future of American Corrections: Punishment or Reform?" *Federal Probation,* 57:3–9.

Byrne, James M., Arthur J. Lurigio, and Joan Petersilia (eds.). (1992). *Smart Sentencing: The Emergence of Intermediate Sanctions.* Newbury Park, CA: Sage.

Byrne, James M., and Faye S. Taxman (1994). "Crime Control Policy and Community Corrections Practice." *Evaluation and Program Planning,* 17:227–233.

Byrne, James M. et al. (1989). "The Effectiveness of the New Intensive Supervision Programs." *Research in Corrections,* 2:1–75.

Cahalan, Margaret W. (1986). *Historical Corrections Statistics in the United States, 1850–1984.* Washington, DC: U.S. Department of Justice.

Calder, James D. (1993). *The Origins and Development of Federal Crime Control Policy.* Westport, CT: Praeger.

Call, Jack E. (1995a). "Prison Overcrowding Cases in the Aftermath of *Wilson v. Seiter.*" *Prison Journal,* 75:390–405.

Call, Jack E. (1995b). "The Supreme Court and Prisoners' Rights." *Federal Probation,* 59:36–46.

Capodanno, Daniel J., and Frederick R. Chavaria (1991). "Polysubstance Abuse: The Interaction of Alcohol and Other Drugs." *Federal Probation,* 55:24–27.

Camp, Camille G., and George M. Camp (1995a). *Adult Corrections.* South Salem, NY: Criminal Justice Institute.

Camp, Camille G., and George M. Camp (1995b). *Jail Systems.* South Salem, NY: Criminal Justice Institute.

Camp, Camille G., and George M. Camp (1995c). *Juvenile Corrections.* South Salem, NY: Criminal Justice Institute.

Camp, Camille G., and George M. Camp (1995d). *Probation and Parole.* South Salem, NY: Criminal Justice Institute.

Carini, Gary (1986). *The Use of Assessment Centers in Corrections.* Philadelphia: Program on Correctional Leadership and Innovation, Wharton Center for Applied Research, University of Pennsylvania.

Carlson, Eric W., and Evalyn Parks (1979). *Critical Issues in Adult Probation: Issues in Probation Management.* Washington, DC: U.S. Department of Justice.

Carlson, Eric W. et al. (1977). *Halfway Houses: National Evaluation Program: Phase 1 Summary Report.* Columbus, OH: Ohio State University Program for the Study of Crime and Delinquency.

Carns, Teresa White, and John Kruse (1991). *Alaska's Plea Bargaining Re-Evaluated: Executive Summary.* Anchorage, AK: Alaska Judicial Council.

Carp, Scarlett V., and Joyce A. David (1991). *Design Considerations in the Building of Women's Prisons.* Boulder, CO: U.S. National Institute of Corrections.

Carp, Scarlett V., and Linda S. Schade (1992). "Tailoring Facility Programming to Suit Female Offenders' Needs." *Corrections Today,* 54:152–159.

Carroll, Leo (1974). *Hacks, Blacks, and Cons: Race Relations in a Maximum-Security Prison.* Lexington, MA: Lexington Books.

Carter, Diane (1991). "The Status of Education and Training in Corrections." *Federal Probation,* 55:17–26.

Carter, Robert M., Jack Cocks, and Daniel Glaser (1987). "Community Service: A Review of the Basic Issues." *Federal Probation,* 51:4–10.

Carter, Robert M., Daniel Glaser, and Leslie T. Wilkins (1985). *Correctional Institutions* (3rd ed.). New York: Harper and Row.

Cavanagh, D.P., and A.R. Kleiman (1990). *A Cost-Benefit Analysis of Prison Cell Construction and Alternative Sanctions.* Cambridge: Botec Analysis Corporation.

Cavanagh, David P., David Boyum, and Jyothi Nambiar (1993). *Relations Between Increases in the Certainty, Severity and Celerity of Punishment for Drug Crimes and Reductions in the Level of Crime.* Washington, DC: BOTEC Analysis Corporation.

Cavanaugh, Michael J. (1992). "Intensive Supervision in South Carolina: Accountability and Assistance." *Corrections Compendium,* 17:1–6.

Chaiken, Marcia R., and Jan M. Chaiken (1987). *Selecting "Career Criminals" for Priority Prosecution.* Cambridge: Abt Associates.

Champion, Dean J. (1975). *The Sociology of Organizations.* New York: McGraw-Hill.

Champion, Dean J. (1988a). "Child Sexual Abusers and Sentencing Severity: Some Judicial Moral and Ethical Dilemmas and Fair Trials." *Federal Probation,* 52:53–57.

Champion, Dean J. (1988b). "Some Recent Trends in Civil Litigation by Federal and State Prison Inmates." *Federal Probation,* 52:43–47.

Champion, Dean J. (1988c). *Felony Probation: Problems and Prospects.* New York: Praeger.

Champion, Dean J. (ed.). (1989). *The U.S. Sentencing Guidelines: Implications for Criminal Justice.* New York: Praeger.

Champion, Dean J. (1992). *The Juvenile Justice System: Delinquency, Processing and the Law.* Upper Saddle River, NJ: Prentice-Hall.

Champion, Dean J. (1994). *Measuring Offender Risk: A Criminal Justice Sourcebook.* Westport, CT: Greenwood Press.

Champion, Dean J. (1996). *Probation, Parole and Community Corrections.* Upper Saddle River, NJ: Prentice-Hall.

Champion, Dean J., and G. Larry Mays (1991). *Transferring Juveniles to Criminal Court.* New York: Praeger.

Cheek, Frances E., and G. M. Nouri (1980). "Coping with Stress and Burnout for Members of the Caring Profession." 1980 Eastern Regional Conference on the Association for Humanistic Psychology, Philadelphia, PA.

Chesney-Lind, Meda (1987). *Prisoners in Paradise: Women's Prison Problems in Hawaii.* Honolulu, HI: Youth Development and Research Center, University of Hawaii.

Chessman, Caryl (1954). *Cell 2455 Death Row.* New York: Bantam Books.

Chung, Kristina H. (1991). "Kids Behind Bars: The Legality of Incarcerating Juveniles in Adult Jails." *Indiana Law Journal,* 66:999–1030.

Chung, Woo Sik, and John T. Pardeck (1994). "An Empirical Validation of a Theory of Punishment." *International Journal of Comparative and Applied Criminal Justice,* 18:221–248.

Claggett, Arthur F. et al. (1992). "Corrections: Innovative Practices, Inmate Behavior Dynamics, Policy Analysis, and Personnel." *Journal of Offender Rehabilitation,* 17:1–211.

Clark, Cherie L., David W. Aziz, and Doris Layton MacKenzie (1994). *Shock Incarceration in New York: Focus on Treatment.* Washington, DC: National Institute of Justice.

Clark, Frances (1990). "Hands-On Jail Training Puts Officers Above Par." *Corrections Today,* 52:72–75.

Clark, Judith (1995). "The Impact of the Prison Environment on Mothers." *Prison Journal,* 75:306–329.

Clarke, Stevens H., et al. (1994). *National Symposium on Court-Connected Dispute Resolution Research.* Washington, DC: State Justice Institute.

Clarke, Stevens H., and Emily Coleman (1993). "County Jail Population Growth, 1975–1992." *Popular Government,* 59:10–15.

Clarke, Stevens H., Ernest Valente, Jr., and Robyn R. Mace (1992). *Mediation of Interpersonal Disputes: An Evaluation of North Carolina's Programs.* Chapel Hill, NC: Institute of Government, University of North Carolina at Chapel Hill, Mediation Network of North Carolina.

Clear, Todd R. (1994). *Harm in American Penology: Offenders, Victims and Their Communities.* Albany: State University of New York Press.

Clear, Todd R., Val B. Clear, and William D. Burrell (1989). *Offender Assessment and Evaluation: The Presentence Investigation Report.* Cincinnati, OH: Anderson Publishing Company.

Clear, Todd R., and Kenneth W. Gallagher (1985). "Probation and Parole Supervision: A Review of Current Classification Practices." *Crime and Delinquency,* 31:423–444.

Clear, Todd, and Edward J. Latessa (1993). "Probation Officers' Roles in Intensive Supervision: Surveillance Versus Treatment." *Justice Quarterly,* 10:441–462.

Clemmer, D.C. (1940). *The Prison Community.* New York: Holt, Rinehart and Winston.

Clemmer, D.C. (1958). *The Prison Community.* New York: Holt, Rinehart and Winston.

Cockburn, J.S., and Thomas A. Green (eds.). (1988). *Twelve Good Men and True: The Criminal Jury Trial in England, 1200–1800.* Princeton, NJ: Princeton University Press.

Codelia, Eddie, and Jane Willis (1989). "Volunteers: A Catalyst for Change." *Corrections Today,* 51:168–170.

Cohn, Alvin W. (1995). "The Failure of Correctional Management: Recycling the Middle Manager." *Federal Probation,* 59:10–16.

Cohn, Alvin W., and Michael M. Ferriter (1990). "The Presentence Investigation: An Old Saw with New Teeth." *Federal Probation,* 54:15–25.

Cole, George F., Roger A. Hanson, and Jonathan E. Silbert (1984). *Alternative Dispute Resolution Mechanisms for Prisoner Grievances.* Washington, DC: U.S. National Institute of Corrections.

Cole, Richard B., and Jack E. Call (1992). "When Courts Find Jail and Prison Overcrowding Unconstitutional." *Federal Probation,* 56:29–39.

Coles, Frances S. (1987). "The Impact of *Bell v. Wolfish* Upon Prisoner's Rights." *Journal of Crime and Justice,* 10:47–70.

Collins, William C. (1986). *Correctional Law (1986): An Analysis and Discussion of the Key Issues and Developments in Correctional Law Over the Past Year.* Olympia, WA: W. C. Collins.

Collins, William C. (1994). *Jail Design and Operation and the Constitution: An Overview.* Boulder, CO: U.S. National Institute of Corrections.

Collins, William C., and John Hagar (1995). "Jails and the Courts: Issues for Today, Issues for Tomorrow." *American Jails* 9:18–28.

Colorado Department of Corrections (1993). *Colorado Regimented Inmate Training Program: A Legislative Report.* Colorado Springs: Colorado Department of Corrections.

Colorado Parole Guidelines Commission (1988). *Report to the Legislature.* Denver: Colorado Parole Guidelines Commission.

Colson, Charles et al. (1989). "Alternatives to Reduce Prison Crowding." *Journal of State Government,* 62:59–94.

Conley, John A. (1982). "Working in Prisons: Personnel, Politics, and Patronage." *The Prison Journal,* 42:68–84.

Connecticut Board of Parole (1974). *Standards Governing Early Release of Prisoners.* Hartford, CT: Office of Policy and Management.

Conrad, John (1984). "Corrections and Its Constituencies." *The Prison Journal,* 64:47–55.

Contact Center. (1987a). "Survey: Lease Arrangements Help Handle Prison Populations." *Corrections Compendium,* 11:9–12.

Contact Center. (1987b). "Inmate Grievance Procedures." *Corrections Compendium,* 11:9–13.

Cook, Philip J., and Donna B. Slawson (1993). *The Costs of Processing Murder Cases in North Carolina.* Durham, NC: Terry Sanford Institute of Public Policy, Duke University.

Cook, Stephen S. (1996). "Mediation as an Alternative to Probation Revocation Proceedings." *Federal Probation,* 59:48–52.

Corbett, Ronald P., and Gary T. Marx (1994). "Critique: No Soul in the New Machine: Technofallacies in the Electronic Monitoring Movement." *Journal of Offender Monitoring,* 7:1–9.

Cornelius, Gary F. (1994). *Stressed Out: Strategies for Living and Working with Stress in Corrections.* Laurel, MD: American Correctional Association.

Cornelius, Gary F. (1995). "Reducing Inmate Management Problems with the Human Services Approach." *American Jails,* 9:62–63.

Cornelius, Gary F. (1996). *Jails in America: An Overview of Issues* (2nd ed.). Lanham, MD: American Correctional Association.

Corrections Compendium (1990a). "Privatization Gains as Marshals Service Contracts for New Jail." *Corrections Compendium,* 15:21.

Corrections Compendium (1990b). "Use of Prison Alternatives Could Save New York Millions." *Corrections Compendium,* 15:14.

Corrections Compendium (1991a). "Electronic Monitoring Programs Grow Rapidly From 1986 to 1989." *NIJ Reports,* No. 222, *Corrections Compendium,* 16:14.

Corrections Compendium (1992a). "ACA's Medal of Valor Goes to Michigan Parole Officer." *Corrections Compendium,* 17:13–14.

Corrections Compendium (1992b). "Florida Authorizes Probation, Parole Officers to Carry Firearms." *Corrections Compendium,* 17:2.

Corrections Compendium (1993a). "Oregon to Reduce Parole Offices." *Corrections Compendium,* 18:17.

Corrections Compendium (1993b). "Work and Educational Release, 1993." *Corrections Compendium,* 18:5–18.

Corrections Compendium (1994a). "Survey Summary: Hiring of Correctional Officers Increasingly More Selective." *Corrections Compendium,* 19:8–11.

Corrections Compendium (1994b). "Survey Summary: Sentencing Guidelines Determine Penalties in 19 Systems." *Corrections Compendium,* 19:7–14.

Corrections Compendium (1996a). "Survey Summary: Fewer Correctional Officer Positions Created in '96." *Corrections Compendium,* 21:12–29.

Corrections Compendium (1996b). "Survey Summary: Violence on the Rise in U.S. Prisons." *Corrections Compendium,* 21:9–12.

Corrections Digest (1994). "Contracts Awarded for Construction of New Prison in Chester, PA." *Corrections Compendium,* 19:25–27.

Corrections Today (1995). "Virginia Loses Jail Crowding Case." *Corrections Today,* 57:29–30.

Corrigan, Mark (1990, November). "The Use of Community-Based Sentencing Alternatives to Reduce Prison Overcrowding: An Assessment of Policy and Practice." Unpublished paper presented at the annual meetings of the American Society of Criminology, Baltimore, MD.

Cosgrove, Edward J. (1994). "ROBO-PO: The Life and Times of a Federal Probation Officer." *Federal Probation,* 58:29–30.

Costa, Jeralita, and Anne Seymour (1993). "Experienced Volunteers: Crime Victims, Former Offenders Contribute a Unique Perspective." *Corrections Today,* 55:110–111.

Crabtree, John (1993). "Waseca, A Small County Jail." *American Jails,* 7:62–66.

Crane, Richard (1992). "No Noose is Good Noose." *Corrections Compendium,* 17:2.

Creighton, Linda L. (1988). "Nursery Rhymes and Hard Time." *U.S. News and World Report,* August 8, 1988:22–24.

Cromwell, Paul F., and George G. Killinger (1994). *Community-Based Corrections: Probation, Parole and Intermediate Punishments.* Minneapolis: West Publishing Company.

Cronin, Mary (1992). "Gilded Cages: New Designs for Jails and Prisons are Showing Positive Results: The Question Is, Can We Afford Them?" *Time,* May 25, 1992:52–54.

Cronin, Roberta C. (1994). *Boot Camps for Adult and Juvenile Offenders: Overview and Update.* Washington, DC: U.S. National Institute of Justice.

Cullen, Francis T. (1986). "The Privatization of Treatment: Prison Reform in the 1980s." *Federal Probation,* 50:8–16.

Cullen, Francis T. et al. (1985). "The Social Dimensions of Correctional Officer Stress." *Justice Quarterly,* 2:505–533.

Culliver, Concetta C. (1993). *Female Criminality: The State of the Art.* New York: Garland Press.

Curran, Daniel J. (1984). "The Myth of the 'New' Female Delinquent." *Crime and Delinquency,* 30:386–399.

Curran, Debra A. (1984). *Characteristics of the Elderly Shoplifter and the Effect of Sanctions on Recidivism.* Lanham, MD: University Press of America.

Curry, Clifton. (1994). *Federal Crime Bill: What Will It Mean for California?* Sacramento, CA: Governor's Task Force to Study the Influence of the Crime Bill.

Curtin, E.L. (1990). "Day Reporting Centers, A Promising Alternative." *IARCA Journal,* 3:8.

Cushman, Robert C., and Dale Sechrest (1992). "Variations in the Administration of Probation Supervision." *Federal Probation,* 56:19–29.

Dale, Michael J. (1991). "Religion in Jails and Prisons: Defining the Inmate's Legal Rights." *American Jails,* 5:30–34.

D'Allessio, Stewart J., and Lisa Stolzenberg (1995). "The Impact of Sentencing Guidelines on Jail Incarceration in Minnesota." *Criminology,* 33:283–302.

Daly, Kathleen (1994). *Gender, Crime and Punishment.* New Haven, CT: Yale University Press.

Davidson, Howard S. (ed.). (1995). *Schooling in a "Total Institution": Critical Perspectives on Prison Education.* Westport, CT: Bergin & Garvey.

Davis, Keith (1962). *Human Relations at Work.* New York: McGraw-Hill.

Davis, Michael (1992). *To Make the Punishment Fit the Crime: Essays in the Theory of Criminal Justice.* Boulder, CO: Westview Press.

Davis, Robert C., and Arthur J. Lurigio (1992). "Compliance with Court-Ordered Restitution: Who Pays?" *APPA Perspectives,* 16:25–31.

Davis, Robert C., and Barbara Smith (1994). "Victim Impact Statements and Victim Satisfaction: An Unfulfilled Promise?" *Journal of Criminal Justice,* 22:1–12.

Davis, Shirley (1990, April). "Participatory Management: A Technique for Reducing Probation/Parole Officer Burnout." Unpublished paper presented at the annual meeting of the Academy of Criminal Justice Sciences, Denver, CO.

Davis, Simon (1994). "Factors Associated with the Diversion of Mentally Disordered Offenders." *Bulletin of the American Academy of Psychiatry and the Law,* 22:389–397.

Davis, Su Perk (1990a). "Good Time." *Corrections Compendium,* 15:1–6.

Davis, Su Perk (1990b). "Survey: Parole Officers' Roles Changing in Some States." *Corrections Compendium,* 15:7–16.

Davis, Su Perk (1991). "Number of Furloughs Increasing—Success Rates High." *Corrections Compendium,* 16:10–22.

Davis, Su Perk (1992a). "Survey: Number of Offenders Under Intensive Probation Increases." *Corrections Compendium,* 17:9–17.

Davis, Su Perk (1992b). "Survey: Programs and Services for the Female Offender." *Corrections Compendium,* 17:7–20.

Davis, Su Perk (1994). "Mandatory Minimum Sentences." *Corrections Compendium,* 19:4–5.

Dawson, John M., Steven K. Smith, and Carol J. DeFrances (1993). *Prosecutors in State Courts, 1992.* Washington, DC: U.S. Department of Justice.

Dawson, Roger E. (1992). "Opponent Process Theory for Substance Abuse Treatment." *Juvenile and Family Court Journal,* 43:51–59.

DeBerry, Clyde E. (1994). *Blacks in Corrections: Understanding Network Systems in Prison Society.* Bristol, IN: Wyndham Hall Press.

DeCostanzo, Elaine, and Helen Scholes (1988). "Women Behind Bars: Their Numbers Increase." *Corrections Today,* 50:104–108.

Dedischew, Jeffrey M., and W. Garrett Capune (1989). "How Working in the Jail Affects Sheriff Deputies: An Assessment." *Journal of California Law Enforcement,* 23: 106–112.

Deichsel, Wolfgang (1991). "Uberlegungen AnlaBlich des Hamburger Diversionsmodells." *Monantsschrift fu Kriminologie und Strafrechsfrom,* 4:224–235.

DeJong, William, and Stan Franzeen (1993). "On the Role of Intermediate Sanctions in Corrections Reform: The Views of Criminal Justice Professionals." *Journal of Crime and Justice,* 16:47–73.

del Carmen, Rolando V. (1986). *Potential Liabilities of Probation and Parole Officers.* Cincinnati, OH: Anderson Publishing Company.

del Carmen, Rolando V., and James Alan Pilant (1994). "The Scope of Judicial Immunity for Probation and Parole Officers." *APPA Perspectives,* 18:14–21.

del Carmen, Rolando V., and F. Trook-White (1986). *Liability Issues in Community Service Sanctions.* Washington, DC: U.S. National Institute of Corrections.

del Carmen, Rolando V., and Joseph Vaughn (1986). "Legal Issues in the Use of Electronic Surveillance in Probation." *Federal Probation,* 50:60–69.

DeMore, Rosemary (1996). "'I'm Not a Criminal': Working with Low-Risk Supervisees." *Federal Probation,* 59:34–40.

Department of Justice (1996). *Probation and Parole Population Reaches Almost 3.8 Million.* Washington, DC: Bureau of Justice Statistics, Bulletin, June 30, 1996.

Deschenes, Elizabeth, Susan Turner, and Todd Clear (1992, November). "The Effectiveness of ISP for Different Types of Drug Offenders." Unpublished paper presented at the annual meeting of the American Society of Criminology. New Orleans, LA.

Deschenes, Elizabeth, Susan Turner, and Joan Petersilia (1995). "A Dual Experiment in Intensive Community Supervision: Minnesota's Prison Diversion and Enhanced Supervised Release Programs." *Prison Journal,* 73:330–336.

DeWitt, Charles B. (1986a). *Florida Sets Example with Use of Concrete Modules.* Washington, DC: U.S. Department of Justice, National Institute of Justice.

DeWitt, Charles B. (1986b). *New Construction Methods for Correctional Facilities.* Washington, DC: U.S. Department of Justice, National Institute of Justice.

DeWitt, Charles B. (1986c). *Ohio's New Approach to Prison and Jail Financing.* Washington, DC: U.S. Department of Justice, National Institute of Justice.

DeWitt, Charles B. (1987). *Building on Experience: A Case Study of Advanced Construction and Financing Methods for Corrections.* Washington, DC: U.S. National Institute of Corrections.

DeWitt, Charles B., and Cindie A. Unger (1987). *Oklahoma Prison Expansion Saves Time and Money.* Washington, DC: National Institute of Justice.

DiCataldo, Frank, and Thomas Grisso (1995). "A Typology of Juvenile Offenders Based on the Judgments of Juvenile Court Professionals." *Criminal Justice and Behavior,* 22:246–262.

Dickey, Walter J. (1989). *From the Bottom Up: Probation Supervision in a Small Wisconsin Community.* Madison, WI: Continuing Education and Outreach, University of Wisconsin Law School.

Dickey, Walter J., and Dennis Wagner (1990). *From the Bottom Up: The High Risk Offender Intensive Supervision Program.* Madison, WI: Continuing Education and Outreach, University of Wisconsin Law School.

Dickstein, L.J., and C.C. Nadelson (1989). *Family Violence: Emerging Issues of a National Crisis.* Washington, DC: American Psychiatric Press.

Dietz, Park Elliott (1985). "Hypothetical Criteria for the Prediction of Individual Criminality." In Christopher D. Webster, Mark H. Ben-Aron, and Stephen J. Hucker (eds.), *Dangerousness: Probability and Prediction, Psychiatry and Public Policy.* Cambridge: Cambridge University Press.

Diggs, David W., and Stephen L. Pieper (1994). "Using Day Reporting Centers as an Alternative to Jail." *Federal Probation,* 58:9–12.

Ditton, Jason, and Roslyn Ford (1994). *The Reality of Probation: A Formal Ethnography of Process and Practice.* Aldershot, UK: Avebury.

Dixon, Jo (1995). "The Organizational Context of Criminal Sentencing." *American Journal of Sociology,* 100:1157–1198.

Dobash, Russell P. (1983). "Labour and Discipline in Scottish and English Prisons: Moral Correction, Punishment, and Useful Toil." *Sociology,* 17:1–27.

Donnelly, Patrick G., and Brian Forschner (1984). "Client Success or Failure in a Halfway House." *Federal Probation,* 48:38–44.

Donnelly, S.M. (1980). *Community Service Orders in Federal Probation.* Washington, DC: National Institute of Justice.

Dowell, David A., Cecilia Klein, and Cheryl Krichmar (1985). "Evaluation of a Halfway House for Women." *Journal of Criminal Justice,* 13:217–226.

Drapkin, Martin, and Gary T. Klugiewicz (1994a). "Use of Force Training in Jails, Part I." *American Jails,* 7:9–12.

Drapkin, Martin, and Gary T. Klugiewicz (1994b). "Use of Force Training in Jails, Part II." *American Jails,* 7:93–98.

Drass, Kriss A., and William J. Spencer (1987). "Accounting for Pre-Sentencing Recommendations: Typologies and Probation Officers' Theory of Office." *Social Problems,* 34:277–293.
Ducker, W. Marc (1984). "Dispute Resolution in Prisons: An Overview and Assessment." *Rutgers Law Review,* 36:145–178.
Duff, Anthony, and David Garland (eds.). (1994). *A Reader on Punishment.* Oxford, UK: Oxford University Press.
Duggan, Nancy (1993). *So Far So Good: The Experience of Male Ex-Offenders 2–5 Years After Release from Incarceration.* Ann Arbor, MI: University Microfilms International.
Duguid, Stephen (ed.). (1992). *Yearbook of Correctional Education 1992* Burnaby, CAN: Institute for the Humanities, Simon Fraser University.
Durham, Alexis M., III (ed.). (1991). "Privatization." *Journal of Contemporary Criminal Justice,* 7:1–73.
Durham, Alexis M., III (1994). *Crisis and Reform: Current Issues in American Punishment.* Boston: Little, Brown and Company.
Durkee, Daniel (1996). "Local Detention Education and Training: A Program Developed by the Criminal Justice Center, Lansing Community College." *American Jails,* 10:58–60.
Dwyer, Diane C., and Roger B. McNally (1987). "Juvenile Justice: Reform, Retain, and Reaffirm." *Federal Probation,* 51:47–51.
Eckstrand, Laurie E. (1993). *National Crime Information Center: Legislation Needed to Deter Misuse of Criminal Justice Information.* Washington, DC: U.S. General Accounting Office.
Eggleston, Carolyn Rebecca (1989). *Zebulon Brockway and the Elmira Reformatory: A Study of Correctional / Special Education.* Richmond, VA: Virginia Commonwealth University.
Ehrenkrantz Group (1984). *State of Maine, Department of Corrections—Legislation Impact Study.* New York: Ehrenkrantz Group.
Elchardus, Jean Marc et al. (1994). "The Problems of Therapeutic Interventions." *Revue Internationale Criminologie et de Police Technique,* 47:389–507.
Ellis, Stephen D. (1986). "*Hudson v. Palmer:* Prisons and the Fourth Amendment Behind the Constitutional Iron Curtain." *Rutgers Law Review,* 38:303–340.
Ellsworth, John (1985). "Treating Substance Abuse: A Good Approach Is to Combine Urinalysis, Education, and Referral." *Corrections Today,* 47:12–13.
Elrod, H. Preston, and Kevin I. Minor (1992). "Second Wave Evaluation of a Multi-Faceted Intervention for Juvenile Court Probationers." *International Journal of Offender Therapy and Comparative Criminology,* 36:247–262.
Emerick, Jeanette E. (1996). "Raising Morale Through Communication." *American Jails,* 10:53–60.
English, Kim, and Mary J. Mande (1991). *Community Corrections in Colorado: Why Do Some Clients Succeed and Others Fail?* Denver: Department of Public Safety, Colorado Division of Criminal Justice.
Erez, Edna (1988). "The Myth of the New Female Offender: Some Evidence from Attitudes Toward Law Justice." *Journal of Criminal Justice,* 16:499–509.
Erez, Edna, and Pamela Tontodonato (1990). "The Effect of Victim Participation in Sentencing on Sentence Outcome." *Criminology,* 28:451–474.
Erwin, Billie S. (1986). "Turning Up the Heat on Probationers in Georgia." *Federal Probation,* 50:17–24.
Erwin, Billie S., and Lawrence A. Bennett (1987). *New Dimensions in Probation: Georgia's Experience with Intensive Probation Supervision (IPS).* Washington, DC: U.S. Department of Justice, National Institute of Justice.
Ethridge, Philip A., and Stephen W. Liebowitz (1994). "The Attitudes of Sheriffs in Texas." *American Jails,* 8:55–60.
Etter, George W. (1996). "The Shell Game." *American Jails,* 10:73–74.
Etzioni, Amitai (1961). *A Comparative Analysis of Organizations.* New York: Free Press.

Ewing, Martin D. (1985). "Private Industry Opportunity." *Corrections Today,* 47:92–94.

Fabelo, Tony (1994). "Sentencing Reform in Texas: Can Criminal Justice Research Inform Public Policy?" *Crime and Delinquency,* 40:282–294.

Faith, Karlene (1987, November). "Media, Myths, and Masculinization: Images of Women in Prison." Unpublished paper presented at the American Society of Criminology meeting, Montreal, Canada.

Farbstein, Jay, and Richard Wener (1986). *Proceedings of the First Annual Symposium on New Generation Jails.* Boulder, CO: U.S. National Institute of Corrections, Jail Center.

Farmer, J. Forbes (1994). "Decentralized Management in Prison: A Comparative Case Study." *Journal of Offender Rehabilitation,* 20:117–130.

Farnworth, Margaret, and Raymond H.C. Teske, Jr. (1995). "Gender Differences in Felony Court Processing: Three Hypotheses of Disparity." *Women and Criminal Justice,* 6:23–44.

Farrington, David P. (1992). "Criminal Career Research: Lessons for Crime Prevention." *Studies on Crime and Crime Prevention,* 1:7–29.

Federal Bureau of Investigation (1996). *Uniform Crime Reports 1996.* Washington, DC: U.S. Department of Justice, Federal Bureau of Investigation.

Feeney, Renee (1995). "HIV/AIDS Infected Inmates Challenging DOC Policies." *Corrections Compendium,* 22:1–3.

Feinman, Clarice (1986). *Women in the Criminal Justice System* (2nd ed.). New York: Praeger.

Feld, Barry C. (1995). "Violent Youth and Public Policy: A Case Study of Juvenile Justice Law Reform." *Minnesota Law Review,* 79:965–1128.

Fenton, Norman (ed.). (1973). *Human Relations in Adult Corrections.* Springfield, IL: Charles C. Thomas.

Field, Joseph E. (1987). "Making Prisons Private: An Improper Delegation of a Government Power." *Hofstra Law Review,* 15:649–675.

Fields, Lea L. (1994). "Pretrial Diversion: A Solution to California's Drunk-Driving Problem." *Federal Probation,* 58:20–30.

Figueira-McDonough, Josefina (1985). "Gender Differences in Informal Processing: A Look at Charge Bargaining and Sentence Reduction in Washington, DC." *Journal of Research in Crime and Delinquency,* 22:101–133.

Finn, Peter (1984a). "Judicial Responses to Prison Crowding." *Judicature,* 67:318–326.

Finn, Peter (1984b). "Prison Crowding: The Response of Probation and Parole." *Crime and Delinquency,* 30:141–153.

Fischer, Daryl R., and Andy Thaker (1992). *Mandatory Sentencing Study.* Phoenix, AZ: Arizona Department of Corrections.

Fisher, Bonnie S., and John J. Sloan, III (1995). *Campus Crime: Legal, Social and Policy Perspectives.* Springfield, IL: Charles C. Thomas.

Fishman, Joseph F. (1934). *Sex in Prison.* New York: National Liberty Press.

Fitzpatrick, Vincent T., and Patrick M. Thomas (1993). "The Evolution of Fire Protection and Life Safety in Correctional Facilities." *American Jails,* 7:47–52.

Fletcher, Beverly R., Lynda Dixon Shaver, and Drema G. Moon (eds.). (1993). *Women Prisoners: A Forgotten Population.* Westport, CT: Greenwood Press.

Fletcher, Lawrence P. (1984). "Restitution in the Criminal Process: Procedures for Fixing the Offender's Liability." *Yale Law Journal,* 93:505–522.

Florida Advisory Council on Intergovernmental Relations (1993). *Privatization as an Option for Constructing and Operating Local Jails in Florida.* Tallahassee, FL: Florida Advisory Council on Intergovernmental Relations.

Florida Advisory Council on Intergovernmental Relations (1994). *Intergovernmental Impacts of the 1994 Juvenile Justice Reform Bill.* Tallahassee, FL: Florida Advisory Council on Intergovernmental Relations.

Florida Joint Legislative Management Committee (1995). *An Assessment of Vocational Education Needs in Florida's Women's Prisons.* Tallahassee, FL: Florida Joint Legislative Management Committee.

Florida Legislature Advisory Council (1993). *Intergovernmental Relations in Local Jail Finance.* Tallahassee, FL: Florida Legislature Advisory Council.

Flowers, Gerald T., Timothy S. Carr, and Barry R. Ruback (1991). *Special Alternative Incarceration Evaluation.* Atlanta, GA: Georgia Department of Corrections.

Flynn, Leonard E. (1986). "House Arrest: Florida's Alternative Eases Crowding and Tight Budgets." *Corrections Today,* 48:64–68.

Flynt, Charles, and Mickey Ellenbecker (1995). "The Certification Experience at Winona State University." *American Jails,* 9:57–58.

Fogel, David (1975). . . . *We Are the Living Proof. . . : The Justice Model for Corrections.* Cincinnati, OH: Anderson Publishing Company.

Fogel, David (1981). *Justice as Fairness: Perspectives on the Justice Model.* Cincinnati, OH: Anderson Publishing Company.

Ford, David A., and Mary Jean Regoli (1993). *The Indianapolis Domestic Violence Prosecution Experiment: Final Report.* Indianapolis: Indiana University, Department of Sociology.

Ford, Francis R. (1993). "Politics and Jails Part I." *American Jails,* 6:16–20.

Forer, Lois G. (1994). *A Rage to Punish: The Unintended Consequences of Mandatory Sentencing.* New York: W.W. Norton.

Forst, Martin (1995). *The New Juvenile Justice.* Chicago: Nelson-Hall.

Foster, Burk, Wilbert Rideau, and Ron Wikberg (eds.). (1991). *The Wall Is Strong: Corrections in Louisiana.* Lafayette: Center for Louisiana Studies, University of Southwestern Louisiana.

Fox, James G. (1989). "Critical Perspectives on Selective Incapacitation and the Prediction of Dangerousness." In Dean J. Champion (ed.), *The U.S. Sentencing Guidelines: Implications for Criminal Justice.* New York: Praeger.

Frazier, Charles E., and Donna M. Bishop (1990). "Jailing Juveniles in Florida: The Dynamics of Compliance with a Sluggish Federal Reform Initiative." *Crime and Delinquency,* 36:427–442.

Frazier, Mansfield B. (1995). *From Behind the Wall: Commentary on Crime, Punishment, Race and the Underclass by a Prison Inmate.* New York: Paragon House.

Freedman, Estelle B. (1981). *Their Sisters' Keepers: Women's Prison Reform in America, 1830–1930.* Ann Arbor: University of Michigan Press.

French, J. R. P., Jr., J. Israel, and D. Aos (1960). "An Experiment in Participation in a Norwegian Factory." *Human Relations,* 13:3–19.

French, J. R. P., Jr., and B. Raven (1959). *The Bases of Social Power.* Ann Arbor, MI: Institute for Social Research.

French, Laurence (1986). "Treatment Considerations for the Mentally Retarded Inmates." *Corrective and Social Psychiatry and Journal of Behavior Technology and Therapy,* 32:124–129.

Friday, Paul C., and David M. Petersen (1972). "Shock of Imprisonment: Comparative Analysis of Short-Term Incarceration as a Treatment Technique." Paper presented at the annual meeting of the American Society of Criminology, Caracas, VENEZ.

Fuller, John R., and William M. Norton (1993). "Juvenile Diversion: The Impact of Program Philosophy on Net Widening." *Journal of Crime and Justice,* 16:29–45.

Fuller, Lisa G. (1993). "Visitors to Women's Prisons in California: An Exploratory Study." *Federal Probation,* 57:41–47.

Fulton, Betsy (1995). "APPA's Vision: Welcome to the Land of Oz . . . Where Dreams Can Come True." *APPA Perspectives,* 19:6–12.

Fulton, Betsy, and Susan Stone (1993). "Achieving Public Safety Through the Provision of Intense Services: The Promise of a New ISP." *APPA Perspectives,* 17:43–45.

Gable, Ralph Kirkland (1986). "Application of Personal Telemonitoring to Current Problems in Corrections." *Journal of Criminal Justice,* 14:167–176.

Galaway, Burt (1988). "Restitution as Innovation or Unfulfilled Promise?" *Federal Probation,* 52:3–14.

Galvin, John J. et al. (1977). *Alternatives to Prosecution: Instead of Jail.* Washington, DC: U.S. Government Printing Office.

Garbarino, James, Jamis Wilson, and A.C. Garbarino (1986). "The Adolescent Runaway." In James Garbarino et al. (eds.), *Troubled Youths, Troubled Families.* Hawthorne, NY: Aldine Press.

Garcia, Gonzalo (1993). "Culture and Control: Understanding, Managing, and Controlling the Inmate Population in the Santa Ana City Jail." *American Jails,* 7:63–66.

Garrett, C. (1985). "Effects of Residential Treatment on Adjudicated Delinquents: A Meta-Analysis." *Journal of Research on Crime and Delinquency,* 22:287–308.

Garza, Pete, Jr. (1994). "Sunnyside City Jail: Big Problems for a Small Jail." *American Jails,* 8:71–72.

Gatz, Nick, and Chris Murray (1981). "An Administrative Overview of Halfway Houses." *Corrections Today,* 43:52–54.

Gaudin, J.M., Jr. (1993). "Effective Intervention with Neglectful Families." *Criminal Justice and Behavior,* 20:66–89.

Gauger, Glenn, and Curtiss Pulitzer (1991). "Built to Last: Construction and Design Issue." *Corrections Today,* 53:90.

Gendreau, Paul (1993). *Does "Punishing Smarter" Work? An Assessment of the New Generation of Alternative Sanctions.* New Brunswick, CAN: Corrections Research Ministry Secretariat.

Georgia Parole Review (1990). "Georgia Rehabilitation Program Helps Disabled Parolees." *Corrections Today,* 52:174–176.

Gewerth, Kenneth E., and Clifford K. Dorne (1991). "Imposing the Death Penalty on Juvenile Murderers: A Constitutional Assessment." *Judicature,* 75:6–15.

Gilbert, Michael J. (1986). "The Challenge of Professionalism in Correctional Training." In B. I. Wolford and P. Lawrenz (eds.), *Issues in Correctional Training and Casework.* College Park, MD: American Correctional Association.

Gilliard, Darrell K., and Allen J. Beck (1996). *Prison and Jail Inmates, 1995.* Washington, DC: U.S. Department of Justice.

Glade, George H. (1996). "*Washington v. Harper:* An Examination of King County Correctional Facility's Decision to Not Adopt a Compelled Medications Policy." *American Jails,* 10:51–55.

Glaser, Daniel (1987). "Classification for Risk." In Don M. Gottfredson and Michael Tonry (eds.), *Prediction and Classification: Criminal Justice Decision Making.* Chicago: University of Chicago Press.

Glaser, Daniel (1994). "What Works, and Why It Is Important: A Response to Logan and Gaes." *Justice Quarterly,* 11:711–723.

Glick, Barry, and Arnold P. Goldstein (eds.). (1995). *Managing Delinquency: Programs that Work.* Laurel, MD: American Correctional Association.

Goetting, A., and R. M. Howsen (1986). "Correlates of Prisoner Misconduct." *Journal of Quantitative Criminology,* 2:49–67.

Goffman, Erving (1961). *Asylums.* Garden City, NY: Anchor.

Golash, Deirdre (1992). "Race, Fairness and Jury Selection." *Behavioral Sciences and the Law,* 10:155–177.

Goldkamp, John S. (1987). "Prediction in Criminal Justice Policy Development." In Don M. Gottfredson and Michael Tonry (eds.), *Prediction and Classification: Criminal Justice Decision Making.* Chicago: University of Chicago Press.

Goodman, Rebecca (1992). *Pretrial Release Study.* Minneapolis: Hennepin County Bureau of Community Corrections, Planning and Evaluation.

Goodstein, Lynne, and John Hepburn (1985). *Determinate Sentencing and Imprisonment: A Failure of Reform.* Cincinnati, OH: Anderson Publishing Company.

Goodstein, Lynne, and Doris Layton MacKenzie (eds.). (1989). *The American Prison: Issues in Research and Policy.* New York: Plenum Press.

Gordon, Margaret A., and Daniel Glaser (1991). "The Use and Effects of Financial Penalties in Municipal Courts." *Criminology,* 29:651–676.

Gottfredson, Don M., and Michael Tonry (1987). *Prediction and Classification: Criminal Justice Decision Making.* Chicago: University of Chicago Press.

Gottfredson, Michael R., and Don M. Gottfredson (1988). *Decision Making in Criminal Justice: The Rational Exercise of Discretion* (2nd ed). New York: Plenum Press.
Gottfredson, Stephen D. (1984). "Institutional Responses to Prison Overcrowding." *New York University Review of Law and Social Change* 12:259–273.
Gottfredson, Stephen D. (1987). "Prediction: An Overview of Selected Methodological Issues." In Don M. Gottfredson and Michael Tonry (eds.), *Prediction and Classification: Criminal Justice Decision Making.* Chicago: University of Chicago Press.
Gottfredson, Stephen D., and Don M. Gottfredson (1990). *Classification, Prediction, and Criminal Justice Policy: Final Report to the National Institute of Justice.* Washington, DC: U.S. National Institute of Justice.
Gottfredson, Stephen D., and Don M. Gottfredson (1992). *Incapacitation Strategies and the Criminal Career.* Sacramento, CA: Law Enforcement Information Center, California Division of Law Enforcement.
Gottlieb, Barbara, and Phillip Rosen (1984). *Report to the Legislature.* Washington, DC: Toborg Associates.
Gowen, Darren (1996). "Pathological Gambling: An Obscurity in Community Corrections?" *Federal Probation* 60:3–7.
Grapendaal, M. (1990). "The Inmate Subculture of Dutch Prisons." *British Journal of Criminology,* 30:341–357.
Gray, Doug, and Greg Wren (1992). *Pre-Release at South Idaho Correctional Institute: "Something Works."* Boise, ID: South Idaho Correctional Institution.
Greenfeld, Lawrence A. (1988). *Prisoners in 1987.* Washington, DC: U.S. Department of Justice.
Greenfeld, Lawrence A. (1996). *Child Victimizers: Violent Offenders and Their Victims.* Washington, DC: U.S. Department of Justice.
Greenwood, Peter W. (1986). "Promising Approaches for the Rehabilitation and Prevention of Chronic Juvenile Offenders." In Peter W. Greenwood (ed.), *Intervention Strategies for Chronic Juvenile Offenders: Some New Perspectives.* New York: Greenwood Press.
Grieser, Robert C. (1989). "Do Correctional Industries Adversely Impact the Private Sector?" *Federal Probation,* 53:18–24.
Griffiths, Curt Taylor, and Margit Nance (1980). *The Female Offender: Selected Papers from an International Symposium.* Vancouver, BC: Simon Fraser University.
Griffiths, Curt Taylor, and Allan L. Patenaude (1990). "The Use of Community Service Orders and Restitution in the Canadian North." In Burt Galaway and Joe Hudson (eds.), *Criminal Justice, Restitution and Reconciliation.* Monsey, NY: Criminal Justice Press.
Griset, Pamela L. (1991). *Determinate Sentencing: The Promise and the Reality of Retributive Justice.* Albany: State University of New York Press.
Griset, Pamela L. (1995). "Determinate Sentencing and Agenda Building: A Case Study of the Failure of a Reform." *Journal of Criminal Justice,* 23:349–362.
Gross, K. Hawkeye (1995). *Tales from the Joint.* Boulder, CO: Paladin Press.
Gross, Michael (1992). *Electronic Monitoring Systems (EMS) in the Pre-Trial Environment: Constitutionality, Cost-Effectiveness, and Other Factors.* Miami, FL: Metro-Dade Department of Justice Assistance.
Gurian, Michael (1994). "Gender and Sexual Contact Trainings in the Criminal Justice Workplace." *American Jails,* 8:29–32.
Gursky, Dan (1988). "The Aftermath of An Execution—An Interview with Jennie Lancaster." *Corrections Today,* 50:76–84.
Guy, Edward et al. (1985). "Mental Health Status of Prisoners in an Urban Jail." *Criminal Justice and Behavior,* 12:29–53.
Guyon, Lois A., and Helen Fay Green (1990). "Calaboose: Small Town Lockup." *Federal Probation,* 54:58–62.
Haas, Kenneth C. (1994). "The Triumph of Vengeance Over Retribution: The United States Supreme Court and the Death Penalty." *Crime, Law and Social Change,* 21:127–154.

Haddock, Billy D., and Dan Richard Beto (1988). "Assessment of Drug and Alcohol Problems: A Probation Model." *Federal Probation,* 52:10–16.

Harding, Christopher, et al. (1985). *Imprisonment in England and Wales: A Concise History.* Dover, NH: Croom Helm.

Haesler, Walter T. (1992). "The Released Prisoner and His Difficulties To Be Accepted Again as a 'Normal' Citizen." *Euro-Criminology,* 4:61–68.

Haglund, Laurie E. (1993). "The National Crime Information Center (NCIC). Missing and Unidentified Persons System Revisited." *Journal of Forensic Sciences,* 38:365–378.

Hahn, Paul H. (1995). "A Standardized Curriculum for Correctional Officers: History and Rationale." *American Jails,* 9:45–51.

Halford, Sally Chandler (1984). "Kansas Co-Correctional Concept." *Corrections Today,* 46:44–54.

Hall, Andy (1987). *Systemwide Strategies to Alleviate Jail Overcrowding.* Washington, DC: National Institute of Justice.

Hall, Julia (1992, November). "Parole Agents: Casemakers for Elderly Clients: A New Role." Unpublished paper presented at the annual meeting of the American Society of Criminology, New Orleans, LA.

Hammett, Theodore M. (1992, November). "HIV/AIDS in Correctional Institutions: Legal Issues." Unpublished paper presented at the annual meetings of the American Society of Criminology. New Orleans, LA.

Hansen, Evan (1995). "Jail Supervision in the '90s." *American Jails,* 9:37–41.

Hanson, R. Karl, Heather Scott, and Richard A. Steffy (1995). "A Comparison of Child Molesters and Nonsexual Criminals: Risk Predictors and Long-Term Recidivism." *Journal of Research in Crime and Delinquency,* 32:325–337.

Hanson, R. Karl, Richard A. Steffy, and Rene Gauthier (1993). "Long-Term Recidivism of Child Molesters." *Journal of Consulting and Clinical Psychology,* 61:646–652.

Hanson, Roger A., and Henry W.K. Daley (1995). *Challenging the Conditions of Prisons and Jails: A Report on Section 1983 Litigation.* Washington, DC: U.S. Bureau of Justice Statistics.

Harer, Miles D. (1994). *Recidivism Among Federal Prison Releasees in 1987.* Washington, DC: U.S. Federal Bureau of Prisons, Office of Research and Evaluation.

Harlow, Caroline Wolf (1993). *HIV in U.S. Prisons and Jails.* Washington, DC: U.S. Bureau of Justice Statistics.

Harlow, Robert E., John M. Darley, and Paul H. Robinson (1995). "The Severity of Intermediate Penal Sanctions: A Psychophysical Scaling Approach for Obtaining Community Perceptions." *Journal of Quantitative Criminology,* 11:71–95.

Harrington, Christine B., and Sally Engle Merry (1988). "Ideological Production: The Making of Community Mediation." *Law and Society Review,* 22:709–735.

Harris, M. Kay (1984). "Rethinking Probation in the Context of the Justice Model." In P. McAnany, D. Thomson, and D. Fogel (eds.), *Probation and Justice: Reconsideration of a Mission.* Cambridge, MA: Oelgeschlager, Gunn, and Hain.

Harris, M. Kay (1992, November). "Reducing Jail Overcrowding: What Can Be Done after Fifteen Years with a Court-Ordered Population Cap?" Unpublished paper presented at the annual meeting of the American Society of Criminology, New Orleans, LA.

Harris, M. Kay, Peter R. Jones, and Gail S. Funke (1990). *The Kansas Community Corrections Act: An Assessment of a Public Policy Initiative.* Philadelphia: Temple University Press.

Harris, M. Kay et al. (1991). "Judicial Intervention in Local Jails II." *Prison Journal* 71:1–92.

Harris, Patricia M. et al. (1993). "A Wilderness Challenge Program as Correctional Treatment." *Journal of Offender Rehabilitation,* 19:149–164.

Harris-George, Becky, Herbert H. Jarrett, and Richard T. Shigley (1994). "State Jails: Texas' Answer to Overcrowding." *American Jails,* 8:17–20.

Haskell, Martin R., and Lewis Yablonsky (1974). *Criminology: Crime and Criminality.* Chicago: Rand-McNally.

Hawk, Kathleen et al. (1993). "Volunteers: Corrections' Unsung Heroes." *Corrections Today,* 55:63–139.
Hawkes, Mary Ann (1985). "Rhode Island: A Case Study in Compliance." *Corrections Today,* 47:167–183.
Hawkins, Darnell F. (1984). "State vs. County: Prison Policy and Conflicts of Interest in North Carolina." In *Criminal Justice History: An International Annual* (Vol. IV). Westport, CT: Meckler.
Haycock, Joel (1991). "Capital Crimes: Suicides in Jail." *Death Studies,* 15:417–433.
Hayes, Lindsay M. (1983). "And Darkness Closes In . . . A National Study of Jail Suicides." *Criminal Justice and Behavior,* 10:461–484.
Hayes, Lindsay M., and Joseph R. Rowan (1988). *National Study of Jail Suicides.* Alexandria, VA: National Center on Institutions and Alternatives.
Heaney, Gerald W. (1991). "The Reality of Guidelines Sentencing: No End to Disparity." *American Criminal Law Review,* 28:161–232.
Heaney, Gerald W. et al. (1992). "Federal Sentencing Guidelines Symposium." *American Criminal Law Review,* 29:771–932.
Heide, Kathleen M. (1992). *Why Kids Kill Parents: Child Abuse and Adolescent Homicide.* Columbus, OH: Ohio State University Press.
Heim, Ted (1993). "The Washburn Experience: The University Role in Training Jail Personnel." *American Jails,* 7:18–20.
Henderson, Joel H., and David R. Simon (1994). *Crimes of the Criminal Justice System.* Cincinnati, OH: Anderson Publishing Company.
Hengstler, Gary A. et al. (1994). "Troubled Justice." *ABA Journal,* 80:44–61.
Hepburn, John R. et al. (1992). *The Maricopa County Demand Reduction Program: An Evaluation Report.* Phoenix, AZ: Maricopa County Drug Abuse and Addiction Program.
Hess, Albert G., and Priscilla F. Clement (eds.). (1993). *History of Juvenile Delinquency: A Collection of Essays on Crime Committed by Young Offenders* (Vol. 2). Aalen, GER: Scientia Verlag.
Hewitt, Bill (1996). "Mothers Behind Bars." *People,* December 11, 1996:95–102.
Hewitt, John D. (1975). *A Multivariate Analysis of Legal and Extralegal Factors in Judicial Sentencing Disparity.* Ann Arbor, MI: Xerox University Microfilms, Inc.
Hewitt, John D., Eric D. Poole, and Robert M. Regoli (1984). "Self-Reported and Observed Rule-Breaking in Prison: A Look at Disciplinary Response." *Justice Quarterly,* 1:437–447.
Hicks, Nancy (1990). "When the Warden is a Woman." *Corrections Compendium,* 15:1–7.
Higgins, Scott (1996). "Making Sure Tomorrow's Correctional Facilities Stand the Test of Time." *Corrections Today,* 58:8.
Hillsman, Sally T., Joyce L. Sichel, and Barry Mahoney (1984). *Fines in Sentencing: A Study of the Use of the Fine as a Criminal Sanction.* Washington, DC: National Institute of Justice, Vera Institute of Justice and Court Management.
Hirsch, Adam J. (1992). *The Rise of the Penitentiary: Prisons and Punishment in Early America.* New Haven, CT: Yale University Press.
Hoefle, Yvonne (1995). "National Recognition for a Small Jail Meeting Community Needs." *American Jails,* 9:65–72.
Hoffman, Peter B. (1983). "Screening for Risk: A Revised Salient Factor Score, SFS 81." *Journal of Criminal Justice,* 11:539–547.
Hoffman, Peter B. (1994). "Twenty Years of Operational Use of a Risk Prediction Instrument: The United States Parole Commission's Salient Factor Score." *Journal of Criminal Justice,* 22:477–494.
Hokanson, Shirley (1986). *The Woman Offender in Minnesota: Profile, Needs and Future Directions.* St. Paul, MN: Minnesota Department of Corrections.
Holgate, Alina M., and Ian J. Clegg (1991). "The Path to Probation Officer Burnout: New Dogs, Old Tricks." *Journal of Criminal Justice,* 19:325–337.
Holman, John E., and James F. Quinn (1989). "Latent Functions of Therapeutic and Punitive Approaches to Community Corrections: A Theoretical Comparison."

Unpublished paper presented at the annual meetings of the American Society of Criminology, Reno, NV (November).
Holman, John E., and James F. Quinn (1990). "Offender Mental Health Status and Electronic Monitoring." *Journal of Offender Monitoring,* 3:1–6.
Holmes, Malcolm D. et al. (1993). "Judges' Ethnicity and Minority Sentencing: Evidence Concerning Hispanics." *Social Science Quarterly,* 74:496–506.
Holton, C. Lewis (1995). "Once Upon a Time Served: Therapeutic Application of Fairy Tales Within a Correctional Institution." *International Journal of Offender Therapy and Comparative Criminology,* 39:210–221.
Horn, Jim (1992). "Kentucky Officers Get Involved: Political Arena." *APPA Perspectives,* 16:27–28.
Houghtalin, Marilyn, and G. Larry Mays (1991). "Criminal Dispositions of New Mexico Juveniles Transferred to Adult Court." *Crime and Delinquency,* 37:393–407.
Houston, James (1994). *Correctional Management: Functions, Skills and Systems.* Chicago, IL: Nelson-Hall.
Huckabee, Robert G. (1992). "Stress in Corrections: An Overview of the Issues." *Journal of Criminal Justice,* 20:479–486.
Hudson, Joe, and Burt Galaway (1989). "Financial Restitution: Toward an Evaluable Program Model." *Canadian Journal of Criminology,* 31:1–18.
Hughes, Robert (1987). *The Fatal Shore.* New York: Alfred Knopf.
Hunt, Geoffrey et al. (1993). "Changes in Prison Culture: Prison Gangs and the Case of the 'Pepsi Generation.'" *Social Problems,* 40:389–409.
Hunter, Robert J. (1993). *Shock Incarceration: An Impact Assessment Measuring Attitudinal Change in the Harris County Texas Courts Regimented Probation Program—CRIPP.* Ann Arbor, MI: University Microfilms International.
Hunter, Susan M. (1984). "Issues and Challenges Facing Women's Prisons in the 1980s." *The Prison Journal,* 64:129–135.
Huskey, Bobbie L. (1984). "Community Corrections Acts." *Corrections Today,* 46:45.
Huskey, Bobbie L., and Arthur J. Lurigio (1992). "An Examination of Privately Operated Intermediate Sanctions Within the U.S." *Corrections Compendium,* 17:1, 3–8.
Hunzeker, Donna, and Cindy Conger (eds). (1985). *Inmate Lawsuits: A Report on Inmate Lawsuits Against State and Federal Correctional Systems Resulting in Monetary Damages and Settlements.* Lincoln, NE: Contact Center, Inc.
Hutchinson, Virginia (1993). "NIC Update." *Corrections Today,* 55:132–133.
Hutton, Heidi E., and Michael H. Miner (1995). "The Validation of the Megargee-Bohn Typology in African American and Caucasian Forensic Psychiatry Patients." *Criminal Justice and Behavior,* 22:233–245.
Illinois Department of Corrections (1988). *Female Classification, Report 5, Assessment Instrument.* Springfield, IL: Illinois Department of Corrections.
Illinois Office of the Governor (1988). *Mentally Retarded and Mentally Ill Offender Task Force Report.* Springfield, IL: Illinois Office of the Governor.
Immarigeon, Russ (1985a). "Private Prisons, Private Programs, and Their Implications for Reducing Reliance on Imprisonment in the United States." *Prison Journal,* 65:60–74.
Immarigeon, Russ (1985b). *Probation at the Crossroads: Innovative Programs in Massachusetts.* Boston: Massachusetts Council for Public Justice.
Immarigeon, Russ (1986). "Community Service Sentences Pose Problems, Show Potential." *Journal of the National Prison Project,* 10:13–15.
Immarigeon, Russ (1987a). "Privatizing Adult Imprisonment in the U.S.: A Bibliography." *Criminal Justice Abstracts,* March:123–139.
Immarigeon, Russ (1987b). "Few Diversion Programs are Offered Female Offenders." *Journal of the National Prison Project,* 12:9–11.
Immarigeon, Russ, and Meda Chesney-Lind (1992). *Women's Prisons: Overcrowded and Overused.* San Francisco: National Council on Crime and Delinquency.
Inch, Heather, Paul Rowlands, and Ahmed Soliman (1995). "Deliberate Self-Harm in a Young Offenders' Institution." *Journal of Forensic Psychiatry,* 6:161–171.

Inciardi, James A. (1993). "Drug-Involved Offenders." *Prison Journal,* 73:253–422.

Ingley, Stephen J. (1993). "Newly Established AJA Resolutions." *American Jails,* 7:7.

Institute for Rational Public Policy (1991). *Arizona Criminal Code and Corrections Study: Final Report to the Legislative Council.* Phoenix, AZ: Institute for Rational Public Policy.

Iowa Equality in the Courts Task Force (1993). *Final Report of the Equality in the Courts Task Force.* Des Moines, IA: The Supreme Court of Iowa.

Irwin, John (1970). *The Felon.* Berkeley: University of California Press.

Irwin, John (1985). *The Jail: Managing the Underclass in American Society.* Berkeley: University of California Press.

Irwin, John, and Donald R. Cressey (1962). "Thieves, Convicts, and the Inmate Culture." *Social Problems,* 10:142–155.

Jacobs, James B. (1980). "The Prisoners' Rights Movement and Its Impact, 1960–1980." In N. Morris and Michael Tonry, *Crime and Justice: An Annual Review of Research.* Chicago: University of Chicago Press.

Jacobs, Susan (1995). "AIDS in Correctional Facilities: Current Status of Legal Issues Critical to Policy Development." *Journal of Criminal Justice,* 23:209–221.

Jankowski, Louis (1991). *Probation and Parole 1990.* Washington, DC: U.S. Department of Justice, Bureau of Justice Statistics.

Johnson, Elmer H. et al. (1990). "Innovations in Corrections." *Journal of Contemporary Criminal Justice,* 6:113–200.

Johnson, Herbert A., and Nancy Travis Wolfe (1996). *Crime and Privilege: Toward a New Criminology.* Englewood Cliffs, NJ: Prentice Hall.

Johnson, Jan (1984). *The Context for Crisis: Background Report on the Kansas Corrections System.* Topeka: Division of the Budget, Kansas Department of Administration.

Johnson, Judith, Keith McKeown, and Roberta James (1984). *Removing the Chronically Mentally Ill from Jail: Case Studies of Collaboration Between Local Criminal Justice and Mental Health Systems.* Washington, DC: National Coalition for Jail Reform.

Johnson, Robert (1996). *Hard Time: Understanding the Prison* (2nd ed.). Belmont, CA: Brooks/Cole Publishing Company.

Johnson, Wesley W., and Mark Jones (1994). "The Increased Felonization of Probation and Its Impact on the Function of Probation: A Descriptive Look at County Level Data from the 1980s and 1990s." *APPA Perspectives,* 18:42–46.

Johnson, Wesley W. et al. (1994). "Goals of Community Corrections: An Analysis of State Legal Codes." *American Journal of Crime and Justice,* 18:79–93.

Johnston, Norman (1973). *The Human Cage: A Brief History of Prison Architecture.* New York: Walker and Company.

Jolin, Annette, and B. Stipak (1992). "Drug Treatment and Electronically Monitored Home Confinement: An Evaluation of a Community-Based Sentencing Option." *Crime and Delinquency,* 38:158–170.

Jones, Mark, and Steven Cuvelier (1992, November). "Are Boot Camp Graduates Better Probation Risks?" Unpublished paper presented at the annual meeting of the American Society of Criminology, Baltimore, MD.

Jones, Mark, and Rolando V. del Carmen (1992). "When Do Probation and Parole Officers Enjoy the Same Immunity as Judges?" *Federal Probation,* 56:36–41.

Jones, Michael A., and David W. Roush (1995). "Developing the NJDA Care Giver Curriculum." *Journal for Juvenile Justice and Detention Services,* 10:64–72.

Jones, Peter B. (1990). "Community Corrections in Kansas: Extending Community-Based Corrections or Widening the Net?" *Journal of Research in Crime and Delinquency,* 27:79–101.

Joo, Hee Jong (1993). *Parole Release and Recidivism: Comparative Three-Year Survival Analysis of Four Successive Release Cohorts of Property Offenders.* Ann Arbor, MI: University Microfilms International.

Judiscak, Daniel (1995). "Why are the Mentally Ill in Jail?" *American Jails,* 9:9–15.

Jurik, Nancy C. (1983). "The Economics of Female Recidivism: A Study of TARP Women Ex-Offenders." *Criminology,* 21:603–622.

Jurik, Nancy C. (1985). "An Officer and a Lady: Organizational Barriers to Women Working as Correctional Officers in Men's Prisons." *Social Problems,* 32:375–388.

Jurik, Nancy C., and Michael C. Musheno (1986). "The Internal Crisis of Corrections: Professionalization and the Work Environment." *Justice Quarterly,* 3:457–480.

Justice Education Center (1993). *Court Disposition Study: Criminal Offenders in Connecticut's Courts in 1991: An Overview.* Hartford, CT: Justice Education Center.

Kaiser, Doug (1994). "Small Jails—How You Can Survive." *American Jails,* 8:77–87.

Kalinich, David B., and John Klofas (eds.). (1986). *Sneaking Inmates Down the Alley: Problems and Prospects in Jail Management.* Springfield, IL: Charles Thomas.

Kalstein, Michele H., Kirstie A. McCornock, and Seth A. Rosenthal (1992). "Calculating Injustice: The Fixation on Punishment as Crime Control." *Harvard Civil Liberties Law Review,* 27:575–655.

Kaminski, Marek M., and Don C. Gibbons (1994). "Prison Subculture in Poland." *Crime and Delinquency,* 40:105–119.

Kane, Thomas R. (1987, November). "Inmates' Perceptions of Justice in Prison Disciplinary Sanctions." Unpublished paper presented at the American Society of Criminology meeting, Montreal, CAN.

Kapsch, Stefan J., and Diane M. Luther (1985). *Punishment and Risk Management as an Oregon Sanctioning Model.* Portland, OR: Oregon Prison Overcrowding Project.

Kassenaum, Gene, and Susan Meyers Chandler (1994). "Polydrug Use and Self Control Among Men and Women in Prisons." *Journal of Drug Education,* 24:333–350.

Kaune, Michael Merlin (1993). *The Impact of Sentencing Reform on Sentencing Practices in Four States.* Ann Arbor, MI: University Microfilms International.

Kaup, David (1995). "Good and Bad Supervision in Corrections." *American Jails,* 9:21–29.

Keating, J. Michael, Jr., and Matthew A. Lopes, Jr. (1993). "Managing Jail Populations." *American Jails,* 6:35–40.

Keil, Thomas J., and Gennaro F. Vito (1990). "Race and the Death Penalty in Kentucky Murder Trials: An Analysis of Post-*Gregg* Outcomes." *Justice Quarterly,* 7:189–207.

Kellman, Pamela (1983). "County Jails: Who Are the Experts?" *Corrections Today,* 45:32–34.

Kelly, Michael (1996). "A Corrections Career Guide: Is a Career in Corrections for You?" *Corrections Today,* 58:134–136.

Kempf, K. L., and R. L. Austin (1986). "Older and More Recent Evidence on Racial Discrimination in Sentencing." *Journal of Quantitative Criminology,* 2:29–48.

Kennedy, Daniel B., and Robert J. Homant (1988). "Predicting Custodial Suicides: Problems with the Use of Profiles." *Justice Quarterly,* 5:441–456.

Kenney, Dennis Jay, Anthony Michael Pate, and Edwin Hamilton (1990). *Policing Handling of Juveniles: Developing Model Programs of Response.* Washington, DC: The Police Foundation.

Kerle, Kenneth E. (1985). "The American Woman County Jail Officer." In Imogene L. Moyer (ed.), *The Changing Roles of Women in the Criminal Justice System.* Prospect Heights, IL: Waveland Press.

Kerle, Kenneth E. (1995). "Jail Supervision—Past and Present." *American Jails,* 9:5.

Keve, Paul W. (1991). *Prison and the American Conscience: A History of U.S. Federal Corrections.* Carbondale, IL: Southern Illinois University Press.

Keve, Paul W. (1992). "The Costliest Punishment: A Corrections Administrator Contemplates the Death Penalty." *Federal Probation,* 56:11–25.

Key, Clarence, Jr. (1991). *The Desirability and Feasibility of Changing Iowa's Sentencing Practices: Comparison Study of Five States and Their Sentencing Structures.* Des Moines: Division of Criminal Justice and Juvenile Justice Planning, Iowa Department of Human Rights.

Kiekbusch, Richard G. (1985). "Management: One Jail's Experience." *Corrections Today,* 47:134–138.

Kiekbusch, Richard G. (1987). "Small Jails: Ignored and Misunderstood?" *Corrections Today,* 49:14–18.

Kim, Ijoong (1994). "An Econometric Study on the Deterrent Impact of Probation: Correcting Selection and Censoring Biases." *Evaluation Review,* 18:380–410.

L. Robert Kimball & Associates (1991). "Downtown Pittsburgh Site of New 2,400-Bed Allegheny County Jail." *Corrections Compendium,* 16:18.

Kimme, Dennis A. et al. (1986). *Small Jail Special Issues.* Champaign, IL: Kimme Planning and Architecture, U.S. National Institute of Corrections.

Kinkade, Patrick T., and Matthew C. Leone (1992). "The Privatization of Prisons: The Wardens' Views." *Federal Probation,* 56:58–65.

Kinkade, Patrick T., Matthew C. Leone, and Scott Semond (1995). "The Consequences of Jail Crowding." *Crime and Delinquency,* 41:150–161.

Klass, P.A. (1994). *The Costs of Crime to Victims.* Washington, DC: U.S. Department of Justice.

Klausner, Marian L. (1991). *Opening Doors for Change: Alternatives to Incarceration—A Report on Alternative Sentencing for Women.* Boston: Social Justice for Women.

Kline, Susan (1987). *Jail Inmates 1986.* Washington, DC: U.S. Department of Justice, Bureau of Justice Statistics.

Klofas, John M. (1993). "Managing Better with Better Partnerships Between the Jail and the University." *American Jails,* 7:25–28.

Klofas, John M. et al. (1991). "Juveniles and Jails." *American Jails,* 4:8.

Knepper, Paul (1989). "Selective Participation, Effectiveness, and Prison College Programs." *Journal of Offender Counseling, Services, and Rehabilitation,* 14:106–135.

Knight, Barbara B. (1992). "Women in Prison as Litigants: Prospects for Post-Prison Futures." *Women and Criminal Justice,* 4:91–116.

Knight, Barbara B., and Stephen T. Early, Jr. (1986). *Prisoner's Rights in America.* Chicago: Nelson-Hall Publishers.

Koppel, Herbert (1984). *Sentencing Practices in 13 States.* Washington, DC: U.S. Department of Justice, Bureau of Justice Statistics.

Koren, Lawrence (1995). "Jail Officers and Education: A Key to Professionalization." *American Jails,* 9:43–48.

Kratcoski, Peter C. (ed.). (1994). *Correctional Counseling and Treatment* (3rd ed.). Prospect Heights, IL: Waveland Press.

Krause, Jerrald D. (1992). "Policy, Prisons and Communities." *Crime and Delinquency,* 38:3–120.

Kraus, Melvyn B., and Edward P. Lazear (eds.). (1991). *Searching for Alternatives: Drug-Control Policy in the United States.* Stanford, CA: Hoover Institution Press.

Krause, Wesley, and Marilyn D. McShane (1994). "A Deinstitutionalization Retrospective: Relabeling the Status Offender." *Journal of Crime and Justice,* 17:45–67.

Krisberg, Barry (1975). *Crime and Privilege: Toward a New Criminology.* Englewood Cliffs, NJ: Prentice Hall.

Kruttschnitt, Candace (1981). "Social Status and Sentences of Female Offenders." *Law and Society Review,* 15:247–265.

Kuhns, Joseph B., III, and Kathleen M. Heide (1992). "AIDS-Related Issues Among Female Prostitutes and Female Arrestees." *International Journal of Offender Therapy and Comparative Criminology,* 36:231–245.

Kulis, Chester J. (1983). "Profit in the Private Presentence Report." *Federal Probation,* 47:11–16.

Kyle, Daniel G. (1995). *Corrections and Justice.* Baton Rouge, LA: Office of the Legislative Auditor.

Langan, Patrick A. (1994). "Between Prison and Probation: Intermediate Sanctions." *Science,* 262:791–793.

Langan, Patrick A., and Helen A. Graziadei (1995). *Felony Sentences in State Courts, 1992.* Washington, DC: U.S. Department of Justice.

Langan, Patrick A., and Caroline Wolf Harlow (1994). *Child Rape Victims, 1992.* Washington, DC: U.S. Department of Justice.

Langbein, John H. (1976). "The Historical Origins of the Sanction of Imprisonment for Serious Crime." *Journal of Legal Studies,* 5:35–60.

Langston, Denny C. (1988a, April). "The Economic Impact of Probation and Parole Supervision." Unpublished paper presented at the Academy of Criminal Justice Sciences meeting, San Francisco, CA. (April)

Langston, Denny C. (1988b). "Probation and Parole: No More Free Rides." *Corrections Today,* 50:92–93.

Langston, Denny C. et al. (1990). *Probation and Parole.* Laurel, MD: American Correctional Association.

Lanier, Mark M., and Cloud H. Miller, III (1995). "Attitudes and Practices of Federal Probation Officers Toward Pre-Plea/Trial Investigative Report Policy." *Crime and Delinquency,* 41:364–377.

Larsen, Nick (1988). "The Utility of Prison Violence: An A-Causal Approach to Prison Riots." *Criminal Justice Review,* 13:29–38.

Lattimer, H.D., J.C. Curran, and B.D. Tepper (1992). *Home Detention Electronic Monitoring Program.* Nevada City: Nevada County Probation Department Second Floor Courthouse.

Lattimore, Pamela K., Ann Dryden Witt, and Joanna R. Baker (1990). "Experimental Assessment of the Effect of Vocational Training on Youthful Property Offenders." *Evaluation Review,* 14:115–133.

Lauen, Roger J. (1984). "Community Corrections? Not in My Neighborhood!—Developing Legitimacy." *Corrections Today,* 46:117–130.

Law Enforcement Assistance Administration (1977). *Instead of Jail: Pre- and Post-Trial Alternatives to Jail Incarceration.* Washington, DC: Law Enforcement Administration.

Lawrence, Daniel W. (1992). "Constituency-Based Corrections: Oklahoma's Community Work Centers Benefit Both Inmates and the Public." *Corrections Today,* 54:130–134.

Lawrence, Richard A. (1985). "Jail Educational Programs: Helping Inmates Cope With Overcrowded Conditions." *Journal of Correctional Education,* 36:15–20.

Lawrence, Richard A. (1990, April). "Re-Examining Community Corrections Models." Unpublished paper presented at the annual meeting of the Academy of Criminal Justice Sciences, Denver, CO.

Lawrence, Richard A. (1991). "Reexamining Community Corrections Models." *Crime and Delinquency,* 37:449–464.

Lay, Donald P. (1986). "Exhaustion of Grievance Procedures for State Prisoners Under Section 1997e of the Civil Rights Act." *Iowa Law Review,* 71:935–974.

LeClair, Daniel P., and Susan Guarino-Ghezzi (1991). "Does Incapacitation Guarantee Public Safety? Lessons from Massachusetts' Furlough and Prerelease Programs." *Justice Quarterly,* 8:9–36.

Leeke, William D., and Heidi Mohn (1986). "Violent Offenders: AIMS and Unit Management Maintain Control." *Corrections Today,* 48:22–24.

Lees, Linda J., and Elaine T. DeCostanzo (1994). *A Bibliography of Resources Concerning Female Offenders.* Atlanta, GA: Planning, Evaluation and Statistics, Georgia Department of Corrections.

LeFlore, Larry, and Mary Ann Holston (1989). "Perceived Importance of Parenting Behaviors as Reported by Inmate Mothers." *Journal of Offender Counseling Services and Rehabilitation,* 14:5–21.

Leger, Robert G. (1987). "Lesbianism Among Women Prisoners: Participants and Nonparticipants." *Criminal Justice and Behavior,* 14:448–467.

Leger, Robert G., and Harvey Gray Barnes (1986). "Black Attitudes in Prison: A Sociological Analysis." *Journal of Criminal Justice,* 14:105–122.

Lehman, Joseph D. (1993). "A Commissioner's Appreciation: Pennsylvania Volunteers Build Bridges Between Our Prisons and the Community." *Corrections Today,* 55:84–86.

Lieb, Roxanne, Lee Fish, and Todd Crosby (1994). *A Summary of State Trends in Juvenile Justice.* Olympia, WA: Washington State Institute for Public Policy, Evergreen State College.

Leiber, Michael J., and Tina L. Mawhorr (1995). "Evaluating the Use of Social Skills Training and Employment with Delinquent Youth." *Journal of Criminal Justice,* 23:127–141.

Leonardi, Thomas J., and David R. Frew (1991). "Applying Job Characteristics Theory to Adult Probation." *Criminal Justice Policy Review,* 5:17–28.

Levine, James P., Michael C. Musheno, and Dennis J. Palumbo (1986). *Criminal Justice in America: Law in Action.* New York: John Wiley & Sons.

Lewis, Jack (1986). "A New Perspective in Correctional Training." In B. I. Wolford and P. Lorenz (eds.), *Issues in Correctional Training and Casework.* College Park, MD: American Correctional Association.

Lewis, Mary R. (1977). *Children in Need of Supervision (CHINS): A New Concept in Alabama Law.* University, AL: University of Alabama.

Lewis, Mary R. (1980). *Alabama's Juvenile Status Offenders: A Pilot Study.* University, AL: University of Alabama.

Lieberg, Gregory J. (1995). "Supervisors: The Good, the Bad, and the Difference." *American Jails,* 9:32–34.

Lieberman, Jethro K., and James F. Henry (1986). "Lessons from the Alternative Dispute Resolution Movement." *University of Chicago Law Review,* 53:424–439.

Lilly, J. Robert (1992). "Review Essay: Selling Justice: Electronic Monitoring and the Security Industry." *Justice Quarterly,* 9:493–503.

Lilly, J. Robert, Richard A. Ball, and Jennifer Wright (1987). "Home Incarceration with Electronic Monitoring in Kenton County, Kentucky: An Evaluation." In Belinda McCarthy (ed.), *Intermediate Punishments.* Monsey, NY: Criminal Justice Press.

Lilly, J. Robert, and Paul Knepper (1993). "The Corrections-Commercial Complex." *Crime and Delinquency,* 39:150–166.

Lindner, Charles (1991). "The Refocused Probation Home Visit: A Subtle But Revolutionary Change." *Journal of Contemporary Criminal Justice,* 7:115–127.

Lindner, Charles (1992a). "The Probation Field Visit and Office Report in New York State: Yesterday, Today, and Tomorrow." *Criminal Justice Review,* 17:44–60.

Lindner, Charles (1992b). "Probation Officer Victimization: An Emerging Concern." *Journal of Criminal Justice,* 20:53–62.

Lindner, Charles (1992c). "The Refocused Probation Home Visit: A Subtle But Revolutionary Change." *Federal Probation,* 56:16–21.

Lindner, Charles, and Robert L. Bonn (1996). "Probation Officer Victimization and Fieldwork Practices: Results of a National Study." *Federal Probation,* 60:16–23.

Lindner, Charles, and Margaret R. Savarese (1984). "The Evolution of Probation: University Settlement and the Beginning of Statutory Probation in New York City." *Federal Probation,* 48:3–12.

Lloyd, Robin M. (1992). "Negotiating Child Sexual Abuse: The Interactional Character of Investigative Practices." *Social Problems,* 39:109–134.

Locke, Michelle (1996). "Davis Sentenced to Death in Klaas Murder." *Minot (N.D.) Daily News,* August 6, 1996:A1.

Lockwood, Dan (1989, November). "Prison Higher Education and Recidivism: A Review of the Literature." Unpublished paper presented at the annual meeting of the American Society of Criminology, Reno, NV.

Logan, Charles H. (1990). *Private Prisons: Cons and Pros.* New York: Oxford University Press.

Logan, Charles H., and Sharla P. Rausch (1985a). "Why Deinstitutionalizing Status Offenders Is Pointless." *Crime and Delinquency,* 31:501–517.

Logan, Charles H., and Sharla P. Rausch (1985b). "Punishment and Profit: The Emergence of Private Enterprise Prisons." *Justice Quarterly,* 2:303–318.

Logan, Gloria (1992). "In Topeka: Family Ties Take Top Priority in Women's Visiting Program." *Corrections Today,* 54:160–161.

Lohr, Sharon L., and Joanna Liu (1994). "A Comparison of Weighted and Unweighted Analyses in the National Crime Victimization Survey." *Journal of Quantitative Criminology,* 10:343–360.

Lombardi, John H., and Donna M. Lombardi (1986). "Objective Parole Criteria: More Harm than Good?" *Corrections Today,* 48:86–87.

Lotke, Eric (1996). "Sex Offenders: Does Treatment Work?" *Corrections Compendium,* 21:1–3.

Love, Bill (1993). "Volunteers Make a Big Difference Inside a Maximum Security Prison." *Corrections Today,* 55:76–78.

Lucas, Wayne L. (1987). "Staff Perceptions of Volunteers in a Correctional Program." *Journal of Crime and Justice,* 10:63–78.

Lucas, Weldon G. (1996). "Out-of-State Contract Prisoners: A Success Story." *American Jails,* 10:9–14.

Luciani, Fred et al. (1994). "Enhancing Community Corrections." *Forum on Corrections Research,* 6:3–47.

Lupton, Gary L. (1996). "Identifying and Referring Inmates with Mental Disorders: A Guide for Correctional Staff." *American Jails,* 10:49–52.

Lurigio, Arthur J., Gad J. Bensinger, and Anna T. Laszlo (eds.). (1990). *AIDS and Community Corrections: The Development of Effective Policies.* Chicago: Loyola University.

Maahs, Jeffrey R., and Rolando V. del Carmen (1996). "Curtailing Frivolous Section 1983 Inmate Litigation: Laws, Practices, and Proposals." *Federal Probation,* 59:53–61.

MacKenzie, Doris Layton, and DeAnna Bellew Ballow (1989). *Shock Incarceration Programs in State Correctional Jurisdictions—An Update.* Washington, DC: U.S. Department of Justice, Office of Justice Programs.

MacKenzie, Doris Layton, and Claire Souryal (1994). *Researchers Evaluate Eight Shock Incarceration Programs.* Washington, DC: National Institute of Justice.

MacKenzie, Doris Layton et al. (1995). "Boot Camp Prisons and Recidivism in Eight States." *Criminology,* 33:327–357.

MacKenzie, Doris Layton, James W. Shaw, and Voncile B. Gowdy (1993). *An Evaluation of Shock Incarceration in Louisiana.* Washington, DC: U.S. Department of Justice, Office of Justice Programs.

MacKenzie, Doris Layton, James W. Shaw, and Claire Souryal (1992). "Characteristics Associated with Successful Adjustment to Supervision: A Comparison of Parolees, Probationers, Shock Participants, and Shock Dropouts." *Criminal Justice and Behavior,* 19:437–454.

Mactavish, Marie (1992). "Are You an STJ? Examining Correctional Managers' Leadership Styles." *Corrections Today,* 56:162–164.

Maguire, Kathleen, and Ann L. Pastore (1995). *Bureau of Justice Statistics Sourcebook of Criminal Justice Statistics—1994.* Albany: The Hindelang Criminal Justice Research Center, State University of New York at Albany.

Maguire, Kathleen, and Ann L. Pastore (1996). *Bureau of Justice Statistics Sourcebook of Criminal Justice Statistics—1995.* Albany: The Hindelang Criminal Justice Research Center, State University of New York at Albany.

Maguire, Kathleen, Ann L. Pastore, and Timothy J. Flanagan (eds.). (1993). *Sourcebook of Criminal Justice Statistics, 1992.* Washington, DC: U.S. Department of Justice, Bureau of Justice Statistics.

Mahaffey, Katherine J., and David K. Marcus (1995). "Correctional Officers' Attitudes toward AIDS." *Criminal Justice and Behavior,* 22:91–105.

Mahan, Sue (1986). "Co-Corrections: Doing Time Together." *Corrections Today,* 48:134–165.

Maher, Richard J., and Henry Dufour (1987). "Experimenting with Community Service: A Punitive Alternative to Imprisonment." *Federal Probation,* 51:22–28.

Maine Commission to Study the Future of Maine's Courts (1993). *New Dimensions for Justice.* Portland: Maine Commission to Study the Future of Maine's Courts.

Mainprize, Stephen (1992). "Electronic Monitoring in Corrections: Assessing Cost Effectiveness and the Potential for Widening the Net of Social Control." *Canadian Journal of Criminology,* 34:161–180.

Maitland, Angela S., and Richard D. Sluder (1996). "Victimization in Prisons: A Study of Factors Related to the General Well-Being of Youthful Inmates." *Federal Probation,* 60:24–31.

Maltz, Michael D. (1984). *Recidivism.* Orlando, FL: Academic Press.

Mande, Mary J. (1992). *Opinions on Sentencing in Alaska: Results of Five Focus Groups.* Anchorage, AL: Alaska Sentencing Commission.

Mann, Coramae Richey (1984). *Female Crime and Delinquency.* University, AL: University of Alabama Press.

Marcus, David K., Theodore M. Amen, and Roger Bibace (1992). "A Developmental Analysis of Prisoners' Conceptions of AIDS." *Criminal Justice and Behavior,* 19:174–188.

Marcus, David K., and Roger Bibace (1993). "A Developmental Analysis of Female Prisoners' Conceptions of AIDS." *Criminal Justice and Behavior,* 20:240–253.

Marenin, Otwin (1995). "The State of Plea Bargaining in Alaska." *Journal of Crime and Justice,* 18:167–197.

Maricopa County, Arizona, Correctional Health Services (1991). *An Evaluation of Health Care Costs in Jails.* Phoenix, AZ: Maricopa County, Arizona, Correctional Health Services.

Maring, Sheri, and Michael Eisenberg (1993). *Treatment Alternatives to Incarceration Program: Process and Preliminary Outcome Evaluation.* Austin, TX: Criminal Justice Policy Council.

Marlette, Marjorie (1988). "Furloughs for Lifers Successful." *Corrections Compendium,* 13:11–20.

Marlette, Marjorie (1990). "Furloughs Tightened—Success Rates High." *Corrections Compendium,* 15:6–21.

Marley, C.W. (1973). "Furlough Programs and Conjugal Visiting in Adult Correctional Institutions." *Federal Probation,* 37:19–25.

Markley, Greg (1994). "The Role of Mission Statements in Community Corrections." *APPA Perspectives,* 18:47–50.

Marra, Herbert A., David A. Shively, and Jerry Minaker (1989). "Community Mental Health and Prisons: A Model for Constitutionally Adequate Care in Correctional Mental Health." *Journal of Criminal Justice,* 17:501–506.

Marshall, W.L., A. Eccles, and H.E. Barbee (1993). "A Three-Tiered Approach to the Rehabilitation of Incarcerated Sex Offenders." *Behavioral Sciences and the Law,* 11:441–455.

Martin, Randy, and Sherwood Zimmerman (1992, November). "Aids Education in U.S. Prisons." Unpublished paper presented at the annual meeting of the American Society of Criminology, New Orleans, LA.

Martin, Teri K., and John L. Hutzler (1994). *Adult Sex Offenders in Oregon: Trends and Characteristics.* Aloha, OR: Oregon Criminal Justice Council.

Martinson, Robert (1974). "What Works? Questions and Answers about Prison Reform." *The Public Interest,* 35:22–54.

Martinson, Robert (1976). "California Research at the Crossroads." *Crime and Delinquency,* 22:181–189.

Martinson, Robert, and J. Wilks (1977). "Save Parole Supervision." *Federal Probation,* 41:23–27.

Marvell, Thomas B. (1994). "Is Further Prison Expansion Worth the Costs?" *Federal Probation,* 58:59–62.

Marvell, Thomas B. (1996). "Is Further Prison Expansion Worth the Costs?" *Corrections Compendium,* 21:1–4.

Marvell, Thomas B., and C.E. Moody, Jr. (1991). *Ultimate Impacts of Sentencing Reforms and Speedy Trial Laws.* Williamsburg, VA: Justec Institute.
Marvell, Thomas B., and C.E. Moody, Jr. (1994). "Prison Population Growth and Crime Reduction." *Journal of Quantitative Criminology,* 10:109–140.
Maryland Committee on Prison Overcrowding (1984). *Report.* Towson, MD: Maryland Criminal Justice Coordinating Council, Committee on Prison Overcrowding.
Maryland General Assembly Department of Fiscal Services (1994). *Maryland's Criminal Justice Process.* Annapolis, MD: Maryland General Assembly Department of Fiscal Services.
Maryland Governor's Office of Justice Administration (1995). *Report of the State/Local Criminal Justice/Mental Health Task Force.* Baltimore: Maryland Governor's Office of Justice Administration.
Maslach, Christina (1982a). "Understanding Burnout: Definitional Issues in Analyzing a Complex Phenomenon." In W. S. Paine (ed.), *Job Stress and Burnout.* Beverly Hills, CA: Sage.
Maslach, Christina (1982b). *Burnout: The Cost of Caring.* Englewood Cliffs, NJ: Prentice-Hall.
Mathews, Louise E. (1993). "Cook Chill: Centralized Food Service in Corrections." *American Jails,* 7:59–60.
Matthews, Ruth, Jane Kinder Matthews, and Kathleen Speltz (1989). *Female Sexual Offenders: An Exploratory Study.* Orwell, VT: Safer Society Press.
Mauer, Marc (1985). *The Lessons of Marion: The Failure of a Maximum Security Prison: A History and Analysis, with Voices of Prisoners.* Philadelphia, PA: American Friends Services Committee.
Mauer, Marc (1991). *Americans Behind Bars: A Comparison of International Rates of Incarceration.* Washington, DC: Sentencing Project.
Maxey, Joseph W. (1986). "Designing a Women's Prison." *Corrections Today,* 48:138–142.
Maxfield, Michael G., and Terry L. Baumer (1990). "Home Detention with Electronic Monitoring: Comparing Pretrial and Postconviction Programs." *Crime and Delinquency,* 36:521–536.
Mays, G. Larry, and Joel A. Thompson (1988). "Mayberry Revisited: The Characteristics and Operations of America's Small Jails." *Justice Quarterly,* 5:421–440.
McCarthy, Belinda R. (1987a). *Intermediate Punishments: Intensive Supervision, Home Confinement, and Electronic Surveillance.* Monsey, NY: Willow Tree Press.
McCarthy, Belinda R. (1987b). "Preventive Detention and Pretrial Custody in the Juvenile Court." *Journal of Criminal Justice,* 15:185–198.
McCarthy, Belinda R., and Bernard J. McCarthy (1997). *Community-Based Corrections* (3rd ed.). Monterey, CA: Brooks/Cole Publishing Company.
McClellan, Dorothy Spektorov (1994). "Disparity in the Discipline of Male and Female Inmates in Texas Prisons." *Women and Criminal Justice,* 5:71–97.
McConville, Mike, and Chester Mirsky (1995). "Guilty Plea Courts: A Social Disciplinary Model of Criminal Justice." *Social Problems,* 42:216–234.
McCorkle, Richard C. (1992). "Personal Precautions to Violence in Prison." *Criminal Justice and Behavior,* 19:160–173.
McCorkle, Richard C. (1995). "Correctional Boot Camps and Change in Attitude: Is All This Shouting Necessary?—A Research Note." *Justice Quarterly,* 12:365–375.
McCorkle, Richard C., Terance D. Miethe, and Kriss A. Drass (1995). "The Roots of Prison Violence: A Test of the Deprivation, Management, and 'Not-so-Total' Institution Models." *Crime and Delinquency,* 41:317–331.
McCoy, John (1981). *Concrete Mama: Prison Profiles from Walla Walla.* Columbia, MO: University of Missouri Press.
McCulloch, Duncan J. (1990). "Computer-Based Security Systems Save Money and Boost Safety." *Corrections Today,* 52:86–91.

McDonald, Douglas C. (1986). *Punishment Without Walls: Community Service Sanctions in New York City.* New Brunswick, NJ: Rutgers University Press.
McDonald, Douglas C., Judith Greene, and Charles Worzella (1992). *Day Fines in American Courts: The Staten Island and Milwaukee Experiments.* Washington, DC: U.S. Department of Justice, Office of Justice Programs.
McDonald, William F. (1985). *Plea Bargaining: Critical Issues and Common Practices.* Washington, DC: U.S. Department of Justice, National Institute of Justice.
McGee, Richard A., George Warner, and Nora Harlow (1985). *The Special Management Inmate.* Washington, DC: U.S. National Institute of Justice.
McGlone, Jerry, and James Mayer (1987). "Ohio Industries and Education: A Vital Tie." *Corrections Today,* 49:32–34.
McManus, Patrick D., and Lynn Zeller Barclay (1994). *Community Corrections Act: Technical Assistance Manual.* College Park, MD: American Correctional Association.
McShane, Marilyn (1985). *The Effect of the Detainer on Prison Overcrowding.* Huntsville, TX: Criminal Justice Center, Sam Houston State University, Research Bulletin No. 3.
McShane, Marilyn (1987). "Immigration Processing and the Alien Inmate: Constructing a Conflict Perspective." *Journal of Crime and Justice,* 10:171–194.
McShane, Marilyn, and Frank P. Williams, III (eds.). (1996). *Encyclopedia of American Prisons.* New York: Garland.
McWilliams, J. Michael et al. (1993). "Crisis in the Courts?" *Trial,* 29:18–50.
Meachum, Larry R. (1986). "House Arrest: The Oklahoma Experience." *Corrections Today,* 48:102–110.
Megargee, Edwin I., and Joyce L. Carbonell (1985). "Predicting Prison Adjustment with MMPI Correctional Scales." *Journal of Consulting and Clinical Psychology,* 53: 874–883.
Messing, Howard (1991). "AIDS in Jail." *Northern Illinois University Law Review,* 11:297–317.
Metchik, Eric (1992a). "Judicial Views of Parole Decision Processes: A Social Science Perspective." *Journal of Offender Rehabilitation,* 18:135–157.
Metchik, Eric (1992b, November). "Legal Views of Parole Decision Making: A Social Science Perspective." Unpublished paper presented at the annual meeting of the American Society of Criminology, New Orleans, LA.
Michigan Council on Crime and Delinquency (1993). *Trends in the Michigan Criminal Justice System.* Lansing, MI: Michigan Council on Crime and Delinquency.
Middendorf, Kathi, and James Luginbuhl (1995). "The Value of Nondirective *Voir Dire* Style in Jury Selection." *Criminal Justice and Behavior,* 22:129–151.
Miller, J. Mitchell, and Jeffrey P. Rush (eds.). (1996). *Gangs: A Criminal Justice Approach.* Cincinnati, OH: Anderson Publishing Company.
Miller, Marsha L., and Bruce Hobler (1996). "Delaware's Life Skills Program Reduces Inmate Recidivism." *Corrections Today,* 58:114–143.
Miller, Robert D., and Jeffrey L. Metzner (1994). "Psychiatric Stigmas in Correctional Facilities." *Bulletin of the American Academy of Psychiatry and the Law,* 22:621–628.
Miller, Tekla Dennison (1996). *The Warden Wore Pink.* Brunswick, ME: Biddle Publishing Company.
Milling, L. (1978). *Home Furlough Functions and Characteristics.* Hartford: Connecticut Department of Corrections.
Mills, Darrell K. (1990). "Career Issues for Probation Officers." *Federal Probation,* 54:3–7.
Milner, Joel S. (1992). "Sexual Child Abuse." *Criminal Justice and Behavior,* 19:1–792.
Milner, Joel S., and Kevin R. Robertson (1990). "Comparison of Physical Child Abusers, Intrafamilial Sexual Child Abusers, and Child Neglecters." *Journal of Interpersonal Violence,* 5:37–48.
Milovanovic, Dragan (1988). "Jailhouse Lawyers and Jailhouse Lawyering." *International Journal of the Sociology of Law,* 16:455–475.

Milovanovic, Dragan, and Jim Thomas (1989). "Overcoming the Absurd: Prisoner Litigation as Primitive Rebellion." *Social Problems,* 36:48–60.
Minnesota Criminal Justice Statistical Analysis Center (1989). *Violent and Chronic Juvenile Crime.* St. Paul: Minnesota Criminal Justice Statistical Analysis Center.
Minnesota Department of Corrections (1984). *Work / Study Release Report to the Commissioner of Corrections.* St. Paul, MN: Work/Study Release Committee of the Advisory Task Force on the Woman Offender in Corrections.
Minnesota Probation Standards Task Force (1993). *Minnesota Probation: A System in Crisis.* St. Paul, MN: Minnesota Probation Standards Task Force.
Minnesota Program Evaluation Division Office of the Legislative Auditor (1994). *Sex Offender Treatment Programs.* St. Paul, MN: Minnesota Program Evaluation Division Office of the Legislative Auditor.
Mitchell, John J., Jr., and Sharon A. Williams (1986). "SOS: Reducing Juvenile Recidivism." *Corrections Today,* 48:70–71.
Minor, Kevin I., and Preston Elrod (1994). "The Effects of a Probation Intervention on Juvenile Offenders' Self-Concepts, Loci of Control, and Perceptions of Juvenile Justice." *Youth and Society,* 25:499–511.
Minor-Harper, Stephanie, and Christopher A. Innes (1987). *Time Served in Prison and on Parole (1984).* Washington, DC: Bureau of Justice Statistics.
Monahan, John (1984). "The Prediction of Violent Behavior: Toward a Second Generation of Theory and Policy." *American Journal of Psychiatry,* 141:10–15.
Monday Highlights (1993). "Nation's Oldest Jail Closes After 181 Years of Service." *Corrections Compendium,* 18:18.
Montgomery, Imogene M. et al. (1994). *What Works: Promising Interventions in Juvenile Justice—Program Report.* Washington, DC: U.S. Office of Juvenile Justice and Delinquency Prevention.
Moore, Margaret A. (1993). "Corrections Volunteers Deserve Appreciation for a Job Well Done." *Corrections Today,* 55:8.
Moracco, John C. (1985). "Stress: How Corrections Personnel Can Anticipate, Manage, and Reduce Stress on the Job." *Corrections Today,* 47:22–26.
Morash, Merry, Robin N. Haarr, and Lila Rucker (1994). "A Comparison of Programming for Women and Men in U.S. Prisons in the 1980s." *Crime and Delinquency,* 40:197–221.
Morris, Allison, and Chris Wilkinson (1995). "Responding to Female Prisoners' Needs." *Prison Journal,* 75:295–305.
Morris, Norval (1974). *The Future of Imprisonment.* Chicago: University of Chicago Press.
Morris, Norval (1984). "On Dangerousness in the Judicial Process." *The Record of the Association of the Bar of the City of New York,* 39:102–128.
Morris, Norval, and Marc Miller (1985). "Predictions of Dangerousness." In Michael Tonry and Norval Morris (eds.), *Crime and Justice: An Annual Review of Research* (Vol. 6). Chicago: University of Chicago Press.
Morris, Suzanne M., and Henry J. Steadman (1994). "Keys to Successfully Diverting Mentally Ill Jail Detainees." *American Jails,* 8:47–49.
Moses, Marilyn C. (1993). "Girl Scouts Behind Bars: New Program at Women's Prisons Benefits Mothers and Children." *Corrections Today,* 55:132–134.
Motiuk, Michele S., Laurence L. Motiuk, and James Bonta (1992). "A Comparison Between Self-Report and Interview-Based Inventories in Offender Classification." *Criminal Justice and Behavior,* 19:143–159.
Mott, Joy (1989). "Is Criminology Any Use?" *Home Office Research and Planning Unit Research Bulletin,* 26:1–48.
Moyer, Imogene L., and Susan E. Giles (1993, October). "Mothers in Prison: Supporting the Parent-Child Bond." Unpublished paper presented at the annual meeting of the American Society of Criminology, Phoenix, AZ.
Mullen, Joan (1985). "Prison Overcrowding and the Evaluation of Public Policy." *The Annals,* 47:31–46.

Mullen, Rod et al. (1996). "California Program Reduces Recidivism and Saves Tax Dollars." *Corrections Today,* 58:118–124.

Muraskin, Roslyn (1990, November). "Females in Correctional Facilities: Separate But Equal?" Unpublished paper presented at the annual meeting of the American Society of Criminology, Baltimore, MD.

Murphy, Jeffrie G. (1992). *Retribution Reconsidered: More Essays in the Philosophy of Law.* Boston: Kluwer.

Murray, Christopher, and Merlyn Bell (1996). "The 1995 Capacity Study of Offender Placements in Washington State." *American Jails,* 10:59–63.

Murton, Thomas O., and Joe Hyams (1976). *Accomplices to Crime: The Arkansas Prison Scandal.* New York: Grove Press.

Murton, Tom (1976). "Shared Decision-Making As a Treatment Technique in Prison Management." *New England Journal on Prison Law,* 3:97–113.

Myers, Laura B., and Sue Titus Reid (1995). "The Importance of County Context in the Measurement of Sentence Disparity: The Search for Routinization." *Journal of Criminal Justice,* 23:223–241.

Nacci, Peter, and Thomas R. Kane (1983). "Incidence of Sex and Sexual Aggression in Federal Prisons." *Federal Probation,* 47:31–36.

Nadel, Barbara A. (1996). "Designing for Women: Doing Time Differently." *Corrections Compendium,* 21:1–7.

Nagel, William G. (1984). "Corrections and Punishment." *Corrections Today,* 46:32–62.

National Council on Crime and Delinquency (1991). *Juvenile Justice Policy Statement.* San Francisco: National Council on Crime and Delinquency.

National Manpower Survey (1978). *The National Manpower Survey of the Criminal Justice System: Corrections.* Washington, DC: U.S. Government Printing Office.

National Research Council Panel on the Understanding and Control of Violent Behavior (1990). *Sexual Violence.* Washington, DC: National Research Council Panel on the Understanding and Control of Violent Behavior.

Nebraska Governor's Task Force on Prison Alternatives (1993). *Executive Summary.* Lincoln, NE: Governor's Task Force on Prison Alternatives.

Nesbitt, Charlotte A. (1986). "Female Offenders: A Changing Population." *Corrections Today,* 48:76–80.

Nesbitt, Charlotte A. (1992). "The Female Offender: Overview of Facility Planning and Design Issues and Considerations." *Corrections Compendium,* 17:1–7.

New York State Department of Correctional Services Division of Parole (1994). *Shock Incarceration and Shock Parole Supervision: The Sixth Annual Report to the Legislature.* Albany: New York State Department of Correctional Services Division of Parole.

News Reports (1991). "Prisoner Escape from Kansas County Jail Unnoticed for Eight Days." *Corrections Compendium,* 16:19.

Newsweek (1987). "Editorial." *Newsweek,* December 7:38.

Nieto, Marcus (1995). *Boot Camps: An Alternative Punishment Option for the Criminal Justice System.* Sacramento: California Research Bureau, California State Library.

Niskanen, William A. (1994). *Crime, Police and Root Causes.* Washington, DC: Cato Institute.

Nimick, Ellen, Linda Szymanski, and Howard Snyder (1986). *Juvenile Court Waiver: A Study of Juvenile Court Cases Transferred to Criminal Court.* Pittsburgh, PA: National Center for Juvenile Justice.

Norland, Stephen, and Priscilla J. Mann (1984). "Being Troublesome: Women on Probation." *Criminal Justice and Behavior,* 11:115–135.

Norrie, Alan W. (1991). *Law, Ideology and Punishment: Retrieval and Critique of the Liberal Ideal of Criminal Justice.* Dordrecht, NETH: Kluwer.

North Carolina Administrative Office of the Courts (1988). *Presentence Reports to Judges.* Raleigh, NC: North Carolina Administrative Office of the Courts.

Nurco, David, Thomas E. Hanlon, and Richard W. Bateman (1992, November). "Correlates of Parole Outcome Among Drug Abusers." Unpublished paper presented at the annual meeting of the American Society of Criminology, New Orleans, LA.

Oberst, Margaret (1988). *Inmate Literacy Programs: Virginia's 'No Read, No Release' Program.* Lexington, KY: Council of State Governments.

O'Connell, Paul, and Jacquelyn M. Power (1992). "The Power of Partnerships: Establishing Literacy Programs in Community Corrections." *APPA Perspectives,* 16:6–8.

Ogburn, Kevin R. (1993). "Volunteer Program Guide." *Corrections Today,* 55:66–70.

Ogletree, Charles J. (1994). "Just Say No! A Proposal to Eliminate Racially Discriminatory Uses of Peremptory Challenges." *American Criminal Law Review* 31:1099–1151.

Oklahoma Commission on Children and Youth (1988). *Oklahoma Youth in Custody, 1988: Jail Removal Solutions—A Continuum of Care.* Oklahoma City: Oklahoma State Central Printing Office.

Oldenstadt, Steven J. (1994). "Benton County Corrections." *American Jails,* 8:67–69.

O'Leary, Vincent, and Todd R. Clear (1984). *Directions for Community Corrections in the 1990s.* Washington, DC: U.S. Department of Justice, National Institute of Corrections.

Olekalns, M. (1985). "Occupational Stress: You or the Job?" *National Police Research Unit Review,* 1:29–32.

O'Neil, Marion (1990). "Correctional Higher Education: Reduced Recidivism?" *Journal of Correctional Education,* 41:28–31.

Orchowsky, Stan, Nancy Merritt, and Katharine Browning (1994). *Evaluation of the Virginia Department of Corrections Intensive Supervision Program: Executive Summary.* Richmond, VA: Virginia Department of Criminal Justice Services.

Oregon Crime Analysis Center (1991). *Intermediate Sanctions.* Salem, OR: Oregon Crime Analysis Center.

Oregon Department of Corrections (1995). *Sex Offender Community Notification in Oregon.* Dallas, OR: Oregon Department of Corrections.

Osgood, D. Wayne (1983). "Offense History and Juvenile Diversion." *Evaluation Review,* 7:793–806.

Ortega, Sandra, and Carolyn Hardin (1993). "Community Corrections Programs Promoting Safety Through Screening and Structure." *Corrections Compendium,* 18:15–16.

Ortega, Suzanne T., and Cathleen Burnett (1987). "Age Variation in Female Crime: In Search of the New Female Criminal." *Journal of Crime and Justice,* 10:133–169.

Osler, Mark W. (1991). "Shock Incarceration: Hard Realities and Real Possibilities." *Federal Probation,* 55:34–42.

O'Toole, Michael (1993). "The Changing Role of Local Jails." *Corrections Today,* 55:8.

Pabon, Edward (1985). "A Neighborhood Correctional Program for Juvenile Offenders." *Juvenile and Family Court Journal,* 36:43–47.

Page, Brian T. (1995). *Assessment Center Handbook.* Longwood, FL: Gould Publications.

Palmer, John W. (1997). *Constitutional Rights of Prisoners* (5th ed.). Cincinnati, OH: Anderson Publishing Company.

Palmer, Ted B. (1991). "Intervention with Juvenile Offenders: Recent and Long-Term Changes." In Troy L. Armstrong (ed.), *Intensive Interventions with High-Risk Youths: Promising Approaches in Juvenile Probation and Parole.* Monsey, NY: Criminal Justice Press.

Palmer, Ted B. (1992). *The Re-Emergence of Correctional Intervention.* Newbury Park, CA: Sage.

Palmer, Ted B. (1995). "Programmatic and Nonprogrammatic Aspects of Successful Intervention: New Directions for Research." *Crime and Delinquency,* 41:100–131.

Palumbo, Dennis J., Michael Musheno, and Michael Hallett (1994). "The Political Construction of Alternative Dispute Resolution and Alternatives to Incarceration." *Evaluation and Program Planning,* 17:197–203.

Palumbo, Dennis J., and Rebecca D. Peterson (1994). "Evaluating Criminal Justice Programs: Using Policy as Well as Program Theory." *Evaluation and Program Planning,* 17:159–164.

Palumbo, Dennis J., and Zoann Snyder-Joy (1990, November). "From Net-Widening to Intermediate Sanctions: The Transformation of Alternatives to Incarceration from Malevolence to Benevolence." Unpublished paper presented at the annual meeting of the American Society of Criminology, Baltimore, MD.

Paparozzi, Mario A., and Barry B. Bass (1990). "Firearms—Debating the Issues for Probation and Parole." *APPA Perspectives,* 14:8–9.

Parent, Dale G. (1989a). "Probation Supervision Fee Collection in Texas." *APPA Perspectives,* 13:9–12.

Parent, Dale G. (1989b). *Shock Incarceration: An Overview of Existing Programs.* Washington, DC: U.S. Department of Justice, Office of Justice Programs.

Parent, Dale (1990). *Day Reporting Centers for Criminal Offenders: A Descriptive Analysis of Existing Programs.* Washington, DC: U.S. National Institute of Justice.

Parent, Dale (1991). "OJJDP Sponsors Conditions of Confinement Study." *Corrections Today,* 53:46, 77.

Parsonage, William H. (1992, November). "The Impact of Victim Testimony on Parole Decision Making." Unpublished paper presented at the annual meeting of the American Society of Criminology, New Orleans, LA.

Patel, Jody, and Curt Soderlund (1994). "Getting a Piece of the Pie: Revenue Sharing with Crime Victims Compensation Programs." *APPA Perspectives,* 18:22–27.

Patterson, Bernie L. (1992). "Job Experience and Perceived Stress Among Police, Correctional, and Probation/Parole Officers." *Criminal Justice and Behavior,* 19:260–285.

Paulus, Paul B., and Mary T. Dzindolet (1993). "Reactions of Male and Female Inmates to Prison Confinement: Further Evidence for a Two-Component Model." *Criminal Justice and Behavior,* 20:149–166.

Peak, Kenneth J. (1995). *Justice Administration: Police, Courts and Corrections Management.* Englewood Cliffs, NJ: Prentice-Hall.

Pearson, Frank S. (1987). "Taking Quality into Account: Assessing the Benefits and Costs of New Jersey's Intensive Supervision Program." In Belinda R. McCarthy (ed.), *Intermediate Punishments: Intensive Supervision, Home Confinement, and Electronic Surveillance.* Monsey, NY: Criminal Justice Press.

Pearson, Frank S. (1991). *Deterring Drug Use with Intensive Supervision.* New Brunswick, NJ: Rutgers University, Institute for Criminological Research.

Pearson, Frank S., and Daniel B. Bibel (1986). "New Jersey's Intensive Supervision Program: What is it Like? How is it Working?" *Federal Probation,* 50:25–31.

Pelfrey, William V. (1986). "Assessment Centers as a Management Promotion Tool." *Federal Probation,* 50:65–69.

Pellicciotti, Joseph M. (1987). "42 U.S. C. Sec. (1983). & Correctional Officials Liability: A Look to the New Century." *Journal of Contemporary Criminal Justice,* 3:1–9.

Pennock, George A. (1930). "Industrial Research at Hawthorne." *Personnel Journal,* 8:296–313.

Perkins, Craig A., James J. Stephan, and Allen J. Beck (1995). *Jails and Jail Inmates 1993–1994.* Washington, DC: U.S. Bureau of Justice Statistics.

Petersilia, Joan (1985a). "Rand's Research: A Closer Look." *Corrections Today,* 47:37–40.

Petersilia, Joan (1985b). "Community Supervision: Trends and Critical Issues." *Crime and Delinquency,* 31:125–135.

Petersilia, Joan (1985c). *Probation and Felony Offenders.* Washington, DC: Bureau of Justice Statistics.

Petersilia, Joan (1986a). *Exploring the Option of House Arrest.* Santa Monica, CA: Rand Corporation.

Petersilia, Joan (1986b). "Exploring the Option of House Arrest." *Federal Probation,* 50:50–55.

Petersilia, Joan (1986c). *Taking Stock of Probation Reform.* Santa Monica, CA: Rand Corporation.

Petersilia, Joan (1987). *Expanding Options for Criminal Sentencing.* Santa Monica, CA: Rand Corporation.

Petersilia, Joan (1988a). *House Arrest.* Washington, DC: U.S. Department of Justice, National Institute of Justice.

Petersilia, Joan (1988b). "Probation Reform." In Joseph E. Scott and Travis Hirschi (eds.), *Controversial Issues in Crime and Justice.* Beverly Hills, CA: Sage.

Petersilia, Joan, and Susan Turner (1987). "Guideline-Based Justice: Prediction and Racial Minorities." In D. M. Gottfredson and Michael Tonry (eds.), *Prediction and Classification.* Chicago, IL: Univ. of Chicago Press.

Petersilia, Joan, and Susan Turner (1990a). *Diverting Prisoners to Intensive Supervision: Results of an Experiment in Oregon.* Santa Monica, CA: Rand.

Petersilia, Joan, and Susan Turner (1990b). *Intensive Supervision for High-Risk Probationers: Findings from Three California Experiments.* Santa Monica, CA: Rand.

Petersilia, Joan, and Susan Turner (1991). "An Evaluation of Intensive Supervision in California." *Journal of Criminal Law and Criminology,* 882:610–658.

Petersilia, Joan, and Susan Turner (1992). "Focusing on High-Risk Parolees: An Experiment to Reduce Commitments to the Texas Department of Corrections." *Journal of Research in Crime and Delinquency,* 29:34–61.

Petersilia, Joan et al. (1985). *Granting Felons Probation: Public Risks and Alternatives.* Santa Monica, CA: The Rand Corporation.

Phelan, Lynn, Lynn Brown, and Charles Friel (1992). *Community Sanctions Evaluation Project: Final Report.* Austin, TX: U.S. Courts in the Northern District of Texas.

Philliber, Susan (1987). "Thy Brother's Keeper: A Review of the Literature on Correctional Officers." *Justice Quarterly,* 4:9–37.

Pike, Luke O. (1968). *A History of Crime in England.* Montclair, NJ: Patterson Smith.

Pisciotta, Alexander W. (1983). "Scientific Reform: The 'New Penology' at Elmira, 1976–1900." *Crime and Delinquency,* 29:613–630.

Pitts, John (1992). "The End of an Era." *Howard Journal of Criminal Justice,* 31:133–149.

Platek, Monika (1990). "Prison Subculture in Poland." *International Journal of the Sociology of Law,* 18:459–472.

Podkopacz, Marcy R. (1994). *Juvenile Reference Study.* Minneapolis: Hennepin County Department of Community Corrections.

Pogrebin, Mark R., and Eric D. Poole (1988). "The Work Orientation of Jail Personnel: A Comparison of Deputy Sheriffs and Career Line Officers." *Policy Studies Review,* 7:606–614.

Pohlman, H.L. (1995). *Constitutional Debate in Action: Criminal Justice.* New York: HarperCollins College Publishers.

Poklemba, John J. (1988). *Measurement Issues in Prison and Jail Administration.* Albany: New York State Criminal Justice Information System Improvement Program.

Pollack, Harriet, and Alexander B. Smith (1983). "White-Collar v. Street Crime Sentencing Disparity: How Judges See the Problem." *Judicature,* 67:174–182.

Pollock-Byrne, Joycelyn M. (1990). *Women, Prison & Crime.* Pacific Grove, CA: Brooks/Cole Publishing Company.

Polsky, Howard W., and Jonathan Fast (1993). "Boot Camps, Juvenile Offenders and Culture Shock." *Child and Youth Care Forum,* 22:403–414.

Pontell, Henry N., and Wayne N. Welsh (1994). "Incarceration as a Deviant Form of Social Control: Jail Overcrowding in California." *Crime and Delinquency,* 40:18–36.

Poole, Carol, and Peggy Slavick (1995). *Boot Camps: A Washington State Update and Overview of National Findings.* Olympia, WA: Washington State Institute for Public Policy.

Potter, James T. (1991). "Future Trends in Intake and Discharge." *American Jails,* 5:47–50.

Powers, Kevin (1992). *Intensive Supervision in the Northern District of Ohio.* Washington, DC: U.S. Parole Commission.

Probation Association (1939). *John Augustus: The First Probation Officer.* New York: Probation Association.

Purdy, Donald A., Jr., and Jeffrey Lawrence (1990). "Plea Agreements Under the Federal Sentencing Guidelines." *Criminal Law Bulletin,* 26:483–508.

Putnam, Mark L. (1930). "Improving Employee Relations." *Personnel Journal,* 8:314–325.

Pynes, Joan, and John H. Bernardin (1992). "Entry-Level Police Selection: The Assessment Center is an Alternative." *Journal of Criminal Justice,* 20:41–52.

Quay, Herbert C. (1984). *Managing Adult Inmates.* College Park, MD: American Correctional Association.

Quay, Herbert C., and Craig T. Love (1989). *Behavioral Classification for Female Offenders.* Washington, DC: U.S. National Institute of Corrections.

Quay, Herbert C., and L. B. Parsons (1971). *The Differential Behavioral Classification of the Adult Male Offender.* Philadelphia, PA: Temple University [Technical report prepared for the U.S. Department of Justice Bureau of Prisons, Contract J-1C-22, 253].

Quigley, Peter, and Suzanne VanGheem (1992). *Alabama Board of Pardons and Paroles 1992 Workload Study.* San Francisco: National Council on Crime and Delinquency.

Quinlan, Judith et al. (1990). "Standards and Training." *American Jails,* 4:22–58.

Quinlan, J. Michael et al. (1992). "Focus on the Female Offender." *Federal Prisons Journal,* 3:3–68.

Quinn, James F., and John E. Holman (1991). "Intrafamilial Conflict Among Felons Under Community Supervision: An Examination of the Co-Habitants of Electronically Monitored Offenders." *Journal of Offender Rehabilitation,* 16:177–192.

Rackmill, Stephen J. (1993). "Community Corrections and the Fourth Amendment." *Federal Probation,* 57:40–45.

Rackmill, Stephen J. (1994). "An Analysis of Home Confinement as a Sanction." *Federal Probation,* 58:45–52.

Rackmill, Stephen J. (1996). "Printzlein's Legacy, the 'Brooklyn Plan,' A.K.A. Deferred Prosecution." *Federal Probation,* 60:8–15.

Radosh, Polly F. (1988). "Inmate Mothers: Legislative Solutions to a Difficult Problem." *Journal of Crime and Justice,* 11:61–76.

Rafter, Nicole Hahn (1983a). "Prisons for Women: 1790–1980." In Michael Tonry and Norval Morris (eds.), *Crime and Justice: An Annual Review of Research.* Chicago: University of Chicago Press.

Rafter, Nicole Hahn (1983b). "Chastizing the Unchaste: Social Control Functions of a Woman's Reformatory, 1894–1931." In Stanley Cohen and Andrew Scull (eds.), *Social Control and the State.* New York: St. Martin's.

Rafter, Nicole Hahn (1990). *Partial Justice: Women, Prisons and Social Control* (2nd ed.). New Brunswick, NJ: Transaction.

Ragghianti, Marie (1993). *Survey of Substance Abuse Services Provided by Maryland State and County Correctional Facilities.* College Park, MD: University of Maryland at College Park, Center for Substance Abuse Research.

Ralph, H. Paige, and James W. Marquart (1992, November). "Correlates of Gang-Related Homicides in Prison." Unpublished paper presented at the annual meeting of the American Society of Criminology, New Orleans, LA.

Rans, Laurel L. (1984). "The Validity of Models to Predict Violence in Community and Prison Settings." *Corrections Today,* 46:50–63.

Rasmussen, David W., and Bruce L. Benson (1994). *Intermediate Sanctions: A Policy Analysis Based on Program Evaluations.* Washington, DC: The Collins Center for Public Policy.

Ray, Garold T. (1994). "The Feasibility of Establishing Probation Field Offices in the District of Minnesota." *Federal Probation,* 58:10–17.

Reaves, Brian A. (1993). *Census of State and Local Law Enforcement Agencies, 1992.* Washington, DC: U.S. Department of Justice.

Reaves, Brian A., and Jacob Perez (1994). *Pretrial Release of Felony Defendants, 1992.* Washington, DC: U.S. Bureau of Justice Statistics.

Reaves, Brian A., and Pheny Z. Smith (1996). *Sheriff's Departments 1993.* Washington, DC: U.S. Department of Justice.

Reckless, Walter C. (1961). *The Crime Problem.* New York: Appleton-Century-Crofts.

Reeves, R. (1992). "Approaching 2000: Finding Solutions to the Most Pressing Issues Facing the Corrections Community." *Corrections Today,* 54:74, 76–79.

Reid, Sue Titus (1987). *Criminal Justice: Procedures and Issues.* St. Paul, MN: West Publishing Company.

Reiss, Albert J., Jr., and Jeffrey A. Roth (eds.). (1993). *Understanding and Preventing Violence.* Washington, DC: National Academy Press.

Remington, Bob, and Marina Remington (1987). "Behavior Modification in Probation Work: A Review and Evaluation." *Criminal Justice and Behavior,* 14:156–174.

Rhine, Edward E., William R. Smith, and Ronald W. Jackson (1991). *Paroling Authorities: Recent History and Current Practice.* Laurel, MD: American Correctional Association.

Richeson, Kent, and John Klofas (1990). "The Politics of Removing Juveniles from Jails: An Illinois Study." *International Journal of Offender Therapy and Comparative Criminology,* 34:57–65.

Richmond, C. (1970). "Expanding the Concepts of the Halfway House: A Satellite Housing Program." *International Journal of Social Psychiatry,* 16:986–102.

Robbins, Ira P. (1988). *The Legal Dimensions of Private Incarceration.* Washington, DC: American Bar Association.

Roberts, Albert R. (ed.). (1994). *Critical Issues in Crime and Justice.* Thousand Oaks, CA: Sage.

Roberts, John W. (ed.). (1994). *Escaping Prison Myths: Selected Topics in the History of Federal Corrections.* Washington, DC: American University Press.

Robins, Arthur J. et al. (1986). "The Missouri Classification System Applied to Female Offenders: Reliability and Validity." *Corrective and Social Psychiatry and Journal of Behavior Technology Methods and Therapy,* 32:21–30.

Robinson, Dinah A., and Otis H. Stephens (1992). "Patterns of Mitigating Factors in Juvenile Death Penalty Cases." *Criminal Law Bulletin,* 28:246–275.

Rocheleau, Ann Marie (1987a, November). "Visiting Programs for Inmate Mothers and Their Children: A Steppingstone Toward United Families." Unpublished paper presented at the American Society of Criminology meeting, Montreal, CAN.

Rocheleau, Ann Marie (1987b). *Joining Incarcerated Mothers with Their Children: Evaluation of the Lancaster Cottage Program.* Boston: Massachusetts Department of Corrections.

Rockowitz, Ruth J. (1986). "Developmentally Disabled Offenders: Issues in Developing and Maintaining Services." *The Prison Journal,* 66:19–23.

Rodriguez-Labarca, Jorge, and John P. O'Connell (1993). *Mandatory Sentencing in Delaware, 1981–1991.* Dover, DE: Delaware Statistical Analysis Center.

Roethlisberger, Fritz J., and William J. Dickson (1939). *Management and the Worker.* Cambridge: Harvard University Press.

Rogers, Joseph W., and G. Larry Mays (1987). *Juvenile Delinquency and Juvenile Justice.* New York: John Wiley & Sons.

Rogers, Robert (1993). "Solitary Confinement." *International Journal of Offender Therapy and Comparative Criminology,* 37:339–349.

Rose, Tracy (1988). "Volunteers in Prison: The Community Link." *Corrections Today,* 50:216–218.

Ross, Robert R., and Elizabeth A. Fabiano (1985). *Correctional Afterthoughts: Programs for Female Offenders.* Ottawa: Ministry of the Solicitor General of Canada.

Rothman, David J. (1983). "Sentencing Reforms in Historical Perspective." *Crime and Delinquency,* 29:631–647.

Roush, David W., and Michael A. Jones (1996). "Juvenile Detention Training: A Status Report." *Federal Probation,* 60:54–60.

Roush, Richard W. (1993). "How to Cost Justify Computer Hardware and Software." *American Jails,* 7:54–57.

Rowan, Joseph R. (1989). "Jail/Correctional Officers with 'Street Attitudes' Incur Lawsuits." *American Jails,* 3:13–17.

Roy, Sudipto (1995). "Juvenile Offenders in an Electronic Home Detention Program: A Study on Factors Related to Failure." *Journal of Offender Monitoring,* 8:9–17.

Roy, Sudipto and Michael Brown (1992, November). "Victim-Offender Reconciliation Project for Adults and Juveniles: A Comparative Study in Elkhart County, Indiana." Unpublished paper presented at the annual meeting of the American Society of Criminology, San Francisco, CA.

Royse, David, and Steven A. Buck (1991). "Evaluating a Diversion Program for First-Time Shoplifters." *Journal of Offender Rehabilitation,* 17:147–158.

Ruback, R. Barry, and Timothy S. Carr (1993). "Prison Crowding Over Time: The Relationship of Density and Changes in Density to Infraction Rules." *Criminal Justice and Behavior,* 20:130–148.

Runda, John C., Edward E. Rhine, and Robert E. Wetter (1994). *The Practice of Parole Boards.* Lexington, KY: Council of State Governments.

Rusche, George, and Otto Kirchheimer (1939). *Punishment and Social Structure.* New York: Columbia University Press.

Russell, Jeanne, Robert A. Nicholson, and Rudy Buigas (1990). *Evaluation of the Female Offender Regimented Treatment Program at Eddie Warrior Correctional Center.* Tulsa, OK: University of Tulsa.

Ryan, T.A. (1984). *State of the Art Analysis of Adult Female Offenders and Institutional Programs.* Washington, DC: U.S. National Institute of Corrections.

Ryan, T.A., and James B. Grassano (1992). "Taking a Progressive Approach to Treating Pregnant Offenders." *Corrections Today,* 54:184–186.

Sagatun, Inger, Loretta L. McCollum, and Leonard P. Edwards (1985). "The Effect of Transfers from Juvenile to Criminal Court: A Loglinear Analysis." *Journal of Crime and Justice,* 8:65–92.

St. Paul Police Department (1991). *Placement of Released Inmates in Private Employment: Executive Summary.* St. Paul, MN: St. Paul Police Department.

Salive, Marcel E., Gordon B. Smith, and T. Fordham Brewer (1990). "Death in Prison: Changing Mortality Patterns Among Male Prisoners in Maryland, 1979–1987." *American Journal of Public Health* 80:1479–1480.

Sametz, Lynn, Joseph Ahren, and Steven Yuan (1994). "Rehabilitating Youth Through Housing Rehabilitation." *Journal of Correctional Education,* 45:142–150.

Sametz, Lynn, Joseph Ahern, and Steven Yuan (1994). "Rehabilitating Youth Through Housing Rehabilitation." *Journal of Correctional Education,* 45:142–150.

Sandys, Marla, and Edmund F. McGarrell (1995). "Attitudes Toward Capital Punishment: Preference for the Penalty or Mere Acceptance?" *Journal of Research in Crime and Delinquency,* 32:191–213.

Santa Clara County Office of the County Executive Center for Urban Analysis (1994). *Assessing the Impact of AB971: "Three Strikes, You're Out" On the Justice System in Santa Clara County California.* Santa Clara County, CA: Santa Clara County Board of Supervisors.

Sapers, Howard (1990, November). "The Fine Options Program in Alberta." Unpublished paper presented at the annual meeting of the American Society of Criminology, Baltimore, MD.

Sapp, Allen D., and Michael Vaughn (1989, November). "Sex Offender Treatment Programs: An Evaluation." Unpublished paper presented at the annual meeting of the American Society of Criminology, Reno, NV.

Saunders, Daniel G., and Sandra T. Azar (1989). "Treatment Programs for Family Violence." In Lloyd Ohlin and Michael Tonry (eds.), *Family Violence.* Chicago: University of Chicago Press.

Saxton, Samuel F. (1987). "Prince George's County, Maryland: A New Generation." *Corrections Today,* 49:28–29.

Saxton, Samuel F. (1988). "Privatization in Corrections." *Corrections Today,* 50:16–22.

Saylor, William G., and Gerald G. Gaes (1991). *PREP Study Links UNICOR Work Experience with Successful Post-Release Outcome.* Washington, DC: U.S. Federal Bureau of Prisons.

Schaar, Jill A. (1985). "Prisoners' Fourth Amendment Right to Privacy: Expanding a Constricted View." *Houston Law Review,* 22:1065–1091.

Schafer, N.E. (1986). "Discretion, Due Process, and the Prison Discipline Committee." *Criminal Justice Review,* 11:37–46.

Schellman, George (1996). "Housing State Offenders in a County Correction Center: The Shelby County Experience." *American Jails,* 10:27–31.

Schiff, Martha F. (1990, November). "Shifting Paradigms from a Presumption of Incarceration to Community Based Supervision and Sanctioning." Unpublished paper presented at the annual meeting of the American Society of Criminology, Baltimore, MD.

Schlossman, Steven, and Joseph Spillane (1992). *Bright Hopes, Dim Realities: Vocational Innovation in American Correctional Education.* Santa Monica, CA: Rand.

Schmidt, Anne (1986). *Electronic Monitoring Equipment.* Washington, DC: U.S. National Institute of Justice.

Schneider, Anne L. (1984). "Divesting Status Offenses from Juvenile Court Jurisdiction." *Crime and Delinquency,* 30:347–370.

Schmidt, Annesley K., and Christine E. Curtis (1987). "Electronic Monitors." In Belinda R. McCarthy (ed.), *Intermediate Punishments: Intensive Supervision, Home Confinement, and Electronic Surveillance.* Monsey, NY: Criminal Justice Press.

Schneider, Hans Joachim (1989). "Crime and Its Control in Japan and in the Federal Republic of Germany." *Indian Journal of Criminology,* 17:31–41.

Schrag, Clarence (1961). "Some Foundations for a Theory of Corrections." In Donald R. Cressey (ed.), *The Prison: Studies in Institutional Organization.* New York: Holt, Rinehart, and Winston.

Schram, Donna D., and Cheryl Darling Milloy (1993). *Specialized Supervision of Sex Offenders: Program and Evaluation.* Seattle, WA: Urban Policy Research, Washington State Institute for Public Policy.

Schuman, Alan M., and Tamara Holden (1989). "Point and Counterpoint: Firearms—Debating the Issues for Probation and Parole." *APPA Perspectives,* 13:6–8.

Schwartz, Ira M., and Chang Ming Hsieh (1994). *Juveniles Confined in the United States: 1979–1991.* Philadelphia: Center for the Study of Youth Policy.

Scully, Diana (1990). *Understanding Sexual Violence: A Study of Convicted Rapists.* Boston: Unwin Hyman.

Sechrest, Dale K. (1991). "The Effects of Density on Jail Assaults." *Journal of Criminal Justice,* 19:211–223.

Sechrest, Lee (1987). "Classification for Treatment." In Don M. Gottfredson and Michael Tonry (eds.), *Prediction and Classification: Criminal Justice Decision Making.* Chicago: University of Chicago Press.

Seis, Mark C., and Kenneth L. Elbe (1991). "The Death Penalty for Juveniles: Bridging the Gap Between an Evolving Standard of Decency and Legislative Policy." *Justice Quarterly,* 8:465–487.

Selke, William L. (1993). *Prisons in Crisis.* Bloomington, IN: Indiana University Press.

Sellin, Thorsten (1980). *The Penalty of Death.* Beverly Hills, CA: Sage.

Selye, Hans (1976). *The Stress of Life* (2nd ed.). New York: McGraw-Hill.

Semanchik, David A. (1990). "Prison Overcrowding in the United States: Judicial and Legislative Remedies." *New England Journal on Criminal and Civil Confinement,* 16:67–88.

Senese, Jeffrey D. (1991). "Jail Utilization Over Time: An Assessment of the Patterns in Male and Female Populations." *Criminal Justice Policy Review,* 5:241–255.

Senese, Jeffrey D. et al. (1992). "Evaluating Jail Reform: Inmate Infractions and Disciplinary Response in a Traditional and a Podular/Direct Supervision Jail." *American Jails,* 6:14–23.

Sepejack, Diana S., Christopher D. Webster, and R. J. Menzies (1984). "The Clinical Prediction of Dangerousness: Getting Beyond the Basic Questions." In Dave J. Muller, Derek E. Blackman, and Anthony J. Chapman (eds.), *Psychology and Law: Topics from an International Conference.* Chichester, UK: John Wiley & Sons.

Serin, Ralph C. (1994). *Treating Violent Offenders: A Review of Current Practices.* Washington, DC: Research Report No. R-38. National Institute of Justice.

Shaffer, C. Edward, David Bluoin, and Gary C. Pettigrew (1985). "Assessment of Prison Escape Risk." *Journal of Police and Criminal Psychology,* 1:42–48.

Shandy, Steven G., Brian M. Gardner, and Elizabeth A. Lyons (1987). *A Jail Management Study of the County Jail in Caroline County, Maryland.* College Park, MD: Institute for Governmental Service, University of Maryland.

Shane-DuBow, Sandra, Alice P. Brown, and Eric Olsen (1985). *Sentencing Reform in the United States: History, Content, and Effect.* Washington, DC: U.S. Department of Justice.

Shannon, Douglas (1987). "Correctional Executives: Who's Leading the Way?" *Corrections Today,* 49:48, 94.

Shapiro, C. (1982). "Creative Supervision: An Underutilized Antidote." In W. Paine (ed.), *Job Stress and Burnout: Research, Theory, and Intervention Perspectives.* Beverly Hills, CA: Sage.

Sharbaro, Edward, and Robert Keller (eds.). (1995). *Prison Crisis: Critical Readings.* Albany, NY: Harrow and Heston.

Shelden, Randall G., and William B. Brown (1991). "Correlates of Jail Overcrowding: A Case Study of a County Detention Center." *Crime and Delinquency,* 37:347–362.

Shichor, David (1995). *Punishment for Profit: Private Prisons/Public Concerns.* Thousand Oaks, CA: Sage.

Shilton, Mary K. et al. (1994). "Mandatory Minimum Sentencing." *IARCA Journal on Community Corrections,* 6:4–35.

Shockley, Carol (1988). "The Federal Presentence Investigation Report: Postsentence Disclosure Under the Freedom of Information Act." *Administrative Law Review,* 40:79–119.

Sickmund, Melissa (1994). *How Juveniles Get to Criminal Court.* Washington, DC: U.S. Office of Juvenile Justice and Delinquency Prevention.

Siedschlaw, Kurt (1992). "A Case Study: Small Jail Information Needs Assessment." *American Jails,* 5:41–46.

Sieh, Edward W. (1990, April). "Role Perception Among Probation Officers." Unpublished paper presented at the annual meeting of the Academy of Criminal Justice Sciences, Denver, CO.

Sigler, Robert T., and David Lamb (1995). "Community-Based Alternatives to Prison: How the Public and Court Personnel View Them." *Federal Probation,* 59:3–9.

Sigurdson, Herbert R. (1996). "A Difference That Made a Difference in the Administration of Justice." *American Jails,* 10:9–21.

Silberman, Matthew (1995). *A World of Violence: Corrections in America.* Belmont, CA: Wadsworth Publishing Company.

Simonet, L. John (1995). "Diverting the Mentally Ill from Jail." *American Jails,* 9:30.

Skibinski, Gregory J. (1992). "Intrafamilial Child Sexual Abuse Intervention: The Impact of Juvenile Court Hearings and Felony Trial Diversions." *Juvenile and Family Court Journal,* 43:41–48.

Skolnick, Jerome H. (1995). "What Not to Do About Crime." *Criminology,* 33:1–15.

Skotnicki, Andrew (1991). *Religion and the Development of the American Penal System.* Ann Arbor, MI: University Microfilms International.

Skovron, Sandra Evans, and Brian Simms (1990). "The Use of Task Forces to Develop Strategies to Alleviate Prison Crowding: An Analysis of Their Recommendations and . . . a Typology . . . of Activities." *Journal of Crime and Justice,* 12:1–28.

Slatkin, Art (1994). "A Bad Officer is Hard to Find." *American Jails,* 7:77–80.

Slatkin, Art, Vicki Wimbs, and Kevin Sidebottom (1994). "Jail Inspections and Audits Division: A Model for Practice." *American Jails,* 8:47–51.

Slotnick, M. (1976). *Evaluating Demonstration Programs: Two Case Studies (Drug Treatment in a Parish Prison and a Community-Based Residential Facility).* New Orleans, LA: New Orleans Mayor's Criminal Justice Coordinating Council.

Sluder, Richard D., and Rolando V. del Carmen (1990). "Are Probation and Parole Officers Liable for Injuries Caused by Probationers and Parolees?" *Federal Probation,* 54:3–12.

Sluder, Richard D., Anne Garner, and Kevin Cannon (1995). "The Fusion of Ideology and Technology: New Directions for Probation in the 21st Century." *Journal of Offender Monitoring,* 8:1–7.

Sluder, Richard D., and Allen D. Sapp (1994). "Peering Into the Crystal Ball to Examine the Future of America's Jails." *American Jails,* 7:81–89.

Sluder, Richard D., Allen D. Sapp, and Denny C. Langston (1994). "Guiding Philosophies for Probation in the 21st Century." *Federal Probation,* 58:29–30.

Sluder, Richard D., Robert A. Shearer, and Dennis W. Potts (1991). "Probation Officers' Role Perceptions and Attitudes Toward Firearms." *Federal Probation,* 55:3–12.

Smith, Albert G. (1991a). "Arming Officers Doesn't Have to Change an Agency's Mission." *Corrections Today,* 53:114–124.

Smith, Albert G. (1991b). "The California Model: Probation and Parole Safety Training." *APPA Perspectives,* 15:38–41.

Smith, Barbara E. (1995). *Prosecuting Child Physical Abuse Cases: A Case Study in San Diego.* Washington, DC: Office of Justice Programs.

Smith, Harry E. (1984). "Officer Evaluations: An Important Program Tool." *Corrections Today,* 46:24–26.

Smith, Kelly R., Patrick L. Imhof, and Laura E. Taylor (1994). *Oversight Report on Nontraditional Vocational Training for Female Inmates.* Tallahassee, FL: Florida House of Representatives.

Smykla, John Ortiz (1978). *Co-Corrections: A Case Study of a Coed Federal Prison.* Washington, DC: University Press of America.

Smykla, John Ortiz (1980). *Coed Prison.* New York: Human Sciences Press.

Smykla, John Ortiz (1981). *Community-Based Corrections: Principles and Practices.* New York: Macmillan.

Smykla, John Ortiz, and William Selke (1982). "The Impact of Home Detention: A Less Restrictive Alternative to the Detention of Juveniles." *Juvenile and Family Court Journal,* 33:3–9.

Smykla, John Ortiz, and William Selke (1995). *Intermediate Sanctions: Sentencing in the 1990s.* Cincinnati, OH: Anderson Publishing Company.

Snell, Tracy L., and Danielle C. Morton (1994). *Women in Prison.* Washington, DC: U.S. Department of Justice, Office of Justice Programs.

Snellenberg, Sidney C. (1986, October). "A Normative Alternative to the Death Penalty." Unpublished paper presented at the Southern Association of Criminal Justice Educators, Atlanta, GA.

Snyder, Howard N., Melissa Sickmund, and Eileen Poe-Yamagata (1996). *Juvenile Offenders and Victims: 1996 Update on Violence: Statistics Summary.* Pittsburgh: National Center for Juvenile Justice.

Soma, Jerry (1994). "Group Reporting: A Sensible Way to Manage High Caseloads." *Federal Probation,* 58:26–28.

Song, Lin, and Roxanne Lieb (1995). *Washington State Sex Offenders: Overview of Recidivism Studies.* Olympia, WA: Washington State Institute for Public Policy.

South Carolina Department of Probation, Parole, and Pardon Services (1993). *Violations Guidelines and Administrative Hearings.* Columbia, SC: South Carolina Department of Probation, Parole, and Pardon Services, Unpublished report.

South Carolina State Reorganization Commission (1990). *Evaluation of the Omnibus Criminal Justice Improvement Act of 1986, Section 3, 4 and 5 Second Year Report.* Columbia, SC: South Carolina State Reorganization Commission.

South Carolina State Reorganization Commission (1991). *Prison Crowding in South Carolina: Is There a Solution?* Columbia, SC: South Carolina State Reorganization Commission.

Sparks, J.R., and A.E. Bottoms (1995). "Legitimacy and Order in Prisons." *British Journal of Sociology,* 46:45–62.

Spelman, William (1994). *Criminal Incapacitation.* New York: Plenum Press.

Spelman, William (1995). "The Severity of Intermediate Sanctions." *Journal of Research in Crime and Delinquency,* 32:107–135.

Spieker, Diane J., and Timothy A. Pierson (1989). *Adult Internal Management System (AIMS): Implementation Manual.* Washington, DC: U.S. Department of Justice, National Institute of Corrections (National Institute of Corrections Grant #87-N081).

Spierenburg, Pieter (1991). *The Prison Experience: Disciplinary Institutions and Their Inmates in Early Modern Europe.* New Brunswick, NJ: Rutgers University Press.

Springer, Charles E. (1987). *Justice for Juveniles.* Washington, DC: Office of Juvenile Justice and Delinquency Prevention.

Stack, William R., and Frank A. Dixon (1990). "Behavior Alert Classification Identification System." *American Jails,* 3:45–47.

Stalans, Loretta J., and Gary T. Henry (1994). "Societal Views of Justice for Adolescents Accused of Murder: Inconsistency Between Community Sentiment and Automatic Legislative Transfers." *Law and Human Behavior,* 18:675–696.

Stan, Adele M. (ed.). (1995). *Debating Sexual Correctness: Pornography, Sexual Harassment, Date Rape and the Politics of Sexual Equality.* New York: Dell.

Steffensmeier, Darrell J., and Cathy Streifel (1989, November). "Indicators of Female Status and Trends in Female Crime 1960–1980." Unpublished paper presented at the annual meeting of the American Society of Criminology, Reno, NV.

Steffensmeier, Darrell J., John Kramer, and Cathy Streifel (1993). "Gender and Imprisonment Decisions." *Criminology,* 31:411–446.

Stephan, James J. (1989). *Prison Rule Violators.* Washington, DC: U.S. Department of Justice, Bureau of Justice Statistics.

Stephan, James J., and Louis W. Jankowski (1991). *Jail Inmates, 1990.* Washington, DC: Bureau of Justice Statistics.

Stephan, James J., and Tracy L. Snell (1996). *Capital Punishment 1994.* Washington, DC: U.S. Department of Justice, Office of Justice Programs.

Stevens, Dennis J. (1994). "The Depth of Imprisonment and Prisonization: Levels of Security and Prisoners' Anticipation of Future Violence." *Howard Journal of Criminal Justice,* 33:137–157.

Stinchcomb, Jeanne B. (1985). "Why Not the Best? Using Assessment Centers for Officer Selection." *Corrections Today,* 47:120–124.

Stinchcomb, Jeanne B. (1986). "Correctional Officer Stress: Is Training Missing the Target?" *Issues in Correctional Training and Casework.* College Park, MD: American Correctional Association.

Stohr, Mary K., and Linda L. Zupan (1992). "Street-Level Bureaucrats and Service Provision in Jails: The Failure of Officers to Identify the Needs of Inmates." *American Journal of Criminal Justice,* 16:75–94.

Stohr, Mary K., Michael W. Stohr-Gillmore, and Nicholas P. Lovrich (1990). "Sifting the Gold from the Pebbles: Using Situational Interviews to Select Correctional Officers for Direct Supervision Jails." *American Jails,* 3:29–34.

Stojkovic, Stan (1986). "Social Bases of Power and Control Mechanisms Among Correctional Administrators in a Prison Organization." *Journal of Criminal Justice,* 14:157–166.

Stolzenberg, Lisa Ann (1993). *Unwarranted Disparity and Determinate Sentencing: A Longitudinal Study of Presumptive Sentencing Guidelines in Minnesota.* Ann Arbor, MI: University Microfilms International.

Stone, William E. (1990). "Means of the Cause of Death in Texas Jail Suicides, 1986–1988." *American Jails,* 4:50–53.

Stratton, Neil R.M. (1988). *How Will California Handle Spousal Abuse Incidents by the Year 2000?* Walnut Creek, CA: California Commission on Peace Officer Standards and Training.

Strazzella, James A. (ed.). (1996). "The Federal Role in Criminal Law." *Annals of the American Academy of Political and Social Sciences,* 543:15–166.

Streib, Victor L. (1983). "Death Penalty for Children: The American Experience with Capital Punishment for Crimes Committed While Under Age Eighteen." *Oklahoma Law Review,* 36:613–641.

Streib, Victor L. (1987). *Death Penalty for Juveniles.* Bloomington, IN: Indiana University Press.

Streib, Victor L., and Lynn Sametz (1989). "Executing Female Juveniles." *Connecticut Law Review,* 22:3–59.

Sullivan, Larry E. (1990). *The Prison Reform Movement: Forlorn Hope.* Boston: Twayne.

Sutherland, Edwin H. (1972/1937). *The Professional Thief.* Chicago: University of Chicago Press.

Swanson, Cheryl G., and Daniel M. Ward (1993). "Enforcement Issues in Electronic Monitoring of Probationers." *Journal of Offender Monitoring,* 6:1–13.

Sweet, Joseph (1988). "Probation as Therapy." *Corrections Today,* 47:89–90.

Sweet, Robert W., Jr. (1991). "Beyond the Mandates: The Chronic Offender." *Juvenile and Family Court Journal,* 42:1–7.

Sykes, Gresham (1958). *The Society of Captives.* Princeton, NJ: Princeton University Press.

Syracuse/Onondaga County Youth Bureau (1984). *Onondaga County Interagency Coordination Project: Alternatives for Youths at Risk—A Final Report: Recommendations and Community Action Plan.* Syracuse, NY: Office of the Onondaga County Executive.

Szostak, Edward W. (1996). "Jails and the Management of Other Agencies' Prisoners." *American Jails,* 10:22–24.

Tartaglini, Aldo J., and David A. Safran (1996). "Occupational Functioning of Correctional Officers: Job-Related, Organizational, and Social Considerations." *American Jails,* 10:42–44.

Taylor, Jon Marc (1996). "Violence in Prison: A Personal Perspective." *Corrections Compendium,* 21:1–12.

Teplin, Linda A., Karen M. Abram, and Gary M. McClelland (1994). "Does Psychiatric Disorder Predict Violent Crime Among Released Jail Detainees? A Six-Year Longitudinal Study." *American Psychologist,* 49:335–342.

Tewksbury, Richard A. (1994). "Improving the Educational Skills of Jail Inmates: Preliminary Program Findings." *Federal Probation,* 58:55–59.

Texas Criminal Justice Policy Council (1993). *Jail Backlog Projection for Fiscal Years 1993–2000.* Austin, TX: Texas Criminal Justice Policy Council.

Texas Criminal Justice Policy Council (1993). *Mentally Retarded and Mentally Ill Criminal Offenders: Effectiveness of Community Intervention Programs.* Austin, TX: Texas Criminal Justice Policy Council.

Texas Criminal Justice Task Force (1989). *Report of the Texas Criminal Justice Task Force: A Summary of Findings and Recommendations.* Austin, TX: Texas Criminal Justice Task Force.

Thomas, Andrew Peyton (1994). *Crime and the Sacking of America: The Roots of Chaos.* McLean, VA: Brassey's.

Thomas, Charles W. (1991a). "How Correctional Privatization Defines the Legal Rights of Prisoners." *Privatization Review,* 6:38–58.

Thomas, Charles W. (1991b). "Prisoners' Rights and Correctional Privatization: A Legal and Ethical Analysis." *Business and Professional Ethics Journal,* 10:3–45.

Thomas, Fate (1988). "The Crisis in Our Jails: Overcrowded Beds or Underused Resources." *American Jails,* 2:60–62.

Thomas, Robert L. (1988). "Stress Perception Among Select Federal Probation and Pretrial Services Officers and Their Supervisors." *Federal Probation,* 52:48–58.

Thompson, Joel A. (1986). "The American Jail: Problems, Politics, Prospects." *American Journal of Criminal Justice,* 10:205–221.

Thompson, Joel A., and G. Larry Mays (eds.). (1991). *American Jails: Public Policy Issues.* Chicago: Nelson-Hall.

Thornberry, Terence P., Stewart E. Tolnay, and Timothy J. Flanagan (1991). *Children in Custody, 1987: A Comparison of Public and Private Juvenile Custody Facilities.* Washington, DC: U.S. Office of Juvenile Justice and Delinquency Prevention.

Thornton, William E., Jr., Lydia Voigt, and William G. Doerner (1987). *Delinquency and Justice* (2nd ed.). New York: Random House.

Tobolowsky, Peggy M., James F. Quinn, and John E. Holman (1991). "Participation of Incarcerated High School Dropouts in County Jail Programs." *Journal of Correctional Education,* 42:142–145.

Toch, Hans (1994). "Democratizing Prisons." *Prison Journal,* 74:62–72.

Toch, Hans, and Kenneth Adams (1986). "Pathology and Disruptiveness Among Prison Inmates." *Journal of Research in Crime and Delinquency,* 23:7–21.

Tonry, Michael (1993). "Sentencing Commissions and Their Guidelines." *Crime and Justice: A Review of Research* (Vol. 17). Chicago: University of Chicago Press.

Tonry, Michael, and Kate Hamilton (eds.). (1995). *Intermediate Sanctions in Overcrowded Times.* Boston: Northeastern University Press.

Torres, Donald A. (1985). *Handbook of Federal Police and Investigative Agencies.* Westport, CT: Greenwood Press.

Townsend, Gail (1991). "Kansas Community Corrections Programs." *American Jails,* 5:26–30.

Tracy, Alice (1993). "Literacy Volunteers Share a Belief in Rehabilitative Effect of Education." *Corrections Today,* 55:102–112.

Travis, Lawrence F., III (1985). *Probation, Parole, and Community Corrections.* Prospect Heights, IL: Waveland Press.

Travisono, Anthony P. (1990). "Development of Standards and Accreditation." *American Jails,* 4:59–62.

Troia, Nina (1993). *Correctional Institution Recidivism Among Youth Released from DYS Institutions 1986 to 1990.* Madison, WI: Department of Health and Social Services, Office of Policy and Budget.

Tunis, Sandra et al. (1996). *Evaluation of Drug Treatment in Local Corrections.* Washington, DC: National Institute of Justice.

Turner, James Roger (1985). *Can Inmate Grievance Procedures Assist Management Decision-Making? The Case of Florida's Prisons.* Tallahassee, FL: Florida State University, Department of Public Administration.

Turner, Susan, and Joan M. Petersilia (1996). "Work Release in Washington: Effects on Recidivism and Corrections Costs." *Prison Journal,* 76:138–164.

Turturici, Jack, and Gregory Sheehy (1993). "How Direct Supervision Jail Design Affects Inmate Behavior Management." *Corrections Today,* 55:102–106.

Umbreit, Mark S. (1986). "Victim/Offender Mediation: A National Survey." *Federal Probation,* 50:53–56.

Umbreit, Mark S. (1991). "Restorative Justice: Having Offenders Meet with Their Victims Offers Benefits for Both Parties." *Corrections Today,* 53:164–165.

Umbreit, Mark S. (1994). "Victim Empowerment Through Mediation: The Impact of Victim Offender Mediation in Four Cities." *APPA Perspectives,* 18:25–28.

Unsinger, Peter Charles, and Harry W. More (eds.). (1990). *Criminal Justice Induction Training: The Field Training Concept.* Springfield, MO: Charles C. Thomas.

Uriell, Patricia (1984). *The Furlough Program: An Evaluation.* Manoa, HI: Youth Development and Research Center, School of Social Work, University of Hawaii, Manoa.

U.S. Bureau of Justice Assistance (1988). *Urinalysis as Part of a Treatment Alternative to Street Crime (TASC) Program.* Washington, DC: U.S. Bureau of Justice Assistance.

U.S. Bureau of Justice Statistics (1994). *Violent Crime.* Washington, DC: U.S. Bureau of Justice Statistics.

U.S. Code (1996). *United States Code Annotated.* St. Paul, MN: West.

U.S. Code (1997). *United States Code Annotated.* St. Paul, MN: West.

U.S. Department of Health and Human Services (1992). *Control of Tuberculosis in Correctional Facilities: A Guide for Health Care Workers.* Washington, DC: U.S. Department of Health and Human Services.

U.S. Federal Bureau of Prisons (1991). *The June 7, 1991 Forum on Issues in Corrections: A Record and Proceedings on "Female Prisoners."* Washington, DC: U.S. Federal Bureau of Prisons.

U.S. Federal Bureau of Prisons (1994). *State of the Bureau: Emergency Preparedness and Response.* Washington, DC: U.S. Federal Bureau of Prisons.

U.S. General Accounting Office (1985a). *UNICOR Products: Federal Prison Industries Can Further Ensure Customer Satisfaction.* Washington, DC: U.S. General Accounting Office.

U.S. General Accounting Office (1985b). *Juvenile Justice: Detention Using Staff Provision Rather Than Architectural Barriers.* Washington, DC: U.S. General Accounting Office.

U.S. General Accounting Office (1995). *Juvenile Justice: Minimal Gender Bias Occurred in Processing Noncriminal Juveniles.* Washington, DC: U.S. General Accounting Office.

U.S. Government Printing Office (1993). *Prisoners in State and Federal Institutions.* Washington, DC: U.S. Government Printing Office.

U.S. National Commission on Acquired Immune Deficiency Syndrome (1991). *Report: HIV Disease in Correctional Facilities.* Washington, DC: U.S. National Commission on Acquired Immune Deficiency Syndrome.

U.S. National Institute of Corrections (1991). *Management Strategies in Disturbances with Gangs/Disruptive Groups.* Washington, DC: U.S. National Institute of Corrections.

U.S. News & World Report (1987). "The Toughest Prison in America." *U.S. News and World Report,* July 27:23–24.

U.S. Sentencing Commission (1987). *The U.S. Sentencing Guidelines.* Washington, DC: U.S. Government Printing Office.

U.S. Sentencing Commission (1991). *The Federal Sentencing Guidelines: A Report on the Operation of the Guidelines System and Short-Term Impacts.* Washington, DC: U.S. Sentencing Commission.

Vachss, Alice (1994). "How to Keep Dangerous Animals Behind Bars." *Parade Magazine,* September 25, 1994:4–5.

Van Voorhis, Patricia (1993). "Psychological Determinants of the Prison Experience." *Prison Journal,* 73:72–102.

Van Voorhis, Patricia (1994). "Measuring Prison Disciplinary Problems: A Multiple Indicators Approach to Understanding Prison Adjustment." *Justice Quarterly,* 11: 679–709.

Vanyur, John M. (1995). "In Colorado: Design Meets Mission at New Federal Max Facility." *Corrections Today,* 58:90–96.

Vaughn, Michael S. (1993). "Listening to the Experts: A National Study of Correctional Administrators' Responses to Prison Overcrowding." *Criminal Justice Review,* 18:12–25.

Velt, Edward, and Albert G. Smith (1993). "A Primer: The Arming of Probation and Parole Officers." *APPA Perspectives,* 17:17–20.

Vicary, Judith R., Linda R. Klingaman, and William L. Harkness (1995). "Risk Factors Associated with Date Rape and Sexual Assault of Adolescent Girls." *Journal of Adolescence,* 18:289–306.

Vigdal, Gerald L., and Donald W. Stadler (1994). "Alternative to Revocation Program Offers Offenders a Second Chance." *Corrections Today,* 56:44–47.

Virginia Commission on Youth (1994). *Report on the Study of Serious Juvenile Offenders.* Richmond: Virginia Commission on Youth.

Virginia Department of Corrections (1987). *Adult Probation and Parole Services: Workload Measurement Study.* Richmond, VA: Division of Adult Community Corrections.

Vito, Gennaro F. (1978). "Shock Probation in Ohio: A Re-Examination of the Factors Influencing the Use of an Early Release Program." *Journal of Offender Rehabilitation,* 3:123–132.

Vito, Gennaro F. (1984). "Developments in Shock Probation: A Review of Research Findings and Policy Implementations." *Federal Probation,* 48:22–27.

Vito, Gennaro F., and Harry E. Allen (1981). "Shock Probation in Ohio: A Comparison of Outcomes." *International Journal of Offender Therapy and Comparative Criminology,* 25:70–75.

Vito, Gennaro F. et al. (1989). "Death Penalty Issues." *Journal of Contemporary Criminal Justice,* 5:181–255.

Vogel, Brenda (1995a). "Meeting Court Mandates: The CD-ROM Solution." *Corrections Today,* 57:158–160.

Vogel, Brenda (1995b). "Ready or Not, Computers are Here." *Corrections Today,* 57:160–162.

von Hirsch, Andrew (1985). *Past or Future Crimes: Deservedness and Dangerousness in the Sentencing of Criminals.* New Brunswick, NJ: Rutgers University Press.

Wahler, Cindy, and Paul Gendreau (1985). "Assessing Correctional Officers." *Federal Probation,* 49:70–74.

Waite, Robert G. (1993). *From Penitentiary to Reformatory . . . The Road to Prison Reform—New South Wales, Ireland, and Elmira, New York, 1840–1970.* Westport, CT: Greenwood Press.

Wagner, Dennis, and Christopher Baird (1993). *Evaluation of the Florida Community Control Program.* Washington, DC: U.S. Department of Justice, Office of Justice Programs.

Wakefield, Hollida, and Ralph Underwager (1991). "Female Child Sexual Abusers: A Critical Review of the Literature." *American Journal of Forensic Psychology,* 9:43–69.

Waley-Cohen, Joanna (1991). *Exile in Mid-Qing, China: Banishment to Xinjiang, 1758–1820.* New Haven, CT: Yale University Press.

Walker, Samuel (1989). *Sense and Nonsense About Crime: A Policy Guide* (2nd ed.). Monterey, CA: Brooks/Cole Publishing Company.

Walker, S. Anne (1993). "Alston Wilkes Society: South Carolina Volunteer Agency Plays Vital Role in Corrections." *Corrections Today,* 55:94–100.

Walters, Glenn D. (1991). "Predicting the Disciplinary Adjustment of Maximum and Minimum Security Prison Inmates Using the Lifestyle Criminality Screening Form." *International Journal of Offender Therapy and Comparative Criminology,* 35:63–71.

Walters, Glenn D. et al. (1992). "The Choice Program: A Comprehensive Residential Treatment Program for Drug Involved Offenders." *International Journal of Offender Therapy and Comparative Criminology,* 36:21–29.

Walters, Stephen (1987, April). "Correctional Officers' Perceptions of Powerlessness." Unpublished paper presented at the Academy of Criminal Justice Sciences meeting, St. Louis, MO.

Walters, Stephen (1993a). "Changing the Guard: Male Correctional Officers' Attitudes Toward Women as Co-Workers." *Journal of Offender Rehabilitation,* 20:47–60.

Walters, Stephen (1993b). "Gender, Job Satisfaction, and Correctional Officers: A Comparative Analysis." *Justice Professional,* 7:23–33.

Ward, David A., and Gene G. Kassebaum (1965). *Women's Prison: Sex and Social Structure.* Chicago, IL: Aldine.

Ward, Sally K., and Jennifer Dzuiba-Leatherman (1994). *Acquaintance and Date Rape.* Westport, CT: Greenwood Press.

Washington State Department of Corrections (1993). *An Integrated Approach to Education, Work, and Offender Reintegration.* Olympia, WA: Washington State Department of Corrections.

Watson, Robin J., and Lana E. Stermac (1994). "Cognitive Group Counseling for Sexual Offenders." *International Journal of Offender Therapy and Comparative Criminology,* 38:259–270.

Watterson, Kathryn (1996). *Women in Prison: Inside the Concrete Womb* (Rev. ed.). Boston: Northeastern University Press.

Watts, Robert (1993). *Study of Alternative Punishment Programs for Offenders.* Richmond, VA: Virginia Department of Planning and Budget.

Webb, Dennis, and Sonny Alicie (1994). "Tactical Response Team." *American Jails,* 7:15–19.

Webb, S.R. (1995). "The Art of Grantsmanship." *Sheriff,* 47:10–12.

Weber, Donald E., and William H. Burke (1986). "An Alternative Approach to Treating Delinquent Youth." *Residential Group Care and Treatment,* 3:65–86.

Webster, Christopher D. et al. (1994). *The Violence Prediction Scheme: Assessing Dangerousness in High Risk Men.* Toronto, CAN: Centre of Criminology, University of Toronto.

Wees, Greg (1996a). "Inmate Population Expected to Increase 43% by 2002." *Corrections Compendium,* 21:1–6.

Wees, Greg (1996b). "Survey Summary: Fewer Correctional Officer Positions Created in '96." *Corrections Compendium,* 21:12–29.

Wehmhoefer, Richard A. (1993). "Ethics in the Probation and Parole Profession: A Vision for the Future." *APPA Perspectives,* 17:8–9.

Weisheit, Ralph, and Sue Mahan (1988). *Women, Crime and Justice.* Cincinnati, OH: Anderson Publishing Company.

Welch, Michael (1995). "Rehabilitation: Holding Its Ground in Corrections." *Federal Probation,* 59:3–8.

Welch, Randy (1990). "Private Prisons—Profitable and Growing." *Corrections Compendium,* 15:1–8.

Wells, Dave, and Tim Brennan (1992). "The Michigan Classification Project: Jail Inmate Classification System." *American Jails,* 6:59–62.

Wells, L. Edward, and Joseph H. Rankin (1995). "Juvenile Victimization: Convergent Validation of Alternative Measurements." *Journal of Research in Crime and Delinquency,* 32:287–307.

Welsh, Wayne N. (1990). "Jail Overcrowding: An Analysis of Policy Makers' Perceptions." *Justice Quarterly,* 7:341–370.

Wener, Richard E., and Christopher Keys (1988). "The Effects of Changes in Jail Population Densities on Crowding, Sick Call, and Spatial Behavior." *Journal of Applied Social Psychology,* 18:852–866.

Wheeler, Pat et al. (1987, November). "The Woman Jailhouse Lawyer." Unpublished paper presented at the American Society of Criminology meeting, Montreal, CAN.

Wheeler, William L. (1993). "Gentle Gestures: Inmates in Connecticut Comfort At-Risk Babies Through Quilting Program." *Corrections Today,* 55:138–139.

Whitehead, John T. (1989). *Burnout in Probation and Corrections.* New York: Praeger.

Whitehead, John T., and Susan Gunn (1988). "Probation Employee Job Attitudes: A Qualitative Analysis." *Journal of Crime and Justice,* 11:143–164.

Whitmore, Robert C. (1995). "Tasks and Duties of Superintendents and Wardens in Pennsylvania." *American Jails,* 9:53–58.

Wicharya, Tamasak (1995). *Simple Theory, Hard Reality: The Impact of Sentencing Reforms on Courts, Prisons, and Crime.* Albany: State University of New York Press.

Widom, Cathy Spatz (1995). *Victims of Childhood Sexual Abuse—Later Criminal Consequences.* Washington, DC: U.S. Department of Justice.

Wiebush, Richard G. (1991). *Evaluation of the Lucas County Intensive Supervision Unit: Diversionary Impact and Youth Outcomes.* Columbus, OH: Governor's Office of Criminal Justice Services.

Wiebush, Richard G. (1993). *At the Crossroads: Juvenile Corrections in the District of Columbia—Profiles of Committed Youth in Secure Care.* Washington, DC: Robert F. Kennedy Memorial.

Wilbur, Richard S. (1991). "AIDS and the Federal Bureau of Prisons: A Unique Challenge." *Northern Illinois University Law Review,* 11:275–295.

Wilkins, Leslie T. (1985). "The Politics of Prediction?" In David Farrington and Roger Tarling (eds.), *Prediction in Criminology.* Albany: State University of New York Press.

Wilkinson, Reginald A. et al. (1994). "Stemming the Violence." *Corrections Today,* 56:64–153.

Williams, D.R., D.P. Callaghan, and I.H. Scheier (1974). *Volunteers in the Criminal Justice System: Rights and Legal Liability.* Washington, DC: American Bar Association.

Williams, Susan Darst (1986). "AIDS in Prison: Coping with a Strange New Death Penalty." *Corrections Compendium,* 10:1–9.

Williams, Susan Darst (1987). "Corrections New Balancing Act: AIDS." *Corrections Compendium,* 10:1–9.

Williams, Susan Darst (1990). "The Invisible Jail: Day Reporting Centers." *Corrections Compendium,* 15:1–7.

Williams, Vergil L., and Mary Fish (1985). "Women's Prisons." In Robert M. Carter, Daniel Glaser, and Leslie T. Wilkins (eds.), *Correctional Institutions* (3rd ed.). New York: Harper and Row.

Wilson, George P. (1985). "Halfway House Programs for Offenders." In Lawrence Travis III (ed.), *Probation, Parole, and Community Corrections.* Prospect Heights, IL: Waveland Press.

Winifred, Sister Mary (1996). "Vocational and Technical Training Programs for Women in Prison." *Corrections Today,* 58:168–170.

Winter, Bill (1993). "Does Corrections Need Volunteers?" *Corrections Today,* 55:20–22.

Wisconsin Department of Health and Social Services (1978). *Huber Law and Work Release Program 1976.* Madison, WI: Wisconsin Health and Social Services Department.

Wisconsin Department of Health and Social Services (1989). *Reducing Criminal Risk: An Evaluation of the High Risk Offender Intensive Supervision Project.* Madison, WI: Wisconsin Department of Health and Social Services, Office of Policy and Budget.

Witte, Ann D. (1973). *Work Release in North Carolina: The Program and the Process.* Chapel Hill, NC: Institute of Government.

Wittenberg, Peter M. (1996). "Power, Influence and the Development of Correctional Policy." *Federal Probation,* 60:43–48.

Wolfe, Manuel, Manuel Vega, and William R. Blount (1992, November). "The Relationship Between Education and Degree of Racial-Ethnic Bias in Inmates." Unpublished paper presented at the annual meeting of the American Society of Criminology, New Orleans, LA.

Wood, Lee F., and Barbara R. Darbey (1987). *The Effects of Treatment Modality on Recidivism with Multiple DWI Offenders in Pretrial Diversion.* Rochester, NY: Pretrial Services Corporation, Monroe County Bar Association.

Wood, William T. (1991). "Multnomah County Sheriff's Office: Population Release Matrix System." *American Jails,* 5:52–53.

Wood, William T. (1995). "Special Management Inmates in Multnomah County." *American Jails,* 9:22–26.

Woodruff, Lary (1993). "Occupational Stress for Correctional Personnel." *American Jails,* 7:71–76.

Woodward, Bill, and Kim English (1993). *Juvenile Intensive Supervision Probation Pilot Project: Phase One Study.* Denver, CO: Department of Public Safety.

Wooldredge, John (1996). "Research Note: A State-Level Analysis of Sentencing Policies and Inmate Crowding in State Prisons." *Crime and Delinquency,* 42:456–466.

World Almanac Books (1996). *The World Almanac and Book of Facts, 1996.* Mahwah, NJ: Funk & Wagnalls Corporation.

Wright, Kevin N. (1991). "A Study of Individual, Environmental and Interactive Effects in Explaining Adjustment to Prison." *Justice Quarterly,* 8:217–242.

Wright, Kevin N., and William G. Saylor (1991). "Male and Female Employees' Perceptions of Prison Work: Is There a Difference?" *Justice Quarterly,* 8:505–524.

Wright, Richard A. (1995). "Rehabilitation, Affirmed, Rejected, and Reaffirmed: Assessments of the Effectiveness of Offender Treatment Programs in Criminology Textbooks." *Journal of Criminal Justice Education,* 6:21–39.

Wright, Thomas A. (1993). "Correctional Employee Turnover: A Longitudinal Study." *Journal of Criminal Justice,* 21:131–142.

Wright, Thomas A., and Dennis Sweeney (1990). "Correctional Institutional Workers' Coping Strategies and Their Effect on Diastolic Blood Pressure." *Journal of Criminal Justice,* 18:161–169.

Yeager, Matthew G. (1992). "Client-Specific Planning: A Status Report." *Criminal Justice Abstracts,* September:537–549.

Yurkanin, Ann (1988). "Trend Toward Shock Incarceration Increasing Among States." *Corrections Today,* 50:87.

Zamble, Edward, and Vernon L. Quinsey (1991). *Dynamic and Behavioral Antecedents to Recidivism: A Retrospective Analysis.* Ottawa, CAN: Correctional Services of Canada, Research Branch.

Zimmer, Lynn E. (1986). *Women Guarding Men.* Chicago: University of Chicago Press.

Zimring, Franklin E., and Gordon Hawkins (1992). *Prison Population and Criminal Justice Policy in California.* Berkeley, CA: Institute of Governmental Studies Press.

Name Index

Subject Index

Cases Cited

Anderson v. Vasquez, N.D.Cal., 827 F.Supp. 617 (1992), 317
Austin v. Pennsylvania Department of Corrections, 876 F.Supp. 1437 (11th Cir. 1991), 287
Avery v. Powell, 806 F.Supp. 7 (1992), 324
Baker v. State, 616 So.2d 571 (1993), 410
Baldwin v. New York, 399 U.S. 66 (1970), 574
Battle v. Anderson, 447 F.Supp. 516 (1977), 328
Bearden v. Georgia, 461 U.S. 660 (1983), 409, 411
Bell v. Wolfish, 441 U.S. 520 (1979), 329–330, 343–345
Bettis v. Delo, 14 F.3d 22 (1994), 325
Black v. Romano, 471 U.S. 606 (1985), 409
Blackburn v. Snow, 771 F.2d 556 (1985), 327
Booth v. Maryland, 107 S.Ct. 2529 (1987), 103
Bordenkircher v. Hayes, 434 U.S. 357 (1978), 79–80
Bounds v. Smith, 430 U.S. 817 (1977), 330
Bowling v. Enomoto, 514 F.Supp. 201 (1981), 484
Brady v. United States, 397 U.S. 742 (1970), 76, 79
Bryson v. Iowa Dist. Court, Iowa, 515 N.W.2d 10 (1994), 324
Burnette v. Phelps, 621 F.Supp. 1157 (1985), 361
California v. Lovercamp, 118 Cal. Rptr. 110 (1974), 531
Cannon v. State, 624 So.2d 238 (1993), 412
Carroll v. Board of Parole, 859 P.2d 1203 (1993), 413
Coffin v. Reichard, 143 F.2d 443 (1944), 322
Coker v. Georgia, 433 U.S. 584 (1977), 360
Cook v. City of New York, 578 F.Supp. 179 (1984), 361
Cooper v. Pate, 382 F.2d 518 (1967), 325
Duncan v. Louisiana, 391 U.S. 145 (1968), 574
Eddings v. Oklahoma, 455 U.S. 104 (1982), 602–603
Enmund v. Florida, 458 U.S. 782 (1982), 344
Escobar v. Landwehr, 837 F.Supp. 284 (1993), 325
Estelle v. Gamble, 429 U.S. 97 (1976), 53, 328, 543
Ex Parte Hull, 312 U.S. 546 (1941), 322, 332
Ex Parte Karstendick, 93 U.S. 396 (1876), 244
Ex Parte Shores, 195 F. 627 (1912), 244
Fisher v. Winter, 564 F.Supp. 281 (1983), 328
Friedman v. State of Arizona, 912 F.2d 328 (1990), 326
Furman v. Georgia, 408 U.S. 238 (1972), 348, 356–357, 386
Gagnon v. Scarpelli, 411 U.S. 788 (1973), 191, 408–409
Galvin v. Carothers, 855 F.Supp. 285 (1994), 329
Gardner v. Johnson, 429 F.Supp. 432 (1977), 361
Gates v. Rowland, 39 F.3d 1439 (9th Cir. 1994), 287
Gettleman v. Werner, 377 F.Supp. 22 (1974), 327

Glover v. Johnson, 478 F.Supp. 1075 (1979), 330, 527
Goldman v. United States, 316 U.S. 129 (1942), 427
Goss v. Sullivan, D.Wyo., 839 F.Supp. 1532 (1993), 317
Gregg v. Georgia, 428 U.S. 153 (1976) 348, 357
Hackett v. United States, 606 F.2d 319, (1978), 347
Hanrahan v. Lane, 747 F.2d. 1137 (1984), 361
Harry v. Smith, 561 N.Y.S.2d 374, 148 Misc.2d 629 (1990), 316
Hause v. Vaught, 993 F.2d 1079 (1993), 332
Holt v. Sarver, 306 F.Supp. 362 (1970), 320
Housely v. Dodson, 41 F.3d 597 (1994), 332
Hudson v. Goodlander, 494 F.Supp. 890 (1980), 484
Hudson v. Palmer, 468 U.S. 517 (1984), 326, 343
Hutto v. Finney, 98 S. Ct. 2565 (1978), 361
Inmates, Washington County Jail v. England, 659 F.2d 1081 (1980), 325
In re Gault, 387 U.S. 1 (1967), 573–574
In re Green, 669 F.2d 779 (1981), 318, 321
In re Winship, 397 U.S. 358 (1970), 574
Johnson v. Avery, 393 U.S. 483 (1969), 332–334
Katz v. United States, 389 U.S. 347 (1967), 427
Kennedy v. New York State Department of Correctional Services, (NYS Division of Human Rights, Case No. 3-E-5084-100365E (May, 1990), 484
Kent v. United States, 383 U.S. 541 (1966), 572–573
Lemon v. State, 861 S.W.2d 249 (1993), 412
Loggins v. Delo, C.A.8 (Mo.), 999 F.2d 364 (1993), 316
Martinez Rodriguez v. Jimenez, 409 F.Supp. 582 (1976), 361
Martyr v. Bachik, 755 F.Supp. 825 (1991), 324
McClafin v. Pearce, 743 F.Supp. 1981 (1990), 325
McGautha v. California, 402 U.S. 183 (1971), 355
McKeiver v. Pennsylvania, 403 U.S. 528 (1971), 574–575
McKnight v. State, 616 So.2d 31 (1993), 412
Medina v. O'Neill, 589 F.Supp. 1028 (1984), 310
Mempa v. Rhay, 389 U.S. 128 (1967), 406–407
Milonas v. Williams, 691 F.2d 931 (1982), 311
Moore v. State, 623 So.2d 842 (1993), 411
Morrissey v. Brewer, 408 U.S. 471 (1972), 191, 406–408
Munir v. Scott, 792 F.Supp. 1472 (1992), 326
North Carolina v. Alford, 400 U.S. 25 (1970), 79
Novak v. Beto, 453 F.2d 661 (1972), 333–334
Olmstead v. United States, 227 U.S. 438 (1928), 427
On Lee v. United States, 343 U.S. 747 (1952), 427
Oviatt v. Pierce, 50 CrL 1426 (1992), 201
Owens v. Brierley, 452 F.2d 640 (1971), 361
Payne v. Tennessee, 501 U.S. 808 (1991), 102–103
People v. Lewis, 502 N.E. 2d 988 (1986), 326
People v. Hipp, 861 S.W.2d 377 (1993), 411–412
People v. Lovercamp, 118 Cal. Rptr. 1 (1974)
People v. Ramos, 48 CrL 1057 (Ill. S.Ct.) (1990), 433
Preiser v. Rodriguez, 429 U.S. 475 (1973), 335
Procunier v. Martinez, 416 U.S. 396 (1974), 324
Pugh v. Locke, 406 F.Supp. 318 (1976), 361
Quinones v. Nettleship, 773 F.2d 10 (1985), 347
Reynolds v. Sheriff, City of Richmond, 574 F.Supp. 90 (1983), 361
Rhodes v. Chapman, 452 U.S. 337 (1981) 329–330, 344–345
Richardson v. New York State Executive Department, 602 N.Y.S.2d 443 (1993), 413–414

Ruffin v. Commonwealth, 62 Va. (21 Gratt) 790 (1871), 319, 321, 406
Rummel v. Estelle, 445 U.S. 263 (1980), 344
Sample v. Borg, 675 F.Supp. 574 (1987), 325
Sands v. Lewis, C.A.9(Ariz.), 878 F.2d 1188 (1989), 317
Schall v. Martin, 104 S. Ct. 2403 (1984), 34, 188, 190
Security and Law Enforcement Employees District Council #82 v. Carey, 737 F.2d 187 (1984), 327, 343
Smith v. Montgomery County, MD, 643 F.Supp. 435 (1986), 361
Smothers v. Gibson, 778 F.2d 470 (1985), 327
Stanford v. Kentucky, 492 U.S. 361 (1989), 353, 559, 603–604
Star v. Gramley, C.D.Ill. 815 F.Supp. 276 (1993), 316
State v. Bergman, 147 CrL 1475 (Ind.Ct.App., 2nd District) (1990), 410
State v. Hayes, 437 S.E.2d 717 (N.C.App.Dec.) (1993), 410
State v. Jimenez, 49CrL 1140 [NM SupCt] (1991), 141
State v. Lubus, 48 CrL 1173 (Conn. SupCt.) (1990), 433
Stone v. San Francisco, 51 CRL 1406 (1992), 201
Strickler v. Waters, 989 F.2d 1375 (1993), 332
Sypert v. United States, 559 F.Supp. 546 (1983), 346
Tarlton v. Clark, 441 F.2d. 384 (1971), 392
Thompson v. Oklahoma, 108 S. Ct. 2687 (1988), 559, 603
Thongvanh v. Thalacker, C.A.8 (Iowa), 17 F.3rd 256 (1994), 316
Timm v. Gunter, 913 F.2d 1093 (8th Cir.) (1990), 484
Tisdale v. Dobbs, 807 F.2d 734 (1986), 325
Tittle v. Jefferson County Commission, 966 F.2d 606 (1992), 178
Turner v. Safley, 107 S.Ct. 2254 (1987), 324
Udey v. Kastner, 805 F.2d 1218 (1986), 325
United States v. Arch John Drummond, 967 F.2d 593 (1992), 433
United States v. Bachsian, 4 F.3rd 288 (1993), 409–410
United States v. Cohen, 796 F.2d 20 (1986), 326
United States v. Dawson, 423 U.S. 855 (1975), 326
United States v. Edwards, 960 F.2d 278 (1992), 433
United States v. Insley, 927 F.2d 185 (1991), 433
United States v. Levi, 2 F.2d 842 (1993), 412
United States v. Mills, 704 F.2d 1553 (1983), 326
United States v. Muniz, 374 U.S. 150 (1963), 335
United States v. Noonan, 47 CrL 1287 (3d Cir.) (1990), 410
United States v. Salerno, 481 U.S. 739 (1987), 34, 190
United States v. Wickman, 955 F.2d 828 (1992), 433
United States v. Zackular, 945 F.2d 23 (1991), 433
Vandelft v. Moses, 31 F.3d 794 (1994), 331
Walker v. United States, 437 F.Supp. 1081 (1977), 346
Washington v. Harper, 110 S.Ct. 1028 (1990), 191
Wilkins v. Missouri, 492 U.S. 361 (1989), 353, 559, 603
Williams v. Puckett, 624 So.2d 496 (1993), 413
Witherspoon v. Illinois, 391 U.S. 510 (1968), 355
Wolff v. McDonnell, 418 U.S. 539 (1974), 324
Woodson v. North Carolina, 428 U.S. 280 (1976), 357